BASIC PROBLEMS
OF
PHILOSOPHY

Fourth edition

BASIC PROBLEMS
OF
PHILOSOPHY

Edited by

DANIEL J. BRONSTEIN
City College of New York

YERVANT H. KRIKORIAN
City College of New York (emeritus)

PHILIP P. WIENER
Temple University

PRENTICE-HALL, INC. *Englewood Cliffs, New Jersey*

ISBN: 0-13-067637-3

Library of Congress Catalog Card Number 79-179449

10   9   8   7

Printed in the United States of America

PRENTICE-HALL INTERNATIONAL, INC., *London*
PRENTICE-HALL OF AUSTRALIA, PTY. LTD., *Sydney*
PRENTICE-HALL OF CANADA, LTD., *Toronto*
PRENTICE-HALL OF INDIA PRIVATE LIMITED, *New Delhi*
PRENTICE-HALL OF JAPAN, INC., *Tokyo*

PREFACE

More than an anthology of philosophical writings, *Basic Problems of Philosophy* seeks to enlighten the beginner, to clarify his understanding, and to stimulate thoughtful discussion. In our fourth edition, we have again balanced classical with contemporary material, grouping the selections around the major areas in philosophy. Among the new selections you will find Plato's *Euthyphro,* Aristotle on Tragedy, Kant's *Perpetual Peace,* and Gilson's *What Is Christian Philosophy?* The views of Ludwig Wittgenstein are presented by Friedrich Waismann; Martin Luther King, Louis Waldman, and Isaiah Berlin discuss relevant political issues; R. B. Perry analyzes the relation of art to morality; Morris Ginsberg discusses the psychoanalytic approach to ethics.

Our aim has been to present diverse views on the basic problems of philosophy in order to encourage the reader to do his own thinking. Each chapter begins with an introductory section in which the historic setting and some of the salient ideas of the selections are pointed out. In addition, we have provided questions at the end of each selection which we hope the student will find challenging. We have also included a glossary of philosophic terms, and biographical data on each of the authors represented in the volume. The bibliographies have been revised and updated. We trust that these reference materials will be helpful to the reader. It is our hope that he will soon discern the breadth of vision and consecutiveness of thought that characterize philosophy.

Although we share in the overall responsibility, particular sections of the volume were prepared as follows:

Chapters 1, 2, and 6 by Daniel J. Bronstein
Chapters 3, 4, and 5 by Philip P. Wiener
Chapters 7, 8, and 9 by Yervant H. Krikorian

CONTENTS

BASIC PROBLEMS
OF
PHILOSOPHY

Chapter 1

WHAT IS PHILOSOPHY?

INTRODUCTION

Many definitions of philosophy have been given. It has been defined as a search for wisdom, or for the truth, or for the goals of human existence; sometimes it is defined as a study of the most general categories of being, such as reality, existence, causality, life, matter, mind. But these concepts are themselves in need of explanation, so they are not useful in clarifying the nature of philosophy. The only way to find out what philosophy is really all about is to observe how philosophers go about the business of philosophizing.

In the selections of this volume you will become acquainted with the thoughts of many philosophers. With Plato and Kant you will study the nature of right and wrong; with Hobbes and John Stuart Mill you will consider the relation of the individual to society and the state; you will find various interpretations of art, science, and religion, and their significance for human endeavor. Berkeley's and Hume's investigations into the nature of knowledge will provide plenty of food for thought.

You may be disappointed to find that there is much less agreement among philosophers than among scholars in other disciplines. Even on the subject of what constitutes philosophy itself, there are basic differences of opinion. Each school of philosophy has its own conception of what philosophy is and how it should be practiced. In this chapter we will consider a few of the many different points of view.

The Platonic-Aristotelian Tradition

The goal of philosophy, for Plato, is the attainment of wisdom through a vision of the absolute ideas: *beauty, truth, piety, justice*, etc. Because of his notion that the body, with its passions and earthly desires, is a constant

1

hindrance to the philosopher in the pursuit of his goal, Plato distinguishes sharply the life of contemplation (pure thought) from the active life (in which the body plays the leading role). How does the philosopher go about searching for wisdom? Plato's answer is that one must try to escape from the sensuous limitations of the body. Socrates even says (or Plato makes him say) that the true philosopher will not only accept death with equanimity, but welcome it as the final liberation of the soul from the body (*Phaedo*).

Some would argue that this is only *one* of Plato's answers. They think it possible to detach this other-worldliness from the rest of Plato's thought and to interpret the attainment of wisdom as a process of discovery and clarification of ideas by the methods of discussion and analysis. An adequate treatment of Plato's theory of knowledge and wisdom, however, would soon become involved in his doctrine of *ideas*—those forms or eternal archetypes which are, according to Plato, a necessary ingredient in all knowledge. These forms, or universals, have a life of their own, an ontological being which transcends the world of sensible experience.[1] They are the realities of which the things we see and hear and touch are only images or imperfect copies. Human knowledge here and now is only a stepping-stone to the apprehension of these absolute realities in and for themselves (*Symposium*). And the soul can only reach those pure and immutable forms, which shine by the light of The Good, if it turns its back on "the twilight of becoming and perishing" (*Republic*, VI). The interpreter of Plato would again be confronted by two distinct and separated realms—the temporal world of change in which our bodies move, and the realm of absolute and timeless forms beckoning those who would become true philosophers, that is, lovers of wisdom.

Though Aristotle criticizes the ontological separation of the two realms, he too establishes a dichotomy between theoretical and practical knowledge, and subordinates the latter to the former:

> It is right also that philosophy should be called knowledge of the truth. For the end of theoretical knowledge is truth, while that of practical knowledge is action (for even if they consider how things are, practical men do not study the eternal, but what is relative and in the present).[2]

According to Aristotle, philosophy had its origin when men began to wonder about the world and tried to explain its phenomena. They did this to escape from ignorance; and since their aim was knowledge, he says that the pursuit of philosophy was not for a utilitarian end. This is confirmed by the

---

[1] Thus, Socrates wants Euthyphro (selection 2.1) to tell him what makes all pious acts pious. Socrates says: "Tell me what is the nature of this form, and then I shall have a standard to which I may look, and by which I may measure actions, whether yours or those of anyone else, and then I shall be able to say that such and such an action is pious, such another impious."

[2] Aristotle, *Metaphysics*, Book *a*.

fact that it was only after most of the necessities of life had been secured that this knowledge began to be sought. A man who is hungry or who cannot find a place to live in peace will find it difficult to philosophize. Philosophy is not desired for any advantage other than that of knowledge itself,[3] and it is Aristotle's view that it alone exists for its own sake. As William James's essay, "Philosophy and Its Critics," (selection 1.1) makes clear, in Aristotle's day, when philosophy was not separated from such sciences as physics and biology, the observations and speculations which constituted knowledge in these fields were considered as belonging to philosophy. Although Aristotle says that it is the function of the philosopher to investigate all things, he tends to think of philosophy as a fundamental science, in which man, using his own powers of thought, attempts to discern the nature of being, substance, unity, plurality, causality, change, and other such theoretical notions which are basic to the other sciences. In this investigation the extent of his knowledge is limited only by the powers of his own rational faculty.

The views of Plato and Aristotle on philosophy have had an incomparable influence on human thought for over two thousand years. Their conception of philosophy has shaped the dominant tradition of western thought and their influence continues to manifest itself in the work of contemporary philosophers. However, the traditional view of philosophy has not remained unchallenged. Discussed below are the three principal challenges: the pragmatists, who challenge the position that philosophy is an abstract and theoretical science; the Thomists, who revised the doctrine that philosophy is an autonomous discipline; and the analytic school, which rejects the notion that the aim of philosophy is to construct a system of "philosophical" truths about a special subject matter.

The Pragmatic Conception

The notion of philosophy as a theoretical science whose goal is the discovery of eternal truths and whose function is to satisfy a natural intellectual curiosity has been challenged by critics with different points of view and for a variety of reasons. It was to be expected that the steady progress of science side by side with the apparent stagnancy and unending conflicts in philosophy should sooner or later lead to a reconsideration of the goal and function of philosophy. This change in our conception of philosophy can be traced back to David Hume, who showed that there are good grounds for doubting the validity of any of the so-called eternal truths or laws of nature which philosophers had been discovering. Kant tried to circumvent Hume's arguments by developing what he called "critical philosophy." Idealistic philosophers subsequent to Kant took their cue from him and it was not until the end of the nineteenth century that the importance of Hume's arguments was

---

[3] Contrast this with Francis Bacon's view that knowledge is power.

fully realized, when his position was further developed by the positivists and the pragmatists.

Pragmatism, as originally conceived by Peirce (see selection 2.5), is a method of determining the *meaning* of ideas and of clarifying them. Even William James, who radically altered the doctrine by shifting the emphasis from logic to psychology, refers to it as a method of settling philosophical disputes. However, James expanded pragmatism until it embraced a theory of truth and metaphysics.

> Grant an idea or belief to be true . . . what concrete difference will its being true make in any one's actual life? What experiences will be different from those which would obtain if the belief were false? What, in short, is the truth's cash-value in experiential terms?

In another place he says: "The true is only the expedient in the way of our thinking." And again:

> But if you follow the pragmatic method . . . you must bring out of each word its practical cash value, set it at work within the stream of your experience. It appears less as a solution then, than as a program for more work, and more particularly as an indication of the ways in which existing realities may be *changed. Theories thus become instruments, not answers to enigmas, in which we can rest.*[4]

James is combating the traditional conception by maintaining that philosophy is a practical venture, not a theoretical science. He has redefined "truth" so that it no longer signifies something independent of human thought which it is the goal of philosophy to discover. For him, the goal of philosophy is the transformation of existing realities.

Though the pragmatism of William James had many loose ends and vulnerable points which critics lost no time in attacking, it had a vitality which could not be argued away; there were many followers and pragmatism soon became a movement. The doctrine has been modified many times since its beginnings over ninety years ago, each new exponent presenting his own ver-

---

[4] All quotations from William James, *Pragmatism*, 1907, italics in original. The view expressed by James in the above quotation has been compared with the following from Karl Marx:

"The question whether objective truth can be attributed to human thinking is not a question of theory but is a practical question. . . . The philosophers have only *interpreted* the world in various ways; the point however is to *change* it." (*Theses on Feuerbach*, 1845.)

There is, indeed, a striking similarity here; but there is also a difference. James was interested in clarifying ideas, molding them to suit human purposes and to serve the end of human satisfaction. Under the fire of criticism he explained that in saying that truths should have *practical* consequences, he did not mean to restrict consequences to those which were physical, but to count mental effects as well. Thus, in saying that a philosophy, to be significant, must ensue in action, he at least sometimes included reflection as a mode of action. The *action* that Marx was interested in, on the other hand, was political and social action, directed toward specified goals; and he proposed to convert philosophy into an instrument for the attainment of these goals.

sion of its main themes. But one fundamental idea running through all versions is the stress on the intimate relation between theory and practice. The conception of philosophy as a theoretical enterprise which can be engaged in and understood without reference to the vicissitudes of time and place is constantly under attack by the pragmatists.

From the beginning of the century until his death in 1951, John Dewey developed the philosophy of pragmatism, eliminating many of its early weaknesses and enlarging its scope. Freeing himself from the early identification by pragmatism of the *true* with the *useful* or the *personally satisfying*, which occasioned so much criticism of James's doctrines, Dewey arrived at a view much closer to the original pragmatism of Peirce, which is a theory of meaning. The consequences of this theory for the interpretation of philosophy are shown in the following quotation:

> A first-rate test of the value of any philosophy which is offered to us is this: Does it end in conclusions which, when they are referred back to ordinary life-experiences and their predicaments, render them more significant, more luminous to us, and make our dealings with them more fruitful? [5]

Dewey's conception of philosophy is that it is one phase of the history of culture; and that philosophers, present as well as past, however much they may strive to attain objectivity and to discover ultimate truth, cannot help reflecting a certain climate of opinion—the cultural milieu of their times. Dewey considers it a mistake, in interpreting the history of philosophy, to *dwell* on the question of the truth of doctrines. The main questions for him are:

> What are the cultural conditions, social, political, artistic, economic, which set the problems for the philosopher and influenced his thinking on them?

and,

> What alterations, if any, in the stream of culture were effected by the contributions of the philosopher?

If this sounds more like a theory concerning the role of philosophy in the history of civilization than a conception of the nature of philosophy itself, Dewey's answer is that

> there is no specifiable difference between philosophy and its role in the history of civilization. Discover and define some characteristic, some unique function in civilization, and you have defined philosophy itself.

It is worth noticing that here Dewey is not saying merely that philosophy is closely interrelated with other aspects of civilization and that its history cannot fruitfully be interpreted when treated in isolation from the cultural flux in which it arose. He is saying more. In the above quotation he is expressing the view that there is not one identifiable feature of civilization

---

[5] John Dewey, *Experience and Nature*.

called "philosophy," which can be distinguished from other characteristics of civilization—from which it would follow that, for Dewey, there are no problems of philosophy peculiarly its own.

Dewey is challenging not only the traditional conception of philosophy as theoretical knowledge; he is also challenging the *substantive* conception of philosophy as a specialized discipline with a distinctive subject matter.

The Thomistic Conception

Plato and Aristotle think of the philosopher as one who uses his reason to investigate the most sublime subjects. In this investigation, the conclusion is something to be discovered; the philosopher is not obliged to conform to dogmas of any sort. He is a servant of the truth and of nothing else. But to the Christian philosopher another element enters the picture—revealed truth. This truth is handed down to all men by God. But what if revealed truth and truth attainable by reason are opposed to each other? The answer is that they cannot be in conflict, since reason itself has its source in God.

There are revealed truths which are beyond the reach of "natural reason." By embracing these truths, the Christian philosopher believes he is possessed of truths that are unavailable to one who relies on reason alone. Revealed truths also include truths that are not beyond the capability of human reason to discover for itself. This gives the Christian philosopher two advantages. First, those who are too young or too busy to devote themselves to the study of metaphysics can be taught the revealed truths at an early age; no need to rely on metaphysicians, some of whom have even disputed the validity of revealed truths. Second, when philosophers claim to discover or rationally demonstrate certain truths, their results can be measured against the revealed truths. Needless to say, any discrepancy would have to be settled in favor of revelation.

As Gilson points out, the reason Descartes' *Discourse on Method* is still prohibited reading for Catholics is that he believed in the separation of philosophy and theology. The Thomistic position is that there can be no autonymous discipline of philosophy. The correct and proper way to philosophize, as practiced by St. Thomas and described by Pope Leo XIII is "to unite obedience to the Christian faith, to the study of philosophy."

In summarizing his position, Gilson says that "the Christian way of philosophizing protects philosophical research against the risks of error and the evil of useless dispersion," while "it in no way deprives it of its necessary freedom of investigation."

The Analytic Conception

With regard to the subject matter of philosophy, several positions can be taken. It can be said, and has been, first, that the subject matter of philosophy is the same as that of the sciences, or secondly, that the subject matter of philosophy is different from that of the sciences. A third position would be that philosophy has no special subject matter of its own—but that anything can be investigated philosophically. It is this last view, which may be called the adverbial conception of philosophy as opposed to the first two views, which are substantive, that we wish to consider now.

This doctrine takes many forms. Indeed, the pragmatic conception found in the philosophy of Peirce is one of them. A similar view is expressed by Whitehead, when he says: "No one truth, thoroughly understood in all the infinitude of its bearings, is more or less philosophical than any other truth." But the most radical form of this doctrine concerning the nature of philosophy is to be found among the analytic philosophers and the logical positivists. We have chosen a selection from Waismann's *Principles of Linguistic Philosophy*. Waismann was a friend and follower of Wittgenstein [6] and also a member of the Vienna Circle (the womb of logical positivism in the 1920s). Wittgenstein held that the metaphysical statements of the philosopher were often expressions of a deep-seated puzzlement. By developing the puzzle, Wittgenstein hoped to explain the purpose or the use, that is, the meaning of the metaphysical statements. The logical positivists, on the other hand, held that the problems of the metaphysician were pseudo-problems and that his statements were literally meaningless. Carnap, speaking for the positivists, advocated the "elimination" of metaphysics, a remedy which, from the point of view of Wittgenstein and Waismann, was tantamount to throwing the baby out with the bath water.

The taunt against philosophy that it is concerned with the same old insoluble problems is no longer valid. Progress in philosophy may be slower than in science; but there is progress. Sometimes such progress must wait for advances in logical and scientific techniques, which have proved useful in helping to solve many of the problems of philosophy. This has happened, for example, in those fields where concepts like infinity, continuity, space, time, and number have played a key role.

But the enterprise of philosophy cannot be evaluated solely in terms of solutions given to various problems. Since the content of human knowledge as achieved by the sciences at any period in history is bound to be fragmentary, and since man's intellectual curiosity outstrips his knowledge, he will construct hypotheses concerning the relations of the sciences, for example, biology and physics, psychology and medicine, the natural sciences and the social sciences; he will try to show the relevance of such knowledge as can be acquired, to human values and the ends of life; and he will try, by insight and analysis, to extend and deepen human understanding in fields

---

[6] Perhaps no other philosopher has had such a profound influence on contemporary Western thought.

as yet uncharted. Beginning at the last bastion conquered by the scientists, the philosopher will make his guesses at the riddle, perchance presenting the starting point in the creation of new sciences. This is what is known as speculative philosophy.

There has been considerable debate among philosophers concerning the value and significance of speculative philosophy. At its worst it has been an undisciplined wandering of the philosopher's fancy through worlds of his own creation which have little, if any, relevance to anything actual or even possible. At its best speculative philosophy can push back our intellectual horizons, revealing unsuspected possibilities which lend new meanings to our old ideas.

There is one duty to his readers and to himself which the speculative philosopher has not always fulfilled. He should acknowledge frankly the speculative character of his venture and not advance claims that he has by superior insight or special revelations obtained an exclusive preview of the Ultimate Truth.

There are other views of the nature of philosophy [7] besides those presented here. For, as we have already mentioned, every type of philosophy has its own unique conception of philosophy. Naturalists,[8] for example, hold that the aim of philosophy is to understand and explain the nature of the world and of man by the methods of hypothesis, observation, and experimentation which have already proved so fruitful in the natural sciences. But a Bergsonian would say that one who thus restricts himself to the methods of science can never truly understand nature.[9] The philosopher, he believes, must strive for insights into reality which spring from sympathy and appreciation. Philosophy, according to this view, should be based primarily on feeling, rather than on reason or intellect. By others, Santayana for example, philosophy has been understood in another sense—as a personal expression of one's reactions to the world and of his reflections on the value of art, science, and religion in achieving whatever happiness is possible for man. Conceived in this sense, a philosophical system is an aesthetic creation and the categories of truth and falsehood are hardly applicable to it as a whole. Two such systems of philosophy may diverge and we may prefer one to another, without being compelled to reject either. They are not incompatible with one another any more than are different photographs of the same scene taken with different lenses and from different vantage points. Some of the so-called conflicts in philosophy don't need to be resolved because they are not really conflicts. Critics who ask: "Why can't philosophers agree?" might, in turn, be asked: "Why is agreement desirable in philosophy?" What such critics overlook is that while agreement is desirable concerning questions of

---

[7] For the existentialist point of view, see Sartre, selection 9.7.

[8] This includes pragmatists and positivists.

[9] Cf. the Bergson selection, 2.4.

fact, provided that such agreement has been reached as the result of free discussion and experimentation, in philosophy agreement might betoken nothing so much as a paucity of philosophical ideas. And where, in the past and in our own day, doctrinal uniformity has been achieved by the imposition of authority, philosophy has degenerated, becoming little more than textual exposition, and philosophers have produced few, if any, important ideas.

If the structure of the universe were revealed all at once and in all its aspects to all men in the same way, we might be expected to share a single all-inclusive philosophy. Or perhaps, since in such a world there would be no room for ignorance, there would also be no philosophy (see Whitehead, selection 1.3). The variety of philosophical systems is due, in part, to the inexhaustibility of knowledge and to the necessarily partial viewpoint of any one philosopher or generation of philosophers. Such variety, far from signifying a sad state of affairs needing correction, as some are suggesting today, is only a natural and desirable consequence of the subtlety of nature, and of freedom of the mind and fertility of the imagination—the fountainhead of all genuine philosophy.

William James (1842-1910)

1.1   Philosophy and Its Critics

The progress of society is due to the fact that individuals vary from the human average in all sorts of directions, and that the originality is often so attractive or useful that they are recognized by their tribe as leaders, and become objects of envy or admiration, and setters of new ideals.

Among the variations, every generation of men produces some individuals exceptionally preoccupied with theory. Such men find matter for puzzle and astonishment where no one else does. Their imagination invents explanations and combines them. They store up the learning of their time, utter prophecies and warnings, and are regarded as sages. Philosophy, etymologically meaning the love of wisdom, is the work of this class of minds, regarded with an indulgent relish, if not with admiration, even by those who do not understand them or believe much in the truth which they proclaim.

Philosophy, thus become a race-heritage, forms in its totality a monstrously unwieldy mass of learning. So taken, there is no reason why any special science like chemistry or astronomy should be excluded from it.

From *Some Problems of Philosophy* (New York: David McKay Co., Inc., 1911).

By common consent, however, special sciences are today excluded, for reasons presently to be explained; and what remains is manageable enough to be taught under the name of philosophy by one man if his interests be broad enough.

If this were a German textbook I should first give my abstract definition of the topic, thus limited by usage, then proceed to display its *"Begriff und Einteilung,"* and its *"Aufgabe und Methode."* But as such displays are usually unintelligible to beginners, and unnecessary after reading the book, it will conduce to brevity to omit that chapter altogether, useful though it might possibly be to more advanced readers as a summary of what is to follow.

I will tarry a moment, however, over the matter of definition. Limited by the omission of the special sciences, the name of philosophy has come more and more to denote ideas of universal scope exclusively. The principles of explanation that underlie all things without exception, the elements common to gods and men and animals and stones, the first *whence* and the last *whither* of the whole cosmic procession, the conditions of all knowing, and the most general rules of human action—

these furnish the problems commonly deemed philosophic *par excellence;* and the philosopher is the man who finds the most to say about them. Philosophy is defined in the usual scholastic textbooks as "the knowledge of things in general by their ultimate causes, so far as natural reason can attain to such knowledge." This means that explanation of the universe at large, not description of its details, is what philosophy must aim at; and so it happens that a view of anything is termed philosophic just in proportion as it is broad and connected with other views, and as it uses principles not proximate, or intermediate, but ultimate and all-embracing, to justify itself. Any very sweeping view of the world is a philosophy in this sense, even though it may be a vague one. It is a *Weltanschauung,* an intellectualized attitude towards life. Professor Dewey well describes the constitution of all the philosophies that actually exist, when he says that philosophy expresses a certain attitude, purpose, and temper of conjoined intellect and will, rather than a discipline whose boundaries can be neatly marked off.[1]

To know the chief rival attitudes towards life, as the history of human thinking has developed them, and to have heard some of the reasons they can give for themselves, ought to be considered an essential part of liberal education. Philosophy, indeed, in one sense of the term is only a compendious name for the spirit in education which the word "college" stands for in America. Things can be taught in dry dogmatic ways or in a philosophic

way. At a technical school a man may grow into a first-rate instrument for doing a certain job, but he may miss all the graciousness of mind suggested by the term liberal culture. He may remain a cad and not a gentleman, intellectually pinned down to his one narrow subject, literal, unable to suppose anything different from what he has seen, without imagination, atmosphere, or mental perspective.

Philosophy, beginning in wonder, as Plato and Aristotle said, is able to fancy everything different from what it is. It sees the familiar as if it were strange, and the strange as if it were familiar. It can take things up and lay them down again. Its mind is full of air that plays round every subject. It rouses us from our native dogmatic slumber and breaks up our caked prejudices. Historically it has always been a sort of fecundation of four different human interests—science, poetry, religion, and logic—by one another. It has sought by hard reasoning for results emotionally valuable. To have some contact with it, to catch its influence, is thus good for both literary and scientific students. By its poetry it appeals to literary minds; but its logic stiffens them up and remedies their softness. By its logic it appeals to the scientific; but softens them by its other aspects, and saves them from too dry a technicality. Both types of student ought to get from philosophy a livelier spirit, more air, more mental background. "Hast any philosophy in thee, Shepherd?"—this question of Touchstone's is the one with which men should always meet one another. A man with no philosophy in him is the most inauspicious and unprofitable of all possible social mates.

I say nothing in all this of what

---

[1] Compare the article "Philosophy" in Baldwin's *Dictionary of Philosophy and Psychology.*

may be called the gymnastic use of philosophic study, the purely intellectual power gained by defining the high and abstract concepts of the philosopher and discriminating between them.

In spite of the advantages thus enumerated, the study of philosophy has systematic enemies, and they were never as numerous as at the present day. The definite conquests of science and the apparent indefiniteness of philosophy's results partly account for this; to say nothing of man's native rudeness of mind, which maliciously enjoys deriding long words and abstractions. "Scholastic jargon," "medieval dialectics," are for many people synonyms of the word philosophy. With his obscure and uncertain speculations as to the intimate nature and causes of things, the philosopher is likened to a "blind man in a dark room looking for a black cat that is not there." His occupation is described as the art of "endlessly disputing without coming to any conclusion," or more contemptuously still as the *"systematische Missbrauch einer eben zu diesem Zwecke erfundenen Terminologie"* ["systematic misuse of a special terminology invented for this very purpose"].

Only to a very limited degree is this sort of hostility reasonable. I will take up some of the current objections in successive order, since to reply to them will be a convenient way of entering into the interior of our subject.

Objection 1. Whereas the sciences make steady progress and yield applications of matchless utility, philosophy makes no progress and has no practical applications.

Reply. The opposition is unjustly founded, for the sciences are them-selves branches of the tree of philosophy. As fast as questions got accurately answered, the answers were called "scientific," and what men call "philosophy" today is but the residuum of questions still unanswered. At this very moment we are seeing two sciences, psychology and general biology, drop off from the parent trunk and take independent root as specialties. The more general philosophy cannot as a rule follow the voluminous details of any special science.

A backward glance at the evolution of philosophy will reward us here. The earliest philosophers in every land were encyclopedic sages, lovers of wisdom, sometimes with and sometimes without a dominantly ethical or religious interest. They were just men curious beyond immediate practical needs, and no particular problems, but rather the problematic generally, was their specialty. China, Persia, Egypt, India had such wise men, but those of Greece are the only sages who until very recently have influenced the course of western thinking. The earlier Greek philosophy lasted, roughly speaking, for about two hundred and fifty years, say from 600 B.C. onwards. Such men as Thales, Heraclitus, Pythagoras, Parmenides, Anaxagoras, Empedocles, Democritus were mathematicians, theologians, politicians, astronomers, and physicists. All the learning of their time, such as it was, was at their disposal. Plato and Aristotle continued their tradition, and the great medieval philosophers only enlarged its field of application. If we turn to Saint Thomas Aquinas' great *Summa,* written in the thirteenth century, we find opinions expressed about literally everything, from God down to matter, with angels, men, and demons taken in on the way. The relations of almost everything with everything else, of the creator with his creatures, of the knower with the known, substances with forms, of mind with body, of sin with salvation, come successively up for treatment. A theology, a psychology, a system of duties and morals, are given in fullest detail, while physics and logic are established in their universal principles. The impression made on the reader is of almost superhuman intellectual resources. It is true that Saint Thomas' method of handling the mass of fact, or supposed fact, which he treated, was different from that to which we are accustomed. He deduced and proved everything, either from fixed principles of reason, or from holy Scripture. The properties and changes of bodies, for example, were explained by the two principles of matter and form, as Aristotle had taught. Matter was the quantitative, determinable, passive element; form the qualitative, unifying, determining, and active principle. All activity was for an end. Things could act on each other only when in contact. The number of species of things was determinate, and their differences discrete, etc., etc.[2]

By the beginning of the seventeenth century, men were tired of the elaborate *a priori* methods of scholasticism. Suarez's treatises availed not to keep them in fashion. But the new philosophy of Descartes, which displaced the scholastic teaching, sweeping over Europe like wildfire,

----

2 J. Rickaby's *General Metaphysics* (New York: David McKay Co., Inc.) gives a popular account of the essentials of St. Thomas' philosophy of nature. Thomas J. Harper's *Metaphysics of the School* (New York: The Macmillan Company) goes into minute detail.

preserved the same encyclopedic character. We think of Descartes nowadays as the metaphysician who said "*Cogito, ergo sum,*" separated mind from matter as two contrasted substances, and gave a renovated proof of God's existence. But his contemporaries thought of him much more as we think of Herbert Spencer in our day, as a great cosmic evolutionist who explained, by "the redistribution of matter and motion," and the laws of impact, the rotations of the heavens, the circulation of the blood, the refraction of light, apparatus of vision and of nervous action, the passions of the soul, and the connection of the mind and body.

Descartes died in 1650. With Locke's *Essay Concerning Human Understanding,* published in 1690, philosophy for the first time turned more exclusively to the problem of knowledge, and became "critical." This subjective tendency developed; and although the school of Leibnitz, who was the pattern of a universal sage, still kept up the more universal tradition—Leibnitz's follower Wolff published systematic treatises on everything, physical as well as moral. Hume, who succeeded Locke, woke Kant "from his dogmatic slumber," and since Kant's time the word "philosophy" has come to stand for mental and moral speculations far more than for physical theories. Until a comparatively recent time, philosophy was taught in our colleges under the name of "mental and moral philosophy," or "philosophy of the human mind," exclusively, to distinguish it from "natural philosophy."

But the older tradition is the better as well as the completer one. To know the actual peculiarities of the world we are born into is surely as important as to know what makes worlds any-how abstractly possible. Yet this latter knowledge has been treated by many since Kant's time as the only knowl-edge worthy of being called philo-sophical. Common men feel the ques-tion "What is Nature like?" to be as meritorious as the Kantian question "How is Nature possible?" So philos-ophy, in order not to lose human re-spect, must take some notice of the actual constitution of reality. There are signs to-day of a return to the more objective tradition.[3]

Philosophy in the full sense is only *man thinking*, thinking about gener-alities rather than about particulars. But whether about generalities or particulars, man thinks always by the same methods. He observes, discrimi-nates, generalizes, classifies, looks for causes, traces analogies, and makes hypotheses. Philosophy, taken as some-thing distinct from science or from practical affairs, follows no method peculiar to itself. All our thinking to-day has evolved gradually out of primitive human thought, and the only really important changes that have come over its manner (as distinguished from the matters in which it believes) are a greater hesitancy in asserting its convictions, and the habit of seek-ing verification [4] for them whenever it can.

It will be instructive to trace very briefly the origins of our present habits of thought.

Auguste Comte, the founder of a philosophy which he called "posi-tive," [5] said that human theory on any subject always took these forms in succession. In the theological stage of theorizing, phenomena are ex-plained by spirits producing them; in the metaphysical stage, their essential feature is made into an abstract idea, and this is placed behind them as if it were an explanation; in the positive stage, phenomena are simply de-scribed as to their coexistences and successions. Their "laws" are formu-lated, but no explanation of their na-tures or existence is sought after. Thus a *"spiritus rector"* would be a theo-logical—a "principle of attraction" a metaphysical—and "a law of the squares" would be a positive theory of the planetary movements.

Comte's account is too sharp and definite. Anthropology shows that the earliest attempts at human theorizing mixed the theological and metaphys-ical together. Common things needed no special explanation; remarkable things alone, odd things, especially deaths, calamities, diseases, called for it. What made things act was the mys-terious energy in them, and the more awful they were, the more of this *mana* they possessed. The great thing was to acquire *mana* oneself. "Sympathetic magic" is the collective name for what seems to have been the primitive phi-losophy here. You could act on any-thing by controlling anything else that either was associated with it or resembled it. If you wished to injure an enemy, you should either make an image of him, or get some of his hair or other belongings, or get his name written. Injuring the substitute, you thus made him suffer correspondingly. If you wished the rain to come, you

---

[3] For an excellent defense of it I refer my readers to Paulsen's *Introduction to Phi-losophy* (translated by Thilly), 1895, pp. 19-44.

[4] Compare G. H. Lewes, *Aristotle*, 1864, Chap. 4.

[5] *Cours de philosophie positive*, 6 vols., Paris, 1830-1842.

sprinkled the ground, if the wind, you whistled, etc. If you would have yams grow well in your garden, put a stone there that looks like a yam. Would you cure jaundice, give tumeric, that makes things look yellow; or give poppies for troubles of the head, because their seed vessels form a "head." This "doctrine of signatures" played a great part in early medicine. The various "-mancies" and "-mantics" come in here, in which witchcraft and incipient science are indistinguishably mixed. "Sympathetic" theorizing persists to the present day. "Thoughts are things" for a contemporary school—and on the whole a good school—of practical philosophy. Cultivate the thought of what you desire, affirm it, and it will bring all similar thoughts from elsewhere to reinforce it, so that finally your wish will be fulfilled.

Little by little, more positive ways of considering things began to prevail. Common elements in phenomena began to be singled out and to form the basis of generalizations. But these elements at first had necessarily to be the more dramatic or humanly interesting ones. The hot, the cold, the wet, the dry in things explained their behavior. Some bodies were naturally warm, others cold. Motions were natural or violent. The heavens moved in circles because circular motion was the most perfect. The lever was explained by the greater quantity of perfection embodied in the movement of its longer arm. The sun went south in winter to escape the cold. Precious or beautiful things had exceptional properties. Peacock's flesh resisted putrefaction. The lodestone would drop the iron which it held, if the superiorly powerful diamond was brought near, etc.

Such ideas sound to us grotesque, but imagine no tracks made for us by scientific ancestors, and what aspects would we single out from nature to understand things by? Not till the beginning of the seventeenth century did the more insipid kinds of regularity in things abstract men's attention away from the properties originally picked out. Few of us realize how short the career of what we know as "science" has been. Three hundred and fifty years ago hardly anyone believed in the Copernican planetary theory. Optical combinations were not discovered. The circulation of the blood, the weight of air, the conduction of heat, the laws of motion were unknown; the common pump was inexplicable; there were no clocks; no thermometers; no general gravitation; the world was five thousand years old; spirits moved the planets; alchemy, magic, astrology, imposed on everyone's belief. Modern science began only after 1600, with Kepler, Galileo, Descartes, Torricelli, Pascal, Harvey, Newton, Huygens, and Boyle. Five men telling one another in succession the discoveries which their lives had witnessed, could deliver the whole of it into our hands: Harvey might have told Newton, who might have told Voltaire; Voltaire might have told Dalton, who might have told Huxley, who might have told the readers of this book.

The men who began this work of emancipation were philosophers in the original sense of the word, universal sages. Galileo said that he had spent more years on philosophy than months on mathematics. Descartes was a universal philosopher in the fullest sense of the term. But the fertility of the newer conceptions made special departments of truth grow at such a rate that they became too unwieldy with details for the more universal minds to carry them, so the special sciences of mechanics, astronomy, and physics began to drop off from the parent stem.

No one could have foreseen in advance the extraordinary fertility of the more insipid mathematical aspects which these geniuses ferreted out. No one could have dreamed of the control over nature which the search for their concomitant variations would give. "Laws" describe these variations; and all our present laws of nature have as their model the proportionality of v to t, and of s to t^2 which Galileo first laid bare. Pascal's discovery of the proportionality of altitude to barometric height, Newton's of acceleration to distance, Boyle's of air-volume to pressure, Descartes' of sine to cosine in the refracted ray, were the first fruits of Galileo's discovery. There was no question of agencies, nothing animistic or sympathetic in this new way of taking nature. It was description only, of concomitant variations, after the particular quantities that varied had been successfully abstracted out. The result soon showed itself in a differentiation of human knowledge into two spheres, one called "Science," within which the more definite laws apply, the other "General Philosophy," in which they do not. The state of mind called positivistic is the result. "Down with philosophy!" is the cry of innumerable scientific minds. "Give us measurable facts only, phenomena, without the mind's additions, without entities or principles that pretend to explain." It is largely from this kind of mind that the objection that philosophy has made no progress, proceeds.

It is obvious enough that if every step forward which philosophy makes, every question to which an accurate answer is found, gets accredited to science the residuum of unanswered problems will alone remain to constitute the domain of philosophy, and will alone bear her name. In point of fact this is just what is happening. Philosophy has become a collective name for questions that have not yet been answered to the satisfaction of all by whom they have been asked. It does not follow, because some of these questions have waited two thousand years for an answer, that no answer will ever be forthcoming. Two thousand years probably measure but one paragraph in that great romance of adventure called the history of the intellect of man. The extraordinary progress of the last three hundred years is due to a rather sudden finding of the way in which a certain order of questions ought to be attacked, questions admitting of mathematical treatment. But to assume, therefore, that the only possible philosophy must be mechanical and mathematical, and to disparage all inquiry into the other sorts of questions, is to forget the extreme diversity of aspects under which reality undoubtedly exists. To the spiritual questions the proper avenues of philosophic approach will also undoubtedly be found. They have, to some extent, been found already. In some respects, indeed, "science" has made less progress than "philosophy"—its most general conceptions would astonish neither Aristotle nor Descartes, could they revisit our earth. The composition of things from elements, their evolution, the conservation of energy, the idea of a universal determinism, would seem to them commonplace enough—the little things, the microscopes, electric lights, telephones, and details of the sciences, would be to them the awe-inspiring things. But if they opened our books on metaphysics, or visited a philosophic lecture room, everything would sound strange. The whole idealistic or "critical" attitude of our time would be novel, and it would be long before they took in it.[6]

Objection 2. Philosophy is dogmatic, and pretends to settle things by pure reason, whereas the only fruitful mode of getting at truth is to appeal to concrete experience. Science collects, classifies, and analyzes facts, and thereby far outstrips philosophy.

Reply. This objection is historically valid. Too many philosophers have aimed at closed systems, established *a priori*, claiming infallibility, and to be accepted or rejected only as totals. The sciences on the other hand, using hypotheses only, but always seeking to verify them by experiment and observation, open a way for indefinite self-correction and increase. At the present day, it is getting more and more difficult for dogmatists claiming finality for their systems, to get a hearing in educated circles. Hypothesis and verification, the watchwords of science, have set the fashion too strongly in academic minds.

Since philosophers are only men thinking about things in the most comprehensive possible way, they can use any method whatsoever freely. Philosophy must, in any case, complete the sciences, and must incorporate their methods. One cannot see why, if such a policy should appear advisable, philosophy might not end

by forswearing all dogmatism whatever, and become as hypothetical in her manners as the most empirical science of them all.

Objection 3. Philosophy is out of touch with real life, for which it substitutes abstractions. The real world is various, tangled, painful. Philosophers have almost without exception, treated it as noble, simple, and perfect, ignoring the complexity of fact, and indulging in a sort of optimism that exposes their systems to the contempt of common men, and to the satire of such writers as Voltaire and Schopenhauer. The great popular success of Schopenhauer is due to the fact that, first among philosophers, he spoke the concrete truth about the ills of life.

Reply. This objection also is historically valid, but no reason appears why philosophy should keep aloof from reality permanently. Her manners may change as she successfully develops. The thin and noble abstractions may give way to more solid and real constructions, when the materials and methods for making such constructions shall be more and more securely ascertained. In the end philosophers may get into as close contact as realistic novelists with the facts of life.

In conclusion. In its original acceptation, meaning the completest knowledge of the universe, philosophy must include the results of all the sciences, and cannot be contrasted with the latter. It simply aims at making of science what Herbert Spencer calls a "system of completely unified knowledge."[7] In the more modern

---

[6] The reader will find all that I have said, and much more, set forth in an excellent article by James Ward in *Mind*, XV, 58: "The Progress of Philosophy."

[7] See the excellent chapter in Spencer's *First Principles* entitled "Philosophy Defined."

sense, of something contrasted with the sciences, philosophy means "metaphysics." The older sense is the more worthy sense, and as the results of the sciences get more available for co-ordination, and the conditions for finding truth in different kinds of questions get more methodically defined, we may hope that the term will revert to its original meaning. Science, metaphysics, and religion may then again form a single body of wisdom, and lend each other mutual support. At present this hope is far from its fulfillment.

QUESTIONS FOR DISCUSSION

1. James says that the study of philosophy has "systematic enemies" and that they were never as numerous as when he was writing (at the end of the 19th century). Why do you suppose the study of philosophy met so much opposition then? Are there enemies to the study of philosophy today? If so, who are they? If not, how and why have things changed?
2. Do you think the goals of philosophy today are the same as those of sciences like physics, biology, chemistry?
3. How does James reply to the objection that philosophy makes no progress while the sciences make many useful discoveries?
4. During the second half of the 20th century in this country, there has been an enormous increase in the number of teachers and students of philosophy in our colleges and universities. Textbooks and books of readings in philosophy both at the elementary and more advanced level are appearing in greater numbers each year. How do you account for this sudden quantum jump in the attention given to the study of philosophy?
5. The problems that interest most of us today, whether we are philosophy students or not, are generated by the existence of certain evils that we would like to eradicate. These include war, poverty, inequality resulting from discriminatory practices, unemployment, inflation, pollution of the environment, overpopulation. Many of these evils and the associated problems have been with us for a long time. Why do you suppose they have suddenly come to the forefront of public attention? The third objection to philosophy considered by James says: "Philosophy is out of touch with real life . . ." Do you think a study of philosophy can contribute to the solution of these problems, or should their consideration be left to scientists, economists, politicians?

Charlie Dunbar Broad (1887-)

1.2 What Is Speculative Philosophy?

It is certainly held to be the function of a philosopher to discuss the nature of Reality as a whole, and to consider the position and prospects of men in it. In a sense Critical Philosophy presupposes a certain view on this question. It assumes that our minds are so far in accord with the rest of Reality that by using them carefully and critically we approach nearer to the truth. But it is still clear that Speculative Philosophy presupposes a considerable amount of Critical Philosophy. Its business is to take over all aspects of human experience, to reflect upon them, and to try to think out a view of Reality as a whole which shall do justice to all of them. Now it is perfectly useless to take over the scientific, social, ethical, aesthetic, and religious experiences of mankind in their crude, unanalyzed form. We do not know what they mean or what weight to attach to various parts of the whole mass till we have submitted them to a critical analytic investigation. Two results follow at once from this consideration. (i) We cannot admit the claim of any system of Speculative Philosophy to be the final truth. The best of them will be guesses at truth, and will be subject to modification as more facts are known, and as known facts become more and more fully analyzed and criticized. (ii) We must always admit the possibility that Critical Philosophy has not yet been carried far enough to make any attempt at Speculative Philosophy profitable.

There is another general point which it seems important to notice. I think that, in different forms, it plays a vital part in such different philosophies as those of Mr. Bradley and M. Bergson, and in the thought of most great theologians, whether Christian or non-Christian. This is the question how far the discursive form of cognition by means of general concepts can ever be completely adequate to the concrete Reality which it seeks to describe. Thought must always be "about" its objects; to speak metaphorically, it is a transcription of the whole of Reality into a medium which is itself one aspect of Reality. We are bound to think of Reality as a complex of terms having various qualities and standing in various relations; because, if we do not think of it on these lines, we can-

From "Critical and Speculative Philosophy," in *Contemporary British Philosophy*, John H. Muirhead, ed. (New York: The Macmillan Company, 1924). Reprinted by permission of The Macmillan Company.

not think of it at all. With Mr. Bradley's attempt to show that this scheme
involves *internal* contradictions I do
not agree. But I do see clearly that
we have only to compare a tune, as
heard, or an emotion, as felt, with
any conceptual description which we
can give them, to recognize how inadequate every conceptual description of Reality must be to Reality itself. When we can *both* be acquainted
with something as a whole *and* can
analyze and describe it conceptually,
this difficulty is at its minimum. But
we cannot be acquainted with Reality as a whole, as we can with a tune
or an emotion, and therefore the difficulty is at a maximum in Speculative
Philosophy. This limitation of the
whole conceptual scheme is one which
we must simply recognize once and
for all and then ignore. We cannot
avoid it in detail, and we cannot understand in outline any other kind of
cognition. Since it is perfectly general, it applies equally to *every* system of Speculative Philosophy, and
therefore gives us no ground for preferring one to another.

It has been held by many philosophers, e.g., Spinoza and Hegel in the
past and Dr. McTaggart at present,
that important results about the structure of Reality as a whole can be
reached by deductive arguments from
self-evident premises. The best general account of such a view will be
found in Dr. McTaggart's *Nature of
Existence*. I do not think that this
view can be refuted; it *is* theoretically possible, so far as I can see. But
I am completely sceptical about its
practicability. I feel pretty certain that
all known attempts to elaborate a
system of Speculative Philosophy on
these lines either contain logical fallacies, or introduce premises which

are ambiguous and only become self-
evident when so interpreted as to be
trivial. And I have not the slightest
expectation that future essays in this
direction will be any more successful.

It seems to me that the main value
of Speculative Philosophy lies, not in
its conclusions, but in the collateral
effects which it has, or ought to have,
on the persons who pursue it. The
speculative philosopher is forced to
look at the world synoptically, and
anyone who does not do this at some
time in his life is bound to hold a
very narrow and inadequate idea of
Reality. This is a danger to which
the natural scientist is peculiarly liable. The extraordinary success of
physics and chemistry within their
own sphere tempts men to think that
the world is simply a physico-chemical
system. These sciences, quite rightly
for their own purposes, ignore the
existence of minds; and scientists are
liable to forget that somehow minds
have grown up in a world of matter,
and that it is by means of their activities that matter and its laws have
become known. If a man referred to
his brother or his cat as "an ingenious
mechanism" we should know that he
was either a fool or a physiologist. No
one in practice treats himself or his
fellow men or his pet animals as
machines, but scientists who have
never made a study of Speculative
Philosophy seem often to think it
their duty to hold in theory what no
one outside a lunatic asylum would
accept in practice. If we remember
that physics and chemistry are simply
constructed to unify the correlations
which we find among a selection of
the sensa of three or four senses, the
idea that these sciences give a complete account of the structure of all
Reality becomes ludicrous. Thus our

inability to explain the facts of life and mind in purely physico-chemical terms is not a paradox to be explained away, but is what might reasonably have been expected from the outset.

On the other hand, the man who starts from the side of mind is equally liable to fail to do justice to the facts. The properties with which physics and chemistry deal *are* very pervasive, and we *do* know them more accurately and thoroughly than we know anything else. And minds *are* very closely bound up with certain bits of matter, viz., our brains and nervous systems, and they *do* seem to have gradually developed in a world which once contained nothing but matter. The characteristic fault of Idealism is to be unable to see the trees for the wood, and the characteristic fault of Realism is to be unable to see the wood for the trees. The great merit of Idealism is that it really has tried to do justice to the social, ethical, aesthetic, and religious facts of the world. The great merit of Realism is that it really has tried to face in a patient and detailed way the problem of matter and of our perception of it. But neither of these activities is a substitute for the other, and a genuine Speculative Philosophy must combine the detailed study of the lower categories with the due recognition of the higher categories, and must try to reconcile the pervasiveness of the former with the apparently growing importance of the latter.

There is one thing which Speculative Philosophy must take into most serious consideration, and that is the religious and mystical experiences of mankind. These form a vast mass of facts which obviously deserve at least as careful attention as the sensations of mankind. They are, of course, less uniform than our sensations; many people, of whom I am one, are practically without these experiences. But probably most people have them to some extent, and there is a considerable amount of agreement between these people of all nations and ages, who have them to a marked degree. Of course, the theoretical interpretations which have been put upon them are very varied, and it is obvious that they depend largely on the traditions of the time, place, and society in which the experient lives. I have compared the experiences themselves with sensations; we might compare the common features in the interpretations which have been put upon them with our ordinary common-sense beliefs about matter; and elaborate systems of theology might be compared with big scientific theories, like the wave theory of light. Obviously there remains a further step to be taken, comparable with the philosophic criticism and interpretation of scientific theories about matter. It seems reasonable to suppose at the outset that the whole mass of mystical and religious experience brings us into contact with an aspect of Reality which is not revealed in ordinary sense-perception, and that any system of Speculative Philosophy which ignores it will be extremely one-sided. In fact it cannot safely be ignored. If we count all such experiences as purely delusive, we must explain how such a widespread and comparatively coherent mass of illusion arose. And, if we find it impossible to take this view, we must try to understand and criticize these experiences; to sift away those factors in them which are of merely local and temporary interest; and to see what the residuum has to tell us about the probable nature of

Reality. The great practical difficulty here is that those who have the experiences most vividly are seldom well fitted for the task of philosophical criticism and construction; whilst those who are fitted for the latter task are not often mystics or persons of religious genius. It is alleged, and it may well be true, that the capacity for such experiences can be cultivated by a suitable mode of life and a suitable system of training and meditation. In so far as this can be done without detriment to the critical faculties, it deserves the serious attention of philosophers; for theories which are built on experiences known only by description are always unsatisfactory.

QUESTIONS FOR DISCUSSION

1. What is the relation between critical philosophy and speculative philosophy?
2. Of what value is speculative philosophy?
3. Why, according to Broad, would it be one-sided on the part of philosophy to ignore the religious and mystical experience of mankind?

Alfred North Whitehead (1861-1947)

1.3   The Aim of Philosophy

The task of a University is the creation of the future, so far as rational thought, and civilized modes of appreciation, can affect the issue. The future is big with every possibility of achievement and of tragedy.

Amid this scene of creative action, What is the special function of philosophy?

In order to answer this question, we must first decide what constitutes

From *Modes of Thought* by Alfred North Whitehead. © 1938 by The Macmillan Company, renewed 1966 by T. North Whitehead. Reprinted by permission of The Macmillan Company.

the philosophic character of any particular doctrine. What makes a doctrine philosophical? No one truth, thoroughly understood in all the infinitude of its bearings, is more or less philosophical than any other truth. The pursuit of philosophy is the one avocation denied to omniscience.

Philosophy is an attitude of mind towards doctrines ignorantly entertained. By the phrase "ignorantly entertained" I mean that the full meaning of the doctrine in respect to the infinitude of circumstances to which it is relevant, is not understood. The philosophic attitude is a resolute attempt to enlarge the understanding of the scope of application of every notion which enters into our current thought. The philosophic attempt takes every word, and every phrase, in the verbal expression of thought, and asks, What does it mean? It refuses to be satisfied by the conventional presupposition that every sensible person knows the answer. As soon as you rest satisfied with primitive ideas, and with primitive propositions, you have ceased to be a philosopher.

Of course you have got to start somewhere for the purposes of discourse. But the philosopher, as he argues from his premises, has already marked down every word and phrase in them as topics for enquiry. No philosopher is satisfied with the concurrence of sensible people, whether they be his colleagues, or even his own previous self. He is always assaulting the boundaries of finitude.

The scientist is also enlarging knowledge. He starts with a group of primitive notions and of primitive relations between these notions, which defines the scope of his science. For example, Newtonian dynamics assumes Euclidean space, massive matter, motion, stresses and strains, and the more general notion of force. There are also the laws of motion, and a few other concepts added later. The sciences consisted in the deduction of consequences, presupposing the applicability of these ideas.

In respect to Newtonian Dynamics, the scientist and the philosopher face in opposite directions. The scientist asks for the consequences in the universe. The philosopher asks for the meaning of these ideas in terms of the welter of characterizations which infest the world.

It is evident that scientists and philosophers can help each other. For the scientist sometimes wants a new idea, and the philosopher is enlightened as to meanings by the study of the scientific consequences. Their usual mode of intercommunication is by sharing in the current habits of cultivated thought.

There is an insistent presupposition continually sterilizing philosophic thought. It is the belief, the very natural belief, that mankind has consciously entertained all the fundamental ideas which are applicable to its experience. Further, it is held that human language, in single words or in phrases, explicitly expresses these ideas. I will term this presupposition, The Fallacy of the Perfect Dictionary.

It is here that the philosopher, as such, parts company with the scholar. The scholar investigates human thought and human achievement, armed with a dictionary. He is the main support of civilized thought. Apart from scholarship, you may be moral, religious, and delightful. But you are not wholly civilized. You will lack the power of delicate accuracy of expression.

It is obvious that the philosopher needs scholarship, just as he needs science. But both science and scholarship are subsidiary weapons for philosophy.

The Fallacy of the Perfect Dictionary divides philosophers into two schools, namely, the "Critical School" which repudiates speculative philosophy, and the "Speculative School" which includes it. The critical school confines itself to verbal analysis within the limits of the dictionary. The speculative school appeals to direct insight, and endeavors to indicate its meanings by further appeal to situations which promote such specific insights. It then enlarges the dictionary. The divergence between the schools is the quarrel between safety and adventure.

The strength of the critical school lies in the fact that the doctrine of evolution never entered, in any radical sense, into ancient scholarship. Thus there arises the presupposition of a fixed specification of the human mind; and the blueprint of this specification is the dictionary.

I appeal to two great moments of philosophy. Socrates spent his life in analyzing the current presuppositions of the Athenian world. He explicitly recognized that his philosophy was an attitude in the face of ignorance. He was critical and yet constructive.

Harvard is justly proud of the great period of its philosophic department about thirty years ago. Josiah Royce, William James, Santayana, George Herbert Palmer, Münsterberg, constitute a group to be proud of. Among them Palmer's achievements center chiefly in literature and in his brilliance as a lecturer. The group is a group of men individually great. But as a group they are greater still. It is a group of adventure, of speculation, of search for new ideas. To be a philosopher is to make some humble approach to the main characteristic of this group of men.

The use of philosophy is to maintain an active novelty of fundamental ideas illuminating the social system. It reverses the slow descent of accepted thought towards the inactive commonplace. If you like to phrase it so, philosophy is mystical. For mysticism is direct insight into depths as yet unspoken. But the purpose of philosophy is to rationalize mysticism: not by explaining it away, but by the introduction of novel verbal characterizations, rationally co-ordinated.

Philosophy is akin to poetry, and both of them seek to express that ultimate good sense which we term civilization. In each case there is reference to form beyond the direct meaning of words. Poetry allies itself to meter, philosophy to mathematic pattern.

QUESTIONS FOR DISCUSSION

1. What makes a doctrine philosophical?
2. What is the fallacy of the perfect dictionary?
3. Compare the attitudes of the philosopher and the scientist.

Bertrand Russell (1872-1970)

1.4   The Value of Philosophy

Having now come to the end of our brief and very incomplete review of the problems of philosophy, it will be well to consider, in conclusion, what is the value of philosophy and why it ought to be studied. It is the more necessary to consider this question, in view of the fact that many men, under the influence of science or of practical affairs, are inclined to doubt whether philosophy is anything better than innocent but useless trifling, hair-splitting distinctions, and controversies on matters concerning which knowledge is impossible.

This view of philosophy appears to result, partly from a wrong conception of the ends of life, partly from a wrong conception of the kind of goods which philosophy strives to achieve. Physical science, through the medium of inventions, is useful to innumerable people who are wholly ignorant of it; thus the study of physical science is to be recommended, not only, or primarily, because of the effect on the student, but rather because of the effect on mankind in general. This utility does not belong to philosophy.

From *Problems of Philosophy* (London: Oxford University Press, 1912). Reprinted by permission of the Oxford University Press.

If the study of philosophy has any value at all for others than students of philosophy, it must be only indirectly, through its effects upon the lives of those who study it. It is in these effects, therefore, if anywhere, that the value of philosophy must be primarily sought.

But further, if we are not to fail in our endeavor to determine the value of philosophy, we must first free our minds from the prejudices of what are wrongly called "practical" men. The "practical" man, as this word is often used, is one who recognizes only material needs, who realizes that men must have food for the body, but is oblivious of the necessity of providing food for the mind. If all men were well off, if poverty and disease had been reduced to their lowest possible point, there would still remain much to be done to produce a valuable society; and even in the existing world the goods of the mind are at least as important as the goods of the body. It is exclusively among the goods of the mind that the value of philosophy is to be found; and only those who are not indifferent to these goods can be persuaded that the study of philosophy is not a waste of time.

Philosophy, like all other studies, aims primarily at knowledge. The knowledge it aims at is the kind of knowledge which gives unity and system to the body of the sciences, and the kind which results from a critical examination of the grounds of our convictions, prejudices, and beliefs. But it cannot be maintained that philosophy has had any very great measure of success in its attempts to provide definite answers to its questions. If you ask a mathematician, a mineralogist, a historian, or any other man of learning, what definite body of truths has been ascertained by his science, his answer will last as long as you are willing to listen. But if you put the same question to a philosopher, he will, if he is candid, have to confess that his study has not achieved positive results such as have been achieved by other sciences. It is true that this is partly accounted for by the fact that, as soon as definite knowledge concerning any subject becomes possible, this subject ceases to be called philosophy, and becomes a separate science. The whole study of the heavens, which now belongs to astronomy, was once included in philosophy; Newton's great work was called "the mathematical principles of natural philosophy." Similarly, the study of the human mind, which was, until very lately, a part of philosophy, has now been separated from philosophy and has become the science of psychology. Thus, to a great extent, the uncertainty of philosophy is more apparent than real: those questions which are already capable of definite answers are placed in the sciences, while those only to which, at present, no definite answer can be given, remain to form the residue which is called philosophy.

This is, however, only a part of the truth concerning the uncertainty of philosophy. There are many questions —and among them those that are of the profoundest interest to our spiritual life—which, so far as we can see, must remain insoluble to the human intellect unless its powers become of quite a different order from what they are now. Has the universe any unity of plan or purpose, or is it a fortuitous concourse of atoms? Is consciousness a permanent part of the universe, giving hope of indefinite growth in wisdom, or is it a transitory accident on a small planet on which life must ultimately become impossible? Are good and evil of importance to the universe or only to man? Such questions are asked by philosophy, and variously answered by various philosophers. But it would seem that, whether answers be otherwise discoverable or not, the answers suggested by philosophy are none of them demonstrably true. Yet, however slight may be the hope of discovering an answer, it is part of the business of philosophy to continue the consideration of such questions, to make us aware of their importance, to examine all the approaches to them, and to keep alive that speculative interest in the universe which is apt to be killed by confining ourselves to definitely ascertainable knowledge.

Many philosophers, it is true, have held that philosophy could establish the truth of certain answers to such fundamental questions. They have supposed that what is of most importance in religious beliefs could be proved by strict demonstrations to be true. In order to judge of such attempts, it is necessary to take a survey of human knowledge, and to form an opinion as to its methods and its limitations. On such a subject it would be unwise to pronounce dogmatically;

but if the investigations of our previous chapters have not led us astray, we shall be compelled to renounce the hope of finding philosophical proofs of religious beliefs. We cannot, therefore, include as part of the value of philosophy any definite set of answers to such questions. Hence, once more, the value of philosophy must not depend upon any supposed body of definitely ascertainable knowledge to be acquired by those who study it.

The value of philosophy is, in fact, to be sought largely in its very uncertainty. The man who has no tincture of philosophy goes through life imprisoned in the prejudices derived from common sense, from the habitual beliefs of his age or his nation, and from convictions which have grown up in his mind without the co-operation or consent of his deliberate reason. To such a man the world tends to become definite, finite, obvious; common objects rouse no questions, and unfamiliar possibilities are contemptuously rejected. As soon as we begin to philosophize, on the contrary, we find . . . that even the most everyday things lead to problems to which only very incomplete answers can be given. Philosophy, though unable to tell us with certainty what is the true answer to the doubts which it raises, is able to suggest many possibilities which enlarge our thoughts and free them from the tyranny of custom. Thus, while diminishing our feeling of certainty as to what things are, it greatly increases our knowledge as to what they may be; it removes the somewhat arrogant dogmatism of those who have never travelled into the region of liberating doubt, and it keeps alive our sense of wonder by showing familiar things in an unfamiliar aspect.

Apart from its utility in showing unsuspected possibilities, philosophy has a value—perhaps its chief value—through the greatness of the objects which it contemplates, and the freedom from narrow and personal aims resulting from this contemplation. The life of the instinctive man is shut up within the circle of his private interests: family and friends may be included, but the outer world is not regarded except as it may help or hinder what comes within the circle of instinctive wishes. In such a life there is something feverish and confined, in comparison with which the philosophic life is calm and free. The private world of instinctive interests is a small one, set in the midst of a great and powerful world which must, sooner or later, lay our private world in ruins. Unless we can so enlarge our interests as to include the whole outer world, we remain like a garrison in a beleaguered fortress, knowing that the enemy prevents escape and that ultimate surrender is inevitable. In such a life there is no peace, but a constant strife between the insistence of desire and the powerlessness of will. In one way or another, if our life is to be great and free, we must escape this prison and this strife.

One way of escape is by philosophic contemplation. Philosophic contemplation does not, in its widest survey, divide the universe into two hostile camps—friends and foes, helpful and hostile, good and bad—it views the whole impartially. Philosophic contemplation, when it is unalloyed, does not aim at proving that the rest of the universe is akin to man. All acquisition of knowledge is an enlargement of the Self, but this enlargement is best attained when it is not directly sought. It is obtained when the desire for knowledge is alone operative, by a study which does not wish in advance that its objects should have this or that character, but adapts the Self to the characters which it finds in its objects. This enlargement of Self is not obtained when, taking the Self as it is, we try to show that the world is so similar to this Self that knowledge of it is possible without any admission of what seems alien. The desire to prove this is a form of self-assertion, and like all self-assertion, it is an obstacle to the growth of Self which it desires, and of which the Self knows that it is capable. Self-assertion, in philosophic speculation as elsewhere, views the world as a means to its own ends; thus it makes the world of less account than Self, and the Self sets bounds to the greatness of its goods. In contemplation, on the contrary, we start from the not-Self, and through its greatness the boundaries of Self are enlarged; through the infinity of the universe the mind which contemplates it achieves some share in infinity.

For this reason greatness of soul is not fostered by those philosophies which assimilate the universe to Man. Knowledge is a form of union of Self and not-Self; like all union, it is impaired by dominion, and therefore by any attempt to force the universe into conformity with what we find in ourselves. There is a widespread philosophical tendency towards the view which tells us that man is the measure of all things, that truth is man-made, that space and time and the world of universals are properties of the mind, and that, if there be anything not created by the mind, it is unknowable and of no account for us. This view, if our previous discussions were correct, is untrue; but in addi-

tion to being untrue, it has the effect of robbing philosophic contemplation of all that gives it value, since it fetters contemplation to Self. What it calls knowledge is not a union with the not-Self, but a set of prejudices, habits, and desires, making an impenetrable veil between us and the world beyond. The man who finds pleasure in such a theory of knowledge is like the man who never leaves the domestic circle for fear his word might not be law.

The true philosophic contemplation, on the contrary, finds its satisfaction in every enlargement of the not-Self, in everything that magnifies the objects contemplated, and thereby the subject contemplating. Everything, in contemplation, that is personal or private, everything that depends upon habit, self-interest, or desire, distorts the object, and hence impairs the union which the intellect seeks. By thus making a barrier between subject and object, such personal and private things become a prison to the intellect. The free intellect will see as God might see, without a *here* and *now*, without hopes and fears, without the trammels of customary beliefs and traditional prejudices, calmly, dispassionately, in the sole and exclusive desire of knowledge—knowledge as impersonal, as purely contemplative, as it is possible for man to attain. Hence, also, the free intellect will value more the abstract and universal knowledge into which the accidents of private history do not enter, than the knowledge brought by the senses, and dependent, as such knowledge must be, upon an exclusive and personal point of view and a body whose sense-organs distort as much as they reveal.

The mind which has become accustomed to the freedom and impartiality of philosophic contemplation will preserve something of the same freedom and impartiality in the world of action and emotion. It will view its purposes and desires as parts of the whole, with the absence of insistence that results from seeing them as infinitesimal fragments in a world of which all the rest is unaffected by any one man's deeds. The impartiality which, in contemplation, is the unalloyed desire for truth, is the very same quality of mind which, in action, is justice, and in emotion is that universal love which can be given to all, and not only to those who are judged useful or admirable. Thus contemplation enlarges not only the objects of our thoughts, but also the objects of our actions and our affections: it makes us citizens of the universe, not only of one walled city at war with all the rest. In this citizenship of the universe consists man's true freedom, and his liberation from the thraldom of narrow hopes and fears.

Thus, to sum up our discussion of the value of philosophy: Philosophy is to be studied, not for the sake of any definite answers to its questions, since no definite answers can, as a rule, be known to be true, but rather for the sake of the questions themselves; because these questions enlarge our conception of what is possible, enrich our intellectual imagination, and diminish the dogmatic assurance which closes the mind against speculation; but above all because, through the greatness of the universe which philosophy contemplates, the mind also is rendered great, and becomes capable of that union with the universe which constitutes its highest good.

QUESTIONS FOR DISCUSSION

1. According to Bertrand Russell, what is the value of philosophy?
2. Compare Russell's view of the relation of philosophy to science with William James's view in selection 1.1.
3. Russell says: "If our life is to be great and free, we must escape this prison and this strife." Explain what he means by "this prison" and "this strife."
4. Explain what Russell means by the union of the self with the not-self.
5. What do you think Russell would say of the view that "man is the measure of all things"?

Etienne Gilson (1884-   )

1.5   What Is Christian Philosophy?

According to its etymology, the word "philosophy" means "the love of wisdom." As it used to be understood by the ancient Greeks, philosophy was less a doctrine or a knowledge than the pursuit of a certain doctrine or knowledge which, precisely, was wisdom. Each Greek philosopher entertained his own notion of wisdom; when several of them found themselves in general agreement about this notion, they were considered as constituting a philosophical school, such as that of Plato, of Aristotle and other ones. However deeply they might differ on secondary issues, all these schools agreed on the main characteristics of wisdom. They all considered it to be the supreme knowledge which, accessible only to men already possessed of the other sciences, enabled its owners to order and purify them, and to unify in its light the whole body of speculative and practical knowledge. Hence the now commonly received expression: the light of wisdom, and its traditional definition as the science of the first principles and of the first causes.

All love of wisdom so understood

is philosophy. There are, therefore, a great many different ways of philosophizing, and many of them are unrelated to Christianity. This simply is a fact. The whole body of Greek philosophical speculation, from the fourth century B.C. to the beginning of the Christian era, came too soon to be able to see the world in the light of the Christian revelation. In our own day, a great many men choose to philosophize, as they say, in the light of natural reason alone, unaided by any sort of religious belief or revelation. The ancient Greeks had no choice, so that problem does not arise in so far as they are concerned; today we do have a choice, and there is for us a problem that deserves to be investigated.

A

The attitude of the early Christians was naturally different according to their individual differences in personal temperament, in intellectual formation, and in philosophical learning. By and large, however, they seem to have agreed on three points.

First, Christianity was going to be their own philosophy, meaning thereby that, from that time onward, Christians would no longer have to worry about what, until then, the pagans had

From *A Gilson Reader* by Anton C. Pegis. © 1957 by Doubleday & Co., Inc. Reprinted by permission of Doubleday & Co., Inc.

called philosophy. In other words, had he been asked the question: Have you a philosophy? a Christian would then have answered: I do have a philosophy indeed! Its name is Christianity.[1]

To this answer it was sometimes objected that philosophy and religion are two entirely different things, since philosophy is the quest of wisdom in the light of human reason alone, whereas religion, particularly Christianity, rests upon the acceptance by faith of a divinely revealed truth. But there was a remarkable answer to the objection. It was that, in point of fact, on all the points covered in common by philosophy and by revelation, rationality stood on the side of revelation much more than on that of philosophy. A single God, creator of heaven and earth, Ruler of the world and its Providence, a God Who made man in His own image and revealed to him, along with his last end, the way to attain it—where, in the splendid achievements of Greek philosophy, could one find a view of the world as clear and as perfectly satisfactory to the mind as the one revealed to men by Holy Scripture? Clearly, on all these problems, the teaching of revelation was incomparably more rational than the conclusions of reason.

A third characteristic of revealed truth further enhanced the already paradoxical nature of the second one. The conclusions of philosophy had been unsafe, mutually contradictory, and, even when they happened to hit the truth, always mixed with a measure of error. Moreover, this rather dubious learning was always the privi-

lege of a small number of men living the leisurely life of scholars and endowed with the talent required to make good use of it. Not so with Christian revelation. God has spoken to all men, and He has done so in simple terms, so that all men can understand His words, provided only they be granted the grace of hearing them.

To sum up, since God Himself had spoken, what was thus revealed to mankind was certainly and completely true; it was more satisfying to reason than reason's own conclusions; and it was being offered to all men, irrespective of color, of race, of nation, as well as of social or economic conditions. No wonder, then, that Christians took to calling this revealed truth *their own philosophy;* by simply believing what God had said, they were finding themselves possessed of all that which they needed in the way of philosophical truth.

This memorable experience of the early Christians was not forgotten by their successors. Let us call it the notion of Christianity conceived as the philosophy of the Christians. Even today it represents a possible attitude; it is, in fact, the attitude of the great majority of Christians, who are not philosophers in the technical sense of the word, but who find in the Christian revelation a view of the world, of man, and of his destiny that gives full satisfaction to their reason. Today, as in the second century after Christ, the teaching of Catholic truth by missionaries provides men of all degrees of culture, or of the lack of it, with a perfect substitute for a philosophical view of the world. In the sixteenth century, the Catechism of the Council of Trent gave a name to revealed truth considered as fulfilling this particular function; the writers of the Catechism

---

[1] See *The History of Christian Philosophy,* pp. 11-14 and pp. 554-555. The case of St. Justin is representative of several other ones.

called it *Christian philosophy*. We still have a right to use the same expression, in the very same sense, provided we give it the same precise meaning.

B

The progressive constitution of the Christian theology in the middle ages brought about a new situation. What is now called scholastic theology has not been the work of any single man, and it has found several great exponents. Still, since we must single out one of them as representative of scholasticism in general, our best choice is St. Thomas Aquinas.

At the beginning of his great work *On the Truth of the Catholic Faith (Summa Contra Gentiles)*,[2] the Master recalls the distinction between the two modes of truth about God, those that exceed the ability of the human reason (such as the Trinity), and those "which the natural reason also is able to reach. Such are that God exists, that He is one, and the like." In point of fact, Thomas adds, "such truths about God have been proved demonstratively by the philosophers, guided by the light of the natural reason" (I, 3, 2).

There is no difficulty in establishing the point that the truth about God that natural reason is not able to investigate is fittingly revealed to men and proposed to them as our object of belief. If the knowledge of such truth is necessary to man in view of salvation, and if God intends to make human salvation possible, there is no

other way for such truth to become accessible to men than through the channel of divine revelation.

On the contrary, it is not immediately clear why God should have revealed to men the truth about Himself that is not beyond the reach of natural reason. Is it not at least superfluous to offer us as an object of belief what we are able to know?

Yet Thomas Aquinas enumerates a long series of reasons why even the truth about God that reason can investigate had to be revealed to men. The fourth chapter of Book I of the *Summa Contra Gentiles* is entirely devoted to the question. This chapter has been analyzed time and again, but even a careful analysis is bound to leave out a great deal of its content. Let us therefore recommend its careful reading [3] and content ourself with pointing out its significance for the problem under discussion.

In order to understand Thomas Aquinas on this point, one should remember that he is a theologian discussing this eminently theological problem: What was it fitting that God should reveal to men in view of their salvation? Related to our own problem, the question becomes: What would it mean for human salvation if, instead of revealing to us His existence, His unicity, and other such truths about Himself without whose knowledge no man can be saved, God had left the philosophers in charge of proving them demonstratively by the light of the natural reason?

The proper answer to this question is given to us in the spectacle of the philosophical teaching now distributed to students by countless good masters

---

[2] This work will be quoted from its English translation by Prof. A. C. Pegis [Doubleday, N.Y., 1955], *Book One: God*. Following the division of the text adopted by Prof. Pegis, we shall quote, for instance: I, 3, 2, meaning *Summa Contra Gentiles*, Book I, chapter 3, par. 2.

[3] *Summa Contra Gentiles*, I, 4, pp. 66-68.

of philosophy, sometimes even by great philosophers, in modern colleges and universities. Some of them say there is no God; others say that there is a God but that His existence cannot be demonstrated; still others say there is a God and they can prove His existence, but their demonstrations fail to carry conviction, or else what they call God in no way resembles the object of our religious worship. There is no reason to wonder what would happen to our knowledge of God if it had been entrusted to the sole care of philosophy and the philosophers. We know it, we see it, and the answer is that philosophers have simply brought the problem to a chaotic condition.

Strangely enough, Thomas Aquinas himself placed more hope in philosophers than we do. The reason probably is that he had not seen anything like the condition of metaphysics in our own time. On the contrary, we rather seem to consider anybody as qualified to become a metaphysician, and the usual training required to this end, in modern philosophical factories, averages a duration of three to eight years.

This is a point on which Thomas Aquinas seems to have had misgivings. According to him, few men would possess the knowledge of God if the only source of such knowledge were philosophy. Some are not intellectually qualified for philosophical studies; others, because they are in business or in an office, lack the leisure of contemplative inquiry; above all, the knowledge of metaphysics presupposes a great deal of already acquired knowledge, which means much labor spent in study: "Now, those who wish to undergo such a labor for the mere love of knowledge are few"; in short,

"if the only way open to us for the knowledge of God were solely that of reason, the human race would remain in the blackest shadows of ignorance" (I, 4, 3, and 4).

The attitude of Thomas Aquinas is simple. All men stand in need of salvation and, therefore, they need to know God's existence, His unicity, and the like; this knowledge is naturally acquired through the study of metaphysics, which "is the last part of philosophy to be learned" (I, 4, 3). Now, even among the few men who are able to learn philosophy, how many will live long enough to have time to become metaphysicians? All men need to know the existence of God from the earliest time of their lives. Unless we pretend that boys and girls seven years old are able to grasp metaphysical demonstrations, it must be conceded that rationally demonstrable conclusions had to be revealed by God in view of human salvation. The plain Thomistic truth of the case is that *all men*, without exception, must believe in the existence of God, and hold it true on faith, before being able to understand its demonstration. It also is that, were it necessary to hold such a truth on the strength of demonstration alone, very few could acquire it, and even these could not do so before a long time. Let us note the very words of Thomas Aquinas: very few men (*paucissimi*), and these only after a long time (*et hi etiam non nisi post longum tempus*).[4]

---

[4] *Quaestiones Disputatiae de Veritate*, q. 14, art. 10 Resp. According to Thomas Aquinas, *everybody* is held *explicitly* and *always* to believe that God is and that He aims at the good of man. These two notions are quoted by Thomas as those that every Christian must explicitly believe. This teaching rests upon the authority of the Apostle,

The *Summa Theologiae* assumes its full meaning in the light of these considerations. It contains an elementary exposition of all the truth revealed to men in view of their salvation. The part of that truth that is accessible to the light of natural reason is stated on the authority of revelation and accompanied by its philosophical demonstrations. In other words, that which either has actually been demonstrated by philosophers or, at least, can be demonstrated in a philosophical way, receives in the *Summa* the full benefit of rational demonstration.

We are not now concerned with the generous use that Thomas makes of philosophy in defining, explaining, and defending even that part of revealed truth that exceeds the reach of human reason. But the way he fulfilled the first part of his program is of primary importance for a correct understanding of the notion of Christian philosophy. True enough, Thomas himself never used the expression, but he left philosophy, particularly metaphysics, in a condition very different from that in which he had found it. After him, each and every revealed truth concerning God, if it was demonstrable to all, now was presenting itself along with its philosophical demonstration. Thomas himself would have been very much surprised to hear that, in giving philosophical demonstrations of philosophically demonstrable truths revealed by

Hebr. xi, 6. There is no reason to think that Thomas is here forgetting his other thesis, that one cannot know and believe one and the same thing at one and the same time (*Qu. Disp. de Veritate*, q. 14, a. 9, *Sed contra*); but very few men can acquire demonstrative knowledge of such truth and all the others are held, always and explicitly, to believe them as revealed of God. Cf. *In Boethium de Trinitate*, q. 3, a. 1.

God to men, he was, although commenting upon the word of God, indulging in a non-theological activity. In the first place, it should be obvious that all which is found in the *Summa Theologiae* is theological; on the other hand, it is no less obvious that when a theologian deems it fit to give a rational demonstration, the only way for him to do so is to proceed as would any philosopher undertaking to do the same thing. From the time of Thomas Aquinas onward, there has existed a body of truth, revealed to men by God, but rationally demonstrable and, in the mind of the Angelic Doctor at least, philosophically demonstrated.

c

As has been said, Thomas Aquinas did not give this body of truth about God any special name. He had no need for any such name. To him all these philosophically demonstrated conclusions were part and parcel of Sacred Doctrine; the Doctor of revealed truth took them in stride; their existence simply raised no problem for the theologian.

The sixteenth century marked the beginning of a new era with respect to our problem, but the decisive turning point was reached with Descartes. In his *Discourse on Method,* the young reformer announced his intention to leave theology and revelation to theologians, who are in charge of leading us all to heaven, scholars and ignorant alike; as to himself, he would deal with problems related to the nature of things and deal with them in the light of natural reason alone. This regime of the separation of theology and philosophy, or of revelation and reason, was an attempt to return in Christian times to the pre-Christian position of the problem. This was an impossible thing to do, and, in point of fact, Descartes did not accomplish it. Himself a Catholic, he never seems to have wondered how it was that, philosophizing wholly apart from theology, he was spontaneously rediscovering the main conclusions about God and man already demonstrated by the theologians of the middle ages, particularly by Thomas Aquinas. At the same time, he was laying down the principles of his own mechanistic physics, but his way of doing so first supposed the demonstration of a God known from His creatures, Creator of heaven and earth, as well as of man, a strange being made of the substantial union of body and soul. Incidentally, since this soul is really distinct from its body, nothing prevents it from being immortal.

All these philosophical conclusions were established by Descartes in a most un-Thomistic way, but they all were Thomistic conclusions. Today, the *Discourse on the Method* still is on the *Index Prohibitorum Librorum*, but a great many Catholic professors of philosophy, while denouncing the philosophical errors of Descartes, in practice subscribe to his own notion of a philosophy separated from theology. To them, as to Descartes himself, where theology begins, philosophy comes to an end. If we philosophize, we cannot be theologizing at the same time. There are no available statistics, but were it possible to know how many priests, monks, or Catholic laymen in charge of teaching philosophy completely imitate the attitude of Descartes in this matter, it probably would appear that the author of the *Discourse* has carried the day.

The reason for this is apparent.

Nearly all the philosophers who followed in the wake of Descartes [5] subscribed to the principle that philosophy has nothing to do with theology, or reason with revelation. Obviously, such was not the case with the philosophical speculation included in the theological works of the great scholastics. Consequently, if a scholastic theologian pretended to argue and to reach conclusions as a philosopher, his opponent would simply object that a scholastic master might well have a theology, but he certainly had no philosophy. The controversy was not a new one. Already in the middle ages, Averroes had reproached Avicenna with teaching revelation in philosophical garb; among the Latins, the Averroists had not only declared their intention to keep philosophy apart from revelation, they had fought, and suffered, to do what they had announced they would do. What was new after Descartes was the generalization of this attitude. This time, the representatives of medieval scholasticism realized that the new philosophical situation could not be ignored.

By and large, the sixteenth- and seventeenth-century scholastics followed the line of least resistance. To the objection: You have no philosophy of your own, their answer was: Yes, we do have a philosophy. In order to prove it, they simply extracted from the *Summae* and the Commentaries on Peter Lombard what of philosophical speculation their medieval predecessors had inserted within them. This philosophical material was set up and organized as an independent body of

---

[5] Nearly all, not all, for indeed Malebranche was a clear case of Christian philosophy.

philosophical speculation to be taught as a philosophical introduction to the study of theology. The only alternative was to follow the example of the medieval Averroists: that is, to identify philosophy with Aristotle and to teach to the young Christians of the sixteenth century a revised version of Aristotelianism in which the worst discrepancies between his authentic doctrine and the Catholic faith were toned down and, wherever it was possible to do so, eliminated.

The consequences were to be damaging to the future of Christian thought. Instead of opposing the onslaught of Cartesianism with the deep metaphysics of Thomas Aquinas, an ever-present truth, the scholastics met it with school versions of the philosophy of Aristotle, and they did so at the very moment when the scientific basis of Aristotelianism, from biology to astronomy, was crumbling down under the impact of the new science. There was not even a battle. From that time onward, scholastic philosophy has survived under the form of textbooks, in which a philosophy using the language of Aristotle miraculously agrees with the conclusions of Catholic theology, from which, however, it is supposed to be specifically distinct.

Owing to this decision, Catholics and their schools could now boast of having a philosophy properly so called, separated from revelation and faith as every true philosophy should be, and fully qualified to claim a place of its own in the philosophical movement of the age. The only tie of this neo-scholastic philosophy with theology and revelation was its professed resolve never to contradict, in philosophical matters, the theological teaching of the Church. What happened to this neo-scholastic philosophy during the seventeenth and the eighteenth centuries is a matter of historical record. The purely negative pact of non-aggression, which was its only tie with the Sacred Doctrine, was not enough to prevent this school philosophy from absorbing strong doses of Descartes, Leibniz, Locke, Condillac, Victor Cousin, even Kant. In the thirteenth century, while philosophy was still part and parcel of theological speculation, the theologians had been the acknowledged leaders in the philosophical world; from the seventeenth century and onward, neo-scholasticism did little else than to contract temporary alliances with any form of philosophical thought that could be reconciled with the teachings of Revelation.

This is the reason that prompted some Italian theologians in the first half of the nineteenth century to advocate a return to the philosophical positions of St. Thomas Aquinas. Only, keeping in mind the desire of their contemporaries to have a philosophy of their own, these theologians called this philosophy a *philosophia christiana*, a Christian philosophy. This move culminated in the encyclical letter *Aeterni Patris* published on August 4, 1879, by Pope Leo XIII, "On the Restoration of Christian Philosophy in Schools." [6]

To the question: What is Christian philosophy? the shortest answer now is: If you read the encyclical letter *Aeterni Patris* you will find there the most highly authorized answer to your

---

[6] *The Church Speaks to the Modern World. The Social Teachings of Leo XIII* [Doubleday, N.Y., 1954], pp. 29-51. An apostolic letter published in 1880 refers to *Aeterni Patris* as to "Our Letter on the Restoring in Catholic Schools of the Christian Philosophy in the Spirit of St. Thomas Aquinas."

question. Reduced to its essentials, the answer is as follows.

In the first third of his encyclical Leo XIII recalls, along with the doctrinal function of the Church and the teaching office of the popes, the services rendered to theology by philosophy, but he does not forget to recall as well the benefits philosophy has always derived in the past from its close association with theology. In carefully weighted words, Leo XIII observes that "the human mind, being confined within certain limits, and these narrow enough, is exposed to many errors and is ignorant of many things . . . Those, therefore, who to the study of philosophy unite obedience to the Christian faith, are philosophizing in the best possible way; for the splendor of the divine truths, received into the mind, helps the understanding, and not only detracts in no wise from its dignity, but adds greatly to its nobility, keenness, and stability." [7]

Obviously we are here returning, under a new name, to the very same situation occupied by philosophy with respect to Christian faith from the time of St. Justin up to the Cartesian philosophical reformation. Nor is it only a question for philosophy not to disagree with faith; a positive influence of faith over the human reason is here advocated not only as the best safeguard against error but also as a remedy to human ignorance.

It is no wonder, then, that instead of sketching a system of Christian philosophy, Leo XIII devotes the middle section of his encyclical to a truly admirable history of what happened to philosophy during the many centuries of its association with faith in the doctrines of the early Apologists, the Fathers of the Church, and the scholastic Doctors. Clearly, what Leo XIII calls Christian philosophy cannot be reduced to the content of any single philosopher; it is neither a system nor even a doctrine. Rather, it is a way of philosophizing; namely, the attitude of those who "to the study of philosophy unite obedience to the Christian faith." [8] This philosophical method, or attitude—*philosophandi institutum* —is *Christian philosophy* itself.

It should now be clear that under the name of Christian philosophy Pope Leo XIII simply is sending us back to the method of handling philosophical problems traditional in the history of patristic and of scholastic theology; that is, to what the encyclical itself calls the "right use of that philosophy which the scholastic teachers have been accustomed carefully and prudently to make use of even in theological disputations." [9] The panegyric of the "philosophy" of St. Thomas that fills up the last third of *Aeterni Patris*, not to the exclusion of other Doctors, but praising it as the very model and idea of the Christian way of philosophizing, is enough to assure us of what Christian philosophy truly was in the mind of Pope Leo XIII. Before anything else, it was the investigation, by means of philosophy, of the saving truth revealed by God and accessible to the light of natural reason.[10]

---

[7] *Aeterni Patris*, p. 38. Cf. (p. 39) the quotation from the Vatican Council: "Faith frees and saves reason from error, and endows it with manifold knowledge."

[8] *Aeterni Patris*, p. 52, note 4.

[9] *Aeterni Patris*, p. 43.

[10] The encyclical of 1879 goes even farther than this; it does not seem to consider philosophy as losing its specific character in helping theology to "assume the nature, form and genius of a true science."

D

Thus understood, Christian philosophy naturally centers around a core of problems perfectly summarized in the famous prayer of St. Augustine to God: "That I may know Thee, that I may know myself." Many modern philosophers would consider this as a sufficient reason to hold Christian philosophy as philosophically disqualified, but all that philosophers say is not necessarily true. On the contrary, Thomas Aquinas always insisted that, Christian or otherwise, all philosophy worthy of the name had in fact posited the knowledge of God as its last end. In this respect, Christian philosophy is like any other right-minded philosophy, with the only difference that it is better equipped than they to fulfill what has always been the common ambition of philosophical speculation.

This final orientation of Christian philosophy entails no *a priori* exclusion of any field of philosophical research. What can there be in the whole world that is irrelevant to the knowledge of God and man? Since the invisible of God is known from His creatures, there is no creature—that is to say, no thing—whose knowledge is unrelated to the knowledge of God; and since the world of knowledge is the work of man, it can be said of man that, in the last analysis, all his acquired knowledge is about himself. Leo XIII has stressed with great insistence the fact that thus to order all the sciences under the leadership of true philosophy is not to do away with them. On the contrary, "all studies ought to find hope of advancement

and promise of assistance in this restoration of philosophic discipline which We have proposed." [11] In short, while the Christian way of philosophizing protects philosophical research against the risks of error and the evil of useless dispersion, it in no way deprives it of its necessary freedom of investigation.

A last benefit of the Christian attitude in philosophical matters is overlooked in our own days. This is the more curious as our contemporaries are acting in a way that makes it imperative for us to exploit it to the limit. In listing the reasons why God deemed it fitting to reveal to men some truths accessible to philosophical knowledge, Thomas Aquinas stressed the fact that many men die, if not young, at least years before reaching the age of philosophical maturity. As he himself saw it, philosophy was a lifetime pursuit, requiring a great liberty of mind, much intellectual leisure, and many years of work spent on the sciences whose knowledge is a necessary prerequisite to the study of natural theology. On the contrary, Thomas added, revelation and faith offer to human understanding the ready knowledge of the highest metaphysical truths under a form that makes them accessible to all.

Today the reverse seems to be considered true. Modern educators speak and act as if they thought that boys and girls are qualified students in metaphysics and, at the same time, they make a profession of teaching a philosophy which, careful as it is never to contradict the Christian revelation, is no less careful not to undergo its influence. The paradoxical nature of the situation scarcely needs to be

---

Aeterni Patris, p. 36. This aspect of the problem is left out as relevant to the notion of theology rather than to that of philosophy.

[11] *Aeterni Patris*, p. 49.

stressed. In his *Summa Contra Gentiles*, a theological work so full of philosophy that it is often mistaken for a philosophical work, Thomas Aquinas makes no effort to conceal his indebtedness to revelation. Nay, he forcefully stresses the universality of the end pursued by God in presenting to men by way of faith the pure truth about Himself: "In this way, all men would easily be able to have a share in the knowledge of God, and this without uncertainty and error." In support of this conclusion, Thomas Aquinas quotes Isaiah, 56:13: "All thy children shall be taught of the Lord." [12] The younger the children, the more necessary it should seem to rely on the teaching of the Lord in order to make them share in the knowledge of God without uncertainty and error. On the contrary, to teach them a systematically non-Christian philosophy is to impose on them all the obligation of reaching in their youth a faultless metaphysical knowledge which, in the past, was the privilege of very few great philosophers, if any.

There would not be much point in explaining these things to non-Christian philosophers; but it is somewhat strange that such a philosophical attitude should be considered paradoxical, if not downright contradictory, by representatives of the Christian tradition. After all, it says only what Thomas Aquinas has done and it does no more than recommend a way of cultivating philosophy prescribed as the only safe one by Pope Leo XIII. The most serious obstacle to the acceptance of the method advocated—nay, prescribed—by Leo XIII to all Christian schools wherein philosophy is taught under any form is the extraordinary ignorance (in which so many Christians still live) of the philosophical principles of St. Thomas Aquinas. The name of the Common Doctor of the Church is frequently quoted; it is to be found on the title pages of many books and there have always been able interpreters of his doctrine; still, it too often happens that what is taught under the name of Thomism has little in common with the authentic philosophy of the saint. It has been our conviction that we must relearn the meaning of the notion of *being* proper to Thomas Aquinas and to follow it in its application to the main problems of Christian philosophy. Unless we are mistaken, this notion is the master key to the metaphysics of the saint, and it is better to have at least striven to master it than, without it, to have covered a vast ground in a theology where it is everywhere present.

---

[12] *On the Truth of the Catholic Faith*, I, 4, 6, and 7.

QUESTIONS FOR DISCUSSION

1. According to Gilson, what was the monumental error committed by Descartes that proved to be so damaging to Christian thought? Show why it had this effect, according to Gilson.
2. Why, according to Gilson (who is presenting the view of St. Thomas Aqui-

nas), is it desirable, even necessary, for all men to be taught the revealed truths of theology at an early age?

3. ". . . on all the points covered in common by philosophy and by revelation, rationality stood on the side of revelation much more than on the side of philosophy. A single God, creator of heaven and earth, Ruler of the world and its Providence, a God Who made man in His own image and revealed to him, along with his last end, the way to attain it — where in the splendid achievements of Greek philosophy, could one find a view of the world as clear and as perfectly satisfactory to the mind as the one revealed to men by Holy Scripture? Clearly, on all these problems, the teaching of revelation was incomparably more rational than the conclusions of reason." Explain what Gilson means in this passage when he uses the words "rational" and "rationality." Can you suggest alternative meanings of these terms?

4. Gilson says that "while the Christian way of philosophizing protects philosophical research against the risks of error and the evil of useless dispersion, it in no way deprives it of its necessary freedom of investigation."

   a) How does the Christian way of philosophy protect philosophical research against the risks of error? Just what is meant by an *error;* how is it decided, and by whom, when an error has been made?

   b) Examine just what is meant in the above quotation by "freedom of investigation."

Friedrich Waismann (1896-1959)

1.6   What Is a Philosophical Problem?

THE INFLUENCE OF LOGIC
UPON PHILOSOPHY

It is characteristic of philosophy that every great turning-point in its history is greeted by many as its

From *The Principles of Linguistic Philosophy* by Friedrich Waismann, chaps. 1 and 2. Reprinted by permission of St. Martin's Press, Inc. and Macmillan & Co., Ltd.

rebirth. Great thinkers of all times have refused to accept the ideas of their predecessors as unquestionable truths; they have preferred to try to reach the foundations of knowledge by their own labours. Descartes, Locke and Kant each felt himself to be a turning-point, the beginning of a new philosophy; they were not mistaken in so thinking, for each made a step which we can never go back upon.

The philosophy of the last eighty years contains almost more contradictions and diverging opinions than ever before.

Some philosophers, discouraged by the collapse of the great metaphysical systems of the nineteenth century, believe that they have found a solution in a return to Kant; others try to construct a picture of the universe from the results of science, drawing from scientific knowledge conclusions about our position in the universe and the meaning of life. A third group rejects the sovereignty of science, believing that only intuition can help us to understand the essence of being. Yet others, tired of these conflicting opinions, say that philosophy can provide no objective knowledge; it is to be understood merely as the expression of personality, of psychological type. This leaves to the philosopher only the task of cataloguing the works of his predecessors, without hoping or wishing to find *the* solution to the problems that exercised them.

This chorus of conflicting opinions, each claiming to be the sole possessor of the truth, is undoubtedly a sign of serious crisis and has been widely recognized as such. We have mentioned it here only in order to emphasize that at the present day a new trend has come into philosophy. What this trend is will be made clear in the course of this book; at the moment we will give merely a preliminary outline of its character.

Previous philosophers have almost always directed their attention to the *answers* given in reply to philosophical questions. Their disputes were all concerned with these answers, their truth or falsity, their proof or refutation. The new point of view differs from all the others in that, from the start,

it ignores the answers and directs all its attention towards the questions. It is well known that we often think that we understand precisely what is meant by a question, whereas further examination shows us that we have deceived ourselves in thinking this and have been led astray by superficial linguistic analogies. The great mistake of philosophers up to now, which has led to so many misunderstandings, is that they have produced answers before seeing clearly the nature of the questions they have been asking. They seem to have been quite unaware of the possibility that the form of the question itself might conceal an error. This has meant that they have never reached the roots of the intellectual discomfort which they have felt; they have been satisfied by pseudo-solutions which, though they dazzled the mind for a little while, could not stand the test of time.

The change, when it came, was from quite a new direction. Without many being aware of it, logic had developed in the hands of mathematicians into an instrument which far surpassed the logic of the Schools in delicacy and expressive power. Though originally made for the purpose of analysing mathematical inferences, logic did not remain restricted to that field. Frege made a remark in his *Begriffsschrift* which today has the air of a prophecy. Logic, he said, will perhaps one day be of use to philosophy in the task of 'breaking the tyranny of words over thought, by bringing to light the confusions which are almost unavoidable in the use of language'. What Frege predicted has been realized by Russell, Moore and Wittgenstein. They used the recently discovered methods and ideas to illuminate the structure of language, and through their work it became apparent how much the logical structure of thought is concealed and misrepresented in the verbal form in which it is expressed. These investigations led to a much clearer understanding of the character of philosophical questions. Such problems disturb us only if we do not see how language functions; if we think we are discussing questions of fact, when we are merely being misled by peculiarities of linguistic form. The danger is that there are innumerable ways of being misled by the analogies, metaphors and similes of language, and even if we are constantly on the watch we are continually being caught in a linguistic snare.

We come, then, to an entirely new solution of philosophical questions, one very different from what had been expected. It had been expected that such questions should be answered either by 'yes' or 'no'. Instead of this the analytic method leads us to the view that the questions themselves rest upon misunderstandings; it frees us from them by making the meaning of our words and the way they are combined in language so clear that we no longer feel driven to ask the questions.

THE NATURE OF A
PHILOSOPHICAL PROBLEM

Everyone understands what is meant, for instance, by the unsolved problem of the origin of life, or by saying that there are still many problems about prehistoric times remaining to be solved. Solving these problems consists in gaining new information, which is expressed and communicated in sentences. We are so used to this sort of problem that it never occurs to us that the problems of philosophy might be quite different. Yet in fact 'problem' and 'solution' are often used in quite different ways. If we talk of the problem of the transmission of force by radio the solution we want is a technical discovery, a piece of practical activity, which is connected with our knowledge of physics only by being suggested and prepared for by the latter. No one would hold that solving a social question consists in acquiring some theoretical ideas about it. The problem of depicting movement in modern painting introduces yet another sense of 'problem'. If we consider these examples, one after the other, it becomes clear that very different sorts of things are collected under the name 'problem'.

The first thing that strikes us is that philosophy does not deal with one homogeneous sort of object in the way that, for instance, history or astronomy does. In fact, from any question, if we follow it far enough back, we can reach a typical philosophical question. For example, from the question whether a judge has decided justly in a particular case—that is to say, has given a judgement in accordance with the law—we can pass to the question whether the laws themselves are just; from the question how a particular natural phenomenon is to be explained we can pass to what is meant by explanation and whether all that explanations achieve is merely to push back the inexplicable a step further; from the question whether a particular story is true we can pass to the problem of the nature of truth. In these cases we can perceive dimly that the direction of the question has changed, that we move, as it were, in a new dimension.

It seems then that what gives a problem its peculiarly philosophical air lies less in its subject-matter than in the way it is put; in what direction we are forced to move when we try to solve it.

At this point we might be tempted to say that philosophical questions are those which are the most general. In daily life we are interested, for example, in the purpose of a particular action, but the philosopher examines the nature of purpose in general, the concept of purpose. The scientist looks for explanations of facts, but according to this view the meaning of explanation is itself a problem for the philosopher. The legal philosopher examines the essence of justice, the philosopher of languages the essence of language and so on. The most general concepts of science—space and time, chance and law, life and consciousness, meaning and purpose—can only be illuminated philosophically.

Though there is doubtless some truth in this opinion, it is not an adequate account of the matter. In the first place, there are philosophical questions which, far from being general, are particular. For instance: How does it come about that, although the image on the retina is the wrong way up, we see things the right way up? and, how does it come about that, in a mirror, things are still the right way up although left and right are the wrong way round? What is even more significant is that there are questions of a very general nature in science and mathematics which are not philosophical. Certain present-day investigations in mathematics (e.g. the theory of sets, the theory of abstract groups, modern algebra) can hardly be surpassed in generality. Yet there is a quite unphilosophical way of dealing with these questions. So generality alone cannot be the differentiating mark of philosophical questions.

From Plato to Schopenhauer all philosophers were agreed that wonder is the source of philosophizing. This wonder is not directed towards extraordinary and rare happenings but towards just those things which are familiar to everyone. The philosopher might be described as the type of man who is given to wonder about the things of everyday knowledge. Consider, for example, the amazement with which Augustine contemplated the fact of memory. It was not exceptional achievements of memory which amazed Augustine, but the fact that there is such a thing as memory at all. His dilemma can be put in the following way: a sense impression, a smell or a taste, lasts for a moment and then disappears. It is now here, now gone. Yet in the halls of memory copies of the vivid impressions of the moment are stored up. From these I draw each one out as I wish. But the copy is not transitory like the sensation it mirrors; it has a continued existence. It is the same as, yet different from, the sensation. The past is preserved as it was, yet it is intrinsically different. How can such a thing come about?

Here the fact of memory itself becomes a problem. The philosopher, as he ponders over a question, has the appearance of a man who is disturbed and irritated by something. He seems to be struggling to do something which is beyond his strength. The words in which such a problem is expressed do not reveal its true meaning. If we try to penetrate into the disturbed background from which the question arises and takes shape, we come upon something else which it is difficult to express in words. We might perhaps call it alarm on coming up against the inconceivable. We can try, by various examples, to get ourselves nearer to this queer state of mind. If while walking alone we saw the place which we had just left suddenly appearing again in front of us, we should feel a sort of dizziness, we should say in bewilderment 'But how can this be?' Similarly the philosopher says to himself 'Certainly there is such a thing as memory, but how is it possible?'

Everyone who has brooded over a philosophical question is familiar with the experience that his mind seems to become blurred, that everything, even the apparently most certain and self-evident, takes on a new and puzzling air. Plato experienced this astonishment when general ideas suddenly became a problem for him. He started from the question: What is meant by a general term? What, for example, does the word 'horse' mean? Does it mean a single particular horse? Clearly not, for the word can be used to refer to this or that or any horse. Then does it mean all horses? No, for even if there were no horses, the word would still have a meaning. But if it means neither a single horse nor all horses what does it mean?

The idealist knows the shock of realizing for the first time that the world is merely an idea in his mind, that he 'knows neither a sun nor an earth but only an eye that sees a sun, a hand that feels an earth' (Schopenhauer). Does anything, then, exist besides individual consciousness? Kant must have felt this sort of thing when the existence of mathematcis suddenly became a riddle to him. How is it possible, he thought, that geometry, which is independent of all experi-

ence, should agree so miraculously with reality? Can mind, without the assistance of experience, fathom the properties of real things merely by cogitation?

A peculiar mental unrest arises from considering such questions as these. It seems as if we had previously passed carelessly over difficulties which we now notice. We ask ourselves in horror 'But how can such a thing be?' We ask this question only if the facts astonish us, if something about them seems to us out of place, incredible, even absurd.

What we can do to overcome this sensation of unanswerable difficulties we shall see presently. We shall see also why our philosophical disturbance cannot be quieted by winning fresh knowledge. We shall be forced to the opinion that philosophy is not a temple of knowledge, that in it there are neither suppositions nor affirmations, that it is something fundamentally different from these, namely the clarification of thought. Wittgenstein was the first to reach this opinion and we can use his words as a motto for this book:

'Philosophy is not one of the natural sciences. . . . The object of philosophy is the logical clarification of thoughts. Philosophy is not a theory but an activity. . . . The result of philosophy is not a number of "philosophical propositions", but to make propositions clear. Philosophy should make clear and delimit sharply the thoughts which otherwise are, as it were, opaque and blurred.' [1]

As we have said, the sense of these words will gradually become more comprehensible to us. Even now we

---

[1] *Tractatus Logico-Philosophicus* (London, 1922, new trans., 1961), 4. 111, 4. 112.

can mention certain general facts which point towards our view of philosophy. First of all, we have often experienced the difficulty of explaining to a practical man the *meaning* of a philosophical question. This cannot be because he lacks some necessary technical knowledge, for many philosophical questions can be put in the simplest words of everyday language. What he lacks is the capacity to share the bewilderment which the philosopher feels at the question. Another important sign is the prevalence of misunderstanding in a philosophical argument, the danger of the parties speaking at cross purposes. Everyone who has to speak to an audience on a philosophical subject feels at a certain loss; he feels that arranging ideas in a logical sequence is not quite the right way to communicate his views to his listeners. All he can do is to conduct them through the ideas in the way he went through them himself, so that they feel for themselves the mental discomfort which he felt, so that the doubts rise before them as they rose before him and they make the same attempts at solution which he has made. Then step by step they may become clearer until they see the affair with his eyes. A philosophical opinion cannot be communicated like a dead formula. The best part of philosophy consists in training the intellect, not in communicating ready-made truths. Outstanding thinkers have always felt this to be so. Thus Kant, for example, said that he did not wish to teach philosophy but philosophizing.

Another sign that our view is correct can be found in the history of philosophy. For though the sceptic makes out that philosophy is merely a disheartening swaying between one system and another, this is not the case. If we look into the matter carefully, we find, under the contradictions on the surface, a continuous development, a gradual progress of views. This change is not so much in the assertions made as in the attitude adopted to the questions, a change in what are looked upon as problems and what are regarded as unfruitful questions. For example, what Hume, in his famous critique of the concept of causality, showed most plainly was that we perceive only the succession of events and not an inner connection joining cause and effect together. The tangible gain in this idea lay not in any philosophical axiom giving rise to further propositions, but in the clarification of the meaning of causal sentences; not in adding to the number of our propositions, but in cutting it down; in getting rid of the pseudo-truths and fancied knowledge which accompany the idea of an inner connection in causality.

WHAT IS LACK OF CLARITY?

What do we mean by saying that someone is unclear about something? Do we mean that he is in a certain peculiar mental state? Is becoming clear the beginning of a new mental state, as it were a ray of light in the mind?

In order to understand the meaning of the words 'clear' and 'unclear' we shall start by looking at typical examples of their use. When do we say that someone is unclear about something? Is it when he lacks certain knowledge? Can his confusion be removed by extending his field of knowledge? We should not say that Newton was unclear about Optics although he knew far less about it than is known by present-day physicists. But we should say that he was unclear about the differential calculus, that, for example, he had nebulous notions of 'infinitely small' quantities. This is shown by the fact that it is very easy, from the point of view adopted by Newton, to ask questions which make us feel perplexed. We will not, however, discuss Newton's confusion in detail, but will turn instead to a simpler example of lack of clarity. Suppose we consider the infinite series $1 - 1 + 1 - 1 + 1 - \ldots$. The question which leads us at once to a difficulty is this: 'What is the sum of the series?' We might first of all say 'It is zero, since the numbers can be paired so that each pair gives zero and the sum of zeros is zero'. We could, on the other hand, say 'The sum is 1'; for we can begin with the first number and then pair off the successive numbers in this way:

$$1 - (1 - 1) - (1 - 1) \ldots$$

Euler, applying the formula for obtaining the sum of a geometrical progression, suggested that the sum is ½ and gave the following justification of his procedure: If you end the series after an even number of terms the sum is zero, and after an odd number it is 1. Since the series has an infinite number of terms and infinity is neither even nor odd, the sum is neither zero nor 1 but their mean.

Here we have a problem which differs from a mathematical problem in a typical way. This difference may be revealed by the curious discomfort which arguments like Euler's produce in us. It is evident that our question cannot be answered by doing further calculations. The calculations lie before us, but they contradict each other, and we must now try to see how this comes about. We are not dealing with a calculation to be performed but with the *meaning* of a calculation.

The first step in resolving the conflict lies in turning from the question 'What is the sum of this series?' to the question 'What does it mean to say that a number is the sum of an infinite series?' As soon as we have made this transition, as soon as we no longer ask whether what is disputed is true or false, but ask what it *means*, we have passed from the domain of calculation to that of clarification, from mathematics to philosophy. Here we have a characteristic example of that change in direction of attention of which we have so often spoken.

The next step consists in seeing that the word 'sum', first of all explained only for a finite number of terms, has as yet no meaning when applied to an infinite series. We must first *define* what we wish to understand by the sum of an infinite series. If we give a definition, such as the usual one, which defines the sum as the limit to which the partial sums taken successively tend, the problem disappears. It then becomes evident that the series under consideration has no sum at all.[2]

In what, therefore, does the solution of the problem consist? It consists in explaining exactly how we operate with a finite and with an infinite series, in stating precisely and completely the rules for manipulating each of these types of series and in comparing these rules. This comparison then shows indeed how far a finite series is *similar* to an infinite one.

Suppose it is now asked how this

_____

[2] But one can apply a number to the series as a sum, if one uses another definition of 'sum'.

confusion can have arisen or why the correct way of escape was not obvious from the start? The answer is that the lack of clarity has its roots deep in the forms of expression of our language. For with both finite and infinite we use the expressions 'sum', 'series', 'addition'; with both we use the plus sign and other mathematical symbols. These facts conceal the fundamental difference in logic between finite and infinite series, so that we do not suspect that in going from one to the other we pass to quite another region. We are amazed to learn that an infinite series obeys quite different laws from those obeyed by a finite series, that, for example, it may happen that its sum can be altered simply by changing the order of its terms. We are in the habit of reading into the infinite series the properties of the finite.

The difficulty in such a problem is to avoid applying the wrong system of concepts. It is always language which leads us into the fallacy of misapplied concepts and which as *a matter of course* uses the same words with different meanings. The effect of this is the effect of a conjuring trick; the change occurs so innocently that it escapes attention. We apply the word 'sum' quite as a matter of course, both to finite and to infinite forms. All the traps are camouflaged by our use of words. . . .

THE PROBLEM OF TRUST-WORTHINESS OF MEMORY

To develop the main principles of our method we shall now take as models some typical philosophical problems and their clarification; these examples are not artificially constructed, but actually occur in the history of philosophic thought, and are chosen here because they can be explained with comparatively little difficulty.

Let us ask, for example: What right have we to believe what our memory tells us?

This question, as is well known, often arises out of Descartes's more general question: Have we any knowledge which is infallible? If there were any such knowledge, it would show itself as infallible in that it would be impossible even to doubt it. Now is there anything which cannot possibly be doubted? Let us review the various departments of knowledge and see which of them can significantly be doubted. This method of doubt is like a sieve which retains only absolutely certain knowledge. It is clear that the general propositions of Physics and the Laws of Nature are excluded; for everyone admits that they are, without exception, hypotheses which can at any time be overthrown by further experiments. The propositions of history are no better since they rest upon tradition, and the same applies to most of our everyday knowledge as far as it relies on the evidence of other people. The situation seems to be different with regard to propositions of whose truth I am convinced by my own observation. For example, if I say 'That rose is red', it does seem as if what I say is beyond all doubt. But do not people now and then have illusions and hallucinations? May not I be only dreaming of seeing a rose? However, what I cannot doubt is that I have the sense-impression of a rose now, whether it is a dream or not. Do we not seem to have reached the point at which all doubt is silenced? Yet a really determined sceptic could, even at this point, find something to attack. He might say 'Be this as it may, even if this moment I have perhaps before me a wholly definite picture, even so my problem is not affected. For the question was whether there is any absolutely certain knowledge? But a perception cannot be called knowledge until it is expressed in words. And to do this presupposes a correct use of words which depends, like all things learned, on memory. So if I look at a rose and say I see a rose, the truth of what I say depends upon my remembering correctly what each word I say means. I must know what the words "rose", "red", "see" mean. Plainly, all speaking, thinking, and formulating presupposes that we can store up the meanings of words in our memories. Yet we know that memory *can* deceive us. What guarantees that it does not *always* deceive us, even when we make the simplest perceptual judgement? Does not certainty seem to dissolve into nothing?'

This train of thought exposes even analytic judgements (which consist merely in the analyses of concepts) to doubt. That certain things follow from the definition of a word cannot be doubted; what can, however, be doubted is our capacity to hold a concept in mind long enough to enable us to infer anything from its definition with certainty. It is not the logical connection, but our psychological capacity to hold it in mind, that is open to doubt. However cogently the steps in a mathematical proof may follow from each other, I can never be sure that my proof is correct, that during the short time that elapses between the first and last steps I have not forgotten, or slightly altered, the meaning of the symbols involved; so that the symbols which I write down as

the final stage in the proof may not *mean* anything that in fact follows from the data with which I started. Whether it is *probable* or not that our memory deceives us in this way is not relevant here; it is sufficient that it should be *possible* to doubt the reliability of memory, for this leads at once to the question, how far, in principle, memory is trustworthy.

At first sight this seems a question that can be answered without much difficulty; for I can easily check whether I am using my words correctly by asking whether their usage is the same, or by consulting various written explanations of our language. But even such practical aids, it might be said, do not in principle exclude possibilities of error. For in what other people say and in the written explanations, dictionaries, etc., there will again occur words whose meaning needs to be determined, and the same sceptical doubts can be raised about this interpretation; not to mention the fact that among fundamental presuppositions of knowledge we cannot include the assumption that the physical marks preserve their shape and could not for some mysterious reason change from one moment to another. How can you tell that there is not an arch-deceiver, who alters the shape of the letters whenever you close the book or look away from the page for an instant? That such things do not happen is already the conclusion of an inference from our experiences in the past; but how can we appeal to these experiences when we are suspicious about the trustworthiness of memory?

So doubt can corrode all certainty. And in fact the situation is exceedingly odd. We cannot go back into the past and hold our present memories alongside it for comparison. We have only our memories to rely upon, and they now seem suspect. Every attempt to prove the reliability of memory at the decisive point makes use of memory, so that we go hopelessly round in a circle. Anyone who broods on this process will soon be overtaken by a kind of giddiness. It is as if a bottomless abyss opened before him. Is there no escape from this desperate situation?

Some philosophers have attempted a solution by saying that we must trust our memories. Memory may now and then deceive us, but that it is in the main trustworthy is a belief which cannot be proved, for it belongs, they say, to the fundamental presuppositions of all knowledge. We must accept these presuppositions or stop thinking altogether.

If I had to take sides in this question I would rather be with those who attack our beliefs than with those who defend. For to forbid a question is not to liquidate it. Yet this is done by those whose defence of memory we have described. For an appeal to belief is only an exhortation to suppress the doubts which perplex us. Such an exhortation in no way shows whether these doubts are unjustified, which is what we want to know. The doubt is suppressed but not disarmed; and, in fact, where is the sceptic who has ever been convinced by such an argument?

Attempts have also been made to still repressed doubt in the following way. To 'prove' the trustworthiness of memory, we are told, is of no avail; for every proof consists in a chain of deductions, and thus would only present new points of attack to the radical sceptic. No, if there is anything that can help us, it can only be an appeal to a datum which is beyond reach of doubt.

It seems that there actually is a datum to which we can appeal. This datum is more primitive than doubting and thinking, for it underlies every mental activity. It is the simple fact that is called the *unity of consciousness*. What is meant by this cannot be expressed in a definition or description; we can only, by the aid of certain circumlocutions, point to certain facts which everyone experiences in his own consciousness. W. James has emphasized that 'consciousness does not appear to itself chopped up in bits. Such words as "chain" or "train" do not describe it fitly as it presents itself in the first instance. It is nothing jointed; it flows. A "river" or a "stream" are the metaphors by which it is most naturally described'. Our consciousness is not a mere bundle or collection of different perceptions, as Hume believed. The mere succession of experiences is not sufficient to make them into parts or states of one and the same consciousness; something more must be added on, and this additional element is nothing but the unity of consciousness. Though it cannot be precisely stated what this is, its existence is a fundamental fact. To fully realize it, we may picture to ourselves what a bundle of psychic elements would look like if this unity were absent.

Suppose I shake hands with somebody, then both of us have certain sensations of touch. In such a case there is certainly a coexistence of psychic data, and yet what is lacking is that peculiar connection which can only be experienced and not described; this lack is expressed by saying that the two sensations belong to *different* consciousnesses. And continuity of consciousness does not consist merely in the uninterruptedness of the succession of experiences; rather the latter must be united by a particular kind of connection if they are to be experiences of the same consciousness; to realize this we need only imagine that the continuous experiences are distributed among different individuals.

If the constitution of consciousness were that of a series of mental states, all perfectly insulated, 'we never could have any knowledge except that of the present instant. The moment each of our sensations ceased it would be gone for ever; and we should be as if it had never been. . . . One idea, upon this supposition, would follow another. But that would be all. Each of our successive states of consciousness, the moment it ceased, would be gone for ever. Each of these momentary states would be our whole being'.[3] W. James remarks on this: 'Our consciousness would be like a glow-worm spark, illuminating the point it immediately covered, but leaving all beyond in total darkness.'[4] In such a case we should have no right to speak of a single consciousness, for the choice of this term implies that there is some sort of connection between those momentary states. What has been described would better be expressed by saying that we have been thinking of a *series of consciousnesses*, each one arising, lasting for an instant, and vanishing into nothingness, and none knowing anything of the others. But what is it we are here imagining? A consciousness vanishing

the moment it arises, a consciousness without duration? How odd to use the word 'consciousness' like this! What we have tried to imagine is entirely different from what is commonly called 'consciousness'.

We made the fanciful hypothesis merely to set off our real nature by the contrast. The constitution of consciousness is such that it is not a 'string of bead-like sensations and images, all separate'. Our experiences 'are not thus contracted, and our consciousness never shrinks to the dimensions of a glow-worm spark'.[5] It cannot so shrink unless it ceases to be consciousness.

Thus we see: where unity of consciousness is wanting there is no such thing as consciousness. In other words, it lies in the nature of consciousness to be a unity. This connection, indescribable and yet so familiar to us, contains already what is called memory. 'Any state of mind which is shut up to its own moment and fails to become an object for succeeding states of mind, is as if it belonged to another stream of consciousness. Or rather, it belongs only physically, not intellectually, to its own stream, forming a bridge from one segment of it to another, but not being appropriated inwardly by other segments.'[6]

The upshot of this discussion seems to be: In a case like this we cannot speak of one consciousness; for what gives that unity to consciousness and binds it together in spite of the ever-changing flow of its content is nothing but memory itself. In the idea of consciousness itself memory is already involved in that the separate moments of consciousness, as it were, cleave to-

---

[3] James Mill, *Analysis* (London, 1829), i. 319.

[4] *Principles of Psychology* (London 1890), i. 606.

[5] Ibid.

[6] Ibid., p. 644.

gether by the power of memory. So the fundamental fact which is called the unity of consciousness in itself provides the assurance we need.

There is certainly some truth in these remarks; but, unfortunately, if we pursue the matter farther we again become uncertain. From what has been said follows only that we cannot conceive any consciousness devoid of memory. But does this entail that memory is reliable? There seems nothing impossible in the idea that although I remember the past, my memory may always present a distorted picture of it in some way or other. In this case my consciousness would not fall apart into isolated instants of consciousness following one another without connection; each element would in fact be connected with and refer back to the previous one; that specific relation which constitutes the unity of consciousness would still bind the whole together; and in spite of this, memory would not be a trustworthy witness. Unity of consciousness does not mean reliability of memory. Again at the crucial point, our attempt has failed.

I believe that the right way out lies close at hand, and that it has been overlooked for so long only because people have not tried to see exactly what is meant by the question. It is only necessary to alter the direction of one's attention in the way we have spoken of earlier to see how a solution is to be found. If we want to understand the meaning of a question, we must know under what circumstances it should be answered by 'yes', and under what circumstances it should be answered by 'no'. So we ask the doubter 'What does it mean to say that my memory deceives me? What are the criteria for this being

the case?' He may make some such answer as: 'My memory deceives me when it disagrees about a past event either with what most other people say really happened or with what is written in reliable documents, diaries, letters, etc.' In this case his question has a clear meaning. I can tell whether specific memories, e.g. of my childhood, are, or are not correct. There is, if *this* is what the sceptic means, no further problem to perplex us. It is a matter of experience how far memory can be trusted. But this is obviously not the sense in which the sceptic doubts the certainty of memory. For what he asks is whether *all* memory is unreliable, including the memory we normally call reliable. So we ask him again: 'What do you now mean by the word "unreliable"? At any rate you do not mean what is normally understood by it. You must therefore explain what you mean by this word; that is, you must say in what circumstances you call memory "reliable", and in what "unreliable".' If he gives us a criterion, such as comparison with a certain document, we can understand precisely what his question means. In this case, however, it is not a philosophical question but one of everyday life. There is nothing exciting about his question but he fails to mention any criterion whatever (and this, of course, is usual with the radical philosophic sceptic), in such a case he does not know himself what he is asking. He does not know how a case of reliable memory is to be distinguished from one of unreliable memory. He draws, in fact, no distinction between these concepts. The question 'Is not all memory (including that which we call reliable) perhaps unreliable?' is thus on a level with 'Are not all notes including those

which we call low perhaps high?'
This question is a misuse of language,
nothing more.

We can now see how the problem dissolves. We do not say to the
doubter, 'You are mistaken, for what
you doubt is something which is a
matter of fact'. We tell him instead,
'Your question has no meaning, for
you have failed to give a meaning to
the words of which it is made up'.
Our conclusion would be in no way
affected, however much he persisted
that he meant something definite by
his question. We should reply: 'Then
tell us what it is that you mean. If
you cannot do this, then do not
imagine that there is a question.'

But what are we to do if the sceptic
contends that the criterion for the reliability of a memory is that it should
agree with the facts of the past? Does
saying this give a sense to his question? It is like somebody supposing
'The criterion for whether a man is
dead or not is whether or not his body
and soul have parted'. It is obvious
that this is not a criterion. (And saying that it is not a criterion is nothing
more than a remark about the use of
the word 'criterion'. It should remind
us of the way in which we actually
use this word.) A criterion for whether a man is dead or not must be something to which we can refer in cases
in which it is difficult to decide
whether he is really dead or only appears to be dead. It must therefore
be a state of affairs whose existence
or non-existence can be ascertained
with a minimum of doubt. 'The part-
ing of body and soul' is not such a
state of affairs, because we at once
want to ask how we know when they
part. Similarly, saying that a memory
is reliable 'when it agrees with the
facts of the past' gets us no farther,

for it does not tell us how we are to
find out whether such an agreement
exists or not. We have not formulated
any criterion but simply replaced the
old words with new ones whose meaning is as much in need of explanation
as the old. Hence the sceptic deceives
himself if he thinks his question has
been given a clear meaning.

This example shows very clearly
how a philosophical problem arises.
We first of all learn to use the word
'unreliable' in cases where it has a
clear meaning, where it means the
opposite of 'reliable'. Thinking that
we understand the word, we then use
it in the question 'Is *all* memory unreliable?' But in this case what does
calling a memory unreliable distinguish it from? We have failed to notice
how, by asking, just this question, we
have destroyed the meaning of the
word 'reliable'.

Somebody might object, 'But surely
I know what the word "unreliable"
means. I need not give an explanation. I am just asking whether all
memory may not turn out to be unreliable. So it is not a matter of how
I am going to use the word, but a
question concerning the facts'. To this
we should reply, 'You are asking the
question whether a memory which is
normally called reliable cannot turn
out to be in fact unreliable. So you
deviate from the ordinary use of language; you cannot mean by "unreliable" what the plain man means. So
will you please explain to us *what* you
mean'.

In order to avoid misunderstandings it must be remarked that it is
not because it is *general* that the
sceptic's question is mistaken. Once
we know under what circumstances
a memory is to be called reliable, it
might well be that the memories of

someone during a certain period of time were all unreliable. Experiences could even be described which (if they occurred) would show that the memory of *all* men during a certain time was unreliable. But then such a case could be contrasted with the case in which this was not so. But if and only if the sceptic rejects this and every other criterion which we may suggest, if for instance he refuses to allow that either introspective knowledge, or the testimony of others, or written documents, or causal effects, e.g. vestiges, can be sufficient to show whether or not a memory is reliable, then his constantly reiterated question: 'But are not all memories unreliable?' is merely a logical confusion dressed up as a problem.

QUESTIONS FOR DISCUSSION

1. Waismann says: "We come to an entirely new solution of philosophical questions." What is the "entirely new" solution? Is it entirely new?
2. It is sometimes held that philosophical questions are those which are the most general. Does Waismann agree?
3. Doubts may be suppressed or they may be disarmed. What is the difference? Does Waismann try to suppress doubts or to disarm them?
4. Show how Waismann deals with the skeptic who asks: "Isn't it possible that all memory is unreliable?"
5. According to Waismann what are the typical characteristics of a philosophical problem?

FURTHER READINGS FOR CHAPTER 1

*Aristotle, *Metaphysics*, Richard Hope, trans. Ann Arbor: University of Michigan Press, 1960.

Cohen, Morris R., "Vision and Technique in Philosophy," in *The Faith of a Liberal: Selected Essays*. New York: Holt, Rinehart & Winston, 1946.

Dewey, John, *Intelligence in the Modern World*. New York: Modern Library, 1939.

Edman, Irwin, *Four Ways of Philosophy*. New York: Holt, Rinehart & Winston, 1937.

*Plato, *Republic*. (Numerous editions available.)

*Spinoza, Benedict de, *On the Improvement of the Understanding*, J. Katz, trans. Indianapolis: Bobbs-Merrill, 1958.

*Whitehead, Alfred North, *Adventures of Ideas*. New York: New American Library of World Literature, n.d.

Wittgenstein, Ludwig, *Philosophical Investigations*, G. E. M. Anscombe, trans. New York: Macmillan, 1953.

---

* Paperback edition.

Chapter 2

METHODOLOGY

INTRODUCTION

An experienced mountain climber planning to ascend a difficult peak makes a survey of the existing trails before starting out. He may find that one trail goes only part of the way up, that another is dangerous in wet weather, or that a third requires special climbing equipment. After trying all the trails, he may blaze a new one better than the others.

A mouse in a maze doesn't pause to examine alternative routes to see which will lead most rapidly to his goal. Confronted by a problem beyond his capacity to solve except by the "method of trial and error," he enters and re-enters the same blind alleys until he finally "learns" the maze.

In our search for knowledge we try to emulate the mountain climber, but there are times when, because of a lack of systematic knowledge, we can do no better than to adopt the tactics of the mouse.

The selections that follow illustrate or describe some of the methods philosophers and scientists have developed to reach the goals they set themselves. It is important to be aware of these ends before evaluating the methods used in attaining them. Just as one mountain climber may prefer a winding scenic trail which does not reach the highest point, while another is intent on reaching the top by the shortest route, so one philosopher may devote his energies to the clarification of such fundamental common notions as virtue, knowledge, justice, and human happiness, as Socrates did, while another, Descartes, for example, is satisfied with nothing less than the reconstruction of the entire edifice of human knowledge on secure foundations. Others may be primarily interested in a correct understanding of natural phenomena, as Bacon was, or in the genesis and justification of human beliefs, like Peirce.

Amidst this diversity of subject matter it may be asked: What is the unifying feature of this chapter? It is the concern with those procedures and techniques which have been devised to aid us in extending our knowledge—that is to say, in clarifying and justifying what we already know, as well as in discovering what is still unknown. This is what we shall mean by *methodology*.

In this sense, methodological issues may arise not only in the context of philosophical discussion but in mathematics, natural science, law, economics, and so on. They arise most conspicuously where two competing methodologies both claim dominion over an area of human experience. In such a case, a methodological conflict occurs, as, for example, the one between religion and science. Each of the sciences, for example, astronomy, geology, medicine, biology (the theory of evolution), has had to establish its claims and vindicate its methods against the opposition of an entrenched theology. The sciences were victorious, but the conflict continues today in such fields as ethics and social policy. Still unsettled is a question such as, "Is right conduct to be determined by standards laid down in sacred texts, or by the laws and customs of a particular community, or by the dictates of individual conscience, or by some other method?" Such a question shows the interrelations of methodology with other branches of philosophy treated in this book, for example, with the philosophy of religion, the philosophy of politics, and ethics.

In selection 2.6, on ethical relativity, we have a prime example of competing methodologies. The ethical absolutists usually appeal to religious tradition to support their position, and the relativists often try to buttress their arguments by citing anthropological and other scientific data. A number of confusions must be clarified before the real issues can emerge. But difficulties may remain. It would be naive to expect, and we are not trying to maintain, that there is some magic method that is guaranteed to resolve every conflict. Sometimes the best we can do is to remove ambiguities and eliminate false issues. After stating the arguments pro and con we are sometimes left with questions rather than with final answers. But, as Waismann has pointed out in selection 1.6, to have found and clearly formulated the genuine questions is often the most important contribution we can make.[1]

In Plato's dialogues Socrates often spends a good deal of time asking questions and rejecting answers. A number of dialogues end without Socrates offering any definitive answer of his own. In fact, the Socratic method has sometimes been criticized on the ground that Socrates is a destructive critic who makes no positive contribution to the discussion. But let us see whether such a conception can be justified by Socrates' actual performance. What kind of question does he ask to open the discussion? How does he proceed when it is answered, as it usually is, in the conventional manner? We will

---

[1] Bertrand Russell makes a similar point in selection 1.4.

find that he starts with some innocent sounding but difficult question such as, "What is piety?" or "Do you think that it is worse to commit, or to suffer, injustice?" The answer is likely to be an ill-considered generalization of ordinary experience. Socrates continues by asking leading questions about our ordinary experience, which, because they appear unrelated to the original hypothesis, catch his companion off guard; eventually the answers reveal an inconsistency between the generalization and the admitted facts of experience. This is likely to lead to a redefinition of the fundamental concept, whether it is knowledge, justice, piety, courage, friendship, or pleasure. The new definition is then subjected to the same sort of critical examination as the old one. Often all proposed definitions are found wanting. Although the reader may be dissatisfied because of the negative character of the results, Socrates considers it no small achievement to produce an awareness of the inadequacy of commonly accepted notions, for such an awareness is a prerequisite to the search for satisfactory definitions. Perhaps Socrates' most notable contribution to logic and methodology was his emphasis on the importance of clearly defined concepts.

The attempt to clarify fundamental ideas is an arduous undertaking, and most people are not likely to engage in it voluntarily. As self-appointed gadfly, challenging the conventional but unexamined opinions held by his fellow Athenians, Socrates induced them to think about such things as the meaning of justice and the function of a state. The clarification of ethical and political concepts was the immediate goal of the Socratic inquiry. But in the broader context of enlightened action, the analysis served as a guide for personal and social conduct. Socrates, and his disciples too, did not hesitate to carry his principles into the political arena. For his interest, despite appearances to the contrary, was not primarily in the meaning of words, but rather in the creation of a just state and the realization of the good life.

The didactic function of the Socratic method, in aiding us to probe beneath clichés and conventional dogmas, has long been recognized. In the hands of a skillful teacher it can be of great assistance, enabling the student to cultivate a critical attitude towards generalizations and to discover for himself why his position is untenable and how to reformulate it more adequately. It can easily be abused, however, and often is by self-styled dialecticians whose sole purpose is to create confusion and to heap ridicule on an opponent. If Socrates himself appears, on occasion, to be doing this (for example, when questioning Euthyphro or Thrasymachus), it should be recalled that he was often arguing with clever Sophists whose bluster and cunning would otherwise have carried the audience, and that his main purpose, in such cases, was to help lift the fog which the Sophists had knowingly spread over fundamental ideas. When dealing with the Athenian youths who were interested in knowledge, his manner and method were noticeably mellower.

Descartes (1596-1650), like Socrates before him, felt the need of exposing the vain pretensions mistaken by his contemporaries for genuine knowledge. But for him no piecemeal reforms would suffice—only a general overhauling of all his beliefs "so that they might later on be replaced either by others which were better, or by the same, when I had made them conform to the uniformity of a rational scheme."

In describing his "method of arriving at a knowledge of all the things of which my mind was capable," Descartes says he saw no reason why the method of mathematics, the deductive method, could not be applied to all the fields of human knowledge. This notion of a "Universal Mathematics" as the key to nature, which was suggested to Descartes by his invention of analytic geometry, did not seem extravagant in the seventeenth century. The discoveries of Kepler, Galileo, and Newton all seemed to substantiate it, and even in such fields as metaphysics, ethics, and jurisprudence writers attempted, following the pattern of Euclid's geometry, to derive a systematic body of truths from (so-called) self-evident axioms.

Descartes' universal doubt has been derided as both futile and disingenuous. Yet, if conscientiously carried out, a critical review of our opinions in the Cartesian fashion can have a healthy effect in unearthing prejudice and other ill-founded notions which we are all too prone to adopt without sufficient scrutiny. However, we must be courageous enough to be patient in the face of ignorance and not in too much of a hurry to substitute new dogmas for the old.

Another rebel against the teaching of the Schools, Francis Bacon (1561-1626), an older contemporary of Descartes, also proposed a program of intellectual reconstruction. Unlike the French philosopher, however, Bacon had no use for a method that starts with *a priori* principles [2] and attempts from them to deduce the nature of the world. His new method of investigation (the "inductive method"), which stressed the importance of an observation of nature unfettered by preconceived notions, was developed in conscious opposition to the untested theorizing about nature so common among the ancients and scholastics. But in his anxiety to combat the tendency of the latter to discover natural laws by appealing to Aristotle instead of nature, he was led to undervalue the role of the mind in selecting and interpreting the raw data of experience. There are passages in Bacon's writings in which he pays his respects to the interpretation of the understanding (hypothesis), but he thinks of this as the last stage of the process of inquiry rather than

---

[2] By an *a priori* principle is meant one which appears to be so clear and rational that no sense experience is needed to establish it. An example would be Aristotle's belief that *nature does nothing in vain*. Another would be that *every triangle has three sides*. A *priori* principles or propositions are contrasted with *a posteriori* propositions, which can only be discovered and verified by experience. Examples would be that *the earth is round*, or that *malaria is transmitted by a mosquito*. (See selection 5.3 and footnotes on page 353.)

its guiding principle. He insists on a careful tabulation of all observed data as a prerequisite to the discovery of correct laws and sound principles. And his descriptions of experiments would lead us to suppose that the method of scientific discovery is a laborious but uninspired digging for facts, from which true generalizations and laws of nature would flow as a matter of course, even as water does from the ground when we have done enough digging. If this were all there is to scientific method, we should not have had to wait for the scientific genius of a Galileo or a Newton to discover the laws of dynamics. Their fruitful hypotheses suggested experiments which would not otherwise have been performed; these led to new and improved hypotheses which were in turn verified by further observations and experiments. If their original hypotheses were not to be found in the works of Aristotle or his scholastic interpreters, neither were they gleaned from Bacon's tables of Inclusion and Exclusion. No neat formulae or shortcuts have ever been devised which can cause such hypotheses to arise in the mind. They are the product of a fertile mind that has proper regard for the facts, but that is also capable of reading a new meaning in them.

Bacon's chief contribution to philosophy was not his analysis of the method of science, which he oversimplified, but his acute dissection of the errors and fallacies of human reasoning (the famous Idols) and his recognition that the method of authority would have to be replaced by a new method before the scientific awakening which he correctly foresaw could become a reality.

Whereas Bacon was one of the most famous of the advocates of the method of science, Henri Bergson (1860-1941) was one of its most popular disparagers. To him it was a feeble instrument incapable of revealing what he considered the essence of reality, that is, change and continuity. Genuine knowledge, he held, is attainable only by a "kind of intellectual sympathy" called *intuition*. An illustration may serve to suggest what Bergson had in mind: a shipwrecked sailor writes a book describing his experiences. These may be vividly and dramatically portrayed; but printed words, though they may evoke vicarious emotions, cannot impart the sense of reality felt by the author. He first has to reconstruct a continuous series of events from memory and at a distance. Then he has to select and describe those portions which he considers worth reporting. The result is a number of fragmentary glimpses, a poor substitute for the immediate experience of a flux of events. If this is true of descriptions in our everyday language, Bergson believed it all the more true of scientific writing, where the scientist consciously abstracts from those features of experience which do not interest him. This conceptual analysis, according to Bergson, yields only static, quantitative, abstract symbols, which have merely practical value; whereas intuition can reveal the dynamic, qualitative, concrete reality. But it is difficult to gather from Bergson's writings the precise nature of this intuitive apprehension which he so exalted, calling it the ideal method of metaphysics; perhaps it is essentially indescribable. Although he thought of his philosophy as a purified empiricism, Bergson's attempt to grasp the essence of reality by immediate insight is regarded by many critics as belonging to the tradition of mysticism.

Bergson's glowing account of the virtues of the intuitive method of discerning the nature of the real is in sharp contrast to the sober, devastating analysis which Charles Peirce (1839-1914) gives of this method in his classic essay, "The Fixation of Belief," written in 1877. Peirce shows the advantages and disadvantages of the various methods practiced by men in "fixing" their beliefs—the methods of tenacity (not a method of reaching, but rather of retaining a belief), authority, intuition (which he calls the *a priori* method), and the method of science. As he points out, there is a fatal weakness in the first three methods, for whoever relies on them in forming his opinions cannot reasonably be surprised if those opinions turn out to be erroneous.

Moreover, there is nothing in these three methods which would lead anyone employing them to discover his error or even to suspect its presence. A glance at the conflicting faiths and ideologies in the world today shows that beliefs reached by appealing to authority (or to intuition) are at variance with the beliefs at which others have arrived by the same method. To resolve these differences, further reliance on the same method is futile, because in each case it will re-enforce the old opinion. Thus, discussion is at a standstill until a method is invoked which can distinguish the true from the false. The method of science can do this because it has been designed to produce beliefs which are in conformity with the facts. Not that it cannot lead to erroneous beliefs. It can. It is not unusual for two investigators, both using scientific method, to reach divergent conclusions, in which case at least one of them must be in error. But—and this is the point—the error can be discovered and the disagreement overcome by the continued use of scientific method, by which we mean constructing hypotheses, testing them by careful observations and controlled experiments, and employing all the other devices (such as analogy and sampling techniques) that have made scientific investigations so fruitful. Thus, what Peirce refers to briefly as the method of science, has one critical advantage over its rivals—it is *self-corrective.*

Does this mean that we have a ground for assurance that all differences of opinion can be resolved by the method of science? Peirce's answer would probably be: "Yes, ultimately"—since he defines the truth as that upon which all who investigate will ultimately agree.[3] But this answer, it should be noted, is compatible with the existence of unresolved differences at any specified

---

[3] There is something unsatisfactory, as Peirce realized, in his statement that "the sole object of inquiry is the settlement of opinion." Psychologically, this is correct, but it will not do as an account of the logic of inquiry. Since Peirce wants inquiry to serve a normative function, its goal must be not merely the settlement of opinion, but the attainment of true belief.

time, so that it actually offers scant hope for the termination of philosophical and religious conflicts in the near future.

But can we resolve differences between those who do not acknowledge the authority of the method of science and those who do? Is there any answer to the critic who claims that the very procedure we have instituted for investigating the methods of authority, intuition, revelation, and for comparing them with the method of science, commits us at the start to the method of science? Have we not decided that the methods of authority and intuition are inadequate because they violate certain conditions set up as necessary by the method of science? And if we thus assume that the method of science can be the arbiter of all methods including itself, are we not convicted of circular reasoning?

This is another way of asking how we *justify* our commitment to the method of science. The answer can only be in terms of what we hope to accomplish by using any of these methods. Do we want comfortable beliefs? Do we want beliefs that will stack up well with those of our social set? Do we want a method that will make it unnecessary for us ever to change our minds? Then one of the other methods would be preferable to the method of science. Or do we want a method which is most likely to lead to beliefs that are true? People tend to choose that method which they think can best accomplish the end they desire.[4] The methods of science, conceived broadly as the methods of rational inquiry, have been constructed, and are constantly being improved, for the precise purpose of leading men to those beliefs which are true—or most probable in the face of all the discoverable evidence. When scientific method is understood in this way, there can be no neutral canons of reasonableness to which we can appeal for adjudication of a contest between the advocates of faith or intuition and the defenders of scientific method. And the intuitionists might reject such canons if they did exist. Our choice of the method of science is a *decision* in terms of a goal, and it can only be sensibly challenged by showing that there are better ways of reaching *that goal*. Such challenges have been made, for example by Bergson, who would attribute Galileo's discoveries to an intuition of pure duration, which was not vouchsafed to Aristotle. This challenge can be met only by a careful study of Galileo's actual procedure and his analysis of his own experiments. It might also require a clearer statement of the process of intuition than is supplied by Bergson. Finally, if a critic should question our right to claim that the methods of science are most likely to lead to true beliefs, we could only refer him to the history of thought.

Many discussions among philosophers concerning the adequacy of scientific method bog down because there is no agreed interpretation of that phrase, *scientific method*. Critics are inclined to identify scientific method

---

[4] Of course, none of these methods can tell us what end to desire.

with some doctrinaire *philosophical* interpretation like behaviorism, pragmatism, positivism, physicalism, or one of the many types of naturalism. But one who chooses scientific method in preference to its alternatives is not *necessarily* committed to *any* of these philosophies. Nor can *scientific method* be identified with the various interpretations of their procedure which have been given by physicists, biologists, or other scientists. In the "Fixation of Belief" Peirce has done no more than contrast scientific method with some competing methods of stabilizing belief. A great deal needs to be said in explanation of such elements of scientific method as *observation, verification, probability, proof, hypothesis, induction,* and *deduction.*[5]

If it is difficult to meet the demand of critics that we demonstrate the *adequacy* of scientific method in all domains of human interest, it is well to remember that a preference for scientific method need not rest on such a demonstration. It can be defended, as we have seen, on two grounds, one logical and one historical: namely, (1) scientific method, in contrast to its alternatives, is self-corrective, and (2) with many notable triumphs to its credit in the natural sciences, it now bids fair to extend and deepen man's knowledge in related fields.

Methodology is far from being a completed structure set forth satisfactorily in a number of canons or rules. A great deal of work needs to be done in clarifying the concepts and methods of science and in applying them to fields in which more profound knowledge is of great urgency to the human race. This presents a challenge to any student interested in philosophy.

---

[5] For a discussion of these topics refer to Chapter 5 and to the bibliography at the end of this chapter.

Plato (427-347 b.c.)

2.1   The Socratic Method

EUTHYPHRO *

Persons of the Dialogue

SOCRATES   EUTHYPHRO

Scene: A portico before the King Archon's office

Euthyphro. What can have happened, Socrates, to bring you away from the Lyceum? and what are you doing in the Porch of the King Archon? Surely you cannot be concerned in a suit before the King, like myself?

Socrates. Not in a suit, Euthyphro; prosecution is the word which the Athenians use.

Euth. What! I suppose that someone has been prosecuting you, for I cannot believe that you are the prosecutor of another.

Soc. Certainly not.

Euth. Then someone else has been prosecuting you?

Soc. Yes.

Euth. And who is he?

Soc. A young man who is little known, Euthyphro; and I hardly know him: his name is Meletus, and he is of the deme of Pitthis. Perhaps you may remember his appearance; he has a

beak, and straight hair, and a beard which is ill grown.

Euth. No, I do not remember him, Socrates. But what is the charge which he brings against you?

Soc. What is the charge? Well, rather a grand one, which implies a degree of discernment far from contemptible in a young man. He says he knows how the youth are corrupted and who are their corruptors. I fancy that he must be a wise man, and seeing that I am the reverse of a wise man, he has found me out, and is going to accuse me of corrupting his generation. And of this our mother the state is to be the judge. Of all our political men he is the only one who seems to me to begin in the right way, with the cultivation of virtue in youth; like a good husbandman, he makes the young shoots his first care, and clears away us whom he accuses of destroying them. This is only the first step; afterwards he will assuredly attend to the elder branches; and if he goes on as he has begun, he will be a very great public benefactor.

---

* From *The Dialogues of Plato* translated by Benjamin Jowett, 1953. Reprinted by permission of The Clarendon Press, Oxford.

Euth. I hope that he may; but I rather fear, Socrates, that the opposite will turn out to be the truth. My opinion is that in attacking you he is simply aiming a blow at the heart of the state. But in what way does he say that you corrupt the young?

Soc. In a curious way, which at first hearing excites surprise: he says that I am a maker of gods, and that I invent new gods and deny the existence of the old ones; this is the ground of his indictment.

Euth. I understand, Socrates; he means to attack you about the familiar sign which occasionally, as you say, comes to you. He thinks that you are a neologian, and he is going to have you up before the court for this. He knows that such a charge is readily received by the world, as I myself know too well; for when I speak in the assembly about divine things, and foretell the future to them, they laugh at me and think me a madman. Yet every word that I say is true. But they are jealous of us all; and we must be brave and go at them.

Soc. Their laughter, friend Euthyphro, is not a matter of much consequence. For a man may be thought clever; but the Athenians, I suspect, do not much trouble themselves about him until he begins to impart his wisdom to others; and then for some reason or other, perhaps, as you say, from jealousy, they are angry.

Euth. I have no great wish to try their temper towards me in this way.

Soc. No doubt they think you are reserved in your behaviour, and unwilling to impart your wisdom. But I have a benevolent habit of pouring out myself to everybody, and would even pay for a listener, and I am afraid that the Athenians may think me too talkative. Now if, as I was say-ing, they would only laugh at me, as you say that they laugh at you, the time might pass gaily enough with jokes and merriment in the court; but perhaps they may be in earnest, and then what the end will be you soothsayers only can predict.

Euth. I dare say that the affair will end in nothing, Socrates, and that you will win your cause; and I think that I shall win my own.

Soc. And what is your suit, Euthyphro? are you the pursuer or the defendant?

Euth. I am the pursuer.

Soc. Of whom?

Euth. When I tell you, you will perceive another reason why I am thought mad.

Soc. Why, has the fugitive wings?

Euth. Nay, he is not very volatile at his time of life.

Soc. Who is he?

Euth. My father.

Soc. My dear Sir! Your own father?

Euth. Yes.

Soc. And of what is he accused?

Euth. Of murder, Socrates.

Soc. Good heavens! How little, Euthyphro, does the common herd know of the nature of right and truth! A man must be an extraordinary man, and have made great strides in wisdom, before he could have seen his way to bring such an action.

Euth. Indeed, Socrates, he must.

Soc. I suppose that the man whom your father murdered was one of your family—clearly he was; for if he had been a stranger you would never have thought of prosecuting him.

Euth. I am amused, Socrates, at your making a distinction between one who is a member of the family and one who is not; for surely the pollution is the same in either case, if you knowingly associate with the mur-

derer when you ought to clear yourself and him by proceeding against
him. The real question is whether the
murdered man has been justly slain.
If justly, then your duty is to let the
matter alone; but if unjustly, then proceed against the murderer, if, that is
to say, he lives under the same roof
with you and eats at the same table.
In fact, the man who is dead was a
poor dependent of mine who worked
for us as a field labourer on our farm
in Naxos, and one day in a fit of
drunken passion he got into a quarrel
with one of our domestic servants and
slew him. My father bound him hand
and foot and threw him into a ditch,
and then sent to Athens to ask an expositor of religious law what he should
do with him. Meanwhile he never
attended to him and took no care
about him, for he regarded him as
a murderer; and thought that no
great harm would be done even if he
did die. Now this was just what happened. For such was the effect of cold
and hunger and chains upon him, that
before the messenger returned from
the expositor, he was dead. And my
father and family are angry with me
for taking the part of the murderer
and prosecuting my father. They say
that he did not kill him, and that if
he did, the dead man was but a murderer, and I ought not to take any
notice, for that a son is impious who
prosecutes a father for murder. Which
shows, Socrates, how little they know
what the gods think about piety and
impiety.

Soc. Good heavens, Euthyphro!
and is your knowledge of religion and
of things pious and impious so very
exact, that, supposing the circumstances to be as you state them, you
are not afraid lest you too may be

doing an impious thing in bringing an
action against your father?

Euth. The best of Euthyphro, that
which distinguishes him, Socrates,
from the common herd, is his exact
knowledge of all such matters. What
should I be good for without it?

Soc. Rare friend! I think that I cannot do better than be your disciple.
Then before the trial with Meletus
comes on I shall challenge him, and
say that I have always had a great interest in religious questions, and now,
as he charges me with rash imaginations and innovations in religion, I
have become your disciple. You, Meletus, as I shall say to him, acknowledge
Euthyphro to be a great theologian,
and so you ought to approve of me,
and not have me into court; otherwise
you should begin by indicting him
who is my teacher, and who will be
the ruin, not of the young, but of the
old; that is to say, of myself whom he
instructs, and of his old father whom
he admonishes and chastises. And if
Meletus refuses to listen to me, but
will go on, and will not shift the indictment from me to you, I cannot do
better than repeat this challenge in
the court.

Euth. Yes, indeed, Socrates; and if
he attempts to indict me I am mistaken if I do not find a flaw in him;
the court will be occupied with him
long before it comes to me.

Soc. And I, my dear friend, knowing this, am desirous of becoming
your disciple. For I observe that no
one appears to notice you—not even
this Meletus; but his sharp eyes have
found me out at once, and he has in-
dicted me for impiety. And therefore,
I adjure you to tell me the nature of
piety and impiety, which you said that
you knew so well, in their bearing on

murder and generally on offences against the gods. Is not piety in every action always the same? and impiety, again—is it not always the opposite of piety, and also the same with itself, having, as impiety, one notion or form which includes whatever is impious?

Euth. To be sure, Socrates.

Soc. And what is piety, and what is impiety?

Euth. Piety is doing as I am doing; that is to say, prosecuting anyone who is guilty of murder, sacrilege, or of any similar crime—whether he be your father or mother, or whoever he may be—that makes no difference; and not to prosecute them is impiety. And please to consider, Socrates, what a notable proof I will give you that this is the law, a proof which I have already given to others:—of the principle, I mean, that the impious, whoever he may be, ought not to go unpunished. For do not men acknowledge Zeus as the best and most righteous of the gods?—and yet they admit that he bound his father (Cronos) because he wickedly devoured his sons, and that he too had punished his own father (Uranus) for a similar reason, in a nameless manner. And yet when I proceed against my father, they are angry with me. So inconsistent are they in their way of talking when the gods are concerned, and when I am concerned.

Soc. May not this be the reason, Euthyphro, why I am charged with impiety—that I cannot away with these stories about the gods? that, I suppose is where people think I go wrong. But as you who are well informed about them approve of them, I cannot do better than assent to your superior wisdom. What else can I say, confessing as I do, that I know noth-

ing about them? Tell me, for the love of Zeus, whether you really believe that they are true.

Euth. Yes, Socrates; and things more wonderful still, of which the world is in ignorance.

Soc. And do you really believe that the gods fought with one another, and had dire quarrels, battles, and the like, as the poets say, and as you see represented in the works of great artists? The temples are full of them; and notably the robe of Athene, which is carried up to the Acropolis at the great Panathenaea, is embroidered with them throughout. Are all these tales of the gods true, Euthyphro?

Euth. Yes, Socrates; and, and as I was saying, I can tell you, if you would like to hear them, many other things about the gods which would quite amaze you.

Soc. I dare say; and you shall tell me them at some other time when I have leisure. But just at present I would rather hear from you a more precise answer, which you have not as yet given, my friend, to the question, 'What is "piety"?' When asked, you only replied, 'Doing as you do, charging your father with murder'.

Euth. And what I said was true, Socrates.

Soc. No doubt, Euthyphro; but you would admit that there are many other pious acts?

Euth. There are.

Soc. Remember that I did not ask you to give me two or three examples of piety, but to explain the general form which makes all pious things to be pious. Do you not recollect saying that one and the same form made the impious impious, the pious pious?

Euth. I remember.

Soc. Tell me what is the nature of

this form, and then I shall have a standard to which I may measure actions, whether yours or those of anyone else, and then I shall be able to say that such and such an action is pious, such another impious.

Euth. I will tell you, if you like.

Soc. I should very much like.

Euth. Piety, then, is that which is dear to the gods, and impiety is that which is not dear to them.

Soc. Very good, Euthyphro; you have now given me the sort of answer which I wanted. But whether what you say is true or not I cannot as yet tell, although I make no doubt that you will go on to prove the truth of your words.

Euth. Of course.

Soc. Come, then, and let us examine what we are saying. That thing or person which is dear to the gods is pious, and that thing or person which is hateful to the gods is impious, these two being the extreme opposites of one another. Was not that said?

Euth. It was.

Soc. And well said?

Euth. Yes, Socrates, I think so.

Soc. And further, Euthyphro, the gods were admitted to have enmities and hatreds and differences?

Euth. Yes, that was also said.

Soc. And what sort of difference creates enmity and anger? Suppose for example that you and I, my good friend, differ on the question which of two groups of things is more numerous; do differences of this sort make us enemies and set us at variance with one another? Do we not proceed at once to counting, and put an end to them?

Euth. True.

Soc. Or suppose that we differ about magnitudes, do we not quickly end the difference by measuring?

Euth. Very true.

Soc. And we end a controversy about heavy and light by resorting to a weighing machine?

Euth. To be sure.

Soc. But what are the matters about which differences arise that cannot be thus decided, and therefore make us angry and set us at enmity with one another? I dare say the answer does not occur to you at the moment, and therefore I will suggest that these enmities arise when the matters of difference are the just and unjust, good and evil, honourable and dishonourable. Are not these the subjects about which men differ, and about which when we are unable satisfactorily to decide our differences, you and I and all of us quarrel, when we do quarrel?

Euth. Yes, Socrates, the nature of the differences about which we quarrel is such as you describe.

Soc. And the quarrels of the gods, noble Euthyphro, when they occur, are of a like nature?

Euth. Certainly they are.

Soc. They have differences of opinion, as you say, about good and evil, just and unjust, honourable and dishonourable: there would be no quarrels among them, if there were no such differences—would there now?

Euth. You are quite right.

Soc. Does not each part of them love that which they deem noble and just and good, and hate the opposite?

Euth. Very true.

Soc. But, as you say, one party regards as just the same things as the other thinks unjust,—about these they dispute, and so there arise wars and fighting among them.

Euth. Very true.

Soc. Then the same things are hated by the gods and loved by the gods, and are both hateful and dear to them?

Euth. It appears so.

Soc. And upon this view the same things, Euthyphro, will be pious and also impious?

Euth. So I should suppose.

Soc. Then, my friend, I remark with surprise that you have not answered the question which I asked. For I certainly did not ask you to tell me what action is both pious and impious; but now it would seem that what is loved by the gods is also hated by them. And therefore, Euthyphro, in thus chastising your father you may very likely be doing what is agreeable to Zeus but disagreeable to Cronos or Uranus, and what is acceptable to Hephaestus but unacceptable to Hera, and there may be other gods who have similar differences of opinion.

Euth. But, I believe, Socrates, that all the gods would be agreed as to the propriety of punishing a murderer: there would be do difference of opinion about that.

Soc. Well, but speaking of men, Euthyphro, did you ever hear anyone arguing that a murderer or any sort of evil-doer ought to be let off?

Euth. I should rather say that these are the questions which they are always arguing, especially in courts of law: they commit all sorts of crimes, and there is nothing which they will not do or say in their own defence.

Soc. But do they admit their guilt, Euthyphro, and yet say that they ought not to be punished?

Euth. No; they do not.

Soc. Then there are some things which they do not venture to say and do: for they do not venture to argue that if guilty they are to go unpunished, but they deny their guilt, do they not?

Euth. Yes.

Soc. Then they do not argue that the evil-doer should not be punished, but they argue about the fact of who the evil-doer is, and what he did and when?

Euth. True.

Soc. And the gods are in the same case, if as you assert they quarrel about just and unjust, and some of them say while others deny that injustice is done among them. For surely neither god nor man will ever venture to say that the doer of injustice is not to be punished?

Euth. That is true, Socrates, in the main.

Soc. But they join issue about the particulars—gods and men alike, if indeed the gods dispute at all; they differ about some act which is called in question, and which by some is affirmed to be just, by others to be unjust. Is not that true?

Euth. Quite true.

Soc. Well then, my dear friend Euthyphro, do tell me, for my better instruction and information, what proof have you that in the opinion of all the gods a servant who is guilty of murder, and is put in chains by the master of the dead man, and dies because he is put in chains before he who bound him can learn from the expositors of religious law what he ought to do with him, is killed unjustly; and that on behalf of such an one a son ought to proceed against his father and accuse him of murder. How would you show that all the gods absolutely agree in approving of his act? Prove to me that they do, and I will applaud your wisdom as long as I live.

Euth. No doubt it will be a difficult task; though I could make the matter very clear indeed to you.

Soc. I understand; you mean to say that I am not so quick of apprehension as the judges: for to them you will be sure to prove that the act is unjust, and hateful to all the gods.

Euth. Yes indeed, Socrates; at least if they will listen to me.

Soc. But they will be sure to listen if they find that you are a good speaker. There was a notion that came into my mind while you were speaking; I said to myself: 'Well, and what if Euthyphro does prove to me that all the gods regarded the death of the serf as unjust, how do I know anything more of the nature of piety and impiety? for granting that this action may be hateful to the gods, still piety and impiety are not adequately defined by these distinctions, for that which is hateful to the gods has been shown to be also dear to them.' And therefore, Euthyphro, I do not ask you to prove this; I will suppose, if you like, that all the gods condemn and abominate such an action. But I will amend the definition so far as to say that what all the gods hate is impious, and what they love pious or holy; and what some of them love and others hate is both or neither. Shall this be our definition of piety and impiety?

Euth. Why not, Socrates?

Soc. Why not! certainly, as far as I am concerned, Euthyphro, there is no reason why not. But whether this premiss will greatly assist you in the task of instructing me as you promised, is a matter for you to consider.

Euth. Yes, I should say that what all the gods love is pious and holy, and the opposite which they all hate, impious.

Soc. Ought we to inquire into the truth of this, Euthyphro, or simply to accept it on our own authority and that of others—echoing mere assertions? What do you say?

Euth. We should inquire; and I believe that the statement will stand the test of inquiry.

Soc. We shall soon be better able to say, my good friend. The point which I should first wish to understand is whether the pious or holy is beloved by the gods because it is holy, or holy because it is beloved of the gods.

Euth. I do not understand your meaning, Socrates.

Soc. I will endeavour to explain: we speak of carrying and we speak of being carried, of leading and being led, seeing and being seen. You know that in all such cases there is a difference, and you know also in what the difference lies?

Euth. I think that I understand.

Soc. And is not that which is beloved distinct from that which loves?

Euth. Certainly.

Soc. Well; and now tell me, is that which is carried in this state of carrying because it is carried, or for some other reason?

Euth. No; that is the reason.

Soc. And the same is true of what is led and of what is seen?

Euth. True.

Soc. And a thing is not seen because it is visible, but conversely, visible because it is seen; nor is a thing led because it is in the state of being led, or carried because it is in the state of being carried, but the converse of this. And now I think, Euthyphro, that my meaning will be intelligible; and my meaning is, that any state of action or passion implies previous action or passion. It does not become because it is becoming, but it is in a state of becoming because it becomes; neither does it suffer because it is in a state of suffering, but it is in a state of suffering because it suffers. Do you not agree?

Euth. Yes.

Soc. Is not that which is loved in some state either of becoming or suffering?

Euth. Yes.

Soc. And the same holds as in the previous instances; the state of being loved follows the act of being loved, and not the act the state.

Euth. Certainly.

Soc. And what do you say of piety, Euthyphro: is not piety, according to your definition, loved by all the gods?

Euth. Yes.

Soc. Because it is pious or holy, or for some other reason?

Euth. No, that is the reason.

Soc. It is loved because it is holy, not holy because it is loved?

Euth. Apparently

Soc. And it is the object of the gods' love, and is dear to them, because it is loved of them?

Euth. Certainly.

Soc. Then that which is dear to the gods, Euthyphro, is not holy, nor is that which is holy dear to the gods, as you affirm; but they are two different things.

Euth. How do you mean, Socrates?

Soc. I mean to say that the holy has been acknowledged by us to be loved because it is holy, not to be holy because it is loved.

Euth. Yes.

Soc. But that which is dear to the gods is dear to them because it is loved by them, not loved by them because it is dear to them.

Euth. True.

Soc. But, friend Euthyphro, if that which is holy were the same with that which is dear to the gods, and were loved because it is holy, then that

which is dear to the gods would be loved as being dear to them; but if that which is dear to them were dear to them because loved by them, then that which is holy would be holy because loved by them. But now you see that the reverse is the case, and that the two things are quite different from one another. For one (θεοφιλές) [*theophiles*] is of a kind to be loved because it is loved and the other (ὅσιον) [*hosion*] is loved because it is of a kind to be loved. Thus you appear to me, Euthyphro, when I ask you what is the nature of holiness, to offer an attribute only, and not the essence —the attribute of being loved by all the gods. But you still do not explain to me the nature of holiness. And therefore, if you please, I will ask you not to hide your treasure, but to start again, and tell me frankly what holiness or piety really is, whether dear to the gods or not (for that is a matter about which we will not quarrel); and what is impiety?

Euth. I really do not know, Socrates, how to express what I mean. For somehow or other the definitions we propound, on whatever bases we rest them, seem always to turn round and walk away from us.

Soc. Your words, Euthyphro, are like the handiwork of my ancestor Daedalus; and if I were the sayer or propounder of them, you might scoffingly reply that the products of my reasoning walk away and will not remain fixed where they are placed because I am a descendant of his. But now, since these propositions are your own, you must find some other gibe, for they certainly, as you yourself allow, show an inclination to be on the move.

Euth. Nay, Socrates, I think the gibe is much to the point, for you are the Daedalus who sets arguments in motion; not I, certainly, but you make them move or go round, for they would never have stirred, as far as I am concerned.

Soc. Then I must be greater than Daedalus: for whereas he only made his own inventions to move, I move those of other people as well. And the beauty of it is, that I would rather not: for I would give the wisdom of Daedalus, and the wealth of Tantalus, to be able to detain them and keep them fixed. But enough of this. As I perceive that you are spoilt, I will myself endeavour to show you how you might instruct me in the nature of piety; and I hope that you will not begrudge your labour. Tell me, then, —Is not all that is pious necessarily just?

Euth. Yes.

Soc. And is, then, all which is just pious? or, is that which is pious all just, but that which is just is only in part, and not all, pious?

Euth. I do not understand you, Socrates.

Soc. And yet I know that you are as much wiser than I am, as you are younger. But, as I was saying, revered friend, you are spoilt owing to the abundance of your wisdom. Please to exert yourself, for there is no real difficulty in understanding me. What I mean I may explain by an illustration of what I do not mean. The poet (Stasinus) sings—

Of Zeus, the author and creator of all these things,
He will not speak reproach: for where there is fear there is also reverence.

Now I disagree with this poet. Shall I tell you in what respect?

Euth. By all means.

Soc. I should not say that where there is fear there is also reverence; for I am sure that many persons fear poverty and disease, and the like evils, but I do not perceive that they reverence the objects of their fear.

Euth. Very true.

Soc. But where reverence is, there is fear; for he who has a feeling of reverence and shame about the commission of any action, fears and is afraid of an ill reputation.

Euth. No doubt.

Soc. Then we are wrong in saying that where there is fear there is also reverence; and we should say, where there is reverence there is also fear. But there is not always reverence where there is fear; for fear is a more extended notion, and reverence is a part of fear, just as the odd is a part of number, and number is a more extended notion than the odd. I suppose that you follow me now?

Euth. Quite well.

Soc. That was the sort of question which I meant to raise when I asked whether the just is always the pious, or whether it is not the case that where there is piety there is always justice, but there may be justice where there is not piety; for justice is the more extended notion of which piety is only a part. Do you dissent?

Euth. No, I think that you are quite right.

Soc. Then, if piety is a part of justice, I suppose that we should inquire what part? If you had pursued the inquiry in the previous cases; for instance, if you had asked me what is an even number, and what part of number the even is, I should have had no difficulty in replying, a number which is not lopsided, so to speak, but represents a figure having two equal sides. Do you not agree?

Euth. Yes, I quite agree.

Soc. In like manner, I want you to tell me what part of justice is piety or holiness, that I may be able to tell Meletus not to do me injustice, or indict me for impiety, as I am now adequately instructed by you in the nature of piety or holiness, and their opposites.

Euth. Piety or holiness, Socrates, appears to me to be that part of justice which attends to the gods, as there is the other part of justice which attends to men.

Soc. That is good, Euthyphro; yet still there is a little point about which I should like to have further information, What is the meaning of 'attention'? For attention can hardly be used in the same sense when applied to the gods as when applied to other things. We do so apply it, do we not? for instance, horses are said to require attention, and not every person is able to attend to them, but only a person skilled in horsemanship. Is it not so?

Euth. Certainly.

Soc. I should suppose that the art of horsemanship is the art of attending to horses?

Euth. Yes.

Soc. Nor is everyone qualified to attend to dogs, but only the huntsman?

Euth. True.

Soc. And I should also conceive that the art of the huntsman is the art of attending to dogs?

Euth. Yes.

Soc. As the art of the oxherd is the art of attending to oxen?

Euth. Very true.

Soc. In like manner holiness or piety is the art of attending to the gods? —that would be your meaning, Euthyphro?

Euth. Yes.

Soc. And is not attention always designed for the good or benefit of that to which the attention is given? As in the case of horses, you may observe that when attended to by the horseman's art they are benefited and improved, are they not?

Euth. True.

Soc. As the dogs are benefited by the huntsman's art, and the oxen by the art of the oxherd, and all other things are tended or attended for their good and not for their hurt?

Euth. Certainly, not for their hurt.

Soc. But for their good?

Euth. Of course.

Soc. And does piety or holiness, which has been defined to be the art of attending to the gods, benefit or improve them? Would you say that when you do a holy act you make any of the gods better?

Euth. No, no; that was certainly not what I meant.

Soc. And I, Euthyphro, never supposed that you did. I asked you the question about the nature of the attention, because I thought that you did not.

Euth. You do me justice, Socrates; that is not the sort of attention which I mean.

Soc. Good: but I must still ask what is this attention to the gods which is called piety?

Euth. It is such, Socrates, as servants show to their masters.

Soc. I understand—a sort of ministration to the gods.

Euth. Exactly.

Soc. Medicine is also a sort of ministration or service, having in view the attainment of some object—would you not say of health?

Euth. I should.

Soc. Again, there is the art which ministers to the ship-builder with a view to the attainment of some result?

Euth. Yes, Socrates, with a view to the building of a ship.

Soc. As there is an art which ministers to the house-builder with a view to the building of a house?

Euth. Yes.

Soc. And now tell me, my good friend, about the art which ministers to the gods: what work does that help to accomplish? For you must surely know if, as you say, you are of all men living the one who is best instructed in religion.

Euth. And I speak the truth, Socrates.

Soc. Tell me then, oh tell me—what is that fair work which the gods do by the help of our ministrations?

Euth. Many and fair, Socrates, are the works which they do.

Soc. Why, my friend, and so are those of a general. But the sum of them is easily told. Would you not say that the sum of his works is victory in war?

Euth. Certainly.

Soc. Many and fair, too, are the works of the husbandman, if I am not mistaken; but their sum is the production of food from the earth?

Euth. Exactly.

Soc. And of the many and fair things done by the gods, what is the sum?

Euth. I have told you already, Socrates, that to learn all these things accurately will be very tiresome. Let me simply say that piety or holiness is learning how to please the gods in word and deed, by prayers and sacrifices. Such piety is the salvation of families and states, just as impiety, which is unpleasing to the gods, is their ruin and destruction.

Soc. I think that you could have answered in much fewer words the substance of my questions if you had

chosen. But I see plainly that you are not disposed to instruct me—clearly not: else why, when we reached the point, did you turn aside? Had you only answered me I should have truly learned of you by this time the nature of piety. But I must follow you as a lover must follow the caprice of his beloved, and therefore can only ask again, what is the pious, and what is piety? Do you mean that they are a sort of science of praying and sacrificing?

Euth. Yes, I do.

Soc. And sacrificing is giving to the gods, and prayer is asking of the gods?

Euth. Yes, Socrates.

Soc. Upon this view, then, piety is a science of asking and giving?

Euth. You understand me capitally, Socrates.

Soc. Yes, my friend; the reason is that I am a votary of your science, and give my mind to it, and therefore nothing which you say will be thrown away upon me. Please then to tell me, what is the nature of this service to the gods? Do you mean that we prefer requests and give gifts to them?

Euth. Yes, I do.

Soc. Is not the right way of asking to ask of them what we want?

Euth. Certainly.

Soc. And the right way of giving is to give to them in return what they want of us. There would be no meaning in an art which gives to anyone that which he does not want.

Euth. Very true, Socrates.

Soc. Then piety, Euthyphro, is an art which gods and men have of trafficking with one another?

Euth. That is an expression which you may use, if you like.

Soc. But I have no particular liking for anything but the truth. I wish, however, that you would tell me what benefit accrues to the gods from our gifts. There is no doubt about what they give to us, for there is no good thing which they do not give; but how they get any benefit from our gifts to them, is far from being equally clear. If they give everything and get from us nothing, that must be a traffic in which we have very greatly the advantage of them.

Euth. And do you imagine, Socrates, that any benefit accrues to the gods from our gifts?

Soc. But if not, Euthyphro, what is the meaning of the gifts we offer to the gods?

Euth. What else but tributes of honour; and, as I was just now saying, what pleases them?

Soc. Piety, then, is pleasing to the gods, but not beneficial or dear to them?

Euth. I should say that nothing could be dearer.

Soc. Then once more the assertion is repeated that piety is that which is dear to the gods?

Euth. Certainly.

Soc. And when you say this, can you wonder at your words not standing firm, but walking away? Will you accuse me of being the Daedalus who makes them walk away, not perceiving that there is another and far greater artist than Daedalus who makes things that go round in a circle, and he is yourself; for the argument, as you will perceive, comes round to the same point. Were we not saying that the holy or pious was not the same with that which is loved of the gods? Have you forgotten?

Euth. I quite remember.

Soc. And are you not now saying that what is dear to the gods is holy; and is not this the same as what is loved of them—do you see?

Euth. True.

Soc. Then either we were wrong in our former assertion; or, if we were right then, we are wrong now.

Euth. It appears so.

Soc. Then we must begin again and ask, What is piety? That is an inquiry which I shall never be weary of pursuing as far as in me lies; and I entreat you not to scorn me, but to apply your mind to the utmost, and tell me the truth. For, if any man knows, you are he; and therefore I must hold you fast, like Proteus, until you tell. If you had not certainly known the nature of piety and impiety, I am confident that you would never, on behalf of a serf, have charged your aged father with murder. You would not have run such a risk of doing wrong in the sight of the gods, and you would have had too much respect for the opinions of men. I am sure, therefore, that you know the nature of piety and impiety. Speak out then, my dear Euthyphro, and do not hide your knowledge.

Euth. Another time, Socrates; for I am in a hurry, and must go now.

Soc. Alas! my friend, and will you leave me in despair? I was hoping that you would instruct me in the nature of piety and impiety; and then I might have cleared myself of Meletus and his indictment. I would have told him that I had been enlightened by Euthyphro, and had given up rash innovations and speculations in which I had indulged only through ignorance, and that now I am about to lead a better life.

QUESTIONS FOR DISCUSSION

1. State each definition of piety given by Euthyphro, and indicate why Socrates feels he cannot accept it.
2. What is the significance of the question posed by Socrates when he asks: "Is the pious, or holy, beloved of the gods because it is holy, or holy because it is beloved of the gods?"
3. What is meant by inquiring as to whether a definition is true? Aren't definitions arbitrary?
4. What methods or techniques does Socrates use to show that a proposed definition is unsatisfactory?
5. Why is it unsatisfactory to define piety in terms of what the gods do or do not approve?
6. Is Socrates justified in demanding that Euthyphro produce a satisfactory definition of piety? Why doesn't he offer one himself?

Francis Bacon (1561-1626)

2.2   The Inductive Method

APHORISMS

39. There are four classes of Idols which beset men's minds. To these for distinction's sake I have assigned names—calling the first class *Idols of the Tribe;* the second, *Idols of the Cave;* the third, *Idols of the Market Place;* the fourth, *Idols of the Theatre.*

40. The formation of ideas and axioms by true induction is no doubt the proper remedy to be applied for the keeping off and clearing away of

---

From "Aphorisms Concerning the Interpretation of Nature and the Kingdom of Man," in *Novum Organum* (1620).

idols. To point them out, however, is of great use; for the doctrine of Idols is to the Interpretation of Nature what the doctrine of the refutation of Sophisms is to common Logic.

41. The Idols of the Tribe have their foundation in human nature itself, and in the tribe or race of men. For it is a false assertion that the sense of man is the measure of things. On the contrary, all perceptions as well of the sense as of the mind are according to the measure of man and not according to the measure of the universe. And the human understanding is like a false mirror, which, receiving rays irregularly, distorts and discolors

the nature of things by mingling its own nature with it.

42. The Idols of the Cave are the idols of the individual man. For everyone (besides the errors common to human nature in general) has a cave or den of his own, which refracts and discolors the light of nature; owing either to his own proper and peculiar nature; or to his education and conversation with others; or to the reading of books, and the authority of those whom he esteems and admires; or to the differences of impressions, accordingly as they take place in a mind preoccupied and predisposed or in a mind indifferent and settled; or the like. So that the spirit of man (according as it is meted out to different individuals) is in fact a thing variable and full of perturbation, and governed as it were by chance. Whence it was well observed by Heraclitus that men look for sciences in their own lesser worlds, and not in the greater or common world.

43. There are also Idols formed by the intercourse and association of men with each other, which I call Idols of the Market Place, on account of the commerce and consort of men there. For it is by discourse that men associate; and words are imposed according to the apprehension of the vulgar. And, therefore, the ill and unfit choice of words wonderfully obstructs the understanding. Nor do the definitions or explanations, wherewith in some things learned men are wont to guard and defend themselves, by any means set the matter right. But words plainly force and overrule the understanding, and throw all into confusion, and lead men away into numberless empty controversies and idle fancies.

44. Lastly, there are Idols which have immigrated into men's minds from the various dogmas of philosophies, and also from wrong laws of demonstration. These I call Idols of the Theatre; because in my judgment all the received systems are but so many stage plays, representing worlds of their own creation after an unreal and scenic fashion. Nor is it only of the systems now in vogue, or only of the ancient sects and philosophies, that I speak; for many more plays of the same kind may yet be composed and in like artificial manner set forth; seeing that errors the most widely different have nevertheless causes for the most part alike. Neither again do I mean this only of entire systems, but also of many principles and axioms in science, which by tradition, credulity, and negligence have come to be received.

But of these several kinds of Idols I must speak more largely and exactly, that the understanding may be duly cautioned.

52. Such then are the idols, which I call *Idols of the Tribe;* and which take their rise either from the homogeneity of the substance of the human spirit, or from its preoccupation, or from its narrowness, or from its restless motion, or from an infusion of the affections, or from the incompetency of the senses, or from the mode of impression.

53. The *Idols of the Cave* take their rise in the peculiar constitution, mental or bodily, of each individual; and also in education, habit, and accident. Of this kind there is a great number and variety; but I will instance those the pointing out of which contains the most important caution, and which have most effect in disturbing the clearness of the understanding.

54. Men become attached to certain particular sciences and speculations,

either because they fancy themselves the authors and inventors thereof, or because they have bestowed the greatest pains upon them and become most habituated to them. But men of this kind, if they betake themselves to philosophy and contemplations of a general character, distort and color them in obedience to their former fancies; a thing especially to be noticed in Aristotle, who made his natural philosophy a mere bond-servant to his logic, thereby rendering it contentious and well-nigh useless. The race of chemists again out of a few experiments of the furnace have built up a fantastic philosophy, framed with reference to a few things; and Gilbert also, after he had employed himself most laboriously in the study and observation of the loadstone, proceeded at once to construct an entire system in accordance with his favorite subject.

58. Let such be our provision and contemplative prudence for keeping off and dislodging the *Idols of the Cave,* which grow for the most part either out of the predominance of a favorite subject, or out of an excessive tendency to compare or to distinguish, or out of partiality for particular ages, or out of the largeness or minuteness of the objects contemplated. And generally, let every student of nature take this as a rule—that whatever his mind seizes and dwells upon with peculiar satisfaction is to be held in suspicion, and that so much the more care is to be taken in dealing with such questions to keep the understanding even and clear.

59. But the *Idols of the Market Place* are the most troublesome of all: idols which have crept into the understanding through the alliances of words and names. For men believe that their reason governs words; but

it is also true that words react on the understanding; and this it is that has rendered philosophy and the sciences sophistical and inactive. . . .

60. The idols imposed by words on the understanding are of two kinds. They are either names of things which do not exist (for as there are things left unnamed through lack of observation, so likewise are there names which result from fantastic suppositions and to which nothing in reality corresponds), or they are names of things which exist, but yet confused and ill-defined, and hastily and irregularly derived from realities. Of the former kind are Fortune, the Prime Mover, Planetary Orbits, Element of Fire, and like fictions which owe their origin to false and idle theories. And this class of idols is more easily expelled, because to get rid of them it is only necessary that all theories should be steadily rejected and dismissed as obsolete.

61. But the *Idols of the Theatre* are not innate, nor do they steal into the understanding secretly, but are plainly impressed and received into the mind from the play books of philosophical systems and the perverted rules of demonstration. To attempt refutations in this case would be merely inconsistent with what I have already said: for since we agree neither upon principles nor upon demonstrations, there is no place for argument. And this is so far well, inasmuch as it leaves the honor of the ancients untouched. For they are nowise disparaged—the question between them and me being only as to the way. For as the saying is, the lame man who keeps the right road outstrips the runner who takes a wrong one. Nay, it is obvious that when a man runs the wrong way, the more active and swift

he is the further he will go astray.

But the course I propose for the discovery of sciences is such as leaves but little to the acuteness and strength of wits, but places all wits and understandings nearly on a level. For, as in the drawing of a straight line or a perfect circle, much depends on the steadiness and practice of the hand, if it be done by aim of hand only, but if with the aid of rule or compass, little or nothing; so is it exactly with my plan. But though particular confutations would be of no avail, yet touching the sects and general divisions of such systems I must say something; something also touching the external signs which show that they are unsound; and finally, something touching the causes of such great infelicity and of such lasting and general agreement in error; that so the access to truth may be made less difficult, and the human understanding may the more willingly submit to its purgation and dismiss its idols.

62. *Idols of the Theatre*, or of *Systems*, are many, and there can be, and perhaps will be, yet many more. For were it not that now for many ages men's minds have been busied with religion and theology; and were it not that civil governments, especially monarchies, have been averse to such novelties, even in matters speculative; so that men labor therein to the peril and harming of their fortune—not only unrewarded, but exposed also to contempt and envy; doubtless there would have arisen many other philosophical sects like to those which in great variety flourished once among the Greeks. For as on the phenomena of the heavens many hypotheses may be constructed, so likewise (and more also) many various dogmas may be set up and established on the phenomena of

philosophy. And in the plays of this philosophical theatre you may observe the same thing which is found in the theatre of the poets, that stories invented for the stage are more compact and elegant, and more as one would wish them to be, than true stories out of history.

In general, however, there is taken for the material of philosophy either a great deal out of a few things, or a very little out of many things; so that on both sides philosophy is based on too narrow a foundation of experiment and natural history, and decides on the authority of too few cases. For the Rational School of philosophers snatches from experience a variety of common instances, neither duly ascertained nor diligently examined and weighed, and leaves all the rest to meditation and agitation of wit.

There is also another class of philosophers, who, having bestowed much diligent and careful labor on a few experiments, have thence made bold to educe and construct systems; wresting all other facts in a strange fashion to conformity therewith.

And there is yet a third class, consisting of those who, out of faith and veneration, mix their philosophy with theology and traditions; among whom the vanity of some has gone so far aside as to seek the origin of sciences among spirits and genii. So that this parent stock of errors—this false philosophy—is of three kinds; the Sophistical, the Empirical, and the Superstitious.

95. Those who have handled sciences have been either men of experiment or men of dogmas. The men of experiment are like the ant; they only collect and use; the reasoners resemble spiders, who make cobwebs out of their own substance. But the bee

takes a middle course; it gathers its material from the flowers of the garden and of the field, but transforms and digests it by a power of its own. Not unlike this is the true business of philosophy; for it neither relies solely or chiefly on the powers of the mind, nor does it take the matter which it gathers from natural history and mechanical experiments and lay it up in the memory whole, as it finds it; but lays it up in the understanding, altered and digested. Therefore, from a closer and purer league between these two faculties, the experimental and the rational (such as has never yet been made), much may be hoped.

96. We have as yet no natural philosophy that is pure; all is tainted and corrupted: in Aristotle's school by logic; in Plato's by natural theology; in the second school of Platonists, such as Proclus and others, by mathematics, which ought only to give definiteness to natural philosophy, not to generate or give it birth. From a natural philosophy pure and unmixed, better things are to be expected.

97. No one has yet been found so firm of mind and purpose as resolutely to compel himself to sweep away all theories and common notions, and to apply the understanding, thus made fair and even, to a fresh examination of particulars. Thus it happens that human knowledge, as we have it, is a mere medley and ill-digested mass, made up of much credulity and much accident, and also of the childish notions which we at first imbibed.

Now if anyone of ripe age, unimpaired senses, and well-purged mind, apply himself anew to experience and particulars, better hopes may be entertained of that man. In which point I promise to myself a like fortune to that of Alexander the Great; and let no man tax me with vanity till he have heard the end; for the thing which I mean tends to the putting off of all vanity. For of Alexander and his deeds Aeschines spake thus: "Assuredly we do not live the life of mortal men; but to this end were we born, that in after ages wonders might be told of us;" as if what Alexander had done seemed to him miraculous. But in the next age Titus Livius took a better and a deeper view of the matter, saying in effect, that Alexander, "had done no more than take courage to despise vain apprehensions." And a like judgment I suppose may be passed on myself in future ages: that I did no great things, but simply made less account of things that were accounted great. In the meanwhile, as I have already said, there is no hope except in a new birth of science; that is, in raising it regularly up from experience and building it afresh; which no one (I think) will say has yet been done or thought of.

98. Now for grounds of experience —since to experience we must come— we have as yet had either none or very weak ones; no search has been made to collect a store of particular observations sufficient either in number, or in kind, or in certainty, to inform the understanding, or in any way adequate. On the contrary, men of learning, but easy withal and idle, have taken for the construction or for the confirmation of their philosophy certain rumors and vague fames or airs of experience, and allowed to these the weight of lawful evidence. And just as if some kingdom or state were to direct its counsels and affairs, not by letters and reports from ambassadors and trustworthy messengers, but by the gossip of the streets; such

exactly is the system of management introduced into philosophy with relation to experience. Nothing duly investigated, nothing verified, nothing counted, weighed, or measured, is to be found in natural history: and what in observation is loose and vague, is in information deceptive and treacherous. And if anyone thinks that this is a strange thing to say, and something like an unjust complaint, seeing that Aristotle, himself so great a man, and supported by the wealth of so great a king, has composed so accurate a history of animals; and that others with greater diligence, though less pretense, have made many additions; while others, again, have compiled copious histories and descriptions of metals, plants, and fossils; it seems that he does not rightly apprehend what it is that we are now about. For a natural history which is composed for its own sake is not like one that is collected to supply the understanding with information for the building up of philosophy. They differ in many ways, but especially in this; that the former contains the variety of natural species only, and not experiments of the mechanical arts. For even as in the business of life a man's disposition and the secret workings of his mind and affections are better discovered when he is in trouble than at other times; so likewise the secrets of nature reveal themselves more readily under the vexations of art than when they go their own way. Good hopes may therefore be conceived of natural philosophy, when natural history, which is the basis and foundation of it, has been drawn up on a better plan; but not till then.

99. Again, even in the great plenty of mechanical experiments, there is yet a great scarcity of those which are of most use for the information of the understanding. For the mechanic, not troubling himself with the investigation of truth, confines his attention to those things which bear upon his particular work, and will not either raise his mind or stretch out his hand for anything else. But then only will there be good ground of hope for the further advance of knowledge, when there shall be received and gathered together into natural history a variety of experiments, which are of no use in themselves, but simply serve to discover causes and axioms; which I call *experimenta lucifera,* experiments of *light,* to distinguish them from those which I call *fructifera,* experiments of *fruit.*

Now experiments of this kind have one admirable property and condition; they never miss or fail. For since they are applied, not for the purpose of producing any particular effect, but only of discovering the natural cause of some effect, they answer the end equally well whichever way they turn out; for they settle the question.

100. But not only is a greater abundance of experiments to be sought for and procured, and that too of a different kind from those hitherto tried; an entirely different method, order, and process for carrying on and advancing experience must also be introduced. For experience, when it wanders in its own track, is, as I have already remarked, mere groping in the dark, and confounds men rather than instructs them. But when it shall proceed in accordance with a fixed law, in regular order, and without interruption, then may better things be hoped of knowledge.

103. But after this store of particulars has been set out duly and in order before our eyes, we are not to pass at

once to the investigation and discovery of new particulars or works; or at any rate if we do so we must not stop there. For although I do not deny that when all the experiments of all the arts shall have been collected and digested, and brought within one man's knowledge and judgment, the mere transferring of the experiments of one art to others may lead, by means of that experience which I term *literate,* to the discovery of many new things of service to the life and state of man; yet it is no great matter that can be hoped from that; but from the new light of axioms, which having been educed from those particulars by a certain method and rule, shall in their turn point out the way again to new particulars, greater things may be looked for. For our road does not lie on a level, but ascends and descends; first ascending to axioms, then descending to works.

104. The understanding must not however be allowed to jump and fly from particulars to remote axioms and of almost the highest generality (such as the first principles, as they are called, of arts and things), and taking stand upon them as truths that cannot be shaken, proceed to prove and frame the middle axioms by reference to them: which has been the practice hitherto; the understanding being not only carried that way by a natural impulse, but also by the use of syllogistic demonstration trained and inured to it. But then, and then only, may we hope well of the sciences, when in a just scale of ascent, and by successive steps not interrupted or broken, we rise from particulars to lesser axioms; and then to middle axioms, one above the other; and last of all to the most general. For the lowest axioms differ but slightly from bare experience,

while the highest and most general (which we now have) are notional and abstract and without solidity. But the middle are the true and solid and living axioms, on which depend the affairs and fortunes of men; and above them again, last of all, those which are indeed the most general,—such I mean as are not abstract, but of which those intermediate axioms are really limitations.

The understanding must not therefore be supplied with wings, but rather hung with weights, to keep it from leaping and flying. Now this has never yet been done; when it is done, we may entertain better hopes of the sciences.

105. In establishing axioms, another form of induction must be devised than has hitherto been employed; and it must be used for proving and discovering not first principles (as they are called) only, but also the lesser axioms, and the middle, and indeed all. For the induction which proceeds by simple enumeration is childish; its conclusions are precarious, and exposed to peril from a contradictory instance; and it generally decides on too small a number of facts, and on those only which are at hand. But the induction which is to be available for the discovery and demonstration of sciences and arts, must analyze nature by proper rejections and exclusions; and then, after a sufficient number of negatives, come to a conclusion on the affirmative instances: which has not yet been done or even attempted, save only by Plato, who does indeed employ this form of induction to a certain extent for the purpose of discussing definitions and ideas. But in order to furnish this induction or demonstration well and duly for its work, very many things are to be provided which

no mortal has yet thought of; inso-much that greater labor will have to be spent in it than has hitherto been spent on the syllogism. And this in-duction must be used not only to discover axioms, but also in the for-mation of notions. And it is in this induction that our chief hope lies.

106. But in establishing axioms by this kind of induction, we must also examine and try whether the axiom so established be framed to the measure of those particulars only from which it is derived, or whether it be larger and wider. And if it be larger and wider, we must observe whether by indicating to us new particulars it con-firm that wideness and largeness as by a collateral security: that we may not either stick fast in things already known, or loosely grasp at shadows and abstract forms; not at things solid and realized in matter. And when this process shall have come into use, then at last shall we see the dawn of a solid hope.

QUESTIONS FOR DISCUSSION

1. Are the kinds of idols Bacon described prevalent today? If so, give some present day illustrations of what he called (1) idols of the cave, (2) idols of the tribe, (3) idols of the theater, and (4) idols of the market place. If not, explain how, in your view, they have been avoided.
2. According to Bacon, how can we counteract, if not eliminate, the effects of the idols?
3. Which idols are the most troublesome? Why?
4. Do you think Bacon was oversanguine in his belief that he had a method which could exorcise the idols?
5. Can you think of an idol of a type not mentioned by Bacon that is particu-larly in evidence today? If so, give illustrations.
6. What explanation does Bacon give to account for the popular belief in as-trology? What kind of idol is found here?
7. Explain Bacon's analogy of the ant, the spider, and the bee.
8. Bacon says (in Aphorism 105): "In establishing axioms, another form of in-duction must be devised than has hitherto been employed . . . and this in-duction must be used not only to discover axioms, but also in the formation of notions. And it is in this induction that our chief hope lies."
   a) Explain what Bacon means by "*another* form of induction."
   b) How can induction be used to "discover axioms"?
   c) How can it be used in "the formation of notions"?

René Descartes (1596-1650)

2.3   The Deductive Method

SYNOPSIS OF THE SIX
FOLLOWING MEDITATIONS

In the first Meditation I set forth the reasons for which we may, generally speaking, doubt about all things and especially about material things, at least so long as we have no other foundations for the sciences than those which we have hitherto possessed. But although the utility of a Doubt which is so general does not at first appear, it is at the same time very great, inasmuch as it delivers us from every kind of prejudice, and sets out for us a very simple way by which the mind may detach itself from the senses; and finally it makes it impossible for us ever to doubt those things which we have once discovered to be true.

In the second Meditation, mind, which making use of the liberty which pertains to it, takes for granted that all those things of whose existence it has the least doubt, are non-existent, recognizes that it is however absolutely impossible that it does not itself exist. This point is likewise of the

greatest moment, inasmuch as by this means a distinction is easily drawn between the things which pertain to mind—that is to say to the intellectual nature—and those which pertain to body.

But because it may be that some expect from me in this place a statement of the reasons establishing the immortality of the soul, I feel that I should here make known to them that having aimed at writing nothing in all this Treatise of which I do not possess very exact demonstrations, I am obliged to follow a similar order to that made use of by the geometers, which is to begin by putting forward as premises all those things upon which the proposition that we seek depends, before coming to any conclusion regarding it. Now the first and principal matter which is requisite for thoroughly understanding the immortality of the soul is to form the clearest possible conception of it, and one which will be entirely distinct from all the conceptions which we may have of body; and in this Meditation this has been done. In addition to this it is requisite that we may be assured that all the things which we conceive clearly and distinctly are true in the very way in which we think them; and this could not be proved previously to the Fourth Meditation. Fur-

From René Descartes, *Meditations on First Philosophy, in which the Existence of God and the Distinction between Mind and Body Are Demonstrated* (1641). Trans. by E. S. Haldane and G. R. T. Ross (London: Cambridge University Press, 1912).

ther we must have a distinct conception of corporeal nature, which is given partly in this second, and partly in the Fifth and Sixth Meditations. And finally we should conclude from all this, that those things which we conceive clearly and distinctly as being diverse substances, as we regard mind and body to be, are really substances essentially distinct one from the other; and this is the conclusion of the Sixth Meditation. This is further confirmed in this same Meditation by the fact that we cannot conceive of body excepting in so far as it is divisible, while the mind cannot be conceived of excepting as indivisible. For we are not able to conceive of the half of a mind as we can do of the smallest of all bodies; so that we see that not only are their natures different but even in some respects contrary to one another. . . .

In the third Meditation it seems to me that I have explained at sufficient length the principal argument of which I make use in order to prove the existence of God. But none the less, because I did not wish in that place to make use of any comparisons derived from corporeal things, so as to withdraw as much as I could the minds of readers from the senses, there may perhaps have remained many obscurities which, however, will, I hope, be entirely removed by the Replies which I have made to the Objections which have been set before me. Amongst others there is, for example, this one, 'How the idea in us of a being supremely perfect possesses so much objective reality [that is to say participates by representation in so many degrees of being and perfection] that it necessarily proceeds from a cause which is absolutely perfect. This is illustrated in these Replies by the com-

parison of a very perfect machine, the idea of which is found in the mind of some workman. For as the objective contrivance of this idea must have some cause, i.e. either the science of the workman or that of some other from whom he has received the idea, it is similarly impossible that the idea of God which is in us should not have God himself as its cause.

In the fourth Meditation it is shown that all these things which we very clearly and distinctly perceive are true, and at the same time it is explained in what the nature of error or falsity consists. This must of necessity be known both for the confirmation of the preceding truths and for the better comprehension of those that follow. (But it must meanwhile be remarked that I do not in any way there treat of sin—that is to say of the error which is committed in the pursuit of good and evil, but only of that which arises in the deciding between the true and the false. And I do not intend to speak of matters pertaining to the Faith or the conduct of life, but only of those which concern speculative truths, and which may be known by the sole aid of the light of nature.)

In the fifth Meditation corporeal nature generally is explained, and in addition to this the existence of God is demonstrated by a new proof in which there may possibly be certain difficulties also, but the solution of these will be seen in the Replies to the Objections. And further I show in what sense it is true to say that the certainty of geometrical demonstrations is itself dependent on the knowledge of God.

Finally in the Sixth I distinguish the action of the understanding from that of the imagination; the marks by which this distinction is made are de-

scribed. I here show that the mind of man is really distinct from the body, and at the same time that the two are so closely joined together that they form, so to speak, a single thing. All the errors which proceed from the senses are then surveyed, while the means of avoiding them are demonstrated, and finally all the reasons from which we may deduce the existence of material things are set forth. Not that I judge them to be very useful in establishing that which they prove, to wit, that there is in truth a world, that men possess bodies, and other such things which never have been doubted by anyone of sense; but because in considering these closely we come to see that they are neither so strong nor so evident as those arguments which lead us to the knowledge of our mind and of God; so that these last must be the most certain and most evident facts which can fall within the cognisance of the human mind. And this is the whole matter that I have tried to prove in these Meditations, for which reason I here omit to speak of many other questions with which I dealt incidentally in this discussion.

MEDITATION I

Of the Things Which May Be Brought Within the Sphere of the Doubtful

It is now some years since I detected how many were the false beliefs that I had from my earliest youth admitted as true, and how doubtful was everything I had since constructed on this basis; and from that time I was convinced that I must once for all seriously undertake to rid myself of all the opinions which I had formerly accepted, and commence to build anew from the foundation, if I wanted to establish any firm and permanent structure in the sciences. But as this enterprise appeared to be a very great one, I waited until I had attained an age so mature that I could not hope that at any later date I should be better fitted to execute my design. This reason caused me to delay so long that I should feel that I was doing wrong were I to occupy in deliberation the time that yet remains to me for action. Today, then, since very opportunely for the plan I have in view I have delivered my mind from every care [and am happily agitated by no passions] and since I have procured for myself an assured leisure in a peaceable retirement, I shall at last seriously and freely address myself to the general upheaval of all my former opinions.

Now for this object it is not necessary that I should show that all of these are false—I shall perhaps never arrive at this end. But inasmuch as reason already persuades me that I ought no less carefully to withhold my assent from matters which are not entirely certain and indubitable than from those which appear to me manifestly to be false, if I am able to find in each one some reason to doubt, this will suffice to justify my rejecting the whole. And for that end it will not be requisite that I should examine each in particular, which would be an endless undertaking; for owing to the fact that the destruction of the foundations of necessity brings with it the downfall of the rest of the edifice, I shall only in the first place attack those principles upon which all my former opinions rested.

All that up to the present time I

have accepted as most true and certain I have learned either from the senses or through the senses; but it is sometimes proved to me that these senses are deceptive, and it is wiser not to trust entirely to any thing by which we have once been deceived.

But it may be that, although the senses sometimes deceive us concerning things which are hardly perceptible, or very far away, there are yet many others to be met with as to which we cannot reasonably have any doubt, although we recognize them by their means. For example, there is the fact that I am here, seated by the fire, attired in a dressing gown, having this paper in my hands, and other similar matters. And how could I deny that these hands and this body are mine, were it not perhaps that I compare myself to certain persons, devoid of sense, whose cerebella are so troubled and clouded by the violent vapors of black bile, that they constantly assure us that they think they are kings when they are really quite poor, or that they are clothed in purple when they are really without covering, or who imagine that they have an earthenware head or are nothing but pumpkins or are made of glass. But they are mad, and I should not be any the less insane were I to follow examples so extravagant.

At the same time I must remember that I am a man, and that consequently I am in the habit of sleeping, and in my dreams representing to myself the same things or sometimes even less probable things, than do those who are insane in their waking moments. How often has it happened to me that in the night I dreamt that I found myself in this particular place, that I was dressed and seated near the fire, whilst in reality I was lying undressed in bed! At this moment it does indeed seem to me that it is with eyes awake that I am looking at this paper; that this head which I move is not asleep, that it is deliberately and of set purpose that I extend my hand and perceive it; what happens in sleep does not appear so clear nor so distinct as does all this. But in thinking over this I remind myself that on many occasions I have in sleep been deceived by similar illusions, and in dwelling carefully on this reflection I see so manifestly that there are no certain indications by which we may clearly distinguish wakefulness from sleep that I am lost in astonishment. And my astonishment is such that it is almost capable of persuading me that I now dream.

Now let us assume that we are asleep and that all these particulars, e.g., that we open our eyes, shake our head, extend our hands, and so on, are but false delusions; and let us reflect that possibly neither our hands nor our whole body are such as they appear to us to be. At the same time we must at least confess that the things which are represented to us in sleep are like painted representations which can only have been formed as the counterparts of something real and true, and that in this way those general things at least, i.e., eyes, a head, hands, and a whole body, are not imaginary things, but things really existent. For, as a matter of fact, painters, even when they study with the greatest skill to represent sirens and satyrs by forms the most strange and extraordinary, cannot give them natures which are entirely new, but merely make a certain medley of the members of different animals; or if their imagination is extravagant enough to invent something so novel that nothing similar has ever before been seen, and that their work represents a thing purely fictitious and absolutely false, it is certain all the same that the colors of which this is composed are necessarily real. And for the same reason, although these general things, to wit, [a body], eyes, a head, and such like, may be imaginary, we are bound at the same time to confess that there are at least some other objects yet more simple and more universal, which are real and true; and of these just in the same way as with certain real colors, all these images of things which dwell in our thoughts, whether true and real or false and fantastic, are formed.

To such a class of things pertains corporeal nature in general, and its extension, the figure of extended things, their quantity or magnitude and number, as also the place in which they are, the time which measures their duration, and so on.

That is possibly why our reasoning is not unjust when we conclude from this that Physics, Astronomy, Medicine, and all other sciences which have as their end the consideration of composite things, are very dubious and uncertain; but that Arithmetic, Geometry, and other sciences of that kind which only treat of things that are very simple and very general, without taking great trouble to ascertain whether they are actually existent or not, contain some measure of certainty and an element of the indubitable. For whether I am awake or asleep, two and three together always form five, and the square can never have more than four sides, and it does not seem possible that truths so clear and apparent can be suspected of any falsity [or uncertainty].

Nevertheless, I have long had fixed in my mind the belief that an all-powerful God existed by whom I have been created such as I am. But how do I know that He has not brought it to pass that there is no earth, no heaven, no extended body, no magnitude, no place, and that nevertheless [I possess the perceptions of all these things and that] they seem to me to exist just exactly as I now see them? And besides, as I sometimes imagine that others deceive themselves in the things which they think they know best, how do I know that I am not deceived every time that I add two and three, or count the sides of a square, or judge of things yet simpler, if anything simpler can be imagined? But possibly God has not desired that I should be thus deceived, for He is said to be supremely good. If, however, it is contrary to His goodness to have made me such that I constantly deceive myself, it would also appear to be contrary to His goodness to permit me to be sometimes deceived, and nevertheless I cannot doubt that He does permit this.

There may, indeed, be those who would prefer to deny the existence of a God so powerful, rather than believe that all other things are uncertain. But let us not oppose them for the present, and grant that all that is said of a God is a fable; nevertheless, in whatever way they suppose that I have arrived at the state of being that I have reached—whether they attribute it to fate or to accident, or make out that it is by a continual succession of antecedents, or by some other method—since to err and deceive oneself is a defect, it is clear that the greater will

be the probability of my being so imperfect as to deceive myself ever, as
is the Author to whom they assign my
origin the less powerful. To these
reasons I have certainly nothing to
reply, but at the end I feel constrained
to confess that there is nothing in all
that I formerly believed to be true, of
which I cannot in some measure
doubt, and that not merely through
want of thought or through levity, but
for reasons which are very powerful
and maturely considered; so that
henceforth I ought not the less carefully to refrain from giving credence
to these opinions than to that which
is manifestly false, if I desire to arrive
at any certainty [in the sciences].

But it is not sufficient to have made
these remarks; we must also be careful to keep them in mind. For these
ancient and commonly held opinions
still revert frequently to my mind,
long and familiar custom having given
them the right to occupy my mind
against my inclination and rendered
them almost masters of my belief; nor
will I ever lose the habit of deferring
to them or of placing my confidence
in them, so long as I consider them as
they really are, i.e., opinions in some
measure doubtful, as I have just
shown, and at the same time highly
probable, so that there is much more
reason to believe than to deny them.
That is why I consider that I shall not
be acting amiss, if, taking of set purpose a contrary belief, I allow myself
to be deceived, and for a certain time
pretend that all these opinions are entirely false and imaginary, until at
last, having thus balanced my former
prejudices with my latter [so that they
cannot divert my opinions more to
one side than to the other], my judgment will no longer be dominated by

bad usage or turned away from the
right knowledge of the truth. For I
am assured that there can be neither
peril nor error in this course, and that
I cannot at present yield too much to
distrust, since I am not considering
the question of action, but only of
knowledge.

I shall then suppose, not that God,
who is supremely good and the foun-
tain of truth, but some evil genius not
less powerful than deceitful, has employed his whole energies in deceiving me; I shall consider that the
heavens, the earth, colors, figures,
sound, and all other external things
are nought but the illusions and
dreams of which this genius has
availed himself in order to lay traps
for my credulity; I shall consider myself as having no hands, no eyes, no
flesh, no blood, nor any senses, yet
falsely believing myself to possess all
these things; I shall remain obstinately
attached to this idea, and if by this
means it is not in my power to arrive
at the knowledge of any truth, I may
at least do what is in my power [i.e.,
suspend my judgment], and with firm
purpose avoid giving credence to any
false thing, or being imposed upon by
this arch deceiver, however powerful
and deceptive he may be. But this
task is a laborious one, and insensibly
a certain lassitude leads me into the
course of my ordinary life. And just
as a captive who in sleep enjoys
imaginary liberty, when he begins to
suspect that his liberty is but a dream,
fears to awaken, and conspires with
these agreeable illusions that the de-
ception may be prolonged, so insensibly of my own accord I fall back
into my former opinions, and I dread
awakening from this slumber, lest the
laborious wakefulness which would

follow the tranquillity of this repose should have to be spent, not in daylight, but in the excessive darkness of the difficulties which have just been discussed.

MEDITATION II

Of the Nature of the Human Mind; and That It Is More Easily Known Than the Body

The Meditation of yesterday filled my mind with so many doubts that it is no longer in my power to forget them. And yet I do not see in what manner I can resolve them; and, just as if I had all of a sudden fallen into very deep water, I am so disconcerted that I can neither make certain of setting my feet on the bottom, nor can I swim and so support myself on the surface. I shall, nevertheless, make an effort and follow anew the same path as that on which I yesterday entered, i.e., I shall proceed by setting aside all that in which the least doubt could be supposed to exist, just as if I had discovered that it was absolutely false; and I shall ever follow in this road until I have met with something which is certain, or at least, if I can do nothing else, until I have learned for certain that there is nothing in the world that is certain. Archimedes, in order that he might draw the terrestrial globe out of its place, and transport it elsewhere, demanded only that one point should be fixed and immovable; in the same way, I shall have the right to conceive high hopes if I am happy enough to discover one thing only which is certain and indubitable.

I suppose, then, that all the things that I see are false; I persuade myself that nothing has ever existed of all that my fallacious memory represents to me. I consider that I possess no senses; I imagine that body, figure, extension, movement, and place are but the fictions of my mind. What, then, can be esteemed as true? Perhaps nothing at all, unless that there is nothing in the world that is certain.

But how can I know there is not something different from those things that I have just considered, of which one cannot have the slightest doubt? Is there not some God, or some other being by whatever name we call it, who puts these reflections into my mind? That is not necessary, for is it not possible that I am capable of producing them myself? I myself, am I not at least something? But I have already denied that I had senses and body. Yet I hesitate, for what follows from that? Am I so dependent on body and senses that I cannot exist without these? But I was persuaded that there was nothing in all the world, that there was no heaven, no earth, that there were no minds, nor any bodies: was I not then likewise persuaded that I did not exist? Not at all; of a surety I myself did exist since I persuaded myself of something [or merely because I thought of something]. But there is some deceiver or other, very powerful and very cunning, who ever employs his ingenuity in deceiving me. Then, without doubt, I exist also if he deceives me, and let him deceive me as much as he will, he can never cause me to be nothing so long as I think that I am something. So that, after having reflected well and carefully examined all things, we must come to the definite conclusion that this proposition: I am, I exist, is necessarily true each time that I pronounce it, or that I mentally conceive it.

But I do not yet know clearly enough what I am, I who am certain that I am; and hence I must be careful to see that I do not imprudently take some other object in place of myself, and thus that I do not go astray in respect of this knowledge that I hold to be the most certain and most evident of all that I have formerly learned. That is why I shall now consider anew what I believed myself to be before I embarked upon these last reflections; and of my former opinions I shall withdraw all that might even in a small degree be invalidated by the reasons which I have just brought forward, in order that there may be nothing at all left beyond what is absolutely certain and indubitable.

What then did I formerly believe myself to be? Undoubtedly I believed myself to be a man. But what is a man? Shall I say a reasonable animal? Certainly not; for then I should have to inquire what an animal is, and what is reasonable; and thus from a single question I should insensibly fall into an infinitude of others more difficult; and I should not wish to waste the little time and leisure remaining to me in trying to unravel subtleties like these. But I shall rather stop here to consider the thoughts which of themselves spring up in my mind, and which were not inspired by anything beyond my own nature alone when I applied myself to the consideration of my being. In the first place, then, I considered myself as having a face, hands, arms, and all that system of members composed of bones and flesh as seen in a corpse which I designated by the name of body. In addition to this I considered that I was nourished, that I walked, that I felt, and that I thought, and I referred all these actions to the soul: but I did not stop to consider what the soul was, or if I did stop, I imagined that it was something extremely rare and subtle like a wind, a flame, or an ether, which was spread throughout my grosser parts. As to body, I had no manner of doubt about its nature, but thought I had a very clear knowledge of it; and if I had desired to explain it according to the notions that I had then formed of it, I should have described it thus: By the body I understand all that which can be defined by a certain figure: something which can be confined in a certain place, and which can fill a given space in such a way that every other body will be excluded from it; which can be perceived either by touch, or by sight, or by hearing, or by taste, or by smell: which can be moved in many ways not, in truth, by itself, but by something which is foreign to it, by which it is touched [and from which it receives impressions]: for to have the power of self-movement, as also of feeling or of thinking, I did not consider to appertain to the nature of body: on the contrary, I was rather astonished to find that faculties similar to them existed in some bodies.

But what am I, now that I suppose that there is a certain genius which is extremely powerful, and, if I may say so, malicious, who employs all his powers in deceiving me? Can I affirm that I possess the least of all those things which I have just said pertain to the nature of body? I pause to consider, I revolve all these things in my mind, and find none of which I can say that it pertains to me. It would be tedious to stop to enumerate them. Let us pass to the attributes of soul and see if there is any one which is in me? What of nutrition or walking [the first mentioned]? But if it is so that I have no body, it is also true that I can neither walk nor take nourishment. Another attribute is sensation. But one cannot feel without body, and besides, I have thought I perceived many things during sleep that I recognized in my waking moments as not having been experienced at all. What of thinking? I find here that thought is an attribute that belongs to me; it alone cannot be separated from me. I am, I exist, that is certain. But how often? Just when I think; for it might possibly be the case if I ceased entirely to think, that I should likewise cease altogether to exist. I do not now admit anything which is not necessarily true: to speak accurately I am not more than a thing which thinks, that is to say a mind or a soul, or an understanding, or a reason, which are terms whose significance was formerly unknown to me. I am, however, a real thing and really exist; but what thing? I have answered: a thing which thinks.

And what more? I shall exercise my imagination [in order to see if I am not something more]. I am not a collection of members which we call the human body; I am not a subtle air distributed through these members; I am not a wind, a fire, a vapor, a breath, nor anything at all which I can imagine or conceive; because I have assumed that all these were nothing. Without changing that supposition I find that I only leave myself certain of the fact that I am somewhat. But perhaps it is true that these same things which I supposed were non-existent because they are unknown to me, are really not different from the self which I know. I am not sure about this; I shall not dispute about it now; I can only give judgment on things that are known

to me. I know that I exist, and I inquire what I am, I whom I know to exist. But it is very certain that the knowledge of my existence taken in its precise significance does not depend on things whose existence is not yet known to me; consequently, it does not depend on those which I can feign in imagination. And, indeed, the very term *feign* in imagination proves to me my error, for I really do this if I image myself a something, since to imagine is nothing else than to contemplate the figure or image of a corporeal thing. But I already know for certain that I am, and that it may be that all these images, and, speaking generally, all things that relate to the nature of body are nothing but dreams [and chimeras]. For this reason I see clearly that I have as little reason to say, "I shall stimulate my imagination in order to know more distinctly what I am," than if I were to say, "I am now awake, and I perceive somewhat that is real and true: but because I do not yet perceive it distinctly enough, I shall go to sleep of express purpose, so that my dreams may represent the perception with greatest truth and evidence." And, thus, I know for certain that nothing of all that I can understand by means of my imagination belongs to this knowledge which I have of myself, and that it is necessary to recall the mind from this mode of thought with the utmost diligence in order that it may be able to know its own nature with perfect distinctness.

But what then am I? A thing which thinks. What is a thing which thinks? It is a thing which doubts, understands, [conceives], affirms, denies, wills, refuses, which also imagines and feels.

Certainly it is no small matter if all

these things pertain to my nature. But why should they not so pertain? Am I not that being who now doubts nearly everything, who nevertheless understands certain things, who affirms that one only is true, who denies all the others, who desires to know more, is averse from being deceived, who imagines many things, sometimes indeed despite his will, and who perceives many likewise, as by the intervention of the bodily organs? Is there nothing in all this which is as true as it is certain that I exist, even though I should always sleep and though he who has given me being employed all his ingenuity in deceiving me? Is there likewise any one of these attributes which can be distinguished from my thought, or which might be said to be separated from myself? For it is so evident of itself that it is I who doubt, who understand, and who desire, that there is no reason here to add anything to explain it. And I have certainly the power of imagining likewise; for although it may happen (as I formerly supposed) that none of the things which I imagine are true, nevertheless this power of imagining does not cease to be really in use, and it forms part of my thought. Finally, I am the same who feels, that is to say, who perceives certain things, as by the organs of sense, since in truth I see light, I hear noise, I feel heat. But it will be said that these phenomena are false and that I am dreaming. Let it be so; still it is at least quite certain that it seems to me that I see light, that I hear noise, and that I feel heat. That cannot be false; properly speaking it is what is in me called feeling; and used in this precise sense that is no other thing than thinking.

From this time I begin to know

what I am with a little more clearness and distinctness than before; but nevertheless it still seems to me, and I cannot prevent myself from thinking, that corporeal things, whose images are framed by thought, which are tested by the senses, are much more distinctly known than that obscure part of me which does not come under the imagination. Although really it is very strange to say that I know and understand more distinctly these things whose existence seems to me dubious, which are unknown to me, and which do not belong to me, than others of the truth of which I am convinced, which are known to me and which pertain to my real nature, in a word, than myself. But I see clearly how the case stands: my mind loves to wander, and cannot yet suffer itself to be retained within the just limits of truth. Very good, let us once more give it the freest rein, so that, when afterwards we seize the proper occasion for pulling up, it may the more easily be regulated and controlled.

Let us begin by considering the commonest matters, those which we believe to be the most distinctly comprehended, to wit, the bodies which we touch and see; not indeed bodies in general, for these general ideas are usually a little more confused, but let us consider one body in particular. Let us take, for example, this piece of wax: it has been taken quite freshly from the hive, and it has not yet lost the sweetness of the honey which it contains; it still retains somewhat of the odor of the flowers from which it has been culled; its color, its figure, its size are apparent; it is hard, cold, easily handled, and if you strike it with the finger, it will emit a sound. Finally, all the things which are requisite to cause us distinctly to recognize a body, are met within it. But notice that while I speak and approach the fire what remained of the taste is exhaled, the smell evaporates, the color alters, the figure is destroyed, the size increases, it becomes liquid, it heats, scarcely can one handle it, and when one strikes it, no sound is emitted. Does the same wax remain after this change? We must confess that it remains; none would judge otherwise. What then did I know so distinctly in this piece of wax? It could certainly be nothing of all that the senses brought to my notice, since all these things which fall under taste, smell, sight, touch, and hearing, are found to be changed, and yet the same wax remains.

Perhaps it was what I now think, viz., that this wax was not that sweetness of honey, nor that agreeable scent of flowers, nor that particular whiteness, nor that figure, nor that sound, but simply a body which a little before appeared to me as perceptible under these forms, and which is now perceptible under others. But what, precisely, is it that I imagine when I form such conceptions? Let us attentively consider this, and, abstracting from all that does not belong to the wax, let use see what remains. Certainly nothing remains excepting a certain extended thing which is flexible and movable. But what is the meaning of flexible and movable? Is it not that I imagine that this piece of wax being round is capable of becoming square and of passing from a square to a triangular figure? No, certainly it is not that, since I imagine it admits of an infinitude of similar changes, and I nevertheless do not know how to compass the infinitude by my imagination, and consequently this conception which I have of the

wax is not brought about by the faculty of imagination. What now is this extension? Is it not also unknown? For it becomes greater when the wax is melted, greater when it is boiled, and greater still when the heat increases; and I should not conceive [clearly] according to truth what wax is, if I did not think that even this piece that we are considering is capable of receiving more variations in extension than I have ever imagined. We must then grant that I could not even understand through the imagination what this piece of wax is, and that it is my mind alone which perceives it. I say this piece of wax in particular, for as to wax in general it is yet clearer. But what is this piece of wax which cannot be understood excepting by the [understanding or] mind? It is certainly the same that I see, touch, imagine, and finally it is the same which I have always believed it to be from the beginning. But what must particularly be observed is that its perception is neither an act of vision, nor of touch, nor of imagination, and has never been such although it may have appeared formerly to be so, but only an intuition of the mind, which may be imperfect and confused as it was formerly, or clear and distinct as it is at present, according as my attention is more or less directed to the elements which are found in it, and of which it is composed.

Yet in the meantime I am greatly astonished when I consider [the great feebleness of mind] and its proneness to fall [insensibly] into error; for although, without giving expression to my thoughts, I consider all this in my own mind, words often impede me and I am almost deceived by the terms of ordinary language. For we say that we see the same wax, if it is present, and not that we simply judge that it is the same from its having the same color and figure. From this I should conclude that I knew the wax by means of vision and not simply by the intuition of the mind; unless by chance I remember that, when looking from a window and saying I see men who pass in the street, I really do not see them, but infer that what I see is men, just as I say that I see wax. And yet what do I see from the window but hats and coats which may cover automatic machines? Yet I judge these to be men. And similarly, solely by the faculty of judgment which rests in my mind, I comprehend that which I believed I saw with my eyes.

A man who makes it his aim to raise his knowledge above the common should be ashamed to derive the occasion for doubting from the forms of speech invented by the vulgar; I prefer to pass on and consider whether I had a more evident and perfect conception of what the wax was when I first perceived it, and when I believed I knew it by means of the external senses or at least by the common sense as it is called, that is to say by the imaginative faculty, or whether my present conception is clearer now that I have most carefully examined what it is, and in what way it can be known. It would certainly be absurd to doubt as to this. For what was there in this first perception which was distinct? What was there which might not as well have been perceived by any of the animals? But when I distinguish the wax from its external forms, and when, just as if I had taken from it its vestments, I consider it quite naked, it is certain that although some error may still be

found in my judgment, I can nevertheless not perceive it thus without a human mind.

But finally, what shall I say of this mind, that is, of myself, for up to this point I do not admit in myself anything but mind? What then, I who seem to perceive this piece of wax distinctly, do I not know myself, not only with much more truth and certainty, but also with much more distinctness and clearness? For if I judge that the wax is or exists from the fact that I see it, it certainly follows much more clearly that I am or that I exist myself from the fact that I see it. For it may be that what I see is not really wax; it may also be that I do not possess eyes with which to see anything; but it cannot be that when I see, or (for I no longer take account of the distinction) when I think I see, that I myself who think am nought. So if I judge that the wax exists from the fact that I touch it, the same thing will follow, to wit, that I am; and if I judge that my imagination, or some other cause, whatever it is, persuades me that the wax exists, I shall still conclude the same. And what I have here remarked of wax may be applied to all other things which are external to me [and which are met with outside of me]. And further, if the [notion or] perception of wax has seemed to me clearer and more distinct, not only after the sight or the touch, but also after many other causes have rendered it quite manifest to me, with how much more [evidence] and distinctness must it be said that I now know myself, since all the reasons which contribute to the knowledge of wax, or any other body whatever, are yet better proofs of the nature of my mind! And there are so many other things in the mind itself which may contribute to the elucidation of its nature, that those which depend on body such as these just mentioned, hardly merit being taken into account.

But finally here I am, having insensibly reverted to the point I desired, for, since it is now manifest to me that even bodies are not, properly speaking, known by the senses or by the faculty of imagination, but by the understanding only, and since they are not known from the fact that they are seen or touched, but only because they are understood, I see clearly that there is nothing which is easier for me to know than my mind. But because it is difficult to rid oneself so promptly of an opinion to which one was accustomed for so long, it will be well that I should halt a little at this point, so that by the length of my meditation I may more deeply imprint on my memory this new knowledge.

QUESTIONS FOR DISCUSSION

1. Why does Descartes resolve to doubt his former beliefs?
2. Is this an easy thing to do? Do you think Descartes succeeds in setting aside all his former beliefs?
3. Do you know any other philosophers who have made doubt a cornerstone of their philosophy? Look up *skepticism* in the Encyclopedia Britannica, in the Encyclopedia of Philosophy edited by Paul Edwards, and in Baldwin's Dictionary of Philosophy and Psychology.
4. Is it possible to doubt everything? Almost everything? Just how far do you think a skeptic can go? Are there psychological barriers to thoroughgoing skepticism? Are there logical limits to doubt? If so what are they?
5. Some philosophers have made a distinction between real doubt and pseudo-doubt. How do you think such a distinction can be made?
6. In the Synopsis of the Six Meditations, Descartes says that no one of sound mind has ever doubted the existence of a world, that men have bodies, and so forth. Doesn't he doubt these very things in the First Meditation?
7. Why does Descartes call his little essays *Meditations?*
8. Are there any beliefs that Descartes takes for granted without being aware of them, and hence without explicitly mentioning them?
9. Where is the evidence in Descartes' writing that he is using a deductive method? Cite at least three places.

Henri Bergson (1860-1941)

2.4 The Intuitive Method

A comparison of the definitions of metaphysics and the various conceptions of the absolute leads to the discovery that philosophers, in spite of their apparent divergencies, agree in distinguishing two profoundly different ways of knowing a thing. The first implies that we move round the object; the second that we enter into it. The first depends on the point of view at which we are placed and on the symbols by which we express ourselves. The second neither depends on a point of view nor relies on any symbol. The first kind of knowledge may be said to stop at the *relative;* the second, in those cases where it is possible, to attain the *absolute.*

Consider, for example, the movement of an object in space. My perception of the motion will vary with the point of view, moving or stationary, from which I observe it. My expression of it will vary with the systems of axes, or the points of reference, to which I relate it; that is, with the symbols by which I translate it. For this double reason I call such motion *relative:* in the one case, as in the other, I am placed outside the object

itself. But when I speak of an *absolute* movement, I am attributing to the moving object an interior and, so to speak, states of mind; I also imply that I am in sympathy with those states, and that I insert myself in them by an effort of imagination. Then, according as the object is moving or stationary, according as it adopts one movement or another, what I experience will vary. And what I experience will depend neither on the point of view I may take up in regard to the object, since I am inside the object itself, nor on the symbols by which I may translate the motion, since I have rejected all translations in order to possess the original. In short, I shall no longer grasp the movement from without, remaining where I am, but from where it is, from within, as it is in itself. I shall possess an absolute.

Consider, again, a character whose adventures are related to me in a novel. The author may multiply the traits of his hero's character, may make him speak and act as much as he pleases, but all this can never be equivalent to the simple and indivisible feeling which I should experience if I were able for an instant to identify myself with the person of the hero himself. Out of that indivisible feeling, as from a spring, all the words,

From *An Introduction to Metaphysics.* Trans. by T. E. Hulme (New York: G. P. Putnam's Sons, 1912).

gestures, and actions of the man would appear to me to flow naturally. They would no longer be accidents which, added to the idea I had already formed of the character, continually enriched that idea, without ever completing it. The character would be given to me all at once, in its entirety, and the thousand incidents which manifest it, instead of adding themselves to the idea and so enriching it, would seem to me, on the contrary, to detach themselves from it, without, however, exhausting it or impoverishing its essence. All the things I am told about the man provide me with so many points of view from which I can observe him. All the traits which describe him, and which can make him known to me only by so many comparisons with persons or things I know already, are signs by which he is expressed more or less symbolically. Symbols and points of view, therefore, place me outside him; they give me only what he has in common with others, and not what belongs to him and to him alone. But that which is properly himself, that which constitutes his essence, cannot be perceived from without, being internal by definition, nor be expressed by symbols, being incommensurable with everything else. Description, history, and analysis leave me here in the relative. Coincidence with the person himself would alone give me the absolute.

It is in this sense, and in this sense only, that *absolute* is synonymous with *perfection*. Were all the photographs of a town, taken from all possible points of view, to go on indefinitely completing one another, they would never be equivalent to the solid town in which we walk about. Were all the translations of a poem into all possible languages to add together their various shades of meaning and, correcting each other by a kind of mutual retouching, to give a more and more faithful image of the poem they translate, they would yet never succeed in rendering the inner meaning of the original. A representation taken from a certain point of view, a translation made with certain symbols, will always remain imperfect in comparison with the object of which a view has been taken, or which the symbols seek to express. But the absolute, which is the object and not its representation, the original and not its translation, is perfect, by being perfectly what it is.

It is doubtless for this reason that the *absolute* has often been identified with the *infinite*. Suppose that I wished to communicate to someone who did not know Greek the extraordinarily simple impression that a passage in Homer makes upon me; I should first give a translation of the lines, I should then comment on my translation, and then develop the commentary; in this way, by piling up explanation on explanation, I might approach nearer and nearer to what I wanted to express; but I should never quite reach it. When you raise your arm, you accomplish a movement of which you have, from within, a simple perception; but for me, watching it from the outside, your arm passes through one point, then through another, and between these two there will be still other points; so that, if I began to count, the operation would go on for ever. Viewed from the inside, then, an absolute is a simple thing; but looked at from the outside, that is to say, relatively to other things, it becomes, in relation to these signs which express it, the gold coin for which we never seem able to finish giving small change. Now, that which lends itself at the same time both to an indivisible apprehension and to an inexhaustible enumeration, is, by the very definition of the word, an infinite.

It follows from this that an absolute could only be given in an *intuition,* while everything else falls within the province of *analysis.* By intuition is meant the kind of *intellectual sympathy* by which one places oneself within an object in order to coincide with what is unique in it and consequently inexpressible. Analysis, on the contrary, is the operation which reduces the object to elements already known, that is, to elements common both to it and other objects. To analyze, therefore, is to express a thing as a function of something other than itself. All analysis is thus a translation, a development into symbols, a representation taken from successive points of view from which we note as many resemblances as possible between the new object which we are studying and others which we believe we know already. In its eternally unsatisfied desire to embrace the object around which it is compelled to turn, analysis multiplies without end the number of its points of view in order to complete its always incomplete representation, and ceaselessly varies its symbols that it may perfect the always imperfect translation. It goes on, therefore, to infinity. But intuition, if intuition is possible, is a simple act.

Now it is easy to see that the ordinary function of positive science is analysis. Positive science works, then, above all, with symbols. Even the most concrete of the natural sciences, those concerned with life, confine themselves to the visible form of living beings, their organs and anatomical elements.

They make comparisons between these forms, they reduce the more complex to the more simple; in short, they study the workings of life in what is, so to speak, only its visual symbol. If there exists any means of possessing a reality absolutely instead of knowing it relatively, of placing oneself within it instead of looking at it from outside points of view, of having the intuition instead of making the analysis: in short, of seizing it without any expression, translation, or symbolic representation—metaphysics is that means. *Metaphysics, then, is the science which claims to dispense with symbols.*

There is one reality, at least, which we all seize from within, by intuition and not by simple analysis. It is our own personality in its flowing through time—our self which endures. We may sympathize intellectually with nothing else, but we certainly sympathize with our own selves.

When I direct my attention inward to contemplate my own self (supposed for the moment to be inactive), I perceive at first, as a crust solidified on the surface, all the perceptions which come to it from the material world. These perceptions are clear, distinct, juxtaposed, or juxtaposable one with another; they tend to group themselves into objects. Next, I notice the memories which more or less adhere to these perceptions and which serve to interpret them. These memories have been detached, as it were, from the depth of my personality, drawn to the surface by the perceptions which resemble them; they rest on the surface of my mind without being absolutely myself. Lastly, I feel the stir of tendencies and motor habits—a crowd of virtual actions, more or less firmly bound to these perceptions and memories. All these clearly defined elements appear more distinct from me, the more distinct they are from each other. Radiating, as they do, from within outwards, they form, collectively, the surface of a sphere which tends to grow larger and lose itself in the exterior world. But if I draw myself in from the periphery toward the center, if I search in the depth of my being that which is most uniformly, most constantly, and most enduringly myself, I find an altogether different thing.

There is, beneath these sharply cut crystals and this frozen surface, a continuous flux which is not comparable to any flux I have ever seen. There is a succession of states, each of which announces that which follows and contains that which precedes it. They can, properly speaking, only be said to form multiple states when I have already passed them and turn back to observe their track. While I was experiencing them they were so solidly organized, so profoundly animated with a common life, that I could not have said where any one of them finished or where another commenced. In reality no one of them begins or ends, but all extend into each other.

This inner life may be compared to the unrolling of a coil, for there is no living being who does not feel himself coming gradually to the end of his role; and to live is to grow old. But it may just as well be compared to a continual rolling up, like that of a thread on a ball, for our past follows us, it swells incessantly with the present that it picks up on its way; and consciousness means memory.

But actually it is neither an unrolling nor a rolling up, for these two similes evoke the idea of lines and surfaces whose parts are homogeneous

and superposable on one another. Now, there are no two identical moments in the life of the same conscious being. Take the simplest sensation, suppose it constant, absorb in it the entire personality: the consciousness which will accompany this sensation cannot remain identical with itself for two consecutive moments, because the second moment always contains, over and above the first, the memory that the first has bequeathed to it. A consciousness which could experience two identical moments would be a consciousness without memory. It would die and be born again continually. In what other way could one represent unconsciousness?

It would be better, then, to use as a comparison the myriad-tinted spectrum, with its insensible gradations leading from one shade to another. A current of feeling which passed along the spectrum, assuming in turn the tint of each of its shades, would experience a series of gradual changes, each of which would announce the one to follow and would sum up those which preceded it. Yet even here the successive shades of the spectrum always remain external one to another. They are juxtaposed; they occupy space. But pure duration, on the contrary, excludes all idea of juxtaposition, reciprocal externality, and extension.

Let us, then, rather, imagine an infinitely small elastic body, contracted, if it were possible, to a mathematical point. Let this be drawn out gradually in such a manner that from the point comes a constant lengthening line. Let us fix our attention not on the line as a line, but on the action by which it is traced. Let us bear in mind that this action, in spite of its duration, is indivisible if accomplished without stopping, that if a stopping point is inserted, we have two actions instead of one, that each of these separate actions is then the indivisible operation of which we speak, and that it is not the moving action itself which is divisible, but, rather, the stationary line it leaves behind it as its track in space. Finally, let us free ourselves from the space which underlies the movement in order to consider only the movement itself, the act of tension or extension; in short, pure mobility. We shall have this time a more faithful image of the development of our self in duration.

However, even this image is incomplete, and, indeed, every comparison will be insufficient, because the unrolling of our duration resembles in some of its aspects the unity of an advancing movement and in others the multiplicity of expanding states; and, clearly, no metaphor can express one of these two aspects without sacrificing the other. If I use the comparison of the spectrum with its thousand shades, I have before me a thing already made, while duration is continually in the making. If I think of an elastic which is being stretched, or of a spring which is extended or relaxed, I forget the richness of color, characteristic of duration that is lived, to see only the simple movement by which consciousness passes from one shade to another. The inner life is all this at once: variety of qualities, continuity of progress, and unity of direction. It cannot be represented by images.

But it is even less possible to represent it by *concepts,* that is, by abstract, general, or simple ideas. It is true that no image can reproduce exactly the original feeling I have of the flow of my own conscious life. But it is not even necessary that I should attempt to render it. If a man is incapable of getting for himself the intuition of the constitutive duration of his own being, nothing will ever give it to him, concepts no more than images. Here the single aim of the philosopher should be to promote a certain effort, which in most men is usually fettered by habits of mind more useful to life. Now the image has at least this advantage, that it keeps us in the concrete. No image can replace the intuition of duration, but many diverse images, borrowed from very different orders of things, may, by the convergence of their action, direct consciousness to the precise point where there is a certain intuition to be seized. By choosing images as dissimilar as possible, we shall prevent any one of them from usurping the place of the intuition it is intended to call up, since it would then be driven away at once by its rivals. By providing that, in spite of their differences of aspect, they all require from the mind the same kind of attention, and in some sort the same degree of tension, we shall gradually accustom consciousness to a particular and clearly defined disposition—that precisely which it must adopt in order to appear to itself as it really is, without any veil. But, then, consciousness must at least consent to make the effort. For it will have been shown nothing: it will simply have been placed in the attitude it must take up in order to make the desired effort, and so come by itself to the intuition. Concepts on the contrary—especially if they are simple—have the disadvantage of being in reality symbols substituted for the object they symbolize, and demand no effort on our part. Examined closely, each of them, it would be seen, retains only that part of the object which is common to it and to others, and expresses, still more than the image does, a *comparison* between the object and others which resemble it. But as the comparison has made manifest a resemblance, as the resemblance is a property of the object, and as a property has every appearance of being a *part* of the object which possesses it, we easily persuade ourselves that by setting concept beside concept we are reconstructing the whole of the object with its parts, thus obtaining, so to speak, its intellectual equivalent. In this way we believe that we can form a faithful representation of duration by setting in line the concepts of unity, multiplicity, continuity, finite or infinite divisibility, etc. There precisely is the illusion. There also is the danger. Just insofar as abstract ideas can render service to analysis, that is, to the scientific study of the object in its relations to other objects, so far are they incapable of replacing intuition, that is, the metaphysical investigation of what is essential and unique in the object. For on the one hand these concepts, laid side by side, never actually give us more than an artificial reconstruction of the object, of which they can only symbolize certain general, and, in a way, impersonal aspects; it is, therefore, useless to believe that with them we can seize a reality of which they present to us the shadow alone. And, on the other hand, besides the illusion there is also a very serious danger. For the concept generalizes at the same time as it abstracts. The concept can only symbolize a particular property by making it common to an infinity of things. It therefore always more or less de-

forms the property by the extension it gives to it. Replaced in the metaphysical object to which it belongs, a property coincides with the object, or at least moulds itself on it, and adopts the same outline. Extracted from the metaphysical object, and presented in a concept, it grows indefinitely larger, and goes beyond the object itself, since henceforth it has to contain it, along with a number of other objects. Thus the different concepts that we form of the properties of a thing inscribe round it so many circles, each much too large and none of them fitting it exactly. And yet, in the thing itself the properties coincided with the thing, and coincided consequently with one another. So that, if we are bent on reconstructing the object with concepts, some artifice must be sought whereby this coincidence of the object and its properties can be brought about. For example, we may choose one of the concepts and try, starting from it, to get round to the others. But we shall then soon discover that, according as we start from one concept or another, the meeting and combination of the concepts will take place in an altogether different way. According as we start, for example, from unity or from multiplicity, we shall have to conceive differently the multiple unity of duration. Everything will depend on the weight we attribute to this or that concept, and this weight will always be arbitrary, since the concept extracted from the object has no weight, being only the shadow of a body. In this way, as many different *systems* will spring up as there are external points of view from which the reality can be examined, or larger circles in which it can be enclosed. Simple concepts have, then, not only the inconvenience of dividing the concrete unity of the object into so many symbolical expressions; they also divide philosophy into distinct schools, each of which takes its seat, chooses its counters, and carries on with the others a game that will never end. Either metaphysics is only this play of ideas, or else, if it is a serious occupation of the mind, if it is a science and not simply an exercise, it must transcend concepts in order to reach intuition. Certainly, concepts are necessary to it, for all the other sciences work as a rule with concepts, and metaphysics cannot dispense with the other sciences. But it is only true itself when it goes beyond the concept, or at least when it frees itself from rigid and ready-made concepts in order to create a kind very different from those which we habitually use; I mean supple, mobile, and almost fluid representations, always ready to mould themselves on the fleeting forms of intuition. We shall return later to this important point. Let it suffice us for the moment to have shown that our duration can be presented to us directly in an intuition, that it can be suggested to us indirectly by images, but that it can never—if we confine the word concept to its proper meaning—be enclosed in a conceptual representation.

Let us try for an instant to consider our duration as a multiplicity. It will then be necessary to add that the terms of this multiplicity, instead of being distinct, as they are in any other multiplicity, encroach on one another; and that, while we can no doubt, by an effort of imagination, solidify duration once it has elapsed, divide it into juxtaposed portions and count all these portions, yet this operation is accomplished on the frozen memory of the duration, on the stationary trace which the mobility of duration leaves behind it, and not on the duration itself. We must admit, therefore, that if there is a multiplicity here, it bears no resemblance to any other multiplicity we know. Shall we say, then, that duration has unity? Doubtless, a continuity of elements which prolong themselves into one another participates in unity as much as in multiplicity; but this moving, changing, colored, living unity has hardly anything in common with the abstract, motionless, and empty unity which the concept of pure unity circumscribes. Shall we conclude from this that duration must be defined as unity and multiplicity at the same time? But singularly enough, however much I manipulate the two concepts, portion them out, combine them differently, practice on them the most subtle operations of mental chemistry, I never obtain anything which resembles the simple intuition that I have of duration; while, on the contrary, when I replace myself in duration by an effort of intuition, I immediately perceive how it is unity, multiplicity, and many other things besides. These different concepts, then, were only so many standpoints from which we could consider duration. Neither separated nor reunited have they made us penetrate into it.

We do penetrate into it, however, and that can only be by an effort of intuition. In this sense, an inner, absolute knowledge of the duration of the self by the self is possible. But if metaphysics here demands and can obtain an intuition, science has none the less need of an analysis. Now it is a confusion between the function of analysis and that of intuition which gives birth to the discussions between the schools and the conflicts between systems.

Psychology, in fact, proceeds like all the other sciences by analysis. It resolves the self, which has been given to it at first in a simple intuition, into sensations, feelings, ideas, etc., which it studies separately. It substitutes, then, for the self a series of elements which form the facts of psychology. But are these *elements* really *parts?* That is the whole question, and it is because it has been evaded that the problem of human personality has so often been stated in insoluble terms.

It is incontestable that every psychical state, simply because it belongs to a person, reflects the whole of a personality. Every feeling, however simple it may be, contains virtually within it the whole past and present of the being experiencing it, and, consequently, can only be separated and constituted into a "state" by an effort of abstraction or of analysis. But it is no less incontestable that without this effort of abstraction or analysis there would be no possible development of the science of psychology. What, then, exactly, is the operation by which a psychologist detaches a mental state in order to erect it into a more or less independent entity? He begins by neglecting that special coloring of the personality which canot be expressed in known and common terms. Then he endeavors to isolate, in the person already thus simplified, some aspect which lends itself to an interesting inquiry. If he is considering inclination, for example, he will neglect the inexpressible shade which colors it, and which makes the inclination mine and not yours; he will fix his attention on the movement by which our personal-

ity *leans towards* a certain object: he will isolate this attitude, and it is this special aspect of the personality, this snapshot of the mobility of the inner life, this "diagram" of concrete inclination, that he will erect into an independent fact. There is in this something very like what an artist passing through Paris does when he makes, for example, a sketch of a tower of Notre Dame. The tower is inseparably united to the building, which is itself no less inseparably united to the ground, to its surroundings, to the whole of Paris, and so on. It is first necessary to detach it from all these; only one aspect of the whole is noted, that formed by the tower of Notre Dame. Moreover, the special form of this tower is due to the grouping of the stones of which it is composed; but the artist does not concern himself with these stones, he notes only the silhouette of the tower. For the real and internal organization of the thing he substitutes, then, an external and schematic representation. So that, on the whole, his sketch corresponds to an observation of the object from a certain point of view and to the choice of a certain means of representation. But exactly the same things holds true of the operation by which the psychologist extracts a single mental state from the whole personality. This isolated psychical state is hardly anything but a sketch, the commencement of an artificial reconstruction; it is the whole considered under a certain elementary aspect in which we are specially interested and which we have carefully noted. It is not a part, but an element. It has not been obtained by a natural dismemberment, but by analysis.

Now beneath all the sketches he has made at Paris the visitor will probably, by way of memento, write the word "Paris." And as he has really seen Paris, he will be able, with the help of the original intuition he had of the whole, to place his sketches therein, and so join them up together. But there is no way of performing the inverse operation; it is impossible, even with an infinite number of accurate sketches, and even with the word "Paris" which indicates that they must be combined together, to get back to an intuition that one has never had, and to give oneself an impression of what Paris is like if one has never seen it. This is because we are not dealing here with real *parts*, but with mere *notes* of the total impression. To take a still more striking example, where the notation is more completely symbolic, suppose that I am shown, mixed together at random, the letters which make up a poem I am ignorant of. If the letters were *parts* of the poem, I could attempt to reconstitute the poem with them by trying the different possible arrangements, as a child does with the pieces of a Chinese puzzle. But I should never for a moment think of attempting such a thing in this case, because the letters are not *component parts*, but only *partial expressions*, which is quite a different thing. That is why, if I know the poem, I at once put each

of the letters in its proper place and join them up without difficulty by a continuous connection, while the inverse operation is impossible. Even when I believe I am actually attempting this inverse operation, even when I put the letters end to end, I begin by thinking of some plausible meaning. I thereby give myself an intuition, and from this intuition I attempt to redescend to the elementary symbols which would reconstitute its expression. The very idea of reconstituting a thing by operations practiced on symbolic elements alone implies such an absurdity that it would never occur to anyone if [he] recollected that [he was] not dealing with fragments of the thing, but only, as it were, with fragments of its symbol.

Such is, however, the undertaking of the philosophers who try to reconstruct personality with psychical states, whether they confine themselves to those states alone, or whether they add a kind of thread for the purpose of joining the states together. Both empiricists and rationalists are victims of the same fallacy. Both of them mistake *partial notations* for *real parts*, thus confusing the point of view of analysis and of intuition, of science and metaphysics.

QUESTIONS FOR DISCUSSION

1. What is the distinction that Bergson makes between absolute and relative knowledge?
2. What does he consider the shortcomings of analysis to be?
3. Can you explain in your own words what Bergson means by intuition?
4. "Metaphysics," says Bergson, "is the science which claims to dispense with symbols." How can the metaphysician express his thoughts if he is forbidden to use symbols?

5. In the same vein, if the unique quality of an object is, as Bergson says, inexpressible, how can the metaphysician convey in writing that which is inexpressible?

6. Bergson doesn't make a distinction between experiencing an object and knowing it. Do you think it is valuable to make such a distinction?

Charles S. Peirce (1839-1914)

2.5   The Scientific Method

Few persons care to study logic, because everybody conceives himself to be proficient enough in the art of reasoning already. But I observe that this satisfaction is limited to one's own ratiocination, and does not extend to that of other men.

We come to the full possession of our power of drawing inferences, the last of all our faculties, for it is not so much a natural gift as a long and difficult art. The history of its practice would make a grand subject for a book. The medieval schoolman, following the Romans, made logic the earliest of a boy's studies after grammar, as being very easy. So it was, as they understood it. Its fundamental principle, according to them, was that all knowledge rests on either authority or reason; but that whatever is deduced by reason depends ultimately on a premise derived from authority. Accordingly, as soon as a boy was

perfect in the syllogistic procedure, his intellectual kit of tools was held to be complete.

To Roger Bacon, that remarkable mind who in the middle of the thirteenth century was almost a scientific man, the schoolmen's conception of reasoning appeared only an obstacle to truth. He saw that experience alone teaches anything—a proposition which to us seems easy to understand, because a distinct conception of experience has been handed down to us from former generations; which to him also seemed perfectly clear, because its difficulties had not yet unfolded themselves. Of all kinds of experience, the best, he thought, was interior illumination, which teaches many things about Nature which the external senses could never discover, such as the transubstantiation of bread.

Four centuries later, the more celebrated Bacon, in the first book of his *Novum Organum*, gave his clear account of experience as something which must be opened to verification

First published in *Popular Science Monthly* (1877), with the title: "The Fixation of Belief."

and reexamination.[1] But, superior as Lord Bacon's conception is to earlier notions, a modern reader who is not in awe of his grandiloquence is chiefly struck by the inadequacy of his view of scientific procedure. That we have only to make some crude experiments, to draw up briefs of the results in certain blank forms, to go through these by rule, checking off everything disproved and setting down the alternatives, and that thus in a few years physical science would be finished up —what an idea! "He wrote on science like a Lord Chancellor," indeed.

The early scientists, Copernicus, Tycho Brahe, Kepler, Galileo, and Gilbert, had methods more like those of their modern brethren. Kepler undertook to draw a curve through the places of Mars; and his greatest service to science was in impressing on men's minds that this was the thing to be done if they wished to improve astronomy; that they were not to content themselves with inquiring whether one system of epicycles was better than another but that they were to sit down by the figures and find out what the curve, in truth, was. He accomplished this by his incomparable energy and courage, blundering along in the most inconceivable way (to us), from one irrational hypothesis to another, until, after trying twenty-two of these, he fell, by the mere exhaustion of his invention, upon the orbit which a mind well furnished with the weapons of modern logic would have tried almost at the outset.[2]

In the same way, every work of science great enough to be remembered for a few generations affords some exemplification of the defective state of the art of reasoning of the time when it was written; and each chief step in science has been a lesson in logic. It was so when Lavoisier and his contemporaries took up the study of chemistry. The old chemist's maxim had been, *"Lege, lege, lege, labora, ora, et relege."* [3] Lavoisier's method was not to read and pray, not to dream that some long and complicated chemical process would have a certain effect, to put it into practice with dull patience, after its inevitable failure, to dream that with some modification it would have another result, and to end by publishing the last dream as a fact: his way was to carry his mind into his laboratory, and to make of his alembics and cucurbits instruments of thought, giving a new conception of reasoning as something which was to be done with one's eyes open, by manipulating real things instead of words and fancies. . . .

The object of reasoning is to find out, from the consideration of what we already know, something else which we do not know. Consequently, reasoning is good if it be such as to give a true conclusion from true premises, and not otherwise. Thus, the question of validity is purely one of fact and not of thinking. A being the premises and B being the conclusion, the question is whether these facts are really so related that if A is, B is. If so, the inference is valid; if

---

[1] See selection 2.2.

[2] Twenty-one years after writing this comment on Kepler, that is, in 1893, Peirce retracted it, saying it was a "foolish remark" which he made because he had not

then read the original work of Kepler. He now believed (in 1893) that it was a "marvelous piece of inductive reasoning." [D. J. B.]

[3] "Read, read, read, work, pray, and reread."

not, not. It is not in the least the question whether, when the premises are accepted by the mind, we feel an impulse to accept the conclusion also. It is true that we do generally reason correctly by nature. But that is an accident; the true conclusion would remain true if we had no impulse to accept it; and the false one would remain false, though we could not resist the tendency to believe in it.

We are, doubtless, in the main logical animals, but we are not perfectly so. Most of us, for example, are naturally more sanguine and hopeful than logic would justify. We seem to be so constituted that, in the absence of any facts to go upon, we are happy and self-satisfied; so that the effect of experience is continually to counteract our hopes and aspirations. Yet a lifetime of the application of this corrective does not usually eradicate our sanguine disposition. Where hope is unchecked by any experience, it is likely that our optimism is extravagant. Logicality in regard to practical matters is the most useful quality an animal can possess, and might, therefore, result from the action of natural selection; but outside of these, it is probably of more advantage to the animal to have his mind filled with pleasing and encouraging visions, independently of their truth; and thus, upon unpractical subjects, natural selection might occasion a fallacious tendency of thought.

That which determines us, from given premises, to draw one inference rather than another, is some habit of mind, whether it be constitutional or acquired. The habit is good or otherwise, according as it produces true conclusions from true premises or not; and an inference is regarded as valid or not, without reference to the truth or falsity of its conclusion specially, but according as the habit which determines it is such as to produce true conclusions in general or not. The particular habit of mind which governs this or that inference may be formulated in a proposition whose truth depends on the validity of the inferences which the habit determines; and such a formula is called a *guiding principle* of inference. Suppose, for example, that we observe that a rotating disk of copper quickly comes to rest when placed between the poles of a magnet, and we infer that this will happen with every disk of copper. The guiding principle is, that what is true of one piece of copper is true of another. Such a guiding principle with regard to copper would be much safer than with regard to many other substances—brass, for example.

A book might be written to signalize all the most important of these guiding principles of reasoning. It would probably be, we must confess, of no service to a person whose thought is directed wholly to practical subjects, and whose activity moves along thoroughly beaten paths. The problems which present themselves to such a mind are matters of routine which he has learned once for all to handle in learning his business. But let a man venture into an unfamiliar field, or where his results are not continually checked by experience, and all history shows that the most masculine intellect will ofttimes lose his orientation and waste his efforts in directions which bring him no nearer to his goal, or even carry him entirely astray. He is like a ship on the open sea, with no one on board who understands the rules of navigation. And in such a case some general study of the guiding principles of reasoning would be sure to be found useful.

The subject could hardly be treated, however, without being first limited; since almost any fact may serve as a guiding principle. But it so happens that there exists a division among facts, such that in one class are all those which are absolutely essential as guiding principles, while in the other are all those which have any other interest as objects of research. This division is between those which are necessarily taken for granted in asking whether a certain conclusion follows from certain premises, and those which are not implied in that question. A moment's thought will show that a variety of facts are already assumed when the logical question is first asked. It is implied, for instance, that there are such states of mind as doubt and belief—that a passage from one to the other is possible, the object of thought remaining the same, and that this transition is subject to some rules which all minds are alike bound by. As these are facts which we must already know before we can have any clear conception of reasoning at all, it cannot be supposed to be any longer of much interest to inquire into their truth or falsity. On the other hand, it is easy to believe that those rules of reasoning which are deduced from the very idea of the process are the ones which are the most essential; and, indeed, that so long as it conforms to these it will, at least, not lead to false conclusions from true premises. In point of fact, the importance of what may be deduced from the assumptions involved in the logical question turns out to be greater than might be sup-

posed, and this for reasons which it is difficult to exhibit at the outset. The only one which I shall here mention is, that conceptions which are really products of logical reflections, without being readily seen to be so, mingle with our ordinary thoughts, and are frequently the causes of great confusion. This is the case, for example, with the conception of quality. A quality as such is never an object of observation. We can see that a thing is blue or green, but the quality of being blue and the quality of being green are not things which we see; they are products of logical reflections. The truth is, that common sense, or thought as it first emerges above the level of the narrowly practical, is deeply imbued with that bad logical quality to which the epithet *metaphysical* is commonly applied; and nothing can clear it up but a severe course of logic.

We generally know when we wish to ask a question and when we wish to pronounce a judgment, for there is a dissimilarity between the sensation of doubting and that of believing.

But this is not all which distinguishes doubt from belief. There is a practical difference. Our beliefs guide our desires and shape our actions. The Assassins, or followers of the Old Man of the Mountain, used to rush into death at his least command, because they believed that obedience to him would insure everlasting felicity. Had they doubted this, they would not have acted as they did. So it is with every belief, according to its degree. The feeling of believing is a more or less sure indication of there being established in our nature some habit which will determine our actions. Doubt never has such an effect.

Nor must we overlook a third point of difference. Doubt is an uneasy and dissatisfied state from which we struggle to free ourselves and pass into the state of belief; while the latter is a calm and satisfactory state which we do not wish to avoid, or to change to a belief in anything else. On the contrary, we cling tenaciously, not merely to believing, but to believing just what we do believe.

Thus, both doubt and belief have positive effects upon us, though very different ones. Belief does not make us act at once, but puts us into such a condition that we shall behave in a certain way, when the occasion arises. Doubt has not the least effect of this sort, but stimulates us to action until it is destroyed. This reminds us of the irritation of a nerve and the reflex action produced thereby; while for the analogue of belief, in the nervous system, we must look to what are called nervous associations—for example, to that habit of the nerves in consequence of which the smell of a peach will make the mouth water.

The irritation of doubt causes a struggle to attain a state of belief. I shall term this struggle *inquiry,* though it must be admitted that this is sometimes not a very apt designation.

The irritation of doubt is the only immediate motive for the struggle to attain belief. It is certainly best for us that our beliefs should be such as may truly guide our actions so as to satisfy our desires; and this reflection will make us reject any belief which does not seem to have been so formed as to insure this result. But it will only do so by creating a doubt in the place of that belief. With the doubt, therefore, the struggle begins, and with the cessation of doubt it ends.

Hence, the sole object of inquiry is the settlement of opinion.[4] We may fancy that this is not enough for us, and that we seek, not merely an opinion, but a true opinion. But put this fancy to the test, and it proves groundless; for as soon as a firm belief is reached we are entirely satisfied, whether the belief be false or true. And it is clear that nothing out of the sphere of our knowledge can be our object, for nothing which does not affect the mind can be a motive for mental effort. The most that can be maintained is that we seek for a belief that we shall *think* to be true. But we think each one of our beliefs to be true, and, indeed, it is mere tautology to say so.

That the settlement of opinion is the sole end of inquiry is a very important proposition. It sweeps away, at once, various vague and erroneous conceptions of proof. A few of these may be noticed here.

1. Some philosophers have imagined that to start an inquiry it was only necessary to utter a question or set it down on paper, and have even recommended us to begin our studies with questioning everything! But the mere putting of a proposition into the interrogative form does not stimulate the mind to any struggle after belief. There must be a real and living doubt, and without this all discussion is idle.

2. It is a very common idea that a demonstration must rest on some ultimate and absolutely indubitable propositions. These, according to one school, are first principles of a general nature; according to another, are

---

[4] In later life Peirce changed his mind about this. See his *Collected Papers,* vol. VI, paragraph 485. [D. J. B.]

first sensations. But, in point of fact, an inquiry, to have that completely satisfactory result called demonstration, has only to start with propositions perfectly free from all actual doubt. If the premises are not in fact doubted at all, they cannot be more satisfactory than they are.

3. Some people seem to love to argue a point after all the world is fully convinced of it. But no further advance can be made. When doubt ceases, mental action on the subject comes to an end; and, if it did go on, it would be without a purpose.

If the settlement of opinion is the sole object of inquiry, and if belief is of the nature of a habit, why should we not attain the desired end by taking any answer to a question, which we may fancy, and constantly reiterating it to ourselves, dwelling on all which may conduce to that belief, and learning to turn with contempt and hatred from anything which might disturb it? This simple and direct method is really pursued by many men. I remember once being entreated not to read a certain newspaper lest it might change my opinion upon free trade. "Lest I might be entrapped by its fallacies and misstatements," was the form of expression. "You are not," my friend said, "a special student of political economy. You might, therefore, easily be deceived by fallacious arguments upon the subject. You might, then, if you read this paper, be led to believe in protection. But you admit that free trade is the true doctrine; and you do not wish to believe what is not true." I have often known this system to be deliberately adopted. Still oftener, the instinctive dislike of an undecided state of mind, exaggerated into a vague dread of doubt,

makes men cling spasmodically to the views they already take. The man feels that, if he only holds to his belief without wavering, it will be entirely satisfactory. Nor can it be denied that a steady and immovable faith yields great peace of mind. It may, indeed, give rise to inconveniences, as if a man should resolutely continue to believe that fire would not burn him, or that he would be eternally damned if he received his *ingesta* otherwise than through a stomach-pump. But then the man who adopts this method will not allow that its inconveniences are greater than its advantages. He will say, "I hold steadfastly to the truth and the truth is always wholesome." And in many cases it may very well be that the pleasure he derives from his calm faith overbalances any inconveniences resulting from its deceptive character. Thus, if it be true that death is annihilation, then the man who believes that he will certainly go straight to heaven when he dies, provided he have fulfilled certain simple observances in this life, has a cheap pleasure which will not be followed by the least disappointment. A similar consideration seems to have weight with many persons in religious topics, for we frequently hear it said, "Oh, I could not believe so-and-so, because I should be wretched if I did." When an ostrich buries its head in the sand as danger approaches, it very likely takes the happiest course. It hides the danger, and then calmly says there is no danger; and, if it feels perfectly sure there is none, why should it raise its head to see? A man may go through life systematically keeping out of view all that might cause a change in his opinions, and if he only succeeds—basing his method, as he does, on two fundamental psychological laws—I do not see what can be said against his doing so. It would be an egotistical impertinence to object that his procedure is irrational, for that only amounts to saying that his method of settling belief is not ours. He does not propose to himself to be rational, and, indeed, will often talk with scorn of man's weak and illusive reason. So let him think as he pleases.

But this method of fixing belief, which may be called the method of tenacity, will be unable to hold its ground in practice. The social impulse is against it. The man who adopts it will find that other men think differently from him, and it will be apt to occur to him in some saner moment that their opinions are quite as good as his own, and this will shake his confidence in his belief. This conception, that another man's thought or sentiment may be equivalent to one's own, is a distinctly new step, and a highly important one. It arises from an impulse too strong in man to be suppressed without danger of destroying the human species. Unless we make ourselves hermits, we shall necessarily influence each other's opinions; so that the problem becomes how to fix belief, not in the individual merely, but in the community.

Let the will of the state act, then, instead of that of the individual. Let an institution be created which shall have for its object to keep correct doctrines before the attention of the people, to reiterate them perpetually, and to teach them to the young; having at the same time power to prevent contrary doctrines from being taught, advocated, or expressed. Let all possible causes of a change of mind be removed from men's apprehensions.

Let them be kept ignorant, lest they should learn of some reason to think otherwise than they do. Let their passions be enlisted, so that they may regard private and unusual opinions with hatred and horror. Then, let all men who reject the established belief be terrified into silence. Let the people turn out and tar-and-feather such men, or let inquisitions be made into the manner of thinking of suspected persons, and, when they are found guilty of forbidden beliefs, let them be subjected to some signal punishment. When complete agreement could not otherwise be reached, a general massacre of all who have not thought in a certain way has proved a very effective means of settling opinion in a country. If the power to do this be wanting, let a list of opinions be drawn up, to which no man of the least independence of thought can assent, and let the faithful be required to accept all these propositions, in order to segregate them as radically as possible from the influence of the rest of the world.

This method has, from the earliest times, been one of the chief means of upholding correct theological and political doctrines, and of preserving their universal or catholic character. In Rome, especially, it has been practiced from the days of Numa Pompilius to those of Pius Nonus. This is the most perfect example in history; but wherever there is a priesthood—and no religion has been without one—this method has been more or less made use of. Wherever there is an aristocracy, or a guild, or any association of a class of men whose interests depend, or are supposed to depend, on certain propositions, there will be inevitably found some traces of this natural product of social feeling. Cruelties always accompany this system; and when it is consistently carried out, they become atrocities of the most horrible kind in the eyes of any rational man. Nor should this occasion surprise, for the officer of a society does not feel justified in surrendering the interests of that society for the sake of mercy, as he might his own private interests. It is natural, therefore, that sympathy and fellowship should thus produce a most ruthless power.

In judging this method of fixing belief, which may be called the method of authority, we must, in the first place, allow its immeasurable mental and moral superiority to the method of tenacity. Its success is proportionately greater; and, in fact, it has over and over again worked the most majestic results. The mere structures of stone which it has caused to be put together—in Siam, for example, in Egypt, and in Europe—have many of them a sublimity hardly more than rivalled by the greatest works of Nature. And, except the geological epochs, there are no periods of time so vast as those which are measured by some of these organized faiths. If we scrutinize the matter closely, we shall find that there has not been one of their creeds which has remained always the same; yet the change is so slow as to be imperceptible during one person's life, so that individual belief remains sensibly fixed. For the mass of mankind, then, there is perhaps no better method than this. If it is their highest impulse to be intellectual slaves, then slaves they ought to remain.

But no institution can undertake to regulate opinions upon every subject. Only the most important ones can be attended to, and on the rest

men's minds must be left to the action of natural causes. This imperfection will be no source of weakness so long as men are in such a state of culture that one opinion does not influence another—that is, so long as they cannot put two and two together. But in the most priest-ridden states some individuals will be found who are raised above that condition. These men possess a wider sort of social feeling; they see that men in other countries and in other ages have held to very different doctrines from those which they themselves have been brought up to believe; and they cannot help seeing that it is the mere accident of their having been taught as they have, and of their having been surrounded with the manners and associations they have, that has caused them to believe as they do and not far differently. Nor can their candor resist the reflection that there is no reason to rate their own views at a higher value than those of other nations and other centuries; thus giving rise to doubts in their minds.

They will further perceive that such doubts as these must exist in their minds with reference to every belief which seems to be determined by the caprice either of themselves or of those who originated the popular opinions. The willful adherence to a belief, and the arbitrary forcing of it upon others, must, therefore, both be given up. A different new method of settling opinions must be adopted, that shall not only produce an impulse to believe, but shall also decide what proposition it is which is to be believed. Let the action of natural preferences be unimpeded, then, and under their influence let men, conversing together and regarding matters in different lights, gradually develop beliefs in harmony with natural causes. This method resembles that by which conceptions of art have been brought to maturity. The most perfect example of it is to be found in the history of metaphysical philosophy. Systems of this sort have not usually rested upon any observed facts, at least not in any great degree. They have been chiefly adopted because their fundamental propositions seemed "agreeable to reason." This is an apt expression; it does not mean that which agrees with experience, but that which we find ourselves inclined to believe. Plato, for example, finds it agreeable to reason that the distances of the celestial spheres from one another should be proportional to the different lengths of strings which produce harmonious chords. Many philosophers have been led to their main conclusions by considerations like this; but this is the lowest and least developed form which the method takes, for it is clear that another man might find Kepler's theory, that the celestial spheres are proportional to the inscribed and circumscribed spheres of the different regular solids, more agreeable to *his* reason. But the shock of opinions will soon lead men to rest on preferences of a far more universal nature. Take, for example, the doctrine that man only acts selfishly—that is, from the consideration that acting in one way will afford him more pleasure than acting in another. This rests on no fact in the world, but it has had a wide acceptance as being the only reasonable theory.

This method is far more intellectual and respectable from the point of view of reason than either of the others which we have noticed. But its failure has been the most manifest. It makes of inquiry something similar to the development of taste; but taste, unfortunately, is always more or less a matter of fashion, and accordingly metaphysicians have never come to any fixed agreement, but the pendulum has swung backward and forward between a more material and a more spiritual philosophy, from the earliest times to the latest. And so from this, which has been called the *a priori* method, we are driven, in Lord Bacon's phrase, to a true induction. We have examined into this *a priori* method as something which promised to deliver our opinions from their accidental and capricious element. But development, while it is a process which eliminates the effect of some casual circumstances, only magnifies that of others. This method, therefore, does not differ in a very essential way from that of authority. The government may not have lifted its finger to influence my convictions; I may have been left outwardly quite free to choose, we will say, between monogamy and polygamy, and, appealing to my conscience only, I may have concluded that the latter practice is in itself licentious. But when I come to see that the chief obstacle to the spread of Christianity among a people of as high culture as the Hindus has been a conviction of the immorality of our way of treating women, I cannot help seeing that, though governments do not interfere, sentiments in their development will be very greatly determined by accidental causes. Now, there are some people, among whom I must suppose that my reader is to be found, who, when they see that any belief of theirs is determined by any circumstance extraneous to the facts, will from that moment not merely admit in words that that belief is doubtful, but will experience a real doubt of it, so that it ceases in some degree to be a belief.

To satisfy our doubts, therefore, it is necessary that a method should be found by which our beliefs may be caused by nothing human, but by some external permanency—by something upon which our thinking has no effect. Some mystics imagine that they have such a method in a private inspiration from on high. But that is only a form of the method of tenacity, in which the conception of truth as something public is not yet developed. Our external permanency would not be external, in our sense, if it was restricted in its influence to one individual. It must be something which affects, or might affect, every man. And, though these affections are necessarily as various as the individual conditions, yet the method must be such that the ultimate conclusion of every man shall be the same. Such is the method of science. Its fundamental hypothesis, restated in more familiar language, is this: There are Real things, whose characters are entirely independent of our opinions about them; those realities affect our senses according to regular laws, and, though our sensations are as different as are our relations to the objects, yet, by taking advantage of the laws of perception, we can ascertain by reasoning how things really are; and any man, if he have sufficient experience and he reason enough about it, will be led to the one True conclusion. The new conception here involved is that of Reality. It may be asked how I know that there are any realities. If this hypothesis is the sole support of my method of inquiry, my method of inquiry must not be used to support my hypothesis. The reply

is this: 1. If investigation cannot be regarded as proving that there are Real things, it at least does not lead to a contrary conclusion; but the method and the conception on which it is based remain ever in harmony. No doubts of the method, therefore, necessarily arise from its practice, as is the case with all the others. 2. The feeling which gives rise to any method of fixing belief is a dissatisfaction at two repugnant propositions. But here already is a vague concession that there is some *one* thing to which a proposition should conform. Nobody, therefore, can really doubt that there are realities, for, if he did, doubt would not be a source of dissatisfaction. The hypothesis, therefore, is one which every mind admits. So that the social impulse does not cause men to doubt it. 3. Everybody uses the scientific method about a great many things, and only ceases to use it when he does not know how to apply it. 4. Experience of the method has not led us to doubt it, but, on the contrary, scientific investigation has had the most wonderful triumphs in the way of settling opinion. These afford the explanation of my not doubting the method or the hypothesis which it supposes; and not having any doubt, nor believing that anybody else whom I could influence has, it would be the merest babble for me to say more about it. If there be anybody with a living doubt upon the subject, let him consider it. . . .

This is the only one of the four methods which presents any distinction of a right and a wrong way. If I adopt the method of tenacity, and shut myself out from all influences, whatever I think necessary to doing this, is necessary according to that method. So with the method of authority: the state may try to put down heresy by means which, from a scientific point of view, seem very ill-calculated to accomplish its purposes; but the only test *on that method* is what that state thinks; so that it cannot pursue the method wrongly. So with the *a priori* method. The very essence of it is to think as one is inclined to think. All metaphysicians will be sure to do that, however they may be inclined to judge each other to be perversely wrong. The Hegelian system recognizes every natural tendency of thought as logical, although it is certain to be abolished by counter-tendencies. Hegel thinks there is a regular system in the succession of these tendencies, in consequence of which, after drifting one way and the other for a long time, opinion will at last go right. And it is true that metaphysicians get the right ideas at last; Hegel's system of Nature represents tolerably the science of that day; and one may be sure that whatever scientific investigation has put out of doubt will presently receive *a priori* demonstration on the part of the metaphysicians. But with the scientific method the case is different. I may start with known and observed facts to proceed to the unknown; and yet the rules which I follow in doing so may not be such as investigation would approve. The test of whether I am truly following the method is not an immediate appeal to my feelings and purposes, but, on the contrary, itself involves the application of the method. Hence it is that bad reasoning as well as good reasoning is possible; and this fact is the foundation of the practical side of logic.

It is not to be supposed that the first three methods of settling opinion present no advantage whatever over the scientific method. On the contrary, each has some peculiar convenience of its own. The *a priori* method is distinguished for its comfortable conclusions. It is the nature of the process to adopt whatever belief we are inclined to, and there are certain flatteries to the vanity of man which we all believe by nature, until we are awakened from our pleasing dream by rough facts. The method of authority will always govern the mass of mankind; and those who wield the various forms of organized force in the state will never be convinced that dangerous reasoning ought not to be suppressed in some way. If liberty of speech is to be untrammelled from the grosser forms of constraint, then uniformity of opinion will be secured by a moral terrorism to which the respectability of society will give its thorough approval. Following the method of authority is the path of peace. Certain non-conformities are permitted; certain others (considered unsafe) are forbidden. These are different in different countries and in different ages; but, wherever you are, let it be known that you seriously hold a tabooed belief, and you may be perfectly sure of being treated with a cruelty less brutal but more refined than hunting you like a wolf. Thus, the greatest intellectual benefactors of mankind have never dared, and dare not now, to utter the whole of their thought; and thus a shade of *prima facie* doubt is cast upon every proposition which is considered essential to the security of society. Singularly enough, the persecution does not all come from without; but a man torments himself and is oftentimes most distressed at finding himself believing propositions which he has been brought up to regard with aversion.

The peaceful and sympathetic man will, therefore, find it hard to resist the temptation to submit his opinions to authority. But most of all I admire the method of tenacity for its strength, simplicity, and directness. Men who pursue it are distinguished for their decision of character, which becomes very easy with such a mental rule. They do not waste time in trying to make up their minds what they want, but, fastening like lightning upon whatever alternative comes first, they hold it to the end, whatever happens, without an instant's irresolution. This is one of the splendid qualities which generally accompany brilliant, unlasting success. It is impossible not to envy the man who can dismiss reason, although we know how it must turn out at last.

Such are the advantages which the other methods of settling opinion have over scientific investigation. A man should consider well of them; and then he should consider that, after all, he wishes his opinions to coincide with the fact, and that there is no reason why the results of those three methods should do so. To bring about this effect is the prerogative of the method of science. Upon such considerations he has to make his choice—a choice which is far more than the adoption of any intellectual opinion, which is one of the ruling decisions of his life, to which, when once made, he is bound to adhere. The force of habit will sometimes cause a man to hold on to old beliefs, after he is in a condition to see that they have no sound basis. But reflection upon the state of the case will overcome these habits, and he ought to allow reflection its full weight. People sometimes shrink from doing this, having an idea that beliefs are

wholesome which they cannot help feeling rest on nothing. But let such persons suppose an analogous though different case from their own. Let them ask themselves what they would say to a reformed Mussulman who should hesitate to give up his old notions in regard to the relations of the sexes; or to a reformed Catholic who should still shrink from reading the Bible. Would they not say that these persons ought to consider the matter fully, and clearly understand the new doctrine, and then ought to embrace it, in its entirety? But, above all, let it be considered that what is more wholesome than any particular belief is integrity of belief, and that to avoid looking into the support of any belief from a fear that it may turn out rotten is quite as immoral as it is disadvantageous. The person who confesses that there is such a thing as truth, which is distinguished from falsehood simply by this, that if acted on it will carry us to the point we aim at and not astray, and then, though convinced of this, dares not know the truth and seeks to avoid it, is in a sorry state of mind indeed.

Yes, the other methods do have their merits: a clear logical conscience does cost something—just as any virtue, just as all that we cherish, costs us dear. But we should not desire it to be otherwise. The genius of a man's logical method should be loved and reverenced as his bride, whom he has chosen from all the world. He need not contemn the others; on the contrary, he may honor them deeply, and in doing so he only honors her the more. But she is the one that he has chosen, and he knows that he was right in making that choice. And having made it, he will work and fight for her, and will not complain that there are blows to take, hoping that knight and champion of her from the blaze of whose splendors he draws his inspiration and his courage. there may be as many and as hard to give, and will strive to be the worthy

QUESTIONS FOR DISCUSSION

1. What does Peirce mean by "inquiry"?
2. What role in inquiry is played by doubt? Compare Peirce's view of doubt with that of Bertrand Russell in selection 1.4.
3. According to Peirce, what is the sole object of inquiry?
4. Why does the method of tenacity break down, according to Peirce?
5. Is there a difference between authority and authoritarianism? Which one does Peirce have in mind when he discusses the "method of authority"? What are his criticisms of the method?
6. Why does Peirce reject the *a priori* method" (believing what is "agreeable to reason") sometimes called the intuitive method?
7. What is the fundamental hypothesis upon which the method of science is based?
8. Give three reasons for preferring the method of science to the others, according to Peirce.
9. Do you think there are cases where one of the other methods would be preferable to the method of science? If so, explain why.

Walter T. Stace (1886-   )

2.6   *Ethical Relativity and Ethical Absolutism: A Methodological Conflict in Ethics*

There is an opinion widely current nowadays in philosophical circles which passes under the name of "ethi-

cal relativity." Exactly what this phrase means or implies is certainly far from clear. But unquestionably it stands as a label for the opinions of a group of ethical philosophers whose position is roughly on the extreme left wing among the moral theorizers of the day. And perhaps one may best

From *The Concept of Morals* by Walter T. Stace. © 1937 by The Macmillan Company, renewed 1965. Reprinted by permission of the publisher. The title of this selection has been supplied by the editors.

understand it by placing it in contrast with the opposite kind of extreme view against which, undoubtedy, it has arisen as a protest. For among moral philosophers one may clearly distinguish a left and a right wing. Those of the left wing are the ethical relativists. They are the revolutionaries, the clever young men, the up to date. Those of the right wing we may call the ethical absolutists. They are the conservatives and the old-fashioned.

According to the absolutists there is but one eternally true and valid moral code. This moral code applies with rigid impartiality to all men. What is a duty for me must likewise be a duty for you. And this will be true whether you are an Engishman, a Chinaman, or a Hottentot. If cannibalism is an abomination in England or America, it is an abomination in central Africa, notwithstanding that the African may think otherwise. The fact that he sees nothing wrong in his cannibal practices does not make them for him morally right. They are as much contrary to morality for him as they are for us. The only difference is that he is an ignorant savage who does not know this. There is not one law for one man or race of men, another for another. There is not one moral standard for Europeans, another for Indians, another for Chinese. There is but one law, one standard, one morality, for all men. And this standard, this law, is absolute and unvarying.

Moreover, as the one moral law extends its dominion over all the corners of the earth, so too it is not limited in its application by any considerations of time or period. That which is right now was right in the centuries of Greece and Rome, nay,

in the very ages of the cave man. That which is evil now was evil then. If slavery is morally wicked today, it was morally wicked among the ancient Athenians, notwithstanding that their greatest men accepted it as a necessary condition of human society. Their opinion did not make slavery a moral good for them. It only showed that they were, in spite of their otherwise noble conceptions, ignorant of what is truly right and good in this matter.

The ethical absolutist recognizes as a fact that moral customs and moral ideas differ from country to country and from age to age. This indeed seems manifest and not to be disputed. We think slavery morally wrong, the Greeks thought it morally unobjectionable. The inhabitants of New Guinea certainly have very different moral ideas from ours. But the fact that the Greeks or the inhabitants of New Guinea think something right does not make it right, even for them. Nor does the fact that we think the same things wrong make them wrong. They are in *themselves* either right or wrong. What we have to do is to discover which they are. What anyone thinks makes no difference. It is here just as it is in matters of physical science. We believe the earth to be a globe. Our ancestors may have thought it flat. This does not show that it *was* flat, and is *now* a globe. What it shows is that men having in other ages been ignorant about the shape of the earth have now learned the truth. So if the Greeks thought slavery morally legitimate, this does not indicate that it was for them and in that age morally legitimate, but rather that they were ignorant of the truth of the matter.

The ethical absolutist is not indeed

committed to the opinion that his own, or our own, moral code is the true one. Theoretically at least he might hold that slavery is ethically justifiable, that the Greeks knew better than we do about this, that ignorance of the true morality lies with us and not with them. All that he is actually committed to is the opinion that, whatever the true moral code may be, it is always the same for all men in all ages. His view is not at all inconsistent with the belief that humanity has still much to learn in moral matters. If anyone were to assert that in five hundred years the moral conceptions of the present day will appear as barbarous to the people of that age as the moral conceptions of the middle ages appear to us now, he need not deny it. If anyone were to assert that the ethics of Christianity are by no means final, and will be superseded in future ages by vastly nobler moral ideals, he need not deny this either. For it is of the essence of his creed to believe that morality is in some sense objective, not man-made, not produced by human opinion; that its principles are real truths about which men have to learn—just as they have to learn about the shape of the world—about which they may have been ignorant in the past, and about which therefore they may well be ignorant now.

Thus although absolutism is conservative in the sense that it is regarded by the more daring spirits as an out of date opinion, it is not necessarily conservative in the sense of being committed to the blind support of existing moral ideas and institutions. If ethical absolutists are sometimes conservative in this sense too, that is their personal affair. Such conservatism is accidental, not essential to the absolutist's creed. There is no logical reason, in the nature of the case, why an absolutist should not be a communist, an anarchist, a surrealist, or an upholder of free love. The fact that he is usually none of these things may be accounted for in various ways. But it has nothing to do with the sheer logic of his ethical position. The sole opinion to which he is committed is that whatever is morally right (or wrong)—be it free love or monogamy or slavery or cannibalism or vegetarianism—is morally right (or wrong) for all men at all times.

Usually the absolutist goes further than this. He often maintains, not merely that the moral law is the same for all the men on this planet—which is, after all, a tiny speck in space—but that in some way or in some sense it has application everywhere in the universe. He may express himself by saying that it applies to all "rational beings"—which would apparently include angels and the men on Mars (if they are rational). He is apt to think that the moral law is a part of the fundamental structure of the universe. But with this aspect of absolutism we need not, at the moment, concern ourselves. At present we may think of it as being simply the opinion that there is a single moral standard for all human beings.

This brief and rough sketch of ethical absolutism is intended merely to form a background against which we may the more clearly indicate, by way of contrast, the theory of ethical relativity. Up to the present, therefore, I have not given any of the reasons which the absolutist can urge in favour of his case. It is sufficient for my purpose at the moment to state *what* he believes, without going into the question of *why* he believes it.

But before proceeding to our next step—the explanation of ethical relativity—I think it will be helpful to indicate some of the historical causes (as distinguished from logical reasons) which have helped in the past to render absolutism a plausible interpretation of morality as understood by European peoples.

Our civilization is a Christian civilization. It has grown up, during nearly two thousand years, upon the soil of Christian monotheism. In this soil our whole outlook upon life, and consequently all our moral ideas, have their roots. They have been moulded by this influence. The wave of religious scepticism which, during the last half century, has swept over us, has altered this fact scarcely at all. The moral ideas even of those who most violently reject the dogmas of Christianity with their intellects are still Christian ideas. This will probably remain true for many centuries even if Christian theology, as a set of intellectual beliefs, comes to be wholly rejected by every educated person. It will probably remain true so long as our civilization lasts. A child cannot, by changing in later life his intellectual creed, strip himself of the early formative moral influences of his childhood, though he can no doubt modify their results in various minor ways. With the outlook on life which was instilled into him in his early days he, in large measure, lives and dies. So it is with a civilization. And our civilization, whatever religious or irreligious views it may come to hold or reject, can hardly escape within its lifetime the moulding influences of its Christian origin. Now ethical absolutism was, in its central ideas, the product of Christian theology.

The connection is not difficult to detect. For morality has been conceived, during the Christian dispensation, as issuing from the will of God. That indeed was its single and all-sufficient source. There would be no point, for the naive believer in the faith, in the philosopher's questions regarding the foundations of morality and the basis of moral obligation. Even to ask such questions is a mark of incipient religious scepticism. For the true believer the author of the moral law is God. What pleases God, what God commands—that is the definition of right. What displeases God, what he forbids, that is the definition of wrong. Now there is, for the Christian monotheist, only one God ruling over the entire universe. And this God is rational, self-consistent. He does not act upon whims. Consequently his will and his commands must be the same everywhere. They will be unvarying for all peoples and in all ages. If the heathen have other moral ideas than ours—inferior ideas—that can only be because they live in ignorance of the true God. If they knew God and his commands, their ethical precepts would be the same as ours.

Polytheistic creeds may well tolerate a number of diverse moral codes. For the God of the western hemisphere might have different views from those entertained by the God of the eastern hemisphere. And the God of the north might issue to his worshippers commands at variance with the commands issued to other peoples by the God of the south. But a monotheistic religion implies a single universal and absolute morality.

This explains why ethical absolutism, until very recently, was not only believed by philosophers but *taken for granted without any argument*. . . .

We can now turn to the consideration of ethical relativity. . . . The revolt of the relativists against absolutism is, I believe, part and parcel of the general revolutionary tendency of our times. In particular it is a result of the decay of belief in the dogmas of orthodox religion. Belief in absolutism was supported, as we have seen, by belief in Christian monotheism. And now that, in an age of widespread religious scepticism, that support is withdrawn, absolutism tends to collapse. Revolutionary movements are as a rule, at any rate in their first onset, purely negative. They attack and destroy. And ethical relativity is, in its essence, a purely negative creed. It is simply a denial of ethical absolutism. That is why the best way of explaining it is to begin by explaining ethical absolutism. If we understand that what the latter asserts the former denies, then we understand ethical relativity.

Any ethical position which denies that there is a single moral standard which is equally applicable to all men at all times may fairly be called a species of ethical relativity. There is not, the relativist asserts, merely one moral law, one code, one standard. There are many moral laws, codes, standards. What morality ordains in one place or age may be quite different from what morality ordains in another place or age. The moral code of Chinamen is quite different from that of Europeans, that of African savages quite different from both. Any morality, therefore, is relative to the age, the place, and the circumstances in which it is found. It is in no sense absolute.

This does not mean merely—as one might at first sight be inclined to suppose—that the very same kind of action which is *thought* right in one country and period may be *thought* wrong in another. This would be a mere platitude, the truth of which everyone would have to admit. Even the absolutist would admit this— would even wish to emphasize it— since he is well aware that different peoples have different sets of moral ideas, and his whole point is that some of these sets of ideas are false. What the relativist means to assert is, not this platitude, but that the very same kind of action which *is* right in one country and period may *be* wrong in another. And this, far from being a platitude, is a very startling assertion.

It is very important to grasp thoroughly the difference between the two ideas. For there is reason to think that many minds tend to find ethical relativity attractive because they fail to keep them clearly apart. It is so very obvious that moral ideas differ from country to country and from age to age. And it is so very easy, if you are mentally lazy, to suppose that to say this means the same as to say that no universal moral standard exists,—or in other words that it implies ethical relativity. We fail to see that the word "standard" is used in two different senses. It is perfectly true that, in one sense, there are many variable moral standards. We speak of judging a man by the standard of his time. And this implies that different times have different standards. And this, of course, is quite true. But when the word "standard" is used in this sense it means simply the set of moral ideas current during the period in question. It means what people *think* right, whether as a matter of fact it *is* right or not. On the other hand when the absolutist asserts that there exists a single universal moral "standard," he is not using the word in this sense at all. He means by "standard" what *is* right as distinct from what people merely think right. His point is that although what people think right varies in different countries and periods, yet what actually is right is everywhere and always the same. And it follows that when the ethical relativist disputes the position of the absolutist and denies that any universal moral standard exists he too means by "standard" what actually is right. But it is exceedingly easy, if we are not careful, to slip loosely from using the word in the first sense to using it in the second sense; and to suppose that the variability of moral beliefs is the same thing as the variability of what really is moral. And unless we keep the two senses of the word "standard" distinct, we are likely to think the creed of ethical relativity much more plausible than it actually is.

The genuine relativist, then, does not merely mean that Chinamen may think right what Frenchmen think wrong. He means that what is wrong for the Frenchman may *be* right for the Chinaman. And if one enquires how, in those circumstances, one is to know what actually is right in China or in France, the answer comes quite glibly. What is right in China is the same as what people think right in China; and what is right in France is the same as what people think right in France. So that, if you want to know what is moral in any particular country or age all you have to do is to ascertain what are the moral ideas current in that age or country. Those ideas are, *for that age or country*, right. Thus what is morally right is identified with what is thought to be morally right, and the distinction which we made above between these

two is simply denied. To put the same thing in another way, it is denied that there can be or ought to be any distinction between the two senses of the word "standard." There is only one kind of standard of right and wrong, namely, the moral ideas current in any particular age or country.

Moral right *means* what people think morally right. It has no other meaning. What Frenchmen think right is, therefore, right *for Frenchmen*. And evidently one must conclude—though I am not aware that relativists are anxious to draw one's attention to such unsavoury but yet absolutely necessary conclusions from their creed—that cannibalism is right for people who believe in it, that human sacrifice is right for those races which practice it, and that burning widows alive was right for Hindus until the British stepped in and compelled the Hindus to behave immorally by allowing their widows to remain alive.

When it is said that, according to the ethical relativist, what is thought right in any social group is right for that group, one must be careful not to misinterpret this. The relativist does not, of course, mean that there actually is an objective moral standard in France and a different objective standard in England, and that French and British opinions respectively give us correct information about these different standards. His point is rather that there are no objectively true moral standards at all. There is no single universal objective standard. Nor are there a variety of local objective standards. All standards are subjective. People's subjective feelings about morality are the only standards which exist.

To sum up. The ethical relativist

consistently denies, it would seem, whatever the ethical absolutist asserts. For the absolutist there is a single universal moral standard. For the relativist there is no such standard. There are only local, ephemeral, and variable standards. For the absolutist there are two senses of the word "standard." Standards in the sense of sets of current moral ideas are relative and changeable. But the standard in the sense of what is actually morally right is absolute and unchanging. For the relativist no such distinction can be made. There is only one meaning of the word standard, namely, that which refers to local and variable sets of moral ideas. Or if it is insisted that the word must be allowed two meanings, then the relativist will say that there is at any rate no actual example of a standard in the absolute sense, and that the word as thus used is an empty name to which nothing in reality corresponds; so that the distinction between the two meanings becomes empty and useless. Finally— though this is merely saying the same thing in another way—the absolutist makes a distinction between what actually is right and what is thought right. The relativist rejects this distinction and identifies what is moral with what is thought moral by certain human beings or groups of human beings. . . .

The first [argument] is that which relies upon the actual varieties of moral "standards" found in the world. It was easy enough to believe in a single absolute morality in older times when there was no anthropology, when all humanity was divided clearly into two groups, Christian peoples and the "heathen." Christian peoples knew and possessed the one true morality. The rest were savages whose

moral ideas could be ignored. But all this is changed. Greater knowledge has brought greater tolerance. We can no longer exalt our own morality as alone true, while dismissing all other moralities as false or inferior. The investigations of anthropologists have shown that there exist side by side in the world a bewildering variety of moral codes. On this topic endless volumes have been written, masses of evidence piled up. Anthropologists have ransacked the Melanesian Islands, the jungles of New Guinea, the steppes of Siberia, the deserts of Australia, the forests of central Africa, and have brought back with them countless examples of weird, extravagant, and fantastic "moral" customs with which to confound us. We learn that all kinds of horrible practices are, in this, that, or the other place, regarded as essential to virtue. We find that there is nothing, or next to nothing, which has always and everywhere been regarded as morally good by all men. Where then is our universal morality? Can we, in face of all this evidence, deny that it is nothing but an empty dream?

This argument, taken by itself, is a very weak one. It relies upon a single set of facts—the variable moral customs of the world. But this variability of moral ideas is admitted by both parties to the dispute, and is capable of ready explanation upon the hypothesis of either party. The relativist says that the facts are to be explained by the non-existence of any absolute moral standard. The absolutist says that they are to be explained by human ignorance of what the absolute moral standard is. And he can truly point out that men have differed widely in their opinions about all manner of topics including the subject-matters of the physical sciences—just as much as they differ about morals. And if the various different opinions which men have held about the shape of the earth do not prove that it has no one real shape, neither do the various opinions which they have held about morality prove that there is no one true morality.

Thus the facts can be explained equally plausibly on either hypothesis. There is nothing in the facts themselves which compels us to prefer the relativistic hypothesis to that of the absolutist. And therefore the argument fails to prove the relativist conclusion. If that conclusion is to be established, it must be by means of other considerations.

This is the essential point. But I will add some suplementary remarks. The work of the anthropologists, upon which ethical relativists seem to rely so heavily, has as a matter of fact added absolutely nothing *in principle* to what has always been known about the variability of moral ideas. Educated people have known all along that the Greeks tolerated sodomy, which in modern times has been regarded in some countries as an abominable crime; that the Hindus thought it a sacred duty to burn their widows; that trickery, now thought despicable, was once believed to be a virtue; that terrible torture was thought by our own ancestors only a few centuries ago to be a justifiable weapon of justice; that it was only yesterday that western peoples came to believe that slavery is immoral. Even the ancients knew very well that moral customs and ideas vary—witness the writings of Herodotus. Thus the principle of the variability of moral ideas was well understood long before modern anthropology was ever heard of. Anthro-

pology has added nothing to the knowledge of this principle except a mass of new and extreme examples of it drawn from very remote sources. But to multiply examples of a principle already well known and universally admitted adds nothing to the argument which is built upon that principle. The discoveries of the anthropologists have no doubt been of the highest importance in their own sphere. But in my considered opinion they have thrown no new light upon the special problems of the moral philosopher.

Although the multiplication of examples has no logical bearing on the argument, it does have an immense *psychological* effect upon people's minds. These masses of anthropological learning are impressive. They are propounded in the sacred name of "science." If they are quoted in support of ethical relativity—as they often are—people *think* that they must prove something important. They bewilder and over-awe the simple-minded, batter down their resistance, make them ready to receive humbly the doctrine of ethical relativity from those who have acquired a reputation by their immense learning and their claims to be "scientific." Perhaps this is why so much ado is made by ethical relativists regarding the anthropological evidence. But we must refuse to be impressed. We must discount all this mass of evidence about the extraordinary moral customs of remote peoples. Once we have admitted—as everyone who is instructed must have admitted these last two thousand years without any anthropology at all—the principle that moral ideas vary, all this new evidence adds nothing to the argument. And the argument itself proves nothing for the reasons already given. . . .

[Another] argument in favour of ethical relativity . . . consists in alleging that no one has ever been able to discover upon what foundation an absolute morality could rest, or from what source a universally binding moral code could derive its authority.

If, for example, it is an absolute and unalterable moral rule that all men ought to be unselfish, from whence does this *command* issue? For a command it certainly is, phrase it how you please. There is no difference in meaning between the sentence "You ought to be unselfish" and the sentence "Be unselfish." Now a command implies a commander. An obligation implies some authority which obliges. Who is this commander, what this authority? Thus the vastly difficult question is raised of *the basis of moral obligation.* Now the argument of the relativist would be that it is impossible to find any basis for a universally binding moral law; but that it is quite easy to discover a basis for morality if moral codes are admitted to be variable, ephemeral, and relative to time, place, and circumstance.

. . . I am assuming that it is no longer possible to solve this difficulty by saying naively that the universal moral law is based upon the uniform commands of God to all men. There will be many, no doubt, who will dispute this. But I am not writing for them. I am writing for those who feel the necessity of finding for morality a basis independent of particular religious dogmas. And I shall therefore make no attempt to argue the matter.

The problem which the absolutist has to face, then, is this. The religious basis of the one absolute morality having disappeared, can there be found for it any other, any secular, basis? If not, then it would seem that we cannot any longer believe in absolutism. We shall have to fall back upon belief in a variety of perhaps mutually inconsistent moral codes operating over restricted areas and limited periods. No one of these will be better, or more true, than any other. Each will be good and true for those living in those areas and periods. We shall have to fall back, in a word, on ethical relativity. . . .

Ethical relativity, in asserting that the moral standards of particular social groups are the only standards which exist, renders meaningless all propositions which attempt to compare these standards with one another in respect of their moral worth. And this is a very serious matter indeed. We are accustomed to think that the moral ideas of one nation or social group may be "higher" or "lower" than those of another. We believe, for example, that Christian ethical ideals are nobler than those of the savage races of central Africa. Probably most of us would think that the Chinese moral standards are higher than those of the inhabitants of New Guinea. In short we habitually compare one civilization with another and judge the sets of ethical ideas to be found in them to be some better, some worse. The fact that such judgments are very difficult to make with any justice, and that they are frequently made on very superficial and prejudiced grounds, has no bearing on the question now at issue. The question is whether such judgments have any *meaning*. We habitually assume that they have.

But on the basis of ethical relativity they can have none whatever. For the relativist must hold that there is no *common* standard which can be applied to the various civilizations judged. Any such comparison of moral standards implies the existence of some superior standard which is applicable to both. And the existence of any such standard is precisely what the relativist denies. According to him the Christian standard is applicable only to Christians, the Chinese standard only to Chinese, the New Guinea standard only to the inhabitants of New Guinea.

What is true of comparisons between the moral standards of different races will also be true of comparisons between those of different ages. It is not unusual to ask such questions as whether the standard of our own day is superior to that which existed among our ancestors five hundred years ago. And when we remember that our ancestors employed slaves, practiced barbaric physical tortures, and burnt people alive, we may be inclined to think that it is. At any rate we assume that the question is one which has meaning and is capable of rational discussion. But if the ethical relativist is right, whatever we assert on this subject must be totally meaningless. For here again there is no common standard which could form the basis of any such judgments.

This in its turn implies that the whole notion of moral *progress* is a sheer delusion. Progress means an advance from lower to higher, from worse to better. But on the basis of ethical relativity it has no meaning to say that the standards of this age are better (or worse) than those of a previous age. For there is no common standard by which both can be measured. Thus it is nonsense to say that the morality of the New Testament is higher than that of the Old. And Jesus Christ, if he imagined that he was introducing into the world a

higher ethical standard than existed before his time, was merely deluded.

There is indeed one way in which the ethical relativist can give some sort of meaning to judgments of higher or lower as applied to the moral ideas of different races or ages. What he will have to say is that we assume *our* standards to be the best simply because they are ours. And we judge other standards by our own. If we say that Chinese moral codes are better than those of African cannibals, what we *mean* by this is that they are better *according to our standards*. We mean, that is to say, that Chinese standards are *more like our own* than African standards are. "Better" accordingly *means* "more like us." "Worse" means "less like us." It thus becomes clear that judgments of better and worse in such cases do not express anything that is really true at all. They merely give expression to our perfectly groundless satisfaction with our own ideas. In short, they give expression to nothing but our egotism and self-conceit. Our moral ideals are not really better than those of the savage. We are simply deluded by our egotism into thinking they are. The African savage has just as good a right to think his morality the best as we have to think ours the best. His opinion is just as well grounded as ours, or rather both opinions are equally groundless. And on this view Jesus Christ can only have been led to the quite absurd belief that his ethical precepts were better than those of Moses by his personal vanity. If only he had read Westermarck and Dewey he would have understood that, so long as people continued to believe in the doctrine of an eye for an eye and a tooth for a tooth, that doctrine was morally *right*; and that

there could not be any point whatever in trying to make them believe
in his new-fangled theory of loving
one's enemies. True, the new morality
would *become* right as soon as people
came to believe in it, for it would then
be the accepted standard. And what
people think right is right. But then,
if only Jesus Christ and persons with
similar ideas had kept these ideas to
themselves, people might have gone
on believing that the old morality was
right. And in that case it would have
been right, and would have remained
so till this day. And that would have
saved a lot of useless trouble. For the
change which Jesus Christ actually
brought about was merely a change
from one set of moral ideas to another. And as the new set of ideas was
in no way better than the set it displaced—to say that it was better would
be meaningless for the reasons already given—the change was really a
sheer waste of time. And of course it
likewise follows that anyone who in
the future tries to improve the moral
ideas of humanity will also be wasting
his time.

Thus the ethical relativist must
treat all judgments comparing different moralities as either entirely meaningless; or, if this course appears too
drastic, he has the alternative of declaring that they have for their mean-
ing-content nothing except the vanity
and egotism of those who pass them.
We are asked to believe that the highest moral ideals of humanity are not
really any better than those of an
Australian bushman. But if this is so,
why strive for higher ideals? Thus the
heart is taken out of all effort, and the
meaning out of all human ideals and
aspirations. . . .

We have abandoned, perhaps with
good reason, the oracles of the past.

Every age, of course, does this. But in
our case it seems that none of us
knows any more whither to turn. We
do no know what to put in the place
of that which has gone. What ought
we, supposedly civilized peoples, to
aim at? What are to be our ideals?
What is right? What is wrong? What
is beautiful? What is ugly? No man
knows. We drift helplessly in this direction and that. We know not where
we stand nor whither we are going.

There are, of course, thousands of
voices frantically shouting directions.
But they shout one another down,
they contradict one another, and the
upshot is mere uproar. And because
of this confusion there creeps upon us
an insidious scepticism and despair.
Since no one knows what the truth is,
we will deny that there is any truth.
Since no one knows what right is, we
will deny that there is any right. Since
no one knows what the beautiful is,
we will deny that there is any beauty.
Or at least we will say—what comes to
the same thing—that what people (the
people of any particular age, region,
society)—think to be true is true *for
them;* that what people think morally
right is morally right *for them;* that
what people think beautiful is beautiful *for them.* There is no common and
objective standard in any of these
matters. Since all the voices contradict one another, they must be all
equally right (or equally wrong, for it
makes no difference which we say).
It is from the practical confusion of
our time that these doctrines issue.
When all the despair and defeatism
of our distracted age are expressed in
abstract concepts, are erected into a
philosophy, it is then called relativism
—ethical relativism, esthetic relativism, relativity of truth. Ethical relativity is simply defeatism in morals.

And the diagnosis will proceed. Perhaps, it will say, the current pessimism as to our future is unjustified. But there is undoubtedly a widespread feeling that our civilization is rushing downwards to the abyss. If this should be true, and if nothing should check the headlong descent, then perhaps some historian of the future will seek to disentangle the causes. The causes will, of course, be found to be multitudinous and enormously complicated. And one must not exaggerate the relative importance of any of them. But it can hardly be doubted that our future historian will include somewhere in his list the failure of the men of our generation to hold steadfastly before themselves the notion of an (even comparatively) unchanging moral idea. He will cite that feebleness of intellectual and moral grasp which has led them weakly to harbour the belief that no one moral aim is really any better than any other, that each is good and true for those who entertain it. This meant, he will surely say, that men had given up in despair the struggle to attain moral truth. Civilization lives in and through its upward struggle. Whoever despairs and gives up the struggle, whether it be an individual or a whole civilization, is already inwardly dead.

And the philosophers of our age, where have they stood? They too, as is notorious, speak with many voices. But those who preach the various relativisms have taken upon themselves a heavy load of responsibility. By formulating abstractly the defeatism of the age they have made themselves the aiders and abettors of death. They are injecting poison into the veins of civilization. Their influence upon practical affairs may indeed be small. But it counts for something. And they cannot avoid their share of the general responsibility. They have failed to do what little they could to stem the tide. They have failed to do what Plato did for the men of his own age—find a way out of at least the intellectual confusions of the time.

We may now sum up the criticisms which have been made of ethical relativity. According to the anti-relativist, the doctrine of the relativist logically implies:

(1) That all propositions which adjudge the moral standards of one civilization to be better or worse than the moral standards of another civilization are either meaningless or express nothing except the groundless self-satisfaction of the person making the judgment.

(2) That all propositions which adjudge the moral standards of one age to be better or worse than those of another age are either meaningless or express only self-satisfaction.

(3) That the notion of progress in moral ideals (as distinguished from moral practice) is meaningless.

(4) That it is consequently useless for people to strive for higher moral ideals than those they already possess.

(5) That it is usually meaningless to judge that any one human being is morally better or worse than any other, for example that Jesus was better than Judas. Such judgments are only meaningful if one can be certain that the two persons compared hold exactly the same moral beliefs. In practice one can almost never be certain of this, and one can usually be fairly certain of the opposite.

QUESTIONS FOR DISCUSSION

1. Ethical relativity can mean a number of different things. What are some of its possible meanings?
2. The same is true for ethical absolutism. What are some of its possible meanings?
3. What are Stace's principal objections to ethical absolutism?
4. What are Stace's principal objections to ethical relativity?
5. Why is the conflict between ethical absolutism and ethical relativity called a methodological conflict?
6. If the religious basis of absolutism is removed, can any sense be made of the notion of universal values or absolute values, for example like justice or equality?
7. Suppose we found that there were values that were universally approved, say courage, while their opposites, in this case cowardice, were everywhere condemned or frowned upon. What bearing would this have on the thesis of ethical relativity as you defined it in your answer to question 1?
8. What do you consider the most telling argument in favor of ethical relativity? Why?
9. What do you consider the most telling argument against ethical relativity?
10. What is the strongest argument in favor of ethical absolutism?
11. What is the strongest argument against ethical absolutism?

FURTHER READINGS FOR CHAPTER 2

Aristotle, *Works,* J. A. Smith and W. D. Ross, eds., vol. I. New York: Oxford University Press, 1910-1952.

Blanshard, Brand, *The Nature of Thought.* New York: Macmillan, 1940.

*Bridgman, Percy W., *The Logic of Modern Physics,* Chap. 1. New York: Macmillan, 1946.

*Broad, C. D., *Scientific Thought.* Paterson, N.J.: Littlefield, Adams & Co., 1959.

*Campbell, Norman, *Foundations of Experimental Science.* New York: Dover Publications, 1957.

*————, *What Is Science?* New York: Dover Publications, n.d.

*Carnap, Rudolf, *Foundations of Logic and Mathematics.* University of Chicago Press, 1939.

————, *The Unity of Science,* M. Black, trans. London: Routledge & Kegan Paul, 1934.

Cohen, Morris R., *Reason and Nature,* rev. ed., Book I, Chap. 3. New York: Free Press, 1953.

Dewey, John, *How We Think.* Boston: D. C. Heath, 1933.

---

* Paperback edition.

*Galilei, Galileo, *Dialogues Concerning Two New Sciences*, Henry Crew and Alfonso de Salvio, trans. New York: Dover Publications, 1953.

*Jevons, W. Stanley, *Principles of Science*, Chaps. 21 and 23. New York: Dover Publications, n.d.

Kaplan, Abraham, *The Conduct of Inquiry*. San Francisco: Chandler, 1964.

*Lenzen, Victor F., *Procedures of Empirical Science*. University of Chicago Press, 1938.

Mach, Ernst, *The Science of Mechanics*, 6th ed., T. J. McCormack, trans. La-Salle, Ill.: Open Court, 1960.

Mill, John Stuart, *System of Logic*, Books III and VI. New York: McKay, 1930.

Murphy, Arthur E., *The Uses of Reason*. New York: Macmillan, 1943.

Nagel, Ernest, *The Structure of Science*. New York: Harcourt Brace Jovanovich, 1961.

Peirce, Charles S., *Collected Papers*, Charles Hartshorne, Paul Weiss, and Arthur W. Burks, eds., vols. I and V. Cambridge: Harvard University Press, 1960.

*Poincaré, Henri, *Science and Hypothesis*, G. B. Halsted, trans. New York: Dover, n.d.

*———, *Science and Method*, Francis Maitland, trans. New York: Dover, n.d.

*———, *The Value of Science*, G. B. Halsted, trans. New York: Dover, n.d.

*Reichenbach, Hans, *Experience and Prediction*. University of Chicago Press, 1938.

Russell, Bertrand, *Principles of Mathematics*. New York: Norton, 1938.

Schiller, F. C. S., "Hypothesis," in *Studies in the History and Methods of Science*, Charles Singer, ed., vol. II. New York: Oxford University Press, 1921.

Veblen, Thorstein, *The Place of Science in Modern Civilization*. New York: Russell & Russell, 1961.

Chapter 3

PROBLEMS OF ETHICS

INTRODUCTION

The various professions of law, medicine, teaching, and so on, have certain "codes of ethics." A lawyer should not accept bribes to conceal or distort evidence; a physician should treat his patients with equal care regardless of their economic status; a teacher should not simply impose his personal opinions on his students; a minister should practice what he preaches. Every religion has ethical commandments: "Thou shalt not kill"; "Do unto others as you would have them do unto you." Ethical notions are implicit even in everyday phrases: "The end justifies the means," "Might makes right," "Every man for himself," "My country, right or wrong," "Good neighbor policy," "Fair play," and so on.

Consider an ethical problem that has affected the lives of many thinking persons who regard themselves as pacifists on religious or other grounds. They are, during wartime, faced with the choice of declaring themselves conscientious objectors or participating in a "justifiable" war. There are different kinds of pacifists, and some governments permit religious pacifists exemption from military conscription. But for all people, the fundamental question is the justification for war. In thinking through such a momentous question, we make certain assumptions about what is "justifiable" in general; for example, we may believe that taking arms against an aggressor is always the "right" course of action. But consider an extreme pacifist who clings to the principle of passive resistance on the ground that it is always wrong to kill a human being, even in self-defense. As moral philosophers, we ask if this view would make it wrong for anybody to kill a ruthless murderer in self-defense or to save innocent persons, for the state to inflict capital punishment, for a physician to put to death mercifully an incurable patient suffering great pain, or for a person facing excruciating torture to commit suicide.

In any case, the general principles which are assumed in coming to a decision as to what choice among alternative courses of conduct one *ought* to make are the subject matter of ethics or moral philosophy. This branch of philosophy is concerned with the understanding of what is meant by such terms as "good," "right," "justifiable," "duty," "responsibility," and so on, in judgments about how persons *ought* to conduct themselves when confronted with a choice of alternatives. Such "value judgments" are implicit in praising or blaming others or ourselves. Though we are usually quick to blame others for not choosing what we consider right, we are rarely clear about the reasons for our own assurance that we know what is "right." It is not an easy matter to make explicit the meaning of ethical terms so that even all intelligent persons will agree, especially when their own interests and beliefs are at stake. Our understanding of what is good or bad, right or wrong, is entangled by conflicting ideas derived from diverse sources that influence us: parents, teachers, ministers, friends, favorite authors, movie stars. A young person's choice of a life career will often depend on whose ideals of living he holds highest in esteem. It has taken a lifetime of experience and reflection for the great moral teachers of mankind to come to certain conclusions about the good life in their search for a "way of life." Such was the case with Confucius, Laotze, Buddha, Zoroaster, Socrates, Epicurus, Epictetus, Jesus, Spinoza, Kant, Dewey, and other moral philosophers who sought answers to ethical problems.

In Western civilization we find contrasting ways of life and conflicting ethical ideals: the this-worldliness of classical and Renaissance culture opposed to the other-worldliness of medieval and mystic renunciation of all earthly desires, the Catholic ethic of Aquinas and the Protestant ethic of Kant, the evolutionary ethics of social reform, and the revolutionary ethics of violent seizure of power. Conflicts between established traditions and changing social conditions are among the chief sources of ethical reflection over the meaning of accepted or socially sanctioned standards of good and bad. Coming in contact with other cultures different from our own, we are likely to wonder whether there is any common morality, but the problems of future international relations lead us to seek a just "bill of rights" for all peoples.

Ethical principles are assumed in making a choice between alternative possibilities in terms of better or worse. It is the aim of moral philosophy to clarify ethical choice by bringing to light the ethical principles assumed in any decision or proposed action and by examining them critically for their consistency and viability.

It may be objected that reflection over abstract ethical principles such as are discussed in the selections below does not make one "a good person," that good character is a product of good breeding, good habits, good education, and good religious training (whereas ethics is just a verbal and intellectual exercise) and that what can be said about good in general is good for nothing in particular. There are certain confusions in this objection. First, it assumes that we already know what good character, good breeding, good habits, good education, and good religious training are. This assumption is doubtful, since there are so many different opinions about what is good in regard to character, breeding, habits, etc. Second, ethical theory does not claim to be a *sufficient* basis for molding character. Aristotle, in fact, in the first chapter of his *Ethics,* notes the importance of a stable set of habits for the formation of character and even regards young persons ruled by uncontrolled impulses as not yet ready for the study of ethics. Of course, Aristotle means by "young" not simply youthful in years, but in maturity of habits of self-control and of reflection over one's experiences.

Professional codes of ethics, religious commandments, and other practical precepts of conduct belong to the study of applied ethics or homiletics. The latter presupposes some ethical theory, as engineering presupposes physical theory, or medicine, biology, though we are far from having reached the same degree of agreement and exactness in ethics as in physics and biology. Furthermore, the problems of ethics do not generally call for the precise quantitative laws of physical science. Aristotle makes it clear that each discipline has its own problems and degree of exactness relevant to those problems. It was a great enough step forward in the progress of ethics as a rational discipline for Socrates to have asked people to define the meanings of their ideas about justice, courage, friendship, and to show the need for greater clarity concerning these ideas.

Socrates' claim that "Virtue is Knowledge" may seem to some to stress unduly the power of clear ideas in guiding conduct, but it has appealed to thinking persons as much sounder than the romantic slogan "Ignorance is Bliss." It has been observed that if the latter were true, many people would be happier than they are.

Greek Rationalism and Naturalism

Socrates was born in 469 B.C. and died in 399 B.C. following a state trial for his alleged atheism, immoral teachings, and corruption of the youth. As a young stone-cutter and humble citizen of Athens, he had been stimulated by the Sophists, the first non-slave teachers of ancient Greece. They questioned the traditional beliefs concerning the nature of justice and the grounds of "law and order," challenging ancient supernatural claims, and arguing for the secular view that "man is the measure of all things." Thrasymachus and Glaucon represent the young cynics who had gone to the extreme of defining justice as simply the selfish interest of those in power.

Socrates was Plato's spokesman and model philosophical mind, pictured as devoted to the relentless search for moral truth. Socrates' method was to start a discussion by claiming ignorance of such basic concepts as say, justice, and inquiring of those who were sure they knew to explain their views to him so that he might learn from them. However, he would continue by questioning the meaning of the terms used in the answers in order to reveal inconsistencies or contradictions between the cocksure answers and the way terms were commonly applied to the activities of such members of society as the physician, ship's pilot, shepherd, etc. When such men were said to be "just" or to be doing their jobs well, were they concerned about the subjects in their care or were they merely interested in their own advancement? What is the true meaning of "interest of the stronger or powerful" when we consider how an intelligent worker shows his strength in the ways he can benefit his subject?

Nearly all ethical systems aim at an ordering of the goods of life in accordance with some notion of what "good" means. If we take stock of the things we call good, we find, among the diverse assortment, the music we enjoy in relaxation, the view from a mountain top, the laughter of children at play— these are examples of simple enjoyments or harmless pleasures which would be classified by Socrates, in selection 3.1, as things good in themselves. Let us call them *intrinsic* goods and note their aesthetic character.

There is another kind of good which is the opposite of being enjoyable in itself but is often regarded as a necessary means to the enjoyment of other things; for example, a severe course of physical training and dietary regimen is a means of restoring bodily health. Socrates placed such means in the class of irksome but needed activities. Let us call this class *instrumental* goods. The highest goods are those which are good both intrinsically and instrumentally. For examples, Socrates mentions intelligence, sight, and health, for these are enjoyed in themselves and also as means for securing other goods. The aim of Plato's *Republic* was to prove that justice belonged to this highest class of goods, contrary to the common opinion that it belongs to the lowest class of painful, but apparently necessary, instrumental means of preserving order. Would anybody really care for law or justice if he could get away with murder, rapine, and theft by the possession of the mythical ring of Gyges that makes its wearer invisible at will? The sceptical Glaucon thus challenges Socrates to prove that justice is more than an instrumental good to further the interests of those who seek to acquire the benefits of fame, wealth, and power "by hook or crook." A similar problem is raised by Plato when he asks whether it is better to do an injustice than to suffer one. It is obvious that such problems are social as well as individual. That is why Plato went on to answer the sceptical query of Glaucon, "Why is justice better than injustice?" by drawing up an ideal state in the *Republic*, for "the state is the individual writ in large characters." That is to say, Plato's problem of proving that the just man's life was more harmonious and happier than the unjust man's life was translated into the larger political problem of justice as the basis of social harmony. Likewise, Aristotle regarded man as a "political animal" and ethics as a preface to politics. But let us return to our problem of the meaning of good by consulting the opening chapter of Aristotle's *Nicomachean Ethics*.

Here we find Aristotle accepting the distinction between instrumental and intrinsic goods and associating them with the specific purposes or ends of human activities in society. These are as diverse as the occupations, arts, and sciences of men in any society. Within and among them there is a subordination of means and ends; for example, bricklaying is instrumental in building a house, and a house is a means to the end of family living. The latter is a means to maintaining a community. There must be some end, however, which is not regarded as a means to anything else, but is the common end of all human activities. That supreme end is called by Aristotle happiness or well-being, and whoever enjoys it for the greater part of his life is said to have a good life or to live well.

The meaning of good is then the same as that of happiness, and if Aristotle were merely looking for a verbal solution to the problem, there would have been no need for his writing ten chapters analyzing moral and intellectual virtues, pleasure, types of friendship, and the relation of the practical to the theoretical uses of the mind. The fact is, Aristotle recognizes, that there is little agreement about what constitutes happiness.

Various opinions identify happiness with the enjoyment of sensory pleasures, of public honor or fame, of wealth, of intellectual excellence. Is pleasure or the balance of pleasure over pain the only meaning of what is good? If so, how can we compare or measure pleasures and pains either in ourselves or in others without some definable unit or standard of comparison or measurement? How can one choose between the pleasure of games and that of serious study? Are there not some unpleasant tasks that *ought* to be done? These are crucial questions for the hedonist, and we are all hedonists whenever we regard only the pleasure of an activity as the sign of its moral value.

It is not pleasure in the abstract that people desire, but pleasurable activities or objects. Such objects seem to fall into three classes: objects that afford sensory excitation (food, drink, sex); the accumulation of wealth and the power that goes with it; and the social fame, public prestige, and praise that are often sought by persons who will sacrifice everything else for their sake. Most people desire all three of these kinds of "goods," but some regard one as more important to them than the others. Aristotle thought that a rational and moderate enjoyment of all these goods entered into that harmonious realization of a person's desires during the whole course of his life which is called happiness (contrasted with momentary pleasure). Though the specific forms of happiness will vary with each person, the meaning of "the good life" is none other than the life which contains such pervasive happiness. Three kinds of lives—the sensual, the political, and the speculative—show how varied the problem is.

It is well to examine people's lives to test these opinions, Aristotle believes, rather than to try to discover what happiness is in some purely abstract way by establishing an absolute cause of all goodness, as Plato tried to do. Aristotle thus adopts an empirical approach to ethical problems. This becomes clear in his criticism of Plato's theory that there is a single Form of the Good which is the absolute source of all earthly goods. How can knowledge of such a transcendent Good make a man a better carpenter or physician? asks Aristotle. It is the *practicable* or realizable good that makes for happiness and not some purely theoretical possibility, humanly unattainable.

A good knife is one that cuts well, for the function of a knife is to cut. Aristotle generalizes this functional sense of goodness and arrives at the notion that the good of man, his happiness, must be inseparable from the function or activity peculiar to his nature. Now what distinguishes man (*Homo sapiens*) from all other creatures is his reason or intelligence. Hence, the good man is one whose activity is guided by reason. It is only by making the most of his rational powers that man can live well. Aristotle, in fact, went so far at the end of his *Ethics* as to make philosophical contemplation the highest good.

The use of reason in ethical problems is not that of the mathematician or pure theoretician who seeks to demonstrate his conclusions with logical certainty. Each subject requires its own degree of certainty, and, considering the variability, diversity, and complexity of human nature and its activities, Aristotle repeatedly reminds us that we can indicate only approximately what it means to be reasonable in human affairs and that we must be guided by careful observation and practical experience. The reasonable course, he observes, is not simply an arithmetic mean, but falls somewhere between the extremes of too much and too little; temperance is found empirically to be an avoidance of the ill effects of overindulgence and those of complete abstinence; courage is a mean between foolhardy exposure to danger and timid fear of all risks. There is historical evidence that Aristotle's ethical rule of the mean was suggested to him by the dietary rules of Greek physicians. The moral philosopher in this naturalistic type of ethics is "the physician of the soul."

But every honest physician knows how complex and varied are the causes of the derangements of human life. Besides physiological injuries, there are psychological and social maladjustments. Plato sought to put man's house in order by reference to an absolute Form of the Good. Aristotle and other naturalists, like Dewey, regard the good as relative to man's native endowments, interests, and abilities. They also emphasize the importance of habits in steadying the emotions and ordering the desires that motivate human conduct. And all of them realize that the social aspects of man's life bring ethics and politics together, so that a further discussion of the merits of their ethical systems would lead us into their theories of human nature, social classes, and the functions of the state. We shall have to postpone the political aspects of ethics to the next chapter and now go on to consider other approaches to ethical problems tied up with different conceptions of human nature and its possibilities for good.

Spinoza's Rationalism

Spinoza's main work on *Ethics,* to which selection 3.3 from the *Improvement of the Understanding* may be read as a prelude, was written in the deductive form of Euclid's *Elements.* The idea was to treat human nature and ethical problems as calmly and thoughtfully as we consider a geometrical figure or problem, the elements being man's emotions, interests, and ideas instead of points, lines, and planes. Thus Spinoza hoped to introduce scientific objectivity and rational methods of proof into a subject ridden with prejudice, partiality, and rhetoric.

Spinoza's *Improvement of the Understanding* begins with an autobiographical account of how he arrived at the severely rational result of his quest for the highest good that the mind can attain with utmost certainty, the good that Aristotle had identified with lasting happiness or well being. Spinoza found the key principle to ethical problems in the idea that the quality of experienced values depends on the quality of the objects to which the mind is attached. He found out that the usual attachment of persons to objects of sensory pleasure, to the pursuit of wealth and fame were too ephemeral to provide the more enduring inner peace and happiness that he sought. Like Aristotle, Spinoza advocated the moderate enjoyment of sense pleasures, a modest income, and only enough social recognition as is needed to preserve one's physical and mental health. However, he explains why the highest good is attainable only by living under the guidance of reason, devoted primarily to the mind's efforts to understand and love the source of all things.

Spinoza's geometric method, common to much of science and philosophy in the seventeenth century, is an a priori method of deducing conclusions from definitions and axioms. Applied to ethics, it presupposes fixed, universal traits in all human beings and simple uniform laws governing their behavior under the influence of emotions. Emotions are regarded as confused ideas, and so long as they remain confused, human nature is slave to their strength, subject to the vicissitudes of external forces, and compelled to suffer accordingly. The only salvation lies in the use of Reason, embodied in Euclid's geometric method. Reason can clarify the direction and end of each emotion and its relation to other emotions. Reason can discover the way to guide the expression of these emotions so as to avoid painful conflicts and mutual frustration. In Spinoza, Reason includes knowledge of the human mind and its relation to the whole of nature. Such knowledge is not only useful to man, but also constitutes his freedom from the bondage of blind passions and his highest good. In fact, such knowledge, for Spinoza, is divine. We must omit discussion of the metaphysics that goes with Spinoza's ethics and simply note the question: To what extent is ethics dependent on metaphysics?

Kant's Ethics of Formal Duty

Kant maintained that morality was impossible without freedom of will or choice, since we do not condemn a person's action as immoral if he could not have considered acting otherwise; for example, consider the destructive acts of an infant, of a mentally sick person, or of someone drugged. An intoxicated driver, however, is held responsible for his recklessness since he was free not to become intoxicated before driving.

Now Kant believed on metaphysical grounds that physical nature was completely determined by universal and necessary laws, so that freedom of the will had to be grounded in another realm, in a higher moral world not limited by space or time as the natural world is. We know the laws governing that moral world through what Kant called the "faculty of practical reason." This faculty prescribes formal rules to a dutiful will whose universal aim is to respect persons as ends in themselves. Kant formulated this rule in a "categorical imperative": Act so that the principle of your action can be generalized by practical reason. A soldier's guerrilla tactics are not acceptable after his return to civilian life in a peaceful, rational society.

Kant rejected the condoning of "white lies" or the breaking of a promise by appealing to empirical consequences or social inclination because he regarded such consequences as not totally foreseeable and inclinations as transitory, whereas the moral law should be certain and eternally binding. That is why he attacked social utility and pleasure as inadequate ethical standards or guides to the individual's sense of duty.

The good, then, for Kant is absolutely independent of the empirical facts or laws which the scientist reports in his accounts of nature, and proceeds categorically only from "the good will" or sense of duty. Kant insists that nothing in the laws of natural sciences tells us that we ought to treat human beings as moral ends in themselves and not merely as a means for the gratification of our personal desires. "Good will" is the sterling quality of all ethical character, and "good faith" the moral basis of legal contracts.

Now, we often do have to depend on people as necessary means; for example, if X wants to apply for a position requiring references, then X must use persons Y and Z, who know his qualifications, as means for securing the desired position. Kant calls such means-ends propositions "hypothetical imperatives" and distinguishes them sharply from what he considers to be the essentially ethical rule or "categorical imperative." Kant would say: X ought to apply for the position because X is one of the most qualified persons and because it is universally good for such persons to make themselves available to fill a vacancy; it is the duty of X to apply for the position, and of Y and Z to recommend him, regardless of what happens to other applicants.

One may question this Kantian cleavage between formal ethical rules and factual, scientific considerations. The empiricist would point out that the only reason for accepting any *application* of the categorical imperative lies in the empirical fact that violatons of such maxims of conduct too often lead to disastrous social consequences. The empiricist, however, assumes that the formal ethical law has no meaning apart from its applications, which is tantamount to denying that ethical rules are purely formal. But the great contribution of Kant's ethics is its emphasis on the intrinsic value of individuals as ends in themselves and on the idea that being *worthy of* social approval is higher than merely selfish pleasure.

Hedonistic Calculus of Happiness and Utilitarian Ethics

The ethics of Hedonism is based on a calculus of pleasures and pains which teaches us what to seek and what to avoid in our private and public lives. The good is whatever promotes the happiness (measured by the predominance of pleasures over pains) of an individual or of the community (never more than a sum of its individual members). An attempt was made by Bentham to measure pleasures and pains by considering their various aspects or dimensions, e.g., intensity, duration, and so forth.

Apart from the psychological difficulties of measuring pleasures and pains, there are other problems for this bold attempt to reduce ethics to a calculus. How can we foresee all the pleasurable and painful consequences of our actions or decisions which need to be guided by principles while we are not fully certain of the future? Are not pleasure and pain *too* variable and lacking in any verifiable common denominator to provide general rules of conduct or units of measurement of values? Can we dissociate our individual preferences from our relations to our fellow beings, and how can we calculate their pleasures as well as ours in arriving at a social policy? Some recent mathematical methods of considering a rational basis for justifying value judgments or social policies raise similar problems.

John Stuart Mill was raised in the tenets of Bentham, but introduced the important point of distinguishing *qualities* of higher and lower among the desires that enter into moral choice. The "higher" discontent of a Socrates was for Mill an integral part of the greater freedom enjoyed by a mind not content with merely a quantity of pleasures of any kind.

The utilitarians rejected the two worlds of Kant, the natural and the moral, the physical and the spiritual, the temporal and the eternal, to which body and soul belong separately. They wished to bring ethics closer to the natural and social sciences. All ethical problems for them are natural and social problems, and the same intelligence that is used in the latter can be and should be used in the former. We have no higher faculties of moral intuition or infallible guides to conduct. The experimental reasoning of natural science and the trial-and-error habits of practical experience constitute the sole reliable means of resolving human problems. These problems occur in and because of changing social conditions. Accordingly, our moral conceptions and standards must be continually subject to revision. The aristocratic ethics of Plato and Aristotle, the a priori ethics of Spinoza, the supernatural revelations of medieval moralists, the intuitions of Protestant ethics, the two-worldly system of Kant—these all belong to past or passing cultures and require drastic modification in the scientific, technological, atomic era in which we are now living. The difference between the fact that we like or desire something and the value judgment that we *ought* to desire it or that it is *desirable* goes to the heart of the ethical problem. That is, the judgment "I like driving at very high speed" expresses a particular fact, but most pedestrians would not like the generalization "I *ought to* drive at very high speed." Is it necessary to invoke Kant's transcendental "good will" in order to justify moral intelligence? The utilitarians believe that the same intelligence that enables us in common sense and science to act in accordance with the connections and consequences of our decisions suffices for moral problems.

John Dewey's discussion of the question "Does Human Nature Change?" attempts to distinguish the aspects of human behavior which appear to be fairly universal from those that depend upon historical circumstances, social conditions, and especially cultural and educational factors. If, as Spinoza showed, the essence of human nature is desire, it is biologically and psychologically evident that the desire for food, sensory pleasures, companionship, aesthetic and intellectual satisfactions are constant. Yet the particular forms of satisfying these constant desires vary in different cultural environments. Against the old psychology of "instincts" (e.g., bellicosity, avarice, etc.), which have been used to justify the inevitability of war and exploitation, Dewey stresses the force of habits acquired through home and school training, propaganda, and outmoded ideas of "original sin" and innately fixed moral inclinations. Even the innate aggressive impulses are not inflexibly bound to produce hate and destruction; such impulses may be channeled through intelligent home and school guidance to constructive and cooperative activities organized to combat the prevalence of hunger, disease, ignorance, bigotry, and war. (Dewey here supported William James's famous essay on "The Moral Equivalents of War.")

Even a political conservative admits the force of habits when he appeals to social customs or established traditions; Dewey's argument insists on the urgent need to modify habits that are no longer useful for solving man's problems and to introduce new habits that will be more helpful in adapting men to a rapidly changing world.

Professor Morris Ginsberg, as a sociologist and moral philosopher, is concerned with Freud's great influence on sex mores and ethical attitudes. Freud's application of scientific objectivity to many of man's inner conflicts and frustrations led the physician beyond subjective reports of mental disturbances to deeper subliminal forces affecting both conscious and unconscious behavior. Early childhood repressions of these forces, especially those surrounding the sexual taboos, were explored by psychoanalytical techniques based on new conceptions of the self as a complex stratified structure of "id," "ego," and "superego." Psychoanalysis is a method of guiding persons to understanding their own desires and states of mind through analysis and self-analysis, not unlike the Socratic method. As Dr. Ginsberg states in selection 3.7, "the function of analysis is to extend the area of conscious control by bringing what was unconscious into consciousness. . . . The ultimate ideal is the 'primacy of reason' and on the moral side 'the brotherhood of man and the reduction of suffering.'"

It is not clear that all forms of repression are morally wrong. Should we not restrain aggressive impulses to ruin persons or destroy hated objects? Are there not unjustified hates, and cannot understanding and love overcome such hatred? Dr. Ginsberg also suggests that the ethical tendency of Freud is one of enlightened self-interest, which often fails to take into account our dependency on the interests of others. Such regard for the interests and rights of others leads to consideration of the ethical problem of social justice. Dr. Ginsberg finds Freud's psychoanalysis weakest in dealing with the problems of social justice. Erich Fromm, Karen Horney, and others have tried to improve on Freud's theory by emphasizing man's social nature and his need to be mindful of the respect and happiness of others in order to fulfill the nature of his "true self." But more is required than the blind aim of self-realization, namely, the knowledge of our social dependency and of the kind of social institutions that can best realize the harmonious fulfillment of all concerned. Psychoanalysis has provided a means for better knowledge of our selves through frank and open discussion and understanding, but it leaves many psychological and ethical problems still to be explored.

Nominalism and New Linguistic Approaches

R. M. Hare's approach to ethical problems is a good example of the method of linguistic analysis made famous at Oxford and Cambridge not only in recent years (e.g., by G. E. Moore, J. L. Austin, G. Ryle, H. L. A. Hart, A. J. Ayer) but by traditional nominalists (e.g., Ockham, Hobbes, Locke, Berkeley, Hume). Nominalists and linguistic analysts find in the structure of language, in its syntax and usage, the key to understanding philosophical concepts in general and moral issues in particular. Vague, ill-defined, or obscure language used in discussion with others or introspectively with one's self is usually an indication of confused thought, and confusion in thought often leads to disorganized living.

Moral language, Hare shows, is not descriptive of mental states but prescriptive of what we ought to do. The moral condemnation of war or of the murder of innocent people is not equivalent to a description of the feelings of pacifists or to an analysis of the causes of crime; the moral judgment prescribes, condemns, and disapproves actions after understanding why they ought or ought not be done. Not all prescriptive language is moral; imperative sentences (e.g., "Don't touch bare high-voltage lines!"), commands to obey orders, or instructions in a manual are neither indicative pronouncements nor moral judgments. Hence, Hare divides value judgments into imperatives that are nonmoral (e.g., "Eat moderately and stay slim and beautiful") and those that are moral (e.g., "Never condemn an innocent person"). The logical question for ethics remains: Are moral judgments merely expressions of mental states or prescriptive value judgments subject to critical analysis?

Plato (427-347 B.C.)

3.1 Republic I and II

BOOK I °

. . . All this time Thrasymachus had been trying more than once to break in upon our conversation; but his neighbors had restrained him, wishing to hear the argument to the end. In the pause after my last words he could keep quiet no longer; but gathering himself up like a wild beast he sprang at us as if he would tear us in pieces. Polemarchus and I were frightened out of our wits, when he burst out to the whole company:

What is the matter with you two, Socrates? Why do you go on in this imbecile way, politely deferring to each other's nonsense? If you really want to know what justice means, stop asking questions and scoring off the answers you get. You know very well it is easier to ask questions than to answer them. Answer yourself, and tell us what you think justice means. I won't have you telling us it is the same as what is obligatory or useful or advantageous or profitable or expedient; I want a clear and precise statement; I won't put up with that sort of verbiage.

I was amazed by this onslaught and looked at him in terror. If I had not seen this wolf before he saw me, I really believe I should have been struck dumb; [1] but fortunately I had looked at him earlier, when he was beginning to get exasperated with our argument; so I was able to reply, though rather tremulously:

Don't be hard on us, Thrasymachus. If Polemarchus and I have gone astray in our search, you may be quite sure the mistake was not intentional. If we had been looking for a piece of gold, we should never have deliberately allowed politeness to spoil our chance of finding it; and now when we are looking for justice, a thing much more precious than gold, you cannot imagine we should defer to each other in that foolish way and not do our best to bring it to light. You must believe we are in earnest, my friend; but I am afraid the task is beyond our powers, and we might expect a man of your ability to pity us instead of being so severe.

Thrasymachus replied with a burst of sardonic laughter.

Good Lord, he said; Socrates at his old trick of shamming ignorance! I

° From *Republic*. Trans. by Francis M. Cornford (Oxford: The Clarendon Press, 1941). Reprinted by permission of The Clarendon Press.

[1] A popular superstition, that if a wolf sees you first, you become dumb.

knew it; I told the others you would refuse to commit yourself and do anything sooner than answer a question.

Yes, Thrasymachus, I replied; because you are clever enough to know that if you asked someone what are the factors of the number twelve, and at the same time warned him: "Look here, you are not to tell me that 12 is twice 6, or 3 times 4, or 6 times 2, or 4 times 3; I won't put up with any such nonsense"—you must surely see that no one would answer a question put like that. He would say: "What do you mean, Thrasymachus? Am I forbidden to give any of these answers, even if one happens to be right? Do you want me to give a wrong one?" What would you say to that?

Humph! said he. As if that were a fair analogy!

I don't see why it is not, said I; but in any case, do you suppose our barring a certain answer would prevent the man from giving it, if he thought it was the truth?

Do you mean that you are going to give me one of those answers I barred?

I should not be surprised, if it seemed to me true, on reflection.

And what if I give you another definition of justice, better than any of those? What penalty are you prepared to pay?[2]

The penalty deserved by ignorance, which must surely be to receive instruction from the wise. So I would suggest that as a suitable punishment.

I like your notion of a penalty! he

said; but you must pay the costs as well.

I will, when I have any money.

That will be all right, said Glaucon; we will all subscribe for Socrates. So let us have your definition, Thrasymachus.

Oh yes, he said; so that Socrates may play the old game of questioning and refuting someone else, instead of giving an answer himself!

But really, I protested, what can you expect from a man who does not know the answer or profess to know it, and, besides that, has been forbidden by no mean authority to put forward any notions he may have? Surely the definition should naturally come from you, who say you do know the answer and can tell it us. Please do not disappoint us. I should take it as a kindness, and I hope you will not be chary of giving Glaucon and the rest of us the advantage of your instruction.

Glaucon and the others added their entreaties to mine. Thrasymachus was evidently longing to win credit, for he was sure he had an admirable answer ready, though he made a show of insisting that I should be the one to reply. In the end he gave way and exclaimed:

So this is what Socrates' wisdom comes to! He refuses to teach, and goes about learning from others without offering so much as thanks in return.

I do learn from others, Thrasymachus; that is quite true; but you are wrong to call me ungrateful. I give in return all I can—praise; for I have no money. And how ready I am to applaud any idea that seems to me sound, you will see in a moment, when you have stated your own; for I am sure that will be sound.

---

[2] In certain lawsuits the defendant, if found guilty, was allowed to propose a penalty alternative to that demanded by the prosecution. The judges then decided which should be inflicted. The "costs" here means the fee which the sophist, unlike Socrates, expected from his pupils.

Listen then, Thrasymachus began. What I say is that "just" or "right" means nothing but what is to the interest of the stronger party. Well, where is your applause? You don't mean to give it me.

I will, as soon as I understand, I said. I don't see yet what you mean by right being the interest of the stronger party. For instance, Polydamas, the athlete, is stronger than we are, and it is to his interest to eat beef for the sake of his muscles; but surely you don't mean that the same diet would be good for weaker men and therefore be right for us?

You are trying to be funny, Socrates. It's a low trick to take my words in the sense you think will be most damaging.

No, no, I protested; but you must explain.

Don't you know, then, that a state may be ruled by a despot, or a democracy, or an aristocracy?

Of course.

And that the ruling element is always the strongest?

Yes.

Well then, in every case the laws are made by the ruling party in its own interest; a democracy makes democratic laws, a despot autocratic ones, and so on. By making these laws they define as "right" for their subjects whatever is for their own interest, and they call anyone who breaks them a "wrongdoer" and punish him accordingly. That is what I mean: in all states alike "right" has the same meaning, namely what is for the interest of the party established in power, and that is the strongest. So the sound conclusion is that what is "right" is the same everywhere: the interest of the stronger party.

Now I see what you mean, said I; whether it is true or not, I must try to make out. When you define right in terms of interest, you are yourself giving one of those answers you forbade to me; though, to be sure, you add "to the stronger party."

An insignificant addition, perhaps!

Its importance is not clear yet; what is clear is that we must find out whether your definition is true. I agree myself that right is in a sense a matter of interest; but when you add "to the stronger party," I don't know about that. I must consider.

Go ahead, then.

I will. Tell me this. No doubt you also think it is right to obey the men in power?

I do.

Are they infallible in every type of state, or can they sometimes make a mistake?

Of course they can make a mistake.

In framing laws, then, they may do their work well or badly?

No doubt.

Well, that is to say, when the laws they make are to their own interest; badly, when they are not?

Yes.

But the subjects are to obey any law they lay down, and they will then be doing right?

Of course.

If so, by your account, it will be right to do what is not to the interest of the stronger party, as well as what is so.

What's that you are saying?

Just what you said, I believe; but let us look again. Haven't you admitted that the rulers, when they enjoin certain acts on their subjects, sometimes mistake their own best interests, and at the same time that it is right for the subjects to obey, whatever they may enjoin?

Yes, I suppose so.

Well, that amounts to admitting that it is right to do what is not to the interest of the rulers or the stronger party. They may unwittingly enjoin what is to their own disadvantage; and you say it is right for the others to do as they are told. In that case, their duty must be the opposite of what you said, because the weaker will have been ordered to do what is against the interest of the stronger. You with your intelligence must see how that follows.

Yes, Socrates, said Polemarchus, that is undeniable.

No doubt, Cleitophon broke in, if you are to be a witness on Socrates' side.

No witness is needed, replied Polemarchus; Thrasymachus himself admits that rulers sometimes ordain acts that are to their own disadvantage, and that it is the subjects' duty to do them.

That is because Thrasymachus said it was right to do what you are told by the men in power.

Yes, but he also said that what is to the interest of the stronger party is right; and, after making both these assertions, he admitted that the stronger sometimes command the weaker subjects to act against their interests. From all which it follows that what is in the stronger's interest is no more right than what is not.

No, said Cleitophon; he meant whatever the stronger *believes* to be in his own interest. That is what the subject must do, and what Thrasymachus meant to define as right.

That was not what he said, rejoined Polemarchus.

No matter, Polemarchus, said I; if Thrasymachus says so now, let us take him in that sense. Now, Thrasymachus, tell me, was that what you intended to say—that right means what the stronger thinks is to his interest, whether it really is so or not?

Most certainly not, he replied. Do you suppose I should speak of a man as "stronger" or "superior" at the very moment when he is making a mistake?

I did think you said as much when you admitted that rulers are not always infallible.

That is because you are a quibbler, Socrates. Would you say a man deserves to be called a physician at the moment when he makes a mistake in treating his patient and just in respect of that mistake; or a mathematician, when he does a sum wrong and just insofar as he gets a wrong result? Of course we do commonly speak of a physician or a mathematician or a scholar having made a mistake; but really none of these, I should say, is ever mistaken, insofar as he is worthy of the name we give him. So, strictly speaking—and you are all for being precise—no one who practices a craft makes mistakes. A man is mistaken when his knowledge fails him; and at that moment he is no craftsman. And what is true of craftsmanship or any sort of skill is true of the ruler: he is never mistaken so long as he is acting as a ruler; though anyone might speak of a ruler making a mistake, just as he might of a physician. You must understand that I was talking in that loose way when I answered your question just now; but the precise statement is this. The ruler, insofar as he is acting as a ruler, makes no mistakes and consequently enjoins what is best for himself; and that is what the subject is to do. So, as I said at first, "right" means doing what is to the interest of the stronger.

Very well, Thrasymachus, said I. So you think I am quibbling?

I am sure you are.

You believe my questions were maliciously designed to damage your position?

I know it. But you will gain nothing by that. You cannot outwit me by cunning, and you are not the man to crush me in the open.

Bless your soul, I answered, I should not think of trying. But, to prevent any more misunderstanding, when you speak of that ruler or stronger party whose interest the weaker ought to serve, please make it clear whether you are using the words in the ordinary way or in that strict sense you have just defined.

I mean a ruler in the strictest possible sense. Now quibble away and be as malicious as you can. I want no mercy. But you are no match for me.

Do you think me mad enough to beard a lion or try to outwit a Thrasymachus?

You did try just now, he retorted, but it wasn't a success.

Enough of this, said I. Now tell me about the physician in that strict sense you spoke of: is it his business to earn money or to treat his patients? Remember, I mean your physician who is worthy of the name.

To treat his patients.

And what of the ship's captain in the true sense? Is he a mere seaman or the commander of the crew?

The commander.

Yes, we shall not speak of him as a seaman just because he is on board a ship. That is not the point. He is called captain because of his skill and authority over the crew.

Quite true.

And each of these people has some special interest? [3]

No doubt.

And the craft in question exists for the very purpose of discovering that interest and providing for it?

Yes.

Can it equally be said of any craft that it has an interest, other than its own greatest possible perfection?

What do you mean by that?

Here is an illustration. If you ask me whether it is sufficient for the human body just to be itself, with no need of help from without, I should say, Certainly not; it has weaknesses and defects, and its condition is not all that it might be. That is precisely why the art of medicine was invented: it was designed to help the body and provide for its interests. Would not that be true?

It would.

But now take the art of medicine itself. Has that any defects or weaknesses? Does any art stand in need of some further perfection, as the eye would be imperfect without the power of vision or the ear without hearing, so that in their case an art is required that will study their interests and provide for their carrying out those functions? Has the art itself any corresponding need of some further art to remedy its defects and look after its

---

[3] All the persons mentioned have some interest. The craftsman *qua* craftsman has an interest in doing his work as well as possible, which is the same thing as serving the interest of the subjects on whom his craft is exercised: and the subjects have their interest, which the craftsman is there to promote.

interests; and will that further art require yet another, and so on for ever? Or will every art look after its own interests? Or, finally, is it not true that no art needs to have its weaknesses remedied or its interests studied either by another art or by itself, because no art has in itself any weakness or fault, and the only interest it is required to serve is that of its subject matter? In itself, an art is sound and flawless, so long as it is entirely true to its own nature as an art in the strictest sense—and it is the strict sense that I want you to keep in view. Is not that true?

So it appears.

Then, said I, the art of medicine does not study its own interest, but the needs of the body, just as a groom shows his skill by caring for horses, not for the art of grooming. And so every art seeks, not its own advantage—for it has no deficiencies—but the interest of the subject on which it is exercised.

It appears so.

But surely, Thrasymachus, every art has authority and superior power over its subject.

To this he agreed, though very reluctantly.

So far as arts are concerned, then, no art ever studies or enjoins the interest of the superior or stronger party, but always that of the weaker over which it has authority.

Thrasymachus assented to this at last, though he tried to put up a fight. I then went on:

So the physician, as such, studies only the patient's interest, not his own. For as we agreed, the business of the physician, in the strict sense, is not to make money for himself, but to exercise his power over the patient's body; and the ship's captain, again, considered strictly as no mere sailor, but in command of the crew, will study and enjoin the interest of his subordinates, not his own.

He agreed reluctantly.

And so with government of any kind: no ruler, insofar as he is acting as ruler, will study or enjoin what is for his own interest. All that he says and does will be said and done with a view to what is good and proper for the subject for whom he practices his art.

At this point, when everyone could see that Thrasymachus' definition of justice had been turned inside out, instead of making any reply, he said:

Socrates, have you a nurse?

Why do you ask such a question as that? I said. Wouldn't it be better to answer mine?

Because she lets you go about sniffling like a child whose nose wants wiping. She hasn't even taught you to know a shepherd when you see one, or his sheep either.

What makes you say that?

Why, you imagine that a herdsman studies the interests of his flocks or cattle, tending and fattening them up with some other end in view than his master's profit or his own; and so you don't see that, in politics, the genuine ruler regards his subjects exactly like sheep, and thinks of nothing else, night and day, but the good he can get out of them for himself. You are so far out in your notions of right and wrong, justice and injustice, as not to know that "right" actually means what is good for someone else, and to be "just" means serving the interest of the stronger who rules, at the cost of the subject who obeys; whereas injustice is just the reverse, asserting its authority over those innocents who are called just, so that they minister solely to their master's advantage and happiness, and not in the least degree to their own. Innocent as you are yourself, Socrates, you must see that a just man always has the worst of it. Take a private business: when a partnership is wound up, you will never find that the more honest of two partners comes off with the larger share; and in their relations to the state, when there are taxes to be paid, the honest man will pay more than the other on the same amount of property; or if there is money to be distributed, the dishonest will get it all. When either of them holds some public office, even if the just man loses in no other way, his private affairs at any rate will suffer from neglect, while his principles will not allow him to help himself from the public funds; not to mention the offense he will give to his friends and relations by refusing to sacrifice those principles to do them a good turn. Injustice has all the opposite advantages. I am speaking of the type I described just now, the man who can get the better of other people on a large scale: you must fix your eye on him, if you want to judge how much it is to one's own interest not to be just. You can see that best in the most consummate form of injustice, which rewards wrongdoing with supreme welfare and happiness and reduces its victims, if they won't retaliate in kind, to misery. That form is despotism, which uses force or fraud to plunder the goods of others, public or private, sacred or profane, and to do it in a wholesale way. If you are caught committing any one of these crimes on a small scale, you are punished and disgraced; they call it sacrilege, kidnapping, burglary, theft, and brigandage.

But if, besides taking their property, you turn all your countrymen into slaves, you will hear no more of those ugly names; your countrymen themselves will call you the happiest of men and bless your name, and so will everyone who hears of such a complete triumph of injustice; for when people denounce injustice, it is because they are afraid of suffering wrong, not of doing it. So true is it, Socrates, that injustice, on a grand enough scale, is superior to justice in strength and freedom and autocratic power; and "right," as I said at first, means simply what serves the interest of the stronger party; "wrong" means what is for the interest and profit of oneself.

Having deluged our ears with this torrent of words, as the man at the baths might empty a bucket over one's head, Thrasymachus meant to take himself off; but the company obliged him to stay and defend his position. I was specially urgent in my entreaties.

My good Thrasymachus, said I, do you propose to fling a doctrine like that at our heads and then go away without explaining it properly or letting us point out to you whether it is true or not? Is it so small a matter in your eyes to determine the whole course of conduct which every one of us must follow to get the best out of life?

Don't I realize it is a serious matter? he retorted.

Apparently not, said I; or else you have no consideration for us, and do not care whether we shall lead better or worse lives for being ignorant of this truth you profess to know. Do take the trouble to let us into your secret; if you treat us handsomely, you may be sure it will be a good investment; there are so many of us to show our gratitude. I will make no secret of my own conviction, which is that injustice is not more profitable than justice, even when left free to work its will unchecked. No; let your unjust man have full power to do wrong, whether by successful violence or by escaping detection; all the same he will not convince me that he will gain more than he would by being just. There may be others here who feel as I do, and set justice above injustice. It is for you to convince us that we are not well advised.

How can I? he replied. If you are not convinced by what I have just said, what more can I do for you? Do you want to be fed with my ideas out of a spoon?

God forbid! I exclaimed; not that. But I do want you to stand by your own words; or, if you shift your ground, shift it openly and stop trying to hoodwink us as you are doing now. You see, Thrasymachus, to go back to your earlier argument, in speaking of the shepherd you did not think it necessary to keep to that strict sense you laid down when you defined the genuine physician. You represent him, in his character of shepherd, as feeding up his flock, not for their own sake but for the table or the market, as if he were out to make money as caterer or a cattle-dealer, rather than a shepherd. Surely the sole concern of the shepherd's art is to do the best for the charges put under its care; its own best interest is sufficiently provided for, so long as it does not fall short of all that shepherding should imply. On that principle it followed, I thought, that any kind of authority, in the state or in private life, must, in its character of authority, consider solely what is best for those under its care. Now what is your opinion? Do you think that the men who govern states—I mean rulers in the strict sense—have no reluctance to hold office?

I don't think so, he replied; I know it.

Well, but haven't you noticed, Thrasymachus, that in other positions of authority no one is willing to act unless he is paid wages, which he demands on the assumption that all the benefit of his action will go to his charges? Tell me: Don't we always distinguish one form of skill from another by its power to effect some particular result? Do say what you really think, so that we may get on.

Yes, that is the distinction.

And also each brings us some benefit that is peculiar to it: medicine gives health, for example; the art of navigation, safety at sea; and so on.

Yes.

And wage-earning brings us wages; that is its distinctive product. Now, speaking with that precision which you proposed, you would not say that the art of navigation is the same as the art of medicine, merely on the ground that a ship's captain regained his health on a voyage, because the sea air was good for him. No more would you identify the practice of medicine with wage-earning because a man may keep his health while earning wages, or a physician attending a case may receive a fee.

No.

And, since we agreed that the benefit obtained by each form of skill is peculiar to it, any common benefit enjoyed alike by all these practitioners must come from some further practice common to them all?

It would seem so.

Yes, we must say that if they all earn wages, they get that benefit insofar as they are engaged in wage-earning as well as in practicing their several arts.

He agreed reluctantly.

This benefit, then—the receipt of wages—does not come to a man from his special art. If we are to speak strictly, the physician, as such, produces health; the builder, a house; and then each, in his further capacity of wage-earner, gets his pay. Thus every art has its own function and benefits its proper subject. But suppose the practitioner is not paid; does he then get any benefit from his art?

Clearly not.

And is he doing no good to anyone either, when he works for nothing?

No, I suppose he does some good.

Well then, Thrasymachus, it is now clear that no form of skill or authority provides for its own benefit. As we were saying some time ago, it always studies and prescribes what is good for its subject—the interest of the weaker party, not of the stronger. And that, my friend, is why I said that no one is willing to be in a position of authority and undertake to set straight other men's troubles without demanding to be paid; because, if he is to do his work well, he will never, in his capacity of ruler, do, or command others to do, what is best for himself, but only what is best for the subject. For that reason, if he is to consent, he must have his recompense, in the shape of money or honor, or of punishment in case of refusal.

What do you mean, Socrates? asked Glaucon. I recognize two of your three kinds of reward; but I don't understand what you mean by speaking of punishment as a recompense.

Then you don't understand the recompense required by the best type of men, or their motive for accepting authority when they do consent. You surely know that a passion for honors or for money is rightly regarded as something to be ashamed of.

Yes I do.

For that reason, I said, good men are unwilling to rule, either for money's sake or for honor. They have no wish to be called mercenary for demanding to be paid, or thieves for making a secret profit out of their office; nor yet will honors tempt them, for they are not ambitious. So they must be forced to consent under threat of penalty; that may be why a readiness to accept power under no such constraint is thought discreditable. And the heaviest penalty for declining to rule is to be ruled by some one inferior to yourself. That is the fear, I believe, that makes decent people accept power; and when they do so, they face the prospect of authority with no idea that they are coming into the enjoyment of a comfortable berth; it is forced upon them because they can find no one better than themselves, or even as good, to be entrusted with power. If there could ever be a society of perfect men, there might well be as much competition to evade office as there now is to gain it; and it would then be clearly seen that the genuine ruler's nature is to seek only the advantage of the subject, with the consequence that any man of understanding would sooner have another to do the best for him than be at the pains to do the best for that other himself. On this point, then, I entirely disagree with Thrasymachus' doctrine that right means what is to the interest of the stronger.

BOOK II [*]

When I had made these remarks I thought we had done with discussing: whereas it seems it was only a prelude. For Glaucon, with that eminent courage which he displays on all occasions, would not acquiesce in the retreat of Thrasymachus, and began thus: Socrates, do you wish really to convince us that it is on every account better to be just than to be unjust, or only to seem to have convinced us?

If it were in my power, I replied, I should prefer convincing you really.

Then, he proceeded, you are not doing what you wish. Let me ask you: Is there, in your opinion, a class of good things of such a kind that we are glad to possess them, not because we desire their consequences, but simply welcoming them for their own sake? Take, for example, the feelings of enjoyment and all those pleasures that are harmless, and that are followed by no result in the after time, beyond simple enjoyment in their possession.

Yes, I certainly think there is a class of this description.

Well, is there another class, do you think, of those which we value, both for their own sake and for their results, such as intelligence, and sight, and health; all of which are welcome, I apprehend, on both accounts?

Yes.

And do you further recognize a third class of good things, which would include gymnastic training, and submission to medical treatment in illness, as well as the practice of medicine, and all other means of making money? Things like these we should

describe as irksome, and yet beneficial to us; and while we should reject them viewed simply in themselves, we accept them for the sake of the emoluments, and of the other consequences which result from them.

Yes, undoubtedly there is such a third class also; but what then?

In which of these classes do you place justice?

I should say in the highest; that is, among the good things which will be valued by one who is in the pursuit of true happiness, alike for their own sake and for their consequences.

Then your opinion is not that of the many, by whom justice is ranked in the irksome class, as a thing which in itself, and for its own sake, is disagreeable and repulsive, but which it is well to practice for the credit of it, with an eye to emolument and a good name.

I know it is so; and under this idea Thrasymachus has been for a long time disparaging justice and praising injustice. But apparently I am a dull scholar.

Pray then listen to my proposal, and tell me whether you agree to it. Thrasymachus appears to me to have yielded like a snake to your fascination sooner than he need have done; but for my part, I am not satisfied as yet with the exposition that has been given of justice and injustice; for I long to be told what they respectively are, and what force they exert, taken simply by themselves, when residing in the soul, dismissing the consideration of their rewards and other consequences. This shall be my plan then, if you do not object: I will revive Thrasymachus' argument, and will first state the common view respecting the nature and origin of justice; in the second place, I will maintain that

[*] Trans. by John L. Davies and David M. Vaughan (1866).

all who practice it do so against their will, because it is indispensable, not because it is a good thing; and thirdly, that they act reasonably in so doing, because the life of the unjust man is, as men say, far better than that of the just. Not that I think so myself, Socrates; only my ears are so dinned with what I hear from Thrasymachus and a thousand others, that I am puzzled. Now I have never heard the argument for the superiority of justice over injustice maintained to my satisfaction; for I should like to hear a panegyric upon it, considered simply in itself; and from you if from anyone, I should expect such a treatment of the subject. Therefore, I will speak as forcibly as I can in praise of an unjust life, and I shall thus give you a specimen of the manner in which I wish to hear you afterwards censure injustice and commend justice. See whether you approve of my plan.

Indeed I do; for on what other subject could a sensible man like better to talk and to hear others talk, again and again?

Admirably spoken! So now listen to me while I speak on my first theme, the nature and the origin of justice.

To commit injustice is, they say, in its nature, a good thing, and to suffer it an evil thing; but the evil of the latter exceeds the good of the former; and so, after the twofold experience of both doing and suffering injustice, those who cannot avoid the latter and compass the former find it expedient to make a compact of mutual abstinence from injustice. Hence arose legislation and contracts between man and man, and hence it became the custom to call that which the law enjoined just, as well as lawful. Such, they tell us, is justice, and so it came into being; and it stands midway between that which is best, to commit injustice with impunity, and that which is worst, to suffer injustice without any power of retaliating. And being a mean between these two extremes, the principle of justice is regarded with satisfaction, not as a positive good, but because the inability to commit injustice has rendered it valuable; for they say that one who had it in his power to be unjust, and who deserved the name of a man, would never be so weak as to contract with anyone that both the parties should abstain from injustice. Such is the current account, Socrates, of the nature of justice, and of the circumstances in which it originated.

The truth of my second statement—that men practice justice unwillingly, and because they lack the power to violate it, will be most readily perceived, if we make a supposition like the following. Let us give full liberty to the just man and to the unjust alike, to do whatever they please, and then let us follow them, and see whither the inclination of each will lead him. In that case we shall surprise the just man in the act of travelling in the same direction as the unjust, owing to that covetous desire, the gratification of which every creature naturally pursues as a good, only that it is forced out of its path by law, and constrained to respect the principle of equality. That full liberty of action would, perhaps, be most effectually realized if they were invested with a power which they say was in old time possessed by the ancestor of Gyges the Lydian. He was a shepherd, so the story runs, in the service of the reigning sovereign of Lydia, when one day a violent storm of rain fell, the ground was rent asunder by an earthquake, and a yawning gulf appeared on the spot where he was feeding his flocks. Seeing what had happened, and wondering at it, he went down into the gulf, and among other marvellous objects he saw, as the legend relates, a hollow brazen horse, with windows in its sides, through which he looked, and beheld in the interior a corpse, apparently of superhuman size; from which he took nothing but a golden ring off the hand, and therewith made his way out. Now when the usual meeting of the shepherds occurred, for the purpose of sending to the king their monthly report on the state of his flocks, this shepherd came with the rest, wearing the ring. And, as he was seated with the company, he happened to turn the hoop of the ring round towards himself, till it came to the inside of his hand. Whereupon he became invisible to his neighbors, who fell to talking about him as if he were gone away. While he was marvelling at this, he again began playing with the ring, and turned the hoop to the outside, upon which he became once more visible. Having noticed this effect, he made experiments with the ring, to see whether it possessed this virtue; and so it was, that when he turned the hoop inwards he became invisible, and when he turned it outwards he was again visible. After this discovery, he immediately contrived to be appointed one of the messengers to carry the report to the king; and upon his arrival he seduced the queen, and, conspiring with her, slew the king, and took possession of the throne.

If then there were two such rings in existence, and if the just and the unjust man were each to put on one, it is to be thought that no one would be so steeled against temptation as to abide in the practice of justice, and resolutely to abstain from touching the property of his neighbors, when he had it in his power to help himself without fear to anything he pleased in the market, or to go into private houses and have intercourse with whom he would, or to kill and release from prison according to his own pleasure, and in everything else to act among men with the power of a god. And in thus following out his desires the just man will be doing precisely what the unjust man would do; and so they would both be pursuing the same path. Surely this will be allowed to be strong evidence that none are just willingly, but only by compulsion, because to be just is not a good to the individual; for all violate justice whenever they imagine that there is nothing to hinder them. And they do so because everyone thinks that, in the individual case, injustice is much more profitable than justice; and they are right in so thinking, as the advocate of this doctrine will maintain. For if anyone having this license within his grasp were to refuse to do any injustice, or to touch the property of others, all who were aware of it would think him a most pitiful and irrational creature, though they would praise him before each other's faces, to impose on one another, through their fear of being treated with injustice. And so much for this topic.

[Thus ends Glaucon's case *vs.* Socrates.]

QUESTIONS FOR DISCUSSION

1. Compare various definitions of justice:
   a) an eye for an eye (retribution)
   b) giving each man his due (paying one's debts)
   c) enlightened *self*-interest
   d) interest of the stronger (ruling class)
   e) obedience to the laws
   f) equality in pursuit of life, liberty, and property
   g) minding one's own business
   h) greatest happiness for the greatest number
   If you were Socrates, how would you criticize each?
   (Criticism may be either favorable or rejection or questioning.)
2. What ambiguities does Socrates find in Thrasymachus' definition of justice as "the interest of the stronger"? In what sense does Socrates in the end reject this definition as inconsistent?
3. Do you agree with Thrasymachus that there is no difference in justice under despotism, democracy, or aristocracy?
4. Is it always right or just to obey the laws of rulers even if they are not infallible? If rulers can make mistakes, what follows logically concerning Thrasymachus' definition of justice?
5. How does Socrates criticize Thrasymachus by reasoning from the analogies of the physician in relation to his patients, the ship's captain in relation to his crew, the shepherd in relation to his flock, and any wage earner in relation to his work?
6. Explain: "Good men are unwilling to rule either for money's sake or for honor. . . . And the heaviest penalty for declining to rule is to be ruled by some one inferior to one's self."
7. In order to answer the question whether it is always good to be just (do the right thing) rather than to be unjust, what idea must be understood first?
8. Define and illustrate three classes of good things. To which does justice belong?
9. How does Glaucon propose to prove that injustice is better than justice (which men do unwillingly)? Explain the myth of Gyges and its relevance to Glaucon's argument.
10. What is your own present opinion about the meaning of justice and the validity of Socrates' view that it is better to be just than unjust?

Aristotle (384-322 B.C.)

3.2   Nicomachean Ethics

Every art and every scientific inquiry, and similarly every action and
purpose, may be said to aim at some
good. Hence, the good has been well
defined as that at which all things
aim. But it is clear that there is a
difference in the ends; for the ends
are sometimes activities, and sometimes results beyond the mere activities. Also, where there are certain
ends beyond the actions, the results
are naturally superior to the activities.

As there are various actions, arts,
and sciences, it follows that the ends
are also various. Thus health is the
end of medicine, a vessel of shipbuild-
ing, victory of strategy, and wealth
of domestic economy. It often happens
that there are a number of such arts
or sciences which fall under a single
faculty, as the art of making bridles,
and all such other arts as make the
instruments of horsemanship, under
horsemanship, and this again as well
as every military action under strategy, and in the same way other arts
or sciences under other faculties. But
in all these cases the ends of the architectonic arts or sciences, whatever they

From *Nicomachean Ethics,* Book I.
Trans. by J. E. C. Welldon (London: Macmillan & Co., Ltd., 1927). Reprinted by
permission of Macmillan & Co., Ltd.

may be, are more desirable than those
of the subordinate arts or sciences, as
it is for the sake of the former that the
latter are themselves sought after. It
makes no difference to the argument
whether the activities themselves are
the ends of the actions, or something
else beyond the activities as in the
above-mentioned sciences.

If it is true that in the sphere of
action there is an end which we wish
for its own sake, and for the sake of
which we wish everything else, and
that we do not desire all things for
the sake of something else (for, if that
is so, the process will go on *ad infinitum,* and our desire will be idle and
futile), it is clear that this will be the
good or the supreme good. Does it
not follow then that the knowledge
of this supreme good is of great importance for the conduct of life, and
that, *if we know it,* we shall be like
archers who have a mark at which to
aim, we shall have a better chance of
attaining what we want? But, if this
is the case, we must endeavor to comprehend, at least in outline, its nature,
and the science or faculty to which
it belongs.

It would seem that this is the most
authoritative or architectonic science
or faculty, and such is evidently the
political; for it is the political science

or faculty which determines what sciences are necessary in states, and what kind of sciences should be learnt, and how far they should be learnt by particular people. We perceive, too, that the faculties which are held in the highest esteem, e.g., strategy, domestic economy, and rhetoric, are subordinate to it. But as it makes use of the other practical sciences, and also legislates upon the things to be done and the things to be left undone, it follows that its end will comprehend the ends of all the other sciences, and will therefore be the true good of mankind. For although the good of an individual is identical with the good of a state, yet the good of the state, whether in attainment or in preservation, is evidently greater and more perfect. For while in an individual by himself it is something to be thankful for, it is nobler and more divine in a nation or state.

These then are the objects at which the present inquiry aims, and it is in a sense a political inquiry. But our statement of the case will be adequate, if it be made with all such clearness as the subject-matter admits; for it would be as wrong to expect the same degree of accuracy in all reasonings as in all manufactures. Things noble and just, which are the subjects of investigation in political science, exhibit so great a diversity and uncertainty that they are sometimes thought to have only a conventional, and not a natural existence. There is the same sort of uncertainty in regard to good things, as it often happens that injuries result from them; thus there have been cases in which people were ruined by wealth, or again by courage. As our subjects then and our premises are of this nature, we must be content to indicate the truth roughly and in

outline; and as our subjects and premises are true generally *but not universally*, we must be content to arrive at conclusions which are only generally true. It is right to receive the particular statements which are made in the same spirit; for an educated person will expect accuracy in each subject only so far as the nature of the subject allows; he might as well accept probable reasoning from a mathematician as require demonstrative proofs from a rhetorician. But everybody is competent to judge the subjects which he understands, and is a good judge of them. It follows that in particular subjects it is a person of *special* education, and in general a person of universal education, who is a good judge. Hence, the young are not proper students of political science, as they have no experience of the actions of life which form the premises and subjects of the reasonings. Also, it may be added that, from their tendency to follow their emotions, they will not study the subject to any purpose or profit, as its end is not knowledge but action. It makes no difference whether a person is young in years or youthful in character; for the defect *of which I speak* is not one of time but is due to the emotional character of his life and pursuits. Knowledge is as useless to such a person as it is to an intemperate person. But where the desires and actions of people are regulated by reason, the knowledge of these subjects will be extremely valuable.

But having said so much by way of preface as to the students of political science, the spirit in which it should be studied, and the object which we set before ourselves, let us resume our argument as follows:

As every knowledge and moral purpose aspires to some good, what is in our view the good at which the political science aims, and what is the highest of all practical goods? As to its name there is, I may say, a general agreement. The masses and the cultured classes agree in calling it happiness, and conceive that "to live well" or "to do well" is the same thing as "to be happy." But as to the nature of happiness they do not agree, nor do the masses give the same account of it as the philosophers. The former define it as something visible and palpable, e.g., pleasure, wealth, or honor; different people give different definitions of it, and often the same person gives different definitions at different times; for when a person has been ill, it is health; when he is poor, it is wealth; and, if he is conscious of his own ignorance, he envies people who use grand language above his own comprehension. Some philosophers, on the other hand, have held that, besides these various goods, there is an absolute good which is the cause of goodness in them all. It would perhaps be a waste of time to examine all these opinions; it will be enough to examine such as are most popular or as seem to be more or less reasonable.

. . . It seems not unreasonable that people should derive their conception of the good or of happiness from men's lives. Thus ordinary or vulgar people conceive it to be pleasure, and accordingly approve a life of enjoyment. For there are practically three prominent lives, the sensual, the political, and, thirdly, the speculative. Now the mass of men present an absolutely slavish appearance, as choosing the life of brute beasts, but they meet with consideration because so many persons in authority share the tastes of Sardanapalus. Cultivated and practical people, on the other hand, identify happiness with honor, as honor is the general end of political life. But this appears too superficial for our present purpose; for honor seems to depend more upon the people who pay it than upon the person to whom it is paid, and we have an intuitive feeling that the good is something which is proper to a man himself and cannot easily be taken away from him. It seems too that the reason why men seek honor is that they may be confident of their own goodness. Accordingly they seek it at the hands of the wise and of those who know them well, and they seek it on the ground of virtue; hence, it is clear that in their judgment, at any rate, virtue is superior to honor. It would perhaps be right then to look upon virtue rather than honor as being the end of the political life. Yet virtue again, it appears, lacks completeness; for it seems that a man may possess virtue and yet be asleep or inactive throughout life, and not only so, but he may experience the greatest calamities and misfortunes. But nobody would call such a life a life of happiness, unless he were maintaining a paradox. It is not necessary to dwell further on this subject, as it is sufficiently discussed in the popular philosophical treatises. The third life is the speculative which we will investigate hereafter.

The life of money-making is in a sense a life of constraint, and it is clear that wealth is not the good of which we are in quest; for it is useful in part as a means to something else. It would be a more reasonable view, therefore, that the things mentioned before, viz., *sensual pleasure, honor, and virtue,* are ends than that wealth is, as they are things which are desired on their own account. Yet these, too, are apparently not ends, although much argument has been employed to show that they are.

We may now dismiss this subject; but it will perhaps be best to consider the universal *good,* and to discuss the meaning in which the phrase is used, although there is this difficulty in such an inquiry, that the *doctrine of* ideas has been introduced by our friends.[1] Yet it will perhaps seem the best and, indeed, the right course, at least when the truth is at stake, to go so far as to sacrifice what is near and dear to us, especially as we are philosophers. For friends and truth are both dear to us, but it is a sacred duty to prefer the truth.

Now the authors of this theory did not make ideas of things in which they predicated priority and posteriority. Hence, they did not constitute an idea of numbers. But good is predicated equally of substance, quality, and relation; and the absolute or essential, *i.e., substance,* is in its nature prior to the relative, as relativity is like an offshoot or accident of existence; hence, there cannot be an idea which is common to them both. Again, there are as many ways of predicating good as of predicating existence; for it is predicated of substance as, e.g., of God or the mind, or of quality as of the virtues, or of quantity as of the mean, or of relativity as of the useful, or of time as of opportunity, or of place as of a habitation, and so on. It is clear then that it cannot be a common universal idea or a unity; other-

---

[1] Aristotle is referring to Plato and his school (the Academy) in which he had been a student for nearly twenty years. What follows is Aristotle's criticism of the Platonic theory that there is only one *Form* of *Good.* [P.P.W.]

wise it would not be predicated in all the categories but only in one. Thirdly, as there is a single science of all such things as fall under a single idea, there would have been a single science of all good things, *if the idea of "good" were single;* but, in fact, there are many sciences even of such good things as fall under a single category, strategy, e.g., being the science of opportunity in war, and medicine the science of opportunity in disease, medicine again being the science of the mean in respect of food, and gymnastic the science of the mean in respect of exercise. It would be difficult, too, to say what is meant by the "absolute" in anything, if in "absolute man" and in "man" there is one and the same conception of man. For there will be no difference between them in respect of manhood, and, if so, neither will there be any difference between "absolute good" and "good" in respect of goodness. Nor again will good be more good if it is eternal, since a white thing which lasts for a long time is not whiter than that which lasts for a single day. . . . However, these are questions which may be deferred to another occasion; but there is an objection to my arguments which suggests itself, viz., that the *Platonic* theory does not apply to every good, that the things which in themselves are sought after and welcomed are reckoned as one species, and the things which tend to produce or in any sense preserve these or to prevent their opposites are reckoned as goods in a secondary sense as being means to these. It is clear then that there will be two kinds of goods, some being absolute goods, and others secondary. Let us then separate goods which are merely serviceable from absolute goods and consider if they are conceived as falling under a single idea. But what kind of things is it that may be defined as absolute goods? Will it be all such as are sought after independently of their consequences, e.g., wisdom, sight, and certain pleasures and honors? For granting that we seek after these sometimes as means to something else, still we may define them as absolute goods. Or is none of these things an absolute good, nor anything else except the idea? But then the type *or idea* will be purposeless, *i.e., it will not comprise any particulars.* If, on the other hand, these things, too, are absolute goods, the conception of the good will necessarily appear the same in them all, as the conception of whiteness appears the same in snow and in white lead. But the conceptions of honor, wisdom, and pleasure, are distinct and different in respect of goodness. "Good" then is not a common term falling under one idea. But in what sense is the term used? For it does not seem to be an accidental homonymy. Is it because all goods issue from one source or all tend to one end; or is it rather a case of analogy? for as the sight is to the body, so is the mind to the soul, *i.e., the mind may be called the eye of the soul, and so on.* But it will perhaps be well to leave this subject for the present, as an exact discussion of it would belong rather to a different branch of philosophy. But the same is true of the idea; for even if there is some one good which is predicated of all these things, or some abstract and absolute good, it will plainly not be such as a man finds practicable and attainable, and, therefore, will not be such a good as we are in search of. It will possibly be held, however, that it is worthwhile to apprehend this *universal good,* as

having a relation to the goods which are attainable and practicable; for if we have this as a model, we shall be better able to know the things which are good relatively to ourselves, and, knowing them, to acquire them. Now, although there is a certain plausibility in this theory, it seems not to harmonize with scientific experience; for while all sciences aim at a certain good and seek to supply a deficiency, they omit the knowledge of the universal good. Yet it is not reasonable to suppose that what would be so extremely helpful is ignored, and not sought at all by artists generally. But it is difficult to see what benefit a cobbler or carpenter will get in reference to his art by knowing the absolute good, or how the contemplation of the absolute idea will make a person a better physician or general. For it appears that a physician does not regard health abstractly, but regards the health of man or rather perhaps of a particular man, as he gives his medicine to individuals.

But, leaving this subject for the present, let us revert to the good of which we are in quest and consider what its nature may be. For it is clearly different in different actions or arts; it is one thing in medicine, another in strategy, and so on. What then is the good in each of these instances? It is presumably that for the sake of which all else is done. This in medicine is health; in strategy, victory; in domestic architecture, a house; and so on. But in every action and purpose it is the end, as it is for the sake of the end that people all do everything else. If then there is a certain end of all action, it will be this which is the practicable good; and if there are several such ends, it will be these.

Our argument has arrived by a different path at the same conclusion as before; but we must endeavor to elucidate it still further. As it appears that there are more ends than one, and some of these, e.g., wealth, flutes, and instruments, generally we desire as means to something else, it is evident that they are not all final ends. But the highest good is clearly something final. Hence, if there is only one final end, this will be the object of which we are in search, and if there are more than one, it will be the most final of them. We speak of that which is sought after for its own sake as more final than that which is sought after as a means to something else; we speak of that which is never desired as a means to something else as more final than the things which are desired both in themselves and as means to something else; and we speak of a thing as absolutely final, if it is always desired in itself and never as a means to something else.

It seems that happiness pre-eminently answers to this description, as we always desire happiness for its own sake and never as a means to something else, whereas we desire honor, pleasure, intellect, and every virtue, partly for their own sakes (for we should desire them independently of what might result from them) but partly also as being means to happiness, because we suppose they will prove the instruments of happiness. Happiness, on the other hand, nobody desires for the sake of these things, nor indeed as a means to anything else at all.

We come to the same conclusion if we start from the consideration of self-sufficiency, if it may be assumed that the final good is self-sufficient. But when we speak of self-sufficiency, we do not mean that a person leads a solitary life all by himself, but that he has parents, children, wife, and friends, and fellow citizens in general, as man is naturally a social being. But here it is necessary to prescribe some limit; for if the circle be extended so as to include parents, descendants, and friends' friends, it will go on indefinitely. Leaving this point, however, for future investigation, we define the self-sufficient as that which, taken by itself, makes life desirable, and wholly free from want, and this is our conception of happiness.

Again, we conceive happiness to be the most desirable of all things, and that not merely as one among other good things. If it were one among other good things, the addition of the smallest good would increase its desirableness; for the accession makes a superiority of goods, and the greater of two goods is always the more desirable. It appears then that happiness is something final and self-sufficient, being the end of all action.

Perhaps, however, it seems a truth which is generally admitted, that happiness is the supreme good; what is wanted is to define its nature a little more clearly. The best way of arriving at such a definition will probably be to ascertain the function of Man. For, as with a flute-player, a statuary, or any artisan, or in fact anybody who has a definite function and action, his goodness or excellence seems to lie in his function, so it would seem to be with Man, if indeed he has a definite function. Can it be said then that, while a carpenter and a cobbler have definite functions and actions, Man, unlike them, is naturally functionless? The reasonable view is that, as the eye, the hand, the foot, and similarly each several part of the body has a definite function, so Man may be regarded as having a definite function apart from all these. What then, can this function be? It is not life; for life is apparently something which man shares with the plants; and it is something peculiar to him that we are looking for. We must exclude, therefore, the life of nutrition and increase. There is next what may be called the life of sensation. But this too, is apparently shared by Man with horses, cattle, and all other animals. There remains what I may call the practical life of the rational part of *Man's being.* But the rational part is twofold; it is rational partly in the sense of being obedient to reason, and partly in the sense of possessing reason and intelligence. The practical life, too, may be conceived of in two ways, *viz., either as a moral state, or as a moral activity:* but we must understand by it the life of activity, as this seems to be the truer form of the conception.

The function of Man then is an activity of soul in accordance with reason, or not independently of reason. Again, the functions of a person of a certain kind, and of such a person who is good of his kind, e.g., of a harpist and a good harpist, are in our view generically the same, and this view is true of people of all kinds without exception, the superior excellence being only an addition to the function; for it is the function of a harpist to play the harp, and of a good harpist to play the harp well.

This being so, if we define the function of Man as a kind of life, and this life as an activity of soul, or a course of action in conformity with reason, if the function of a good man is such activity or action of a good and noble kind, and if everything is successfully performed when it is performed in accordance with its proper excellence, it follows that the good of Man is an activity of soul in accordance with virtue or, if there are more virtues than one, in accordance with the best and most complete virtue. But it is necessary to add the words "in a complete life." For as one swallow or one day does not make a spring, so one day or a short time does not make a fortunate or happy man.

This may be taken as a sufficiently accurate sketch of the good; for it is right, I think, to draw the outlines first and afterwards to fill in the details. It would seem that anybody can carry on and complete what has been satisfactorily sketched in outline, and that time is a good inventor or co-operator in so doing. This is the way in which the arts have made their advances, as anybody can supply a deficiency.

But bearing in mind what has been already said, we must not look for the same degree of accuracy in all subjects; we must be content in each class of subjects with accuracy of such a kind as the subject-matter allows, and to such an extent as is proper to the inquiry.

QUESTIONS FOR DISCUSSION

1. Aristotle defines the good as "that at which all things aim" (a *teleological* generalization of all natural processes and human actions). Does this definition imply that there are no differences among the ends (purposes, aims) of the arts, sciences, and other activities of men? Illustrate.

2. What relation do instrumental goods have to the ends to which they are subordinate? Illustrate.

3. Why is political science the highest science, even if it cannot yield universally necessary conclusions but only probable ones? Why must it be different in method than mathematical reasoning? Why are the young "not proper students of political science"?

4. Why is happiness or well being the highest of all practical goods, such as pleasure, wealth, or honor (which nearly all men strive for)? Why is the life of money-making not the highest end? Nor that of sensual pleasures or honor (fame)?

5. How does Aristotle criticize Plato's theory of the eternal idea of a single good as the only final end?

6. How does Aristotle relate self-sufficient happiness to man's functions or activities "in accordance with reason . . . in a complete life"? What does he mean by adding: "For one swallow or one day does not make a spring"?

Benedict de Spinoza (1632-1677)

3.3   On the Improvement of the Understanding

After experience has taught me that all the usual surroundings of social life are vain and futile; seeing that none of the objects of my fears contained in themselves anything either good or bad, except in so far as the mind is affected by them, I finally resolved to inquire whether there might be some real good having power to communicate itself, which would affect the mind singly, to the exclusion of all else; whether, in fact,

there might be anything of which the discovery and attainment would enable me to enjoy continuous, supreme, and unending happiness. I say "I FINALLY resolved," for at first sight it seemed unwise willingly to lose hold on what was sure for the sake of something then uncertain. I could see the benefits which are acquired through fame and riches, and that I should be obliged to abandon the quest of such objects, if I seriously devoted myself to the search for something different and new. I perceived that, if true happiness chanced to be placed in the former, I should neces-

From *The Chief Works of Benedict de Spinoza,* vol. II. Trans. by R. H. M. Elwes (1887).

sarily miss it; while if, on the other hand, it were not so placed, and I gave them my whole attention, I should equally fail.

I therefore debated whether it would not be possible to arrive at the new principle, or, at any rate, at a certainty concerning its existence, without changing the conduct and usual plan of my life; with this end in view, I made many efforts, but in vain. For the ordinary surroundings of life which are esteemed by men (as their actions testify) to be the highest good, may be classed under the three heads—Riches, Fame, and the Pleasures of Sense: with these three the mind is so absorbed that it has little power to reflect on any different good. By sensual pleasure the mind is enthralled to the extent of quiescence, as if the supreme good were actually attained, so that it is quite incapable of thinking of any other object; when such pleasure has been gratified it is followed by extreme melancholy, whereby the mind, though not enthralled, is disturbed and dulled.

The pursuit of honors and riches is likewise very absorbing, especially if such objects be sought simply for their own sake, inasmuch as they are then supposed to constitute the highest good. In the case of fame, the mind is still more absorbed, for fame is conceived as always good for its own sake, and as the ultimate end to which all actions are directed. Further, the attainment of riches and fame is not followed as in the case of sensual pleasures by repentance, but, the more we acquire, the greater is our delight, and, consequently, the more we are incited to increase both the one and the other; on the other hand, if our hopes happen to be frustrated we are plunged into the deep-est sadness. Fame has the further drawback that it compels its votaries to order their lives according to the opinions of their fellow men, shunning what they usually shun, and seeking what they usually seek.

When I saw that all these ordinary objects of desire would be obstacles in the way of a search for something different and new—nay, that they were so opposed thereto, that either they or it would have to be abandoned, I was forced to inquire which would prove the most useful to me: for, as I say, I seemed to be willingly losing hold on a sure good for the sake of something uncertain. However, after I had reflected on the matter, I came in the first place to the conclusion that by abandoning the ordinary objects of pursuit, and betaking myself to a new quest, I should be leaving a good, uncertain by reason of its own nature, as may be gathered from what has been said, for the sake of a good, not uncertain in its nature (for I sought for a fixed good) but only in the possibility of its attainment.

Further reflection convinced me, that, if I could really get to the root of the matter, I should be leaving certain evils for a certain good. I thus perceived that I was in a state of great peril, and I compelled myself to seek with all my strength for a remedy, however uncertain it might be; as a sick man struggling with a deadly disease, when he sees that death will surely be upon him unless a remedy be found, is compelled to seek such a remedy, although it may be uncertain, with all his strength, inasmuch as his whole hope lies therein. All the objects pursued by the multitude, not only bring no remedy that tends to preserve our being, but even act as

hindrances, causing the death not seldom of those who possess them, and
always of those who are possessed by
them. There are many examples of
men who have suffered persecution
even to death for the sake of their
riches, and of men who in pursuit of
wealth have exposed themselves to so
many dangers that they have paid
away their life as a penalty for their
folly. Examples are no less numerous
of men who have endured the utmost
wretchedness for the sake of gaining or preserving their reputation.
Lastly, there are innumerable cases
of men who have hastened their death
through overindulgences in sensual
pleasure. All these evils seem to have
arisen from the fact that happiness
or unhappiness is made wholly to depend on the quality of the object
which we love. When a thing is not
loved, no quarrels will arise concerning it—no sadness will be felt if it
perishes—no envy if it is possessed by
another—no fear, no hatred, in short,
no disturbances of the mind. All these
arise from the love of what is perishable, such as the objects already
mentioned. But love toward a thing
eternal and infinite feeds the mind
wholly with joy, and is itself unmin-
gled with any sadness, wherefore it is
greatly to be desired and sought for
with all our strength. Yet it was not
at random that I used the words, "If
I could go to the root of the matter,"
for, though what I have urged was
perfectly clear to my mind, I could
not forthwith lay aside all love of
riches, sensual enjoyment, and fame.
One thing was evident, namely, that
while my mind was employed with
these thoughts it turned away from
its former objects of desire, and seriously considered the search for a new
principle; this state of things was a

great comfort to me, for I perceived
that the evils were not such as to resist all remedies. Although these intervals were at first rare and of very
short duration, yet afterward, as the
true good became more and more discernible to me, they became more
frequent and more lasting; especially
after I had recognized that the acquisition of wealth, sensual pleasure,
or fame, is only a hindrance, so long
as they are sought as ends not as
means; if they be sought as means,
they will be under restraint, and, far
from being hindrances, will further
not a little the end for which they are
sought, as I will show in due time.

I will here only briefly state what I
mean by true good, and also what is
the nature of the highest good. In order that this may be rightly understood, we must bear in mind that the
terms good and evil are only applied
relatively, so that the same thing may
be called both good and bad, according to the relations in view, in the
same way as it may be called perfect
or imperfect. Nothing regarded in its
own nature can be called perfect or
imperfect; especially when we are
aware that all things which come to
pass, come to pass according to the
eternal order and fixed laws of nature.
However, human weakness cannot attain to this order in its own thoughts,
but meanwhile man conceives a human character much more stable than
his own, and sees that there is no
reason why he should not himself acquire such a character. Thus he is
led to seek for means which will
bring him to this pitch of perfection,
and calls everything which will serve
as such means a true good. The chief
good is that he should arrive, together
with other individuals if possible, at
the possession of the aforesaid charac-

ter. What that character is we shall show in due time, namely, that it is the knowledge of the union existing between the mind and the whole of nature. This, then, is the end for which I strive, to attain to such a character myself, and to endeavor that many should attain to it with me. In other words, it is part of my happiness to lend a helping hand, that many others may understand even as I do, so that their understanding and desire may entirely agree with my own. In order to bring this about, it is necessary to understand as much of nature as will enable us to attain to the aforesaid character, and also to form a social order such as is most conducive to the attainment of this character by the greatest number with the least difficulty and danger. We must seek the assistance of Moral Philosophy [1] and the Theory of Education; further, as health is no insignificant means for attaining our end, we must also include the whole science of Medicine; and, as many difficult things are by contrivance rendered easy, and we can in this way gain much time and convenience, the science of Mechanics must in no way be despised. But, before all things, a means must be devised for improving the understanding and purifying it, as far as may be at the outset, so that it may apprehend things without error, and in the best possible way.

Thus it is apparent to everyone that I wish to direct all sciences to

one end and aim, so that we may attain to the supreme human perfection which we have named; and, therefore, whatsoever in the sciences does not serve to promote our object will have to be rejected as useless. To sum up the matter in a word, all our actions and thoughts must be directed to this one end. Yet, as it is necessary that, while we are endeavoring to attain our purpose and bring the understanding into the right path, we should carry on our life, we are compelled first of all to lay down certain rules of life as provisionally good, to wit, the following:

I. To speak in a manner intelligible to the multitude, and to do all those things that do not hinder the attainment of our purpose. For we can gain from the multitude no small advantages, provided that we strive to accommodate ourselves to its understanding as far as possible: moreover, we shall in this way gain a friendly audience for the reception of the truth.

II. To indulge ourselves with pleasures only in so far as they are necessary for preserving health.

III. Lastly, to endeavor to obtain only sufficient money or other commodities to enable us to preserve our life and health, and to follow such general customs as are consistent with our purpose.

Having laid down these preliminary rules, I will betake myself to the first and most important task, namely, the amendment of the understanding, and the rendering it capable of understanding things in the manner necessary for attaining our end. . . .

---

[1] I do no more here than enumerate the sciences necessary for our purpose; I lay no stress on their order.

QUESTIONS FOR DISCUSSION

1. Explain: No objects of fear are either good or bad except insofar as the mind is affected by them.
2. What three classes of good things are ordinarily esteemed to be the highest values? What states of mind usually follow the exclusive pursuit and enjoyment of each?
3. What fourth alternative does Spinoza advocate, and how did he arrive at it? Does it exclude the other three, and how does it differ from them?
4. What subjects need to be studied in order to assist the mind to achieve Spinoza's highest good? Is everyone capable of learning them?
5. What practical rules are provisionally good as preliminary means of living?

Immanuel Kant (1724-1804)

3.4   The Metaphysic of Morals

Nothing can possibly be conceived in the world, or even out of it, which can be called good without qualification, except a Good Will. Intelligence, wit, judgment, and the other *talents* of the mind, however they may be named, or courage, resolution, perseverance, as qualities of temperament, are undoubtedly good and desirable in many respects; but these gifts of nature may also become extremely bad and mischievous if the will which is to make use of them, and which, therefore, constitutes what is called *character*, is not good. It is the same with the *gifts of fortune*.

Power, riches, honor, even health, and the general well-being and contentment with one's condition which is called *happiness*, inspire pride, and often presumption, if there is not a good will to correct the influence of these on the mind, and with this also to rectify the whole principle of acting, and adapt it to its end. The sight of a being who is not adorned with a single feature of a pure and good will, enjoying unbroken prosperity, can never give pleasure to an impartial rational spectator. Thus a good will appears to constitute the indispensable condition even of being worthy of happiness.

There are even some qualities which are of service to this good will itself, and may facilitate its action,

From *Fundamental Principles of the Metaphysic of Morals.* Trans. by T. K. Abbott (1907).

yet which have no intrinsic unconditional value, but always presuppose a good will, and this qualifies the esteem that we justly have for them, and does not permit us to regard them as absolutely good. Moderation in the affections and passions, self-control and calm deliberation are not only good in many respects, but even seem to constitute part of the intrinsic worth of the person; but they are far from deserving to be called good without qualification, although they have been so unconditionally praised by the ancients. For without the principles of a good will, they may become extremely bad, and the coolness of a villain not only makes him far more dangerous, but also directly makes him more abominable in our eyes than he would have been without it.

A good will is good, not because of what it performs or effects, not by its aptness for the attainment of some proposed end, but simply by virtue of the volition; that is, it is good in itself, and considered by itself is to be esteemed much higher than all that can be brought about by it in favor of any inclination, nay even of the sum total of all inclinations. Even if it should happen that, owing to special disfavor of fortune, or the niggardly provision of a stepmotherly nature, this will should wholly lack power to accomplish its purpose, if with its greatest efforts it should yet achieve nothing, and there should remain only the good will (not, to be sure, a mere wish, but the summoning of all means in our power), then, like a jewel, it would still shine by its own light, as a thing which has its whole value in itself. Its usefulness or fruitlessness can neither add to nor take away anything from this value.

It would be, as it were, only the setting to enable us to handle it the more conveniently in common commerce or to attract to it the attention of those who are not yet connoisseurs, but not to recommend it to true connoisseurs, or to determine its value.

There is, however, something so strange in this idea of the absolute value of the mere will, in which no account is taken of its utility, that notwithstanding the thorough assent of even common reason to the idea, yet a suspicion must arise that it may perhaps really be the product of mere high-flown fancy, and that we may have misunderstood the purpose of nature in assigning reason as the governor of our will. Therefore, we will examine this idea from this point of view.

In the physical constitution of an organized being, that is, a being adapted suitably to the purposes of life, we assume it as a fundamental principle that no organ for any purpose will be found but what is also the fittest and best adapted for that purpose. Now in a being which has reason and a will, if the proper object of nature were its *conservation*, its *welfare*, in a word, its *happiness*, then nature would have hit upon a very bad arrangement in selecting the reason of the creature to carry out this purpose. For all actions which the creature has to perform with a view to this purpose, and the whole rule of its conduct, would be far more surely prescribed to it by instinct, and that end would have been attained thereby much more certainly than it ever can be by reason. Should reason have been communicated to this favored creature over and above, it must only have served it to contemplate the happy constitution of its nature, to admire it, to congratulate itself thereon, and to feel thankful for it to the beneficent cause, but not that it should subject its desires to that weak and delusive guidance, and meddle bunglingly with the purpose of nature. In a word, nature would have taken care that reason should not break forth into *practical exercise,* nor have the presumption, with its weak insight, to think out for itself the plan of happiness, and of the means of attaining it. Nature would not only have taken on herself the choice of the ends, but also of the means, and with wise foresight would have entrusted both to instinct.

And, in fact, we find that the more a cultivated reason applies itself with deliberate purpose to the enjoyment of life and happiness, so much the more does the man fail of true satisfaction. And from this circumstance there arises in many, if they are candid enough to confess it, a certain degree of *misology,* that is, hatred of reason, especially in the case of those who are most experienced in the use of it, because after calculating all the advantages they derive, I do not say from the invention of all the arts of common luxury, but even from the sciences (which seem to them to be after all only a luxury of the understanding), they find that they have, in fact, only brought more trouble on their shoulders, rather than gained in happiness; and they end by envying, rather than despising, the more common stamp of men who keep closer to the guidance of mere instinct, and do not allow their reason much influence on their conduct. And thus we must admit that the judgment of those who would very much lower the lofty eulogies of the advantages which reason gives us in regard to the happiness

and satisfaction of life, or who would even reduce them below zero, is by no means morose or ungrateful to the goodness with which the world is governed, but that there lies at the root of these judgments the idea that our existence has a different and far nobler end, for which, and not for happiness, reason is properly intended, and which must, therefore, be regarded as the supreme condition to which the private ends of man must, for the most part, be postponed.

For as reason is not competent to guide the will with certainty in regard to its objects and the satisfaction of all our wants (which it to some extent even multiplies), this being an end to which an implanted instinct would have led with much greater certainty; and since, nevertheless, reason is imparted to us as a practical faculty, i.e., as one which is to have influence on the *will,* therefore, admitting that nature generally in the distribution of her capacities has adapted the means to the end, its true destination must be to produce a *will,* not merely good as a *means* to something else, but *good in itself,* for which reason was absolutely necessary. This will, then, though not indeed the sole and complete good, must be the supreme good and the condition of every other, even of the desire of happiness. Under these circumstances, there is nothing inconsistent with the wisdom of nature in the fact that the cultivation of the reason, which is requisite for the first and unconditional purpose, does in many ways interfere, at least in this life, with the attainment of the second, which is always conditional, namely, happiness. Nay, it may even reduce it to nothing, without nature thereby failing of her purpose. For reason recognizes the establishment of a good will as its highest practical destination, and in attaining this purpose is capable only of a satisfaction of its own proper kind, namely, that from the attainment of an end, which end again is determined by reason only, notwithstanding that this may involve many a disappointment to the ends of inclination.

We have then to develop the notion of a will which deserves to be highly esteemed for itself, and is good without a view to anything further, a notion which exists already in the sound natural understanding, requiring rather to be cleared up than to be taught, and which in estimating the value of our actions always takes the first place, and constitutes the condition of all the rest. In order to do this we will take the notion of duty, which includes that of a good will although implying certain subjective restrictions and hindrances. These, however, far from concealing it, or rendering it unrecognizable, rather bring it out by contrast, and make it shine forth so much the brighter.

I omit here all actions which are already recognized as inconsistent with duty, although they may be useful for this or that purpose, for with these the question whether they are done *from duty* cannot arise at all, since they even conflict with it. I also set aside those actions which really conform to duty, but to which men have *no* direct *inclination*, performing them because they are impelled thereto by some other inclination. For in this case we can readily distinguish whether the action which agrees with duty is done *from duty*, or from a selfish view. It is much harder to make this distinction when the action accords with duty, and the subject has besides a *direct* inclination to it. For example, it is always a matter of duty that a dealer should not overcharge an inexperienced purchaser, and wherever there is much commerce the prudent tradesman does not overcharge, but keeps a fixed price for everyone, so that a child buys of him as well as any other. Men are thus *honestly* served; but this is not enough to make us believe that the tradesman has so acted from duty and from principles of honesty: his own advantage required it: it is out of the question in this case to suppose that he might besides have a direct inclination in favor of the buyers, so that, as it were, from love he should give no advantage to one over another. Accordingly the action was done neither from duty nor from direct inclination, but merely with a selfish view.

On the other hand, it is a duty to maintain one's life; and, in addition, everyone has also a direct inclination to do so. But on this account the often anxious care which most men take for it has no intrinsic worth, and their maxim has no moral import. They preserve their life *as duty requires,* no doubt, but not *because duty requires.* On the other hand, if adversity and hopeless sorrow have completely taken away the relish for life, if the unfortunate one, strong in mind, indignant at his fate rather than desponding or dejected, wishes for death, and yet preserves his life without loving it—not from inclination or fear, but from duty—then this maxim has a moral worth.

To be beneficent when we can is a duty; and besides this, there are many minds so sympathetically constituted that, without any other motive of vanity or self-interest, they find a pleasure in spreading joy around them, and can take delight in the satisfaction of others so far as it is their own work. But I maintain that in such a case an action of this kind, however proper, however amiable it may be, has nevertheless no true moral worth, but is on a level with other inclinations, e.g., the inclination to honor, which, if it is happily directed to that which is in fact of public utility and accordant with duty, and consequently honorable, deserves praise and encouragement, but not esteem. For the maxim lacks the moral import, namely, that such actions be done *from duty,* not from inclination. Put the case that the mind of that philanthropist were clouded by sorrow of his own, extinguishing all sympathy with the lot of others, and that while he still has the power to benefit others in distress, he is not touched by their trouble because he is absorbed with his own; and now suppose that he tears himself out of this dead insensibility, and performs the action without any inclination to it, but simply from duty, then only has his action its genuine moral worth. Further still; if nature has put little sympathy in the heart of this or that man; if he, supposed to be an upright man, is by temperament cold and indifferent to the sufferings of others, perhaps because in respect of his own he is provided with the special gift of patience and fortitude, and supposes, or even requires, that others should have the same—and such a man would certainly not be the meanest product of nature—but if nature had not specially framed him for a philanthropist, would he not still find in himself a source from [which to derive a far] higher worth than [any] that a good-natured temperament [might have]?

Unquestionably. It is just in this that the moral worth of the character is brought out which is incomparably the highest of all, namely, that he is beneficent, not from inclination, but from duty.

To secure one's own happiness is a duty, at least indirectly; for discontent with one's condition, under a pressure of many anxieties and amidst unsatisfied wants, might easily become a great *temptation to transgression of duty.* But here again, without looking to duty, all men have already the strongest and most intimate inclination to happiness, because it is just in this idea that all inclinations are combined in one total. But the precept of happiness is often of such a sort that it greatly interferes with some inclinations, and yet a man cannot form any definite and certain conception of the sum of satisfaction of all of them which is called happiness. It is not then to be wondered at that a single inclination, definite both as to what it promises and as to the time within which it can be gratified, is often able to overcome such a fluctuating idea, and that a gouty patient, for instance, can choose to enjoy what he likes, and to suffer what he may, since, according to his calculation, on this occasion at least, he has [only] not sacrificed the enjoyment of the present moment to a possibly mistaken expectation of a happiness which is supposed to be found in health. But even in this case, if the general desire for happiness did not influence his will, and supposing that in his particular case health was not a necessary element in this calculation, there yet remains in this, as in all other cases, this law, namely, that he should promote his happiness not from inclination but from duty, and by this would his conduct first acquire true moral worth.

It is in this manner, undoubtedly, that we are to understand those passages of Scripture also in which we are commanded to love our neighbor, even our enemy. For love, as an affection, cannot be commanded, but beneficence for duty's sake may; even though we are not impelled to it by any inclination—nay, are even repelled by a natural and unconquerable aversion. This is *practical* love, and not *pathological*—a love which is seated in the will, and not in the propensions of sense—in principles of action and not of tender sympathy; and it is this love alone which can be commanded.

The second [1] proposition is: That an action done from duty derives its moral worth, *not from the purpose* which is to be attained by it, but from the maxim by which it is determined, and therefore does not depend on the realization of the object of the action, but merely on the *principle of volition* by which the action has taken place, without regard to any object of desire. It is clear from what precedes that the purposes which we may have in view in our actions, or their effects regarded as ends and springs of the will, cannot give to actions any unconditional or moral worth. In what, then, can their worth lie, if it is not to consist in the will and in reference to its expected effect? It cannot lie anywhere but in the *principle of the will* without regard to the ends which can be attained by the action. For the will stands between its *a priori* principle, which is formal, and its *a posteriori* spring, which is material, as between two roads, and as it must be determined by something, it follows that it must be determined by the formal principle of volition when an action is done from duty, in which case every material principle has been withdrawn from it.

The third proposition, which is a consequence of the two preceding, I would express thus: *Duty is the necessity of acting from respect for the law.* I may have *inclination* for an object as the effect of my proposed action, but I cannot have *respect* for it, just for this reason, that it is an effect and not an energy of will. Similarly, I cannot have respect for inclination, whether my own or another's; I can at most, if my own, approve it; if another's, sometimes even love it; i.e., look on it as favorable to my own interest. It is only what is connected with my will as a principle, by no means as an effect—what does not subserve my inclination, but overpowers it, or at least in case of choice excludes it from its calculation—in other words, simply the law of itself which can be an object of respect, and hence a command. Now an action done from duty must wholly exclude the influence of inclination, and with it every object of the will, so that nothing remains which can determine the will except objectively the *law,* and subjectively *pure respect* for this practical law, and consequently the maxim [2] that I

---

[1] The first proposition was the law that conduct acquires true moral worth not from inclination or pleasure but from duty, as discussed above. [P.P.W.]

[2] A *maxim* is the subjective principle of volition. The objective principle (i.e., that which would also serve subjectivity as a practical principle to all rational beings if reason had full power over the faculty of desire) is the practical *law*.

should follow this law even to the thwarting of all my inclinations.

Thus the moral worth of an action does not lie in the effect expected from it, nor in any principle of action which requires to borrow its motive from this expected effect. For all these effects—agreeableness of one's condition, and even the promotion of the happiness of others—could have been also brought about by other causes, so that for this there would have been no need of the will of a rational being; whereas, it is in this alone that the supreme and unconditional good can be found. The pre-eminent good which we call moral can, therefore, consist in nothing else than *the conception of law* in itself, *which certainly is only possible in a rational being*, in so far as this conception, and not the expected effect, determines the will. This is a good which is already present in the person who acts accordingly, and we have not to wait for it to appear first in the result.[3]

But what sort of law can that be, the conception of which must determine the will, even without paying any regard to the effect expected from it, in order that this will may be called good absolutely and without qualification? As I have deprived the will of every impulse which could arise to it from obedience to any law, there remains nothing but the universal conformity of its actions to law in general, which alone is to serve the will as a principle, i.e., I am never to act otherwise than so *that I could also will that my maxim should become a universal law*. Here now, it is the simple conformity to law in general, without assuming any particular law applicable to certain actions, that serves the will as its principle, and must so serve it, if duty is not to be a vain delusion and a chimerical notion. The common reason of men in its practical judgments perfectly coincides with this, and always has in view the principle here suggested. Let the question be, for example: May I, when in distress, make a promise with the intention not to keep it? I readily distinguish here between the two significations which the question may

---

[3] It might be here objected to me that I take refuge behind the word *respect* in an obscure feeling, instead of giving a distinct solution of the question by a concept of the reason. But! although respect is a feeling, it is not a feeling *received* through influence, but is *self-wrought* by a rational concept, and, therefore, is specifically distinct from all feelings of the former kind, which may be referred either to inclination or fear. What I recognize immediately as a law for me, I recognize with respect. This merely signifies the consciousness that my will is *subordinate* to a law, without the intervention of other influences on my sense. The immediate determination of the will by the law, and the consciousness of this is called *respect*, so that this is regarded as an *effect* of the law on the subject, and not as the *cause* of it. Respect is properly the conception of a worth which thwarts my self-love. Accordingly it is something which is considered neither as an object of inclination nor

of fear, although it has something analogous to both. The *object* of respect is the *law* only, and that, the law which we impose on *ourselves*, and yet recognize as necessary in itself. As a law, we are subjected to it without consulting self-love; as imposed by us on ourselves, it is a result of our will. In the former aspect, it has an analogy to fear, in the latter to inclination. Respect for a person is properly only respect for the law (of honesty, etc.), of which he gives us an example. Since we also look on the improvement of our talents as a duty, we consider that we see in a person of talents, as it were, the *example of a law* (viz., to become like him in this by exercise), and this constitutes our respect. All so-called moral *interest* consists simply in *respect* for the law.

have: Whether it is prudent, or whether it is right, to make a false promise. The former may undoubtedly often be the case. I see clearly, indeed, that it is not enough to extricate myself from a present difficulty by means of this subterfuge, but it must be well considered whether there may not hereafter spring from this lie much greater inconvenience than that from which I now free myself, and as, with all my supposed *cunning*, the consequences cannot be so easily foreseen but that credit once lost may be much more injurious to me than any mischief which I seek to avoid at present, it should be considered whether it would not be more *prudent* to act herein according to a universal maxim, and to make it a habit to promise nothing except with the intention of keeping it. But it is soon clear to me that such a maxim will still only be based on the fear of consequences. Now it is a wholly different thing to be truthful from duty, and to be so from apprehension of injurious consequences. In the first case, the very notion of the action already implies a law for me; in the second case, I must first look about elsewhere to see what results may be combined with it which would affect myself. For to deviate from the principle of duty is beyond all doubt wicked; but to be unfaithful to my maxim of prudence may often be very advantageous to me, although to abide by it is certainly safer. The shortest way, however, and an unerring one, to discover the answer to this question whether a lying promise is consistent with duty, is to ask myself, Should I be content that my maxim (to extricate myself from difficulty by a false promise) should hold good as a universal law, for myself as well as

for others? and should I be able to say to myself, "Everyone may make a deceitful promise when he finds himself in a difficulty from which he cannot otherwise extricate himself"? Then I presently become aware that while I can will the lie, I can by no means will that lying should be a universal law. For with such a law there would be no promises at all, since it would be in vain to allege my intention in regard to my future actions to those who would not believe this allegation, or if they overhastily did so would pay me back in my own coin. Hence my maxim, as soon as it should be made a universal law, would necessarily destroy itself.

I do not, therefore, need any far-reaching penetration to discern what I have to do in order that my will may be morally good. Inexperienced in the course of the world, incapable of being prepared for all its contingencies, I only ask myself: Canst thou also will that thy maxim should be a universal law? If not, then it must be rejected, and that not because of a disadvantage accruing from it to myself or even to others, but because it cannot enter as a principle into a possible universal legislation, and reason extorts from me immediate respect for such legislation. I do not indeed as yet *discern* on what this respect is based (this the philosopher may inquire), but at least I understand this, that it is an estimation of the worth which far outweighs all worth of what is recommended by inclination, and that the necessity of acting from *pure* respect for the practical law is what constitutes duty, to which every other motive must give place, because it is the condition of a will being good *in itself*, and the

worth of such a will is above everything.

Thus, then, without quitting the
moral knowledge of common human
reason, we have arrived at its principle. And although, no doubt, common men do not conceive it in such
an abstract and universal form, yet
they always have it really before their
eyes, and use it as the standard of
their decision. Here it would be easy
to show how, with this compass in
hand, men are well able to distinguish, in every case that occurs, what
is good, what bad, conformably to
duty or inconsistent with it, if, without in the least teaching them anything new, we only, like Socrates,
direct their attention to the principle
they themselves employ; and that,
therefore, we do not need science and
philosophy to know what we should
do to be honest and good, yea, even
wise and virtuous. Indeed, we might
well have conjectured beforehand
that the knowledge of what every
man is bound to do, and therefore
also to know, would be within the
reach of every man, even the commonest. Here we cannot forbear admiration when we see how great an
advantage the practical judgment has
over the theoretical in the common
understanding of men. In the latter,
if common reason ventures to depart
from the laws of experience and from
the perceptions of the senses it falls
into mere inconceivabilities and self-
contradictions, at least into a chaos
of uncertainty, obscurity, and instabil-
ity. But in the practical sphere, it is
just when the common understanding
excludes all sensible springs from
practical laws that its power of judgment begins to show itself to advantage. It then becomes even subtle,
whether it be that it chicanes with its

own conscience or with other claims
respecting what is to be called right,
or whether it desires for its own instruction to determine honestly the
worth of actions; and, in the latter
case, it may even have as good a hope
of hitting the mark as any philosopher
whatever can promise himself. Nay,
it is almost more sure of doing so,
because the philosopher cannot have
any other principle, while he may
easily perplex his judgment by a multitude of considerations foreign to the
matter, and so turn aside from the
right way. Would it not, therefore, be
wiser in moral concerns to acquiesce
in the judgment of common reason,
or at most, only to call in philosophy
for the purpose of rendering the system of morals more complete and
intelligible, and its rules more convenient for use (especially for disputation), but not so as to draw off the
common understanding from its happy
simplicity, or to bring it by means
of philosophy into a new path of inquiry and instruction?

Innocence is indeed a glorious
thing, only, on the other hand, it is
very sad that it cannot well maintain
itself, and is easily seduced. On this
account even wisdom—which otherwise consists more in conduct than in
knowledge—yet has need of science,
not in order to learn from it, but to
secure for its precepts admission and
permanence. Against all the commands of duty which reason represents to man as so deserving of
respect, he feels in himself a powerful counterpoise in his wants and inclinations, the entire satisfaction of
which he sums up under the name of
happiness. Now reason issues its commands unyieldingly, without promising
anything to the inclinations, and, as
it were, with disregard and contempt

for these claims, which are so impetuous, and at the same time so plausible, and which will not allow themselves to be suppressed by any command. Hence there arises a natural *dialectic,* i.e., a disposition to argue against these strict laws of duty and to question their validity, or at least their purity and strictness; and, if possible, to make them more accordant with our wishes and inclinations, that is to say, to corrupt them at their very source, and entirely to destroy their worth—a thing which even common practical reason cannot ultimately call good.

Thus is the *common reason of man* compelled to go out of its sphere, and to take a step into the field of a *practical philosophy,* not to satisfy any speculative want (which never occurs to it as long as it is content to be mere sound reason), but even on practical grounds, in order to attain in it information and clear instruction respecting the source of its principle, and the correct determination of it in opposition to the maxims which are based on wants and inclinations, so that it may escape from the perplexity of opposite claims, and not run the risk of losing all genuine moral principles through the equivocation into which it easily falls. Thus, when practical reason cultivates itself, there insensibly arises in it a dialectic which forces it to seek aid in philosophy, just as happens to it in its theoretic use; and in this case, therefore, as well as in the other, it will find rest nowhere but in a thorough critical examination of our reason.

QUESTIONS FOR DISCUSSION

1. Contrast Kant's conception of the absolute good of the good will with the ordinary notions that happiness, natural aptitudes, and the pleasures of sense, wealth, or fame constitute the supreme good.
2. What is Kant's view with respect to the relative ranking of instrumental and intrinsic values?
3. We often use people as means to helping us in matters of economic services, learning, health, travel, etc. Does this fact raise any moral problem from the standpoint of Kant's categorical imperative always to treat a person as an end in himself?
4. "Honesty is a good policy because its pays to be honest." Criticize this statement from Kantian ethical principles.
5. Kant's arguments against lying or breaking one's promise seem to appeal to certain undesirable empirical and social consequences. Is Kant inconsistent here?

John Stuart Mill (1806-1873)

3.5   Utilitarianism

There are few circumstances among those which make up the present condition of human knowledge more unlike what might have been expected, or more significant of the backward state in which speculation on the most important subjects still lingers, than the little progress which has been made in the decision of the controversy respecting the criterion of right and wrong. From the dawn of philosophy, the question concerning the *summum bonum,* or, what is the same thing, concerning the foundation of morality, has been accounted the main problem in speculative thought, has occupied the most gifted intellects and divided them into sects and schools, carrying on a vigorous warfare against one another. And after more than two thousand years the same discussions continue, philosophers are still ranged under the same contending banners, and neither thinkers nor mankind at large seem nearer to being unanimous on the subject than when the youth Socrates listened to the old Protagoras, and asserted (if Plato's dialogue be grounded on a real conversation) the theory of utilitarianism against the popular morality of the so-called sophist.

From *Utilitarianism* (1863), Chapters 1, 2, and 4.

It is true that similar confusion and uncertainty and, in some cases, similar discordance exist respecting the first principles of all the sciences, not excepting that which is deemed the most certain of them—mathematics, without much impairing, generally indeed without impairing at all, the trustworthiness of the conclusions of those sciences. An apparent anomaly, the explanation of which is that the detailed doctrines of a science are not usually deduced from, nor depend for their evidence upon, what are called its first principles. Were it not so, there would be no science more precarious, or whose conclusions were more insufficiently made out, than algebra, which derives none of its certainty from what are commonly taught to learners as its elements, since these, as laid down by some of its most eminent teachers, are as full of fictions as English law, and of mysteries as theology. The truths which are ultimately accepted as the first principles of a science are really the last results of metaphysical analysis, practiced on the elementary notions with which the science is conversant; and their relation to the science is not that of foundations to an edifice, but of roots to a tree, which may perform their office equally well though they be never dug down to and exposed to light. But though in science the particular truths precede the general theory, the contrary might be expected to be the case with a practical art, such as morals or legislation. All action is for the sake of some end, and rules of action, it seems natural to suppose, must take their whole character and color from the end to which they are subservient. When we engage in a pursuit, a clear and precise conception of what we are pursuing would seem to be the first thing we need, instead of the last we are to look forward to. A test of right and wrong must be the means, one would think, of ascertaining what is right or wrong, and not a consequence of having already ascertained it.

The difficulty is not avoided by having recourse to the popular theory of a natural faculty, a sense or instinct, informing us of right and wrong. For—besides that the existence of such a moral instinct is itself one of the matters in dispute—those believers in it who have any pretensions to philosophy have been obliged to abandon the idea that it discerns what is right or wrong in the particular case in hand, as our other senses discern the sight or sound actually present. Our moral faculty, according to all those of its interpreters who are entitled to the name of thinkers, supplies us only with the general principles of moral judgments; it is a branch of our reason, not of our sensitive, faculty; and must be looked to for the abstract doctrines of morality, not for perception of it in the concrete. The intuitive, no less than what may be termed the inductive, school of ethics insists on the necessity of general laws. They both agree that the morality of an individual action is not a question of direct perception, but of the application of a law to an individual case. They recognize also, to a great extent, the same moral laws, but differ as to their evidence and the source from which they derive their authority. According to the one opinion, the principles of morals are evident *a priori*, requiring nothing to command assent except that the meaning of the terms be understood. According to the other doctrine, right and wrong, as well as truth and falsehood, are questions of observation and experience. But both hold equally that morality must be deduced from principles; and the intuitive school affirm as strongly as the inductive that there is a science of morals. Yet they seldom attempt to make out a list of the *a priori* principles which are to serve as the premises of the science; still more rarely do they make any effort to reduce those various principles to one first principle, or common ground of obligation. They either assume the ordinary precepts of morals as of *a priori* authority, or they lay down as the common groundwork of those maxims some generalities much less obviously authoritative than the maxims themselves, and which have never succeeded in gaining popular acceptance. Yet to support their pretensions there ought either to be some one fundamental principle or law at the root of all morality, or, if there be several, there should be a determinate order of precedence among them; and the one principle, or the rule for deciding between the various principles when they conflict, ought to be self-evident.

To inquire how far the bad effects of this deficiency have been mitigated in practice, or to what extent the moral beliefs of mankind have been vitiated or made uncertain by the absence of any distinct recognition of an ultimate standard, would imply a complete survey and criticism of past and present ethical doctrine. It would, however, be easy to show that whatever steadiness or consistency these moral beliefs have attained has been mainly due to the tacit influence of a standard not recognized. Although the non-existence of an acknowledged first principle has made ethics not so much a guide as a consecration of men's actual sentiments, still, as men's sentiments, both in favor and of aversion, are greatly influenced by what they suppose to be the effect of things upon their happiness, the principle of utility, or, as Bentham latterly called it, the greatest happiness principle, has had a large share in forming the moral doctrines even of those who most scornfully reject its authority. Nor is there any school of thought which refuses to admit that the influence of actions on happiness is a most material and even predominant consideration in many of the details of morals, however unwilling to acknowledge it as the fundamental principle of morality and the source of moral obligation. I might go much further and say that to all those *a priori* moralists who deem it necessary to argue at all, utilitarian arguments are indispensable. It is not my present purpose to criticize these thinkers; but I cannot help referring, for illustration, to a systematic treatise by one of the most illustrious of them, the *Metaphysics of Ethics* by Kant. This remarkable man, whose system of thought will long remain one of the landmarks in the history of philosophical speculation, does, in the treatise in question, lay down a universal first principle as the origin and ground of moral obligation; it is this: "So act that the rule on which thou actest would admit of being adopted as a law by all rational beings." But when he begins to deduce from this precept any of the actual duties of morality, he fails, almost grotesquely, to show that there would be any contradiction, any logical (not to say physical) impossibility, in the adoption by all rational beings of the most outrageously immoral rules of conduct. All he knows is that the *consequences* of their universal adoption would be such as no one would choose to incur.

On the present occasion, I shall, without further discussion of the other theories, attempt to contribute something towards the understanding and appreciation of the "utilitarian" or "happiness" theory, and towards such proof as it is susceptible of. It is evident that this cannot be proof in the ordinary and popular meaning of the term. Questions of ultimate ends are not amenable to direct proof. Whatever can be proved to be good must be so by being shown to be a means to something admitted to be good without proof. The medical art is proved to be good by its conducing to health; but how is it possible to prove that health is good? The art of music is good, for the reason, among others, that it produces pleasure; but what proof is it possible to give that pleasure is good? If, then, it is asserted that there is a comprehensive formula, including all things which are in themselves good, and that whatever else is good is not so as an end but as a means, the formula may be accepted or rejected, but is not a subject of what is commonly understood by proof. We are not, however, to infer that its acceptance or rejection must depend on blind impulse, or arbitrary choice. There is a larger meaning of the word "proof," in which this question is as amenable to it as any other of the disputed questions of philosophy. The subject is within the cognizance of the rational faculty; and neither does that faculty deal with it solely in the way of intuition. Considerations may be presented capable of determining the intellect either to give or withhold its assent to the doctrine; and this is equivalent to proof. . . .

The creed which accepts as the foundation of morals "utility" or the "greatest happiness principle" holds that actions are right in proportion as they tend to promote happiness, wrong as they tend to produce the reverse of happiness. By happiness is intended pleasure, and the absence of pain; by unhappiness, pain, and the privation of pleasure. To give a clear view of the moral standard set up by the theory, much more requires to be said; in particular, what things it includes in the ideas of pain and pleasure; and to what extent this is left an open question. But these supplementary explanations do not affect the theory of life on which this theory of morality is grounded—namely, that pleasure and freedom from pain are the only things desirable as ends; and that all desirable things (which are as numerous in the utilitarian as in any other scheme) are desirable either for the pleasure inherent in themselves, or as means to the promotion of pleasure and the prevention of pain.

Now such a theory of life excites in many minds, and among them in some of the most estimable in feeling and purpose, inveterate dislike. To suppose that life has (as they express it) no higher end than pleasure—no

better and nobler object of desire and pursuit—they designate as utterly mean and groveling; as a doctrine worthy only of swine, to whom the followers of Epicurus were, at a very early period, contemptuously likened; and modern holders of the doctrine are occasionally made the subject of equally polite comparisons by its German, French, and English assailants.

When thus attacked, the Epicureans have always answered that it is not they, but their accusers, who represent human nature in a degrading light, since the accusation supposes human beings to be capable of no pleasures except those of which swine are capable. If this supposition were true, the charge could not be gainsaid, but would then be no longer an imputation; for if the sources of pleasure were precisely the same to human beings and to swine, the rule of life which is good enough for the one would be good enough for the other. The comparison of the Epicurean life to that of beasts is felt as degrading, precisely because a beast's pleasures do not satisfy a human being's conceptions of happiness. Human beings have faculties more elevated than the animal appetites and, when once made conscious of them, do not regard anything as happiness which does not include their gratification. I do not, indeed, consider the Epicureans to have been by any means faultless in drawing out their scheme of consequences from the utilitarian principle. To do this in any sufficient manner, many Stoic, as well as Christian, elements require to be included. But there is no known Epicurean theory of life which does not assign to the pleasures of the intellect, of the feelings and imagination, and of the moral sentiments, a much higher value of pleasures than to those of mere sensation. It must be admitted, however, that utilitarian writers in general have placed the superiority of mental over bodily pleasures chiefly in the greater permanency, safety, uncostliness, etc., of the former—that is, in their circumstantial advantages rather than in their intrinsic nature. And on all these points utilitarians have fully proved their case; but they might have taken the other and, as it may be called, higher ground with entire consistency. It is quite compatible with the principle of utility to recognize the fact that some kinds of pleasure are more desirable and more valuable than others. It would be absurd that, while, in estimating all other things, quality is considered as well as quantity, the estimation of pleasures should be supposed to depend on quantity alone.

If I am asked what I mean by difference of quality in pleasures, or what makes one pleasure more valuable than another merely as a pleasure, except its being greater in amount, there is but one possible answer. Of two pleasures, if there be one to which all or almost all who have experience of both give a decided preference, irrespective of a feeling of moral obligation to prefer it, that is the more desirable pleasure. If one of the two is, by those who are competently acquainted with both, placed so far above the other that they prefer it, even though knowing it to be attended with a greater amount of discontent, and would not resign it for any quantity of the other pleasure which their nature is capable of, we are justified in ascribing to the preferred enjoyment a superiority in quality so far outweighing quantity as to render it, in comparison, of small account.

Now it is an unquestionable fact that those who are equally acquainted with and equally capable of appreciating and enjoying both, do give a most marked preference to the manner of existence which employs their higher faculties. Few human creatures would consent to be changed into any of the lower animals for a promise of the fullest allowance of a beast's pleasures; no intelligent human being would consent to be a fool, no instructed person would be an ignoramus, no person of feeling and conscience would be selfish and base, even though they should be persuaded that the fool, the dunce, or the rascal is better satisfied with his lot than they are with theirs. They would not resign what they possess more than he for the most complete satisfaction of all the desires which they have in common with him. If they ever fancy they would, it is only in cases of unhappiness so extreme that to escape from it they would exchange their lot for almost any other, however undesirable in their own eyes. A being of higher faculties requires more to make him happy, is capable probably of more acute suffering, and certainly accessible to it at more points, than one of an inferior type; but in spite of these liabilities, he can never really wish to sink into what he feels to be a lower grade of existence. We may give what explanation we please of this unwillingness; we may attribute it to pride, a name which is given indiscriminately to some of the most and to some of the least estimable feelings of which mankind are capable; we may refer it to the love of liberty and personal independence, an appeal to which was with the Stoics one of the most effective means for the inculcation of it; to the love of power or to the love of excitement, both of which do really enter into and contribute to it; but its most appropriate appellation is a sense of dignity, which all human beings possess in one form or other, and in some, though by no means in exact, proportion to their higher faculties, and which is so essential a part of the happiness of those in whom it is strong that nothing which conflicts with it could be otherwise than momentarily an object of desire to them. Whoever supposes that this preference takes place at a sacrifice of happiness—that the superior being, in anything like equal circumstances, is not happier than the inferior—confounds the two very different ideas of happiness and content. It is indisputable that the being whose capacities of enjoyment are low has the greatest chance of having them fully satisfied; and a highly endowed being will always feel that any happiness which he can look for, as the world is constituted, is imperfect. But he can learn to bear its imperfections, if they are at all bearable; and they will not make him envy the being who is indeed unconscious of the imperfections, but only because he feels not at all the good which those imperfections qualify. It is better to be a human being dissatisfied than a pig satisfied; better to be Socrates dissatisfied than a fool satisfied. And if the fool, or the pig, are of a different opinion, it is because they only know their own side of the question. The other party to the comparison knows both sides. . . .

According to the greatest happiness principle, as above explained, the ultimate end, with reference to and for the sake of which all other things are desirable—whether we are considering our own good or that of other people—is an existence exempt as far as possible from pain, and as rich as possible in enjoyments, both in point of quantity and quality; the test of quality and the rule for measuring it against quantity being the preference felt by those who, in their opportunities of experience, to which must be added their habits of self-consciousness and self-observation, are best furnished with the means of comparison. This, being, according to the utilitarian opinion, the end of human action, is necessarily also the standard of morality, which may accordingly be defined "the rules and precepts for human conduct," by the observance of which an existence such as has been described might be, to the greatest extent possible, secured to all mankind; and not to them only, but, so far as the nature of things admits, to the whole sentient creation.

Against this doctrine, however, arises another class of objectors who say that happiness, in any form, cannot be the rational purpose of human life and action; because, in the first place, it is unattainable; and they contemptuously ask, What right hast thou to be happy?—a question which Mr. Carlyle clinches by the addition, What right, a short time ago, hadst thou even *to be?* Next they say that men can do *without* happiness; that all noble human beings have felt this, and could not have become noble but by learning the lesson of *Entsagen,* or renunciation; which lesson, thoroughly learnt and submitted to, they affirm to be the beginning and necessary condition of all virtue.

The first of these objections would go to the root of the matter were it well founded; for if no happiness is to be had at all by human beings, the attainment of it cannot be the end of morality or of any rational conduct. Though, even in that case, something might still be said for the utilitarian theory, since utility includes not solely the pursuit of happiness, but the prevention or mitigation of unhappiness; and if the former aim be chimerical, there will be all the greater scope and more imperative need for the latter, so long at least as mankind think fit to live, and do not take refuge in the simultaneous act of suicide recommended under certain conditions by Novalis. When, however, it is thus positively asserted to be impossible that human life should be happy, the assertion, if not something like a verbal quibble, is at least an exaggeration. If by happiness be meant a continuity of highly pleasurable excitement, it is evident enough that this is impossible. A state of exalted pleasure lasts only moments or in some cases, and with some intermissions, hours, or days, and is the occasional brilliant flash of enjoyment, not its permanent and steady flame. Of this the philosophers who have taught that happiness is the end of life were as fully aware as those who taunt them. The happiness which they meant was not a life of rapture; but moments of such, in an existence made up of few and transitory pains, many and various pleasures, with a decided predominance of the active over the passive, and having as the foundation of the whole not to expect more from life than it is capable of bestowing. A life thus composed, to those who have been fortunate enough to obtain it, has always appeared worthy of the name of happiness. And such an existence is even now the lot of many, during some considerable portion of their lives. The present wretched education and wretched social arrangements are the only real hindrance to its being attainable by almost all.

The objectors perhaps may doubt whether human beings, if taught to consider happiness as the end of life, would be satisfied with such a moderate share of it. But great numbers of mankind have been satisfied with much less. The main constituents of a satisfied life appear to be two, either of which by itself is often found sufficient for the purpose: tranquillity and excitement. With much tranquillity, many find that they can be content with very little pleasure; with much excitement, many can reconcile themselves to a considerable quantity of pain. There is assuredly no inherent impossibility of enabling even the mass of mankind to unite both, since the two are so far from being incompatible that they are in natural alliance, the prolongation of either being a preparation for, and exciting a wish for, the other. It is only those in whom indolence amounts to a vice that do not desire excitement after an interval of repose; it is only those in whom the need of excitement is a disease that feel the tranquillity which follows excitement dull and insipid, instead of pleasurable in direct proportion to the excitement which preceded it. When people who are tolerably fortunate in their outward lot do not find in life sufficient enjoyment to make it valuable to them, the cause generally is caring for nobody but themselves. To those who have neither public nor private affections, the excitements of life are much curtailed, and in any case dwindle in value as the time approaches when all selfish interests must be terminated by death; while those who leave after them objects of personal affection, and especially those who have also cultivated a fellow feeling with the collective interests of mankind, retain as lively an interest in life on the eve of death as in the vigor of youth and health. Next to selfishness, the principal cause which makes life unsatisfactory is want of mental cultivation. A cultivated mind—I do not mean that of a philosopher, but any mind to which the fountains of knowledge have been opened, and which has been taught, in any tolerable degree, to exercise its faculties—finds sources of inexhaustible interest in all that surrounds it: in the objects of nature, the achievements of art, the imaginations of poetry, the incidents of history, the ways of mankind, past and present, and their prospects in the future. It is possible, indeed, to become indifferent to all this, and that too without having exhausted a thousandth part of it, but only when one has had from the beginning no moral or human interest in these things, and has sought in them only the gratification of curiosity.

Now there is absolutely no reason in the nature of things why an amount of mental culture sufficient to give an intelligent interest in these objects of contemplation should not be the inheritance of everyone born in a civilized country. As little is there an inherent necessity that any human being should be a selfish egotist, devoid of every feeling or care but those which center in his own miserable individuality. Something far superior to this is sufficiently common even now, to give ample earnest of what the human species may be made. Genuine private affections and a sincere interest in the public good are possible, though in unequal degrees, to every rightly brought up human being. In a world in which there is so much to interest, so much to enjoy, and so much also to correct and improve, everyone who has this moderate amount of moral and intellectual requisites is capable of an existence which may be called enviable; and unless such a person, through bad laws or subjection to the will of others, is denied the liberty to use the sources of happiness within his reach, he will not fail to find this enviable existence, if he escape the positive evils of life, the great sources of physical and mental suffering—such as indigence, disease, and the unkindness, worthlessness, or premature loss of objects of affection. The main stress of the problem lies, therefore, in the contest with these calamities from which it is a rare good fortune entirely to escape; which, as things now are, cannot be obviated, and often cannot be in any material degree mitigated. Yet no one whose opinion deserves a moment's consideration can doubt that most of the great positive evils of the world are in themselves removable, and will, if human affairs continue to improve, be in the end reduced within narrow limits. Poverty, in any sense implying suffering, may be completely extinguished by the wisdom of society combined with the good sense and providence of individuals. Even that most intractable of enemies, disease, may be indefinitely reduced in dimensions by good physical and moral education and proper control of noxious influences, while the progress of science holds out a promise for the future of still more direct conquests over this detestable foe. And every advance in that direction relieves us from some, not only of the chances which cut short our own lives, but, what concerns us still more, which deprive us of those in whom our happiness is wrapt up. As for vicissitudes of fortune and other disappointments connected with worldly circumstances, these are principally the effect, either of gross imprudence, of ill-regulated desires, or of bad or imperfect social institutions. All the grand sources, in short, of human suffering are in a great degree, many of them almost entirely, conquerable by human care and effort; and though their removal is grievously slow—though a long succession of generations will perish in the breach before the conquest is completed, and this world becomes all that, if will and knowledge were not wanting, it might easily be made —yet every mind sufficiently intelligent and generous to bear a part, however small and inconspicuous, in the endeavor will draw a noble enjoyment from the contest itself, which he would not for any bribe in the form of selfish indulgence consent to be without.

And this leads to the true estimation of what is said by the objectors concerning the possibility and the obligation of learning to do without happiness. Unquestionably it is possible to do without happiness; it is done involuntarily by nineteen-twentieths of mankind, even in those parts of our present world which are least deep in barbarism; and it often has to be done voluntarily by the hero or the martyr, for the sake of something which he prizes more than his individual happiness. But this something, what is it, unless the happiness of others or some of the requisites of happiness? It is noble to be capable of resigning entirely one's own portion of happiness,

or chances of it; but, after all, this self-sacrifice must be for some end; it is not its own end; and if we are told that its end is not happiness but virtue, which is better than happiness, I ask, would the sacrifice be made if the hero or martyr did not believe that it would earn for others immunity from similar sacrifices? Would it be made if he thought that his renunciation of happiness for himself would produce no fruit for any of his fellow creatures, but to make their lot like his, and place them also in the condition of persons who have renounced happiness? All honor to those who can abnegate for themselves the personal enjoyment of life when by such renunciation they contribute worthily to increase the amount of happiness in the world; but he who does it or professes to do it for any other purpose is no more deserving of admiration than the ascetic mounted on his pillar. He may be an inspiriting proof of what men *can* do, but assuredly not an example of what they *should*.

Though it is only in a very imperfect state of the world's arrangements that anyone can best serve the happiness of others by the absolute sacrifice of his own, yet, so long as the world is in that imperfect state, I fully acknowledge that the readiness to make such a sacrifice is the highest virtue which can be found in man. I will add that in this condition of the world, paradoxical as the assertion may be, the conscious ability to do without happiness gives the best prospect of realizing such happiness as is attainable. For nothing except that consciousness can raise a person above the chances of life, by making him feel that, let fate and fortune do their worst, they have not power to subdue him; which, once felt, frees him from excess of anxiety concerning the evils of life, and enables him, like many a Stoic in the worst times of the Roman Empire, to cultivate in tranquillity the sources of satisfaction accessible to him, without concerning himself about the uncertainty of their duration any more than about their inevitable end.

Meanwhile, let utilitarians never cease to claim the morality of self-devotion as a possession which belongs by as good a right to them as either to the Stoic or to the Transcendentalist. The utilitarian morality does recognize in human beings the power of sacrificing their own greatest good for the good of others. It only refuses to admit that the sacrifice is itself a good. A sacrifice which does not increase or tend to increase the sum total of happiness, it considers as wasted. The only self-renunciation which it applauds is devotion to the happiness, or to some of the means of happiness, of others, either of mankind collectively or of individuals within the limits imposed by the collective interests of mankind.

I must again repeat what the assailants of utilitarianism seldom have the justice to acknowledge, that the happiness which forms the utilitarian standard of what is right in conduct is not the agent's own happiness but that of all concerned. As between his own happiness and that of others, utilitarianism requires him to be as strictly impartial as a disinterested and benevolent spectator. In the golden rule of Jesus of Nazareth, we read the complete spirit of the ethics of utility. "To do as you would be done by," and "to love your neighbor as yourself," constitute the ideal perfection of utilitarian morality. As the means of making the nearest approach to this ideal, utility would enjoin, first,

that laws and social arrangements should place the happiness or (as, speaking practically, it may be called) the interest of every individual as nearly as possible in harmony with the interest of the whole; and, secondly, that education and opinion, which have so vast a power over human character, should so use that power as to establish in the mind of every individual an indissoluble association between his own happiness and the good of the whole, especially between his own happiness and the practice of such modes of conduct, negative and positive, as regard for the universal happiness prescribes; so that not only he may be unable to conceive the possibility of happiness to himself, consistently with conduct opposed to the general good, but also that a direct impulse to promote the general good may be in every individual one of the habitual motives of action, and the sentiments connected therewith may fill a large and prominent place in every human being's sentient existence. If the impugners of the utilitarian morality represented it to their own minds in this its true character, I know not what recommendation possessed by any other morality they could possibly affirm to be wanting to it; what more beautiful or more exalted developments of human nature any other ethical system can be supposed to foster, or what springs of action, not accessible to the utilitarian, such systems rely on for giving effect to their mandates. . . .

OF WHAT SORT OF PROOF THE PRINCIPLE OF UTILITY IS SUSCEPTIBLE

It has already been remarked that questions of ultimate ends do not admit of proof, in the ordinary acceptation of the term. To be incapable of proof by reasoning is common to all first principles, to the first premises of our knowledge, as well as to those of our conduct. . . .

Questions about ends are, in other words, questions about what things are desirable. The utilitarian doctrine is that happiness is desirable, as an end; all other things being only desirable as means to that end. What ought to be required of this doctrine, what conditions is it requisite that the doctrine should fulfill—to make good its claim to be believed?

The only proof capable of being given that an object is visible is that people actually see it. The only proof that a sound is audible is that people hear it; and so of the other sources of our experience. In like manner, I apprehend, the sole evidence it is possible to produce that anything is desirable is that people do actually desire it. If the end which the utilitarian doctrine proposes to itself were not, in theory and practice, acknowledged to be an end, nothing could ever convince any person that it was so. No reason can be given why the general happiness is desirable, except that each person, so far as he believes it to be attainable, desires his own happiness. This, however, being a fact, we have not only all the proof which the case admits of, but all which it is possible to require, that happiness is a good; that each person's happiness is a good to that person, and the general happiness, therefore, a good to the aggregate of all persons. Happiness has made out its title as *one* of the ends of conduct, and consequently one of the criteria of morality.

QUESTIONS FOR DISCUSSION

1. Why does Mill regard moral principles based on intuition (or a moral instinct) as *a priori* as those based on observation and experience?
2. On what is Bentham's "greatest happiness" principle of utility based?
3. What is Mill's criticism of Kant's categorical imperative as a universal ethical rule allegedly independent of experience?
4. How does Mill criticize the Epicurean theory of pleasure as the supreme good (*summum bonum*)?
5. Is Mill correct in saying that the spirit of the ethics of utilitarianism is in the golden rule of Jesus?
6. Examine critically Mill's argument from analogy that the only proof that anything is universally desirable is that it is universally desired, just as the only proof that anything is visible is that people actually see it.
7. Compare Mill's utilitarian ethics with Spinoza's definition of the good as relative to what is known to be useful to mankind.

John Dewey (1859-1952)

3.6   Does Human Nature Change?

I have come to the conclusion that those who give different answers to the question I have asked in the title of this article are talking about different things. This statement in itself, however, is too easy a way out of the problem to be satisfactory. For there is a real problem, and so far as the question is a practical one instead of an academic one, I think the proper answer is that human nature *does* change.

By the practical side of the question, I mean the question whether or not important, almost fundamental, changes in the ways of human belief and action have taken place and are capable of still taking place. But to put this question in its proper perspective, we have first to recognize the sense in which human nature does not change. I do not think it can be shown that the innate needs of men have changed since man became man or that there is any evidence that they will change as long as man is on the earth.

By "needs" I mean the inherent demands that men make because of their constitution. Needs for food and

From *The Rotarian* (February, 1938). Reprinted by permission of the editor of *The Rotarian*.

drink and for moving about, for example, are so much a part of our being that we cannot imagine any condition under which they would cease to be. There are other things not so directly physical that seem to me equally engrained in human nature. I would mention as examples the need for some kind of companionship; the need for exhibiting energy, for bringing one's powers to bear upon surrounding conditions; the need for both co-operation with and emulation of one's fellows for mutual aid and combat alike; the need for some sort of aesthetic expression and satisfaction; the need to lead and to follow; etc.

Whether my particular examples are well chosen or not does not matter so much as does recognition of the fact that there are some tendencies so integral a part of human nature that the latter would not be human nature if they changed. These tendencies used to be called instincts. Psychologists are now more chary of using that word than they used to be. But the word by which the tendencies are called does not matter much in comparison to the fact that human nature has its own constitution.

Where we are likely to go wrong after the fact is recognized that there is something unchangeable in the structure of human nature is the inference we draw from it. We suppose that the manifestation of these needs is also unalterable. We suppose that the manifestations we have got used to are as natural and as unalterable as are the needs from which they spring.

The need for food is so imperative that we call the persons insane who persistently refuse to take nourishment. But what kinds of food are wanted and used is a matter of acquired habit influenced by both physical environment and social custom. To civilized people today, eating human flesh is an entirely unnatural thing. Yet there have been peoples to whom it seemed natural because it was socially authorized and even highly esteemed. There are well-accredited stories of persons, needing support from others, who have refused palatable and nourishing foods because they were not accustomed to them; the alien foods were so "unnatural" they preferred to starve rather than eat them.

Aristotle spoke for an entire social order as well as for himself when he said that slavery existed by nature. He would have regarded efforts to abolish slavery from society as an idle and utopian effort to change human nature where it was unchangeable. For according to him it was not simply the desire to be a master that was engrained in human nature. There were persons who were born with such an inherently slavish nature that it did violence to human nature to set them free.

The assertion that human nature cannot be changed is heard when social changes are urged as reforms and improvements of existing conditions. It is always heard when the proposed changes in institutions or conditions stand in sharp opposition to what exists. If the conservative were wiser, he would rest his objections in most cases, not upon the unchangeability of human nature, but upon the inertia of custom; upon the resistance that acquired habits offer to change after they are once acquired. It is hard to teach an old dog new tricks and it is harder yet to teach society to adopt customs which are contrary to those which have long prevailed. Conservatism of this type would be intelligent and it would compel those wanting change not only to moderate their pace, but also to ask how the changes they desire could be introduced with a minimum of shock and dislocation.

Nevertheless, there are few social changes that can be opposed on the ground that they are contrary to human nature itself. A proposal to have a society get along without food and drink is one of the few that are of this kind. Proposals to form communities in which there is no cohabitation have been made and the communities have endured for a time. But they are so nearly contrary to human nature that they have not endured long. These cases are almost the only ones in which social change can be opposed simply on the ground that human nature cannot be changed.

Take the institution of war, one of the oldest, most socially reputable of all human institutions. Efforts for stable peace are often opposed on the ground that man is by nature a fighting animal and that this phase of his nature is unalterable. The failure of peace movements in the past can be cited in support of this view. In fact, however, war is as much a social pattern as is the domestic slavery which the ancients thought to be an immutable fact.

I have already said that, in my opinion, combativeness is a constituent part of human nature. But I have also said that the manifestations of these native elements are subject to change because they are affected by custom and tradition. War does not exist because man has combative instincts, but because social conditions and forces have led, almost forced, these "instincts" into this channel.

There are a large number of other channels in which the need for combat has been satisfied, and there are other channels not yet discovered or explored into which it could be led with equal satisfaction. There is war against disease, against poverty, against insecurity, against injustice, in which multitudes of persons have found full opportunity for the exercise of their combative tendencies.

The time may be far off when men will cease to fulfill their need for combat by destroying each other and when they will manifest it in common and combined efforts against the forces that are enemies of all men equally. But the difficulties in the way are found in the persistence of certain acquired social customs and not in the unchangeability of the demand for combat.

Pugnacity and fear are native elements of human nature. But so are pity and sympathy. We send nurses and physicians to the battlefield and provide hospital facilities as "naturally" as we change bayonets and discharge machine guns. In early times there was a close connection between pugnacity and fighting, for the latter was done largely with the fists. Pug-

nacity plays a small part in generating wars today. Citizens of one country do not hate those of another nation by instinct. When they attack or are attacked, they do not use their fists in close combat, but throw shells from a great distance at persons whom they have never seen. In modern wars, anger and hatred come after the war has started; they are effects of war, not the cause of it.

It is a tough job sustaining a modern war; all the emotional reactions have to be excited. Propaganda and atrocity stories are enlisted. Aside from such extreme measures there has to be definite organization, as we saw in the World War, to keep up the morale of even non-combatants. And morale is largely a matter of keeping emotions at a certain pitch; and unfortunately fear, hatred, suspicion, are among the emotions most easily aroused.

I shall not attempt to dogmatize about the causes of modern wars. But I do not think that anyone will deny that they are social rather than psychological, though psychological appeal is highly important in working up a people to the point where they want to fight and in keeping them at it. I do not think, moreover, that anyone will deny that economic conditions are powerful among the social causes of war. The main point, however, is that whatever the sociological causes, they are affairs of tradition, custom, and institutional organization, and these factors belong among the changeable manifestations of human nature, not among the unchangeable elements.

I have used the case of war as a typical instance of what is changeable and what is unchangeable in human nature, in their relation to schemes of social change. I have selected the case because it is an extremely difficult one in which to effect durable changes, not because it is an easy one. The point is that the obstacles in the way are put there by social forces which do change from time to time, not by fixed elements of human nature. This fact is also illustrated in the failures of pacifists to achieve their ends by appeal simply to sympathy and pity. For while, as I have said, the kindly emotions are also a fixed constituent of human nature, the channel they take is dependent upon social conditions.

There is always a great outburst of these kindly emotions in time of war. Fellow feeling and the desire to help those in need are intense during war, as they are at every period of great disaster that comes home to observation or imagination. But they are canalized in their expression; they are confined to those upon our side. They occur simultaneously with manifestation of rage and fear against the other side, if not always in the same person, at least in the community generally. Hence the ultimate failure of pacifist appeals to the kindly elements of native human nature when they are separated from intelligent consideration of the social and economic forces at work.

William James made a great contribution in the title of one of his essays, *The Moral Equivalents of War*. The very title conveys the point I am making. Certain basic needs and emotions are permanent. But they are capable of finding expression in ways that are radically different from the ways in which they now currently operate.

An even more burning issue emerges when there is proposed any fundamental change in economic institutions and relations. Proposals for such sweeping change are among the commonplaces of our time. On the other hand, the proposals are met by the statement that the changes are impossible because they involve an impossible change in human nature. To this statement, advocates of the desired changes are only too likely to reply that the present system or some phase of it is contrary to human nature. The argument *pro* and *con* then gets put on the wrong ground.

As a matter of fact, economic institutions and relations are among the manifestations of human nature that are most susceptible of change. History is living evidence of the scope of these changes. Aristotle, for example, held that paying interest is unnatural, and the Middle Ages re-echoed the doctrine. All interest was usury, and it was only after economic conditions had so changed that payment of interest was a customary and in that sense a "natural" thing, that usury got its present meaning.

There have been times and places in which land was held in common and in which private ownership of land would have been regarded as the most monstrous of unnatural things. There have been other times and places when all wealth was possessed by an overlord and his subjects held wealth, if any, subject to his pleasure. The entire system of credit so fundamental in contemporary financial and industrial life is a modern invention. The invention of the joint stock company with limited liability of individuals has brought about a great change from earlier facts and conceptions of property. I think the need of owning something is one of the native elements of human nature. But it takes either ignorance or a very lively fancy to suppose that the system of ownership that exists in the United States in 1938, with all its complex relations and its interweaving with legal and political supports, is a necessary and unchangeable product of an inherent tendency to appropriate and possess.

Law is one of the most conservative of human institutions; yet through the cumulative effect of legislation and judicial decisions it changes, sometimes at a slow rate, sometimes rapidly. The changes in human relations that are brought about by changes in industrial and legal institutions then react to modify the ways in which human nature manifests itself, and this brings about still further changes in institutions, and so on indefinitely.

It is for these reasons that I say that those who hold that proposals for social change, even of rather a profound character, are impossible and utopian because of the fixity of human nature, confuse the resistance to change that comes from acquired habits with that which comes from original human nature. The savage, living in a primitive society, comes nearer to being a purely "natural" human being than does civilized man. Civilization itself is the product of altered human nature. But even the savage is bound by a mass of tribal customs and transmitted beliefs that modify his original nature, and it is these acquired habits that make it so difficult to transform him into a civilized human being.

The revolutionary radical, on the other hand, overlooks the force of engrained habits. He is right, in my opinion, about the indefinite plasticity of human nature. But he is wrong in thinking that patterns of desire, be-

lief, and purpose do not have a force comparable to the momentum of physical objects once they are set in motion, and comparable to the inertia, the resistance to movement, possessed by these same objects when they are at rest. Habit, not original human nature, keeps things moving most of the time, about as they have moved in the past.

If human nature is unchangeable, then there is no such thing as education and all our efforts to educate are doomed to failure. For the very meaning of education is modification of native human nature in formation of those new ways of thinking, of feeling, of desiring, and of believing that are foreign to raw human nature. If the latter were unalterable, we might have training but not education. For training, as distinct from education, means simply the acquisition of certain skills. Native gifts can be trained to a point of higher efficiency without that development of new attitudes and dispositions which is the goal of education. But the result is mechanical. It is like supposing that while a musician may acquire by practice greater technical ability, he cannot rise from one plane of musical appreciation and creation to another.

The theory that human nature is unchangeable is thus the most depressing and pessimistic of all possible doctrines. If it were carried out logically, it would mean a doctrine of predestination from birth that would outdo the most rigid of theological doctrines. For according to it, persons are what they are at birth and nothing can be done about it, beyond the kind of training that an acrobat might give to the muscular system with which he is originally endowed. If a person is born with criminal tendencies, a criminal he will become and remain. If a person is born with an excessive amount of greed, he will become a person living by predatory activities at the expense of others; and so on. I do not doubt at all the existence of differences in natural endowment. But what I am questioning is the notion that they doom individuals to a fixed channel of expression. It is difficult indeed to make a silk purse out of a sow's ear. But the particular form which say, a natural musical endowment will take depends upon the social influences to which he is subjected. Beethoven in a savage tribe would doubtless have been outstanding as a musician, but he would not have been the Beethoven who composed symphonies.

The existence of almost every conceivable kind of social institution at some time and place in the history of the world is evidence of the plasticity of human nature. This fact does not prove that all these different social systems are of equal value, materially, morally, and culturally. The slightest observation shows that such is not the case. But the fact in proving the changeability of human nature indicates the attitude that should be taken toward proposals for social changes. The question is primarily whether they, in special cases, are desirable or not. And the way to answer that question is to try to discover what their consequences would be if they were adopted. Then if the conclusion is that they are desirable, the further question is how they can be accomplished with a minimum of waste, destruction, and needless dislocation.

In finding the answer to this ques-

tion, we have to take into account the force of existing traditions and customs; of the patterns of action and belief that already exist. We have to find out what forces already at work can be reinforced so that they move toward the desired change and how the conditions that oppose change can be gradually weakened. Such questions as these can be considered on the basis of fact and reason.

The assertion that a proposed change is impossible because of the fixed constitution of human nature diverts attention from the question of whether or not a change is desirable and from the other question of how it shall be brought about. It throws the question into the arena of blind emotion and brute force. In the end, it encourages those who think that great changes can be produced offhand and by the use of sheer violence.

When our sciences of human nature and human relations are anything like as developed as are our sciences of physical nature, their chief concern will be with the problem of how human nature is most effectively modified. The question will not be whether it is capable of change, but of how it is to be changed under given conditions. This problem is ultimately that of education in its widest sense. Consequently, whatever represses and distorts the processes of education that might bring about a change in human dispositions with the minimum of waste puts a premium upon the forces that bring society to a state of deadlock, and thereby encourages the use of violence as a means of social change.

QUESTIONS FOR DISCUSSION

1. In what specific senses of "innate needs" does human nature *not* change?
2. How does the "manifestation" of need differ from its "innateness"? Illustrate.
3. How common is Aristotle's belief that some men are born to be masters and some slaves? Criticize the evidence or grounds for this belief.
4. Is war inevitable because men are by "nature" or by "instinct" fighting animals? Explain why Dewey's answer is negative.
5. Why does Dewey regard habits as more powerful than instincts in shaping conduct and social institutions? Illustrate from the ways in which customs change in religion, industry, law, and education.

Morris Ginsberg (1889-1970)

3.7   Psychoanalysis and Ethics

We have now to deal with the question whether psychoanalytic theory can provide the basis for a rational ethic. The morality so far discussed is super-ego morality. Its basis is the authority of the father or father-substitute internalized. If all the rules of morals come to us from without as commands, is there any rational method for choosing between them? We have seen that Freud himself nowhere claims to have worked out a rational ethic, yet in various places in his writings he holds out hopes for such an enterprise. In general, he has great faith in the power of rational inquiry. He dismisses subjectivist or

From M. Ginsberg, *On the Diversity of Morals* (London: Heinemann Educational Books, Ltd., 1956), pp. 323-32. Reprinted by permission of the author and publisher.

relativist views of knowledge as 'intellectual nihilism'.[1] Though our knowledge of nature is affected by the structure of the mind, this does not make knowledge necessarily subjective, since the structure of the mind itself can be scientifically investigated, and the errors arising out of subjective factors allowed for. The theory of Psychoanalysis, so often accused of exaggerating the strength of the non-rational elements in human nature, rests in fact on the assumption that these are subject to rational control. The function of analysis is to extend the area of conscious control by bringing what was unconscious into consciousness, to ensure, as we are told, that 'where id was there shall ego be.'

[1] *New Introductory Lectures*, p. 224.

The ultimate ideal is the 'primacy of reason' and on the moral side, 'the brotherhood of man and the reduction of suffering'.[2] An ethic of this sort, it is suggested, requires another foundation than that of religion.[3] Only hints are given, however, where such a foundation is to be sought for. It is suggested, for example, that a scientific ethic might play a therapeutic role analogous to that which the physician plays in dealing with neuroses in the individual. The analyst frequently finds that he has to do battle with the individual's conscience, which is often excessively severe and makes demands which he cannot possibly fulfil and which threaten his happiness. What Freud calls the 'cultural super-ego' as represented, for example, in the ethical injunctions of the higher religions, calls for similar therapy. They set up standards too high for human nature and are therefore easily defeated by those who take a more realistic view. Thus the command to love your neighbour as yourself is no defence against human aggressiveness. 'Such a grandiose inflation of love only lowers its value and cannot remove the evil.' It is not clear, however, by what principles such an examination of idealistic codes is to be guided. The analogy with individual therapy breaks down. In dealing with the individual, the analyst assumes a 'normal' environment and considers behaviour as neurotic which is in conflict with it. No such standard is available for societies, since there exists no scientific, comparative study of the pathology of civilizations, and we therefore cannot tell what is normal and what pathological.

Despite the lack of comparative data Freud has ventured on a general statement of the role of repression in the history of culture. Our civilization, he argued already in his early papers, is in the main founded on the suppression of instincts.[4] The theme is developed more fully in his sombre essay on the Malaise of Culture.[5] Both the libidinal and the aggressive tendencies have to be repressed if civilization is to flourish. Sexual energy has to be diverted from its original object to make possible the formation of wider groups and to keep them together. This is one of the reasons for the rules and regulations by which all known societies seek to control the sexual relations of their members. Another reason is to be found in the fact that love is needed to control hate. The aggressive impulses which, in Freud's view, are an ineradicable and primary element in human nature, could destroy mankind if left to work themselves out. To control them, aim-inhibited sexual energy has had to be used. The process involves the building up of the super-ego by the aid of which aggression is turned inwards and prevented from expressing itself directly. Following this line of thought Freud might have said with Buddha that 'hatred does not cease by hatred; by love alone is hate destroyed.' Freud, however, does not share the hope held out by the spiritual religions of the ultimate triumph of love. Eros is pitted against Thanatos and

---

[2] *The Future of an Illusion*, p. 93.
[3] *New Introductory Lectures on Psycho-Analysis*, p. 215.

[4] *'Civilized' Sexual Morality and Modern Nervousness*, 1908. *Collected Papers* II.
[5] *Das Unbehagen in der Kultur*, 1930. English translation, *Civilization and its Discontents*.

the antagonism between them will in all probability never be overcome.

In urging that the growth of civilization depends on the control or repression of fundamental instinctive drives Freud is saying what, in their different ways, the moralists of all ages have said. From the point of view of ethical theory the important problem is whether it is possible to elicit from his teaching any principles for determining the limits of this inevitable repression or any standards for estimating the loss and gain involved. As regards 'civilized' sexual morality his discussion in the early papers at least is tentative and inconclusive. It is possible, he allows, to maintain that the cultural gains derived from sexual restraint outweigh its manifestly injurious results. But he finds himself unable to balance gain and loss with any precision. And he ends by saying that as judged by individual happiness it is very doubtful whether the sacrifices demanded can be justified—so long, at least, as we are 'still so insufficiently purged of hedonism as to include a certain degree of individual happiness among the aims of our cultural development'.[6] As regards the effect of sexual restraint on cultural activities, Freud's conclusions are equally tentative. He does not, of course, claim to have undertaken any comparative study of moral codes from this point of view. But on the basis of his own personal impressions he believes that 'the relation between possible sublimation and indispensable sexual activity naturally varies very much in different persons, and indeed with the various kinds of occupation.' He does not support the view that 'sexual abstinence helps to shape energetic self-reliant men of action, or original thinkers, bold pioneers and reformers; far more often it produces "good" weaklings who later become lost in the crowd that tend to follow painfully the initiative of strong characters.'[7] In the end it emerges that while Freud is convinced that the code of sexual morality in Western societies urgently needs to be reformed, he is not prepared as a physician to come forward with definite proposals. This was not to be expected. But the discussion throws light on the sort of ethical theory that Freud might have developed, had he chosen to pursue the matter further. It is clear that the ethical criteria to which he appeals in criticizing existing moral codes are individual happiness and cultural advance. Furthermore, he realizes that we have not the knowledge that would be necessary for any accurate application of these criteria, and he is

---

[6] *Sexual Morality and Nervousness*, 1908. *Collected Papers*, II, 99.

[7] Dr J. D. Unwin has produced an elaborate argument to show that in primitive societies there is a definite relation between sexual continence and degree of cultural advance (*Sex and Culture*, 1934). But the criteria which he uses both for cultural condition and sexual regulation are very vague and the evidence he adduces is not sufficient to justify a generalization so far-reaching. (Cf. my review of this book in *Nature*, CXXXV, 1935, p. 205.) Westermarck, who made a very comprehensive survey of the available information, concludes that there is no relation between the toleration of unchastity and the degree of culture, and that on the contrary chastity is more respected in the lowest tribes than in the higher ones. In *The Material Culture and Social Institutions of the Simpler Peoples* (1915), L. T. Hobhouse, G. C. Wheeler and the present writer found that the evidence was not sufficient to establish a universal association between sexual regulation and cultural grade as judged by economic criteria.

obviously disturbed by the fact that gains in one direction are often countered by loss in the other.

In the later writings the problem thus raised reappears in another form. Freud finds that there is a certain antagonism between the growth of culture and the development of the individual. The antagonism results, in the first place, from the struggle between Eros and Thanatos. The aim of cultural development is the unification of all mankind. This can only be achieved by a repression of aggression. But every time we control our aggression, it turns against the self. The result is an increasing tension between the ego and the super-ego which is felt as a sense of guilt. It seems to be assumed that the larger the group, the greater the difficulty of achieving libidinal unity and the greater the cost in human happiness. The progress of mankind can only be achieved at the expense of an intensification of the sense of guilt 'until perhaps it may swell to a magnitude that individuals can hardly support.' [8] No wonder that Freud thought the sense of guilt constituted the most important problem in the evolution of culture.

In the second place, there is, according to Freud, not only this irreconcilable conflict between the life and death instincts but a fissure within the libido itself, which from the ethical point of view is at least as important. The growth of the individual is shaped by the pleasure principle, that is by the desire of the individual for his own happiness. No doubt he can only attain this through membership in a community. But this condition is sometimes represented by

Freud as a sort of unfortunate necessity, as something he would be better without. For culture, as we have seen, is necessarily restrictive of the individual; it demands instinctual renunciation. There is thus, as Freud says,[9] dissension in the camp of the libido itself, a struggle between the striving for happiness and the impulse towards union with others. Freud asserts that this contest will ultimately be resolved in the case of the individual and perhaps also in the future of civilization. But unfortunately the theme is not further developed.

The ethical theory that Freud's discussion suggests is one of enlightened self-interest, that is self-interest purged of unconscious distortions, fears and anxieties not rooted in the objective situation. What such self-interest would require can only emerge after therapeutic analysis both of the individuals and societies. But it is difficult to believe that psychology will ever by itself solve the fundamental problems of human relations, or in the Freudian terminology, the problem of the right apportionment of libidinal attachment as between self and other 'objects'. A theory of ethics which rests on the assumption that in dealing justly with others the individual can after all secure his own happiness has all the air of an 'illusion' which, from the Freudian point of view, should be relegated to the infantile stages of the development of morality.

It is, I think, remarkable that while Freud and his followers have so much to say about love, they pay hardly any attention to justice. The only reference I can find is in Freud's *Group Psychology and the Psychology of the Ego*. 'Social justice', we are told,

---

[8] *Civilization and its Discontents*, p. 116.

[9] Ibid., p. 136.

'means that we deny ourselves many things so that others may have to do without them as well, or what is the same thing, may not be able to ask for them.' The demand for equality among the members of a group is said to be rooted in the jealousy aroused against those who would monopolize the love of the leader, just as their sense of community rests on their common renunciation of his exclusive love. This reduction of humanity and justice to envy and jealousy is somewhat mitigated by his interpretation of Eros as a force working for unity and harmony. But the two sides of his theory, ultimately due to the vagueness and ambiguity of the concept of the libido, are nowhere satisfactorily brought into relation, and on the whole the 'egoistic' trend in his thought predominates. It is difficult to see how such a conception of human nature can ever provide the basis for a rational ethic.

The most important problems of ethics centre round the theory of justice and in dealing with it Psychoanalysis is, I think, at its weakest. I see no reason, from the purely psychological side, for accepting the Freudian view of the origins of the sense of justice. Neither in the history of the individual or of civilization can this be shown to be rooted predominantly in the desire that no one shall fare better than ourselves. It owes at least as much to the power of sympathy, that is the power of entering in imagination into the situation of another and seeing it as though it were our own. Above all there is a rational element in it which the Freudian analysis completely ignores. The core of justice is the demand for equality and this is based at bottom on the rejection of arbitrariness, the recogni-

tion that individuals ought not to be treated differently unless a reasonable ground can be given for so treating them. I can see no ground for regarding this demand as merely emotional. If I say that 'one man's good is of as much intrinsic worth as the like good of another,' I certainly do not mean that 'the emotion which I experience in knowing that one man is benefited or injured is the same as that which I should experience in the case of any other.' This latter statement would be manifestly untrue in many instances but the recognition of its falsity has no bearing on the truth or falsity of my recognition of the principle of equality as binding on me. The difficulties in the theory of equality begin to emerge when we try to think out the grounds which justify differential treatment. On these again psychology may throw some light, but in the end value judgments have to be made, which, though ineffectual if lacking in emotional warmth, do not depend for their validity on the strength of the emotional response.

In sum, the issue that psychoanalytic theories of ethics have to face is that with which all naturalistic ethics are confronted. The problem is whether moral judgements express desires, strivings or emotions, or whether they go beyond what is actually desired to what *ought* to be desired. It seems to me that psychoanalysts suffer from what might be called an 'ought phobia'. They show too great an anxiety to explain the 'ought' away, and they tend to pass from the indicative to the imperative mood without realizing the implications of the transition. Thus, for example, Professor Flugel in his very illuminating study of the psychological basis of morals is in search of an ethic purged of anger and aggression and one that would make its appeal to reason. Yet reason is, in his view, concerned with means and not with ends, which in the last resort are set by 'orexis' or desire. The moral criterion which is finally adopted, however, clearly goes beyond what individuals actually desire to what they ought to desire, or, if you like, to what they would desire if they were rational. This criterion is the free and spontaneous expression of the instincts in so far as this is compatible with harmony not only in the individual but in society. Is this ideal then 'orectic' or cognitive? Again when we are told that increasing sociality and increasing individualization are complementary aspects of moral evolution, is this a statement of fact or of what ought to be fact? We have seen that according to Freud the conflict between individual and social development is far from being resolved, and Professor Flugel also points out that the compromise which has to be effected between socialization and individualization remains one of the most acute problems of modern democracy.[10] To set up social harmony as an ideal is to describe a form of life held to be desirable, not one which is necessarily desired. If the test is to be found in what people actually desire, the impulses making for discord may prove more powerful, or no less powerful, than those making for harmony. Despite a good deal that is attractive in Professor Flugel's exposition I feel that in the end he leaves undefined the relation between the striving and the cognitive elements in the moral judgement. He says that in a scientific handling of human relations 'we must substitute a cognitive

and psychological approach for an emotional and a moral one.'[11] But this, I think, would be not to explain morality, but to explain it away.

I turn now to the views of Erich Fromm, which in important respects involve a departure from Freudian theory. In the first place, his conception of human nature is not as individualistic, or asocial, as he takes Freud's to be. He has a different conception of both the love and hate elements in the human mind. Man is fundamentally social in that he needs to be related to others, to escape aloneness, to belong or to be needed. Destructiveness on the other hand is the result of a baulking of vitality, not an inherent or primary need to hurt or destroy. In the second place, he distinguishes more radically than the Freudians between what he calls an 'authoritarian' conscience and a 'humanistic' conscience. The former is the voice of an internalized external authority, the super-ego of Freudian theory. The latter is not 'the internalized voice of an authority we are eager to please and are afraid of displeasing; it is our own voice, present in every human being and independent of external rewards and sanctions.'[12] It is the expression of our true selves', 'the reaction of our total personality to its proper functioning or disfunctioning'. It bids us develop fully and harmoniously, that is 'to realize ourselves, to become what we potentially are'.

Here we are back full circle to theories long familiar to philosophers, but now claiming to be derived from empirical psychology. While there is

---

[10] *Man, Morals and Society*, p. 253.

[11] *Man, Morals and Society*, p. 255.
[12] *Man for Himself*, p. 158

a great deal that is very helpful in Fromm's analysis of the conditions of harmonious development, he does not seem to succeed any better than the Freudians in making the transition from what is or may be to what ought to be. To say that we should aim at becoming what we potentially are is not illuminating, since we are potentially evil as well as good and what we need is a criterion for distinguishing between them. The appeal to the 'real' or 'true' self is purely verbal, since the real self is not the self as it is but as it ought to be. Furthermore, the formula of self-realization leaves out of consideration the central problem of ethics—that of the relation between self and others. In the end, it is not any form of self-fulfilment that is desirable, but only that which is compatible with the fulfilment of others. Clearly such an end goes far beyond what any particular individuals actually desire, and it may require them to abandon or sacrifice a good deal of what they so desire. The philosophical problem of the principles of justice thus remains. It seems to me that writers like Fromm and Karen Horney are too optimistic in assuming that these can be discovered by 'listening to ourselves'. What we may thus hear may not be very enlightening. The conditions of social harmony have to be discovered; they will not follow automatically from the striving towards self-realization, even if each individual is 'true to himself'.

An interesting approach to the ethical aspects of Psychoanalysis is to be found in the various attempts that have been made to clarify the concept of a 'normal' mind. It soon becomes clear that from the point of view of mental health the 'normal' is not equivalent to the 'well adjusted'. Adjustment is a relation between the individual and his environment, and it is obvious that not every environment is equally likely to elicit what is best in the minds it moulds. . . .

QUESTIONS FOR DISCUSSION

1. What is the rational or scientific function of psychoanalysis with respect to sexual and aggressive impulses, and how is that function related to the religious ethics of love?
2. Is there an inevitable moral conflict between the development of the individual and the evolution of culture, and why did Freud claim that the sense of guilt is so important a problem for cultural growth?
3. What do you think of Ginsberg's criticisms of Freud's theory of "enlightened self-interest" and the "illusion" of altruism as moral guides?
4. How does one distinguish psychological and sociological analysis from ethics? Explain: "Value judgments do not depend for their validity on the strength of emotional response."
5. Do Fromm's and Horney's ideas of "true self-realization" deal adequately with the problems of justice or social harmony? Give the arguments pro and con, and your reasons for favoring either side.

R. M. Hare (1919-   )

3.8   The Language of Morals

PRESCRIPTIVE LANGUAGE

1.1 If we were to ask of a person
'What are his moral principles?' the
way in which we could be most sure
of a true answer would be by studying what he *did*. He might, to be sure,
profess in his conversation all sorts of
principles, which in his actions he
completely disregarded; but it would
be when, knowing all the relevant
facts of a situation, he was faced with
choices or decisions between alternative courses of action, between alternative answers to the question 'What
shall I do?', that he would reveal in
what principles of conduct he really
believed. The reason why actions are
in a peculiar way revelatory of moral
principles is that the function of moral
principles is to guide conduct. The
language of morals is one sort of prescriptive language. And this is what
makes ethics worth studying: for the
question 'What shall I do?' is one that
we cannot for long evade; the problems of conduct, though sometimes
less diverting than crossword puzzles,
have to be solved in a way that crossword puzzles do not. We cannot wait

From R. M. Hare, *The Language of
Morals*, 1952, Chapter I. Reprinted by permission of the Clarendon Press, Oxford.

to see the solution in the next issue,
because on the solution of the problems depends what happens in the
next issue. Thus, in a world in which
the problems of conduct become every
day more complex and tormenting,
there is a great need for an understanding of the language in which
these problems are posed and answered. For confusion about our moral
language leads, not merely to theoretical muddles, but to needless practical
perplexities.

An old-fashioned, but still useful,
way of studying anything is *per genus
et differentiam;* if moral language belongs to the genus 'prescriptive language', we shall most easily understand its nature if we compare and
contrast first of all prescriptive language with other sorts of language,
and then moral language with other
sorts of prescriptive language. That,
in brief, is the plan of this book.
I shall proceed from the simple to the
more complex. I shall deal first with
the simplest form of prescriptive language, the ordinary imperative sentence. The logical behaviour of this
type of sentence is of great interest to
the student of moral language because,
in spite of its comparative simplicity,
it raises in an easily discernible form
many of the problems which have be-

set ethical theory. Therefore, although it is no part of my purpose to 'reduce' moral language to imperatives, the study of imperatives is by far the best introduction to the study of ethics; and if the reader does not at once see the relevance to ethics of the earlier part of the discussion, I must ask him to be patient. Neglect of the principles enunciated in the first part of this book is the source of many of the most insidious confusions in ethics.

From singular imperatives I shall proceed to universal imperatives or principles. The discussion of these, and of how we come to adopt or reject them, will give me an opportunity of describing the processes of teaching and learning, and the logic of the language that we use for these purposes. Since one of the most important uses of moral language is in moral teaching, the relevance of this discussion to ethics will be obvious.

I shall then go on to discuss a kind of prescriptive language which is more nearly related to the language of morals than is the simple imperative. This is the language of non-moral value-judgements—all those sentences containing words like 'ought', 'right', and 'good' which are not moral judgements. I shall seek to establish that many of the features which have caused trouble to students of ethics are also displayed by these sorts of sentence—so much so that a proper understanding of them does much to elucidate the problems of ethics itself. I shall take the two most typical moral words 'good' and 'ought' in turn, and shall discuss first their non-moral uses, and then their moral ones; in each case I hope to show that these uses have many features in common. In conclusion I shall relate the logic of 'ought' and 'good', in both moral and

non-moral contexts, to the logic of imperatives by constructing a logical model in which artificial concepts, which could to some extent do duty for the value-words of ordinary language, are defined in terms of a modified imperative mood. This model is not to be taken too seriously; it is intended only as a very rough schematization of the preceding discussion, which itself contains the substance of what I have to say.

Thus the classification of prescriptive language which I propose may be represented as follows:

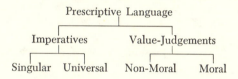

This classification is rough only; it will be made more precise in the course of the book; for example, it will be seen that the so-called 'universal imperatives' of ordinary language are not proper universals. Nor do I wish to suggest that the classification is exhaustive; there are, for example, many different kinds of singular imperatives, and of non-moral value-judgements; and there are other kinds of imperatives besides singular and universal. But the classification is good enough to begin with, and explains the plan of this book [*The Language of Morals*].

1.2 The writers of elementary grammar books sometimes classify sentences according as they express statements, commands, or questions. This classification is not exhaustive or rigorous enough for the logician. For example, logicians have devoted much labour to showing that sentences in the indicative mood may be of very various logical characters, and that the classification of them all under the one name 'statements' may lead to serious error if it makes us ignore the important differences between them. We shall in the later part of this book see how one kind of indicative sentence, that which expresses value-judgements, behaves logically in a quite different way from the ordinary indicative sentence.

Imperatives, likewise, are a mixed bunch. Even if we exclude sentences like 'Would I were in Granchester!' which are dealt with by some grammarians in the same division of their books as imperatives, we still have, among sentences that are in the imperative mood proper, many different kinds of utterance. We have military orders (parade-ground and otherwise), architects' specifications, instructions for cooking omelets or operating vacuum cleaners, pieces of advice, requests, entreaties, and countless other sorts of sentence, many of whose functions shade into one another. The distinction between these various kinds of sentence would provide a nice logician with material for many articles in the philosophical periodicals; but in a work of this character it is necessary to be bold. I shall therefore follow the grammarians and use the single term 'command' to cover all these sorts of thing that sentences in the imperative mood express, and within the class of commands make only some very broad distinctions. The justification for this procedure is that I hope to interest the reader in features that are common to all, or nearly all, these types of sentence; with their differences he is no doubt familiar enough. For the same reason I shall use the word 'statement' to cover whatever is expressed by typical indicative sentences, if there be such. I shall be drawing a contrast, that is to say, between sentences like 'Shut the door' and sentences like 'You are going to shut the door'.

It is difficult to deny that there is a difference between statements and commands; but it is far harder to say just what the difference is. It is not merely one of grammatical form; for if we had to study a newly discovered language we should be able to identify those grammatical forms which were used for expressing statements and commands respectively, and should call these forms 'indicative' and 'imperative' (if the language were constructed in such a way as to make this distinction useful). The distinction lies between the meanings which the different grammatical forms convey. Both are used for talking about a subject-matter, but they are used for talking about it in different ways. The two sentences 'You are going to shut the door' and 'Shut the door' are both about your shutting the door in the immediate future; but what they say about it is quite different. An indicative sentence is used for telling someone that something is the case; an imperative is not—it is used for telling someone to make something the case.

1.3 It is well worth the moral philosopher's while examining some of the theories which have been, or which might be, held about the way in which imperatives have meaning. They offer a most arresting parallel to similar theories about moral judgements, and this parallel indicates that there may be some important logical similarity between the two. Let us first consider two theories, similar to the type of ethical theory to which I shall later give the name 'naturalist' (5.3). Both are attempts to 'reduce' imperatives to indicatives. The first does this by representing them as expressing statements about the mind of the speaker. Just as it has been held that 'A is right' means 'I approve of A', so it might be held that 'Shut the door' means 'I want you to shut the door'. There is on the colloquial plane no harm in saying this; but it may be very misleading philosophically. It has the consequence that if I say 'Shut the door' and you say (to the same person) 'Do not shut the door', we are not contradicting one another; and this is odd. The upholder of the theory may reply that although there is no contradiction, there is a disagreement in wishes, and that this is sufficient to account for the feeling we have that the two sentences are somehow incompatible with one another (that 'not' has the same function as in the sentence 'You are not going to shut the door'). But there remains the difficulty that the sentence 'Shut the door' seems to be about shutting the door, and not about the speaker's frame of mind, just as instructions for cooking omelets ('Take four eggs, etc.') are instructions about eggs, not introspective analyses of the psyche of Mrs. Beeton. To say that 'Shut the door' means the same as 'I want you to shut the door' is like saying that 'You are going to shut the door' means the same as 'I believe that you are going to shut the door'. In both cases it seems strange to represent a remark about shutting the door as a remark about what is going on in my mind. But in fact neither the word 'believe' nor the word 'want' will bear this interpretation. 'I believe that you are going to shut the door' is not (except in a highly figurative way) a statement about my mind; it is a tentative statement about your shutting the door, a more hesitant version of 'You are going to shut the door'; and similarly, 'I want you to shut the door' is not a statement about my mind but a polite way of saying the imperative 'Shut the door'. Unless we understand the logic of 'You are going to shut the door', we cannot understand the logic of 'I believe that you are going to shut the door'; and similarly unless we understand 'Shut the door' we are unlikely to understand 'I want you to shut the door'. The theory, therefore, explains nothing; and the parallel ethical theory is in the same case; for 'I approve of A' is merely a more complicated and circumlocutory way of saying 'A is right'. It is not a statement, verifiable by observation, that I have a recognizable feeling or recurrent frame of mind; it is a value-judgement; if I ask 'Do I approve of A?' my answer is a moral decision, not an observation of introspectible fact. 'I approve of A' would be unintelligible to someone who did not understand 'A is right', and the explanation is a case of *obscurum per obscurius*.[1]

1.4   The second attempt to reduce imperatives to indicatives which I wish to consider is that of Dr. H. G. Bohnert.[2] This interesting suggestion may be summarized (I hope without injustice) by the statement that 'Shut the door' means the same as 'Either you are going to shut the door, or X will happen', where X is understood to be something bad for the person addressed. A similar theory would be that it meant the same as 'If you do

---

[1] Explaining something obscure by means of something even more obscure.

[2] 'The Semiotic Status of Commands', *Philosophy of Science*, XII (1945), p. 302.

not shut the door, X will happen'. This theory is parallel to ethical theories of the sort which equate 'A is right' with 'A is conducive to Y' where Y is something regarded by the generality as good, for example pleasure or the avoidance of pain. We shall see later that value-expressions sometimes acquire—by reason of the constancy of the standards by which they are applied—a certain descriptive force; thus if, in a society whose standards are markedly utilitarian, we say 'The Health Service has done a lot of good', everyone knows that we are implying that the Health Service has averted a lot of pain, anxiety, etc. Similarly, in the case of imperatives which are to a high degree 'hypothetical' (3.2) because we quickly realize, to the attainment of what end, or the prevention of what untoward result, they are directed, Bohnert's analysis is plausible. To take his own example, 'Run', said in a burning house, is somewhat similar in intention to 'Either you run or you burn'. But in cases where the end aimed at is not so easily recognized (the imperative being only to a small degree, or not at all, 'hypothetical') the hearer may be quite at a loss to understand, on this analysis, what he is to supply after the word 'or'. It is very difficult to see how a sentence like 'Please tell your father that I called' would be analysed on Bohnert's theory. It is, of course, always possible to terminate the analysis 'or something bad will happen'; but this expedient succeeds only by reintroducing into the analysis a prescriptive word; for 'bad' is a value-word, and therefore prescriptive. And similarly, teleological theories of ethics which interpret 'right' as 'conducive to Z', where 'Z' is a value-word such as 'satisfaction' or 'happiness', only

store up for themselves the difficulty of analysing such words.

The temptation to reduce imperatives to indicatives is very strong, and has the same source as the temptation to analyse value-words in the way called 'naturalistic'. This is the feeling that the 'proper' indicative sentence, of which there is thought to be only one kind, is somehow above suspicion in a way that other sorts of sentence are not; and that therefore, in order to put these other sorts of sentence above suspicion, it is necessary to show that they are *really* indicatives. This feeling was intensified when the so-called 'verificationist' theory of meaning became popular. This theory, which is in many ways a very fruitful one in its proper sphere, holds, to put it roughly, that a sentence does not have meaning unless there is something that would be the case if it were true. Now this is a very promising account of one of the ways in which a certain class of sentences (the typical indicatives) have meaning. Obviously, if a sentence is claimed to express a statement of fact, and yet we have no idea what would be the case if it were true, then that sentence is (to us) meaningless. But if this criterion of meaningfulness, which is useful in the case of statements of fact, is applied indiscriminately to types of utterance which are not intended to express statements of fact, trouble will result. Imperative sentences do not satisfy this criterion, and it may be that sentences expressing moral judgements do not either; but this only shows that they do not express statements in the sense defined by the criterion; and this sense may be a narrower one than that of normal usage. It does not mean that they are meaningless, or even that their meaning is of such a character that no logical rules can be given for their employment.[3]

1.5 The feeling, that only 'proper indicatives' are above suspicion, can survive (surprisingly) the discovery that there are perfectly good significant sentences of our ordinary speech which are not reducible to indicatives. It survives in the assumption that any meaning which is discovered for these sentences must necessarily be of some logically inferior status to that of indicatives. This assumption has led philosophers such as Professor A. J. Ayer, in the course of expounding their most valuable researches into the logical nature of moral judgements, to make incidental remarks which have raised needless storms of protest.[4] The substance of Ayer's theory is that moral judgements do not ordinarily function in the same way as the class of indicative sentences marked out by his verification-criterion. But by his way of stating his view, and his assimilation of moral judgements to other (quite distinct) types of sentence which are also marked off from typical indicatives by this criterion, he stirred up dust which has not yet subsided. All this might be closely paralleled by a similar treatment of imperatives—and it seems that writers of the same general line of thought as Ayer would have said the same sort of thing about imperatives as they did about moral judgements. Suppose that we recognize the obvious fact that imperatives are not like typical indicatives. Sup-

pose, further, that we regard only typical indicatives as above suspicion. It will be natural then to say 'Imperatives do not state anything, they only express wishes'. Now to say that imperatives express wishes is, like the first theory which we considered, unexceptionable on the colloquial plane; we would indeed say, if someone said 'Keep my name out of this', that he had expressed a wish to have his name kept out of it. But nevertheless the extreme ambiguity of the word 'express' may generate philosophical confusion. We speak of expressing statements, opinions, beliefs, mathematical relations, and so on; and if it is in one of these senses that the word is used, the theory, though it tells us little, is harmless. But unfortunately it is also used in ways which are unlike these; and Ayer's use (in speaking of moral judgements) of the word 'evince' as its rough synonym was dangerous. Artists and composers and poets are said to express their own and our feelings; oaths are said to express anger; and dancing upon the table may express joy. Thus to say that imperatives express wishes may lead the unwary to suppose that what happens when we use one, is this: we have welling up inside us a kind of longing, to which, when the pressure gets too great for us to bear, we give vent by saying an imperative sentence. Such an interpretation, when applied to such sentences as 'Supply and fit to door mortise dead latch and plastic knob furniture', is unplausible. And it would seem that value-judgements also may fail to satisfy the verification-criterion, and indeed be in some sense, like imperatives, prescriptive, without having this sort of thing said about them. It is perfectly unexceptionable, on the colloquial plane, to say that the sen-

---

[3] See my article 'Imperative Sentences', *Mind,* LVIII (1949), p. 21, from which some material is here used.

[4] See especially *Language, Truth and Logic,* 2nd ed., pp. 108-9. For a later and more balanced statement, see 'On the Analysis of Moral Judgments', *Philosophical Essays,* pp. 231 ff.

tence 'A is good' is used to express approval of A *(The Shorter Oxford English Dictionary* says: 'Approve: . . . to pronounce to be good'); but it is philosophically misleading if we think that the approval which is expressed is a peculiar warm feeling inside us. If the Minister of Local Government expresses approval of my town plan by getting his underlings to write to me saying 'The Minister approves of your plan' or 'The Minister thinks your plan is the best one', I shall in no circumstances confirm the letter by getting a private detective to observe the Minister for signs of emotion. In this case, to have such a letter sent *is* to approve.

1.6 There could be no analogue, in the case of singular imperatives, of the 'attitude' variety of the approval theory of value-judgements,[5] but it is possible to construct such a theory about *universal* imperative sentences. If someone said 'Never hit a man when he is down', it would be natural to say that he had expressed a certain attitude towards such conduct. It is extremely hard to define exactly this attitude or give criteria for recognizing it, just as it is difficult to say exactly what *moral* approval is as opposed to other sorts of approval. The only safe way of characterizing the attitude which is expressed by a universal imperative is to say 'The attitude that one should not (or should) do so and so'; and the only safe way of characterizing the attitude which is expressed by a moral judgement is to say 'The attitude that it is wrong (or right) to do so and so'. To maintain an attitude of 'moral' approval' towards a certain practice is to have a

disposition to think, on the appropriate occasions, that it is right; or, if 'think' itself is a dispositional word, it is simply to think that it is right; and our thinking that it is right may be betrayed or exhibited—behaviourists would say constituted—by our acting in certain ways (above all, doing acts of the sort in question when the occasion arises; next, saying that they are right; applauding them in other ways, and so on). But there is in all this nothing to explain just *what* one thinks when one thinks that a certain sort of act is right. And similarly, if we said that 'Never hit a man when he is down' expressed an attitude that one should not hit, etc. (or an attitude of aversion from hitting, or a 'contra-attitude' towards hitting), we should not have said anything that would be intelligible to someone who did not understand the sentence which we were trying to explain.

I wish to emphasize that I am not seeking to refute any of these theories. They have all of them the characteristic that, if put in everyday terms, they say nothing exceptionable so far as their main contentions go; but when we seek to understand how they explain the philosophical perplexities which generated them, we are either forced to interpret them in such a way as to render them unplausible, or else find that they merely set the same problems in a more complicated way. Sentences containing the word 'approve' are so difficult of analysis that it seems perverse to use this notion to explain the meaning of moral judgements which we learn to make years before we learn the word 'approve'; and similarly, it would be perverse to explain the meaning of the imperative mood in terms of wishing or any other feeling or attitude; for we learn how

---

[5] See, for example, C. L. Stevenson, *Ethics and Language.*

to respond to and use commands long before we learn the comparatively complex notions of 'wish', 'desire', 'aversion', etc.

1.7 We must now consider another group of theories which have often been held concurrently with the group just considered. These hold that the function in language of either moral judgements or imperatives (which the theories often equate) is to affect causally the behaviour or emotions of the hearer. Professor R. Carnap writes:

> But actually a value-statement is nothing else than a command in a misleading grammatical form. It may have effects upon the actions of men, and these effects may either be in accordance with our wishes or not; but it is neither true nor false.[6]

and Professor Ayer writes:

> Ethical terms do not serve only to express feeling. They are calculated also to arouse feeling, and so to stimulate action. Indeed some of them are used in such a way as to give the sentences in which they occur the effect of commands.[7]

More recently this sort of view has been elaborated by Professor Stevenson.[8] Here again we have a type of theory which may be on the colloquial plane harmless, but which suggests philosophical errors by seeming to assimilate the processes of using a command or a moral judgement to other processes which are in fact markedly dissimilar.

It is indeed true of imperative sentences that if anyone, in using them, is being sincere or honest, he intends that the person referred to should *do* something (namely, what is commanded). This is indeed a test of sincerity in the case of commands, just as a statement is held to be sincere only if the speaker believes it. And there are similar criteria, as we shall later see, for sincerely assenting to commands and statements that have been given or made by someone else. But this is not quite what the theories suggest. They suggest, rather, that the function of a command is to affect the hearer causally, or get him to do something; and to say this may be misleading. In ordinary parlance there is no harm in saying that in using a command our intention is to get someone to do something; but for philosophical purposes an important distinction has to be made. The processes of *telling* someone to do something, and *getting* him to do it, are quite distinct, logically, from each other.[9] The distinction may be elucidated by considering a parallel one in the case of statements. To tell someone that something is the case is logically distinct from getting (or trying to get) him to believe it. Having told someone that something is the case we may, if he is not disposed to believe what we say, start on a quite different process of trying to get him to believe it (trying to persuade or convince him that what we have said is true). No one, in seeking to explain the function of indicative sentences, would say that they were attempts to persuade someone that something is the case. And there is no more reason for saying that commands are attempts to persuade or

---

[6] *Philosophy and Logical Syntax*, p. 24.
[7] *Language, Truth and Logic*, 2nd ed., p. 108.
[8] *Ethics and Language*, especially p. 21.

[9] For a fuller treatment of this question see my article, "Freedom of the Will," *Aristotelian Society*, Supplementary Vol. XXV (1951), 201, from which I have used some material here.

get someone to do something; here, too, we first tell someone what he is to do, and then, if he is not disposed to do what we say, we may start on the wholly different process of trying to get him to do it. Thus the instruction already quoted 'Supply and fit to door mortise dead latch and plastic knob furniture' is not intended to *galvanize* joiners into activity; for such a purpose other means are employed.

This distinction is important for moral philosophy; for in fact the suggestion, that the function of moral judgements was to persuade, led to a difficulty in distinguishing their function from that of propaganda.[10] Since I am going to draw attention to some similarities between commands and moral judgements, and to classify them both as prescriptions, I require most emphatically to dissociate myself from the confusion of either of these things with propaganda. We have here, as often in philosophy, a mixture of two distinctions. The first is that between the language of statements and prescriptive language. The second is that between telling someone something and getting him to believe or do what one has told him. That these two distinctions are quite different, and overlap each other, should be clear after a moment's consideration. For we may tell someone, either that something is the case, or to do something; here there is no attempt at persuasion (or influencing or inducing or getting to). If the person is not disposed to assent to what we tell him, we may then resort to rhetoric, propaganda, marshalling of additional facts, psychological tricks, threats, bribes, torture, mockery, prom-

ises of protection, and a variety of other expedients. All of these are ways of inducing him or getting him to do something; the first four are also ways of getting him to believe something; none of them are ways of telling him something, though those of them which involve the employment of language may include telling him all sorts of things. Regarded as inducements or expedients for persuasion, their success is judged solely by their effects— by whether the person believes or does what we are trying to get him to believe or do. It does not matter whether the means used to persuade him are fair or foul, so long as they do persuade him. And therefore the natural reaction to the realization that someone is trying to persuade us is 'He's trying to get at me; I must be on my guard; I mustn't let him bias my decision unfairly; I must be careful to make up my own mind in the matter and remain a free responsible agent'. Such a reaction to moral judgements should not be encouraged by philosophers. On the other hand, these are not natural reactions either to someone's telling us that something is the case, or to his telling us to do something (for example, to fit a latch to the door). Telling someone to do something, or that something is the case, is answering the question 'What shall I do?' or 'What are the facts?' When we have answered these questions the hearer knows what to do or what the facts are—if what we have told him is right. He is not necessarily thereby *influenced* one way or the other, nor have we failed if he is not; for he may decide to disbelieve or disobey us, and the mere telling him does nothing—and seeks to do nothing—to prevent him doing this. But persuasion is not directed to a person

---

[10] Cf. Stevenson, *Ethics and Language*, chap. 9.

as a rational agent, who is asking himself (or us) 'What shall I do?'; it is not an answer to this or any other question; it is an attempt to *make* him answer it in a particular way.

It is easy to see, therefore, why the so-called 'imperative theory' of moral judgements raised the protests that it did. Because based on a misconception of the function, not only of moral judgements but also of the commands to which they were being assimilated, it seemed to impugn the rationality of moral discourse. But if we realize that commands, however much they may differ from statements, are like them in this, that they consist in telling someone something, not in seeking to influence him, it does no harm to draw attention to the similarities between commands and moral judgements. For, as I shall show, commands, because they, like statements, are essentially intended for answering questions asked by rational agents, are governed by logical rules just as statements are. And this means that moral judgements may also be so governed. We remember that the greatest of all rationalists, Kant, referred to moral judgements as imperatives; though we must remember also that he was using the latter term in an extended sense, and that moral judgements, though they are like imperatives in some respects, are unlike them in others.

QUESTIONS FOR DISCUSSION

1. Illustrate Hare's statement that we should judge a person's moral principles not from his words but from his deeds. Are there also counter-examples to show that even deeds may not reveal a person's moral principles?
2. Define and illustrate the relevance to ethics of prescriptive language, imperatives (singular and universal), value-judgments (moral and nonmoral).
3. What are the logical difficulties in reducing imperative sentences to indicative sentences? Illustrate.
4. Show why the sentence "A is right" does not mean the same as "I approve of A" or "Most people approve of A."
5. What do you think of Hare's criticisms of the naturalistic and utilitarian attempt to reduce ethical imperatives to indicative or hypothetical statements which are verifiable? (E.g., "Do not lie" means "Lying leads to chaotic consequences which are undesirable for self-knowledge or for social harmony.")

FURTHER READINGS FOR CHAPTER 3

Bible: Books of Isaiah, Job, and the Gospel According to St. Matthew (esp. the Sermon on the Mount).

*Aristotle, *Nicomachean Ethics*, M. Ostwald, trans. Indianapolis: Bobbs-Merrill, n.d.

---

* Paperback edition.

*Augustine, Saint, *Confessions*. (Numerous editions available.)

*Bentham, Jeremy, *Introduction to the Principles of Morals and Legislation*. New York: Hafner, 1948.

*Bergson, Henri, *Two Sources of Morality and Religion*, R. Ashley Audra, *et al.*, trans. New York: Doubleday, 1954.

*Cohen, Felix S., *Ethical Systems and Legal Ideals*. Ithaca: Cornell University Press, 1959.

Darwin, Charles, *The Descent of Man* (esp. Chap. 3). New York: Modern Library, n.d. (Note that this was first published in 1871, twelve years after *The Origin of Species*.)

Dewey, John, *Human Nature and Conduct*. New York: Modern Library, 1930.

Edel, Abraham, *Ethical Judgment*. New York: Free Press, 1955.

Edelstein, Ludwig, *Hippocratic Oath*. Baltimore: Johns Hopkins University Press, 1954.

Epictetus, *Discourses*. Mount Vernon, N.Y.: Peter Pauper Press, n.d.

Epicurus, *Extant Remains*, Cyril Bailey, trans. London: Oxford University Press, 1926.

*Freud, Sigmund, *Civilization and Its Discontents*, Joan Rivière, trans. New York: Doubleday, 1958.

Hare, R. M., *The Language of Morals*. New York: Oxford University Press, 1952.

*Hume, David, *An Inquiry Concerning the Principles of Morals*. Indianapolis: Bobbs-Merrill, 1957.

*Kropotkin, Peter, *Memoirs of a Revolutionist*, James A. Rogers, ed. New York: Doubleday, n.d.

*——, *Mutual Aid*. Boston: Peter E. Sargent, 1955.

Melden, A. I., *Ethical Theories*, 2nd ed. Englewood Cliffs, N.J.: Prentice-Hall, 1955.

*Mill, John Stuart, *Utilitarianism*. Indianapolis: Bobbs-Merrill, 1957.

Moore, George Edward, *Ethics*. New York: Oxford University Press, 1947.

*Nietzsche, Friedrich, *Beyond Good and Evil*. Chicago: Henry Regnery, n.d.

*——, *The Birth of Tragedy; The Genealogy of Morals*, F. Golffing, trans. New York: Doubleday, 1956.

Plato, *Apology*, St. G. Stock, ed. New York: Oxford University Press, 1922.

Ratner, Joseph, *The Philosophy of Spinoza, Selected from His Chief Works*. With a life of Spinoza and an introduction. New York: Modern Library, 1927.

Sartre, Jean-Paul, *Being and Nothingness*, Hazel E. Barnes, trans. New York: Philosophical Library, 1956.

*Stevenson, Charles L., *Ethics and Language*. New Haven: Yale University Press, 1960.

Westermarck, E. A., *Christianity and Morals*. New York: Macmillan, 1939.

*——, *Ethical Relativity*. Paterson, N.J.: Littlefield, Adams & Co., 1960.

Chapter 4

PHILOSOPHY OF
POLITICS AND HISTORY

INTRODUCTION

Just how far government may reasonably control the lives of individuals in their various associations with one another is one of the basic problems of all political theory. Political philosophy is concerned with the principles we assume in order to justify or criticize political controls or laws regulating the lives of members of a state. What are the functions of the state in relation to the ends it serves? The political scientist or sociologist undertakes to answer this question by describing the machinery and operations of government and related institutions as he finds them in different states under different social and historical circumstances. But when he judges their adequacy in relation to the needs and possibilities of enriching the lives of the individuals who constitute society, he is said to be concerned with the philosophical side of politics. It is doubtful whether a political philosophy that disregarded the concrete historical and social circumstances which serve as a testing ground for the desirability of preserving or modfiying existing political ideas would be more than an academic enterprise. Both Hobbes and Hegel aimed to *justify a highly powerful and centralized state*. Neither was content with a mere description of forms of government. Marx's revolutionary politics and Mill's faith in democratic liberalism are both far from being merely descriptions of social and political institutions. They are bold and epochal hypotheses of what man's political life *ought* to be in the light of profound insights into the historical development of man's social existence and the possibilities of transforming it into a richer and fuller life for all. This problem was strikingly expressed in Rousseau's opening statement of his *Social Contract*: "Man is born free, but everywhere he is in chains." What is the social need

211

or justification of the restraints of government on men who desire freedom?

Classical moral philosophers, though mindful of the value of personal freedom, were aware of its natural, social, and political conditions. Plato in his *Republic* pictured the ideal state as "the individual writ large" in order to analyze the conflicting desires and interests within and among men. Plato's ideal state was a perfect system of eternally fixed classes of men. It was intended to serve as the standard for judging existing states. His fixed social classes consisted of an élite ruling group of philosophers guided by pure reason, a soldiery of strength and courage to defend the state, and workers (figuratively representative of man's unruly passions) held in temperate check by obedience to the laws imposed on them. In this scheme, justice was conceived as emerging from the stable and harmonious relations among the three classes, each attending to its own business. Aristotle, judging the practical futility of this perfect state which abolished such age-old institutions as the family and private property among the rulers, constructed his political philosophy with more empirical notions of man's political problems, derived from his study of the different types of political constitutions adopted in the Greek city-states. But both Plato and Aristotle were agreed that some persons are by nature born to be rulers or masters and others to be ruled. If such an antidemocratic assumption is eternally grounded "in the nature of things," it would be foolish (as Hegel later insisted) to ask whether it ought to be so. But those who hold this view that political justice and class distinctions are predetermined once and for all time by "nature" have been challenged on the ground that social and political systems are products of customs, institutions, and conventions which are man-made. Since Plato and Aristotle believed in fixed natures, they were inclined to subordinate the man-made elements of law and politics to the inherent natures of different classes of people.

The metaphysical assumption of "inherent natures" has been used to justify slavery, original sin, the divine right of kings, and the nationalistic notion of a chosen people with a historic mission to perform. We find a much more empirical approach in Machiavelli, the first important modern political philosopher to analyze the state and political history in terms of how rulers and their subjects actually behave in diverse historical circumstances rather than in terms of how they might or should behave under ideal conditions.

Hobbes on Human Nature and the "Social Contract"

Hobbes followed the lead of Machiavelli by attempting to deduce political principles from the actual manifestations of human nature in political relations. He believed that men could not lead a peaceful, civilized life together in society unless they submitted their natural "nasty, brutish, and selfish" impulses to man-made laws and government. These man-made laws are not arbitrary but are determined by the immutable constitution of nature and human nature of which we have some knowledge in physics, psychology, and social science.

"The desires and passions of men are in themselves no sin," declared Hobbes. But, as a matter of objective social fact, men are unable to secure freedom to realize their needs without the restraints of law and a government powerful enough to keep the peace. In the absence of such restraining laws and government, men fall into the insecure and warlike "state of nature" where no man's life or possessions enjoy any protection from the brutish impulses and selfishness of human nature. To say that government is necessary simply means that we cannot reasonably find a way of living freely in society without accepting the restraints of government through laws of our own making, accompanied by penalties severe enough to instill fear in those who are impulsively inclined to disregard the laws.

Hobbes's problem is to show how individual freedom and legal necessity are not only consistent but also inseparable. He tried to incorporate his demonstration in a materialistic and mechanistic system of physical bodies, the human mind, and the state.[1] That was his way of being scientific about politics. In fact, however, his political sagacity owed much more to his psychological observations and long experience with statesmen and political situations in the turbulent civil wars of seventeenth-century England than to his philosophy of physics as a geometric science of matter in motion and of thinking as a form of such motion.

Hobbes's pessimistic view that human nature is essentially antisocial is often contrasted with Rousseau's belief in the innate or primitive goodness and strength of man's inherently social nature. These two opposing views of the characteristics of the state of nature rest on hypotheses about how men would act if they were removed from the restraining influences of social institutions, customs, and laws. Some empirical idea of what this state of nature would be can be gained by considering a shipwrecked crew on an isolated island. How the starving group would behave would depend on the previous habits as well as on the impulses of each person to look out for himself or for his neighbor. As the natural resources of the island became cultivated, there would be further need for some sort of social organization arising from a mutual understanding of the practical advantages of securing mutual protection through law and government. This mutual and, most often, tacit understanding of the need for political and legal organization is what is meant by "the social contract" as the basis of the state. Different

---

[1] A materialistic system of philosophy is one which explains everything in terms of the laws of matter and motion. Hobbes believed, as most thinkers in the seventeenth century, that the physical world was a mechanism of geometric structure. However, the axioms of all deductive systems (mechanics or politics) were for Hobbes man-made conventions; hence, he regarded them as binding on our thoughts only because we have agreed to make them so.

theories exist among political philosophers as to the nature of this contract. That it is not simply a deliberate agreement of individuals to come together to form a state is obvious enough from man's social history. But certain elements of the theory persist in the doctrine that government is dependent on the consent of the governed, and that every man has a natural right to life, liberty, and the pursuit of happiness.

The critical questions here are: What is the extent to which states depend for their existence on coercion and armed force, on the one hand, and the consent of its members, on the other hand? Is government by consent a fact or an ideal? What role do propaganda and state-controlled education play in securing consent to government by a particular group? What role do the diverse historical traditions, cultural customs, and institutional developments of different peoples in different parts of the world play in molding the character of the state or "the spirit of the laws," as Montesquieu called it?

Hobbes paid insufficient attention to the historical and economic factors that preserve and modify the forms of the state. Hegel stressed the historical force of custom and organized authority by attempting to prove an inner necessity controlling the march of history and the state. Marx regarded the state primarily as the weapon of the ruling class. Dewey regards the state as an instrument for social reform. Thus, the differences among the political philosophies of Plato, Hobbes, Kant, Hegel, Marx, and Mill are intimately related to their theories of history and of human nature.

Kant's essay on *Perpetual Peace*, written just after the French Revolution, is still regarded by many delegates to the United Nations as their bible. It not only envisions their goal, the age-old dream of the day when nations will beat their swords into plowshares, but it also formulates the legal and political conditions for the permanent elimination of war. Kant's radical proposal aims at undermining the causes and instruments of war: secret diplomatic intrigues to invade independent states, standing armies, international cartels, conspiracies against the internal republican order of states, imposition of dictatorships, and the imperialistic expansionist ambitions of any single state to dominate the world. Kant's appeal stresses the realistic fact that international commerce and exchange of ideas, which promote the prosperity and culture of all peoples, cannot coexist with war. He urges a world federation of states that would have a republican form of democratic government internally without any standing armies, and would support an international police or military force greater than the power of any state that would endanger world peace.

Hegel's Idealistic Theory of History and of the State

Hegel's philosophy of the state is an outcome of a political conservatism supported by a spiritualistic philosophy of history. His idealism assimilates the nature of the world to the nature of man and interprets human nature in terms of its psychical and cultural manifestations. The physical world becomes merely a means for the realization of ideals of an ethical, political, or religious character. Hegel unifies the purposes or values of the human spirit under a single, rational, universal purpose, as absolute and necessary as God is traditionally supposed to be. Instead of a transcendent Being operating from another world of his own, Hegel's God or Absolute Spirit is present or immanent in all the cultural epochs of history as well as in the "lower order" of inanimate nature. Hegel's philosophy of history is a "higher" science of the manifestations of the human spirit in diverse cultural epochs; in the rise and fall of peoples, nations, and empires; in the succession of different types of art, religion, and philosophy. The history of civilization becomes the actual realization of an infinite, eternal, objective Mind as contrasted with the finite, temporal, subjective passions and interests, which empiricists like Hobbes took to be the foundations of human history and society. The state becomes in Hegel's philosophy of history the most concrete embodiment of the objective purpose or meaning of the world, for the state exists by rational necessity and makes freedom possible for man by overcoming one-sided "natural" passions and individual or group interest. Individuals whose personal ideals are doomed to frustration do not realize, insists Hegel, what the mature philosophy of Hegel teaches, namely, that whatever is, is right. History teaches us what at once is, must, and ought to be the necessary plan of divine and absolute purpose. "The state is the divine idea on earth" means that there are no accidents, no arbitrary or capricious events, although there are disappointed individuals who in their ignorance may imagine otherwise. Hegel's philosophy teaches acceptance of the status quo, for what folly it would be to defy the Absolute.

Beside the logical problem of disentangling the *is,* the *must,* and the *ought,* which Hegel so ingeniously contrives to make identical, there are many other problems raised by Hegel's bold analysis of history as the basis for his justification of the state, which he claimed came to perfection in the Prussian monarchy of his own day. The student should examine critically Hegel's answers to the following questions: Does cultural history fall into the peculiar triadic pattern of the Thesis-Antithesis-Synthesis of Hegel's dialectic? Are the conflicts of vested interests merely logical contradictions? How does each stage of history negate the previous stage and yet salvage the cultural continuity ascribed to world history? How can we reconcile the national spirit of a people with the international spirit of the world-mind? What kinds of freedom do different types of state actually give men? How consistent is Hegel's view of the role of great men in history with his subordination of the individual to the inexorable march of the logic of the Absolute? Can there be any genuine temporal development in history if the Absolute has an eternally immutable and predetermined nature? Why must philosophy culminate in Hegel's system? In dealing with social sciences, must we abandon the empirical logic of the natural sciences with their pluralistic and tentative concepts and probabilities, for the dialectic of Hegel with its monistic and absolute conclusions?

The remarkable organic correlations the Hegelians make among the art, philosophy, religion, and politics of any one culture rest on a great deal of cumulative historical evidence, regardless of whether we accept or reject Hegel's a priori development of his eternal categories. Bereft of its obscure Hegelianism, the Marxian insight into the close connection between economic and political change rests on *historical* studies of agricultural and industrial capitalism, the industrial revolution, the factory system, and political revolutions, regardless of the laws of dialectics. The further claims of Hegelians and Marxists concerning the cultural developments of history, for example, the cultural superiority of the Prussian military class and the advent of socialism in England or its status in the U.S.S.R., can and should be tested by a critical examination of the alleged philosophical necessity of their historical hypotheses. The nineteenth-century logic of science in Hegel's and Marx's time was intimately fused with the rationalistic assumption that some sort of *necessity* holds for material, empirical, or historical phenomena. But what was meant by historical or empirical necessity? This is a historical and philosophical question of utmost significance, for the answers of both Hegel and Marx and their followers today are assumed by many to be a sufficient ground for drawing what they hold to be inevitable political conclusions concerning the necessity for a concentration of political power in the hands of an organized minority.

One of the principal differences between the philosophies of Marx and Dewey is that Marx retained more of the Hegelian dialectical pattern of historical necessity than does Dewey. This is undoubtedly due to the difference between the nineteenth- and twentieth-century conceptions of scientific law. Though Dewey started his philosophic career as a Hegelian, he soon found Hegel's logic incompatible with that of the experimental methods of the natural sciences which Dewey wished to extend to the social sciences.

Marxian Theory of History and of the State

Marx claimed he was turning Hegel upside down by giving reflection a more active role in the making of history by revolutionary manipulation of class struggle. This struggle is due to the relations of production inherent in capitalistic economy, namely, the exploitation of the working class by the ruling class. The exploitation of one class by another is explained as a necessary dialectic relation of the changing mode of production. The historical progress of society is towards a workers' democracy. The revolutionary leader's job is to help the exploited working class to become conscious of its true interests and to overthrow the political power of the exploiting class, which makes use of the state as a weapon for the subjugation of the masses. Though Marx agrees with Hegel that the state has served certain social ends, like education and protection of life and property, he believes the capitalist state cannot continue to make progress and has become, in truth, the armed force of the ruling class. The problem here is to distinguish different functions of the state and their relation to one another in different stages of history; e.g., capitalism today is not what it was in Marx's time.

Marx's chief contribution to the philosophy of politics and of history was in showing by concrete historical studies, for example, of agricultural capitalism and the effects of the British factory system, how specific social and political changes were correlated with the changing means of production; for example, the change from an agricultural, rural economy to an industrial, urban one. As a major result, his analysis showed there were no eternal laws of economics or politics as the classical school of Adam Smith and his followers assumed. Though Locke and Ricardo had pointed out how the exchange value of commodities and land was dependent on the labor that went into production and cultivation, they did not develop the consequences of the labor theory of value as Marx did. Marx and Engels, his life-long collaborator, saw in the exploitation of labor the source of the accrual of surplus-value for the capitalist entrepreneur with an increasing concentration of wealth in their hands and the intensification of class struggle as a result of unemployment. The internal collapse of capitalism was predicted on the basis of crises precipitated by increasing lack of purchasing power on the part of the working population and concentration of wealth by the exploiting class. The middle class, on this theory, was to disappear gradually and take its place on one or another side of the barricades that would inevitably be thrown up by a revolutionary uprising of the oppressed class of industrial workers led by the class-conscious leaders of a revolutionary party. The manifesto of this party is printed below. It emphasizes the inevitability of the collapse of capitalism as a result of the intensified class struggle, to be succeeded by a revolutionary seizure of political power and a dictatorship by the proletariat. Finally, this dictatorship, after liquidating the exploiting capitalist class, would itself "wither away" into a classless society.

Marx's ambiguous term "materialistic dialectics" was meant to be more empirical and scientific in its connotation than Hegel's idealistic dialectic. But another meaning to Marx's materialism lies in his view that history and politics depend on man's economic struggles and class conflicts. The term "economic" is crucial to the Marxist philosophy of history and politics. It ought to be noted that the term covers a broad variety of meanings in Marx's use of it, notably technological means of production, legal relations of private property or ownership of means of production, natural resources, labor, exchange of goods and services, the struggle for existence in human society.

Insofar as technology depends on scientific research, law on social custom, natural resources on geography and climate, labor on reproduction, exchange on supply and demand, and the struggle for existence on social, biological, and physical conditions, we see that "economics" designates a very broad area. Hence, it is not surprising that so much can be claimed for the "economic factor" when so broadly and loosely applied to social and cultural history.

Democratic Liberalism

It is not difficult for liberals to criticize this Hegelian and Marxian doctrine of historical inevitability in the light of the logic of empirical science. It scarcely follows from an historical approach based on empirical method that the state must wither away and a classless society ensue inevitably. The state, for Mill, can and should be democratically converted into an instrument for the social improvement of the living conditions of the masses. The cardinal hypothesis of political liberalism is that the social functions of the state can be democratically developed through experimental and educational agencies. We have already mentioned Dewey's abandonment of Hegel's strait-jacket of dialectics in favor of Mill's extension of the experimental methods of the natural sciences to the social sciences. Against the view of both Hegelians and Marxists that imposes a pattern of certainty and monism on politics and history, Dewey insists that "probability and pluralism are the characteristics of the present state of science."

The theoreticians of the Communist Party in their unquestioning support of every policy of the U.S.S.R. are far from realizing the socialist democracy at which Marx aims. As harbingers of a new type of political authoritarianism, their subordination of individual freedom to the demands of a totalitarian state appears in the one-party system guaranteed by the so-called democratic constitution of the U.S.S.R. Political thinkers indicate the dangers of one-party control of the newspapers, radio, schools, the arts and sciences, which are the principal agencies for the formation of public opinion. To the extent that ideas are used as instruments of political control, to that extent we cannot universally subordinate psychological factors to economic ones in history. Marx himself regarded a highly industrialized country like England a much more probable place for a successful socialistic revolution than an agricultural country like Russia, because industrial workers are much more likely to be conscious of their class status and their need for organization than farm workers or peasants, who see no need for collectivistic enterprises. The important point is that full-fledged social and economic democracy is not guaranteed by a merely formal political democracy which does not provide equality of economic opportunities for all groups, whether in the United States, England, or the U.S.S.R. In any case, the problem of all those who aim at spreading democracy is to provide both the economic and political opportunities that will yield the maximum participation of all in realizing the welfare of all.

The political philosophies outlined above differ not only in the particular political forms favored by each (absolute monarchy by Hobbes, constitutional monarchy by Hegel, dictatorship of the proletariat by Marx, and democracy by Mill), but in their more general conceptions of human nature, history, and science: mechanistic materialism (Hobbes), objective idealism (Hegel) historical materialism (Marx), democratic liberalism (Mill). It is logically possible to accept some parts of these political philosophies without accepting all the more general theories that they advocate. To discriminate the wheat from the chaff requires a fuller understanding of the assumptions of each type of philosophy than can be given here. That such questions are not merely academic exercises is evident from the role that ideological indoctrination and education play in both war and peace.

To what extent have the governments of the world powers been really working for or towards economic and social democracy in their own and less powerful countries?

It is a fact that in every existing state—no matter how democratic its pretensions are—individuals are penalized for expressing certain thoughts in public assemblies or in print, thoughts that are critical of existing governmental policy or of an institution backed by those powerful enough to use the machinery of the law courts and law-enforcing agencies to suppress opposition or criticism. The penalties imposed on the critic need not be direct incarceration or death or deportation—witness Socrates, who was given his choice between the latter two and chose death in order to teach the future citizenry of Athens and, we may add, of the world, a lesson in the political value of free thought and discussion. There are other more indirect forms of political tyranny: social ostracism, deprivation of economic opportunities in private or public employment, character assassination, and threats against the family and friends of the persecuted opposition. The extent to which suppression of such civil and political liberties as free discussion, the right of assembly, freedom of the press, the right of minority groups to organize for their own protection as practiced under different forms of government is part of the subject matter of social science. One of the chief obstacles in the slow progress of the social sciences is the difficulty of getting at the facts of secret inquisitions and star-chamber proceedings aimed at suppressing the opposition of individuals or minority groups. There is, however, the fact that certain methods of violence, like outright seizure of power by a dictatorial minority strong enough to suppress all opposition, are incompatible with the methods and aims of democratic liberalism.

The problem of political philosophy is to find the broad social principles that will guide us in deciding, after we have all the facts, to what extent any individual or group *ought* to be prevented from or penalized for exercising the civil liberties normally guaranteed by a democratic and liberal state. John Stuart Mill's essay *On Liberty* (1859), was published in the heyday of nineteenth-century laissez-faire political economy, which promised indefinite prosperity and "the greatest good for the greatest number" on the basis of unrestricted individual enterprise. Mill feared that too much emphasis on economic self-advancement and freedom would lead to the neglect of moral progress, which to his mind was essentially a matter of individual freedom. However, in his later writings, Mill's democratic liberalism became more socialistic, and he may be regarded as one of the forerunners of moderate British socialism which uses the methods of reform legislation rather than revolution. Political programs are generally linked with changing economic developments, but there are certain continuities in political history that are fundamental for any political philosophy. Of these continuities the civil liberties of freedom of thought, discussion, assembly, press, religious worship, and scientific inquiry are paramount rights of individuals, which no system of political authority can ignore without endangering the very aim of social existence—human welfare. Mill's classic presentation of the arguments for unrestrained freedom for all individual thought and discussion, no matter how completely false or true or partially false and true the opinions in question are, is especially relevant today when authoritarian elements abroad and in our own midst threaten to stifle any hope of realizing a democratic and liberal civilization for mankind.

Mill's essay does, however, also raise further problems for our own age. Is "the tyranny of the majority" an inseparable evil of democracy? Should a minority group that would, in gaining control of a government, refuse democratic liberties to others, be free to gain such control under the protection of these civil liberties at present?

There are also problems connected with the theory of punishment (penology): Is legal punishment justified if it merely satisfies the revenge impulses of the offended or damaged persons? Or does the state merely have to punish criminals in order to deter them and others from violating the law? Or should the state readjust criminals to learning more useful forms of occupation? Or should we not seek also to eliminate the economic and social causes of crime—e.g., illiteracy, poverty, poor housing, racial, religious, and nationalistic hatreds?

In any case, whether our political problem is to justify the very existence of the state on a materialistic (Hobbes) or idealistic (Hegel) basis, or its overthrow by a dictatorship of the proletariat towards a classless society (Marx), or its gradual reform by an enlightened and free citizenry under a liberal democratic state, there is no easy or final settlement of the problem by philosophical principles that provide an absolute mechanical, historical, dialectical, or psychological necessity as a basis on which to meet the complex and variable needs of human beings. This is not a merely negative result, for it should turn our attention to the specific needs of mankind, to the elimination of economic and social inequities, and to the integrity of our own thoughts and lives in sharing the responsibility for the failure to advance human welfare by a more truly democratic way of living.

At this juncture of the world's seething politics, the devastating and horrible effects of atomic warfare should lead the frightened peoples of the world to realize the value of what some philosophers long ago envisaged: the establishment of an equitable system of law and order among nations. As Spinoza and Kant recognized, Hobbes's warlike, predatory "state of nature" is not far from the actual relations of states that refuse to allow their absolute sovereignty to be limited by any international laws when dealing with other states. The stronger states dominate the weaker ones and have often enabled the greedy to thrive on the backs of the others without restraint. Resentment at such injustice, if it does not lead to war eventually, certainly saps all desire for human cooperation on a worldwide scale.

In the political writings of Immanuel Kant, the great eighteenth-century German enlightener, we find a prophetic, cosmopolitan plan for perpetual world peace. Nations, according to Kant, will sooner or later be driven to their senses by their awareness of the futility and waste of wars arising from the clash of powers each seeking its own interests. But a world federation of nations will not serve the ends of world peace unless it operates democratically to protect weaker nations from stronger ones. Furthermore, only when every nation has achieved democratic controls over any ruthless, war-bent group within its own borders will it be possible to nip war in the bud and to realize perpetual peace. Kant did not specify the economic roots of war so vividly and did not insist on an industrial economy as Marx and Dewey did. But he believed that if nations can reach agreements in international trade, they ought also to cooperate on world peace, and he tried to show the rationale of world unity without resorting to a highly abstract metaphysics of history. It remains to be seen whether a more empirical scrutiny of the possibilities of world organization can lead to a feasible solution of the immensely important problem of avoiding future wars that may destroy civilization entirely. There are common enemies against which all nations and peoples may unitedly devote their greatest energies: famine, poverty, disease, ignorance, and injustice.

Problems of the Philosophy of History

Just as knowing a person's habits, background, and education helps us understand much of his behavior and ideas, so historical knowledge of the customs and traditional beliefs of the peoples of various nations can throw light on their present attitudes and conduct. History can thus play an important part in bettering international understanding. Unfortunately, historians have too often presented images of the past colored strongly by nationalistic bias, race prejudice, religious sectarianism, political propaganda, or by commercial and egotistic interests. In fact, the writings of historians are good clues to some of the cultural characteristics of the period in which the historian lives or to the character of the historian himself ("Peter's opinion of Paul tells you more about Peter than about Paul," Spinoza said).

Methodologically, therefore, historiography requires objective testing of statements about the past by referring to the documentary evidence. The historian should be critical of the evidence alleged to support "facts," generalizations, and value judgments imputed to the past, even though it is difficult to avoid subjective bias. It is logically possible and scientifically required to distinguish between the values of the historian and those belonging to past periods. The historian's own values lead him to select certain aspects of the past for study, and it is impossible to avoid selectivity in any subject of inquiry; but selectivity and objectivity are not incompatible. Historical "facts" are not simply sensations (contrary to the theory of knowledge known as "naïve realism"), but are inferences based on documentary evidence, and hence, subject to logical scrutiny. Such historical inferences make use of hypotheses based on some assumed similarity between past characters and presently known or given documents allegedly related to past events by some sort of continuity. "Laws," or inductive generalizations about history, are hazardous because of the large number of uncontrollable variables intersecting in any event. However, generalizations about physical, biological, psychological, economic, etc., factors in history are useful in unearthing new facts, if all such generalizations are treated as hypotheses first, and as limited inductive generalizations requiring documentary verification. Even speculative theories about all history, e.g., Hegel's or Marx's, can be useful if they suggest study of neglected factors in history, but are harmful if they are treated as absolute dogmas.

Professor Berlin's essay brings us to the political philosophies of the twentieth century focused on the way they treat the ideas of liberty and determinism in history and the state. The nineteenth century contributed humanitarian liberalism (e.g., in Bentham and Mill) and romantic nationalism (e.g., Michelet and Mazzini) to political thought. The twentieth century finds democratic ideas on the defensive against the rise of totalitarianism (communism and fascism) in the Soviet Union, Nazi Germany, and Communist China among the great powers. In other countries democratic institutions are threatened by antirational forces seeking to establish totalitarian regimes by violent overthrow of the bourgeois "establishment." Militant racism and jingoistic nationalism often vie with each other in condemning liberal democracy. Unconscious and anti-intellectual influences combat rational efforts to apply planning and science to the resolution of social conflicts of individual and group interests. The appeal to reason is threatened by the resort to violence and brute force as the means of dealing with social and international problems. In this crisis the very survival of civilization is at stake.

Martin Luther King, Jr. was a martyr to the cause of minority rights, so essential to the democratic ideal of freedom. His speech on August 28, 1963, before 200,000 or more people assembled at the Lincoln Memorial in Washington, D.C., was a fervent appeal for justice, denied the Negro people and other minorities with respect to economic, social, and political equality. Dr. King forcefully deplored the great gap between the promise of Lincoln's proclamation of emancipation and continued racial discrimination, repression, and segregation. When his program of nonviolent spiritual resistance to racial repression seemed to have little effect, he was prepared to call for greater resistance to discriminatory laws and government by urging civil disobedience, justified by the cry of conscience and its "higher law."

Louis Waldman, a labor lawyer and expert on civil rights, although sympathetic to the cause of minorities' rights, strongly disagrees with the moral and political wisdom of resorting to civil disobedience. He indicates that the appeal to individual conscience is too subjective, and can be used by anyone who does not wish to obey a law that goes counter to his own or his group's interests. The prejudiced racist or violent vigilante will also feel justified in disobeying legal constraints on his activist expression of hatred. Waldman appeals to people to comply with the democratic process of remedying evils by obeying laws that need to be changed until they are amended or replaced legally. Though slower and more painful at first, Waldman argues, this process will in the long run produce more harmony and steady progress than lack of respect for law, which civil disobedience brings in its wake.

Thomas Hobbes (1588-1679)

4.1   Leviathan

The principal parts of philosophy are two. For two chief kinds of bodies, and very different from one another, offer themselves to such as search after their generation and properties; one whereof being the work of nature, is called a *natural body*, the other is called a *commonwealth*, and is made by the wills and agreement of men. And from these spring the two parts of philosophy, called *natural* and *civil*. But seeing that, for the knowledge of the properties of a commonwealth, it is necessary first to know the dispositions, affections, and manners of men, civil philosophy is again commonly divided into two parts, whereof one, which treats of men's dispositions and manners, is called *ethics;* and the other, which takes cognizance of their civil duties, is called *politics*, or simply *civil philosophy*. In the first place, therefore (after I have set down such premises as appertain to the nature of philosophy in general), I will discourse of *bodies natural;* in the second, of the *dispositions and manners of men;* and in the third, of the *civil duties of subjects*. . . .

So that in the nature of man, we find three principal causes of quarrel.

First, competition; second, diffidence; thirdly, glory.

The first, maketh men invade for gain; the second, for safety; and the third, for reputation. The first use violence to make themselves masters of other men's persons, wives, children, and cattle; the second, to defend them; the third, for trifles, as a word, a smile, a different opinion, and any other sign of undervalue, either direct in their persons, or by reflection in their kindred, their friends, their nation, their profession, or their name.

Hereby it is manifest, that during the time men live without a common power to keep them all in awe, they are in that condition which is called war; and such a war, as is of every man, against every man. For WAR, consisteth not in battle only, or the act of fighting; but in a tract of time, wherein the will to contend by battle is sufficiently known: and therefore the notion of *time* is to be considered in the nature of war, as it is in the nature of weather. For as the nature of foul weather lieth not in a shower or two of rain, but in an inclination thereto of many days together; so the nature of war consisteth not in actual fighting, but in the known disposition thereto, during all the time there is

---

From *The Leviathan* (1651).

no assurance to the contrary. All other time is PEACE.

Whatsoever therefore is consequent to a time of war, where every man is enemy to every man, the same is consequent to the time, wherein men live without other security than what their own strength and their own invention shall furnish them withal. In such condition, there is no place for industry, because the fruit thereof is uncertain: and consequently no culture of the earth; no navigation, nor use of the commodities that may be imported by sea; no commodious building; no instruments of moving, and removing, such things as require much force; no knowledge of the face of the earth; no account of time; no arts; no letters; no society; and which is worst of all, continual fear, and danger of violent death; and the life of man, solitary, poor, nasty, brutish, and short.

It may seem strange to some man that has not well weighed these things, that nature should thus dissociate, and render man apt to invade and destroy one another; and he may, therefore, not trusting to this inference, made from the passions, desire perhaps to have the same confirmed by experience. Let him therefore consider with himself, when taking a journey, he arms himself, and seeks to go well accompanied; when going to sleep, he locks his doors; when even in his house he locks his chests; and this when he knows there be laws, and public officers, armed, to revenge all injuries shall be done him; what opinion he has of his fellow subjects, when he rides armed; of his fellow citizens, when he locks his doors; and of his children, and servants, when he locks his chests. Does he not there as much accuse mankind by his actions, as I

do by my words? But neither of us accuse man's nature in it. The desires and other passions of man are in themselves no sin. No more are the actions that proceed from those passions, till they know a law that forbids them; which till laws be made they cannot know: nor can any law be made, till they have agreed upon the person that shall make it.

It may peradventure be thought there was never such a time nor condition of war as this; and I believe it was never generally so, over all the world: but there are many places where they live so now. But the savage people in many places of America, except the government of small families, the concord whereof dependeth on natural lust, have no government at all; and live at this day in that brutish manner as I said before. Howsoever, it may be perceived what manner of life there would be, where there were no common power to fear, by the manner of life, which men that have formerly lived under a peaceful government, use to degenerate into, in a civil war.

But though there had never been any time, wherein particular men were in a condition of war one against another; yet in all times, kings, and persons of sovereign authority, because of their independency, are in continual jealousies, and in the state and posture of gladiators; having their weapons pointing, and their eyes fixed on one another; that is, their forts, garrisons, and guns upon the frontiers of their kingdoms ; and continual spies upon their neighbors; which is a posture of war. But because they uphold thereby the industry of their subjects, there does not follow from it, that misery, which accompanies the liberty of particular men.

To this war of every man against every man, this also is consequent; that nothing can be unjust. The notions of right and wrong, justice and injustice have there no place. Where there is no common power, there is no law: where no law, no injustice. Force, and fraud, are in war the two cardinal virtues. Justice and injustice are none of the faculties neither of the body, nor mind. If they were, they might be in a man that were alone in the world, as well as his senses and passions. They are qualities that relate to men in society, not in solitude. It is consequent also to the same condition, that there be no propriety, no dominion, no *mine* and *thine* distinct; but only that to be every man's that he can get, and for so long as he can keep it. And thus much for the ill condition, which man by mere nature is actually placed in; though with a possibility to come out of it, consisting partly in the passions, partly in his reason.

The passions that incline men to peace are fear of death, desire of such things as are necessary to commodious living, and a hope by their industry to obtain them. And reason suggesteth convenient articles of peace, upon which men may be drawn to agreement. . . .

The final cause, end, or design of men, who naturally love liberty, and dominion over others, in the introduction of that restraint upon themselves, in which we see them live in commonwealths, is the foresight of their own preservation, and of a more contented life thereby; that is to say, of getting themselves out from that miserable condition of war, which is necessarily consequent . . . to the natural passions of men, when there is no visible power to keep them in awe,

and tie them by fear of punishment to the performance of their covenants, and observation of those laws of nature set down. . . .

It is true, that certain living creatures, as bees, and ants, live sociably one with another, which are therefore by Aristotle numbered amongst political creatures; and yet have no other direction, than their particular judgments and appetites; nor speech, whereby one of them can signify to another what he thinks expedient for the common benefit; and, therefore, some man may perhaps desire to know why mankind cannot do the same. To which I answer:

First, that men are continually in competition for honor and dignity, which these creatures are not; and consequently amongst men there ariseth on that ground envy and hatred, and finally war; but amongst these not so.

Secondly, that amongst these creatures, the common good differeth not from the private; and being by nature inclined to their private, they procure thereby the common benefit. But man, whose joy consisteth in comparing himself with other men, can relish nothing but what is eminent.

Thirdly, that these creatures, having not, as man, the use of reason, do not see, nor think they see any fault in the administration of their common business; whereas amongst men, there are very many that think themselves wiser, and able to govern the public better than the rest; and these strive to reform and innovate, one this way, another that way; and thereby bring it into distraction and civil war.

Fourthly, that these creatures, though they have some use of voice in making known to one another their desires, and other affections; yet they want that art of words, by which some men can represent to others that which is good, in the likeness of evil; and evil, in the likeness of good; and augment, or diminish the apparent greatness of good and evil; discontenting men, and troubling their peace at their pleasure.

Fifthly, irrational creatures cannot distinguish between *injury* and *damage;* and, therefore, as long as they be at ease, they are not offended with their fellows, whereas man is then most troublesome, when he is most at ease: for then it is that he loves to show his wisdom, and control the actions of them that govern the commonwealth.

Lastly, the agreement of these creatures is natural; that of men is by covenant only, which is artificial: and, therefore, it is no wonder if there be somewhat else required, besides covenant, to make their agreement constant and lasting; which is a common power, to keep them in awe and to direct their actions to the common benefit.

The only way to erect such a common power, as may be able to defend them from the invasion of foreigners, and the injuries of one another, and thereby to secure them in such sort, as that by their own industry, and by the fruits of the earth, they may nourish themselves and live contentedly is to confer all their power and strength upon one man, or upon one assembly of men, that may reduce all their wills, by plurality of voices, unto one will: which is as much as to say, to appoint one man, or assembly of men, to bear their person; and every one to own, and acknowledge himself to be author of whatsoever he that so beareth their person, shall act, or cause to be acted, in those things which concern the common peace and safety; and therein to submit their wills, every one to his will, and their judgments, to his judgment. This is more than consent, or concord; it is a real unity of them all, in one and the same person, made by covenant of every man with every man, in such manner, as if every man should say to every man, *I authorize and give up my right of governing myself, to this man, or to this assembly of men, on this condition, that thou give up thy right to him, and authorize all his actions in like manner.* This done, the multitude so united in one person, is called a COMMONWEALTH, in Latin CIVITAS. This is the generation of that great LEVIATHAN, or rather, to speak more reverently, of that *mortal god,* to which we owe under the *immortal God,* our peace and defense. For by this authority, given him by every particular man in the commonwealth, he hath the use of so much power and strength conferred on him, that by terror thereof, he is enabled to perform the wills of them all, to peace at home, and mutual aid against their enemies abroad. And in him consisteth the essence of the commonwealth; which, to define it, is *one person, of whose acts as a great multitude, by mutual covenants one with another, have made themselves every one the author, to the end he may use the strength and means of them all, as he shall think expedient, for their peace and common defense.*

And he that carrieth this person, is called SOVEREIGN, and said to have *sovereign power;* and every one besides, his SUBJECT.

The attaining to this sovereign power is by two ways. One, by natural force; as when a man maketh his children, to submit themselves, and their children, to his government, as being able to destroy them if they refuse; or by war subdueth his enemies to his will, giving them their lives on that condition. The other, is when men agree amongst themselves to submit to some men, or assembly of men, voluntarily, on confidence to be protected by him against all others. This latter my be called a political commonwealth, or commonwealth by *institution;* and the former, a commonwealth by *acquisition.*

Liberty, or Freedom, signifieth, properly, the absence of opposition; by opposition, I mean external impediments of motion; and may be applied no less to irrational, or inanimate creatures, than to rational. For whatsoever is so tied, or environed, as it cannot move but within a certain space, which space is determined by the opposition of some external body, we say it hath not liberty to go further. And so of all living creatures, whilst they are imprisoned, or restrained, with walls, or chains; and of the water whilst it is kept in by banks, or vessels, that otherwise would spread itself into a larger space, we use to say, they are not at liberty, to move in such manner, as without those external impediments they would. But when the impediment of motion is in the constitution of the thing itself, we use not to say: it wants the liberty, but the power, to move; as when a stone lieth still, or a man is fastened to his bed by sickness.

And according to this proper and generally received meaning of the word, a FREEMAN, *is he, that in those things, which by his strength and wit he is able to do, is not hindered to do what he has a will to.* But when the words *free,* and *liberty,* are applied to anything but bodies, they are abused; for that which is not subject to motion is not subject to impediment; and therefore, when it is said, for example, the way is free, no liberty of the way is signified, but of those that walk in it without stop. And when we say a gift is free, there is not meant any liberty of the gift, but of the giver, that was not bound by any law or covenant to give it. So when we *speak freely,* it is not the liberty of voice, or pronunciation, but of the man, whom no law hath obliged to speak otherwise than he did. Lastly, from the use of the word *free-will,* no liberty can be inferred of the will, desire, or inclination, but the liberty of the man; which consisteth in this, that he finds no stop in doing what he has the will, desire, or inclination to do.

Fear and liberty are consistent; as when a man throweth his goods into the sea for *fear* the ship should sink, he doth it nevertheless very willingly, and may refuse to do it if he will; it is therefore the action of one that was *free:* so a man sometimes pays his debt, only for *fear* of imprisonment, which because nobody hindered him from detaining, was the action of a man at *liberty.* And generally all actions which men do in commonwealths, for *fear* of the law, are actions which the doers had *liberty* to omit.

Liberty and *necessity* are consistent: as in the water, that hath not only *liberty,* but a *necessity* of descending by the channel; so likewise in the actions which men voluntarily do; which, because they proceed from their will, proceed from *liberty;* and yet, because every act of man's will, and every desire, and inclination proceedeth from some cause, and that from another cause, in a continual chain, whose first link is in the hand of God the first of all causes, proceed from *necessity*. So that to him that could see the connection of those causes, the *necessity* of all men's voluntary actions would appear manifest. And therefore God, that seeth, and disposeth all things, seeth also that the liberty of man in doing what he will, is accompanied with the *necessity* of doing that which God will, and no more, nor less. For though men may do many things which God does not command, nor is therefore author of them; yet they can have no passion, nor appetite to anything of which appetite God's will is not the cause. And did not his will assure the *necessity* of man's will, and consequently of all that on man's will dependeth, the *liberty* of men would be a contradiction and impediment to the omnipotence and *liberty* of God. And this shall suffice, as to the matter in hand, of that natural *liberty*, which *only* is properly called *liberty*.

But as men, for the attaining of peace, and conservation of themselves thereby, have made an artificial man, which we call a commonwealth; so also have they made artificial chains, called *civil laws*, which they themselves, by mutual covenants, have fastened at one end, to the lips of that man, or assembly, to whom they have given the sovereign power; and at the other end to their own ears. These bonds in their own nature but weak, may nevertheless be made to hold, by the danger, though not by the difficulty of breaking them.

In relation to these bonds only it is, that I am to speak now, of the *liberty* of *subjects*. For seeing there is no commonwealth in the *world*, wherein there be rules enough set down, for the regulating of all the actions and words of men; as being a thing impossible: it followeth necessarily, that in all kinds of actions by the laws praetermitted, men have the liberty of doing what their own reasons shall suggest, for the most profitable to themselves. For if we take liberty in the proper sense, for corporal liberty; that is to say, freedom from chains and prison, it were very absurd for men to clamor as they do for the liberty they so manifestly enjoy. Again, if we take liberty for an exemption from laws, it is no less absurd for men to demand as they do, that liberty by which all other men may be masters of their lives. And yet, as absurd as it is, this is it they demand; not knowing that the laws are of no power to protect them, without a sword in the hands of a man, or men, to cause those laws to be put in execution. The liberty of a subject lieth therefore only in those things, which in regulating their actions, the sovereign hath praetermitted: such as is the liberty to buy, and sell, and otherwise contract with one another; to choose their own abode, their own diet, their own trade of life, and institute their children as they themselves think fit; and the like.

Nevertheless, we are not to understand, that by such liberty the sovereign power of life and death is either abolished, or limited. For it has been already shown that nothing the sovereign representative can do to a subject, on what pretense soever, can properly be called injustice, or injury; because every subject is author of every act the sovereign doth; so that he never wanteth right to anything, otherwise, than as he himself is the subject of God, and bound thereby to observe the laws of nature. And therefore it may, and doth often happen in commonwealths, that a subject may be put to death by the command of the sovereign power; and yet neither do the other wrong; as when Jephtha caused his daughter to be sacrificed: in which, and the like cases, he that so dieth, had liberty to do the action, for which he is nevertheless, without injury put to death. And the same holdeth also in a sovereign prince, that putteth to death an innocent subject. For though the action be against the law of nature, as being contrary to equity, as was the killing of Uriah, by David; yet it was not an injury to Uriah, but to God. Not to Uriah, because the right to do what he pleased was given him by Uriah himself: and yet to God, because David was God's subject, and prohibited all iniquity by the law of nature: which distinction, David himself, when he repented the fact, evidently confirmed, saying, *To thee only have I sinned.* In the same manner, the people of Athens, when they banished the most potent of their commonwealth for ten years, thought they committed no injustice; and yet they never questioned what crime he had done; but what hurt he would do: nay they commanded the banishment of they knew not whom; and every citizen bringing his oystershell into the market place, written with the name of him he desired should be banished, without actually accusing him, sometimes banished an Aristides, for his reputation of justice; and sometimes a scurrilous jester, as Hyperbolus, to make a jest of it. And yet a man cannot say the sovereign people of Athens wanted right to banish them; or an Athenian the liberty to jest, or to be just.

The liberty, whereof there is so frequent and honorable mention, in the histories, and philosophy of the ancient Greeks, and Romans, and in the writings, and discourse of those that from them have received all their learning in the politics, is not the liberty of particular men; but the liberty of the commonwealth: which is the same with that which every man then should have, if there were no civil laws, nor commonwealth at all. And the effects of it also be the same. For as amongst masterless men, there is perpetual war, of every man against his neighbor; no inheritance, to transmit to the son, nor to expect from the father; no propriety of goods, or lands; no security; but a full and absolute liberty in every particular man; so in states and commonwealths not dependent on one another, every commonwealth, not every man, has an absolute liberty to do what it shall judge, that is to say, what that man, or assembly that representeth it, shall judge most conducing to their benefit. But withal, they live in the condition of a perpetual war, and upon the confines of battle, with their frontiers armed, and cannons planted against their neighbors round about. The Athenians, and Romans were free; that is, free commonwealth: not that any particular men had the liberty to resist their own representative; but that their representative had the liberty to resist or invade other people. There is written on the turrets of the city of Lucca in great characters at this day the word LIBERTAS; yet no man can thence infer that a particular man has more liberty, or immunity from the service of the commonwealth there, than in Constantinople. Whether a commonwealth be monarchical, or popular, the freedom is still the same.

But it is an easy thing for men to be deceived, by the specious name of liberty; and for want of judgment to distinguish, mistake that for their private inheritance, and birthright, which is the right of the public only. And when the same error is confirmed by the authority of men in reputation for their writings on this subject, it is no wonder if it produce sedition, and change of government. In these western parts of the world, we are made to receive our opinions concerning the institution, and rights of commonwealths, from Aristotle, Cicero, and other men, Greeks and Romans, that living under popular states, derived those rights, not from the principles of nature, but transcribed them into their books, out of the practice of their own commonwealths, which were popular; as the grammarians describe the rules of language, out of the practice of the time; or the rules of poetry, out of the poems of Homer and Virgil. And because the Athenians were taught to keep them from desire of changing their government, that they were freemen, and all that lived under monarchy were slaves; therefore Aristotle puts it down in his *Politics, (lib. 6 cap. ii.) In democracy,* LIBERTY *is to be supposed: for it is commonly held that no man is* FREE *in any other government.* And as Aristotle, so Cicero and other writers have grounded their civil doctrine on the opinions of the Romans, who were taught to hate monarchy, at first, by them that having deposed their sovereign, shared amongst them the sovereignty of Rome; and afterwards by their successor. And by reading of these Greek and Latin authors, men from their childhood have gotten a habit, under a false show of liberty, of favoring tumults, and of licentious controlling the actions of their sovereigns, and again of controlling those controllers; with the effu-

sion of so much blood, as I think I may truly say, there was never anything so dearly bought, as these western parts have bought the learning of the Greek and Latin tongues.

To come now to the particulars of the true liberty of a subject; that is to say, what are the things, which though commanded by the sovereign, he may nevertheless, without injustice, refuse to do; we are to consider, what rights we pass away, when we make a commonwealth; or, which is all one, what liberty we deny ourselves, by owning all the actions, without exception, of the man, or assembly, we make our sovereign. For in the act of our *submission* consisteth both our *obligation* and our *liberty;* which must therefore be inferred by arguments taken from thence; there being no obligation on any man, which ariseth not from some act of his own; for all men equally, are by nature free. And because such arguments, must either be drawn from the express words, *I authorize all his actions,* or from the intention of him that submitteth himself to his power, which intention is to be understood by the end for which he so submitteth; the obligation, and liberty of the subject, is to be derived, either from those words, or others equivalent; or else from the end of the institution of sovereignty, namely, the peace of the subjects within themselves, and their defense against a common enemy.

First, therefore, seeing sovereignty by institution is by covenant of every one to every one; and sovereignty by acquisition, by covenants of the vanquished to the victor, or child to the parent; it is manifest, that every subject has liberty in all those things, the right whereof cannot by covenant be transferred. . . . Covenants, not to defend a man's own body, are void. Therefore:

If the sovereign command a man, though justly condemned, to kill, wound, or maim himself; or not to resist those that assault him; or to abstain from the use of food, air, medicine, or any other thing, without which he cannot live; yet hath that man the liberty to disobey.

If a man be interrogated by the sovereign, or his authority, concerning a crime done by himself, he is not bound, without assurance of pardon, to confess it; because no man . . . can be obliged by covenant to accuse himself.

Again, the consent of a subject to sovereign power is contained in these words, I authorize, or take upon me, all his actions; in which there is no restriction at all of his own former natural liberty: for by allowing him to kill me, I am not bound to kill myself when he commands me. It is one thing to say, kill me, or my fellow, if you please; another thing to say, I will kill myself, or my fellow. It followeth therefore, that

No man is bound by the words themselves, either to kill himself, or any other man; and consequently, that the obligation a man may sometimes have, upon the command of the sovereign to execute any dangerous, or dishonorable office, dependeth not on the words of our submission; but on the intention, which is to be understood by the end thereof. When therefore our refusal to obey frustrates the end for which the sovereignty was ordained, then there is no liberty to refuse: otherwise there is.

Upon this ground, a man that is commanded as a soldier to fight against the enemy, though his sovereign have right enough to punish his refusal with death, may nevertheless in many cases refuse, without injustice; as when he substituteth a sufficient soldier in his place: for in this case he deserteth not the service of the commonwealth. And there is allowance to be made for natural timorousness; not only to women, of whom no such dangerous duty is expected, but also to men of feminine courage. When armies fight, there is on one side, or both, a running away; yet when they do it not out of treachery, but fear, they are not esteemed to do it unjustly, but dishonorably. For the same reason, to avoid battle is not injustice, but cowardice. But he that inrolleth himself a soldier, or taketh imprest money, taketh away the excuse of a timorous nature; and is obliged, not only to go to the battle, but also not to run from it, without his captain's leave. And when the defense of the commonwealth requireth at once the help of all that are able to bear arms, everyone is obliged; because otherwise the institution of the commonwealth, which they have not the purpose, or courage to preserve, was in vain.

To resist the sword of the commonwealth, in defense of another man, guilty or innocent, no man hath liberty; because such liberty takes away from the sovereign the means of protecting us and is therefore destructive of the very essence of government. But in case a great many men together have already resisted the sovereign power unjustly, or committed some capital crime, for which every one of them expecteth death, whether have they not the liberty then to join together, and assist, and defend one another? Certainly they have: for they but defend their lives, which the guilty man may as well do as the innocent. There was indeed injustice in the first breach of their duty; their bearing of arms subsequent to it, though it be to maintain what they have done, is no new unjust act. And if it be only to defend their persons, it is not unjust at all. But the offer of pardon taketh from them, to whom it is offered, the plea of self-defense, and maketh their perseverance in assisting, or defending, the rest, unlawful.

As for other liberties, they depend on the silence of the law. In cases where the sovereign has prescribed no rule, there the subject hath the liberty to do, or forbear, according to his own discretion. And therefore such liberty is in some places more, and in some less; and in some times more, in other times less, according as they that have the sovereignty shall think most convenient. As for example, there was a time, when in England a man might enter into his own land, and dispossess such as wrongfully possessed it, by force. But in after times, that liberty of forcible entry was taken away by a statute made, by the king, in parliament. And in some places of the world, men have the liberty of many wives; in other places, such liberty is not allowed. . . .

If the sovereign banish his subject, during the banishment, he is not subject. But he that is sent on a message, or hath leave to travel, is still subject; but it is, by contract between sovereigns, not by virtue of the covenant of subjection. For whosoever entereth into another's dominion, is subject to all the laws thereof; unless he have a privilege of the amity of the sovereigns, or by special licence. . . .

The law of nature, and the civil law, contain each other, and are of equal extent. For the laws of nature, which consist in equity, justice, gratitude, and other moral virtues on these depending, in the condition of mere nature . . . are not properly laws, but qualities that dispose men to peace, and to obedience. When a commonwealth is once settled, then are they actually laws, and not before; as being then the commands of the commonwealth; and therefore also civil laws: for it is the sovereign power that obliges men to obey them. For in the differences of private men, to declare what is equity, what is justice, and what is moral virtue, and to make them binding, there is need of the ordinances of sovereign power, and punishments to be ordained for such as shall break them; which ordinances are therefore part of the civil law. The law of nature, therefore, is a part of the civil law in all commonwealths of the world. Reciprocally also, the civil law is a part of the dictates of nature. For justice, that is to say, performance of covenant, and giving to every man his own, is a dictate of the law of nature. But every subject in a commonwealth hath covenanted to obey the civil law, (either one with another, as when they assemble to make a common representative, or with the representative itself one by one, when subdued by the sword they promise obedience, that they may receive life). And therefore obedience to the civil law is part also of the law of nature. Civil and natural law are not different kinds, but different parts of law; whereof one part being written, is called civil, the other unwritten, natural. But the right of nature, that is, the natural liberty of man, may by the civil law be abridged, and restrained: nay, the end of making laws, is no other, but such restraint; without the which there cannot possibly be any peace. And law was brought into the world for nothing else, but to limit the natural liberty of particular men, in such manner, as they might not hurt, but assist one another, and join together against a common enemy.

QUESTIONS FOR DISCUSSION

1. What are the three principal causes of quarrel or civil war among men? How do these causes (for the sake of economic gain, national security, and glory) also explain wars among nations? Define "state of nature."
2. Why does Hobbes say that in this war of every man against every man, nothing can be unjust or just, right or wrong?
3. How does or can a society emerge from the state of nature to a civil state or commonwealth?
4. What does Hobbes mean by "Liberty and necessity are consistent"?
5. Is the social covenant or contract a historical or logical basis of government?

Immanuel Kant (1724-1804)

4.2   Perpetual Peace

FIRST SECTION

CONTAINING THE PRELIMINARY ARTICLES OF PERPETUAL PEACE BETWEEN STATES

1. *No treaty of peace shall be regarded as valid if made with the secret reservation of material for a future war.*

For then it would be a mere truce, a mere suspension of hostilities, not

From *Perpetual Peace* (1796). Translated by M. Campbell Smith (London, 1903).

peace. A peace signifies the end of all hostilities and to attach to it the epithet "eternal" is not only a verbal pleonasm, but matter of suspicion: The causes of a future war existing, although perhaps not yet known to the high contracting parties themselves, are entirely annihilated by the conclusion of peace, however acutely they may be ferreted out of documents in the public archives. There may be a mental reservation of old claims to be thought out at a future time, which are, none of them, mentioned at this stage because both parties are too much exhausted to continue the war, while the evil intention remains of using the first favorable opportunity for further hostilities. Diplomacy of this kind only Jesuitical casuistry can justify: it is beneath the dignity of a ruler, just as acquiescence in such processes of reasoning is beneath the dignity of his minister, if one judges the facts as they really are.

If, however, according to present enlightened ideas of political wisdom, the true glory of a state lies in the uninterrupted development of its power by every possible means, this judgment must certainly strike one as scholastic and pedantic.

2. *No state having an independent existence—whether it be great or small —shall be acquired by another through inheritance, exchange, purchase or donation.*

For a state is not a property, as may be the ground on which its people are settled. It is a society of human beings over whom no one but itself has the right to rule and to dispose. Like the trunk of a tree, it has its own roots, and to graft it on to another state is to do away with its existence as a moral person, and to make of it a thing. Hence it is in contradiction to the idea of the original contract without which no right over a people is thinkable. Everyone knows to what danger the bias in favor of these modes of acquisition has brought Europe (in other parts of the world it has never been known). The custom of marriage between states, as if they were individuals, has survived even up to the most recent times, and is regarded partly as a new kind of industry by which ascendency may be acquired through family alliances, without any expenditure of strength; partly as a device for territorial expansion. Moreover, the hiring out of the troops of one state to another to fight against an enemy not at war with their native country is to be reckoned in this connection; for the subjects are in this way used and abused at will as personal property.

3. *Standing armies shall be abolished in course of time.*

For they are always threatening other states with war by appearing to be in constant readiness to fight. They incite the various states to outrival one another in the number of their soldiers, and to this number no limit can be set. Now, since owing to the sums devoted to this purpose, peace at last becomes even more oppressive than a short war, these standing armies are themselves the cause of wars of aggression, undertaken in order to get rid of this burden. To which we must add the practice of hiring men to kill or to be killed seems to imply a use of them as mere machines and instruments in the hand of another (namely, the state) which cannot easily be reconciled with the right of humanity in our own person. The matter stands quite differently in the case of voluntary periodical military exercise on the part of citizens of the state, who thereby seek to secure themselves and their country against attack from without.

The accumulation of treasure in a state would in the same way be regarded by other states as a menace of war, and might compel them to anticipate this by striking the first blow. For of the three forces, the power of arms, the power of alliance, and the power of money, the last might well become the most reliable instrument of war did not the difficulty of ascertaining the amount stand in the way.

4. *No national debts shall be contracted in connection with the external affairs of the state.*

This source of help is above suspicion where assistance is sought outside or within the state, on behalf of the economic administration of the country (for instance, the improvements of the roads, the settlement and support of new colonies, the establishment of granaries to provide against seasons of scarcity, and so on). But, as a common weapon used by the Powers against one another, a credit system under which debts go on indefinitely increasing and are yet always assured against immediate claims (because all the creditors do not put in their claim at once) is a dangerous money power. This ingenious invention of a commercial people in the present century is, in other words, a treasure for the carrying on of war which may exceed the treasures of all the other states taken together, and can only be exhausted by a threatening deficiency in the taxes—an event, however, which will long be kept off by the very briskness of commerce resulting from the reaction of this system on industry and trade. The ease, then, with which war may be waged, coupled with the inclination of rulers towards it—an inclination which seems to be implanted in human nature—is a great obstacle in the way of perpetual peace. The prohibition of this system must be laid down as a preliminary article of perpetual peace, all the more necessarily because the final inevitable bankruptcy of the state in question must involve in the loss many who are innocent, and this would be a public injury to these states. Therefore other nations are at least justified

in uniting themselves against such an one and its pretensions.

5. *No state shall violently interfere with the constitution and administration of another.*

For what can justify it in so doing? The scandal which is here presented to the subjects of another state? The erring state can much more serve as a warning by exemplifying the great evils which a nation draws on itself through its own lawlessness. Moreover, the bad example which one free person gives another does no injury to the latter. In this connection, it is true we cannot count the case of a state which has become split up through internal corruption into two parts, each of them representing by itself an individual state which lays claim to the whole. Here the yielding of assistance to one faction could not be reckoned as interference on the part of a foreign state with the constitution of another, for here anarchy prevails. So long, however, as the inner strife has not yet reached this stage the interference of other powers would be a violation of the rights of an independent nation which is only struggling with internal disease. It would therefore itself cause a scandal, and make the autonomy of all states insecure.

6. *No state at war with another shall countenance such modes of hostility as would make mutual confidence impossible in a subsequent state of peace: such are the employment of assassins or of poisoners, breaches of capitulation, the instigating and making use of treachery in the hostile state.*

These are dishonorable stratagems. For some kind of confidence in the disposition of the enemy must exist even in the midst of war, as otherwise peace could not be concluded, and the hostilities would pass into a war of extermination. War, however, is only our wretched expedient of asserting a right by force—an expedient adopted in the state of nature where no court of justice exists, which could settle the matter in dispute. In circumstances like these, neither of the two parties can be called an unjust enemy because this form of speech presupposes a legal decision: the issue of the conflict—just as in the case of the so-called judgments of God—decides on which side right is. Between states, however, no punitive war is thinkable because between them a relation of superior and inferior does not exist. Whence it follows that a war of extermination, where the process of annihilation would strike both parties at once and all right as well, would bring about perpetual peace only in the great graveyard of the human race. Such a war, then, and therefore also the use of all means which lead to it, must be absolutely forbidden. That the methods just mentioned do inevitably lead to this result is obvious from the fact that these infernal arts, already vile in themselves, on coming into use, are not long confined to the sphere of war. Take, for example, the use of spies (*uti exploratoribus*). Here only the dishonesty of others is made use of; but vices such as these, when once encouraged, cannot in the nature of things be stamped out and would be carried over into the state of peace, where their presence would be utterly destructive to the purpose of that state.

Although the laws stated are, objectively regarded (i.e., in so far as they affect the action of rulers), purely prohibitive laws, some of them are strictly valid without regard to circumstances and urgently require to be enforced. Such as Nos. 1, 5, 6. Others, again—like Nos. 2, 3, 4—although not indeed exceptions to the maxims of law, yet in respect of the practical application of these maxims, allow subjectively of a certain latitude to suit particular circumstances. The enforcement of these by laws may be legitimately put off, so long as we do not lose sight of the ends at which they aim. This purpose of reform does not permit of the deferment of an act of restitution (as, for example, the restoration to certain states of freedom of which they have been deprived in the manner described in article 2) to an infinitely distant date —as Augustus used to say, to the "Greek Kalends," a day that will never come. This would be to sanction nonrestitution. Delay is permitted only with the intention that restitution should not be made too precipitately and so defeat the purpose we have in view. For the prohibition refers here only to the *mode of acquisition* which is to be no longer valid, and not to the *fact of possession* which, although indeed it has not the necessary title of right, yet at the time of so-called acquisition was held legal by all states, in accordance with the public opinion of the time.

SECOND SECTION

CONTAINING THE DEFINITIVE ARTICLES OF A PERPETUAL PEACE BETWEEN STATES

A state of peace among men who live side by side is not the natural state which is rather to be described as a state of war: that is to say, although there is not perhaps always actual open hostility, yet there is a constant threatening that an outbreak may occur. Thus the state of peace must be established. For the mere cessation of hostilities is no guarantee of continued peaceful relations, and unless this guarantee is given by every individual to his neighbor—which can only be done in a state of society regulated by law—one man is at liberty to challenge another and treat him as an enemy.

1. *The civil constitution of each state shall be republican.*

The only constitution which has its origin in the idea of the original contract, upon which the lawful legislation of every nation must be based, is the republican. It is a constitution, in the first place, founded in accordance with the principle of the freedom of the members of society as human beings: secondly, in accordance with the principle of the dependence of all, as subjects, on a common legislation; and, thirdly, in accordance with the law of the equality of the members as citizens. It is then, looking at the question of right, the only constitution whose fundamental principles lie at the basis of every form of civil constitution. And the only question for us now is whether it is also the one constitution which can lead to perpetual peace.

Now the republican constitution, apart from the soundness of its origin, since it arose from the pure source of the concept of right, has also the prospect of attaining the desired result—namely, perpetual peace. And the reason is this. If, as must be so under this constitution, the consent of the subjects is required to determine whether there shall be war or not, nothing is more natural than that they should weigh the matter well, before undertaking such a bad business. For in decreeing war, they would, of necessity, be resolving to bring down the miseries of war upon their country. This implies: they must fight themselves; they must pay for the costs of the war out of their own property; they must do their poor best to make good the devastation which it leaves behind; and finally, as a crowning ill, they have to accept a burden of debt which will embitter even peace itself, and which they can never pay off on account of the new wars which are always impending. On the other hand, in a government where the subject is not a citizen holding a vote (i.e., in a constitution which is not republican), the plunging into war is the least serious thing in the world. For the ruler is not a citizen but the owner of the state, and does not lose a whit by the war, while he goes on enjoying the delights of his table or sport, or of his pleasure palaces and gala days. He can therefore decide on war for the most trifling reasons, as if it were a kind of pleasure party. Any justification of it that is necessary for the sake of decency he can leave without concern to the diplomatic corps who are always only too ready with their services.

2. *The law of nations shall be founded on a federation of free states.*

Nations, as states, may be judged like individuals who, living in the natural state of society—that is to say, uncontrolled by external law—injure one another through their very proximity. Every state, for the sake of its own security, may—and ought to—demand that its neighbor should submit itself to conditions similar to those of the civil society where the right of every individual is guaranteed. This would give rise to a federation of nations, which, however, would not have to be a "state of nations." That would involve a contradiction. For the term "state" implies the relation of one who rules to those who obey—that is to say, of lawgiver to the subject people: and many nations in one state would constitute only one nation, which contradicts our hypothesis, since here we have to consider the right of one nation against another, in so far as they are so many separate states and are not to be fused into one. . . .

The depravity of human nature shows itself without disguise in the unrestrained relations of nations to each other, while in the law-governed civil state much of this is hidden by the check of government. This being so, it is astonishing that the word "right" has not yet been entirely banished from the politics of war as pedantic, and that no state has yet ventured to publicly advocate this point of view: For Hugo Grotius, Pufendorf, Vattel, and others—Job's comforters, all of them—are always quoted in good faith to justify an attack, although their codes, whether couched in philosophical or diplomatic terms, have not—nor can have—the slightest legal force, because states, as such, are under no common external authority; and there is no instance of a state having ever been moved by argument to desist from its purpose, even when this was backed up by the testimony of such great men. This homage which every state renders—in words at least—to the idea of right proves that, although it may be slumbering, there is, notwithstanding, to be found in man a still higher natural moral capacity by the aid of which he will in time gain the mastery over the evil principle in his nature, the existence of which he is unable to deny. And he hopes the same of others; for otherwise the word "right" would never be uttered by states who wish to wage war, unless to deride it like the Gallic Prince who declared: "The privilege which nature gives the strong is that the weak must obey them."

The method by which states prosecute their rights can never be by process of law—as it is where there is an external tribunal—but only by war. Through this means, however, and its favorable issue, victory, the question of right is never decided. A treaty of peace makes, it may be, an end to the war of the moment, but not to the conditions of war which at any time may afford a new pretext for opening hostilities; and this we cannot exactly condemn as unjust, because under these conditions everyone is his own judge. Notwithstanding, not quite the same rule applies to states according to the law of nations as holds good of individuals in a lawless condition according to the law of nature, namely, "that they ought to advance out of this condition." This is so because, as states, they have already within themselves a legal constitution, and have therefore advanced beyond the stage at which others, in accordance with their ideas of right, can force them to come under a wider legal constitution. Meanwhile, however, reason, from her throne of the supreme lawgiving moral power, absolutely condemns war as a morally lawful proceeding, and makes a state of peace, on the other hand, an immediate duty. Without a compact between the nations, however, this state of peace cannot be established or assured. Hence there must be an alliance of a particular kind which we may call a covenant of peace which would differ from a treaty of peace in this respect that the latter merely puts an end to one war, while the former would seek to put an end to war forever. This alliance does not aim at the gain of any power whatsoever of the state, but merely at the preservation and security of the freedom of the state for itself and of other allied states at the same time. The latter do not, however, require, for this reason, to submit themselves like individuals in the state of nature to public laws and coercion. The practicability or objective reality of this idea of federation, which is to extend gradually over all states and so lead to perpetual peace, can be shown. For, if Fortune ordains that a powerful and enlightened people should form a republic —which by its very nature is inclined to perpetual peace—this would serve as a center of federal union for other states wishing to join, and thus secure conditions of freedom among the states in accordance with the idea of the law of nations. Gradually, through different union of this kind, the federation would extend further and further.

It is quite comprehensible that a people should say: "There shall be no war among us, for we shall form ourselves into a state—that is to say, constitute for ourselves a supreme legislative, administrative, and judicial power which will settle our disputes peaceably." But if this state says: "There shall be no war between me and other states, although I recognize no supreme lawgiving power which will secure me my rights and whose rights I will guarantee"; then it is not at all clear upon what grounds I could base my confidence in my right, unless it were the substitute for that compact on which civil society is based—namely, free federation which reason must necessarily connect with the idea of the law of nations, if indeed any meaning is to be left in that concept at all.

There is no intelligible meaning in the idea of the law of nations as giving a right to make war; for that must be a right to decide what is just, not in accordance with universal, external laws limiting the freedom of each individual, but by means of one-sided maxims applied by force. We must then understand by this that men of such ways of thinking are quite justly served when they destroy one another, and thus find perpetual peace in the wide grave which covers all the abominations of acts of violence as well as the authors of such deeds. For states, in their relation to one another, there can be, according to reason, no other way of advancing from that lawless condition which unceasing war implies, than by giving up their savage lawless freedom, just as individual men have done, and yielding to the coercion of public laws. Thus they can form a State of nations, one, too, which will be ever increasing and would finally embrace all the peoples of the earth. States, however, in accordance with their understanding of the law of nations, by no means desire this, and therefore reject *in hypothesi* what is correct *in thesi*. Hence, instead of the positive idea of a world-republic, if all is not to be lost, only the negative substitute for it, a federation averting war, maintaining its ground, and ever extending over the world, may stop the current of this tendency to war and shrinking from the control of law. But even then there will be a constant danger that this propensity may break out.

3. *The rights of men, as citizens of the world, shall be limited to the conditions of universal hospitality.*

We are speaking here, as in the previous articles, not of philanthropy, but of right; and in this sphere hospitality signifies the claim of a stranger entering foreign territory to be treated by its owner without hostility. The latter may send him away again if this can be done without causing his death; but, so long as he conducts himself peaceably, he must not be treated as an enemy. . . .

The intercourse, more or less close, which has been everywhere steadily increasing between the nations of the earth, has now extended so enormously that a violation of right in one part of the world is felt all over it. Hence the idea of a cosmopolitan right is no fantastical, high-flown notion of right, but a complement of the unwritten code of law—constitutional as well as international law—necessary for the public rights of mankind in general and thus for the realization of perpetual peace. For only by endeavoring to fulfill the conditions laid down by this cosmopolitan law can we flatter ourselves that we are gradually approaching that ideal.

FIRST SUPPLEMENT

CONCERNING THE GUARANTEE OF PERPETUAL PEACE

This guarantee is given by no less a power than the great artist nature in whose mechanical course is clearly exhibited a predetermined design to make harmony spring from human discord, even against the will of man. Now this design, although called "Fate" when looked upon as the compelling force of a cause the laws of whose operation are unknown to us, is, when considered as the purpose manifested in the course of nature, called "Providence," as the deeplying wisdom of a Higher Cause, directing itself towards the ultimate practical end of the human race and predetermining the cause of things with a view to its realization. This Providence we do not, it is true, perceive in the cunning contrivances of nature; nor can we even conclude from the fact of their existence that it is there; but, as in every relation between the form of things and their final cause, we can, and must, supply the thought of a Higher Wisdom, in order that we may be able to form an idea of the possible existence of these products after the analogy of human works of art. The representation to ourselves of the relation and agreement of these formations of nature to the moral purpose for which they were made and which reason directly prescribes to us, is an Idea, it is true, which is in theory superfluous; but in practice it is dogmatic, and its objective reality is well established. Thus we see, for example, with regard to the ideal of perpetual peace, that it is our duty to make use of the mechanism of nature for the realization of that end. Moreover, in a case like this where we are interested merely in the theory and not in the religious question, the use of the word "nature" is more appropriate than that of "providence," in view of the limitations of human reason, which, in considering the relation of effects to their causes, must keep within the limits of possible experience. And the term "nature" is also less presumptuous than the other. To speak of a Providence knowable by us would be boldly to put on the wings of Icarus in order to draw near to the mystery of its unfathomable purpose. . . .

Now comes the question which touches the essential points in this design of a perpetual peace: "What does nature do in this respect with reference to the end which man's own reason sets before him as a duty? and consequently what does she do to further the realization of his moral purpose? How does she guarantee that what man, by the laws of freedom, ought to do and yet fails to do, he will do, without any infringement of his freedom by the compulsion of nature and that, moreover, this shall be done in accordance with the three form of public right—constitutional or political law, international law, and cosmopolitan law?" When I say of nature that she *wills* that this or that should take place, I do not mean that she imposes upon us the duty to do it—for only the free, unrestrained, practical reason can do that—but that she does it herself, whether we will or not.

1. Even if a people were not compelled through internal discord to submit to the restraint of public laws, wars would bring this about, working from without. For, according to the contrivance of nature which we have mentioned, every people finds another tribe in its neighborhood, pressing upon it in such a manner that it is compelled to form itself internally into a state to be able to defend itself as a power should. Now the republican constitution is the only one which is perfectly adapted to the rights of man, but it is also the most difficult to establish and still more to maintain. So generally is this recognized that people often say the members of a republican state would require to be angels, because men, with their self-seeking propensities, are not fit for a constitution of so sublime a form. But now nature comes to the aid of the universal, reason-derived will which, much as we honor it, is in practice powerless. And this she does by means of these very self-seeking propensities, so that it only depends —and so much lies within the power of man—on a good organization of the state for their forces to be so pitted against one another, that the one may check the destructive activity of the other or neutralize its effect. And hence, from the standpoint of reason, the result will be the same as if both forces did not exist, and each individual is compelled to be, if not a morally good man, yet at least a good citizen. The problem of the formation of the state, hard as it may sound, is not insoluble, even for a race of devils, granted that they have intelligence. It may be put thus: "Given a multitude of rational beings who, in a body, require general laws for their own preservation, but each of whom, as an individual, is secretly inclined to exempt himself from this restraint: how are we to order their affairs and how establish for them a constitution such that, although their private dis-

positions may be really antagonistic, they may yet so act as a check upon one another that, in their public relations, the effect is the same as if they had no such evil sentiments." Such a problem must be capable of solution. For it deals, not with the moral reformation of mankind, but only with the mechanism of nature; and the problem is to learn how this mechanism of nature can be applied to men, in order so to regulate the antagonism of conflicting interests in a people that they may even compel one another to submit to compulsory laws and thus necessarily bring about the state of peace in which laws have force. We can see, in states actually existing, although very imperfectly organized, that, in externals, they already approximate very nearly to what the *idea* of right prescribes, although the principle of morality is certainly not the cause. A good political constitution, however, is not to be expected as a result of progress in morality; but rather, conversely, the good moral condition of a nation is to be looked for as one of the first fruits of such a constitution. Hence the mechanism of nature, working through the self-seeking propensities of man (which of course counteract one another in their external effects), may be used by reason as a means of making way for the realization of her own purpose—the empire of right —and, as far as is in the power of the state, to promote and secure in this way internal as well as external peace. We may say, then, that it is the irresistible will of nature that right shall at last get the supremacy. What one here fails to do will be accomplished in the long run, although perhaps with much inconvenience to us. As Bouterwek says, "If you bend the reed too much it breaks: he who would do too much does nothing."

2. The idea of international law presupposes the separate existence of a number of neighboring and independent states; and, although such a condition of things is in itself already a state of war (if a federative union of these nations does not prevent the outbreak of hostilities), yet, according to the *idea* of reason, this is better than that all the states should be merged into one under a power which has gained the ascendancy over its neighbors and gradually become a universal monarchy. For the wider the sphere of their jurisdiction, the more laws lose in force; and soulless despotism, when it has choked the seeds of good, at last sinks into anarchy. Nevertheless, it is the desire of every state, or of its ruler, to attain to a permanent condition of peace in this very way—that is to say, by subjecting the whole world as far as possible to its sway. But nature wills it otherwise. She employs two means to separate nations, and prevent them from intermixing—namely, the differences of language and of religion. These differences bring with them a tendency to mutual hatred, and furnish pretexts for waging war. But, none the less, with the growth of culture and the gradual advance of men to greater unanimity of principle, they lead to concord in a state of peace which, unlike the despotism we have spoken of (the churchyard of freedom), does not arise from the weakening of all forces, but is brought into being and secured through the equilibrium of these forces in their most active rivalry.

3. As nature wisely separates nations which the will of each state, sanctioned even by the principles of

international law, would gladly unite under its own sway by stratagem or force; in the same way, on the other hand, she unites nations whom the principle of a cosmopolitan right would not have secured against violence and war. And this union she brings about through an appeal to their mutual interests. The commercial spirit cannot co-exist with war, and sooner or later it takes possession of every nation. For, of all the forces which lie at the command of a state, the power of money is probably the most reliable. Hence states find themselves compelled—not, it is true, exactly from motives of morality—to further the noble end of peace and to avert war, by means of mediation, wherever it threatens to break out, just as if they had made a permanent league for this purpose. For great alliances with a view to war can, from the nature of things, only very rarely occur, and still more seldom succeed.

In this way nature guarantees the coming of perpetual peace, through the natural course of human propensities: not indeed with sufficient certainty to enable us to prophesy the future of this ideal theoretically, but yet clearly enough for practical purposes. And thus this guarantee of nature makes it a duty that we should labor for this end—an end which is no mere chimera. . . .

QUESTIONS FOR DISCUSSION

1. Why do historical "treaties of peace" never abolish war entirely? State Kant's proposed remedies for such treaties.
2. Compare Hobbes's theory of the social contract and "state of nature" with Kant's view of "the state of nations" bound by no covenant of peace that can be enforced.
3. Why must international law for a "perpetual peace" be founded on a federation of free states?
4. Explain Kant's claim that "reason absolutely condemns war as a morally lawful proceeding, and makes a state of peace . . . an immediate duty," and that without a compact between nations this state of peace cannot be established.
5. Do you agree with Kant that Nature guarantees the coming of perpetual peace? Give your reasons for accepting or rejecting Kant's arguments about Nature coming to the aid of universal reason and its will for eternal peace.

Georg W. F. Hegel (1770-1831)

4.3   Introduction to the
Philosophy of History

The inquiry into the *essential destiny* of Reason—as far as it is considered in reference to the world—is identical with the question, *what is the ultimate purpose of the world?* And the expression implies that that purpose is to be realized. Two points of consideration suggest themselves: first, the *import* of this design—its abstract definition; and secondly, its *realization.*

It must be observed at the outset, that the object we investigate—universal history—belongs to the realm of *Spirit.* The term "world" includes both physical and psychical nature. Physical nature also plays its part in the world's history, and from the very beginning attention will have to be paid to the fundamental natural relations thus involved. But Spirit, and the course of its development, is our substantial object. Our task does not require us to contemplate nature as a rational system in itself—though in its own proper domain it proves itself such—but simply in its relation to *Spirit.* On the stage on which we are observing it—universal history—Spirit displays itself in its most concrete

From *Lectures on the Philosophy of History.* Translated by J. Sibree (1852).

actuality. Notwithstanding this (or rather for the very purpose of comprehending the *general* principles which this, its form of *concrete actuality,* embodies) we must premise some abstract characteristics of the *nature of Spirit.* Such an explanation, however, cannot be given here under any other form than that of bare assertion. The present is not the occasion for unfolding the idea of Spirit speculatively; for whatever has a place in an introduction, must, as already observed, be taken as simply historical; something assumed as having been explained and proved elsewhere; or whose demonstration awaits the sequel of the Science of History itself.

We have therefore to mention here:

1. The abstract characteristics of the nature of Spirit.

2. What means Spirit uses in order to realize its Idea.

3. Lastly, we must consider the shape which the perfect embodiment of Spirit assumes—the state.

The nature of Spirit may be understood by a glance at its direct opposite—*Matter.* As the essence of matter is gravity, so, on the other hand, we may affirm that the substance, the essence of Spirit is freedom. All will readily assent to the doctrine that Spirit, among other properties, is also endowed with freedom; but philosophy teaches that all the qualities of Spirit exist only through freedom; that all are but means for attaining freedom; that all seek and produce this and this alone. And it is a precept of speculative philosophy, that freedom is the sole truth of Spirit. Matter possesses gravity in virtue of its tendency towards a central point. It is essentially composite, consisting of parts that *exclude* each other. It seeks its unity; and therefore exhibits the tendency towards self-destruction, towards its opposite [an indivisible point.] If it could attain this, it would be matter no longer; it would have perished. It strives after the realization of its Idea; for in unity it exists *ideally*. Spirit, on the contrary, may be defined as that which has its center in itself. It has not a unity beyond itself, but has already found it; it exists *in* and *with itself*. Matter has its essence out of itself; Spirit is *self-contained existence* (*Bei-sich-selbst-sein*). Now this is freedom, exactly. For if I am dependent, my being is referred to something else which I am not; I cannot exist independently of something external. I am free, on the contrary, when my existence depends upon myself. This self-contained existence of Spirit is none other than self-consciousness—consciousness of one's own being. Two things must be distinguished in consciousness; first, the fact *that I know;* secondly, *what I know*. In *self*-consciousness these are merged in one; for Spirit *knows itself*. It involves an appreciation of its own nature, as also an energy enabling it to realize itself; to make itself *actually* that which it is *potentially*. According to this abstract definition it may be said of universal history, that it is the exhibition of Spirit in the process of working out the knowledge of that which it is potentially. And as the germ bears in itself the whole nature of the tree, and the taste and form of its fruits, so do the first traces of Spirit virtually contain the whole of that history. The Orientals have not attained the knowledge that Spirit— Man *as such*—is free; and because they do not know this they are not free. They only know that *one is free*. But on this very account, the freedom of that one is only caprice; ferocity—brutal recklessness or passion, or a mildness and tameness of the desires, which is itself only an accident of nature or mere caprice like the former—that *one* is therefore only a despot; not a *free man*. The consciousness of freedom first arose among the Greeks, and therefore they were free; but they, and the Romans likewise, knew only that *some* are free—not man as such. Even Plato and Aristotle did not know this. The Greeks, therefore, had slaves; and their whole life and the maintenance of their splendid liberty was implicated with the institution of slavery: a fact, moreover, which made that liberty on the one hand only an accidental, transient, and limited growth; on the other hand, constituted it a rigorous thraldom of our common nature—of the human. The German nations, under the influence of Christianity, were the first to attain the consciousness, that man, as man, is free: that it is the *freedom* of Spirit which constitutes its essence. This consciousness arose first in religion, the inmost region of Spirit; but to introduce the principle into the various relations of the actual world involves a more extensive problem than its simple implantation; a problem whose solution and application require a severe and lengthened process of culture. As an example of this, we may note that slavery did not cease immediately on the reception of Christianity. Still less did liberty predominate in states; or governments and constitutions adopt a rational organization, or recognize freedom as their basis. That application of the principle to political relations, the thorough molding and interpenetration of the constitution of society by it, is a process identical with history itself. I have already directed attention to the distinction here involved, between a principle as such, and its *application;* i.e., its introduction and carrying out in the actuality of Spirit and life. This is a point of fundamental importance in our science, and one which must be constantly respected as essential. And in the same way as this distinction has attracted attention in view of the *Christian* principle of self-consciousness—freedom, it also shows itself as an essential one, in view of the principle of freedom *generally.* The history of the world is none other than the progress in the consciousness of freedom; a progress whose development according to the necessity of its nature, it is our business to investigate.

The general statement given above, of the various grades in the consciousness of freedom—and which we applied in the first instance to the fact that the Eastern nations knew only *one* is free; the Greek and Roman world only that *some* are free; whilst *we* know that all men absolutely (man *as man*) are free—supplies us with the natural division of univer-

sal history, and suggests the mode of its discussion. This is remarked, however, only incidentally and anticipatively; some other ideas must be first explained.

The destiny of the spiritual world, and—since this is the *substantial world,* while the physical remains subordinate to it, or, in the language of speculation, has no truth *as against* the spiritual—the *final cause of the world at large,* we allege to be the *consciousness* of its own freedom on the part of Spirit, and *ipso facto,* the *reality* of that freedom. But that this term "freedom," without further qualification, is an indefinite and incalculable ambiguous term; and that while that which it represents is the *ne plus ultra* of attainment, it is liable to an infinity of misunderstandings, confusions, and errors, and to become the occasion for all imaginable excesses—has never been more clearly known and felt than in modern times. Yet, for the present, we must content ourselves with the term itself without further definition. Attention was also directed to the importance of the infinite difference between a principle in the abstract, and its actualization in the concrete. In the process before us, the essential nature of freedom—which involves in it absolute necessity—is to be displayed as coming to a consciousness of itself (for it is in its very nature, self-consciousness) and thereby actualizing its existence. Itself is its own object of attainment, and the sole aim of Spirit. This result it is, at which the process of the world's history has been continually aiming; and to which the sacrifices that have ever and anon been laid on the vast altar of the earth, through the long lapse of ages, have been offered. This is the only aim that sees itself realized and fulfilled; the only pole of repose amid the ceaseless change of events and conditions, and the truly efficient principle that pervades them. This final aim is God's purpose with the world; but God is the absolutely perfect being, and can, therefore, will nothing other than himself—his own will. The nature of His will—that is, His nature itself—is what we here call the idea of freedom; translating the language of religion into that of thought. The question, then, which we may next put, is: What means does this principle of freedom use for its realization? This is the second point we have to consider.

The question of the *means* by which freedom develops itself to a world conducts us to the phenomenon of history itself. Although freedom is, primarily, an undeveloped idea, the means it uses are external and phenomenal, presenting themselves in history to our sensuous vision. The first glance at history convinces us that the actions of men proceed from their needs, their passions, their interests, their characters and talents; and impresses us with the belief that such needs, passions, and interest are the sole springs of action—the efficient agents in this scene of activity. Among these may, perhaps, be found aims of a liberal or universal kind—benevolence it may be, or noble patriotism; but such virtues and general views are but insignificant as compared with the world and its doings. We may, perhaps, see the ideal of Reason actualized in those who adopt such aims, and within the spheres of their influence; but they bear only a trifling proportion to the mass of the human race; and the extent of that

influence is limited accordingly. Passions, private aims, and the satisfaction of selfish desires, are on the other hand, most effective springs of action. Their power lies in the fact that they respect none of the limitations which justice and morality would impose on them; and that these natural impulses have a more direct influence over man than the artificial and tedious discipline that tends to order and self-restraint, law and morality. When we look at this display of passions, and the consequences of their violence; the unreason which is associated not only with them, but even (rather we might say *especially*) with *good* designs and righteous aims; when we see the evil, the vice, the ruin that has befallen the most flourishing kingdoms which the mind of man ever created, we can scarce avoid being filled with sorrow at this universal taint of corruption: and, since this decay is not the work of mere nature, but of the human will—a moral embitterment—a revolt of the good spirit (if it have a place within us) may well be the result of our reflections. Without rhetorical exaggeration, a simply truthful combination of the miseries that have overwhelmed the noblest of nations and polities, and the finest exemplars of private virtue—forms a picture of most fearful aspect, and excites emotions of the profoundest and most hopeless sadness, counterbalanced by no consolatory result. We endure in beholding it a mental torture, allowing no defense or escape but the consideration that what has happened could not be otherwise; that it is a fatality which no intervention could alter. And at last we draw back from the intolerable disgust with which these sorrowful reflections threaten us, into the more agreeable environment of our individual life—the present formed by our private aims and interests. In short, we retreat into the selfishness that stands on the quiet shore, and thence enjoy in safety the distant spectacle of "wrecks confusedly hurled." But even regarding history as the slaughter-bench at which the happiness of peoples, the wisdom of states, and the virtue of individuals have been victimized—the question involuntarily arises—to what principle, to what final aim these enormous sacrifices have been offered. From this point the investigation usually proceeds to that which we have made the general commencement of our inquiry. Starting from this we pointed out those events which made up a picture so suggestive of gloomy emotions and thoughtful reflections—as *the very field* which we, for our part, regard as exhibiting only the means for realizing what we assert to be the essential destiny—the absolute aim, or —which comes to the same thing—the true *result* of the world's history. We have all along purposely eschewed "moral reflections" as a method of rising from the scene of particular historical events to the general principles which they embody. Besides, it is not the interest of such sentimentalities, really to rise above those depressing emotions, and to solve the enigmas of providence which the considerations that occasioned them present. It is essential to their character to find a gloomy satisfaction in the empty and fruitless sublimities of that negative result. We return then to the point of view which we have adopted; observing that the successive steps (*Momente*) of the analysis to which it will lead us, will also evolve the conditions requisite for answering the en-

quiries suggested by the panorama of sin and suffering that history unfolds.

The *first* remark we have to make, and which—though already presented more than once—cannot be too often repeated when the occasion seems to call for it—is that what we call *principle, aim, destiny,* or the nature and idea of Spirit, is something merely general and abstract. Principle—plan of existence—law—is an undeveloped essence, which *as such*—however true in itself—is not completely actual. Aims, principles, etc., have a place in our thoughts, in our subjective design only; but not yet in the sphere of actuality. That which exists for itself only, is a possibility, a potentiality; but has not yet emerged into existence. A *second* element must be introduced in order to produce actuality—viz., actuation, realization; and whose principle is the will—the activity of man in the widest sense. It is only by this activity that that Idea, as well as abstract characteristics generally, are realized, actualized; for of themselves they are powerless. The motive power that puts them in operation and gives them determinate existence, is the need, instinct, inclination, and passion of man. That some conception of mine should be developed into act and existence, is my earnest desire: I wish to assert my personality in connection with it: I wish to be satisfied by its execution. If I am to exert myself for any object, it must in some way or other be *my* object. In the accomplishment of such or such designs I must at the same time find *my* satisfaction; although the purpose for which I exert myself includes a complication of results, many of which have no interest for me. This is the absolute right of personal existence—to find *itself* satisfied in its activity and labor. If men are to interest themselves for anything, they must (so to speak) have part of their existence involved in it; find their individuality gratified by its attainment. Here a mistake must be avoided. We intend blame, and justly impute it as a fault, when we say of an individual that he is "interested" (in taking part in such or such transactions), that is, seeks only his private advantage. In reprehending this we find fault with him for furthering his personal aims without any regard to a more comprehensive design; of which he takes advantage to promote his own interest, or which he even sacrifices with this view. But he who is active in *promoting an object* is not simply "interested," but interested in that object itself. Language faithfully expresses this distinction. Nothing therefore happens, nothing is accomplished, unless the individuals concerned seek their own satisfaction in the issue. They are particular units of society; i.e., they have special needs, instincts, and interests generally, peculiar to themselves. Among these needs are not only such as we usually call necessities—the stimuli of individual desire and volition—but also those connected with individual views and convictions; or—to use a term expressing less decision—leanings of opinion, supposing the impulses of reflection, understanding, and reason, to have been awakened. In these cases people demand, if they are to exert themselves in any direction, that the object should commend itself to them; that in point of opinion—whether as to its goodness, justice, advantage, profit,—they should be able to "enter into it" (*dabei sein*). This is a consideration of especial importance in our age, when people are less than

formerly influenced by reliance on others, and by authority; when, on the contrary, they devote their activities to a cause on the ground of their own understanding, their independent conviction and opinion.

We assert then that nothing has been accomplished without interest on the part of the actors; and—if interest be called passion, inasmuch as the whole individuality, to the neglect of all other actual or possible interest and aims, is devoted to an object with every fibre of volition, concentrating all its desires and powers upon it—we may affirm absolutely that *nothing great* in *the world* has been accomplished without *passion*. Two elements, therefore, enter into the object of our investigation; the first the Idea, the second the complex of human passions; the one the warp, the other the woof of the vast tapestry of universal history. The concrete mean and union of the two is liberty, under the conditions of morality in a state. We have spoken of the idea of freedom as the nature of Spirit, and the absolute goal of history. Passion is regarded as a thing of sinister aspect, as more or less immoral. Man is required to have no passions. Passion, it is true, is not quite the suitable word for what I wish to express. I mean here nothing more than human activity as resulting from private interests—special, or if you will, self-seeking designs—with this qualification, that the whole energy of will and character is devoted to their attainment; that other interests (which would in themselves constitute attractive aims), or rather all things else, are sacrificed to them. The object in question is so bound up with the man's will that it entirely and alone determines the "hue of resolution," and is inseparable from it. It has become the very essence of his volition. For a person is a specific existence; not man in general (a term to which no real existence corresponds), but a particular human being. The term "character" likewise expresses the idiosyncrasy of will and intelligence. But *character* comprehends all peculiarities whatever; the way in which a person conducts himself in private relations, etc., and is not limited to his idiosyncrasy in its practical and active phase. I shall, therefore, use the term "passion"; understanding thereby the particular bent of character, as far as the peculiarities of volition are not limited to private interest, but supply the impelling and actuating force for accomplishing deeds shared in by the community at large. Passion is in the first instance the *subjective* and, therefore, the *formal* side of energy, will, and activity—leaving the object or aim still undetermined. And there is a similar relation of formality to reality in merely individual conviction, individual views, individual conscience. It is always a question of essential importance, what is the purport of my conviction, what the object of my passion, in deciding whether the one or the other is of a true and substantial nature. Conversely, if it is so, it will inevitably attain actual existence—be actualized.

From this comment on the second essential element in the historical embodiment of an aim, we infer—glancing at the institution of the state in passing—that a state is then well constituted and internally powerful, when the private interest of its citizens is one with the common interest of the state; when the one finds its gratification and realization in the other—a proposition in itself very important.

But in a state many institutions must be adopted, much political machinery invented, accompanied by appropriate political arrangements—necessitating long struggles of the understanding before what is really appropriate can be discovered—involving, moreover, contentions with private interest and passions, and a tedious discipline of these latter, in order to bring about the desired harmony. The epoch when a state attains this harmonious condition marks the period of its bloom, its virtue, its vigor, and its prosperity. But the history of mankind does not begin with a *conscious* aim of any kind, as it is the case with the particular circles into which men form themselves of set purpose. The mere social instinct implies a conscious purpose of security for life and property; and when society has been constituted, this purpose becomes more comprehensive. The history of the world begins with its general aim—the realization of the idea of Spirit—only in an *implicit* form (*an sich*) that is, as nature; an inmost, unconscious instinct; and the whole process of history (as already observed) is directed to rendering this unconscious impulse a conscious one. Thus appearing in the form of merely natural existence, natural will—that which has been called the subjective, side—physical craving, instinct, passion, private interest, as also opinion and subjective conception—spontaneously present themselves at the very commencement. This vast congeries of volitions, interests, and activities, constitute the instruments and means of the world-spirit for attaining its object; bringing it to consciousness, and realizing it. And this aim is none other than finding itself—coming to itself—and contemplating itself in concrete

actuality. But that those manifestations of vitality on the part of individuals and peoples, in which they seek
and satisfy their own purposes, are, at
the same time, the means and instruments of a higher and broader purpose of which they know nothing—
which they realize unconsciously—
might be made a matter of question;
rather has been questioned, and in
every variety of form negatived, decried, and contemned as mere dreaming and "philosophy." But on this point
I announced my view at the very
outset, and asserted our hypothesis—
which, however, will appear in the
sequel, in the form of a legitimate
inference—and our belief that Reason
governs the world, and has consequently governed its history. In relation to this independently universal
and substantial existence—all else is
subordinate, subservient to it, and the
means for its development. But moreover this Reason is immanent in historical existence and attains to its own
perfection in and through that existence. The union of universal abstract
existence generally with the individual—the subjective—that in this alone
is truth, belongs to the department
of speculation, and is treated in this
general form in logic. But in the process of the world's history itself—as still
incomplete—the abstract final aim of
history is not yet made the distinct
object of desire and interest. While
these limited sentiments are still unconscious of the purpose they are fulfilling, the universal principle is implicit in them, and is realizing itself
through them. The question also assumes the form of the union of *freedom and necessity;* the latent abstract
process of Spirit being regarded as
necessity, while that which exhibits
itself in the conscious will of men, as

their interest, belongs to the domain
of *freedom.* As the metaphysical connection (i.e., the connection in the
Idea) of these forms of thought belongs to logic, it would be out of place
to analyze it here.

It is quite otherwise with the comprehensive relations that history has
to do with. In this sphere are presented those momentous collisions between existing, acknowledged duties,
laws, and rights, and those contingencies which are adverse to this fixed
system; which assail and even destroy
its foundations and existence; whose
tenor may nevertheless seem good—
on the large scale advantageous—yes,
even indispensable and necessary.
These contingencies realize themselves
in history; they involve a general principle of a different order from that
on which depends the *permanence* of
a people or a state. This principle is
an essential phase in the development
of the *creating* Idea, of truth striving
and urging towards [consciousness of]
itself. Historical men—*world-historical
individuals*—are those in whose aims
such a general principle lies.

Caesar, in danger of losing a position, not perhaps at that time of superiority, yet at least of equality with
the others who were at the head of
the state, and of succumbing to those
who were just on the point of becoming his enemies—belongs essentially to
this category. These enemies—who
were at the same time pursuing *their*
personal aims—had the form of the
constitution, and the power conferred
by an appearance of justice, on their
side. Caesar was contending for the
maintenance of his position, honor,
and safety; and, since the power of
his opponents included the sovereignty over the provinces of the Roman Empire, his victory secured for

him the conquest of that entire empire and he thus became—though leaving the form of the constitution—the autocrat of the state. That which secured for him the execution of a design, which in the first instance was of negative import—the autocracy of Rome—was, however, at the same time an independently necessary feature in the history of Rome and of the world. It was not, then, his private gain merely, but an unconscious impulse that occasioned the accomplishment of that for which the time was ripe. Such are all great historical men, whose own particular aims involve those large issues which are the will of the world-spirit. They may be called heroes, inasmuch as they have derived their purposes and their vocation, not from the calm, regular course of things, sanctioned by the existing order, but from a concealed fount—one which has not attained to phenomenal, present existence—from that inner Spirit, still hidden beneath the surface, which, impinging on the outer world as on a shell, bursts it in pieces, because it is another kernel than that which belonged to the shell in question. They are men, therefore, who appear to draw the impulse of their life from themselves; and whose deeds have produced a condition of things and a complex of historical relations which appear to be only *their* interest and *their* work.

Such individuals had no consciousness of the general Idea they were unfolding, while prosecuting those aims of theirs; on the contrary, they were practical, political men. But at the same time they were thinking men, who had an insight into the requirements of the time—*what was ripe for development*. This was the very truth for their age, for their world; the

species next in order, so to speak, and which was already formed in the womb of time. It was theirs to know this nascent principle; the necessary, directly sequent step in progress, which their world was to take; to make this their aim, and to expend their energy in promoting it. World-historical men—the heroes of an epoch —must, therefore, be recognized as its clear-sighted ones; *their* deeds, *their* words are the best of that time. Great men have formed purposes to satisfy themselves, not others. Whatever prudent designs and counsels they might have learned from others would be the more limited and inconsistent features in their career; for it was they who best understood affairs; from whom *others* learned, and approved, or at least acquiesced in their policy. For that Spirit which had taken this fresh step in history is the inmost soul of all individuals; but in a state of unconsciousness which the great men in question aroused. Their fellows, therefore, follow these soul-leaders, for they feel the irresistible power of their own inner spirit thus embodied. If we go on to cast a look at the fate of these world-historical persons, whose vocation it was to be the agents of the world-spirit, we shall find it to have been no happy one. They attained no calm enjoyment; their whole life was labor and trouble; their whole nature was nought else but their master-passion. When their object is attained they fall off like empty hulls from the kernel. They die early, like Alexander; they are murdered, like Caesar; transported to St. Helena, like Napoleon. This fearful consolation, that historical men have not enjoyed what is called happiness, and of which only private life (and this may be passed under very various external

circumstances) is capable—this consolation those may draw from history
who stand in need of it; and it is
craved by envy—vexed at what is great
and transcendent—striving, therefore,
to depreciate it, and to find some flaw
in it. Thus in modern times it has
been demonstrated *ad nauseam* that
princes are generally unhappy on their
thrones; in consideration of which the
possession of a throne is tolerated, and
men acquiesce in the fact that not
themselves but the personages in question are its occupants. The free man,
we may observe, is not envious, but
gladly recognizes what is great and
exalted, and rejoices that it exists.

It is in the light of those common
elements which constitute the interest and therefore the passions of individuals, that these historical men
are to be regarded. They are *great*
men, because they willed and accomplished something great; not a mere
fancy; a mere intention, but that
which met the case and fell in with
the needs of the age. This mode of
considering them also excludes the
so-called "psychological" view, which
—serving the purpose of envy most
effectually—contrives so to refer all actions to the heart, to bring them under
such a subjective aspect as that their
authors appear to have done everything under the impulse of some passion, mean or grand—some *morbid
craving*—and on account of these passions and cravings to have been not
moral men. Alexander of Macedon
partly subdued Greece, and then Asia;
therefore, he was possessed by a *morbid craving* for conquest. He is alleged
to have acted from a craving for fame,
for conquest; and the proof that these
were the impelling motives is that he
did that which resulted in fame. What
pedagogue has not demonstrated of

Alexander the Great—of Julius Caesar
—that they were instigated by such
passions, and were consequently immoral men?—whence the conclusion
immediately follows that he, the
pedagogue, is a better man than
they, because he has not such passions; a proof of which lies in the
fact that he does not conquer Asia—
vanquish Darius and Porus—but while
he enjoys life himself lets others enjoy
it too. These psychologists are particularly fond of contemplating those
peculiarities of great historical figures
which appertain to them as private
persons. Man must eat and drink; he
sustains relations to friends and ac-
quaintances; he has passing impulses
and ebullitions of temper. "No man is
a hero to his valet-de-chambre," is a
well-known proverb; I have added—
and Goethe repeated it ten years later
—"but not because the former is no
hero, but because the latter is a valet."
He takes off the hero's boots, assists
him to bed, knows that he prefers
champagne, etc. Historical personages
waited upon in historical literature
by such psychological valets, come
poorly off; they are brought down by
these their attendants to a level with
—or rather a few degrees below the
level of—the morality of such exquisite
discerners of spirits. The Thersites of
Homer who abuses the kings is a
standing figure for all times. Blows—
that is beating with a solid cudgel—
he does not get in every age, as in the
Homeric one; but his envy, his egotism, is the thorn which he has to
carry in his flesh; and the undying
worm that gnaws him is the tormenting consideration that his excellent
views and vituperations remain absolutely without result in the world. But
our satisfaction at the fate of ther-
sitism also may have its sinister side.

A world-historical individual is not so unwise as to indulge a variety of wishes to divide his regards. He is devoted to the one aim, regardless of all else. It is even possible that such men may treat other great, even sacred interests, inconsiderately; conduct which is indeed obnoxious to moral reprehension. But so mighty a form must trample down many an innocent flower—crush to pieces many an object in its path.

The special interest of passion is thus inseparable from the active development of a general principle; for it is from the special and determinate and from its negation that the universal results. Particularity contends with its like, and some loss is involved in the issue. *It* is not the general idea that is implicated in opposition and combat, and that is exposed to danger. It remains in the background, untouched and uninjured. This may be called the *cunning of reason*—that it sets the passions to work for itself, while that which develops its existence through such impulsion pays the penalty, and suffers loss. For it is *phenomenal* being that is so treated, and of this, part is of no value, part is positive and real. The particular is for the most part of too trifling value as compared with the general; individuals are sacrificed and abandoned. The Idea pays the penalty of determinate existence, and of corruptibility, not from itself, but from the passions of individuals.

But though we might tolerate the idea that individuals, their desires and the gratification of them, are thus sacrificed, and their happiness given up to the empire of chance, to which it belongs; and that as a general rule, individuals come under the category of means to an ulterior end—there is

one aspect of human individuality which we should hesitate to regard in that subordinate light, even in relation to the highest; since it is absolutely no subordinate element, but exists in those individuals as inherently eternal and divine. I mean *morality, ethics, religion*. Even when speaking of the realization of the great ideal aim by means of individuals, the *subjective* element in them—their interest and that of their cravings and impulses, their views and judgments, though exhibited as the merely formal side of their existence—was spoken of as having an infinite right to be consulted. The first idea that presents itself in speaking of *means* is that of something external to the object, and having no share in the object itself. But merely natural things—even the commonest lifeless objects—used as means, must be of such a kind as adapts them to their purpose; they must possess something in common with it. Human beings least of all sustain the bare external relation of mere means to the great ideal aim. Not only do they, in the very act of realizing it, make it the occasion of satisfying personal desires, whose purport is diverse from that aim—but they share in that ideal aim itself, and are for that very reason objects of their own existence; not *formally* merely, as the world of living beings generally is—whose individual life is essentially subordinate to that of man, and is properly used *up* as an instrument. Men, on the contrary, are objects of existence to themselves, as regards the intrinsic import of the aim in question. To this order belongs that in them which we would exclude from the category of mere means— morality, ethics, religion. That is to say, man is an object of existence in himself only in virtue of the divine that is in him—that which was designated at the outset as *Reason;* which, in view of its activity and power of self-determination, was called *freedom.* And we affirm—without entering at present on the proof of the assertion—that religion, morality, etc., have their foundation and source in that principle, and so are essentially elevated above all alien necessity and chance. And here we must remark that individuals, to the extent of their freedom, are responsible for the depravation and enfeeblement of morals and religion. This is the seal of the absolute and sublime destiny of man—that he knows what is good and what is evil; that his destiny *is* his very ability to will either good or evil—in one word, that he is the subject of moral imputation, imputation not only of evil, but of good; and not only concerning this or that particular matter, and all that happens *ab extra,* but *also* the good and evil attaching to his individual freedom. The brute alone is simply innocent. It would, however, demand an extensive explanation—as extensive as the analysis of moral freedom itself—to preclude or obviate all the misunderstandings which the statement that what is called innocent imports the entire unconsciousness of evil, is wont to occasion.

In contemplating the fate which virtue, morality, even piety experience in history, we must not fall into the litany of lamentations, that the good and pious often—or for the most part —fare ill in the world, while the evil-disposed and wicked prosper. The term *prosperity* is used in a variety of meanings—riches, outward honor, and the like. But in speaking of something which in and for itself constitutes an aim of existence, that so-

called well or ill-faring of these or those isolated individuals cannot be regarded as an essential element in the rational order of the universe. With more justice than happiness— or a fortunate environment for individuals—it is demanded of the grand aim of the world's existence, that it should foster, nay, involve the execution and ratification of good, moral, righteous purposes. What makes men morally discontented (a discontent, by the by, on which they somewhat pride themselves), is that they do not find the present adapted to the realization of aims which they hold to be right and just (more especially in modern times, ideals of political constitutions); they contrast unfavorably things as they *are,* with their idea of things as they *ought* to be. In this case it is not private interest nor passion that desires gratification, but reason, justice, liberty; and equipped with this title, the demand in question assumes a lofty bearing, and readily adopts a position, not merely of discontent, but of open revolt against the actual condition of the world. To estimate such a feeling and such views aright, the demands insisted upon, and the very dogmatic opinions asserted, must be examined. At no time so much as in our own, have such general principles and notions been advanced, or with greater assurance. If in days gone by, history seems to present itself as a struggle of passions; in our time—though displays of passion are not wanting—it exhibits partly a predominance of the struggle of notions assuming the authority of principles; partly that of passions and interests essentially subjective, but under the mask of such higher sanctions. The pretensions thus contended for as legitimate in the name of that which has been stated as the ultimate aim of Reason, pass accordingly, for absolute aims—to the same extent as religion, morals, ethics. Nothing, as before remarked, is now more common than the complaint that the *ideals* which imagination sets up are not realized—that these glorious dreams are destroyed by cold actuality. These ideals—which in the voyage of life founder on the rocks of hard reality— may be in the first instance only subjective, and belong to the idiosyncrasy of the individual, imagining himself the highest and wisest. Such do not properly belong to this category. For the fancies which the individual in his isolation indulges, cannot be the model for universal reality; just as *universal* law is not designed for the units of the mass. These as such may, in fact, find their interests decidedly thrust into the background. But by the term "Ideal," we also understand the ideal of reason, of the good, of the true. Poets, as e.g., Schiller, have painted such ideals touchingly and with strong emotion, and with the deeply melancholy conviction that they could not be realized. In affirming, on the contrary that the universal Reason *does* realize itself, we have indeed nothing to do with the individual empirically regarded. That admits of degrees of better and worse, since here chance and particularity have received authority from the Idea to exercise their monstrous power. Much, therefore, in particular aspects of the grand phenomenon might be found fault with. This subjective fault-finding—which, however, only keeps in view the individual and its deficiency, without taking notice of Reason pervading the whole—is easy; and inasmuch as it asserts an excellent intention with regard to the good of the whole, and seems to result from a kindly heart, it feels authorized to give itself airs and assume great consequence. It is easier to discover a deficiency in individuals, in states, and in providence, than to see their real import and value. For in this merely negative fault-finding a proud position is taken—one which overlooks the object, without having entered into it— without having comprehended its positive aspect. Age generally makes men more tolerant; youth is always discontented. The tolerance of age is the result of the ripeness of a judgment which, not merely as the result of indifference, is satisfied even with what is inferior; but, more deeply taught by the grave experience of life, has been led to perceive the substantial, solid worth of the object in question. The insight then to which—in contradistinction from those ideals—philosophy is to lead us is that the actual world is as it ought to be—that the truly good—the universal divine reason—is not a mere abstraction, but a vital principle capable of realizing itself. This *good*, this *Reason*, in its most concrete form, is God. God governs the world; the actual working of his government—the carrying out of his plan —is the history of the world. This plan philosophy strives to comprehend; for only that which has been developed as the result of it possesses *bona fide* reality. That which does not accord with it is negative, worthless existence. Before the pure light of this divine Idea—which is no mere ideal— the phantom of a world whose events are an incoherent concourse of fortuitous circumstances utterly vanishes. Philosophy wishes to discover the substantial purport, the actual side of the divine idea, and to justify the so much despised actuality of things; for Reason is the comprehension of the divine work. But as to what concerns the perversion, corruption, and ruin of religious, ethical, and moral purposes, and states of society generally, it must be affirmed, that in their *essence* these are infinite and eternal; but that the forms they assume may be of a limited order, and consequently belong to the domain of mere nature, and be subject to the sway of chance. They are, therefore, perishable and exposed to decay and corruption. Religion and morality—in the same way as inherently universal essences—have the peculiarity of being present in the individual soul, in the full extent of their Idea, and therefore truly and really; although they may not manifest themselves in it *in extenso,* and are not applied to fully developed relations. The religion, the morality of a limited sphere of life—that of a shepherd or a peasant, e.g.—in its intensive concentration and limitation to a few perfectly simple relations of life—has infinite worth; the same worth as the religion and morality of extensive knowledge, and of an existence rich in the compass of its relations and actions. This inner focus—this simple region of the claims of subjective freedom—the home of volition, resolution, and action—the abstract sphere of conscience—that which comprises the responsibility and moral value of the individual, remains untouched; and is quite shut out from the noisy din of the world's history—including not merely external and temporal changes, but also those entailed by the absolute necessity inseparable from the realization of the Idea of freedom itself. But as a general truth this must be regarded as settled, that whatever in the world possesses claims as noble and glorious, has nevertheless a higher

existence above it. The claim of the world-spirit rises above all special claims.

. . . It must further be understood that all the worth which the human being possesses—all spiritual actuality—he possesses only through the state. For his spiritual actuality consists in this, that his own essence—Reason—is objectively present to him, that it possesses objective immediate existence for him. Thus only is he fully conscious; thus only is he a partaker of morality—of a just and moral social and political life. For truth is the unity of the universal and subjective will; and the universal is to be found in the state, in its laws, its universal and rational arrangements. The state is the divine Idea as it exists on earth. We have in it, therefore, the object of history in a more definite shape than before; that in which freedom obtains objectivity, and lives in the enjoyment of this objectivity. For law is the objectivity of spirit; volition in its true form. Only that will which obeys law, is free; for it obeys itself—it is independent and so free. When the state or our country constitutes a community of existence; when the subjective will of man submits to laws, the contradiction between liberty and necessity vanishes. The rational has necessary existence, as being the reality and substance of things, and we are free in recognizing it as law, and following it as the substance of our own being. The objective and the subjective will are then reconciled, and present one identical homogeneous whole. For the morality *(Sittlichkeit)* of the state is not of that ethical *(moralische)* reflective kind, in which one's own conviction bears sway; this latter is rather the peculiarity of the modern time, while the true ancient morality is based on the principle of abiding by one's duty [to the state at large]. An Athenian citizen did what was required of him, as it were from instinct; but if I reflect on the object of my activity, I must have the consciousness that my will has been called into exercise. But morality is duty—substantial right—a "*second* nature" as it has been justly called; for the *first* nature of man is his primary merely animal existence.

The development *in extenso* of the Idea of the state belongs to the philosophy of jurisprudence; but it must be observed that in the theories of our time various errors are current respecting it, which pass for established truths, and have become fixed prejudices. We will mention only a few of them, giving prominence to such as have a reference to the object of our history.

The error which first meets us is the direct contradictory of our principle that the state presents the realization of freedom; the opinion, viz., that man is free by *nature*, but that in *society*, in the state—to which nevertheless he is irresistibly impelled—he must limit this natural freedom. That man is free by nature is quite correct in one sense; viz., that he is so according to the idea of humanity; but we imply thereby that he is such only in virtue of his destiny—that he has an undeveloped power to become such; for the "nature" of an object is exactly synonymous with its "Idea." But the view in question imports more than this. When man is spoken of as "free by nature," the mode of his existence as well as his destiny is implied. His merely natural and primary condition is intended. In this sense a "state of nature" is assumed in which mankind at large are in the posses-sion of their natural rights with the unconstrained exercise and enjoyment of their freedom. This assumption is not indeed raised to the dignity of the historical fact; it would indeed be difficult, were the attempt seriously made, to point out any such condition as actually existing, or as having ever occurred. Examples of a savage state of life can be pointed out, but they are marked by brutal passions and deeds of violence; while, however rude and simple their conditions, they involve social arrangements which (to use the common phrase) *restrain* freedom. That assumption is one of those nebulous images which theory produces; an idea which it cannot avoid originating, but which it fathers upon real existence, without sufficient historical justification.

What we find such a state of nature to be in actual experience, answers exactly to the idea of a *merely* natural condition. Freedom, as the *ideal* of that which is original and natural, does not exist *as original and natural*. Rather must it be first sought out and won; and that by an incalculable medial discipline of the intellectual and moral powers. The state of nature is, therefore, predominantly that of injustice and violence, of untamed natural impulses, of inhuman deeds and feelings. Limitation is certainly produced by society and the state, but it is a limitation of the mere brute emotions and rude instincts; as also, in a more advanced stage of culture, of the premeditated self-will of caprice and passion. This kind of constraint is part of the instrumentality by which only the consciousness of freedom and the desire for its attainment in its true—that is, rational and ideal form—can be obtained. To the notion of freedom, law and morality are indispensably requisite; and they are, in and for themselves, universal existences, objects, and aims; which are discovered only by the activity of thought, separating itself from the merely sensuous, and developing itself, in opposition thereto; and which must, on the other hand, be introduced into and incorporated with the originally sensuous will, and that contrarily to its natural inclination. The perpetually recurring misapprehension of freedom consists in regarding that term only in its *formal*, subjective sense, abstracted from its essential objects and aims; thus a constraint put upon impulse, desire, passion—pertaining to the particular individual as such —a limitation of caprice and self-will is regarded as a fettering of freedom. We should on the contrary look upon such limitation as the indispensable proviso of emancipation. Society and the state are the very conditions in which freedom is realized.

QUESTIONS FOR DISCUSSION

1. What does Hegel mean by "spirit" (as opposed to what?), and its embodiment in the history of the world (*Weltgeist*) and in peoples (*Volksgeist*)?
2. How does Hegel trace the idea of freedom historically in Orientals (despotism), in the Greeks and Romans, and in the German nations?
3. How does he reconcile the institution of slavery with Christianity in his teleological view of history?
4. Explain *"nothing great in the world* has been accomplished *without passion."* How does Hegel try to reconcile subjective passion with the objective unfolding of the Absolute Idea in history ("cunning of the Absolute")?
5. What role do "world-historical" great men play in history, and what about the ordinary individual's relation to the state?
6. Why does Hegel consider the state as the realization of freedom and its morality (*Sittlichkeit*) above that of individual ethical (*moralische*) reflection?

Karl Marx (1818-1883)

4.4   The Communist Manifesto

A specter is haunting Europe—the specter of Communism. All the powers of old Europe have entered into a holy alliance to exorcise this specter; Pope and Czar, Metternich and Guizot, French radicals and German police spies.

Where is the party in opposition that has not been decried as Communistic by its opponents in power? Where the opposition that has not hurled back the branding reproach of Communism, against the more advanced opposition parties, as well as against its reactionary adversaries?

Two things result from this fact.

I. Communism is already acknowledged by all European powers to be in itself a power.

II. It is high time that Communists should openly, in the face of the whole world, publish their views, their aims, their tendencies, and meet this nursery tale of the Specter of Communism with a Manifesto of the party itself.

To this end the Communists of various nationalities have assembled in London, and sketched the following manifesto to be published in the English, French, German, Italian, Flemish, and Danish languages.

_____

From *The Communist Manifesto* (1848). Edited by Friedrich Engels (1888).

BOURGEOIS AND
PROLETARIANS [1]

The history of all hitherto existing society [2] is the history of class struggles.

Freeman and slave, patrician and

_____

[1] By bourgeoisie is meant the class of modern Capitalists, owners of the means of social production and employers of wage-labor. By proletariat, the class of modern wage-laborers who, having no means of production of their own, are reduced to selling their labor-power in order to live.

[2] That is, all *written* history. In 1847, the pre-history of society, the social organization existing previous to recorded history, was all but unknown. Since then, Haxthausen discovered common ownership of land in Russia, Maurer proved it to be the social foundation from which all Teutonic races started in history, and by and by village communities were found to be, or to have been, the primitive form of society everywhere from India to Ireland. The inner organization of this primitive Communistic society was laid bare, in its typical form, by Morgan's crowning discovery of the true nature of the *Gens* and its relation to the *Tribe*. With the dissolution of these primæval communities society begins to be differentiated into separate and finally antagonistic classes. I have attempted to retrace this process of dissolution in: *Der Ursprung der Familie, des Privateigentums und des Staats*, 2nd ed., Stuttgart, 1886. (English trans., *Origin of the Family, Property, and the State.*)

plebeian, lord and serf, guild master [3] and journeyman, in a word, oppressor and oppressed, stood in constant opposition to one another, carried on an uninterrupted, now hidden, now open fight, that each time ended, either in the revolutionary reconstitution of society at large, or in the common ruin of the contending classes.

In the earlier epochs of history we find almost everywhere a complicated arrangement of society into various orders, a manifold gradation of social rank. In ancient Rome we have patricians, knights, plebeians, slaves; in the middle ages, feudal lords, vassals, guild masters, journeymen, apprentices, serfs; in almost all of these classes, again, subordinate gradations.

The modern bourgeois society that has sprouted from the ruins of feudal society, has not done away with class antagonisms. It has but established new classes, new conditions of oppression, new forms of struggle in place of the old ones.

Our epoch, the epoch of the bourgeois, possesses, however, this distinctive feature: it has simplified the class antagonisms. Society as a whole is more and more splitting up into two great hostile camps, into two great classes directly facing each other: Bourgeoisie and Proletariat.

From the serfs of the middle ages sprang the chartered burghers of the earliest towns. From these burgesses the first elements of the bourgeoisie were developed.

The discovery of America, the rounding of the Cape, opened up fresh ground for the rising bourgeoisie. The East Indian and Chinese markets, the colonization of America, trade with the colonies, the increase in the means of exchange and in commodities generally, gave to commerce, to navigation, to industry, an impulse never before known, and thereby, to the revolutionary element in the tottering feudal society, a rapid development.

The feudal system of industry, under which industrial production was monopolized by closed guilds, now no longer sufficed for the growing wants of the new markets. The manufacturing system took its place. The guild masters were pushed on one side by the manufacturing middle class; division of labor between the different corporate guilds vanished in the face of division of labor in each single workshop.

Meantime the markets kept ever growing, the demand ever rising. Even manufacture no longer sufficed. Thereupon steam and machinery revolutionized industrial production. The place of manufacture was taken by the giant, Modern Industry; the place of the industrial middle class, by industrial millionaires, the leaders of whole industrial armies, the modern bourgeois.

Modern industry has established the world's market, for which the discovery of America paved the way. The market has given an immense development to commerce, to navigation, to communication by land. This development has, in its turn, reacted on the extension of industry; and in proportion as industry, commerce, navigation, and railways extended, in the same proportion the bourgeoisie developed, increased its capital, and pushed into the background every class handed down from the middle ages.

---

[3] Guild master, that is a full member of a guild, a master within, not a head of a guild.

We see, therefore, how the modern bourgeoisie is itself the product of a long course of development, of a series of revolutions in the modes of production and of exchange.

Each step in the development of the bourgeoisie was accompanied by a corresponding political advance of that class. An oppressed class under the sway of the feudal nobility, an armed and self-governing association in the mediæval commune,[4] here independent urban republic (as in Italy and Germany), there taxable "third estate" of the monarchy (as in France), afterwards, in the period of manufacture proper, serving either the semi-feudal or the absolute monarchy as a counterpoise against the nobility, and, in fact, cornerstone of the great monarchies in general, the bourgeoisie has at last, since the establishment of Modern Industry and of the world's market, conquered for itself, in the modern representative State, exclusive political sway. The executive of the modern State is but a committee for managing the common affairs of the whole bourgeoisie.

The bourgeoisie, historically, has played a most revolutionary part.

The bourgeoisie, wherever it has got the upper hand, has put an end to all feudal, patriarchal, idyllic relations. It has pitilessly torn asunder the motley feudal ties that bound man to his "natural superiors," and has left remaining no other nexus between

man and man than naked self-interest, callous "cash payment." It has drowned the most heavenly ecstasies of religious fervor, of chivalrous enthusiasm, of philistine sentimentalism, in the icy water of egotistical calculation. It has resolved personal worth into exchange value, and in place of the numberless indefeasible chartered freedoms, has set up that single, unconscionable freedom—Free Trade. In one word, for exploitation, veiled by religious and political illusions, it has substituted naked, shameless, direct, brutal exploitation.

The bourgeoisie has stripped of its halo every occupation hitherto honored and looked up to with reverent awe. It has converted the physician, the lawyer, the priest, the poet, the man of science, into its paid wage laborers.

The bourgeoisie has torn away from the family its sentimental veil, and has reduced the family relation to a mere money relation.

The bourgeoisie has disclosed how it came to pass that the brutal display of vigor in the middle ages, which Reactionists so much admire, found its fitting complement in the most slothful indolence. It has been the first to show what man's activity can bring about. It has accomplished wonders far surpassing Egyptian pyramids, Roman aqueducts, and Gothic cathedrals; it has conducted expeditions that put in the shade all former Exoduses of nations and crusades.

The bourgeoisie cannot exist without constantly revolutionizing the instruments of production, and thereby the relations of production, and with them the whole relations of society. Conservation of the old modes of production in unaltered forms, was, on the contrary, the first condition of

---

[4] "Commune" was the name taken, in France, by the nascent towns even before they had conquered, from their feudal lords and masters, local self-government and political rights as the "Third Estate." Generally speaking, for the economical development of the bourgeoisie, England is here taken as the typical country; for its political development, France.

existence for all earlier industrial classes. Constant revolutionizing of production, uninterrupted disturbance of all social conditions, everlasting uncertainty and agitation, distinguish the bourgeois epoch from all earlier ones. All fixed, fast-frozen relations, with their train of ancient and venerable prejudices and opinions, are swept away; all new-formed ones become antiquated before they can ossify. All that is solid melts into air, all that is holy is profaned, and man is at last compelled to face with sober senses his real conditions of life and his relations with his kind.

The need of a constantly expanding market for its products chases the bourgeoisie over the whole surface of the globe. It must nestle everywhere, settle everywhere, establish connections everywhere.

The bourgeoisie has through its exploitation of the world's market given a cosmopolitan character to production and consumption in every country. To the great chagrin of Reactionists, it has drawn from under the feet of industry the national ground on which it stood. All old-established national industries have been destroyed or are daily being destroyed. They are dislodged by new industries, whose introduction becomes a life and death question for all civilized nations, by industries that no longer work up indigenous raw material, but raw material drawn from the remotest zones, industries whose products are consumed, not only at home, but in every quarter of the globe. In place of the old wants, satisfied by the productions of the country, we find new wants, requiring for their satisfaction the products of distant lands and climes. In place of the old local and national seclusion and self-sufficiency, we have

intercourse in every direction, universal interdependence of nations. And as in material, so also in intellectual production. The intellectual creations of individual nations become common property. National one-sidedness and narrow-mindedness become more and more impossible, and from the numerous national and local literatures, there arises a world literature.

The bourgeoisie, by the rapid improvement of all instruments of production, by the immensely facilitated means of communication, draws all, even the most barbarian, nations into civilization. The cheap prices of its commodities are the heavy artillery with which it batters down all Chinese walls, with which it forces the barbarians' intensely obstinate hatred of foreigners to capitulate. It compels all nations, on pain of extinction, to adopt the bourgeois mode of production; it compels them to introduce what it calls civilization into their midst, i.e., to become bourgeois themselves. In one word, it creates a world after its own image.

The bourgeoisie has subjected the country to the rule of the towns. It has created enormous cities, has greatly increased the urban population as compared with the rural, and has thus rescued a considerable part of the population from the idiocy of rural life. Just as it has made the country dependent on the towns, so it has made barbarian and semi-barbarian countries dependent on the civilized ones, nations of peasants on nations of bourgeois, the East on the West.

The bourgeoisie keeps more and more doing away with the scattered state of the population, of the means of production, and of property. It has agglomerated population, centralized means of production, and has concentrated property in a few hands. The necessary consequence of this was political centralization. Independent, or but loosely connected provinces, with separate interests, laws, governments, and systems of taxation, became lumped together into one nation, with one government, one code of laws, one national class interest, one frontier, and one customs tariff.

The bourgeoisie, during its rule of scarce one hundred years, has created more massive and more colossal productive forces than have all preceding generations together. Subjection of Nature's forces to man, machinery, application of chemistry to industry and agriculture, steam navigation, railways, electric telegraphs, clearing of whole continents for cultivation, canalization of rivers, whole populations conjured out of the ground— what earlier century had even a presentiment that such productive forces slumbered in the lap of social labor?

We see then: the means of production and of exchange on whose foundation the bourgeoisie built itself up, were generated in feudal society. At a certain stage in the development of these means of production and of exchange, the conditions under which feudal society produced and exchanged, the feudal organization of agriculture and manufacturing industry, in one word, the feudal relations of property, became no longer compatible with the already developed productive forces; they became so many fetters. They had to be burst asunder.

Into their place stepped free competition, accompanied by a social and political constitution adapted to it, and by the economical and political sway of the bourgeois class.

A similar movement is going on before our own eyes. Modern bourgeois society with its relations of production, of exchange, and of property, a society that has conjured up such gigantic means of production and of exchange, is like the sorcerer, who is no longer able to control the powers of the nether world whom he has called up by his spells. For many a decade past the history of industry and commerce is but the history of the revolt of modern productive forces against modern conditions of production, against the property relations that are the conditions for the existence of the bourgeoisie and of its rule. It is enough to mention the commercial crises that by their periodical return put on its trial, each time more threateningly, the existence of the bourgeois society. In these crises a great part not only of the existing products, but also of the previously created productive forces, is periodically destroyed. In these crises there breaks out an epidemic that, in all earlier epochs, would have seemed an absurdity—the epidemic of overproduction. Society suddenly finds itself put back into a state of momentary barbarism; it appears as if a famine, a universal war of devastation had cut off the supply of every means of subsistence; industry and commerce seem to be destroyed; and why? because there is too much civilization, too much means of subsistence, too much industry, too much commerce. The productive forces at the disposal of society no longer tend to further the development of the conditions of bourgeois property; on the contrary, they have become too powerful for these conditions, by which they are fettered, and so soon as they overcome these fetters, they bring disorder into the whole of bourgeois society, endanger the existence of bourgeois property. The conditions of bourgeois society are too narrow to comprise the wealth created by them. And how does the bourgeoisie get over these crises? On the one hand, by enforced destruction of a mass of productive forces; on the other, by the conquest of new markets and by the more thorough exploitation of the old ones. That is to say, by paving the way for more extensive and more destructive crises, and by diminishing the means whereby crises are prevented.

The weapons with which the bourgeoisie felled feudalism to the ground are now turned against the bourgeoisie itself.

But not only has the bourgeoisie forged the weapons that bring death to itself; it has also called into existence the men who are to wield those weapons—the modern working class—the proletarians.

In proportion as the bourgeoisie, i.e., capital, is developed, in the same proportion is the proletariat, the modern working class, developed; a class of laborers, who live only so long as they find work, and who find work only so long as their labor increases capital. These laborers, who must sell themselves piecemeal, are a commodity, like every other article of commerce, and are consequently exposed to all the vicissitudes of competition, to all the fluctuations of the market.

Owing to the extensive use of machinery and to division of labor, the work of the proletarians has lost all individual character, and, consequently, all charm for the workman. He becomes an appendage of the machine, and it is only the most simple, most monotonous, and most easily acquired knack, that is required of him. Hence,

the cost of production of a workman is restricted almost entirely to the means of subsistence that he requires for his maintenance, and for the propagation of his race. But the price of a commodity, and therefore also of labor, is equal, in the long run, to its cost of production. In proportion, therefore, as the repulsiveness of the work increases, the wage decreases. Nay, more, in proportion as the use of machinery and division of labor increase, in the same proportion the burden of toil also increases, whether by prolongation of the working hours, by increase of the work exacted in a given time, or by increased speed of the machinery, etc.

Modern industry has converted the little workshop of the patriarchal master into the great factory of the industry capitalist. Masses of laborers, crowded into the factory, are organized like soldiers. As privates of the industrial army they are placed under the command of a perfect hierarchy of officers and sergeants. Not only are they slaves of the bourgeois State, they are daily and hourly enslaved by the machine, by the overseer, and, above all, by the individual bourgeois manufacturer himself. The more openly this despotism proclaims gain to be its end and aim, the more petty, the more hateful, and the more embittering it is.

The less skill and exertion of strength is implied in manual labor, in other words, the more modern industry becomes developed, the more is the labor of men superseded by that of women. Differences of age and sex have no longer any distinctive social validity for the working class. All are instruments of labor, more or less expensive to use, according to age and sex.

No sooner is the exploitation of the laborer by the manufacturer so far at an end that he receives his wages in cash, than he is set upon by the other portions of the bourgeoisie, the landlord, the shopkeeper, the pawnbroker, etc.

The lower strata of middle class—the small tradespeople, shopkeepers, and retired tradesmen generally, the handicraftsmen and peasants—all these sink gradually into the proletariat, partly because their diminutive capital does not suffice for the scale on which modern industry is carried on, and is swamped in the competition with the large capitalists, partly because their specialized skill is rendered worthless by new methods of production. Thus the proletariat is recruited from all classes of the population.

The proletariat goes through various stages of development. With its birth begins its struggle with the bourgeoisie. At first the contest is carried on by individual laborers, then by the work-people of a factory, then by the operatives of one trade, in one locality, against the individual bourgeois who directly exploits them. They direct their attacks, not against the bourgeois conditions of production, but against the instruments of production themselves; they destroy imported wares that compete with their labor, they smash to pieces machinery, they set factories ablaze, they seek to restore by force the vanished status of the workman of the middle ages.

At this stage the laborers still form an incoherent mass scattered over the whole country, and broken up by their mutual competition. If anywhere they unite to form more compact bodies, this is not yet the consequence of their own active union, but of the union of the bourgeoisie, which class, in order to attain its own political ends, is compelled to set the whole proletariat in motion, and is moreover yet, for a time, able to do so. At this stage, therefore, the proletarians do not fight their enemies, but the enemies of their enemies, the remnants of absolute monarchy, and land owners, the nonindustrial bourgeois, the petty bourgeoisie. Thus the whole historical movement is concentrated in the hands of the bourgeoisie; every victory so obtained is a victory for the bourgeoisie.

But with the development of industry the proletariat not only increases in number; it becomes concentrated in greater masses, its strength grows, and it feels that strength more. The various interests and conditions of life within the ranks of the proletariat are more and more equalized, in proportion as machinery obliterates all distinctions of labor, and nearly everywhere reduces wages to the same low level. The growing competition among the bourgeois, and the resulting commercial crises, make the wages of the workers ever more fluctuating. The unceasing improvement of machinery, ever more rapidly developing, makes their livelihood more and more precarious; the collisions between individual workman and individual bourgeois take more and more the character of collisions between two classes. Thereupon the workers begin to form combinations (Trades' Unions) against the bourgeois; they club together in order to keep up the rate of wages; they found permanent associations in order to make provision beforehand for these occasional revolts. Here and there the contest breaks out into riots.

Now and then the workers are victorious, but only for a time. The real fruit of their battles lies not in the immediate result but in the ever improved means of communication that are created in modern industry and that place the workers of different localities in contact with one another. It was just this contact that was needed to centralize the numerous local struggles, all of the same character, into one national struggle between classes. But every class struggle is a political struggle. And that union, to attain which the burghers of the middle ages, with their miserable highways, required centuries, the modern proletarians, thanks to railways, achieve in a few years.

This organization of the proletarians into a class and consequently into a political party, is continually being upset again by the competition between the workers themselves. But it ever rises up again; stronger, firmer, mightier. It compels legislative recognition of particular interests of the workers, by taking advantage of the divisions among the bourgeoisie itself. Thus the Ten-Hours Bill in England was carried.

Altogether collisions between the classes of the old society further, in many ways, the course of the development of the proletariat. The bourgeoisie finds itself involved in a constant battle. At first with the aristocracy; later on, with those portions of the bourgeoisie itself whose interests have become antagonistic to the progress of industry; at all times with the bourgeoisie of foreign countries. In all these countries it sees itself compelled to appeal to the proletariat, to ask for its help, and thus to drag it into the political arena. The bourgeoisie itself, therefore, supplies the proletariat with weapons for fighting the bourgeoisie.

Further, as we have already seen, entire sections of the ruling classes are, by the advance of industry, precipitated into the proletariat, or are at least threatened in their conditions of existence. These also supply the proletariat with fresh elements of enlightenment and progress.

Finally, in times when the class struggle nears the decisive hour, the process of dissolution going on within the ruling class, in fact within the whole range of old society, assumes such a violent, glaring character, that a small section of the ruling class cuts itself adrift, and joins the revolutionary class, the class that holds the future in its hands. Just as, therefore, at an earlier period, a section of the nobility went over to the bourgeoisie, so now a portion of the bourgeoisie goes over to the proletariat, and in particular, a portion of the bourgeois ideologists, who have raised themselves to the level of comprehending theoretically the historical movement as a whole.

Of all the classes that stand face to face with the bourgeoisie today, the proletariat alone is a really revolutionary class. The other classes decay and finally disappear in the face of modern industry; the proletariat is its special and essential product.

The lower middle class, the small manufacturer, the shopkeeper, the artisan, the peasant, all these fight against the bourgeoisie to save from extinction their existence as fractions of the middle class. They are, therefore, not revolutionary, but conservative. Nay, more, they are reactionary, for they try to roll back the wheel of history. If by chance they are revolutionary, they are so only in view of their impending transfer into the proletariat; they thus defend not their present, but their future interests, they desert their own standpoint to place themselves at that of the proletariat.

The "dangerous class," the social scum, that passively rotting class thrown off by the lowest layers of old society, may, here and there, be swept into the movement by a proletarian revolution; its conditions of life, however, prepare it far more for the part of a bribed tool of reactionary intrigue.

In the conditions of the proletariat, those of the old society at large are already virtually swamped. The proletarian is without property; his relation to his wife and children has no longer anything in common with the bourgeois family relations; modern industrial labor, modern subjection to capital, the same in England as in France, in America as in Germany, has stripped him of every trace of national character. Law, morality, religion, are to him so many bourgeois prejudices, behind which lurk in ambush just as many bourgeois interests.

All the preceding classes that got the upper hand sought to fortify their already acquired status by subjecting society at large to their conditions of appropriation. The proletarians cannot become masters of the productive forces of society, except by abolishing their own previous mode of appropriation, and thereby also every other previous mode of appropriation. They have nothing of their own to secure and to fortify; their mission is to destroy all previous securities for, and insurances of, individual property.

All previous historical movements were movements of minorities, or in the interest of minorities. The prole-tarian movement is the self-conscious, independent movement of the immense majority, in the interest of the immense majority. The proletariat, the lowest stratum of our present society, cannot stir, cannot raise itself up, without the whole superincumbent strata of official society being sprung into the air.

Though not in substance, yet in form, the struggle of the proletariat with the bourgeoisie is at first a national struggle. The proletariat of each country must, of course, first of all settle matters with its own bourgeoisie.

In depicting the most general phases of the development of the proletariat, we traced the more or less veiled civil war, raging within existing society, up to the point where that war breaks out into open revolution, and where the violent overthrow of the bourgeoisie lays the foundation for the sway of the proletariat.

Hitherto every form of society has been based, as we have already seen, on the antagonism of oppressing and oppressed classes. But in order to oppress a class certain conditions must be assured to it under which it can, at least, continue its slavish existence. The serf, in the period of serfdom, raised himself to membership in the commune, just as the petty bourgeois, under the yoke of feudal absolutism, managed to develop into a bourgeois. The modern laborer, on the contrary, instead of rising with the progress of industry, sinks deeper and deeper below the conditions of existence of his own class. He becomes a pauper, and pauperism develops more rapidly than population and wealth. And here it becomes evident that the bourgeoisie is unfit any longer to be the ruling class in society and to impose its conditions of existence upon society as an overriding law. It is unfit to rule because it is incompetent to assure an existence to its slave within his slavery, because it cannot help letting him sink into such a state that it has to feed him instead of being fed by him. Society can no longer live under this bourgeoisie; in other words, its existence is no longer compatible with society.

The essential condition for the existence, and for the sway of the bourgeois class, is the formation and augmentation of capital; the condition for capital is wage-labor. Wage-labor rests exclusively on competition among the laborers. The advance of industry, whose involuntary promoter is the bourgeoisie, replaces the isolation of the laborers, due to competition, by their revolutionary combination, due to association. The development of modern industry, therefore, cuts from under its feet the very foundation on which the bourgeoisie produces and appropriates products. What the bourgeoisie therefore produces, above all, are its own grave diggers. Its fall and the victory of the proletariat are equally inevitable.

QUESTIONS FOR DISCUSSION

1. If historical changes are inevitable, why is any revolutionary propaganda necessary? Why is the victory of the proletarian class "inevitable"?
2. Is capitalism the same today as it was in Marx's time? What difference would any changes today in capitalist economy make to Marxist doctrine?
3. Are there only two classes in the social history of struggles among men? What other divisions divide men? Is it true that the middle class is disappearing?
4. Are the causes of war always and necessarily due to class struggle?
5. What are the various meanings of "economic" and "material" in Marxist philosophy of history?
6. What is meant by saying that all historical change is the result of "internal contradictions" in dialectical materialism?
7. What is the theory of the identity of theory and practice? Criticize.
8. What is the ultimate goal of communism after the dictatorship of the proletariat and socialism? Will the state "wither away" necessarily?
9. What conception of human nature does Marx have? What role can an individual have in history? Can the social environment produce any new kinds of individuals and does heredity play no part?
10. Compare and contrast communist ideology and reform liberalism.

Sir Isaiah Berlin (1909-   )

4.5   Political Ideas
in the Twentieth Century[1]

> Anyone desiring a quiet life has done badly to be born in the
> twentieth century.   —L. TROTSKY

I

Historians of ideas, however scrupulous and minute they may feel it necessary to be, cannot avoid perceiving their material in terms of some kind of pattern. To say this is not necessarily to subscribe to any form of Hegelian dogma about the dominant role of laws and metaphysical principles in history—a view increasingly influential in our time—according to which there is some single explanation of the order and attributes of persons, things, and events. Usually this consists in the advocacy of some fundamental category or principle which claims to act as an infallible guide both to the past and to the future, a magic lens revealing 'inner', inexorable, all-pervasive historical laws, invisible to the naked eye of the mere recorder of events, but capable, when understood, of giving the historian a unique sense of certainty—certainty not only of what in fact occurred, but of the reason why it could not have occurred otherwise, affording a secure knowledge which the mere empirical investigator, with his collections of data, his insecure structure of painstakingly accumulated evidence, his tentative approximations and perpetual liability to error and reassessment, can never hope to attain.[2]

From "Political Ideas in the Twentieth Century" in *Four Essays on Liberty* by Sir Isaiah Berlin, published by Oxford University Press, London, 1969. Reprinted by permission of the publisher.

[1] This article was written in 1949 at the request of the Editor of the American Journal *Foreign Affairs*, for its Mid-century Issue. Its tone was to some extent due to the policies of the Soviet régime during Stalin's last years. Since then a modification of the worst excesses of that dictatorship has fortunately taken place; but the general tendency with which the issue was concerned seems to me, if anything, to have gained, if not in intensity, then in extent: some of the new national states of Asia and Africa seem to show no greater concern for civil liberties, even allowing for the exigencies of security and planning which these states need for their development or survival, than the régimes they have replaced.

[2] I do not, of course, attribute this view either to Hegel or to Marx, whose doctrines are both more complex and far more plausible; only to the *terribles simplificateurs* among their followers.

The notion of 'laws' of this kind is rightly condemned as a species of metaphysical fantasy; but the contrary notion of bare facts—facts which are nothing but facts, hard, inescapable, untainted by interpretation or arrangement in man-made patterns—is equally mythological. To comprehend and contrast and classify and arrange, to see in patterns of lesser or greater complexity, is not a peculiar kind of thinking, it is thinking itself. We accuse historians of exaggeration, distortion, ignorance, bias, or departure from the facts, not because they select, compare, and set forth in a context and order which are in part, at least, of their own choosing, in part conditioned by the circumstances of their material and social environment or their character or purpose—we accuse them only when the result deviates too far, contrasts too harshly with the accepted canons of verification and interpretation which belong to their own time and place and society. These canons and methods and categories are those of the normal rational outlook of a given period and culture, at their best a sharpened, highly trained form of this outlook, which takes cognizance of all the relevant scientific techniques available, but is itself not one of them. All the criticisms directed against this or that writer for an excess of bias or fancy, or too weak a sense of evidence, or too limited a perception of connexions between events, are based not upon some absolute standard of truth, of strict 'factuality', of a rigid adherence to a permanently fixed ideal method of 'scientifically' discovering the past *wie es eigentlich gewesen,* in contrast with mere theories about it, for there is in the last analysis no meaning in the notion of 'objective' criticism in

this timeless sense. They rest rather on the most refined concept of accuracy and objectivity and scrupulous 'fidelity to the facts' which obtain in a given society at a given period, within the subject in question.

When the great romantic revolution in the writing of history transferred emphasis from the achievements of individuals to the growth and influence of institutions conceived in much less personal terms, the degree of 'fidelity to the facts' was not thereby automatically altered. The new kind of history, the account of the development, let us say, of public and private law, or government, or literature, or social habits during some given period of time, was not necessarily less or more accurate or 'objective' than earlier accounts of the acts and fate of Alcibiades or Marcus Aurelius or Calvin or Louis XIV. Thucydides or Tacitus or Voltaire were not subjective or vague or fanciful in a sense in which Ranke or Savigny or Michelet were not. The new history was merely written from what is nowadays called a different 'angle'. The kinds of fact the new history was intended to record were different, the emphasis was different, a shift of interest had occurred in the questions asked and consequently in the methods used. The concepts and terminology reflect an altered view of what constitutes evidence and therefore, in the end, of what are the 'facts'. When the 'romances' of chroniclers were criticized by 'scientific' historians, at least part of the implied reproach lay in the alleged discrepancies in the work of the older writers from the findings of the most admired and trusted sciences of a later period; and these were in their turn due to the change in the prevalent conceptions of the patterns of human development —to the change in the models in terms of which the past was perceived, those artistic, theological, mechanical, biological, or psychological models which were reflected in the fields of inquiry, in the new questions asked and the new types of technique used, to answer questions felt to be more interesting or important than those which had become outmoded.

The history of these changes of 'models' is to a large degree the history of human thought. The 'organic' or the Marxist methods of investigating history certainly owed part of their vogue to the prestige of the particular natural sciences, or the particular artistic techniques, upon whose model they were supposedly or genuinely constructed; the increased interest, for example, both in biology and in music, from which many basic metaphors and analogies derived, is relevant to the historical writing of the nineteenth century, as the new interest in physics and mathematics is to the philosophy and history of the eighteenth; and the deflationary methods and ironical temper of the historians who wrote after the war of 1914–18 were conspicuously influenced by—and accepted in terms of —the new psychological and sociological techniques which had gained public confidence during this period. The relative dominance of, say, social, economic, and political concepts and presuppositions in a once admired historical work throws more light upon the general characteristics of its time and for this reason is a more reliable index to the standards adopted, the questions asked, the respective roles of 'facts' and 'interpretation', and, in effect, to the entire social and political outlook of an age, than the

putative distance of the work in question from some imaginary, fixed, unaltering ideal of absolute truth, metaphysical or scientific, empirical or *a priori*. It is in terms of such shifts in the methods of treating the past (or the present or the future) and of idioms and catchwords, the doubts and hopes, fears and exhortations which they expressed, that the development of political ideas and the conceptual apparatus of a society and of its most gifted and articulate representatives can best be judged. No doubt the concepts in terms of which people speak and think may be symptoms and effects of other processes social, psychological, physical, the discovery of which is the task of this or that empirical science. But this does not detract from their importance and paramount interest for those who wish to know what constitutes the conscious experience of the most characteristic men of an age or a society, whatever its causes and whatever its fate. And we are, of course, for obvious reasons of perspective, in a better situation to determine this in the case of past societies than for our own. The historical approach is inescapable: the very sense of contrast and dissimilarity with which the past affects us provides the only relevant background against which the features peculiar to our own experience stand out in sufficient relief to be adequately discerned and described.

The student of the political ideas of, for example, the midnineteenth century must indeed be blind if he does not, sooner or later, become aware of the profound differences in ideas and terminology, in the general view of things—the ways in which the elements of experience are conceived to be related to one another—which divide that not very distant age from our own. He understands neither that time nor his own if he does not perceive the contrast between what was common to Comte and Mill, Mazzini and Michelet, Herzen and Marx, on the one hand, and to Max Weber and William James, Tawney and Beard, Lytton Strachey and Namier, on the other; the continuity of the European intellectual tradition without which no historical understanding at all would be possible is, at shorter range, a succession of specific discontinuities and dissimilarities. Consequently, the remarks which follow deliberately ignore the similarities in favour of the specific differences in political outlook which characterize our own time, and to a large degree, solely our own.

II

The two great liberating political movements of the nineteenth century were, as every history book informs us, humanitarian individualism and romantic nationalism. Whatever their differences—and they were notoriously profound enough to lead to a sharp divergence and ultimate collision of these two ideals—they had this in common: they believed that the problems both of individuals and of societies could be solved if only the forces of intelligence and of virtue could be made to prevail over ignorance and wickedness. They believed, as against the pessimists and fatalists, both religious and secular, whose voices, audible indeed a good deal earlier, began to sound loudly only toward the end of the century, that all clearly understood questions could be solved by human beings with the moral and intellectual resources at their disposal. No doubt different schools of thought returned different answers to these varying problems; utilitarians said one thing, and neo-feudal romantics—Tory democrats, Christian Socialists, Pan-Germans, Slavophiles—another. Liberals believed in the unlimited power of education and power of rational morality to overcome economic misery and inequality. Socialists, on the contrary, believed that without radical alterations in the distribution and control of economic resources no amount of change of heart or mind on the part of individuals could be adequate; or, for that matter, occur at all. Conservatives and Socialists believed in the power and influence of institutions and regarded them as a necessary safeguard against the chaos, injustice, and cruelty caused by uncontrolled individualism; anarchists, radicals, and liberals looked upon institutions as such with suspicion as being obstructive to the realization of that free (and, in the view of most such thinkers, rational) society which the will of man could both conceive and build, if it were not for the unliquidated residue of ancient abuses (or unreason) upon which the existing rulers of society—whether individuals or administrative machines—leaned so heavily, and of which so many of them indeed were typical expressions.

Arguments about the relative degree of the obligation of the individual to society, and *vice versa,* filled the air. It is scarcely necessary to rehearse these familiar questions, which to this day form the staple of discussion in the more conservative institutions of Western learning, to realize that however wide the disagreements about the proper answers to them, the questions themselves were common to Liberals and Conservatives alike. There were, of course, even at that time isolated irrationalists —Stirner, Kierkegaard, in certain moods Carlyle; but in the main all the parties to the great controversies, even Calvinists and ultramontane Catholics, accepted the notion of man as resembling in varying degrees one or the other of two idealized types. Either he is a creature free and naturally good, but hemmed in and frustrated [3] by obsolete or corrupt or sinister institutions masquerading as saviours, protectors, and repositories of sacred traditions; or he is a being within limits, but never wholly, free, and to some degree, but never entirely, good, and consequently unable to save himself by his own wholly unaided efforts; and therefore rightly seeking salvation within the great frameworks—states, churches, unions. For only these great edifices promote solidarity, security, and sufficient strength to resist the shallow joys and dangerous, ultimately self-destructive, liberties peddled by those conscienceless or self-deceived individualists who, in the name of some bloodless intellectual dogma, or noble enthusiasm for an ideal unrelated to human lives, ignore or destroy the rich texture of social life heavy with treasures from the past—blind leaders of the blind, robbing men of their most precious resources, exposing them again to the perils of a life solitary, brutish, nasty, and short. Yet there was at least one premiss common to all the disputants, namely the belief that the problems were real, that it

took men of exceptional training and intelligence to formulate them properly, and men with exceptional grasp of the facts, will-power, and capacity for effective thought to find and apply the correct solutions.

These two great currents finally ended in exaggerated and indeed distorted forms as Communism and Fascism—the first as the treacherous heir of the liberal internationalism of the previous century, the second as the culmination and bankruptcy of the mystical patriotism which animated the national movements of the time. All movements have origins, forerunners, imperceptible beginnings: nor does the twentieth century seem divided from the nineteenth by so universal an explosion as the French Revolution, even in our day the greatest of all historical landmarks. Yet it is a fallacy to regard Fascism and Communism as being in the main only more uncompromising and violent manifestations of an earlier crisis, the culmination of a struggle fully discernible long before. The differences between the political movements of the twentieth century and the nineteenth are very sharp, and they spring from factors whose full force was not properly realized until our century was well under way. For there is a barrier which divides what is unmistakably past and done with from that which most characteristically belongs to our day. The familiarity of this barrier must not blind us to its relative novelty. One of the elements of the new outlook is the notion of unconscious and irrational influences which outweigh the forces of reason; another the notion that answers to problems exist not in rational solutions, but in the removal of the problems them-

---

[3] According to some, for historically or metaphysically inevitable reasons or causes which, however, soon or late will lose their potency.

selves by means other than thought and argument. The interplay between the old tradition, which saw history as the battle-ground between the easily identifiable forces of light and darkness, reason and obscurantism, progress and reaction; or alternatively between spiritualism and empiricism, intuition and scientific method, institutionalism and individualism—the conflict between this order and, on the other hand, the new factors violently opposed to the humanist psychology of *bourgeois* civilization is to a large extent the history of political ideas in our time.

QUESTIONS FOR DISCUSSION

1. What forms of determinism in history did the philosophies of nationalism, positivism (Comte), Hegel, and Marx take in the nineteenth century that still persist in the twentieth?
2. How do Hegelians differ from Marxists in the application of dialectics to history and politics?
3. How do totalitarian philosophies of the state make use of the "organic model" of society and culture?
4. What model of freedom does the democratic liberal have to offer against totalitarian irrationalism?
5. Evaluate the effectiveness of democratic liberalism in the political world today.

Martin Luther King, Jr. (1929-1968)

4.6   I Have a Dream . . .

Five score years ago, a great American, in whose symbolic shadow we stand, signed the Emancipation Proclamation. This momentous decree

Address delivered at the Lincoln Memorial during the March on Washington, August 28, 1963. © 1963 by Martin Luther King, Jr. Reprinted by permission of Joan Daves.

came as a great beacon light of hope to millions of Negro slaves who had been seared in the flames of withering injustice. It came as a joyous daybreak to end the long night of captivity.

But one hundred years later, we must face the tragic fact that the Negro is still not free. One hundred years later, the life of the Negro is still sadly crippled by the manacles of segregation and the chains of discrimination. One hundred years later, the Negro lives on a lonely island of poverty in the midst of a vast ocean of material prosperity. One hundred years later, the Negro is still languished in the corners of American society and finds himself an exile in his own land. So we have come here today to dramatize an appalling condition.

In a sense we have come to our nation's Capital to cash a check. When the architects of our republic wrote the magnificent words of the Constitution and the Declaration of Independence, they were signing a promissory note to which every American was to fall heir. This note was a promise that all men would be guaranteed the unalienable rights of life, liberty, and the pursuit of happiness.

It is obvious today that America has defaulted on this promissory note insofar as her citizens of color are concerned. Instead of honoring this sacred obligation, America has given the Negro people a bad check; a check which has come back marked "insufficient funds." But we refuse to believe that the bank of justice is bankrupt. We refuse to believe that there are insufficient funds in the great vaults of opportunity of this nation. So we have come to cash this check—a check that will give us upon demand the riches of freedom and the security of justice. We have also come to this hallowed spot to remind America of the fierce urgency of *now*. This is no time to engage in the luxury of cooling off or to take the tranquilizing drug of gradualism. *Now* is the time to make real the promises of Democracy. *Now* is the time to rise from the dark and desolate valley of segrega-

tion to the sunlit path of racial justice. *Now* is the time to open the doors of opportunity to all of God's children. *Now* is the time to lift our nation from the quicksands of racial injustice to the solid rock of brotherhood.

It would be fatal for the nation to overlook the urgency of the moment and to underestimate the determination of the Negro. This sweltering summer of the Negro's legitimate discontent will not pass until there is an invigorating autumn of freedom and equality. 1963 is not an end, but a beginning. Those who hope that the Negro needed to blow off steam and will now be content will have a rude awakening if the nation returns to business as usual. There will be neither rest nor tranquillity in America until the Negro is granted his citizenship rights. The whirlwinds of revolt will continue to shake the foundations of our nation until the bright day of justice emerges.

But there is something that I must say to my people who stand on the warm threshold which leads into the palace of justice. In the process of gaining our rightful place we must not be guilty of wrongful deeds. Let us not seek to satisfy our thirst for freedom by drinking from the cup of bitterness and hatred. We must forever conduct our struggle on the high plane of dignity and discipline. We must not allow our creative protest to degenerate into physical violence. Again and again we must rise to the majestic heights of meeting physical force with soul force. The marvelous new militancy which has engulfed the Negro community must not lead us to a distrust of all white people, for many of our white brothers, as evidenced by their presence here today, have come to realize that their destiny is tied up with our destiny and their freedom is inextricably bound to our freedom. We cannot walk alone.

And as we walk, we must make the pledge that we shall march ahead. We cannot turn back. There are those who are asking the devotees of civil rights, "When will you be satisfied?" We can never be satisfied as long as the Negro is the victim of the unspeakable horrors of police brutality. We can never be satisfied as long as our bodies, heavy with the fatigue of travel, cannot gain lodging in the motels of the highways and the hotels of the cities. We cannot be satisfied as long as the Negro's basic mobility is from a smaller ghetto to a larger one. We can never be satisfied as long as a Negro in Mississippi cannot vote and a Negro in New York believes he has nothing for which to vote. No, no, we are not satisfied, and we will not be satisfied until justice rolls down like waters and righteousness like a mighty stream.

I am not unmindful that some of you have come here out of great trials and tribulations. Some of you have come fresh from narrow jail cells. Some of you have come from areas where your quest for freedom left you battered by the storms of persecution and staggered by the winds of police brutality. You have been the veterans of creative suffering. Continue to work with the faith that unearned suffering is redemptive.

Go back to Mississippi, go back to Alabama, go back to South Carolina, go back to Georgia, go back to Louisiana, go back to the slums and ghettos of our northern cities, knowing that somehow this situation can and will be changed. Let us not wallow in the valley of despair.

I say to you today, my friends, that in spite of the difficulties and frustrations of the moment I still have a dream. It is a dream deeply rooted in the American dream.

I have a dream that one day this nation will rise up and live out the true meaning of its creed: "We hold these truths to be self-evident; that all men are created equal."

I have a dream that one day on the red hills of Georgia the sons of former slaves and the sons of former slaveowners will be able to sit down together at the table of brotherhood.

I have a dream that one day even the state of Mississippi, a desert state sweltering with the heat of injustice and oppression, will be transformed into an oasis of freedom and justice.

I have a dream that my four little children will one day live in a nation where they will not be judged by the color of their skin but by the content of their character.

I have a dream today.

I have a dream that one day the state of Alabama, whose governor's lips are presently dripping with the words of interposition and nullification, will be transformed into a situation where little black boys and black girls will be able to join hands with little white boys and white girls and walk together as sisters and brothers.

I have a dream today.

I have a dream that one day every valley shall be exalted, every hill and mountain shall be made low, the rough places will be made plains, and the crooked places will be made straight, and the glory of the Lord shall be revealed, and all flesh shall see it together.

This is our hope. This is the faith with which I return to the South. With this faith we will be able to hew out of the mountain of despair a stone of hope. With this faith we will be able to transform the jangling discords of our nation into a beautiful symphony of brotherhood. With this faith we will be able to work together, to pray together, to struggle together, to go to jail together, to stand up for freedom together, knowing that we will be free one day.

This will be the day when all of God's children will be able to sing with new meaning

> My country, 'tis of thee,
> Sweet land of liberty,
>   Of thee I sing:
> Land where my fathers died,
> Land of the pilgrims' pride,
> From every mountain-side
> Let freedom ring.

And if America is to be a great nation this must become true. So let freedom ring from the prodigious hilltops of New Hampshire. Let freedom ring from the mighty mountains of New York. Let freedom ring from the heightening Alleghenies of Pennsylvania!

Let freedom ring from the snow-capped Rockies of Colorado!

Let freedom ring from the curvaceous peaks of California!

But not only that; let freedom ring from Stone Mountain of Georgia!

Let freedom ring from Lookout Mountain of Tennessee!

Let freedom ring from every hill and molehill of Mississippi. From every mountainside, let freedom ring.

When we let freedom ring, when we let it ring from every village and every hamlet, from every state and every city, we will be able to speed up that day when all of God's children, black men and white men, Jews and Gentiles, Protestants and Catholics, will be able to join hands and sing in the words of the old Negro spiritual, "Free at last! free at last! thank God almighty, we are free at last!"

Louis Waldman (1892-   )

4.7   Civil Rights—Yes:
Civil Disobedience—No

On Wednesday, April 21, 1965, Dr. Martin Luther King, Jr. addressed a meeting of the Association of the Bar

Reprinted by permission of the author and publisher from *New York State Bar Journal* (August 1965), pp. 331-37.

of the City of New York on the subject "The Civil Rights Struggle in the United States Today." In that address Dr. King made a strong and eloquent plea for civil rights for our fellow citizens of the Negro race. He also dealt with another subject of far-reaching importance, not only to Negroes, but to every single American and to our nation as such, a subject on which he has spoken and written before: his program for civil disobedience as a means of achieving not only civil rights but to remedy all injustice.

In so far as Dr. King made a plea for Negro civil rights, I say with emphasis: Civil Rights—Yes. In so far, however, as Dr. King advocated civil disobedience, I say with equal emphasis: Civil Disobedience—No.

For myself, long before Dr. King was born, I espoused, and still espouse, the cause of civil rights for all people along with causes aimed at abolishing poverty and lifting the standards of workingmen, regardless of race or color, to a higher level of civilized existence, and providing for equality before the law, human dignity, and social and economic justice. In my world we were, and are, color blind. I have never ceased believing in the rightness of these causes. I am happy to say that more and more Americans, not only in the profession of the law, but in every walk of life are enlisting in the realization of these dreams, which are at the heart of the American dream.

The nation's response, and the ever-growing support for civil rights for the Negro, is reflected by the actions of all three branches of our Federal Government, by the United States Supreme Court, beginning with *Brown* v. *Board of Education* in 1954, by the Executive, from the White House down, and by Congress' enactment of new legislation, a process continuing up to the present. And this, it should be recorded in the interest of truth, is also the fact in the overwhelming number of our states, going back many years.

But this must be proclaimed for all to remember: The unanimous decision in *Brown* v. *Board of Education,* which is the foundation for the progress made in the last 10 years, was not achieved by civil disobedience, sit-ins, lie-ins, or marches. On the contrary, it was achieved by reason and the appeal to traditional constitutional principles.

Now the rights of Negroes to enjoy the same civil rights as do other Americans, to equality before the law, to equal opportunity, to an education, to a job, to vote under a system of voter qualifications applied uniformly to all citizens, are all based on our constitutional system of government, and the laws enacted under the Constitution. Those who assert rights under the Constitution and the laws made thereunder must abide by that Constitution and the law, if that Constitution is to survive. They cannot pick and choose; they cannot say that they will abide by those laws which they think are just and refuse to abide by those laws which they think are unjust. And the same is true of decisions on constitutional principles.

The country, therefore, cannot accept Dr. King's doctrine that he and his followers will pick and choose, knowing that it is illegal to do so. I say, such doctrine is not only illegal and for that reason alone should be abandoned, but that it is also immoral, destructive of the principles of democratic government, and a danger to the very civil rights Dr. King seeks to promote.

Stripped of all pejorative rhetoric, what is this program of civil disobedience which Dr. King advocates? In his address on April 21st, Dr. King said the following:

Before I close I feel compelled to comment briefly on the oft-heard charge that we who urge non-cooperation with evil in the form of civil disobedience are equally lawless.

And, continuing, he said:

> . . . the devotees of nonviolent action . . . feel a moral responsibility to obey just laws. But they recognize that there are also unjust laws.

Dr. King then performs intellectual acrobatics by jumping from the premise—that he and his "devotees" . . . "recognize that there are also unjust laws"—to the asserted right to violate such laws "that conscience tells him [are] unjust," that is, in the sole judgment of the violator. He defines "an unjust law" as

> . . . One in which people are required to obey a code that they had no part in making because they were denied the right to vote

and also as being

> . . . One in which the minority is compelled to observe a code that is not binding on the majority.

According to this logic, every person under 21 or the millions of non-citizens, all denied the right to vote, have no obligation to obey the law. Now, as to the minority logic. There are thousands of laws throughout the land which apply only to minorities, and are "not binding on" the majorities. For example, we are all familiar with laws which provide that application is limited to "cities of 1,000,000 or more," or "cities of less than 100,000," or just "cities" as opposed to "towns" or "villages." We all know of laws that apply only to bankers, farmers, trade unions, manufacturers, sailors, or electricians, or other trades or groups, but do not apply to the great bulk of the rest of the nation, to the "majority." May all such laws be ignored by the affected minority because they do not bind the majority?

These glib generalizations in Dr. King's advocacy of civil disobedience are as bad as they are illogical. For when literally applied by many of his followers, who do not have the sophistication and training of Dr. King, such shibboleths lead to an intellectual, religious, and moral justification for doing illegal acts of which violence and lawlessness are but the extreme expressions.

"In disobeying such unjust laws," continues Dr. King, "we do so peacefully, openly, and non-violently. Most important, we willingly accept the penalty, whatever it is."

Apparently Dr. King thinks that in violating laws "openly," he and his followers are more virtuous than those who violate laws secretly. As a matter of fact, the reverse is true. The open violation of law is an open invitation to others to join in such violation. Disobedience to law is bad enough when done secretly, but it is far worse when done openly, especially when accompanied by clothing such acts in the mantle of virtue and organizing well-advertised and financed plans to carry out such violations. The secret violator of law recognizes his act for what it is: an antisocial act; he may even be ashamed of what he is doing and seek to avoid disapprobation of his neighbors. But the open violator, the agitating violator, acts shamelessly, in defiance of his neighbor's judgment and his fellow man's disapproval.

After his address Dr. King was asked questions and he gave answers, all recorded. The answers to some of these questions are most illuminating.

Dr. King was asked whether he thought "there is a right to disobey an unjust law" in those places "where the Negroes actually have the right to vote." This is Dr. King's answer:

> There may be a community where Negroes have the right to vote, but there are still unjust laws in that community. There may be unjust laws in a community where people in large numbers are voting, and I think wherever unjust laws exist people on the basis of conscience have a right to disobey those laws.

There we have it. If this philosophy were accepted and carried out by the twenty million American Negroes, it would be enough to disorganize our entire society and produce an intolerable chaos and a denial of individual liberty to every other American.

But, note carefully, Dr. King does not limit his philosophy to Negroes. He says "wherever unjust laws exist *people* on the basis of conscience have a right to disobey those laws." To this I say that we are all fully aware that human beings, being what they are, "conscience" can be, and sometimes is, elastic, conforming to what people want, both overtly and subconsciously. But, as Dr. King must know, civil disobedience cannot end with Negroes alone. You cannot build a fence around this kind of program. Other people become involved.

The consequences of Dr. King's program, if allowed to continue, would be disastrous to our nation. For example, if Dr. King's erroneous and ill-founded advocacy of civil disobedience were applied, let us say, to the Labor Movement and its fifteen million organized members, think of what

it would mean. It is common knowledge that the Labor Movement is convinced, and in good conscience believes, that Section 14(b) of the Taft-Hartley Law discriminates in favor of states having the so-called "Right-to-Work" laws, and is unjust. What if in the last 18 years the Labor Movement had proceeded with a program of civil disobedience as outlined by Dr. King, and had used its organizational power to stage marches, "non-violent marches" of course, sit-ins, "non-violent sit-ins" of course, and other activities—would not such actions tend to disorient our politically organized society? Let us suppose further that George Meany, his Executive Council, and the AFL-CIO unions did all of these things not only with respect to Section 14(b) of the Taft-Hartley Law, but also with respect to other laws, city, state, or federal, which they honestly and in good conscience believe to be unjust to labor. What would happen to our country, to our industries, to our commerce, to our trade, to our existence as a civilized community?

The same applies to all other segments of the nation, to farmers, to merchants, to bankers, to manufacturers, to pacifists, to Catholics, to Protestants or to Jews. Whatever the group, if they decide in the name of religion, morality or personal conscience that certain laws are unjust, then, according to Dr. King's program, they would be justified in carrying out civil disobedience.

Again I ask: If this be so, where would our nation be? Where would our freedom be? Where would our civil rights be?

Dr. King has, not only at this meeting, but at other meetings recently, referred to Hitler's Germany and said that "everything that Hitler did in Germany was legal."

Apart from the fact that in this bare assertion Dr. King is telling only part of Hitler's role in relation to law, he is making an invidious comparison between Hitler's Germany and the United States. I deeply resent it. Most Americans in their right senses should resent it as well. Hitler's Germany was the product of a vicious megalomaniac who was a curse to Germany and the German people, as he turned out to be a curse to other people, and the world at large.

But I want to remind Dr. King, whenever he makes his next speech and compares Hitler and Hitler's Germany to the United States, to tell his audience also that Hitler, when he began in the middle 20's and until he finally escalated himself into becoming the Chancellor of that unhappy nation, followed a philosophy and practice of direct action and civil disobedience. To Hitler and his devotees the laws of the Weimar Republic and the treaties made thereunder were unjust. And from small beginnings of violating one law after another, he built a movement which was prepared to accept and obey the laws he thought were just and to defy and violate the laws he thought were unjust.

Hitler's Germany and all that it represents in modern experience, with all its tragic consequences, is a most potent argument against civil disobedience. There are any number of other experiences in the world in this century alone, where those who advocated and organized movements to defy the laws made by their governments, particularly democratic governments, have brought evil to their countries and to the world. Numerous

Communist as well as Fascist examples come to mind and should not be passed over.

And let us not think that Dr. King's advocacy of civil disobedience is just for the South. He was asked what are the main differences between North and South in so far as civil rights are concerned, and his answer came in a flash:

> Let me say that the problem in a sense is the same. There may be a difference in degree, but not a difference of kind.

And so, civil disobedience applies to the North as it does to the South, in Dr. King's view. The reason why the North is to be included in the civil disobedience program, according to Dr. King, is that the North is guilty of broad injustice in three areas: unemployment, housing and education. Yet, it is patently obvious that these three problems involve broad social and economic policies, on the justice or injustice of which thousands of laws, touching on these questions, honest men may in good conscience differ.

Then as if to cap the climax of the April 21st meeting, came the last question:

> Dr. King, does your concept of civil disobedience include such tactics as obstructing sites where Negroes are not employed, where those who use such means are willing to accept the consequences, but are not quarreling with the justice of any law?

Dr. King's answer, which is self-revealing, I set forth in full, as follows:

> I think all of our demonstrations and all civil disobedience must be centered on something. In other words, the goals must be clearly stated.

I think we have to face the fact that there are instances where in the process of frustration with the structure of things, people find themselves in positions of not quite being able to see the unjust law. But they see injustice in a very large sense existing. Consequently, they feel the need to engage in civil disobedience to call attention to overall injustice. At that point they are not protesting against an unjust law. I would say that there are very few unjust laws in most of our northern communities. There are some unjust laws, I think, on the housing question and some other, but on the whole the laws are just. But there is injustice, and there are communities which do not work with vigor and with determination to remove that injustice. In such instances I think men of conscience and men of good will will have no alternative but to engage in some kind of civil disobedience in order to call attention to the injustices, so that the society will seek to rid itself of that overall injustice. Again I say that there must be a willingness to accept the penalty.

I think there must be, always, in a nonviolent movement, a sense of political timing. I do not believe in the indiscriminate use of any form of demonstration. I think we must be well disciplined and think through our moves, and we must clearly define our goals. I think some of us, for example, felt that the stall-in at the World's Fair didn't quite meet that test because certain goals had not been clearly defined. On the other hand we understood the discontent and the impatience and the frustration, and the disappointment, that led individuals to feel that in an unfair world, maybe people should not be finding it too easy to get to a World's Fair. But at the same time we must set clearly defined goals, in calling for demonstrations and practicing civil disobedience.

This answer, like many others, is full of holes and dodges. For example, according to Dr. King, as long as there is "discontent" and "disappointment" individuals have a right to "feel that in an unfair world, maybe people should not be finding it too easy to get to a World's Fair." And thus stall-ins to block the road between New York City and the World's Fair on opening day in 1964, instead of being condemned, get to be "*understood.*"

From the same sources came the suggestion that, as a further demonstration of "discontent" and "disappointment" with "an unfair world" people should open their faucets in their private homes and let water run to waste. A simpler name for this conduct is sabotage. Where is the end to this type of civil disobedience? It seems that private sabotage, stall-ins on the highway, lie-ins in the White House, in the offices of governors and mayors, and in the offices of other governmental agencies, do not suggest that the end is in sight.

There is also implied in Dr. King's last answer, that if once you state your goal, then you are justified in proceeding with marches and demonstrations, a point which, it seems to a lawyer, is constitutionally indefensible. Let me illustrate with a graphic example that has only come to the fore in Chicago this very month. In the June 13, 1965, *New York Times*, there appeared a story under the head of "150 Jailed in Chicago Sitdown over Rehiring of School Chief." The repeated demonstrations in Chicago were designed to compel Mayor Richard J. Daley to discharge Dr. Benjamin C. Willis as Superintendent of Schools. The demonstrators stated their goal, "Ben Willis must go." Their demonstrations included lying on the streets to obstruct traffic, sit-ins at City Hall and other familiar techniques.

The demonstrators, according to the *Times,*

> . . . were led today by the Rev. John Porter, a Negro minister who is head of the Chicago affiliate of the Rev. Dr. Martin Luther King's Southern Christian Leadership Conference, and by Robert Lucas, also a Negro and chairman of the Chicago branch of the Congress of Racial Equality.

Unfortunately, we have reached a point where, if you can gather a large enough group who will chant and sing loud enough, and if that group can obstruct the normal operations of life in the community or of agencies of government and that group's actions are carried out repeatedly, then they seem to feel that they have acquired a legal right to do so. Police are "brutal" when they stop such actions; mayors are "unfair" if they seek to protect life and property; and judges and the law are denounced.

Now, why?

Dr. King has written a book called *Why We Can't Wait,* in which he tells us his philosophy and purpose: "The purpose of our direct-action program is to create a situation so crisis-packed that it will inevitably open the door to negotiation."

At another point, he says:

> . . . Actually, we who engage in non-violent direct action are not the creators of tension. We merely bring to the surface the hidden tension that is already alive. We bring it out in the open, where it can be seen and dealt with. . . .

Thus, we have the philosophy and purpose of Dr. King's program. It is to produce "crisis-packed" situations and "tensions." Such a purpose is the very opposite of non-violence, for the atmosphere-of-crisis policy leads to violence by provoking violence. And the provocation of violence is violence. To describe such provocations as "non-violent" is to trifle with the plain meaning of words.

The perpetual crisis technique has been used by the Communist movement throughout the world. Both Communist governments and parties follow it. As I said, it was also used by Hitler in Germany, both on his road to power and after power came to him, as a means of justifying his arbitrary, brutal and barbarous policy. It has been used by every Fascist country we learned to know and abhor in this century. It is disruptive of democratic society and institutions.

Whether Dr. King knows it or not, or wills it or not, the policy of perpetual crisis, of provoking "tensions," as he calls it, and of civil disobedience, are disastrous to the Negro people themselves, to civil liberties and to constitutional government. Such a policy flies in the teeth of the very purpose of our Constitution, which is clearly stated in the preamble to be, among other things, "to insure domestic tranquillity."

It is time that the organized Bar is heard on this question. It is time that we tell Dr. King and his devotees of civil disobedience that the rule of law will and must prevail, that violators of the law, however lofty their aims or position in society, are not above the law. Correction of injustices by intimidation, by extralegal means, or inspired by fear of violence cannot longer be continued. And law enforcement authorities must make it clear that we are a constitutional government and the laws enacted pursuant to our Constitution must be obeyed whether the individuals or groups affected by those laws believe they are just or not.

In absolute as well as relative terms, we in the United States have built a democratic constitutional system second to none. We have done so by recognizing the proper roles, assigned by our history and governmental philosophy, to the separation of powers in our government. This separation recognizes the sovereignty of states and distributes the political and governmental authorities and functions at the Federal level. It lays down the fundamental principles which regulate the relations of government with citizens and inhabitants of our land. It establishes the rule of law through constitutions and the Bill of Rights.

Our nation has survived because of the dedication to these principles. Our nation will continue to live as long as all of us, from lawyer to ditch digger, from judge to police officer, insist on according respect and obedience to these basic values of our society.

QUESTIONS FOR DISCUSSION

1. Define "civil rights" under the Constitution and the laws enacted recently. To what extent are these laws not enforced and what are the causes of their nonenforcement?
2. What program of civil disobedience did Martin Luther King advocate? Compare it with the ideas of Thoreau and Gandhi.
3. What are Waldman's legal and political objections to Dr. King's appeal to the higher law of conscience in justifying some acts of civil disobedience?
4. Give your reasons for agreeing or disagreeing with Waldman.
5. What political issues are involved in resistance to military conscription by those whose conscience condemns a war as "unjust"?

FURTHER READINGS FOR CHAPTER 4

*Aristotle, *Politics*. (Numerous editions available.)
*Bentham, Jeremy, *The Handbook of Political Fallacies*, rev. and ed. by Harold A. Larabee. New York: Harper, Torchbooks, 1962.
*Berlin, Isaiah, *The Hedgehog and the Fox*. New York: New American Library of World Literature, 1957.
*Cohen, Morris R., *The Meaning of Human History*. LaSalle, Ill.: Open Court, 1947.
*Collingwood, R. G., *The Idea of History*, T. M. Knox, ed. New York: Oxford University Press, 1946.

---

* Paperback edition.

Croce, Benedetto, *History as the Story of Liberty*. New York: Humanities Press, 1949.

———, *History: Its Theory and Practice*. New York: Russell & Russell, 1960.

Gandhi, Mohandas K., *Non-Violent Resistance*. New York: Schocken, 1961.

*Grotius, Hugo, *Prolegomena to the Law of War and Peace*. Indianapolis: Bobbs-Merrill, 1957.

*Hegel, Georg Wilhelm Friedrich, *The Philosophy of History*, J. Sibree, trans. New York: Dover Publications, 1956.

———, *The Philosophy of Right*, T. M. Knox, ed. New York: Oxford University Press, 1942.

*Hobbes, Thomas, *Leviathan*. (Numerous editions available.)

Holmes, Oliver Wendell, Jr., *The Common Law*. Boston: Little, Brown & Co., n.d.

Kant, Immanuel, *Essay on Universal History from a Cosmopolitan Viewpoint*, in *On History*, L. W. Beck, trans. Indianapolis: Bobbs-Merrill, 1963.

*———, *Perpetual Peace*, L. W. Beck, trans. Indianapolis: Bobbs-Merrill, 1957.

Kropotkin, Peter, *Mutual Aid*. Boston: Peter E. Sargent, 1955.

*Locke, John, *Of Civil Government*. (Numerous editions available.)

*Machiavelli, Niccolo, *The Prince*. (Numerous editions available.)

Ortega y Gasset, José, *Toward a Philosophy of History*, Helene Weyl, trans. New York: Norton, 1941.

*Orwell, George, *Animal Farm*. New York: New American Library of World Literature, 1954.

*———, *1984*. New York: New American Library of World Literature, 1954.

*Rousseau, Jean-Jacques, *Social Contract*. (Numerous editions available.)

Sabine, George H., *The History of Political Theory*, 3rd ed. New York: Holt, Rinehart & Winston, 1961.

*Smith, Adam, *The Wealth of Nations*. (Numerous editions available.)

Spinoza, Benedict de, *Tractatus Theologico-Politicus*, in *Works of Spinoza*, R. H. M. Elwes, trans. 2 vols. Gloucester, Mass.: Peter Smith, Publisher.

*Thoreau, Henry D., *Civil Disobedience*, in *Civil Disobedience: Theory and Practice*, H. A. Bedau, ed. New York: Pegasus, 1969.

*Tolstoy, Leo, *War and Peace* (Numerous editions available.)

*Toynbee, Arnold J., *A Study of History*, 3 vols. New York: Oxford University Press, n.d.

*Vico, Giambattista, *New Science*, rev. ed., Thomas Bergin and Max H. Fisch, trans. New York: Doubleday & Company, Inc., n.d.

Chapter 5

PHILOSOPHY OF SCIENCE

INTRODUCTION

It was once possible—as late as the seventeenth century—for philosophers to master most of the basic ideas of the sciences, and even to be leaders in one or more other fields of learning. Such was the case with Aristotle, whose scientific texts supplied Western civilization for almost 1,000 years with the foundations of every science. Another classical example of a philosopher-scientist is Leibniz (1646-1716), whose contributions to mathematics and the logic of the sciences were as fruitful as the scientific societies he helped organize all over seventeenth-century Europe. In this classical tradition the love of wisdom and the cultivation of the sciences were inseparable. But the rapid growth of specialized sciences in the last few hundred years makes it practically impossible for one person to keep abreast of all the sciences and to synthesize their results in a philosophical system. Philosophers of science hence nowadays deal with problems underlying (1) the logical structure or common methodological features of the sciences, (2) their interrelations, and (3) the relations of the growing sciences to other phases of civilization, namely, morals, politics, art, and religion. These three sets of problems concerning the rapidly changing sciences require for their solution philosophical principles that are in consonance with the presuppositions and logic of science.

Logic of Science

Despite the great number of specialized branches and sub-branches of every science, each with its own problems, techniques, and nomenclature, there are certain features common to all scientific inquiry in the so-called scientific method. The chief elements of thought operating as common features of scientific method are hypothesis, deduction, and verification. An hypothesis is a tentative or proposed solution to the problem which initiated the inquiry. Suppose the problem is to ascertain the cause of cancer. Then the idea that specific physico-chemical structures and reactions will occur in all cases of cancer would be considered an hypothesis. Deduction would be the drawing of consequences from the hypothesis. For example, if such and such physical or chemical molecular reactions are experimentally induced in the tissues, then cancerous growth will ensue. Experiments are more precisely made when the conditions are defined and the procedure specified. The research scientists need to know how to measure the required reaction and at what rate cancerous growth takes place. Experiment and measurement are thus involved in verification, which is the testing of the consequences deduced from an hypothesis. There are a priori an infinite number of hypotheses the scientist might test, but in practice he limits himself to those grounded in previous knowledge or related by analogy to similar situations, and to tests within his means.

There are many important questions that the philosophic student of scientific method will have to face; for example, What is meant by causation? Hume challenged the idea that there was a *necessary* connection between cause and effect such as we have between a statement and what is logically deduced from it. If empirical relations are contingent but not necessary, then how can we establish a generalization that goes beyond our limited previous experience to an unlimited future, as we do when we say that all men are mortal because men have to date been mortal? This is the problem of induction: How can we logically justify generalizations that refer to more than what has been experienced? To ask whether all statements of empirical fact are probable is to raise another basic question: What do we mean by probability? Some philosophers challenge the theory of knowledge which appeals to the "certainties" of common sense, such as "I know for certain that I see red or feel pain, etc." We shall discuss theories of knowledge in the next chapter, but we shall here note some of the differences between common sense and science that do not preclude their continuity and similarity in other regards.

The scientific method of checking the consequences of hypotheses by experimental verification generally differs in certain respects from common sense; first of all, by specifying the problem and defining the terms of its hypotheses more carefully and exactly; secondly, by the systematic use of experimental controls of isolated factors; thirdly, by free and open discussion of ideas in collaboration with other investigators. Though a scientist may obtain his hypotheses from any source, he has to submit his reasoning and claims of verification to his co-workers. We have already seen in Chapter 2 ("Methodology") how scientific method differs from the more prevailing methods of tenacity, authority, and apriorism. Insofar as the latter three ways of fixing belief and tradition influence common sense, scientific method is more critical, more flexible, and more progressive than the fossilized features of common sense. The common observation of the rising and setting of the sun, moon, and other heavenly bodies led people to cling tenaciously to the view that the earth was stationary until the astronomers showed that patiently accumulated facts about the positions and motions of heavenly bodies required us to abandon the once common belief.

On the other hand, Campbell maintains that common sense is not to be rejected when it practically or crudely but satisfactorily copes with everyday situations and problems, correcting itself, like science, on the basis of well-tried experience and tested habits. Scientists and philosophers both naturally rely on such tested common sense in matters requiring neither the precision nor generality of scientific laws or comprehensive theories. Furthermore, the basic and often concealed assumptions of science and philosophy are subject to critical examination and revision just as those of common sense. Campbell also shows the intertwined nature of pure and applied science. "Laws" are hypotheses confirmed by experiment; "theories" coordinate laws into a system. Laws are predictive; theories are attempted unifications of laws.

The other selections have been written by men also eminent for their scientific and philosophic reflections on the foundations of the sciences.

Poincaré is a mathematical physicist who has thought profoundly about the logical foundations of his science. The problem he discusses is one that occurs in all scientific generalization: how can we make predictions from what we have experienced? We measure the acceleration of falling bodies at different places and times and accept the hypothesis that, under similar conditions, the same results of measurement will be obtained within the limits of error of our measuring instruments. But there is no a priori guarantee that exactly similar conditions will obtain. Hence, our generalization that there is a constant acceleration of freely falling bodies at a given place on the earth contains several general ideas: (1) bodies fall freely; (2) they are accelerated uniformly toward the center of the earth; (3) their constant acceleration is not affected materially by other very distant or remote events. These ideas are not given by direct observation, for the ideas are general while our observations are particular. Are the general ideas mere fictions or figments of the scientist's imagination, or are they representations of objective laws of nature? This is the problem known throughout the history of philosophy as the problem of universals. The medieval "realist" asserted the objective reality of universals in the very fabric of nature, whereas the "nominalist" claimed that universals exist only as names of similarities or uniformities of particular experiences of essentially individual realities. Now, Poincaré's position is an intermediate one, called "conceptualism." It regards generalizations as hypotheses suggested by the uniformities or similarities of experience. But once the generalization is framed as an hypothesis, the mind reasons to certain conclusions that are valid regardless of truth or falsity of the hypothesis. These reasonings, however, are applicable to the phenomena studied only so long as there is a certain uniformity of behavior or homogeneity of structure present throughout the observations.

Charles Peirce was thoroughly grounded in physics and chemistry as well as in logic, metaphysics, and the history of science and philosophy. Specimens of the fruits of his life-long study of the methods and foundations of the sciences appear, respectively, in selection 2.5 and in the following "Notes on Scientific Philosophy." Although he called himself a "laboratory philosopher," he firmly believed that all the sciences rested on categories like causality, quality, relation, which are taken for granted by the scientist but which ought to be logically analyzed by the philosopher of science. The logical analysis of relations and of such concepts as probability, infinity, and continuity of which Peirce gives us a glimpse has been one of the major achievements of modern logic. It encouraged Russell to conceive of logic as the essence of philosophy.

Interrelations of the Sciences

Peirce aimed at a synthesis of physical, biological, and psychological sciences by means of a systematic elaboration of the ideas of chance, continuity, and feeling. Chance designates the absolute spontaneity and variety in nature. There is always an element of unpredictable contingency in natural phenomena that eludes the most exact scientific formulas; besides, probable errors attach to all statements of scientific laws no matter how precise our instruments of measurement. Continuity is employed as a category in order to explain how regularity or law can evolve from chance variations. Belief in the objective reality of general ideas made Peirce a "realist" in the medieval sense, as distinguished from "nominalists," who regard such ideas as mere names or labels for a sum of particular objects of experience. Peirce's illustrations of such objective universal ideas include physical constants, for example, the value of g, and qualities like the hardness of diamonds. There are also, in social studies, more elusive things like the commercial or nationalistic "spirit of an age," which are as real for Peirce as the merchants or rulers of a nation. But the universals of physical or social science do not exist apart from observable individuals. Specialists trained in the exact mathematical and physical sciences may err in extending their authority beyond their fields, for they may not have enough clear knowledge of the more complex phenomena of biology, psychology, and the social sciences to make generalizations that would hold for all the sciences. Peirce exposes himself to criticism in his cosmic speculations on some rather inexact ideas about evolution and habit formation (with which biologists and psychologists are still experimenting) as a basis for metaphysical generalizations about all the sciences, for example, when he describes the laws of nature as "habits," as if nature were an organism that grows and acquires habits. Whether such a vast analogy is sound or not, it illustrates the sort of speculative philosophy of science which has often stimulated more critical studies; no absolute, temporarily fixed distinction between speculative and critical philosophy is tenable. Also, there is no restriction on where a scientist may go to obtain suggestions for his hypotheses. The important concept of probability originated in problems of gambling, and was used at first in sociology (insurance, population changes, and so forth) and biology (birth and death rates, medical statistics) more extensively than in physics, where it plays such a major role today, as Peirce predicted it would.

Are biological, psychological, and social phenomena *reducible* to physical laws? The problem is the logical one of the interrelations of various sciences, and expert knowledge of any one of these sciences cannot settle the question by the sheer weight of specialized authority. In other words, the philosophy of science requires a knowledge of the basic presuppositions and logical interrelations of the sciences, but cannot dictate any final comprehensive interpretation of nature by merely referring to the results of these sciences. It is a common historical fact that the sciences borrow fruitful ideas from one another, but the test of any generalization remains within the logic of consistency and verification. It is in this sense that the philosophy of science is coordinate with scientific method rather than based on a higher authority that can legitimately impose its views on the sciences.

Ernest Nagel offers an analysis of *explanation* in science. First, we cannot and should not assume that science merely describes "how" but does not explain "why" things happen, because every question of "why?" is really an inquiry into more processes of *how* nature behaves. Secondly, Nagel explicates the various patterns of explanation (deductive, probabilistic, teleological, and genetic) which enter in diverse ways into the constructions of scientific concepts, laws, and theories.

One of the most persistent problems in modern philosophy is the "mind-body" problem, the topic of the symposium by three British philosophers on "The Physical Basis of Mind." Not only do all three touch on the relation of physiology to psychology, but they are also concerned with the categories of the physical and the mental, with behavioral and introspective statements, and with the puzzle of a "free will" in a mechanistic framework. Viscount Samuel is impressed by the traditional dualism of mechanism in bodies and voluntary action in minds, and he raises the metaphysical question of their interrelation as one for future science and philosophy to resolve. Sir A. J. Ayer, in a positivistic vein, regards the traditional way of stating the problem as misguided by the metaphysical assumption (due to Descartes in modern philosophy) of body and mind as two distinct substances. The only relevant problem for Ayer is the analysis of statements about thoughts and feelings and how far such statements are equivalent to those about people's behavior. Gilbert Ryle sees the problem as that of "the ghost in the machine" (cf. his book on *The Concept of Mind*). He rejects the Cartesian dualism and regards "Mind" and "Matter" as obsolete "category mistakes" in describing the activities of people "calculating, conjuring, hoping, resolving, tasting, bluffing, fretting, and so on."

Cultural Implications of Scientific Methods

Quite often philosophers seek a superior realm of objects as more permanent or more important than the transitory world of common sense and science. Some of these philosophers follow Plato in placing objects on three different levels: common sense, which deals confusedly with particular things; science, which discovers empirical uniformities; and philosophy, which discovers eternal truth and purpose in a "higher" world order. "Higher" may mean more comprehensive or more important, but the former logical meaning is independent of the latter ethical sense. This hierarchy of common sense, science, and philosophy is acceptable to a theological or metaphysical system which makes philosophy the handmaid of that system and subordinates science to both. Examples of such systems are found not only in those who advocate the medieval and modern subordination of the philosophy of science to theology, but also in those who seek to find an eternal framework of philosophic categories within which to interpret the sciences.

The antimetaphysical viewpoint of modern positivistic philosophy of science goes back historically to Hume, Auguste Comte, and Ernst Mach, although it advances beyond them on the basis of modern logic and physics. Comte distinguished three stages of cultural and intellectual history: the theological, the metaphysical, and the positive or scientific. It would be wrong to regard these as inevitable historical stages, since we find each of them in all periods of intellectual history. Comte also accepted the classical view of nature's laws as necessary relations among observed phenomena, and erected a hierarchy of sciences (mathematics, astronomy, physics, chemistry, biology, and sociology) terminating in a high priesthood of sociologists,[1]

Mach was a more critical scientific thinker, who tried to rid the sciences of all a priori or metaphysical notions like substance, causality, and teleology by offering an "antimetaphysical" view of scientific laws. On this view, a scientific law is simply a functional relation asserted to hold for directly or indirectly observed elements or sensations. Mach followed Hume's analysis of the notion of causality to show there was no proof of necessary connec-

---

[1] Comte's "Temple of Humanity" found a following in Latin America where there are still adherents.

tion between cause and effect beyond the "constant conjunction" of sensed qualities. Today it is said that Mach and Hume did not distinguish clearly enough the logical and the psychological aspects of the problem. Like Mach, modern positivists go back to Galileo's functional descriptions of observed and measured phenomena for the understanding of scientific laws. These empirical descriptions are not intuitions of any necessary causal relations which the classical philosophy of science regarded as purely logical. This is an a priori tendency from which even Galileo is not free in his extrascientific philosophical speculations. If Galileo could have freed his philosophizing from the rationalistic metaphysics of his times, and simply analyzed the experiments by which he established his laws of falling bodies, he would have realized that he had discovered a most probable relation between the distance and time of fall, not because of any a priori rational necessity, but because the relation of uniform acceleration recurs in a constant way, which can be verified by further experimentation. On the frequency theory of probability a statistical view replaces mechanical necessity in their notions of scientific law, which can thus be extended to social sciences, as more recent developments indicate.

The types of relations asserted in a scientific law will depend on the kinds of methods of observation and calculation that are required to establish them. Not all physical or social phenomena are directly observable, but only certain large-scale or macroscopic events like the motions of terrestrial and heavenly bodies or political trends. In the microscopic world of the atom and its subatomic components, we can observe, with the proper instruments, only the net effects of large numbers of minute changes, and only a statistical correlation can serve as the basis of any generalization. The statistical conception of law is applicable to any physical or social phenomena involving large numbers of individuals whose behavior is collectively and not individually observable or predictable. We thus have in the functional, statistical view of scientific laws a logical basis common to the natural and social sciences, and perhaps more fruitful for the further development of both than the traditional metaphysical conceptions of either mechanistic or organismic philosophies of science. In any case, the logical study of the foundations of science makes it obligatory upon students of philosophy to reconsider the traditional theories of knowledge and views of the world which have hitherto dominated our thinking.

The cultural values of science are not limited to the useful products of technology, important as these are for reducing the drudgery of menial labor, for improving the health and living standards of an industrial civilization. The growth of science affects men's lives and minds by "challenging established beliefs about the cosmos and its parts, and inducing emendations in habitual modes of thought." Science has and still can rid us of many superstitions and ungrounded fears that prevent the mind from exercising its creative functions. It can help break down prejudice and hatred in human relations when they rest on ignorance or on false guarantees of certainty about human happiness. The "brave new world" of a scientific society, satirized by Aldous Huxley as leading to a regimented mechanical conformity of belief and taste, is a caricature of the patience, diversity of opinion, and fallibilism that actually characterize the specific practice of science, although it is true to say that the best scientist outside his field of specialization is heir to all the prejudices of laymen. The value of the philosophy of science consists in discouraging such one-sided use of intelligence and in suggesting ways of humanizing the scientific temper of mind. Tolerance of new ideas no matter what race, nation, religion, or social class the originator comes from, freedom to question all beliefs, intellectual honesty, and willingness to submit one's ideas to public criticism—these are some of the cultural values of science without which no liberal culture can thrive.

Norman Campbell (1880-1949)

5.1 The Applications of Science

THE PRACTICAL VALUE
OF SCIENCE

So far we have regarded science as a means of satisfying our purely intellectual desires. And it must be insisted once again that such is the primary and fundamental object of science; if science did not fulfill that purpose, then it could certainly fulfill no other. It has applications to practical life, only because it is true; and its truth arises directly and immediately from its success as an instrument of intellectual satisfaction. Nevertheless, there is no doubt that,

From *What Is Science?*, Chapter 8 (New York: Dover Publications, Inc., 1952). Reprinted by permission of Dover Publications, Inc.

for the world at large—the world which includes those to which this book is addressed—it is the practical rather than the intellectual value of science which makes the greater appeal. I do not mean that they are blind to the things of the mind, and consider only those of the body; I mean merely that science is not for them the most suitable instrument by which they may cultivate their minds. Art, history, and philosophy are competing vehicles of culture; and their sense of the supreme value of their own study should not lead men of science to insist that its value is unique. Indeed, if we are forced to recognize that pure science will always be an esoteric study, it should increase our pride that we are to be found in the inner circle of the elect. On the other hand, since man cannot live by thought alone, the practical value of science makes a universal appeal; it would be pedantic and misleading to omit some consideration of this aspect of science.

The practical value of science arises, of course, from the formulation of laws. Laws predict the behavior of that external world with which our practical and everyday life is an unceasing struggle. Forewarned is forearmed, and we stand a better chance of success in the contest if we know precisely how our adversary may be expected to behave. Knowledge is power and our knowledge of the external world enables us in some measure to control it. So much is obvious; nobody today will be found to deny that science—and it must be remembered that we always use that word to denote the abstract study—might be of great service in practical life. Nor indeed will anybody deny that it has been of great service. We have all heard how the invention of the dynamo—on which is based every industrial use of electricity, without which modern civilization would be impossible—or the discovery of the true nature of ferments—the basis of modern medicine—was the direct outcome of the purest and most disinterested intellectual inquiries. But although this is granted universally, men of science are still heard to complain with ever-increasing vehemence that they are not allotted their due share of influence in the control of industry and of the State, and that science is always suffering from material starvation. It is clear, therefore, that in spite of the superficial agreement on the value of science, there is still an underlying difference of opinion which merits our attention.

The difference is not surprising, for candor compels us to confess that these admitted facts, on which the claims of science to practical value are often based, are not really an adequate basis for those claims. The fact that science might produce valuable results and actually has produced some, is no more justification for our devoting any great part of our energies to its development than the fact that I picked up half a crown in the street yesterday—and might pick up another—would be a justification for my abandoning sober work to search for buried treasure. Moreover, the very people who claim, on the ground of the work of Faraday or Pasteur, that science should receive large endowments and a great share in government, often urge at the same time that Faraday and Pasteur were examples of that genius which cannot be produced by training and can scarcely be stunted by adversity. If it were only these exceptional achievements, occurring two or three times a century, which had practical value, the encouragement of science would be an unprofitable gamble. If we are really to convince the outside world of the need for the closer application of science to practical affairs, we must give reasons for our claim much more carefully and guardedly than has been the custom up to the present. Nothing is more fatal to our cause than to encourage expectations doomed to disappointment.

Accordingly, in this chapter, I propose to diverge entirely from the usual path. I shall not give a single example of practical science. There are plenty of good books which tell what science has achieved in the past, and plenty of newspaper paragraphs to tell us what it is going to achieve in the future. Here I want to inquire carefully what value science might have for practical life, why it has that value, and under what conditions its value is most likely to be realized.

THE LIMITATIONS
OF SCIENCE

It will be well to point out immediately that science, like everything else, has its limitations, and that there are some practical problems which, from its very nature, it is debarred from solving. It must never be forgotten that, though science helps us in controlling the external world, it does not give us the smallest indication in which direction that control should be exercised. Whenever we undertake any practical action, we have two decisions to make; we have to decide what is the *end* of our action, what result we wish to obtain; and we have to decide what is the right *means* to that end, what action will produce the desired result. The distinction between the two decisions can be traced in the simplest as well as (perhaps better than) in the most complex actions. If I go to a meal in a restaurant, I have first to decide whether I want beef or mutton, tea or coffee, and second how I am to get what I want. If I have toothache, I have first to decide whether I want to be cured, and second if I am more likely to be cured if I doctor myself or if I go to a dentist. The fact that there are two decisions is sometimes obscured by the simplicity and obviousness of one of them. In the first example, the decision as to means is liable to be overlooked; for (except in some restaurants) it is obvious that the best way to get the meal I want

is to ask for it. In the second, the decision as to end may be unobserved, because it is so obvious that I want to be cured.

In these simple examples the distinction between the two decisions is clear; in others they are so closely interconnected that care is needed to separate them. Our choice of the ends at which we may aim is often determined in part by the means we have of attaining them; it is foolish to struggle towards a goal that can never be reached. On the other hand, action which is desirable as a means to one end, may be objectionable because it leads at the same time to other results that are undesirable as ends. In all the more complicated decisions of life, such conflicts between ends and means arise, and it is a necessary step towards accuracy of thought to disentangle the conflicting elements. It is all the more necessary, because in controversial matters there is always a tendency to conceal questions of ends and to pretend that every question is one of means only; the reason is that agreement concerning ends is far less easily attainable than agreement concerning means, so that, when we are trying to make converts to our views, we are naturally apt to disguise differences that are irreconcilable.

Political discussion provides examples of this tendency. It is clap-trap to announce portentously that we all desire the welfare of the community and to pretend that we differ only in our view of the best way of attaining it; what we really differ about is our ideas of the welfare of the community; we disagree as to what is the state of society that forms the end of our political action. If we could agree about that, our remaining differences would not excite much heat. As it is, our pretense that we are arguing merely about means often leads us to adopt means which are obviously ill-adapted to secure any of the ends at which any of the contending parties aim.

Since science must always exclude from its province judgments concerning which differences are irreconcilable, it can only guide practical life in the choice of means, and not in the choice of ends. If one course of action is more "scientific" than another, that course is better only in the sense that it is a more efficient means to some end; from the fact that it is indicated as a result of scientific inquiry, it is quite illegitimate to conclude that the action must necessarily be desirable. That conclusion follows only if it can be proved that the end, to which the action is a means, is desirable; such a proof must always lie wholly without the range of science. The neglect to observe this distinction is responsible for much of the disregard, and even actual dislike, of their study in its application to practical life of which men of science so often complain. It was seriously urged in recent years that science, being responsible for the horrors of modern warfare, is a danger to civilization; and I am told that many manual workers are inclined to regard science with hostility because it is associated in their minds with the "scientific" management of industry.[1] Such objections are alto-

gether unjust; science gives to mankind a greater power of control over his environment. He may use that control for good or for ill; and if he uses it for ill, the fault lies in that part of human nature which is most remote from science; it lies in the free exercise of will. To deny knowledge for fear it may be misused is to repeat the errors of the medieval church; thus to deprive men of the power to do evil is to deprive them of the yet greater power to do good. For precisely the same knowledge that has made Europe a desert has given the power to restore her former fertility; and the increase of individual productive power which may be used to rivet more closely the chains of wage-slavery might also give to the worker that leisure from material production which alone can give freedom to the slave.

Men of science themselves are largely to blame for the confusion against which this protest is directed. They are so accustomed to having to force their conclusions on an ignorant and reluctant world, that they are apt to overstep the limits of their special sphere; they sometimes forget that they cease to be experts when they leave their laboratories, and that in deciding questions foreign to science, they have no more (but, of course, no less) claim to attention than anyone else. Like the members of any other trade or profession, they are apt to be affected in their social and political views by the work which is their main occupation, and to lay special stress on the evils which come immediately under their notice.[2] In this respect it is useless to

---

[1] We need not discuss here whether the methods of factory control to which objection is taken have really any claim to be scientific in our sense; whether, that is to say, they are the outcome of such investigation as has been described in the earlier chapters.

[2] I am tempted to describe what are the social and political views which the study

expect them to be more perfect than the rest of mankind. But any danger of paying too much or too little heed to pronouncements put forward on behalf of "science" will be avoided if the distinction on which so much stress has been laid is borne in mind. On questions of means to a given end (if they concern the nature of the external world) science is the one and only true guide; on questions of the ends to which means should be directed, science has nothing to say.

THE CERTAINTY OF SCIENTIFIC KNOWLEDGE

I have thought it better thus to start with a consideration of the limitations of science; not because the greater danger lies in the neglect of those limitations, but merely to convince the reader that I am not blind to their existence. Actually, in this country at least, the greater danger lies in the other direction, in refusing to accept the clear and positive decisions of science on matters which lie wholly within its bounds. Why is there any such danger? It arises, I believe, from two sources not wholly independent. The first source is a disbelief that science is really possessed of any definite knowledge. Scientific experts seem to differ as much as experts in other subjects, and may be heard in any patent litigation swearing cheerfully against each other. The second source is a general distrust of the "theorist" as compared with the "practical man." The chief points that

---

and practice of science tends to inculcate. But this is a matter in which the spectator sees most of the game; if I made the attempt, I should probably be led astray by my own particular opinions.

have to be raised will appear naturally in a discussion of these two errors.

It may be thought that the first "error" has been implicitly confirmed by our previous discussions. For it has been urged that there is a strong personal element in science and that complete agreement is to be found only in its subject matter and not in its conclusions. But while it is perfectly true that a theory, and even to some extent a law, may be an object of contention when it is first proposed, it is equally true that the difference of opinion is always ultimately resolved. A theory may be doubted, but while it is doubted it is not part of the firm fabric of science; but in the end it is always either definitely accepted or definitely rejected. It is in this that science differs from such studies as history or philosophy, in which controversies are perennial. There is an immense body of science concerning which there is no doubt, and that body includes both theories and laws; there is a smaller part concerning which dispute is still continuing. It is only natural that this smaller part should receive the greater share of explicit attention; the other and greater part we learn in our school and university courses and find no need to discuss later, because it is a matter of common knowledge with which all properly informed persons are completely familiar; it is the base from which we proceed to establish new knowledge, and the premise on which we found our arguments concerning it. The distinction between the two parts of scientific knowledge, that which is firmly established, and that which is still doubtful, is perfectly clear and definite to all who have been properly trained. The fact that doctors differ in science, as in other things, does not affect the equally important fact that in much the larger part of their knowledge they agree.

But a more serious objection may be raised, . . . that science draws its subject matter from a limited portion of experience, and that this limited portion necessarily excludes all that part of our life which is of the most intimate interest to us. It may be urged with force that while science may be in possession of perfectly positive knowledge concerning which everyone who has studied the matter is in agreement, yet this knowledge is entirely divorced from all the affairs of practical life; when science attempts to intrude into such affairs it becomes as hesitating and dubitable as any other source of knowledge.

As a formal statement of the position, this objection must be admitted as valid. The uniformly certain and completely universal laws of science can be realized only in the carefully guarded conditions of the laboratory, and are never found in the busy world outside. There is scarcely any event or process of practical importance to which we could point as providing a direct confirmation of any of the propositions of pure science, or which could be described completely in terms of those propositions. In every such event and process, there is involved some element of which science can take no cognizance, and it is usually on account of this element . . . that the event has practical importance. And again, it is the presence of this element which makes it possible for experts, equally well-informed, to differ in their preliminary suggestions of an explanation of the event or of the most suitable means for controlling it. But it does

not follow because practical events do not lie wholly within the realm of science that they lie wholly without it. Indeed, it is from the study of practically important events that many of the results of pure science have actually been derived. Let us examine the matter more carefully.

All the applications of science to practical life depend ultimately on a knowledge of laws. Whether we are asked to explain an event, or to suggest means whereby an event may be produced or prevented, we can meet the demand only if we know the laws of which the event is the consequence. But laws state only relations between events; when we say that an event is the consequence of certain laws, we do not mean that this event must happen in all possible circumstances; we mean only that it is invariably associated with certain other events, and must happen if they happen. The event in question is not only a consequence of the laws, it is a consequence of the laws and of the other events to which it is related by the laws. Again, it must be noted that I have spoken of laws, not "a law." The practical event to which our attention is directed will not be a simple event such as is related by pure science to another simple event; it will be an immensely complicated collection of such events, and these constituent events will be each related to some other event by a separate law. The constituent events will not in general be related to each other by a law, nor will the other events, to which they are so related, be related to each other by a law. The explanation of the events in question will not be complete when we have stated a single law, or even all the many laws in which the constituent events are involved; it is necessary to add that the many events to which they are related by these many laws have actually occurred, and that the many laws are actually in operation.

The last part of the explanation is the part which is not pure science. Science, when it asserts laws, only asserts that, if so-and-so happens, something else will also happen. But in practical matters it is necessary to convert this hypothetical statement into a definite statement, and to assert that something actually has happened. This is often an extremely difficult matter, which may be the subject of much difference of opinion until all the circumstances have been investigated. An obvious example of this difficulty arises in the practice of medicine; diagnosis, the determination of what is wrong with the patient, is a necessary preliminary to his treatment, and is actually the gravest problem with which the physician is faced. And similar problems arise in all other branches of applied science. If we are asked to produce some desired product or to find out why the product of some existing process is not satisfactory, the first part of our task must always be to find out exactly in what the desired product consists, and exactly in what particulars it differs from the unsatisfactory product. This problem of determining precisely what are the existing facts is not strictly one of science at all; the solution of it does not involve the statement of any scientific laws, for laws assert, not what does actually occur, but what will occur if something else occurs. Nevertheless, science and scientific laws are useful, and even indispensable, in the solving of it; for very often the best or only proof that something has oc-

curred is that some other event has occurred with which the first is associated by a law. Thus, the physician bases his diagnosis on his examination of symptoms; he observes that the bodily state of his patient is abnormal in some particulars, and from his knowledge of the laws connecting those parts of the body which are accessible to observation with those that are not, deduces what must be the state of the hidden organs. In the same way the works chemist or physicist is often led to judge what is the source of failure in a product, by examining carefully the process by which it has been produced, and deducing by his knowledge of the laws of chemistry or physics what must be the result of that process.

It is for such reasons that pure science, although it takes no direct cognizance of the actual events of practical life, is of inestimable service in explaining and controlling them. Even though it is impossible to analyze those events completely into laws, it is only by carrying that analysis as far as it will go, and by bringing to light all the laws that are involved, that any explanation or any control can be attained.

These considerations have been suggested by the first of the two errors noted above; they answer the objection that science is not possessed of any positive and certain knowledge, or that, if it has such knowledge, it is not relevant to practical problems. The second error is even more dangerous. Science, it is often urged (perhaps not in these actual words), is all very well; it may even be indispensable; but it must be the right kind of science. The kind of science that is needed in everyday life is not that of the pure theorist, but that which every practical man is bound to acquire for himself in the ordinary conduct of his business.

Again, it will be well to begin by admitting that there is some truth in the contention that the practical man is likely to manage the business in which he has been immersed all his life better than one who has no experience of any conditions more complicated than those of the laboratory. No doubt scientific men of great eminence often prove as great failures in industry as commercial men would in pure science. But we have already noticed that no practical problem is wholly scientific; there are questions of ends as well as of means. The scientific man in industry is doubtless apt to be led astray by forgetting that the object of industry is to produce goods, and that processes, however scientifically interesting they may be, are commercially worthless unless they decrease the expenditure of capital and labor necessary to obtain a given amount of goods. Again, at the present time at least, all questions of means have not been brought within the range of science; the estimation of demand and the foreseeing of supply are matters not yet reduced to any scientific basis. Besides, no man is expert in all sciences, and the fact that he is familiar with one may tend to hide from him his ignorance of another. All this may be readily granted; but all it proves is that something besides scientific knowledge is required for the competent conduct of affairs. Because the man of science needs the help of the man trained in commerce or administration, it does not follow that the latter does not need the help of the former.

The attack on the practical value of science that we are considering is best met by a counter-offensive. It sounds plausible to maintain that those who have had the greatest experience of any matter must know most about it. But, like many other plausible doctrines, this one is absolutely false. No popular saying is more misleading than that we learn from experience; really, the capacity of learning from experience is one of the rarest gifts of genius, attained by humble folk only by long and arduous training. Anyone who examines carefully any subject concerning which popular beliefs are prevalent, will always discover that those beliefs are almost uniformly contradicted by the commonest everyday experience. We shall not waste our time if we devote a few pages to discovering the sources of popular fallacies, and considering in what manner they can be corrected by scientific investigation. When we have established how little worthy of confidence is "practical knowledge" we shall be in a position to see the value of "theory."

POPULAR FALLACIES

The most frequent source of such fallacies is a disposition to accept without inquiry statements made by other people. Error from this source is not wholly avoidable; except in the very few matters in which we can interest ourselves, we must, if we are to avoid blank ignorance, simply believe what we are told by the best authority we can secure. And since nobody is always right, we shall always believe some false doctrines however carefully we choose our authority. But it is very remarkable how people will go on believing things on authority, when the weight of that authority is quite unknown, and when their belief is flatly contradicted by experience. I know a family, not without intelligence, who, until their statement was challenged in a heated argument, always believed, on the authority of some family tradition of unknown origin, that the walk they took every Sunday afternoon was eight miles long; and yet a party which was not specially athletic, starting after three, always accomplished it before five. A glance at a map which was hanging in their house would have shown them it was barely six miles. This will doubtless seem a very extreme example concerning a very trivial matter, but parallels can be found readily in matters of considerable importance. During the war it was almost a sufficient reason for the army chiefs to adopt some device that it was known (or more often believed) that the enemy made use of it; and anyone who comes into contact with unscientific managers of industry will be amazed to find how largely their practice is based on hearsay information, and how little evidence they have that the information was reliable or even given in good faith.

In matters which lie outside their own sphere, men of science are often as credulous as anyone else; but in that sphere, if they are really men of science, intimately acquainted with their study by the actual practice of it, they cannot fail to have learnt how dangerous it is to believe any statement, however firmly asserted by high authority, unless they have tested it for themselves. The necessity for the obtaining of information by direct experiment is embedded in their nature, and no information attained by other means will satisfy them permanently. The determination to believe what is true, and not what other people assert to be true, is the first and not the least important correction applied by science to popular errors.

But if there were no other source of error, reliance on hearsay would not be so dangerous, for our informants would not be so likely to be wrong. There would still be the possibility that they intended to mislead us, though we may neglect that possibility for our purpose. A more serious possibility would remain, namely, that we had misinterpreted their information, and this is actually the greatest danger in knowledge acquired at second-hand. Thus the error about the length of the walk, quoted just now, doubtless arose from the fact that the original Sunday walk was eight miles, and that a weaker generation had abbreviated it to six. However, there are other sources of error; people do draw false conclusions directly from experience; and even if we could be sure that we had rightly understood an honest informant, there would still be a danger that his information was wrong. In discussing these other sources and giving examples of them, it will be impossible to distinguish them wholly from the first, for all popular beliefs (from which many technical and professional beliefs do not differ essentially) derive much of their weight from their general prevalence. We can only ask what fallacies predisposed men to these beliefs, and thus enabled the beliefs to become prevalent.

The most prolific of these fallacies

are false theories. In discussing sci- entific theories . . . we saw that in their ultimate nature they are not very different from any other and unscientific attempt to explain things. A theory which suggests that A and B *might* be connected predisposes to the belief that A and B *are* connected. An extreme example of unscientific theories is provided by the supersti- tions and magical beliefs of primitive civilization. They have ceased to be held explicitly, but they still exert an influence, which is not generally ap- preciated, on popular beliefs. Thus many people believe, and are very indignant when the assertion is de- nied, that the poker laid across the bars of the grate will draw up the fire. The belief is based on the old doctrine of the magical power of the cross, formed in this instance by the poker and the bars; old people can still be found who will say that the poker "keeps the witch up the chimney." Experiment would show that the poker has no effect whatsoever; but it is not easy to undertake seriously because the circumstances of "draw- ing up" a fire are so indeterminate. Most popular weather-lore has a similar origin in false theory; people are ready to think that the weather will change when the moon changes, only because they think that the moon *might* have some effect on the weather. Again, the persistent feeling that there is some intimate connection between names, and the things of which they are names, leads to curious credulity. "Rain before seven, fine before eleven" would never have be- come a popular saying had it not been for the purely verbal jingle.[3]

It is scarcely too much to say that every popular belief concerning such matters is false, and can be refuted by experience which is directly ac- cessible to those who assert it; and that the reason why such beliefs have gained a hold can always be traced to some false theory which, nowadays, only needs to be expressed to be re- jected. Their prevalence indicates clearly how little the majority of mankind can be trusted to analyze their experience carefully, and to base conclusions on that experience and on nothing else. And it has been ad- mitted that the most careful and ac- curate science does not base its conclusions only on experience; in sci- ence, too, analysis is guided by theory. But there is this vast difference: though science may in the first in- stance analyze experience and put forward laws guided by theory and not by simple examination of facts, when the analysis is completed and the laws suggested, it does return and compare them with the facts. It is by this procedure that it has been able to establish true theories which may be trusted, provisionally at least, in new analysis. The practical man is apt to sneer at the theorist; but an examination of any of his most firmly- rooted prejudices would show at once that he himself is as much a theorist as the purest and most academic student; theory is a necessary instru- ment of thought in disentangling the amazingly complex relations of the external world. But while his theories are false because he never tests them

---

[3] There may be this truth in the saying that, in many parts of England, continuous

rain for four hours is unusual at any time of the day or night. But if it is meant, as it usually is meant, that rain at seven is more likely to be followed by fine weather than rain at six or eight, then the saying is cer- tainly false.

properly, the theories of science are continually under constant test and only survive if they are true. It is the practical man and not the student of pure science who is guilty of relying on extravagant speculation, unchecked by comparison with solid fact.

Closely connected with the errors of false theories are those which arise from false, or more often incomplete, laws. Such laws are, of course, in themselves errors, but they often breed errors much more serious. For we have seen that the things between which laws assert relations are themselves interconnected by laws; if we start with false laws we are sure to interpret our experience on the wrong lines, because the things between which we shall try to find laws will be such that no laws can involve them. An example which we have used before will make this source of error clear. The word "steel" is used in all but the strictest scientific circles to denote many different things; or, in other words, there is no law asserting the association of all the properties of all the things which are conventionally called steel. Accordingly there can be no law, strictly true, asserting anything about steel: for though a law may be found which is true of many kinds of steel, some kind of "steel" can almost certainly be found of which it is not true. If we want to find true laws involving the materials all of which are conventionally termed steel, we must first differentiate the various kinds of steel and seek laws which involve each kind separately.

Neglect of this precaution is one of the most frequent causes of a failure to detect and to cure troubles encountered in industrial processes. The unscientific manager regards as iden-

tical everything that is sold to him as steel; he regards as "water" everything that comes out of the water main; and as "gas" everything that comes out of the gas main. He does not realize that these substances, though called by the same name, may have very different properties; and when his customary process does not lead to the usual result, he will probably waste a great deal of time and money on far-fetched ideas before he realizes that he did not get the same result because he did not start with the same materials. He can expect his processes to be governed by laws and to lead invariably to the same result only if all the materials and operations involved in those laws and employed in those processes are themselves invariable; that is to say, if their constituent properties and events are themselves associated by invariable laws. This is a very obvious conclusion when it is pointed out, but there is no conclusion more difficult to impress finally on the practical man ignorant of science. He is misled by words. Words are very useful when they really represent ideas, but are a most terrible danger when they do not. A word represents ideas, in the sense important for the practical applications of science, only when the things which it is used to denote are truly collections of properties or events associated by laws; for it is only then that the word can properly occur in one of the laws on which all those applications depend. Perhaps the most important service which science can render to practical affairs is to insist that laws can only be expected to hold between things which are themselves the expression of laws.

The last of the main sources of popular error is connected with a peculiar form of law which brevity has forbidden us to discuss hitherto. We have spoken of laws as asserting invariable associations. Now, a very slight acquaintance with science will suggest that this view is unduly narrow; it may seem that some laws in almost all sciences (and almost all laws in some sciences) assert that one event is associated with another, not invariably, but usually or nearly always. Thus, if meteorology, the science of weather, has any laws at all, they would seem to be of this type; nobody pretends that it is possible at present, or likely to be possible in the near future, to predict the weather exactly, especially a long time ahead; the most we can hope for is to discover rules which will enable us generally to predict rightly. Another instance may be found in the study of heredity. It is an undoubted fact that, whether in plants, animals, or human beings, children of the same parents generally resemble each other and their parents more than they do others not closely related. But even the great progress in our knowledge of the laws of inheritance which has been made in recent years has not brought us near to a position in which it can be predicted (except in a few very simple cases) what exactly will be the property of each child of known parents. We know some rules, but they are not the exact and invariable rules which we have hitherto regarded as constituting laws.

The pure scientific view of such laws is very interesting. Put briefly it is that in such cases we have a mingling of two opposed agencies. There are laws concerned in such events, laws as strict and as invariable as those which are regarded as typical, but they are acting as it were on

events governed not by law but by chance. The result of any law or set of laws depends not only on the laws but on the events to which they are applied; the irregularity that occurs in the study of the weather or of heredity is an irregularity in such events. Moreover, when science uses the conception of events governed by chance, it means something much more definite than is associated with that word by popular use. We say in ordinary discourse that an event is due to pure chance when we are completely ignorant whether it will or will not happen. But complete ignorance can never be a basis for knowledge, and the scientific conception of chance, which does lead to knowledge, implies only a certain limited degree of ignorance associated with a limited degree of knowledge. It is impossible here to discuss accurately what ignorance and what knowledge are implied, but it may be said roughly that the ignorance concerns each particular happening of the event, while the knowledge concerns a very long series of a great number of happenings. Thus, scientifically, it is an even chance whether a penny falls head or tail, because while we are perfectly ignorant whether on each particular toss it will fall head or tail, we are perfectly certain that in a sufficiently long series of tosses, heads and tails will be nearly equally distributed.

When, therefore, science finds, as in the study of weather or of heredity, phenomena which show some regularity, but not complete regularity, it tries to analyze them into perfectly regular laws acting on "chance" material. And the first step in the analysis is always to examine long series of the phenomena and to try to discover in these long series regularities which are not found in the individual members of them; the regularity will usually consist in each of the alternative phenomena happening in a definite proportion of the trials. When such regularity has been found, a second step can sometimes be taken and an analysis made into strict laws applied to events which are governed by the particular form of regularity which science regards as *pure* chance. If that step can be taken, the scientific problem is solved, for *pure* chance, like strict law, is one of the ultimate conceptions of science. But there is often (as in meteorology) a long interval between the first step and the second, and in that interval all that is known is a regularity in the long series which is usually called a "statistical" law.

This procedure, like most scientific procedure, is borrowed and developed from common sense; but—and this is the reason why it is mentioned here —it is here that modern common sense lags most behind scientific method. It is a familiar saying that statistics can prove anything; and so they can in the hands of those not trained in scientific analysis. Statistical laws are one of the most abundant sources of popular fallacies which arise both from an ignorance of what such a law means and a still greater ignorance of how it is to be established. A statistical law does not state that something always happens, but that it happens more (or less) frequently than something else; the quotation of instances of the thing happening are quite irrelevant to a proof of the law, unless there is at the same time a careful collection of instances in which it does not happen. Moreover, the clear distinction between a true law and a statistical law is not generally appreciated. A statistical law, which is really scientific, is made utterly fallacious in its application because it is interpreted as if it predicted the result of individual trials.

For reasons which have been given already, many of the laws that are most important in their practical application are statistical laws; and anyone, with a little reflection, can suggest any number of examples of them. Those which are generally familiar are usually entirely fallacious (e.g., laws of weather and of heredity), and even those which are true are habitually misapplied. The general misunderstanding of statistical laws renders them peculiarly liable, not only to their special fallacies, but to all those which we have discussed before. False theories and prejudices lead men to notice only those instances which are favorable to the law they want to establish; they fail to see that, if it were a true law, a single contrary instance would be sufficient to disprove it, while, if it is a statistical law, favorable instances prove nothing, unless contrary instances are examined with equal care. They forget, too, that a statistical law can never be the whole truth; it may, for the time being, represent all the truth we can attain; but our efforts should never cease, until the full analysis has been effected, and the domain of strict law carefully separated from that of pure chance. The invention of that method of analysis, which leads to a possibility of prediction and control utterly impossible while knowledge is still in the statistical stage, is one of the things which makes science indispensable to the conduct of the affairs of practical life.

CONCLUSION

Our examination of the errors into which uninstructed reasoning is liable to mislead mankind, affected by so many prejudices and superstitions, shows immediately how and why science is indispensable, if any valuable lessons are to be drawn from the most ordinary experience. In the first place, science brings to the analysis of such experience the conception of definite, positive, and fixed law. For the vague conception of a law as a predominating, though variable, association, always liable to be distorted by circumstances, or even, like the laws of mankind, superseded by the vagaries of some higher authority, science substitutes, as its basic and most important conception, the association which is absolutely invariable, unchanging, universal. We may not always be successful in finding such laws, but our firm belief that they are to be found never wavers; we never have the smallest reason to abandon our fundamental conviction that all events and changes, except in so far as they are the direct outcome of volition (and therefore immediately controllable), can be analyzed into, and interpreted by, laws of the strictest form. It is only those who are guided by such a conviction that can hope to bring order and form into the infinite complexity of everyday experience.

However, such a conviction by itself would probably be of little avail. If we only knew from the outset that the analysis and explanation of experience could not be effected, except by disentangling from it the strict laws of science, every fresh problem would probably have to await solution until it came to the notice of some great genius; for, as we noticed before, the discovery of a *wholly* new law is one of the greatest achievements of mankind. But we know much more; the long series of laws which have been discovered indicate where new laws are to be sought. We know that the terms involved in a new law must themselves be associated by a law. Moreover, the laws which define terms involved in other laws, though numerous, form a well-recognized class; there are the laws defining various kinds of substances or various species of living beings; those defining forces, volumes, electric currents, the many forces of energy, and all the various measurable quantities of physics; a complete list of them would fill a textbook, and yet their number is finite and comprehended by all serious students of the branches of science in which they are involved. Such students know that, when they try to analyze and explain new experience, it is between a definite class of terms that the necessary laws must be sought; and that knowledge reduces the problem to one within the compass of a normal intellect, provided it is well trained. He who seeks to solve the problem without that knowledge and without the training on which it is based, cannot hope for even partial success, unless he can boast the powers of a Galileo or a Faraday.

And science provides yet another clue. It has established theories as well as laws. Its theories do not cover the full extent of its laws, and in some sciences little guidance except that of "empirical" laws is available. But where theories exist, they serve very closely to limit the laws by means of which it is worthwhile to try to analyze experience; no law contradictory of a firmly-rooted theory is worth examining till all other alternatives have been exhausted. Here uninstructed inquirers are at a still greater disadvantage, compared with those familiar with the results of science, for while many of the terms involved in scientific laws are vaguely familiar to everyone, it is only those who have studied seriously, who have any knowledge of theories.

Here a word of warning should be given. . . . When in popular parlance "theory" is contrasted with "practice" it is often not this kind of theory that is meant at all. The plain man—I do not think this is an overstatement—calls a "theory" anything he does not understand, especially if the conclusions it is used to support are distasteful to him. Arguments about matters in which science is concerned, though they are denounced as wildly "theoretical," often depend on nothing but firmly-established law. It is only because he does not understand "theory" that the plain man is apt to compare it unfavorably with "practice," by which he means what he can understand. The idea that something can be "true in theory but false in practice" is due to mere ignorance; if any portion of "practice," about which there is no doubt, is inconsistent with some "theory," then the "theory" (whether it is a law or what we call a theory) is false—and there is an end of it. But it may easily happen, does often happen, that a "theory" is misinterpreted by those who fail to understand it; it appears to predict something inconsistent with practice only because its real meaning is not grasped. It is certainly true that those who do not understand "theory" had better leave it alone; reliance on misunderstood

theory is certainly quite as dangerous as reliance on uninstructed "practice."

And here we come to the conclusion about the relation of science to everyday life, which it seems to me most important to enforce. Those unversed in the ways of science often regard it as a body of fixed knowledge contained in textbooks and treatises, from which anyone who takes the trouble can extract all the information on any subject which science has to offer; they think of it as something that can be learnt as the multiplication table can be learnt, and consider that anyone who has "done" science at school or college is complete master of its mysteries. Nothing could be further from the truth regarding science applied to practical problems. It is scarcely ever possible, even for the most learned student, to offer a complete and satisfying explanation of any difficulty, merely on the basis of established knowledge; there is also some element in the problem which has not yet engaged scientific attention. Applied science, like pure science, is not a set of immutable principles and propositions; it is rather an instrument of thought and a way of thinking. Every practical problem is really a problem in reasearch, leading to the advancement of pure learning as well as to material efficiency; indeed, almost all the problems by the solution of which science has actually advanced have been suggested, more or less directly, by the familiar experiences of everyday life. This tremendous instrument of research can be mastered, this new way of thinking can be acquired, only by long training and laborious exercise. It is not, or it ought not to be, the academic student in the pure refined air of the laboratory who makes the knowledge, and the hard-handed and hard-headed worker who applies it to its needs. The man who can make new knowledge is the man, and the only man, to apply it.

Pure and applied science are the roots and the branches of the tree of experimental knowledge; theory and practice are inseparably interwoven, and cannot be torn asunder without grave injury to both. The intellectual and the material health of society depend on the maintenance of their close connection. A few years ago there was a tendency for true science to be confined to the laboratory, for its students to become thin-blooded, deprived of the invigorating air of industrial life, while industry wilted from neglect. Today there are perhaps some signs of an extravagant reaction; industrial science receives all the support and all the attention, while the universities, the nursing mothers of all science and all learning, are left to starve. The danger of rushing from one extreme to another will not be avoided until there is a general consciousness of what science means, both as a source of intellectual satisfaction and as a means of attaining material desires. We cannot all be—it is not desirable that we all should be—close students of science; but we can all appreciate in some measure what are its aims, its methods, its uses. Science, like art, should not be something extraneous, added as a decoration to the other activities of existence; it should be part of them, inspiring our most trivial actions as well as our noblest thoughts.

QUESTIONS FOR DISCUSSION

1. What is *pure* science? What is technology? Illustrate how historically the two are related.
2. What are the limitations of science with respect to means and ends (values)? Illustrate.
3. What is a scientific law? Illustrate. Do laws of science merely describe events or explain them? Is there an absolute difference between describing and explaining (telling how and why)? Illustrate or explain your answer.
4. What popular fallacies exist about the relation of "practical knowledge" and "theory"? Illustrate from the popular reliance on tradition, hearsay, names, statistics.
5. Illustrate how pure and applied science are "the roots and branches of the tree of experimental knowledge," and how "the intellectual and material health of society depend on the maintenance of their close connection."

Henri Poincaré (1854-1912)

5.2   Science and Hypothesis

HYPOTHESES IN PHYSICS

The Role of Experiment and Generalization

Experiment is the sole source of truth. It alone can teach us anything new; it alone can give us certainty. These are two points that cannot be questioned.

But then, if experiment is everything, what place will remain for mathematical physics? What has experimental physics to do with such an aid, one which seems useless and perhaps even dangerous?

And yet mathematical physics exists, and has done unquestionable service. We have here a fact that must be explained.

The explanation is that merely to observe is not enough. We must use our observations, and to do that we must generalize. This is what men always have done; only as the memory of past errors has made them more and more careful, they have observed more and more, and generalized less and less.

Every age has ridiculed the one before it, and accused it of having generalized too quickly and too naïvely.

From *Science and Hypothesis,* Chapter 9. Translated by G. B. Halsted (1905).

Descartes pitied the Ionians; Descartes, in his turn, makes us smile. No doubt our children will some day laugh at us.

But can we not then pass over immediately to the goal? Is not this the means of escaping the ridicule that we foresee? Can we not be content with just the bare experiment?

No, this is impossible, it would be to mistake utterly the true nature of science. The scientist must set in order. Science is built up with facts, as a house is with stones. But a collection of facts is no more a science than a heap of stones is a house.

And above all the scientist must foresee. Carlyle has somewhere said something like this: "Nothing but facts are of importance. John Lackland passed by here. Here is something that is admirable. Here is a reality for which I would give all the theories in the world." Carlyle was a fellow countryman of Bacon; but Bacon would not have said that. That is the language of the historian. The physicist would say rather: "John Lackland passed by here; that makes no difference to me, for he never will pass this way again."

We all know that there are good experiments and poor ones. The latter will accumulate in vain; though one may have made a hundred or a thousand, a single piece of work by a true master, by a Pasteur, for example, will suffice to tumble them into oblivion. Bacon would have well understood this; it is he who invented the phrase *Experimentum crucis.* But Carlyle would not have understood it. A fact is a fact. A pupil has read a certain number on his thermometer; he has taken no precaution; no matter, he has read it, and if it is only the fact that counts, here is a reality of the same rank as the peregrinations of King John Lackland. Why is the fact that this pupil has made this reading of no interest, while the fact that a skilled physicist had made another reading might be on the contrary very important? It is because from the first reading we could not infer anything. What then is a good experiment? It is that which informs us of something besides an isolated fact; it is that which enables us to foresee, that is, that which enables us to generalize.

For without generalization foreknowledge is impossible. The circumstances under which one has worked will never reproduce themselves all at once. The observed action then will never recur; the only thing that can be affirmed is that under analogous circumstances an analogous action will be produced. In order to foresee, then, it is necessary to invoke at least analogy, that is to say, already then to generalize.

No matter how timid one may be, still it is necessary to interpolate. Experiment gives us only a certain number of isolated points. We must unite these by a continuous line. This is a veritable generalization. But we do more; the curve that we shall trace will pass between the observed points and near these points; it will not pass

through these points themselves. Thus one does not restrict himself to generalizing the experiments, but corrects them; and the physicist, who should try to abstain from these corrections and really be content with the bare experiment, would be forced to enunciate some very strange laws.

The bare facts, then, would not be enough for us; and that is why we must have science ordered, or rather organized.

It is often said experiments must be made without a preconceived idea. That is impossible. Not only would it make all experiment barren, but that would be attempted which could not be done. Everyone carries in his mind his own conception of the world, of which he cannot so easily rid himself. We must, for instance, use language; and our language is made up only of preconceived ideas and cannot be otherwise. Only these are unconscious preconceived ideas, a thousand times more dangerous than the others.

Shall we say that if we introduce others, of which we are fully conscious, we shall only aggravate the evil? I think not. I believe rather that they will serve as counterbalances to each other—I was going to say as antidotes; they will in general accord ill with one another; they will come into conflict with one another, and thereby force us to regard things under different aspects. This is enough to emancipate us. He is no longer a slave who can choose his master.

Thus, thanks to generalization, each fact observed enables us to foresee a great many others; only we must not forget that the first alone is certain, that all others are merely probable. No matter how solidly founded a prediction may appear to us, we are never *absolutely* sure that experiment will not contradict it, if we undertake to verify it. The probability, however, is often so great that practically we may be content with it. It is far better to foresee even without certainty than not to foresee at all.

One must, then, never disdain to make a verification when opportunity offers. But all experiment is long and difficult; the workers are few; and the number of facts that we need to foresee is immense. Compared with this mass the number of direct verifications that we can make will never be anything but a negligible quantity.

Of this few that we can directly attain, we must make the best use; it is very necessary to get from every experiment the greatest possible number of predictions, and with the highest possible degree of probability. The problem is, so to speak, to increase the yield of the scientific machine.

Let us compare science to a library that ought to grow continually. The librarian has at his disposal for his purchases only insufficient funds. He ought to make an effort not to waste them.

It is experimental physics that is entrusted with the purchases. It alone, then, can enrich the library.

As for mathematical physics, its task will be to make out the catalogue. If the catalogue is well made, the library will not be any richer, but the reader will be helped to use its riches.

And even by showing the librarian the gaps in his collections, it will enable him to make a judicious use of his funds; which is all the more important because these funds are entirely inadequate.

Such, then, is the role of mathematical physics. It must direct generalization in such a manner as to increase what I just now called the yield of science. By what means it can arrive at this, and how it can do it without danger, is what remains for us to investigate.

The Unity of Nature

Let us notice first of all, that every generalization implies in some measure the belief in the unity and simplicity of nature. As to the unity there can be no difficulty. If the different parts of the universe were not like the members of one body, they would not act on one another, they would know nothing of each other; and we in particular would know only one of these parts. We do not ask, then, if nature is one, but how it is one.

As for the second point, that is not such an easy matter. It is not certain that nature is simple. Can we without danger act as if it were?

There was a time when the simplicity of Mariotte's [Boyle's] law was an argument invoked in favor of its accuracy; when Fresnel himself, after having said in a conversation with Laplace that nature was not concerned about analytical difficulties, felt himself obliged to make explanations, in order not to strike too hard at prevailing opinion.

Today ideas have greatly changed; and yet, those who do not believe that natural laws have to be simple, are still often obliged to act as if they did. They could not entirely avoid this necessity without making impossible all generalization, and consequently all science.

It is clear that any fact can be generalized in an infinity of ways, and it is a question of choice. The choice can be guided only by considerations of simplicity. Let us take the most commonplace case, that of interpolation. We pass a continuous line, as regular as possible, between the points given by observation. Why do we avoid points making angles, and too abrupt turns? Why do we not make our curve describe the most capricious zigzags? It is because we know beforehand, or believe we know, that the law to be expressed cannot be so complicated as all that.

We may calculate the mass of Jupiter from either the movement of its satellites, or the perturbations of the major planets, or those of the minor planets. If we take the averages of the determinations obtained by these three methods, we find three numbers very close together, but different. We might interpret this result by supposing that the coefficient of gravitation is not the same in the three cases. The observations would certainly be much better represented. Why do we reject this interpretation? Not because it is absurd, but because it is needlessly complicated. We shall only accept it when we are forced to, and that is not yet.

To sum up, ordinarily every law is held to be simple till the contrary is proved.

This custom is imposed upon physicists by the causes that I have just explained. But how shall we justify it in the presence of discoveries that show us every day new details that are richer and more complex? How shall we even reconcile it with the belief in the unity of nature? For if everything depends on everything, relationships where so many diverse factors enter can no longer be simple.

If we study the history of science, we see happen two inverse phenomena, so to speak. Sometimes simplicity hides under complex appearances; sometimes it is the simplicity which is apparent, and which disguises extremely complicated realities.

What is more complicated than the confused movements of the planets? What simpler than Newton's law? Here nature, making sport, as Fresnel said, of analytical difficulties, employs only simple means, and by combining them produces I know not what inextricable tangle. Here it is the hidden simplicity which must be discovered.

Examples of the opposite abound. In the kinetic theory of gases, one deals with molecules moving with great velocities, whose paths, altered by incessant collisions, have the most capricious forms and traverse space in every direction. The observable result is Mariotte's simple law. Every individual fact was complicated. The law of great numbers has reestablished simplicity in the average. Here the simplicity is merely apparent, and only the coarseness of our senses prevents our perceiving the complexity.

Many phenomena obey a law of proportionality. But why? Because in these phenomena there is something very small. The simple law observed, then, is only a result of the general analytical rule that the infinitely small increment of a function is proportional to the increment of the variable. As in reality our increments are not infinitely small, but very small, the law of proportionality is only approximate, and the simplicity is only apparent. What I have just said applies to the rule of the superposition of small motions, the use of which is so fruitful, and which is the basis of optics.

And Newton's law itself? Its simplicity, so long undetected, is perhaps only apparent. Who knows whether it is not due to some complicated mechanism, to the impact of some subtile matter animated by irregular movements, and whether it has not become simple only through the action of averages and of great numbers? In any case, it is difficult not to suppose that the true law contains complementary terms, which would become sensible at small distances. If in astronomy they are negligible as modifying Newton's law, and if the law thus regains its simplicity, it would be only because of the immensity of celestial distances.

No doubt, if our means of investigation should become more and more penetrating, we should discover the simple under the complex, then the complex under the simple, then again the simple under the complex, and so on, without our being able to foresee what will be the last term.

We must stop somewhere, and that science may be possible, we must stop when we have found simplicity. This is the only ground on which we can rear the edifice of our generalizations. But this simplicity being only apparent, will the ground be firm enough? This is what must be investigated.

For that purpose, let us see what part is played in our generalizations by the belief in simplicity. We have verified a simple law in a good many particular cases; we refuse to admit that this agreement, so often repeated, is simply the result of chance, and conclude that the law must be true in the general case.

Kepler notices that a planet's positions, as observed by Tycho, are all on one ellipse. Never for a moment does he have the thought that by a strange play of chance, Tycho never observed the heavens except at a moment when the real orbit of the planet happened to cut this ellipse.

What does it matter then whether the simplicity be real, or whether it covers a complex reality? Whether it is due to the influence of great numbers, which levels down individual differences, or to the greatness or smallness of certain quantities, which allows us to neglect certain terms, in no case is it due to chance. This simplicity, real or apparent, always has a cause. We can always follow, then, the same course of reasoning, and if a simple law has been observed in several particular cases, we can legitimately suppose that it will still be true in analogous cases. To refuse to do this would be to attribute to chance an inadmissible role.

There is, however, a difference. If the simplicity were real and essential, it would resist the increasing precision of our means of measure. If then we believe nature to be essentially simple, we must, from a simplicity that is approximate, infer a simplicity that is rigorous. This is what was done formerly; and this is what we no longer have a right to do.

The simplicity of Kepler's laws, for example, is only apparent. That does not prevent their being applicable, very nearly, to all systems analogous to the solar system; but it does prevent their being rigorously exact.

The Role of Hypothesis

All generalization is an hypothesis. Hypothesis, then, has a necessary role that no one has ever contested. Only, it ought always, as soon as possible and as often as possible, to be subjected to verification. And, of course, if it does not stand this test, it ought to be abandoned without reserve. This is what we generally do, but sometimes with rather an ill humor.

Well, even this ill humor is not justified. The physicist who has just renounced one of his hypotheses ought, on the contrary, to be full of joy; for he has found an unexpected opportunity for discovery. His hypothesis, I imagine, had not been adopted without consideration; it took account of all the known factors that it seemed could enter into the phenomenon. If the test does not support it, it is because there is something unexpected and extraordinary; and because there is going to be something found that is unknown and new.

Has the discarded hypothesis, then, been barren? Far from that, it may be said it has rendered more service than a true hypothesis. Not only has it been the occasion of the decisive experiment, but, without having made the hypothesis, the experiment would have been made by chance, so that nothing would have been derived from it. One would have seen nothing extraordinary; only one fact the more would have been catalogued without deducing from it the least consequence.

Now on what condition is the use of hypothesis without danger?

The firm determination to submit to experiment is not enough; there are still dangerous hypotheses; first, and above all, those which are tacit and unconscious. Since we make them without knowing it, we are powerless to abandon them. Here again, then, is a service that mathematical physics can render us. By the precision that is characteristic of it, it compels us to formulate all the hypotheses that we should make without it, but unconsciously.

Let us notice besides that it is important not to multiply hypotheses beyond measure, and to make them only one after the other. If we construct a theory based on a number of hypotheses, and if experiment condemns it, which of our premises is it necessary to change? It will be impossible to know. And inversely, if the experiment succeeds, shall we believe that we have demonstrated all the hypotheses at once? Shall we believe that with one single equation we have determined several unknowns?

We must equally take care to distinguish between the different kinds of hypotheses. There are first those which are perfectly natural and from which one can scarcely escape. It is difficult not to suppose that the influence of bodies very remote is quite negligible, that small movements follow a linear law, that the effect is a continuous function of its cause. I will say as much of the conditions imposed by symmetry. All these hypotheses form, as it were, the common basis of all the theories of mathematical physics. They are the last that ought to be abandoned.

There is a second class of hypotheses, that I shall term neutral. In most questions the analyst assumes at the beginning of his calculations either that matter is continuous or, on the contrary, that it is formed of atoms. He might have made the opposite assumption without changing his results. He would only have had more trouble to obtain them; that is all. If, then, experiment confirms his conclusions, will he think that he has demonstrated, for instance, the real existence of atoms? . . .

These neutral hypotheses are never dangerous, if only their character is not misunderstood. They may be useful, either as devices for computation, or to aid our understanding by concrete images, to fix our ideas as the saying is. There is, then, no occasion to exclude them.

The hypotheses of the third class are the real generalizations. They are the ones that experiment must confirm or invalidate. Whether verified or condemned, they will always be fruitful. But for the reasons that I have set forth, they will only be fruitful if they are not too numerous.

Origin of Mathematical Physics

Let us penetrate further, and study more closely the conditions that have permitted the development of mathematical physics. We observe at once that the efforts of scientists have always aimed to resolve the complex phenomenon directly given by experiment into a very large number of elementary phenomena.

This is done in three different ways: first, in time. Instead of embracing in its entirety the progressive development of a phenomenon, the aim is simply to connect each instant with the instant immediately preceding it. It is admitted that the actual state of of the world depends only on the immediate past, without being directly influenced, so to speak, by the memory of a distant past. Thanks to this postulate, instead of studying directly the whole succession of phenomena, it is possible to confine ourselves to writing its "differential equation." For Kepler's laws we substitute Newton's law.

Next we try to analyze the phenomenon in space. What experiment gives us is a confused mass of facts presented on a stage of considerable extent. We must try to discover the elementary phenomenon, which will be, on the contrary, localized in a very small region of space.

Some examples will perhaps make my thought better understood. If we wished to study in all its complexity the distribution of temperature in a cooling solid, we could never succeed. Everything becomes simple if we reflect that one point of the solid cannot give up its heat directly to a distant point; it will give up its heat only to the points in the immediate neighborhood, and it is by degrees that the flow of heat can reach other parts of the solid. The elementary phenomenon is the exchange of heat between two contiguous points. It is strictly localized, and is relatively simple, if we admit, as is natural, that it is not influenced by the temperature of molecules whose distance is sensible.

I bend a rod. It is going to take a very complicated form, the direct study of which would be impossible. But I shall be able, however, to attack it, if I observe that its flexure is a result only of the deformation of the very small elements of the rod, and that the deformation of each of these elements depends only on the forces that are directly applied to it, and not at all on those which may act on the other elements.

In all these examples, which I might easily multiply, we admit that there is no action at a distance, or at least at a great distance. This is an hypothesis. It is not always true, as the law of gravitation shows us. It must, then, be submitted to verification. If it is confirmed, even approximately, it is precious, for it will enable us to make mathematical physics, at least by successive approximations.

If it does not stand the test, we must look for something else analogous; for there are still other means of arriving at the elementary phenomenon. If several bodies act simultaneously, it may happen that their actions are independent and are simply added to one another, either as vectors or as scalars. The elementary phenomenon is then the action of an isolated body. Or again, we have to deal with small movements, or more generally, with small variations, which obey the well-known law of superposition. The observed movement will then be decomposed into simple movements, for example, sound into its harmonics, white light into its monochromatic components.

When we have discovered in what direction it is advisable to look for the elementary phenomenon, by what means can we reach it?

First of all, it will often happen that in order to detect it, or rather to detect the part of it useful to us, it will not be necessary to penetrate the mechanism; the law of great numbers will suffice.

Let us take again the instance of the propagation of heat. Every molecule emits rays towards every neighboring molecule. According to what law, we do not need to know. If we should make any supposition in regard to this, it would be a neutral hypothesis and consequently useless and incapable of verification. And, in fact, by the action of averages, and thanks to the symmetry of the medium, all the differences are leveled down, and whatever hypotheses may be made, the result is always the same.

The same circumstance is presented in the theory of electricity and in that of capillarity. The neighboring molecules attract and repel one another. We do not need to know according to what law; it is enough for us that this attraction is sensible only at small distances, that the molecules are very numerous, that the medium is symmetrical, and we shall only have to let the law of great numbers act.

Here again the simplicity of the elementary phenomenon was hidden under the complexity of the resultant observable phenomenon; but, in its turn, this simplicity was only apparent, and concealed a very complex mechanism.

The best means of arriving at the elementary phenomenon would evidently be experiment. We ought by experimental contrivance to dissociate the complex sheaf that nature offers to our researches, and to study with care the elements as much isolated as possible. For example, natural white light would be decomposed into monochromatic lights by the aid of the prism, and into polarized lights by the aid of the polarizer.

Unfortunately that is neither always possible nor always sufficient, and sometimes the mind must outstrip experiment. . . . It may be asked why, in physical sciences, generalization so readily takes the mathematical form. The reason is now easy to see. It is not only because we have numerical laws to express; it is because the observable phenomenon is due to the superposition of a great number of elementary phenomena *all alike.* Thus quite naturally are introduced differential equations. . . .

It is then, thanks to the approximate homogeneity of the matter studied by physicists, that mathematical physics could be born.

In the natural sciences, we no longer find these conditions: homogeneity, relative independence of remote parts, simplicity of the elementary fact; and this is why naturalists are obliged to resort to other methods of generalization.

Morality and Science

The dream of creating a scientific morality appeared often in the last half of the nineteenth century. It was not enough to praise the educational value of science, the benefits obtained by the human mind for its own improvement, thanks to direct commerce with truth. It was expected that science would put moral truths on an indisputable plane, along with mathematical theorems and the laws formulated by physicists.

Religions can wield a great deal of power on believers, but not everybody is a believer, for faith falls only to some, whereas reason should appeal to all. So we must address ourselves to reason, and I do not mean the reason of the metaphysician, whose constructions are brilliant but ephemeral, like soap-bubbles amusing us for an instant and then bursting. Science alone builds solidly; it built astronomy and physics; it is building biology today; by the same procedures it will build morality. Its prescriptions will reign indivisibly; nobody will be able to murmur against them, or dream of rebelling against the moral law any more than of revolting today against the Pythagorean theorem or law of gravitation.

But on the other side, there were people who imputed every evil possible to science and saw in it a school

for immorality. The reason was not merely that science is too materialistic, or that it deprives us of the sense of respect, for we respect highly only the things we dare not look at. But its conclusions seemed to be the negation of morality. As some well-known author, whose name I forget, put it, science goes about to extinguish the lights of heaven or at least rob them of their mystery in order to reduce them to the lowly state of gas jets. Science tends to expose the tricks of the Creator who will thereby lose something of his prestige. It is not good to let children into the wings, for that might inspire doubts in them about the existence of the puppet Croquemitaine. If you let the scientists have their way, it will be the end of morality.

What are we to think of the hopes on one side of the argument and of the fears on the other side? I reply without hesitation: they are both equally vain. There can be no scientific morals; but neither can there be any immoral science. And the reason for this is simple; the reason, how else shall I put it, is simply a grammatical one.

If the premises of a syllogism are both in the indicative mood, the conclusion will also be in the indicative mood. In order for the conclusion to be put into the imperative mood, it would be necessary for at least one of the premises to be in the impera-

From *Dernières Pensées.* Translated by Philip P. Wiener.

tive. Now the principles of science and the postulates of geometry are and can only be in the indicative; this is also the mood in which experimental truths are stated, and at the base of the sciences, there is not and cannot be any other mood. Whence it follows, that no matter how the subtlest dialectician wishes to juggle and combine these principles, one on top of the other, everything he concludes will be in the indicative. He will never obtain a proposition which will say: Do this or do not do that; that is to say, he will not produce a proposition which confirms or contradicts morals.

This difficulty is one that moralists often encounter. They try hard to demonstrate moral law; they must be pardoned because that is their vocation. They wish to rest morals on something, as if it could be made to rest on anything but itself. Science shows us that man can only degrade himself by living in such and such a manner; but what if I don't care about degrading myself, or if what you call degrading I baptize as a mark of progress? Metaphysics invites us to conform to the universal law of the moral order it claims to have discovered; but one can reply, I prefer to obey my own personal law. I don't know what metaphysics will reply, but I can assure you that it will not have the last word.

Will religious ethics be more fortunate than science or metaphysics? Obey because God orders it, and because he is a master who breaks down all resistance. Is that a demonstration, and can we not maintain that it is in vain to stand up against Omnipotence, or that in the duel between Jupiter and Prometheus the true conqueror is the tortured Prometheus? But then to yield to force is not to obey, and the obedience of the heart cannot be coerced.

QUESTIONS FOR DISCUSSION

1. If "experiment is the sole source of truth," why are hypotheses necessary? Illustrate.
2. What is the relation of generalizations to "facts of observation" and to verified laws of science? Illustrate. Explain: "Any fact can be generalized in infinite ways."
3. What is meant by the "unity and simplicity of nature"? Illustrate the rule "not to multiply hypotheses beyond measure" (Ockham's razor).
4. What is the distinction between "natural" and "neutral" hypotheses with respect to continuity and discontinuity?
5. State three different ways of organizing experimental phenomena in mathematical physics (in time, in space, laws of large numbers).
6. Explain: "There can be no scientific morality nor any immoral science." Criticize.

Charles S. Peirce (1839-1914)

5.3   Notes on Scientific Philosophy

LABORATORY AND
SEMINARY PHILOSOPHIES [1]

The kind of philosophy which interests me and must, I think, interest everybody is that philosophy which uses the most rational methods it can devise for finding out the little that can as yet be found out about the universe of mind and matter from those observations which every person can make in every hour of his waking life. It will not include matters which are more conveniently studied by students of special sciences, such as psychology. Thus, everybody has remarked that there are four prominent qualities of the sense of taste, sweet, sour, salt, and bitter. But there may be other tastes, not so readily made out without special study; and in any case tastes are conveniently studied

in connection with flavors and odors, which make a difficult experimental inquiry. Besides the four tastes are altogether special and throw no light on the problems which, on account of their extreme generality, will naturally be examined by a class of researchers of entirely different aptitudes from those which adapt men to the discovery of recondite facts.

If anybody asks what there is in the study of obvious phenomena to make it particularly interesting, I will give two answers. The first is the one which seems to me the strongest; the other is that which nobody can fail to feel the force of. The first answer is that the spirit in which, as it seems to me, philosophy ought to be studied is the spirit in which every branch of science ought to be studied; namely, the spirit of joy in learning ourselves and in making others acquainted with the glories of God. Each person will feel this joy most in the particular branch of science to which his faculties are best adapted. It is not a sin to have no taste for philosophy as I define philosophy. As a matter of fact, however, almost everybody does feel an interest in philosophical problems, especially at that time of life at which he is spoiling for an intellectual tussle.

From Collected Papers of Charles Sanders Peirce, Vol. I, edited by Charles Hartshorne and Paul Weiss (Cambridge: Harvard University Press, 1931). Reprinted by permission of Harvard University Press.

[1] From "Introduction showing the point of view from which Philosophy appears to the author to be an interesting subject to a man of common-sense," in the Notebook, "Sketch of Some Proposed Chapters on the Sect of Philosophy Called Pragmatism," c. 1905.

It is true that philosophy is in a lamentably crude condition at present; that very little is really established about it; while most philosophers set up a pretension of knowing all there is to know—a pretension calculated to disgust anybody who is at home in any real science. But all we have to do is to turn our backs upon all such truly vicious conduct, and we shall find ourselves enjoying the advantages of having an almost virgin soil to till, where a given amount of really scientific work will bring in an extraordinary harvest, and that a harvest of very fundamental truth of exceptional value from every point of view.

This consideration touches upon the second reason for studying laboratory philosophy (as contradistinguished from seminary philosophy). It is that the special sciences are obliged to take for granted a number of most important propositions, because their ways of working afford no means of bringing these propositions to the test. In short, they always rest upon metaphysics. At one time, for example, we find physicists, Kelvin, Maxwell, and others, assuming that a body cannot act where it is not, meaning by "where it is not" where its lines of force do not center. At another time, we find them assuming that the laws of mechanics (including the principles of metric geometry) hold good for the smallest corpuscles. Now it is one thing to infer from the laws of little things how great things, that consist of little things, will act; but it is quite a different thing to infer from the phenomena presented by great things how single things billions of times smaller will act. It is like inferring that because in any country one man in so many will commit suicide, therefore every individual, once in such a period of time, will make an attempt at suicide. The psychical sciences, especially psychology, are, if possible, even more necessitated to assume general principles that cannot be proved or disproved by their ordinary methods of work. The philosopher alone is equipped with the facilities for examining such "axioms" and for determining the degree to which confidence may safely be reposed in them. Find a scientific man who proposes to get along without any metaphysics—not by any means every man who holds the ordinary reasonings of metaphysicians in scorn—and you have found one whose doctrines are thoroughly vitiated by the crude and uncriticized metaphysics with which they are packed. We must philosophize, said the great naturalist Aristotle [2]—if only to avoid philosophizing. Every man of us has a metaphysics, and has to have one; and it will influence his life greatly. Far better, then, that metaphysics should be criticized and not be allowed to run loose. A man may say, "I will content myself with common sense." I, for one, am with him there, in the main. I shall show why I do not think there can be any *direct* profit in going behind common sense —meaning by common sense those ideas and beliefs that man's situation absolutely forces upon him. We shall later see more definitely what is meant. I agree, for example, that it is better to recognize that some things are red and some others blue, in the teeth of what optical philosophers say, that it is merely that some things are resonant to shorter ether waves and some to longer ones. But the dif-

---

[2] *Metaphysics,* Book I, 982b-983a.

ficulty is to determine what really is and what is not the authoritative decision of common sense and what is merely *obiter dictum*. In short, there is no escape from the need of a critical examination of "first principles."

AXIOMS

The science which, next after logic, may be expected to throw the most light upon philosophy, is mathematics. It is historical fact, I believe, that it was the mathematicians Thales, Pythagoras, and Plato who created metaphysics, and that metaphysics has always been the ape of mathematics. Seeing how the propositions of geometry flowed demonstratively from a few postulates, men got the notion that the same must be true in philosophy. But of late, mathematicians have fully agreed that the axioms of geometry (as they are wrongly called) are not by any means evidently true. Euclid, be it observed, never pretended they were evident; he does not reckon them among his κοιναὶ ἔννοιαι or things everybody knows, but among the αἰτήματα, postulates or things the author must beg you to admit, because he is unable to prove them. At any rate, it is now agreed that there is no reason whatever to think the sum of the three angles of a triangle precisely equal to 180 degrees. It is generally admitted that the evidence is that the departure from 180 degrees (if there is any) will be greater the larger the triangle, and in the case of a triangle having for its base the diameter of the earth's orbit and for its apex the furthest star, the sum hardly can differ, according to observation, so much as 0.1″. It is probable the discrepancy

is far less. Nevertheless, there is an infinite number of different possible values, of which precisely 180 degrees is only one; so that the probability is as 1 to ∞ or 0 to 1, that the value is just 180 degrees. In other words, it seems for the present impossible to suppose the postulates of geometry precisely true. The matter is reduced to one of evidence; and as absolute precision [is] beyond the reach of direct observation, so it can never be rendered probable by evidence, which is indirect observation.

Thus, the postulates of geometry must go into the number of things approximately true. It may be thousands of years before men find out whether the sum of the three angles of a triangle is greater or less than 180 degrees; but the presumption is, it is one or the other.

Now what is metaphysics, which has always formed itself after the model of mathematics, to say to this state of things? The mathematical axioms being discredited, are the metaphysical ones to remain unquestioned? I trow not. There is one proposition, now held to be very certain, though denied throughout antiquity, namely, that every event is precisely determined by general laws, which evidently never can be rendered probable by observation, and which, if admitted, must, therefore, stand as self-evident. This is a metaphysical postulate closely analogous to the postulates of geometry. Its fate is sealed. The geometrical axioms being exploded, this is for the future untenable. Whenever we attempt to verify a physical law, we find discrepancies between observation and theory, which we rightly set down as errors of observation. But now it appears we have no reason to deny that there are similar, though no doubt far smaller, discrepancies between the law and the real facts. As Lucretius says,[3] the atoms swerve from the paths to which the laws of mechanics would confine them. I do not now inquire whether there is or not any positive evidence that this is so. What I am at present urging is that this arbitrariness is a conception occurring in logic, encouraged by mathematics, and ought to be regarded as a possible material to be used in the construction of a philosophical theory, should we find that it would suit the facts. We observe that phenomena approach very closely to satisfying general laws; but we have not the smallest reason for supposing that they satisfy them precisely.

THE OBSERVATIONAL PART OF PHILOSOPHY

Every science has a mathematical part, a branch of work that the mathematician is called in to do. We say, "Here, mathematician, suppose such and such to be the case. Never you mind whether it is really so or not; but tell us, supposing it to be so, what will be the consequence." Thus arise mathematical psychology, mathematical stylometry, mathematical economics, mathematical physics, mathematical chemistry, mathematical meteorology, mathematical biology, mathematical geology, mathematical astronomy, etc., etc., etc. But there is none of these mathematical offices which constitutes quite so large a proportion of the whole science to which it is annexed as mathematical philosophy, for the obvious reason

that the observational part of philosophy is a simple business, compared, for example, with that of anatomy or biography, or any other special science.

To assume, however, that the observational part of philosophy, because it is not particularly laborious, is therefore easy, is a dreadful mistake, into which the student is very apt to fall, and which gives the death-blow to any possibility of his success in this study. It is, on the contrary, extremely difficult to bring our attention to elements of experience which are continually present. For we have nothing in experience with which to contrast them; and without contrast, they cannot excite our attention. We can only contrast them with imaginary states of things; but even what we imagine is but a crazy-quilt of bits snipped off from actual experiences. The result is that roundabout devices have to be resorted to, in order to enable us to perceive what stares us in the face with a glare that, once noticed, becomes almost oppressive with its insistency. This circumstance alone would be sufficient to render philosophical observation difficult—much more difficult, for example, than the kind of observation which the painter has to exercise. Yet this is the least of the difficulties of philosophy. Of the various hindrances more serious still, I may mention once more the notion that it is an extremely easy thing to perceive what is before us every day and hour. But quite the worst is, that every man becomes more or less imbued with philosophical opinions, without being clearly aware of it. Some of these, it is true, may be right opinions; if he is a quite uneducated man, they doubtless will be so. But even if they are right, or

---

[3] *De Rerum Natura*, Book II, 1, 216 ff.

nearly right, they prevent true observation as much as a pair of blue spectacles will prevent a man from observing the blue of the sky. The man will hold the right opinion, but not knowing that it might be founded upon direct observation, he will class it among articles of faith of a pretty dubious character. The more a man is educated in other branches, but not trained in philosophy, the more certain it is that two-thirds of his stock of half-conscious philosophical opinions will be utterly wrong, and will completely blind him to the truth, which he will gradually become unable so much as to conceive. I remember a really eminent French *savant,* who had sojourned for very many months in America, but who must have imbibed in his childhood the notion, then common in France, that Englishmen and Americans interject into every second sentence a certain word which the French imagine to be English. He belonged to one of the most observant of races; he was naturally a keen observer; and he was trained in an observational science; and yet, in order to assimilate himself as much as possible to American ways, he used to think it necessary to greet one every morning with a "How do you do, goddam?" and to keep it up all day. He actually believed that he had observed that such was the American style. The educated man who is a beginner in philosophy is just like that man, who (be it remembered) had been moving about in America for years—and by a beginner in philosophy I wish to be understood as meaning, in the case of an educated man, one who has not been seriously, earnestly, and single-mindedly devoted to the study of it for more than six or eight years. For there is no other science for which the preparatory training requires to be nearly so severe and so long, no matter how great the natural genius of the student may be. For a plain man or a boy who should be early taken in hand by an instructor capable of making him comprehend both sides of every question, the time, without doubt, can be greatly reduced, with untiring industry and energy on the pupil's part.

THE FIRST RULE OF REASON

Upon this first, and in one sense this sole, rule of reason, that in order to learn you must desire to learn, and in so desiring not be satisfied with what you already incline to think, there follows one corollary which itself deserves to be inscribed upon every wall of the city of philosophy:
Do not block the way of inquiry.

Although it is better to be methodical in our investigations, and to consider the economics of research, yet there is no positive sin against logic in *trying* any theory which may come into our heads, so long as it is adopted in such a sense as to permit the investigation to go on unimpeded and undiscouraged. On the other hand, to set up a philosophy which barricades the road of further advance toward the truth is the one unpardonable offense in reasoning, as it is also the one to which metaphysicians have in all ages shown themselves the most addicted.

Let me call your attention to four familiar shapes in which this venomous error assails our knowledge:

The first is the shape of absolute assertion. That we can be sure of nothing in science is an ancient truth. The Academy taught it. Yet science has been infested with overconfident assertion, especially on the part of the third-rate and fourth-rate men, who have been more concerned with teaching than with learning, at all times. No doubt some of the geometries still teach as a self-evident truth the proposition that if two straight lines in one plane meet a third straight line so as to make the sum of the internal angles on one side less than two right angles, those two lines will meet on that side if sufficiently prolonged. Euclid, whose logic was more careful, only reckoned this proposition as a *Postulate,* or arbitrary Hypothesis. Yet even he places among his axioms the proposition that a part is less than its whole, and falls into several conflicts with our most modern geometry in consequence. But why need we stop to consider cases where some subtilty of thought is required to see that the assertion is not warranted when every book which applies philosophy to the conduct of life lays down as positive certainty propositions which it is quite as easy to doubt as to believe.

The second bar which philosophers often set up across the roadway of inquiry lies in maintaining that this, that, and the other never can be known. When Auguste Comte was pressed to specify any matter of positive fact to the knowledge of which no man could by any possibility attain, he instanced the knowledge of the chemical composition of the fixed stars; and you may see his answer set down in the *philosophie positive.*[4] But the ink was scarcely dry upon the printed page before the spectroscope

was discovered and that which he had deemed absolutely unknowable was well on the way of getting ascertained. It is easy enough to mention a question the answer to which is not known to me today. But to aver that that answer will not be known tomorrow is somewhat risky; for oftentimes it is precisely the least expected truth which is turned up under the ploughshare of research. And when it comes to positive assertion that the truth never will be found out, that, in the light of the history of our time, seems to me more hazardous than the venture of Andrée.[5]

The third philosophical stratagem for cutting off inquiry consists in maintaining that this, that, or the other element of science is basic, ultimate, independent of aught else, and utterly inexplicable—not so much from any defect in our knowing as because there is nothing beneath it to know. The only type of reasoning by which such a conclusion could possibly be reached is *retroduction.*[6] Now nothing justifies a retroductive inference except its affording an explanation of the facts. It is, however, no explanation at all of a fact to pronounce it *inexplicable.* That, therefore, is a conclusion which no reasoning can ever justify or excuse.

The last philosophical obstacle to the advance of knowledge which I intend to mention is the holding that this or that law or truth has found its

---

[4] Dix-neuvième leçon.

[5] In 1897 Salomon August Andrée attempted to fly over the polar regions in a balloon. He died in the attempt.

[6] "Retroduction" is Peirce's name for the method of reasoning which leads to an explanatory *hypothesis.* Peirce also used the term "abduction" (as the complement of "induction" and "deduction") for reasoning to an hypothesis. [P. P. W.]

last and perfect formulation—and especially that the ordinary and usual course of nature never can be broken through. "Stones do not fall from heaven," said Laplace, although they had been falling upon inhabited ground every day from the earliest times. But there is no kind of inference which can lend the slightest probability to any such absolute denial of an unusual phenomenon.

FALLIBILISM

All positive reasoning is of the nature of judging the proportion of something in a whole collection by the proportion found in a sample. Accordingly, there are three things to which we can never hope to attain by reasoning, namely, absolute certainty, absolute exactitude, absolute universality. We cannot be absolutely certain that our conclusions are even approximately true; for the sample may be utterly unlike the unsampled part of the collection. We cannot pretend to be even probably exact; because the sample consists of but a finite number of instances and only admits special values of the proportion sought. Finally, even if we could ascertain with absolute certainty and exactness that the ratio of sinful men to all men was as 1 to 1; still among the infinite generations of men there would be room for any finite number of sinless men without violating the proportion. The case is the same with a seven-legged calf.

Now if exactitude, certitude, and universality are not to be attained by reasoning, there is certainly no other means by which they can be reached.

Somebody will suggest *revelation*. There are scientists and people influenced by science who laugh at revelation; and certainly science has taught us to look at testimony in such a light that the whole theological doctrine of the "Evidences" seems pretty weak. However, I do not think it is philosophical to reject the possibility of a revelation. Still, granting that, I declare as a logician that revealed truths—that is, truths which have nothing in their favor but revelations made to a few individuals—constitute by far the most uncertain class of truths there are. There is here no question of universality; for revelation is itself sporadic and miraculous. There is no question of mathematical exactitude; for no revelation makes any pretension to that character. But it does pretend to be *certain;* and against that there are three conclusive objections. First, we never can be absolutely certain that any given deliverance really is inspired; for that can only be established by reasoning. We cannot even prove it with any very high degree of probability. Second, even if it is inspired, we cannot be sure, or nearly sure, that the statement is true. We know that one of the commandments was in one of the Bibles printed with[out] a *not* in it.[7] All inspired matter has been subject to human distortion or coloring. Besides, we cannot penetrate the counsels of the most High, or lay down anything as a principle that would govern his conduct. We do not know his inscrutable purposes, nor can we comprehend his plans. We cannot tell but he might see fit to inspire his servants with errors. In the third place, a truth which rests on the authority of inspiration only is of a

---

[7] The "Wicked Bible" of 1631 omitted "not" from the Seventh Commandment.

somewhat incomprehensible nature; and we never can be sure that we rightly comprehend it. As there is no way of evading these difficulties, I say that revelation, far from affording us any certainty, gives results less certain than other sources of information. This would be so even if revelation were much plainer than it is.

But, it will be said, you forget the laws which are known to us *a priori,* the axioms of geometry, the principles of logic, the maxims of *causality,* and the like. Those are absolutely certain, without exception and exact. To this I reply that it seems to me there is the most positive historic proof that innate truths are particularly uncertain and mixed up with error, and therefore *a fortiori* not without exception. This historical proof is, of course, not infallible; but it is very strong. Therefore, I ask *how do you know* that *a priori* truth is certain, exceptionless, and exact? You cannot know it by *reasoning.* For that would be subject to uncertainty and inexactitude. Then, it must amount to this, that you know it *a priori;* that is, you take *a priori* judgments at their own valuation, without criticism or credentials. That is barring the gate of inquiry.

Ah! but it will be said, you forget direct experience. Direct experience is neither certain nor uncertain, because it affirms nothing—it just *is.* There are delusions, hallucinations, dreams. But there is no mistake that such things really do appear, and direct experience means simply the appearance. It involves no error, because it testifies to nothing but its own appearance. For the same reason, it affords no certainty. It is not *exact,* because it leaves much vague; though it is not *inexact* either; that is, it has no false exactitude.

All this is true of direct experience at its first presentation. But when it comes up to be criticized it is past, itself, and is represented by *memory.* Now the deceptions and inexactitude of memory are proverbial.

. . . On the whole, then, we cannot in any way reach perfect certitude nor exactitude. We never can be absolutely sure of anything, nor can we with any probability ascertain the exact value of any measure or general ratio.

This is my conclusion, after many years' study of the logic of science; and it is the conclusion which others, of very different cast of mind, have come to, likewise. I believe I may say there is no tenable opinion regarding human knowledge which does not legitimately lead to this corollary. Certainly there is nothing new in it; and many of the greatest minds of all time have held it for true.

Indeed, most everybody will admit it until he begins to see what is involved in the admission—and then most people will draw back. It will not be admitted by persons utterly incapable of philosophical reflection. It will not be fully admitted by masterful minds developed exclusively in the direction of action and accustomed to claim practical infallibility in matters of business. These men will admit the incurable fallibility of all opinions readily enough; only, they will always make exception of their own. The doctrine of fallibilism will also be denied by those who fear its consequences for science, for religion, and for morality. But I will take leave to say to these highly conservative gentlemen that however competent they may be to direct the affairs of a church or other corporation, they had better not try to manage science in that way. Conservatism—in the sense of a dread of consequences—is altogether out of place in science—which has on the contrary always been forwarded by radicals and radicalism, in the sense of the eagerness to carry consequences to their extremes. Not the radicalism that is cocksure, however, but the *radicalism that tries experiments.* Indeed, it is precisely among men animated by the spirit of science that the doctrine of fallibilism will find supporters.

Still, even such a man as that may well ask whether I propose to say that it is not quite certain that twice two are four—and that it is even not probably quite exact! But it would be quite misunderstanding the doctrine of fallibilism to suppose that it means that twice two is probably not exactly four. As I have already remarked, it

is not my purpose to doubt that people can usually *count* with accuracy. Nor does fallibilism say that men cannot attain a sure knowledge of the creations of their own minds. It neither affirms nor denies that. It only says that people cannot attain absolute certainty concerning questions of fact. Numbers are merely a system of names devised by men for the purpose of counting. It is a matter of real fact to say that in a certain room there are two persons. It is a matter of fact to say that each person has two eyes. It is a matter of fact to say that there are four eyes in the room. But to say that *if* there are two persons and each person has two eyes there *will be* four eyes is not a statement of fact, but a statement about the system of numbers which is our own creation.

QUESTIONS FOR DISCUSSION

1. How does Peirce distinguish "laboratory" from "seminary" philosophies? Illustrate each. What are Peirce's reasons for preferring one to the other? Give your reasons for agreeing or disagreeing.
2. Does every man including every scientist have a metaphysics, even without knowing it? Should he?
3. Define "axioms" and illustrate from mathematics, physics, and metaphysics. Why is "self-evidence" not a necessary or adequate basis for axioms?
4. What does Peirce mean by the "observational part of philosophy"? Illustrate.
5. What is Peirce's "First Rule of Reason" and how is it related to his doctrine of Fallibilism?

Ernest Nagel (1901-   )

5.4   Patterns of Scientific Explanation

ILLUSTRATIONS OF SCIENTIFIC EXPLANATION

Explanations are answers to the question "Why?" However, very little reflection is needed to reveal that the word "why" is not unambiguous and that with varying contexts different sorts of answers are relevant responses to it. The following brief list contains examples of the use of "why," several of which impose certain distinctive restrictions upon admissible answers to questions put with the help of the word.

1. Why is the sum of any number of consecutive odd integers beginning with 1 always a perfect square (for example, $1 + 3 + 5 + 7 = 16 = 4^2$)? Here the "fact" to be explained (called the *explicandum*) will be assumed to be a claimant for the familiar though not transparently clear label of "necessary truth," in the sense that its denial is self-contradictory. A relevant answer to the question is, therefore, a demonstration which establishes not only the universal truth but also the necessity of the explicandum. The explanation will accomplish this if the steps of the demonstration conform to

From *The Structure of Science* by Ernest Nagel, © 1961 by Harcourt Brace Jovanovich, and reprinted with their permission.

the formal requirements of logical proof and if, furthermore, the premises of the demonstration are themselves in some sense necessary. The premises will presumably be the postulates of arithmetic; and their necessary character will be assured if, for example, they can be construed as true in virtue of the meanings associated with the expressions occurring in their formulation.

2. Why did moisture form on the outside of the glass when it was filled with ice water yesterday? Here the fact to be explained is the occurrence of an individual event. Its explanation, in broad outlines, might run as follows: The temperature of the glass after it was filled with ice water was considerably lower than the temperature of the surrounding air; the air contained water vapor, and water vapor in air is in general precipitated as a liquid whenever the air comes into contact with a sufficiently cold surface. In this example, as in the previous one, the formal pattern of the explanation appears to be that of a deduction. Indeed, were the explanatory premises formulated more fully and carefully, the deductive form would be unmistakable. However, the explicandum in this case is not a necessary truth, and on the

face of it neither are the explanatory premises. On the contrary, the premises are statements which are presumably based on pertinent observational or experimental evidence.

3. Why did a smaller percentage of Catholics commit suicide than did Protestants in European countries during the last quarter of the nineteenth century? A well-known answer to the question is that the institutional arrangements under which Catholics lived made for a greater degree of "social cohesion" than did the social organizations of Protestants, and that in general the existence of strongly knit social bonds between members of a community helps to sustain human beings during periods of personal stress. The explicandum in this case is a historical phenomenon that is statistically described, in contrast with the individual event of the previous example; and the proposed explanation does not, therefore, attempt to account for any individual suicide in the period under discussion. Indeed, although the explanatory premises are stated neither precisely nor completely, it is clear that some of them have a statistical content, just as does the explicandum. But, since the premises are not fully formulated, it is not quite clear just what the logical structure of the explanation is. We shall assume, however, that the implicit premises can be made explicit and that, moreover, the explanation then exhibits a deductive pattern.

4. Why does ice float on water? The explicandum in this example is not a historical fact, whether individual or statistical, but a universal law which asserts an invariable association of certain physical traits. It is familiarly explained by exhibiting it as the logical consequence of other laws—the law that the density of ice is less than that of water, the Archimedean law that a fluid buoys up a body immersed in it with a force equal to the weight of the fluid displaced by the body, and further laws concerning the conditions under which bodies subjected to forces are in equilibrium. It is worth noting that in this case, in contrast with the two immediately preceding examples, the explanatory premises are statements of universal law.

5. Why does the addition of salt to water lower its freezing point? The explicandum in this case is once more a law, so that in this respect the present example does not differ from the preceding one. Moreover, its current explanation consists in deducing it from the principles of thermodynamics conjoined with certain assumptions about the composition of heterogeneous mixtures; and in consequence the present example also agrees with the previous one in regard to the formal pattern of the explanation. Nevertheless, the example is included for future reference, because the explanatory premises exhibit certain *prima facie* distinctive features having considerable methodological interest. For the thermodynamical principles included among the explanatory premises in the present example are assumptions much more comprehensive than any of the laws cited in previous examples. Unlike those laws, these assumptions make use of "theoretical" notions, such as energy and entropy, that do not appear to be associated with any overtly fixed experimental procedures for identifying or measuring the physical properties those notions presumably represent. Assumptions of this sort are frequently called "theories" and are sometimes

sharply distinguished from "experimental laws." However, we must postpone for later discussion the question of whether the distinction has any merit, and if so, what is its importance. For the moment, the present example simply puts on record an allegedly distinctive species of deductive explanations in science.

6. Why is it that in the progeny of inbred hybrid peas, obtained by crossing round and wrinkled parents, approximately ¾ of the peas are always round, whereas the remaining ¼ are wrinkled? The explicandum is currently explained by deducing it from the general principles of the Mendelian theory of heredity, coupled with certain further assumptions about the genetic constitution of peas. It is obvious that the fact here explained is a statistical regularity, not an invariable association of attributes, which is formulated as the relative frequency of a given trait in a certain population of elements. Moreover, as becomes evident when the explanatory premises are carefully stated, some of the premises also have a statistical content, since they formulate the probability (in the sense of a relative frequency) with which parent peas transmit determinants of given genetic traits to their offspring. The present example is similar to the preceding one in illustrating a deductive pattern of explanation containing theoretical assumptions among its premises. It is unlike any previous example, however, in that the explicandum as well as some of the premises are ostensibly statistical laws, which formulate statistical rather than invariable regularities.

7. Why did Cassius plot the death of Caesar? The fact to be explained is once more an individual historical occurrence. If we can believe Plutarch, the explanation is to be found in the inbred hatred which Cassius bore toward tyrants. However, this answer is obviously incomplete without a number of further general assumptions, such as some assumption concerning the way hatred is manifested in a given culture by persons of a certain social rank. It is unlikely, however, that such assumptions, if they are to be credible, can be asserted with strict universality. If the assumption is to be in agreement with the known facts, it will at best be only a statistical generalization. For example, a credible generalization may assert that most men (or a certain percentage of men) of a certain sort in a certain kind of society will behave in a certain manner. Accordingly, since the fact to be explained in this example is an individual historical occurrence, while the crucial explanatory assumption is statistical in form, the explicandum is not a deductive consequence of the explanatory premises. On the contrary, the explicandum in this case is simply made "probable" by the latter. This is a distinguishing feature of the present example, and sets it off from the preceding ones. Furthermore, there is an important substantive difference between this and previous examples, in that the explanatory premises in the present instance mention a psychological disposition (e.g., an emotional state or attitude) as one of the springs of an action. Accordingly, if the question "Why?" is raised in order to obtain an answer in terms of psychological dispositions, the question is significant only if there is some warrant for assuming that such dispositions do in fact occur in the subject matter under consideration.

8. Why did Henry VIII of England seek to annul his marriage to Catherine of Aragon? A familiar explanation for this historical occurrence consists in imputing to Henry a consciously entertained objective rather than a psychological disposition, as was the case in the immediately preceding example. Thus historians often account for Henry's efforts to annul his marriage to Catherine by citing the fact that, since she bore him no son, he wished to remarry in order to obtain a male heir. Henry doubtless possessed many psychological dispositions that may have been partly responsible for his behavior toward Catherine. However, in the explanation as just stated such psychological "springs of action" for Henry's conduct are not mentioned, and his efforts at obtaining an annulment are explained as deliberate means instituted for realizing a conscious goal (or end-in-view). Accordingly, the difference between the present and the preceding example hinges on the distinction between a psychological disposition or spring of action (of which an individual may be unaware even though it controls his actions) and a consciously held end-in-view (for the sake of which an individual may adopt certain means). This distinction is commonly recognized. A man's behavior is sometimes explained in terms of springs of action, even when he has no end-in-view for that behavior. On the other hand, no explanation is regarded as satisfactory for a certain class of human actions if the explanation does not refer to some conscious goal for the realization of which those actions are instituted. In consequence, in certain contexts a requirement for the intelligibility of questions introduced by "Why" is that in those con-

texts explicitly entertained objectives can be asserted.

9. Why do human beings have lungs? The question as it stands is ambiguous, for it may be construed either as raising a problem in the historical evolution of the human species or as requesting an account of the function of lungs in the human body at its present stage of evolutionary development. It is in this latter sense that the question is here intended. When so understood, the usual answer as supplied by current physiology calls attention to the indispensability of oxygen for the combustion of food substances in the body, and to the instrumental role of the lungs in conveying oxygen from the air to the blood and so eventually to various cells of the organism. Accordingly, the explanation describes the operation of the lungs as essential for the maintenance of certain biological activities. The explanation thus exhibits a *prima facie* distinctive form. The explanation does not explicitly mention the conditions under which the complex events called "the operation of the lungs" occur. It states rather in what way the lungs, as a specially organized part of the human body, contribute to the continuance of some of the other activities of the body.

10. Why does the English language in its current form have so many words of Latin origin? The historical fact for which an explanation is requested here is a complex set of linguistic habits, manifested by men during a somewhat loosely delimited historical period in various parts of the world. It is also important to note that the question "Why?" in the present example, unlike the questions in preceding ones, tacitly calls for an

account of how a certain system has developed into its current form from some earlier stage of the system. For the system under consideration, however, we do not possess general "dynamical laws of development," such as are available in physics, for example, for the development of a rotating gaseous mass. An admissible explanation for the historical fact in question will, therefore, have to mention sequential changes over a period of time, and not merely a set of occurrences at some antecedent initial time. Accordingly, the standard explanation for that fact includes reference to the Norman Conquest of England, to the speech employed by the victors and vanquished before the Conquest, and to developments in England and elsewhere after the Conquest. Moreover, the explanation assumes a number of more or less vague generalizations (not always explicitly stated, and some of them undoubtedly possessing a statistical content) concerning ways in which speech habits in different linguistic communities are altered when such communities enter into stated relations with each other. In short, the explanation requested in the present example is a genetic one, whose structure is patently more complex than the structure of explanations previously illustrated. The complexity should not be attributed to the circumstance that this explicandum happens to be a fact of human behavior. A comparable complexity is exhibited by a genetic explanation for the fact that the saline content of the oceans is at present about three per cent by volume.

FOUR TYPES
OF EXPLANATION

The above list does not exhaust the types of answers that are some-times called "explanations." It is long enough, however, to establish the important point that even answers to the limited class of questions introduced by "Why" are not all of the same kind. Indeed, the list clearly suggests that explanations offered in various sciences in response to such questions may differ in the way explanatory assumptions are related to their explicanda, so that explanations fall into distinct logical patterns.

We shall proceed on that suggestion, and characterize what appear to be the distinct types of explanation under which the examples in the above list can be classified. However, we shall at this point not engage the issue whether what seem to be different logical patterns of explanation are in fact only imperfectly formulated variants or limiting cases of some common pattern. For the present, at any rate, we identify four major and ostensibly different patterns of explanation.

The Deductive Model

A type of explanation commonly encountered in the natural sciences, though not exclusively in those disciplines, has the formal structure of a deductive argument, in which the explicandum is a logically necessary consequence of the explanatory premises. Accordingly, in explanations of this type the premises state a sufficient (and sometimes, though not invariably, a necessary) condition for the truth of the explicandum. This type has been extensively studied since ancient times. It has been widely regarded as the paradigm for any "genuine" explanation, and has often been adopted as the ideal form to which all efforts at explanation should strive.

The first six examples in the above list are *prima facie* illustrations of this type. Nevertheless, there are significant differences between them that are worth reviewing. In the first example, both the explicandum and the premises are necessary truths. However, although the point will need further discussion, few if any experimental scientists today believe that their explicanda can be shown to be inherently necessary. Indeed, it is just because the propositions (whether singular or general) investigated by the empirical sciences can be denied without logical absurdity that observational evidence is required to support them. Accordingly, the justification of claims as to the necessity of propositions, as well as the explanation of why propositions are necessary, are the business for formal disciplines like logic and mathematics, and not of empirical inquiry.

In both the second and third examples, the explicandum is an historical fact. However, in the second the fact is an individual event, while in the third it is a statistical phenomenon. In both examples the premises contain at least one "lawlike" assumption that is general in form, and at least one singular statement (whether individual or statistical). On the other hand, the explanation of the statistical phenomenon is distinguished by the presence of a statistical generalization in the premises.

In the fourth, fifth, and sixth examples the explicandum is a law—in the fourth and fifth cases a strictly universal statement asserting an invariable association of certain traits, in the sixth case a statistical law. However, the law in the fourth example is explained by deducing it from assumptions each of which is an "ex-perimental law" in the sense already indicated briefly. In the fifth and sixth examples, on the other hand, the explanatory premises include so-called "theoretical" statements; in the sixth example, with a statistical law as the explicandum, the explanatory theory itself contains assumptions of a statistical form.

The differences just noted between explanations conforming to the deductive model have been described only in a schematic way. A fuller account of them will be given subsequently. Moreover, the purely formal requirements which deductive explanations must meet do not exhaust all the conditions that satisfactory explanations of this type are frequently expected to meet; and a number of further conditions will need to be discussed. In particular, although the important role of general laws in deductive explanations has been briefly noticed, the much-debated question remains whether laws can be characterized simply as presumptively true universal statements, or whether in order to serve as a premise in a satisfactory explanation a universal statement must in addition possess a distinctive type of relational structure. Furthermore, while mention has been made of the fact that highly integrated and comprehensive systems of explanation are achieved in science through the use of so-called "theoretical" assumptions, it will be necessary to inquire more closely what are the traits that distinguish theories from other laws, what features in them account for their power to explain a wide variety of facts in a systematic manner, and what cognitive status can be assigned to them.

Probabilistic Explanations

Many explanations in practically every scientific discipline are *prima facie* not of deductive form, since their explanatory premises do not formally imply their explicanda. Nevertheless, though the premises are logically insufficient to secure the truth of the explicandum, they are said to make the latter "probable."

Probabilistic explanations are usually encountered when the explanatory premises contain a statistical assumption about some class of elements, while the explicandum is a singular statement about a given individual member of that class. This type of explanation is illustrated by both the seventh and tenth examples in the above list, though more clearly by the seventh. When this latter is formulated somewhat more explicitly, it runs as follows: In ancient Rome the relative frequency (or probability) was high (e.g., greater than one-half) that an individual belonging to the upper strata of society and possessed by great hatred of tyranny would plot the death of men who were in a position to secure tyrannical power. Cassius was such a Roman and Caesar such a potential tyrant. Hence, though it does not follow that Cassius plotted the death of Caesar, it is highly probable that he did so.

A few observations are in order. It is sometimes maintained that probabilistic explanations are only temporary halfway stations on the road to the deductive ideal, and do not, therefore, constitute a distinct type. All that need be done, so it has been suggested, is to replace the statistical assumptions in the premises of probabilistic explanations by a strictly universal statement—in the above illustration, for example, by a statement asserting an invariable association between certain carefully delimited psychosociological traits (which Cassius presumably possessed) and participation in assassination plots. But, though the suggestion is not necessarily without merit and may be a goad to further inquiry, in point of fact it is extremely difficult in many subject matters to assert with even moderate plausibility strictly universal laws that are not trivial and hence otiose. Often the best that can be established with some warrant is a statistical regularity. Accordingly, probabilistic explanations cannot be ignored, on pain of excluding from the discussion of the logic of explanation important areas of investigation.

It is essential not to confuse the question whether the premises of an explanation are known to be true, with the question whether an explanation is of the probabilistic type. It may well be that in no scientific explanation are the general assumptions contained in the premises known to be true, and that every such assumption can be asserted as only "probable." However, even if this is so, it does not abolish the distinction between deductive and probabilistic types of explanation. For the distinction is based on patent differences in the way the premises and the explicanda are related to one another, and not only any supposed differences in our knowledge of the premises.

It should be noted, finally, that it is still an unsettled question whether an explanation must contain a statistical assumption in order to be a probabilistic one, or whether non-statistical premises may not make an explicandum "probable" in some non-statistical sense of the word. Nor are students of the subject in general agreement as to how the relation between premises and explicanda is to be analyzed, even in those probabilistic explanations in which the premises are statistical and the explicanda are statements about some individual. These questions will receive attention later.

Functional or Teleological Explanations

In many contexts of inquiry—especially, though not exclusively, in biology and in the study of human affairs—explanations take the form of indicating one or more functions (or even dysfunctions) that a unit performs in maintaining or realizing certain traits of a system to which the unit belongs, or of stating the instrumental role an action plays in bringing about some goal. Such explanations are commonly called "functional" or "teleological." It is characteristic of functional explanations that they employ such typical locutions as "in order that," "for the sake of," and the like. Moreover, in many functional explanations there is an explicit reference to some still future state or event, in terms of which the existence of a thing or the occurrence of an act is made intelligible.

It is implicit in what has just been said that two subsidiary cases of functional explanation can be distinguished. A functional explanation may be sought for a particular act, state, or thing occurring at a stated time. This case is illustrated by the eighth example in the above list. Or alternatively, a functional explanation may be given for a feature that is present in all systems of a certain kind, at whatever time such systems

may exist. This case is illustrated by the ninth of the above examples. Both examples exhibit the characteristic features of functional explanations. Thus, Henry's efforts to annul his first marriage are explained by indicating that they were undertaken for the sake of obtaining a male heir in the future; and the occurrence of lungs in the human body is explained by showing that they operate in a stated manner in order to maintain a certain chemical process and thereby to assure a continuance of life for the body into the future.

What the detailed structure of functional explanations is, how they are related to nonteleological ones, and why teleological explanations are frequent in certain areas of inquiry but rare in others are questions which must be reserved for later discussion. However, two common misconceptions concerning teleological explanations require brief notice immediately.

It is a mistaken supposition that teleological explanations are intelligible only if the things and activities so explained are conscious agents or the products of such agents. Thus, in the functional explanation of lungs, no assumption is made, either explicitly or tacitly, that the lungs have any conscious ends-in-view or that they have been devised by any agent for a definite purpose. In short, the occurrence of teleological explanations in biology or elsewhere is not necessarily a sign of anthropomorphism. On the other hand, some teleological explanations patently do assume the existence of deliberate plans and conscious purposes; but such an assumption is not illegitimate when, as in the case of teleological explanations of certain aspects of human behavior, the facts warrant it.

It is also a mistake to suppose that, because teleological explanations contain references to the future in accounting for what already exists, such explanations must tacitly assume that the future acts causally on the present. Thus, in accounting for Henry's efforts at obtaining an annulment of his marriage, no assumption is made that the unrealized future state of his possessing a male heir caused him to engage in certain activities. On the contrary, the explanation of Henry's behavior is entirely compatible with the view that it was his existing desires for a certain kind of future, and not the future itself, which were causally responsible for his conduct. Similarly, no assumption is made in the functional explanation of human lungs that it is the future oxidation of foods in the body which brings lungs into existence or causes them to operate; and the explanation does not depend on denying that the operation of the lungs is causally determined by the existing constitution of the body and its environment. By giving a teleological explanation one is, therefore, not necessarily giving hostages to the doctrine that the future is an agent in its own realization.

Genetic Explanations

One remaining kind of explanation remains to be mentioned, though it is a moot question whether it constitutes a distinctive type. Historical inquiries frequently undertake to explain why it is that a given subject of study has certain characteristics, by describing how the subject has evolved out of some earlier one. Such explanations are commonly called "genetic," and they have been given for animate as well as inanimate things, for traits of an individual as well as for characteristics of a group. The tenth example in the above list illustrates the type.

The task of genetic explanations is to set out the sequence of major events through which some earlier system has been transformed into a later one. The explanatory premises of such explanations will, therefore, necessarily contain a large number of singular statements about past events in the system under inquiry. Two further points about the explanatory premises of genetic explanations should be noted. The first is the obvious one that not every past event in the career of the system will be mentioned. The second is that those events which are mentioned are selected on the basis of assumptions (frequently tacit ones) as to what sorts of events are causally relevant to the development of the system. Accordingly, in addition to the singular statements the premises will also include (whether explicitly or implicitly) general assumptions about the causal dependencies of various kinds of events.

These general assumptions may be fairly precise developmental laws, for which independent inductive evidence is available. (This may happen when the system under study can be regarded for the purposes at hand as a member of a class of similar systems which undergo a similar evolution—for example, in the study of the development of biological traits of an individual member of some species. For it is then often possible to employ methods of comparative analysis to establish such developmental laws.) In other cases, the general assumptions may be only vague generalizations, perhaps statistical in content, and may contain no reference to some of the highly specific features of the subject matter under study. (This often happens when the system investigated is a relatively unique one —for example, when the development of some institution in a particular culture is investigated.) However, in neither case do the explanatory premises in familiar examples of genetic explanations state the sufficient conditions for the occurrence of the fact stated in the explicandum, though the premises often do state some of the conditions which, under the circumstances generally taken for granted, are necessary for the latter. It is, therefore, a reasonable conclusion that genetic explanations are by and large probabilistic. However, further consideration of the structure of genetic explanations—and more generally of historical explanations—must be postponed.

DO THE SCIENCES EXPLAIN?

These four major types of explanation have been distinguished because they appear to correspond to real structural differences in the examples of explanation that have been surveyed, and because the classification provides a convenient framework for examining important issues in the construction of systematic explanations. . . .

But before turning away from the outline of explanatory patterns, . . . a historically influential objection to the claim that the sciences do in fact explain deserves brief comment. No science (and certainly no physical science), so the objection runs, really answers questions as to *why* any event occurs, or *why* things are related in

certain ways. Such questions could be answered only if we were able to show that the events which occur *must* occur and that the relations which hold between things *must* hold between them. However, the experimental methods of science can detect no absolute or logical necessity in the phenomena which are the ultimate subject matter of every empirical inquiry; and, even if the laws and theories of science are true, they are no more than logically contingent truths about the relations of concomitance or the sequential orders of phenomena. Accordingly, the questions which the sciences answer are questions as to *how* (in what manner or under what circumstances) events happen and things are related. The sciences, therefore, achieve what are at best only comprehensive and accurate systems of *description,* not of explanation.[1]

More issues are raised by this argument than can be discussed with profit at this point. In particular, the question whether laws and theories

_____

[1] "The very common idea that it is the function of Natural Science to explain physical phenomena cannot be accepted as true unless the word 'explain' is used in a very limited sense. The notions of efficient causation, and of logical necessity, not being applicable to the world of physical phenomena, the function of Natural Science is to describe conceptually the sequences of events which are to be observed in Nature; but Natural Science cannot account for the existence of such sequences, and therefore cannot explain the phenomena in the physical worlds, in the strictest sense in which the term explanation can be used. Thus Natural Science describes, so far as it can, *how*, or in accordance with what rules, phenomena happen, but it is wholly incompetent to answer the question *why* they happen."—E. W. Hobson, *The Domain of Natural Science* (Cambridge: Cambridge University Press, 1923), pp. 81-82.

are merely formulations of relations of concomitance and sequence between phenomena needs more attention than can now be given to it. But even if this view of laws and theories is granted, it is evident that the argument hinges in some measure on a verbal issue. For the argument assumes that there is just one correct sense in which "why" questions can be raised—namely, the sense in which the proper answer to it is a proof of the inherent necessity of a proposition. However, this is a mistaken assumption, as the above list of examples amply testifies. Accordingly, a sufficient reply to the argument when it is construed as resting on this assumption is that there are in fact well-established uses for the words "why" and "explanation" such that it is entirely appropriate to designate an answer to a "why" question as an explanation, even when the answer does not supply reasons for regarding the explicandum as intrinsically necessary. Indeed, even writers who officially reject the view that the sciences can ever explain anything sometimes lapse into language which describes certain scientific discoveries as "explanations." [2]

---

[2] For example, Mach describes Galileo's analysis of equilibrium on an inclined plane in terms of the principle of the lever, as an explanation of the former. (Ernst Mach, *The Science of Mechanics* (LaSalle, Ill.: The Open Court Publishing Company, 1942), p. 31.

To the extent that the argument rests exclusively on assumptions about linguistic usage, it is neither important nor interesting. In point of fact, however, the argument does have more substance. The objection it voices was originally directed against several targets. One was the surviving anthropomorphisms in physics and biology, some of which lurked in the meanings commonly associated even with technical notions such as force and energy, while others were manifest in the uncritical use of teleological categories. In this respect, the objection was a demand for intellectual house cleaning, and it stimulated a program of careful analysis of scientific ideas that remains an active one. A second target of the objection was a conception of science that was at one time widespread and that continues in variant forms to retain distinguished adherents. According to this conception, it is the business of science to explain phenomena on the basis of laws of nature that codify a necessary order in things, and that are, therefore, more than contingently true. The objection is thus a denial of the claim that laws of nature possess more than a *de facto* universality, a denial which coincides with one major conclusion of David Hume's analysis of causality. The real issue which the argument raises is not a trivial one about linguistic usage, but a substantial one about the adequacy of an essentially Humean account of scientific law.

QUESTIONS FOR DISCUSSION

1. Give illustrations of scientific explanations from arithmetic, physical science, biology, social science, history, and linguistics.

2. Define and illustrate the *deductive model* of explanation, and the difference between *laws* and *theories*.
3. Define and illustrate a probabilistic type of explanation.
4. Define and illustrate a functional or teleological type of explanation.
5. Define and illustrate a genetic explanation.
6. Do the sciences explain? Give reasons why some think not, and your own comments.

Viscount Samuel (1870-1963)

5.5   The Physical Basis of Mind: A Philosophers' Symposium

In so short a broadcast, I can only offer baldly my own conclusions on the question debated in this most interesting, and indeed exciting, discussion, without attempting any survey of the previous contributions.

The discussion has been an approach, from the side of physiology, to one of the oldest and most fundamental of the problems of philosophy —the relation between mind and matter. For centuries, philosophers of different schools have made strenuous efforts to resolve one into the other. Some have sought to show that mind is nothing more than an emanation, in the course of evolution, from matter; others that matter is nothing more than a concept of mind, which alone is real. Those efforts have been un-

successful: neither view has won general assent.

The materialists appear to ignore the obvious lessons of daily experience. We see, every moment, events which cannot be accounted for by derivations, however subtle, from physical or chemical processes. Watch a chess-player deliberating for a quarter of an hour whether to move his queen here or a pawn there. At last he stretches out his hand and does the one or the other: or he may do neither; using his vocal organs, he may say, 'I resign this game.' The physiologist may reveal the nervous and muscular mechanism which operates the hand or the tongue, but not the process which has decided the player's action. Or consider a novelist making up a story, a musician writing a symphony, a scientist engaged in a mathematical calculation; or, indeed, something much simpler, a bird building its nest, and choosing the right materials for each stage; or a cat

From *The Physical Basis of Mind*, A Series of Broadcast Talks (B.B.C. Third Programme), edited by Peter Laslett (Oxford: Basil Blackwell, 1950), pp. 65-79. Reprinted by permission of the publisher.

waiting for a pause in the traffic before crossing the street. All these, and all such, are engaged in some process that is different in kind from electrical attractions and repulsions, or from the processes that unite particles into atoms, atoms into molecules, molecules into objects, and move them about relatively to one another.

The idealists do not account for the fact, which we are bound to accept from astronomy, geology, and anthropology—if we think at all, and if we accept anything at all—that the stars and the planets and this earth existed aeons before man existed; that the universe carried on its activities then—and may properly be assumed to carry them on now—independently of man's perceiving and observing, timing and measuring. The material universe cannot, therefore, be a product of human thought. If it is said that matter may still be an emanation of mind—the mind of God—that is merely an evasion, removing the problem outside the scope of the argument.

The whole effort—to resolve mind into matter or else matter into mind —is the outcome of what T. H. Green called 'the philosophic craving for unity.' But a craving is something irrational, and we had better beware of becoming addicts. What ground is there for requiring any such unification, either of the one kind or of the other? An essential duality in nature is the alternative that is left.

For those who have proceeded on that assumption, it has been natural and usual to regard the living conscious body as the province of mind and the outside material universe as the province of matter. This series of addresses, which is now concluding, has been most valuable in showing that that is an error; it has put the boundary between the two in the wrong place. The eminent scientists who have taken part in it have clearly established that the acceptance of sense stimuli, the transmission of their effects along the nerve fibres, and their activation of different parts of the brain, are mechanical. Whether the approach is from bio-physics or bio-chemistry, anatomy or pathology, the conclusion is the same—these are material activities, obeying mechanical laws. Dr. Russell Brain who spoke on 'Speech and Thought' tells us that 'all stimuli reach the brain as electrical patterns'; Professor Le Gros Clark and others describe with great clarity the mechanism of the nervous system as a whole. We must conclude that these processes, although inside the body, are not essentially different from the physical processes that are going on outside; rather they are a continuation. When we feel an electric shock, the nerve fibres that carry the current are performing a function similar in kind to that of the copper wire between the battery and the hand. When we hear a sound, the mechanism of the auditory organs, including the relevant part of the brain, is specialized, no doubt, but is not fundamentally of a different order from the air-waves which had carried the sound. It follows that the meeting-place between mind and matter in our own experience is not where we had supposed it to be; it is not at the boundary between body and not-body, but is internal.

That, however, does not solve the problem; it merely shifts it. Some meeting-place there must be to account for the brain-mind relation. And we are bound to assume that, although the two are of different orders, they must have something in common, because there is a meeting-place; because the two interconnect and interact; because body (including brain) does in fact condition and influence mind, and mind does in fact condition and influence body.

The painter or sculptor is conditioned and influenced by his materials; the composer by the musical instruments that exist in his time; the architect by the available building materials; the craftsman by his tools; the captain and crew by their ship. But also the artist, composer, architect, craftsman, or navigator chooses the things that he will use and decides the purposes that they shall serve. So with mind and body.

This discussion has helped to clarify the whole problem by establishing the fact that the meeting-place is not at the points where external stimuli impinge upon the nervous system; it is at the points where mind accepts and utilizes the sense-data offered by the brain. But the discussion has not been able to answer the question what it is that takes over at those points; and therefore it could not even begin to consider how the connection may be made.

Here again our scientists are substantially agreed. Professor Le Gros Clark said at the end of his broadcast: 'No more than the physiologist is the anatomist able even to suggest how the physico-chemical phenomena associated with the passage of nervous impulses from one part of the brain to another can be translated into a mental experience.' Dr. Penfield compares the mechanism of nerve-cell connections to a telephone switchboard. He asks: 'What is the real relationship of this mechanism to the mind?' He says that 'there is a difference between automatic action and voluntary action: . . . that something else finds its dwelling-place between the sensory complex and the motor mechanism, that there is a switchboard operator as well as a switchboard.' Sir Charles Sherrington has written elsewhere, 'That our being should consist of *two* fundamental elements offers, I suppose, no greater inherent improbability than that it should rest on one only.' Again, 'We have to regard the relation of mind to brain as still not merely unsolved, but still devoid of a basis for its very beginning.' And he has ended his stimulating contribution to the present discussion by saying, 'Aristotle, 2,000 years ago, was asking how is the mind attached to the body? We are asking that question still.'

That, it seems, is where we are now at a standstill. Until science and philosophy can help us to move on from that position we cannot hope that the universe will, for us, be rationalized.

A. J. Ayer (1910-   )

I wonder if Lord Samuel has made it completely clear what the problem is that the philosophers are here called upon to solve? The scientists who have spoken in this series have shown very fully and convincingly how various mental processes—thinking, feeling, perceiving, remembering—are causally dependent upon processes in the brain, but to some of them at least the character of this connection still appears mysterious. Thus, Sir Charles Sherrington remarks that 'it is a far cry from an electrical reaction in the brain to suddenly seeing the world around one, with all its distances, colours, and chiaroscuro'; and Professor Adrian confesses to the same 'misgivings' when he says that 'the part of the picture of the brain which may always be missing is of course the part which deals with the mind, the part which ought to explain how a particular pattern of nerve impulses can produce an idea; or the other way round, how a thought can decide which nerve cells are to come into action.'

If this is a genuine problem, it is hard to see why further information about the brain should be expected to solve it. For however much we amplify our picture of the brain, it remains still a picture of something physical, and it is just the question how anything physical can interact with something that is not that is supposed to constitute our difficulty. If what we are seeking is a bridge across a seemingly impassable river it will not help us merely to elevate one of the banks. It looks, indeed, as if some of the previous speakers were hoping to discover in the brain something describable as the locus of the mind; as if mind and brain could be conceived as meeting at a point in space or as somehow shading into one another: but to me this is not even an intelligible hypothesis. What would it be like to come upon this junction? By what signs would you recognize it if you found it? Descartes had the same problem, and he met it by suggesting that mind and body came together in the pineal gland; but how this conjecture could con-

ceivably be tested he did not explain. The reason he had the problem—the reason why we have it still—is that matter and mind were conceived by him from the outset as distinct orders of being; it is as if there were two separate worlds, such that every event had to belong to one or other of them, but no event could belong to both. But from these premises it follows necessarily that there can be no bridge or junction; for what would the bridge consist of? Any event that you discovered would have to fall on one or other side of it. So, if there is a difficulty here, it is not because our factual information is scanty, but because our logic is defective. Perhaps this whole manner of conceiving the distinction between mind and matter is at fault. In short, our problem is not scientific but philosophical.

Let us consider, then, what can be meant by saying that a particular pattern of nerve impulses 'produces' an idea, or that 'a thought decides' which nerve cells are to come into action. What are the facts on which such assertions are based? The facts are that the physiologist makes certain observations, and that these observations fall into different categories. On the one hand there are the observations which lead him to tell his story about nerve cells and electrical impulses. That is to say, the story is an interpretation of the observations in question. On the other hand, there are the observations which he interprets by saying that the subject of his experiment is in such and such a 'mental' state, that he is thinking, or resolving to perform some action, or feeling some sensation, or whatever it may be. It is then found to be the case that these two sorts of observations can be correlated with one another; that whenever an observation of the first type can be made, there is good reason to suppose that an observation of the second type can be made also. For example, when the scientists make observations which they interpret by saying that such and such nerve cells are undergoing such and such electrical disturbances, they can also make observations which are interpreted by saying that the subject is having sensations of a certain type. Again, when they are able to make such observations as are interpreted by saying that the subject is resolving to perform some action, they can also make further observations which are interpreted by saying that certain impulses are passing through certain of his nerve fibres. It seems to me that when it is asserted that the two events in question—the mental and the physical—are causally connected, that the pattern of nerve impulses 'produces' the sensation, or that the thought 'decides' which nerve cells are to operate, all that is meant, or at least all that can properly be meant, is that these two sets of observations are correlated in the way that I have described. But if this is so, where is the difficulty? There is nothing especially mysterious about the fact that two different sets of observations are correlated; that, given the appropriate conditions, they habitually accompany one another. You may say that this fact requires an explanation; but such an explanation could only be some theory from which the fact of this correlation could be deduced. And in so far as the theory was not a mere redescription of the facts which it was intended to explain, it would serve only to fit them into a wider context. We should learn from it that not only were these observations correlated, but certain

further types of observation were correlated with them. To ask *why* something occurs, if it is not simply equivalent to asking *how* it occurs, is to ask what other things are associated with it. Once the facts are fully described, there is no mystery left.

If there seems to be a mystery in this case, it is because we are misled by our conceptual systems; not by the facts themselves but by the pictures which we use to interpret the facts. The physiologist's story is complete in itself. The characters that figure in it are nerve cells, electrical impulses, and so forth. It has no place for an entirely different cast, of sensations, thoughts, feelings, and the other *personae* of the mental play. And just because it has no place for them they do not intervene in it. The muddle arises from trying to make them intervene, as I am afraid Lord Samuel does. We then get a confused, indeed an unintelligible, story of electrical impulses being transmuted into sensations, or of mental processes interleaved with disturbances of the nervous cells. The picture we are given is that of messengers travelling through the brain, reaching a mysterious entity called the mind, receiving orders from it, and then travelling on. But since the mind has no position in space—it is by definition not the sort of thing that can have a position in space—it does not literally make sense to talk of physical signals reaching it; nor are there such temporal gaps in the procession of nervous impulses as would leave room for the mental characters to intervene. In short, the two stories will not mix. It is like trying to play *Hamlet,* not without the Prince of Denmark, but with Pericles, the Prince of Tyre. But to say that the two stories will not mix is not to say that either of them is superfluous. Each is an interpretation of certain phenomena and they are connected by the fact that, in certain conditions, when one of them is true, the other is true also.

My conclusion is, then, that mind and body are not to be conceived as two disparate entities between which we have to make, or find, some sort of amphibious bridge, but that talking about minds and talking about bodies are different ways of classifying and interpreting our experiences. I do not say that this procedure does not give rise to serious philosophical problems; how, for example, to analyse statements about the thoughts and feelings of others; or how far statements about people's so-called mental processes are equivalent to statements about their observable behaviour. But once we are freed from the Cartesian fallacy of regarding minds as immaterial substances, I do not think that the discovery of causal connections between what we choose to describe respectively as mental and physical occurrences implies anything by which we need to be perplexed.

Gilbert Ryle (1900-   )

The story is told of some peasants who were terrified at the sight of their first railway-train. Their pastor therefore gave them a lecture explaining how a steam-engine works. One of the peasants then said, 'Yes, pastor, we quite understand what you say about the steam-engine. But there is really a horse inside, isn't there?' So used were they to horse-drawn carts that they could not take in the idea that some vehicles propel themselves.

We might invent a sequel. The peasants examined the engine and peeped into every crevice of it. They then said, 'Certainly we cannot see, feel, or hear a horse there. We are foiled. But we know there is a horse there, so it must be a ghost-horse which, like the fairies, hides from mortal eyes.'

The pastor objected, 'But, after all, horses themselves are made of moving parts, just as the steam-engine is made of moving parts. You know what their muscles, joints, and blood-ves-sels do. So why is there a mystery in the self-propulsion of a steam-engine, if there is none in that of a horse? What do you think makes the horse's hooves go to and fro?' After a pause a peasant replied, 'What makes the horse's hooves go is four extra little ghost-horses inside.'

Poor simple-minded peasants! Yet just such a story has been the official theory of the mind for the last three very scientific centuries. Several, though not all, of the scientists in this series have automatically posed their problem in this very way. I think that Lord Samuel still accepts the whole story, and that Professor Ayer would like to reject it, but does not see how to do so. For the general terms in which the scientists have set their problem of mind and body, we philosophers have been chiefly to blame, though we have been obsessed, not by the rustic idea of horses, but by the newer idea of mechanical contrivances. The legend that we have told and sold runs like this. A person consists of two theatres, one bodily and one non-bodily. In his Theatre A go on the incidents which we can explore by eye and instrument. But a person also incorporates a second theatre, Theatre B. Here there go on incidents which are totally unlike, though synchronized with those that go on in Theatre A. These Theatre B spisodes are changes in the states, not of bits of flesh, but of something called 'consciousness,' which occupies no space. Only the proprietor of Theatre B has first-hand knowledge of what goes on in it. It is a secret theatre. The experimentalist tries to open its doors, but it has no doors. He tries to peep through its windows, but it has no windows. He is foiled.

We tend nowadays to treat it as obvious that a person, unlike a newt, lives the two lives, life 'A' and life 'B,' each completely unlike, though mysteriously geared to the other. In-grained hypotheses do feel obvious, however redundant they may be. The peasants in my story correctly thought that a steam-engine was hugely different from a cart and automatically but incorrectly explained the difference by postulating a ghost-horse inside. So most of us, correctly thinking that there are huge differences between a clock and a person, automatically but incorrectly explain these differences by postulating an extra set of ghost-works inside. We correctly say that people are not like clocks, since people meditate, calculate, and invent things; they make plans, dream dreams, and shirk their obligations; they get angry, feel depressed, scan the heavens, and have likes and dis-likes; they work, play, and idle; they are sane, crazy, or imbecile; they are skilful at some things and bunglers

at others. Where we go wrong is in explaining these familiar actions and conditions as the operations of a sec-ondary set of secret works.

Everybody knows quite well when to describe someone as acting absent-mindedly or with heed, as babbling deliriously or reasoning coherently, as feeling angry but not showing it, as wanting one thing but pretending to want another, as being ambitious, patriotic, or miserly. We often get our accounts and estimates of other people and of ourselves wrong; but we more often get them right. We did not need to learn the legend of the two theatres before we were able to talk sense about people and to deal effectively with them. Nor has this fairly new-fangled legend helped us to do it better.

When we read novels, biographies, and reminiscences, we do not find the chapters partitioned into Section 'A,' covering the hero's 'bodily' doings, and Section 'B,' covering his 'mental' doings. We find unpartitioned ac-counts of what he did and thought and felt, of what he said to others and to himself, of the mountains he tried to climb and the problems he tried to solve. Should an examiner mark the paper written by the candidate's hand but refuse to assess the candidate's wits? Theorists themselves, when actually describing people, sensibly forget Theatre A and Theatre B. Sir Charles Sherrington paid a well-de-served compliment to Professor Adrian, but he did not pay one cool compliment to Professor Adrian 'A' and another warmer compliment to Professor Adrian 'B.'

In saying that a person is not to be described as a mind coupled with a body I am not saying, with some truculent thinkers, that people are just machines. Nor are engines just wagons or live bodies just corpses. What is wrong with the story of the two theatres is not that it reports differences which are not there but that it misrepresents differences which are there. It is a story with the right characters but the wrong plot. It is an attempt to explain a genuine difference—or rather a galaxy of differences—but its effect, like that of the peasants' theory, is merely to reduplicate the thing to be explained. It says, 'The difference between a machine like a human body on the one hand and a human being on the other is that in a human being, besides the organs which we do see, there is a counterpart set of organs which we do not see; besides the causes and effects which we can witness, there is a counterpart series of causes and effects which we cannot witness.' So now we ask, 'But what explains the differences between what goes on in the Theatre B of a sane man and what goes on in that of a lunatic? A third theatre, Theatre C?'

No, what prevents us from examining Theatre B is not that it has no doors or windows, but that there is no such theatre. What prevented the peasants from finding the horse was not that it was a ghost-horse, but that there was no horse. None the less, the engine *was* different from a wagon and ordinary people *are* different not only from machines, but also from animals, imbeciles, infants, and corpses. They also differ in countless important ways from one another. I have not begun to show how we should grade these differences. I have only shown how we should not grade them.

One last word. In ordinary life (save when we want to sound knowing) we seldom use the noun 'Mind' or the adjective 'mental' at all. What we do is to talk of people, of people calculating, conjuring, hoping, resolving, tasting, bluffing, fretting, and so on. Nor, in ordinary life, do we talk of 'Matter' or of things being 'material.' What we do is to talk of steel, granite, and water; of wood, moss, and grain; of flesh, bone, and sinew. The umbrella-titles 'Mind' and 'Matter' obliterate the very differences that ought to interest us. Theorists should drop both these words. 'Mind' and 'Matter' are echoes from the hustings of philosophy and prejudice the solutions of all problems posed in terms of them.

QUESTIONS FOR DISCUSSION

1. What are Viscount Samuel's criticisms of materialism and idealism on the relation of the physiological to the mental?
2. Is there a "fallacy of reductionism" in both materialism and idealism?
3. Do you agree with Ayer's dismissal of the mind-body problem as a "pseudo-problem" or with his restatement of the problem? Explain his position and your reasons for agreeing or disagreeing with it.
4. What is your reaction to Ryle's argument against the use of the categories of Mind and Matter? What seems to be Ryle's preferred category in describing "mental phenomena"?

FURTHER READINGS FOR CHAPTER 5

*Bacon, Francis, *The Advancement of Learning* and *The New Atlantis*. New York: Oxford University Press, 1938.

*Butterfield, Herbert, *The Origins of Modern Science*, rev. ed. New York: Macmillan, 1957.

*Duhem, Pierre, *The Aim and Structure of Physical Theory*. Philip P. Wiener, trans. New York: Atheneum, 1962.

Feigl, Herbert, and May Brodbeck, eds., *Readings in the Philosophy of Science*. New York: Appleton-Century-Crofts, 1953.

*Frank, Philipp, *Modern Science and Its Philosophy*. New York: Collier Books, n.d.

Gillispie, Charles C., *The Edge of Objectivity*. Princeton: Princeton University Press, 1960.

*Mach, Ernst, *The Science of Mechanics*, 6th ed., T. J. McCormack, trans. LaSalle, Ill.: Open Court, 1960.

Mises, Richard von, *Positivism: A Study in Human Understanding*. New York: Braziller, 1956.

Morgenbesser, S., P. Suppes, and M. White, eds. *Philosophy, Science, and Method, Essays in Honor of Ernest Nagel*. New York: St. Martin's Press, 1969.

Nagel, Ernest, *et al.*, *Logic, Methodology and Philosophy of Science: Proceedings of the 1960 International Conference*. Stanford: Stanford University Press, 1962.

*Peirce, Charles S., *Selected Writings*. Philip P. Wiener, ed. New York: Dover, 1965.

*Poincaré, Henri, *Science and Hypothesis*, G. B. Halsted, trans. New York: Dover, n.d.

*———, *Science and Method*, Francis Maitland, trans. New York: Dover, n.d.

*———, *The Value of Science*, G. B. Halsted, trans. New York: Dover, n.d.

*Popper, Karl R., *The Logic of Scientific Discovery*. New York: Revised Torchbook Edition, Harper's, 1965.

*Russell, Bertrand, *Human Knowledge: Its Scope and Limits*. New York: Simon and Schuster, 1962.

Wiener, Philip P., ed., *Readings in Philosophy of Science*. New York: Scribner's, 1953.

—————

* Paperback edition.

Chapter **6**

THEORY OF KNOWLEDGE

INTRODUCTION

We all have a natural desire for knowledge, which is attested by our interest in what is perceived by our senses. Not content, however, with enjoying the sights and sounds that come to us without any effort on our part, we instinctively strive, by coordinating them, to locate their origin in material things—as when we hear the faint drone of a motor, we turn to look for a speck in the sky that we identify as a plane. Then we may be interested in tracing a causal chain and in anticipating the future; where did the plane come from, and what is its mission? In a similar way men have studied eclipses, growth, disease, and so on. Thus there gradually developed the sciences of astronomy, biology, medicine, and the others. Success in the scientific enterprise is rewarded by understanding, which may serve practical purposes, but is also, by the satisfaction it brings, its own reward. And failure, when recognized as such, can be a stimulus to search for hidden causes and to construct subtler explanations. The difficulties encountered in achieving knowledge of natural phenomena were not only a stimulus to the discovery of new scientific techniques; they were also the starting point of an inquiry into the nature of knowledge and how it differs from error. In fact, if nature had not proved baffling and man's grasp limited, the theory of knowledge might never have arisen. For it is the discovery of something apparently inexplicable and the desire to override error in human understanding that gave birth to this branch of philosophy. With error the inquirer into nature is brought up short; and because he wishes to avoid it, he inquires first into the sources of human error and then whether sense-perception or memory can give us genuine knowledge—free from the danger of error. Before long, if he is skeptically inclined, he is likely to find himself considering the question: Is any reliable knowledge of nature possible?

Whoever entertains this question, provided it is prompted by real doubt, or answers it in the negative, has joined the camp of the skeptic. There he will be in the company of many famous philosophers, though most of them remain for only a short visit. Descartes, as we have seen (selection 2.3), adopts universal doubt as a methodological device to help him rid his mind of illusions, prejudices, and the false notions taught him at school. His doubt, however, is only provisional. What he wants to show is that there are items of knowledge so indubitable that they can resist the most radical skepticism. In his theory of knowledge Descartes is anything but skeptical. Once he proves to his own satisfaction that God exists, he casts away doubt, affirming his readiness to believe anything that seems true to him, since he is convinced that God would not deceive him.

Although Descartes begins his philosophy by sweeping the slate clean and resolving to admit nothing about which the least doubt can be raised, he ends by demonstrating an unbounded faith in the power of the human mind to discover the nature of the world. George Berkeley, on the other hand, who proclaims his opposition to the skeptics, aims to convince us that no matter how hard we try to "conceive the existence of external bodies, we are all the while only contemplating our own ideas."

Berkely begins by attacking certain basic assumptions which had been taken for granted by scientists and philosophers for centuries. Among these was the view that we can perceive the existence of material bodies outside and independent of the mind by means of images or mental representations that are more or less faithful copies of the qualities of these bodies. John Locke, who adopted this theory of representative perception (sometimes called "the copy theory of knowledge"), made a distinction between qualities like extension and mobility which inhere in things (the primary or physical qualities), and the qualities like color, sound, taste, and so on, which are not in the objects themselves, but are effects produced by them on the mind (the secondary or sense-qualities).[1]

Locke accepted this view though it presents insuperable problems for his theory of knowledge. This theory contains the two following assumptions:

(1) that the mind can directly perceive only its own contents, which are variously called images, impressions, ideas; and

(2) that these ideas are distinct from one another.

The question that arises is: How can we know that our ideas truly represent the properties of existing things, since we can never perceive the things themselves, but only our own ideas of them? Locke struggled with this difficulty, but confessed he had no solution. He believed that our innate feeling of certainty was a sufficient guarantee of the validity of natural knowledge. As he himself puts it:

---

[1] It is interesting to note that the primary qualities were those which were amenable to the processes of measurement; the secondary qualities were thought to be incapable of measurement, and were regarded as subjective.

The notice we have by our senses, of the existence of things without us, though it be not altogether so certain as our intuitive knowledge, or the deductions of our reason employed about the clear abstract ideas of our own minds; yet it is an assurance that deserves the name of knowledge. If we persuade ourselves that our faculties act and inform us right, concerning the existence of those objects that affect them, it cannot pass for an ill-grounded confidence; for I think nobody can, in earnest, be so skeptical, as to be uncertain of the existence of those things which he sees and feels.

To the two epistemological premises which Locke assumed, Berkeley and Hume added a third, namely:

(3) that the existence of things "out there" which react on one another as well as on our minds can be accepted only if it can be validly inferred from the first two premises. In this respect they were more influenced than was Locke by the Cartesian method of doubt and quest for certainty. For both Berkeley and Hume the mind is encased in a framework of its own sensations and ideas from which it vainly endeavors to escape. Berkeley embraces this skeptical doctrine enthusiastically and with remarkable consistency. Hume, on the contrary, does so regretfully and haltingly. At times his own arguments fail to convince him, but he sees no way of answering them.

Berkeley and Hume did not share the confidence which Locke felt in the validity of our knowledge of nature—Berkeley concluding that there is nothing in the universe but minds, or spirits, and Hume that our knowledge of nature is restricted to a succession of disconnected events. Hume holds that the notion of an order of nature in which events are necessarily connected with other events is an illusion engendered by a mental habit. The seventeenth century British empiricists have a reputation for being hard-headed men of common sense, but the above three epistemological premises had so thoroughly infected their theory of knowledge with the germ of skepticism that the dictates of common sense were all but submerged.

To common sense it seems obvious that the "objects of knowledge" are chairs, tables, rivers and oceans, animals and other men, and not more or less reasonable facsimiles of the same. However, it is one thing to point out where the epistemology of Locke, Berkeley, and Hume does violence to common sense. It is quite another to construct an alternative theory of knowledge, based on common sense, which gives an adequate account of the nature of knowledge in such diverse fields as mathematics, natural science, and history. Many philosophers who have made such an attempt found in the end that they had to depart more or less from common-sense notions. Perhaps the "principles of common sense" are not as clear, when analyzed, as they appear to be. Perhaps they cannot be integrated into a consistent philosophy.

So far we have been discussing one facet of the theory of knowledge—its relation to skepticism. Closely connected with questions concerning the significance and reliability of our knowledge of nature is an issue prominent in the history of philosophy, which has been the subject of a long debate between empiricists, who adhere to the views of Locke, Berkeley, and Hume, and rationalists, who follow Descartes and Kant. Is all knowledge derived from experience as the former maintain, or are there truths known a priori, such as the law of causality [2] and the principle of induction,[3] which are presupposed for the significant interpretation of experience, as the latter insist?

Immanuel Kant, who writes that Hume's skeptical criticism of knowledge awakened him from his dogmatic slumbers, is credited by some with having successfully answered Hume's arguments. Kant's "answer" is in his *Critique of Pure Reason,* a work that has profoundly influenced modern philosophy. The gist of Kant's epistemology (theory of knowledge) is that all knowledge is compounded out of two factors: (1) what is given in experience, and (2) what is contributed by the interpretation of the mind. The "given in experience" is formless and chaotic and can enter into knowledge only by being transformed and ordered by the faculties of the mind. Far from being a blank tablet on which experience writes (Locke's view), the mind, for Kant, is the agency whose activity makes cognitive experience possible. Knowledge is not received by a passive intellect, but must be constructed by the mind, which impresses on the given, its own notions of *space* and *time* (called by Kant forms of intuition) and its own conceptions of *substance, quantity, quality, relation, causality* (categories of the understanding). These forms of intuition and categories of the understanding Kant believed were common possessions of all human minds. Reality can be known only as it is screened through the forms and categories of the mind. It then becomes what Kant calls a *phenomenon.* The "thing-in-itself," something that has an independent existence, is not and cannot be an object of knowledge; it is unknowable. For to know it, the mind would first have to impart to it its own forms of organization, thus transforming it. For this reason, in the opinion of some philosophers, the shadow of doubt that Hume cast over our knowledge of the natural world is not only not removed by Kant, but is converted by him into a curtain effectively placed between the external reality and the mind, thereby making knowledge a delusion. Philosophers have also questioned Kant's right to assume the existence of fixed and permanent faculties in all human minds; for this is an empirical question that Kant is deciding by an *ad hoc* hypothesis, an hypothesis that has not received the needed confirma-

---

[2] The law of causality, which is a favorite example of an a priori law, is difficult to state briefly and precisely; it has usually been taken to mean that every event has a cause and the same cause always has the same effect.

[3] The principle of induction states that repeated association of a group of things, events, or properties in the past affords a ground for believing that they will be so ordered in the future; and that the more often such an association of things has been observed, the stronger is the ground for inferring that they are universally connected in that way. Hume's skepticism is based on his attempt to undermine the law of causality and the principle of induction. See selection 6.2.

tion by psychologists and philosophers outside the Kantian schools. But interpreters of Kant are legion and they are far from unanimous in their reading and evaluation of the master's position. There is no doubt that the active, dominant role in knowledge which Kant assigned to the mind proved to be a needed and welcome change from the Humean conception of the mind as a discontinuous series of inert, momentary perceptions, no one of which contains within itself any inkling of a past or a future. The many post-Kantian and neo-Kantian movements that took their inspiration from Kant's philosophy, even while departing from it in many respects, are, in themselves, evidence enough of the suggestive and stimulating character of his thought.

A challenge of a different kind to skepticism was made by the contemporary British philosopher, G. E. Moore. In his famous "Defence of Common Sense," Moore asserts that he has no doubt whatsoever about the truth of a great many propositions that plain men have always taken for granted but that many philosophers have considered as open to doubt. Moore admits he doesn't know the correct analysis of these common-sense truths, but claims nevertheless that he *understands* them and knows with certainty that they are true.

Bertrand Russell, Moore's friend and colleague, is less concerned with defending common sense and more anxious to square his theory of knowledge with physical theory. Russell believes in the existence of a physical world, independent of our perceptions. He holds that we can know that this world and the world of our percepts have a similar structure; but once we have described the spatio-temporal structure of the world, that is all we can confidently say about it. The qualitative character of physical occurrences is unknown to us. We can infer that the sun is round because it looks round to us. This is because roundness is a structural property. But we can't say the sun is bright because it looks bright, since brightness is not a structural property. This is more than a little reminiscent of Locke's distinction between primary and secondary qualities.

By using ordinary words in unusual ways, Russell is able to say things that seem intended to astound his audience. For example, he holds that when a physiologist looks into a man's brain, he is really seeing an event in his own brain. This of course is not "seeing" as commonly used and understood.

Russell believes that common sense is wrong in thinking that we perceive things and events outside ourselves—that we see and touch physical objects, hear sounds and so forth. What we see, hear, and touch, he calls a *percept*, which is a private datum that no one else perceives. Although we cannot perceive physical objects, we can infer their existence from percepts, on certain conditions. The reason Russell gives for taking issue with common sense is that physics has shown the physical object to be quite different from our percept except in "abstract structural respects." Also, when two people claim they are perceiving the same object, they are actually having percepts that differ qualitatively from each other; one may be brighter, or larger, or look more bluish than greenish, etc., whereas we hold that a physical object cannot be both large and small, blue and green, etc., at the same time.

Knowledge, for Russell, is a matter of degree. The highest degree is found in facts of perception, and these are known without inference. At the other end is our knowledge of physical events, which we acquire by inference and which is restricted to their space-time structure. Clearly, Russell's epistemology belongs to the tradition of seventeenth century British empiricism.

The methodology of Descartes, as we saw in Chapter 2, while resolved to doubt everything, accepted certain beliefs as true. One was the belief that there is some agency responsible for reasoning, remembering, imagining, doubting. And if one accepts that there is thinking, then there must be a thing that does the thinking. Descartes called this thinking thing a *substance,* to show that he believed it existed as a distinct thing and not as a dependent part of a larger whole. But how could this thinking thing act on the body or be affected by it? Descartes' answer tried to describe the body's changes as if they were part of a mechanical system, while the mind belongs to a totally different, spiritual realm. The contemporary British philosopher Gilbert Ryle has labeled Descartes' view "the theory of the ghost in the machine" (selection 6.5). We have long realized that the body is very far from being a machine, and Ryle thinks it is about time we got rid of the ghost.

George Berkeley (1685-1753)

6.1   Of the Principles
of Human Knowledge

1. It is evident to anyone who takes a survey of the *objects of human knowledge,* that they are either *ideas* actually imprinted on the senses; or else such as are perceived by attending to the passions and operations of the mind; or lastly, *ideas* formed by help of memory and imagination—either compounding, dividing, or barely representing those originally perceived in the aforesaid ways. By sight I have the ideas of light and colors, with their several degrees and variations. By touch I perceive hard and soft, heat and cold, motion and resistance; and of all these more and less either as to quantity or degree. Smelling furnishes me with odors; the palate with tastes; and hearing conveys sounds to the mind in all their variety of tone and composition.

And as several of these are observed to accompany each other, they come to be marked by one name, and so to be reputed as one *thing.* Thus, for example, a certain color, taste, smell, figure, and consistence, having been observed to go together, are accounted one distinct thing, signified

From *A Treatise Concerning the Principles of Human Knowledge* (1710).

by the name apple; other collections of ideas constitute a stone, a tree, a book, and the like sensible things; which as they are pleasing or disagreeable excite the passions of love, hatred, joy, grief, and so forth.

2. But, besides all that endless variety of ideas or objects of knowledge, there is likewise Something which knows or perceives them; and exercises diverse operations, as willing, imagining, remembering, about them. This perceiving, active being is what I call *mind, spirit, soul,* or *myself.* By which words I do not denote any one of my ideas, but a thing entirely distinct from them, wherein they exist, or, which is the same thing, whereby they are perceived; for the existence of an idea consists in being perceived.

3. That neither our thoughts, nor passions, nor ideas formed by the imagination, exist without the mind is what everybody will allow. And to me it seems no less evident that the various sensations or ideas imprinted on the Sense, however blended or combined together (that is, whatever objects they compose), cannot exist otherwise than in a mind perceiving them. I think an intuitive knowledge may be obtained of this, by anyone that shall attend to what is meant by

the term *exist* when applied to sensible things. The table I write on I say exists; that is, I see and feel it: and if I were out of my study I should say it existed; meaning thereby that if I was in my study I might perceive it, or that some other spirit actually does perceive it. There was an odor, that is, it was smelt; there was a sound, that is, it was heard; a color or figure, and it was perceived by sight or touch. This is all that I can understand by these and the like expressions. For as to what is said of the *absolute* existence of unthinking things, without any relation to their being perceived, that is to me perfectly unintelligible. Their *esse* is *percipi;* nor is it possible they should have any existence out of the minds or thinking things which perceive them.

4. It is indeed an opinion strangely prevailing amongst men, that houses, mountains, rivers, and in a word all sensible objects, have an existence, natural or real, distinct from their being perceived by the understanding. But with how great an assurance and acquiescence soever this Principle may be entertained in the world, yet whoever shall find in his heart to call it in question may, if I mistake not, perceive it to involve a manifest contradicition. For, what are the forementioned objects but the things we perceive by sense? and what do we perceive besides our own ideas or sensations? and is it not plainly repugnant that any one of these, or any combination of them, should exist unperceived?

5. If we thoroughly examine this tenet it will, perhaps, be found at bottom to depend on the doctrine of *abstract ideas.* For can there be a nicer strain of abstraction than to distinguish the existence of sensible objects from their being perceived, so as to conceive them existing unperceived? Light and colors, heat and cold, extension and figures—in a word, the things we see and feel—what are they but so many sensations, notions, ideas, or impressions on the sense? and is it possible to separate, even in thought, any of these from perception? For my part, I might as easily divide a thing from itself. I may, indeed, divide in my thoughts, or conceive apart from each other, those things which perhaps I never perceived by sense so divided. Thus, I imagine the trunk of a human body without the limbs, or conceive the smell of a rose without thinking on the rose itself. So far, I will not deny, I can abstract; if that may properly be called *abstraction* which extends only to the conceiving separately such objects as it is possible may really exist or be actually perceived asunder. But my conceiving or imagining power does not extend beyond the possibility of real existence or perception. Hence, as it is impossible for me to see or feel anything without an actual sensation of that thing, so is it impossible for me to conceive in my thoughts any sensible thing or object distinct from the sensation or perception of it. (In truth, the object and the sensation are the same thing, and cannot therefore be abstracted from each other.)

6. Some truths there are so near and obvious to the mind that a man need only open his eyes to see them. Such I take this important one to be, viz., that all the choir of heaven and furniture of the earth, in a word, all those bodies which compose the mighty frame of the world, have not any subsistence without a mind; that their *being* is to be perceived or

known; that consequently so long as they are not actually perceived by me, or do not exist in my mind, or that of any other created spirit, they must either have no existence at all, or else subsist in the mind of some Eternal Spirit: it being perfectly unintelligible, and involving all the absurdity of abstraction, to attribute to any single part of them an existence independent of a spirit. (To be convinced of which, the reader need only reflect, and try to separate in his own thoughts the *being* of a sensible thing from its *being perceived.*)

7. From what has been said it is evident there is not any other Substance than *Spirit*, or that which perceives. But, for the fuller proof of this point, let it be considered the sensible qualities are color, figure, motion, smell, taste, and such like, that is, the ideas perceived by sense. Now, for an idea to exist in an unperceiving thing is a manifest contradiction; for to have an idea is all one as to perceive: that therefore wherein color, figure, and the like qualities exist must perceive them. Hence, it is clear there can be no thinking substance or *substratum* of those ideas.

8. But, say you, though the ideas themselves do not exist without the mind, yet there may be things like them, whereof they are copies or resemblances; which things exist without the mind, in an unthinking substance. I answer, an idea can be like nothing but an idea; a color or figure can be like nothing but another color or figure. If we look but never so little into our thoughts, we shall find it impossible for us to conceive a likeness except only between our ideas. Again, I ask whether those supposed *originals*, or external things, of which our ideas are the pictures or representations, be themselves perceivable or no? If they are, then *they* are ideas, and we have gained our point: but if you say they are not, I appeal to anyone whether it be sense to assert a color is like something which is invisible; hard or soft, like something which is intangible; and so of the rest.

9. Some there are who make a distinction betwixt *primary* and *secondary* qualities. By the former they mean extension, figure, motion, rest, solidity or impenetrability, and number; by the latter they denote all other sensible qualities, as colors sounds, tastes, and so forth. The ideas we have of these last they acknowledge not to be the resemblances of anything existing without the mind, or unperceived; but they will have our ideas of the *primary qualities* to be patterns or images of things which exist without the mind, in an unthinking substance which they call Matter. By Matter, therefore, we are to understand an inert, senseless substance, in which extension, figure, and motion do actually subsist. But it is evident, from what we have already shown, that extension, figure, and motion are only ideas existing in the mind, and that an idea can be like nothing but another idea; and that consequently neither they nor their archetypes can exist in an unperceiving substance. Hence, it is plain that the very notion of what is called *Matter*, of *corporeal substance*, involves a contradiction in it. . . .

18. But, though it were possible that solid, figured, movable substances may exist without the mind, corresponding to the ideas we have of bodies, yet how is it possible for us to know this? Either we must know it by Sense or by Reason. As for our

senses, by them we have the knowledge only of our sensations, ideas, or those things that are immediately perceived by sense, call them what you will: but they do not inform us that things exist without the mind, or unperceived, like to those which are perceived. This the materialists themselves acknowledge. It remains, therefore, that if we have any knowledge at all of external things, it must be by reason inferring their existence from what is immediately perceived by sense. But [I do not see] what reason can induce us to believe the existence of bodies without the mind, from what we perceive, since the very patrons of Matter themselves do not pretend there is any necessary connection betwixt them and our ideas? I say it is granted on all hands (and what happens in dream, frenzies, and the like, puts it beyond dispute) that it is possible we might be affected with all the ideas we have now, though no bodies existed without resembling them. Hence, it is evident the supposition of external bodies is not necessary for the producing our ideas; since it is granted they are produced sometimes, and might possibly be produced always, in the same order we see them in at present, without their concurrence.

19. But, though we might possibly have all our sensations without them, yet perhaps it may be thought easier to conceive and explain the manner of their production, by supposing external bodies in their likeness rather than otherwise; and so it might be at least probable there are such things as bodies that excite their ideas in our minds. But neither can this be said. For, though we give the materialists their external bodies, they by their own confession are never the nearer knowing how our ideas are produced; since they own themselves unable to comprehend in what manner body can act upon spirit, or how it is possible it should imprint any idea in the mind. Hence, it is evident the production of ideas or sensations in our minds can be no reason why we should suppose Matter or corporeal substances, since that is acknowledged to remain equally inexplicable with or without this supposition. If, therefore, it were possible for bodies to exist without the mind, yet to hold they do so must needs be a very precarious opinion; since it is to suppose, without any reason at all, that God has created innumerable beings that are entirely useless, and serve to no manner of purpose.

20. In short, if there were external bodies, it is impossible we should ever come to know it; and if there were not, we might have the very same reasons to think there were that we have now. Suppose—what no one can deny possible—an intelligence, without the help of external bodies, to be affected with the same train of sensations or ideas that you are, imprinted in the same order and with like vividness in his mind. I ask whether that intelligence hath not all the reason to believe the existence of Corporeal Substances, represented by his ideas, and exciting them in his mind, that you can possibly have for believing the same thing? Of this there can be no question. Which one consideration were enough to make any reasonable person suspect the strength of whatever arguments he may think himself to have, for the existence of bodies without the mind. . . .

23. But, say you, surely there is nothing easier than for me to imag-

ine trees, for instance, in a park, or books existing in a closet, and nobody by to perceive them. I answer, you may so, there is no difficulty in it. But what is all this, I beseech you, more than framing in your mind certain ideas which you call *books* and *trees,* and at the same time omitting to frame the idea of anyone that may perceive them? But do not you yourself perceive or think of them all the while? This therefore is nothing to the purpose: it only shows you have the power of imagining, or forming ideas in your mind; but it does not show that you can conceive it possible the objects of your thought may exist without the mind. To make out this, it is necessary that you conceive them existing unconceived or unthought of; which is a manifest repugnancy. When we do our utmost to conceive the existence of external bodies, we are all the while only contemplating our own ideas. But the mind, taking no notice of itself, is deluded to think it can and does conceive bodies existing unthought of, or without the mind, though at the same time they are apprehended by, or exist in, itself. A little attention will discover to anyone the truth and evidence of what is here said, and make it unnecessary to insist on any other proofs against the existence of *material substance.* . . .

33. The ideas imprinted on the Senses by the Author of nature are called *real things:* and those excited in the imagination, being less regular, vivid, and constant, are more properly termed *ideas* or *images of* things, which they copy and represent. But then our *sensations,* be they never so vivid and distinct, are nevertheless ideas: that is, they exist in the mind, or are perceived by it, as truly as the ideas of its own framing. The ideas of Sense are allowed to have more reality in them, that is, to be more strong, orderly, and coherent than the creatures of the mind; but this is no argument that they exist without the mind. They are also less dependent on the spirit or thinking substance which perceives them, in that they are excited by the will of another and more powerful Spirit: yet still they are *ideas* and certainly no idea, whether faint or strong, can exist otherwise than in a mind perceiving it.

34. Before we proceed any farther it is necessary we spend some time in answering Objections which may probably be made against the Principles we have hitherto laid down. In doing of which, if I seem too prolix to those of quick apprehensions, I desire I may be excused, since all men do not equally apprehend things of this nature; and I am willing to be understood by everyone.

First, then, it will be objected that by the foregoing principles all that is real and substantial in nature is banished out of the world, and instead thereof a chimerical scheme of *ideas* takes place. All things that exist, exist only in the mind; that is, they are purely notional. What, therefore, becomes of the sun, moon, and stars? What must we think of houses, rivers, mountains, trees, stones; nay, even of our bodies? Are all these but so many chimeras and illusions on the fancy? To all which, and whatever else of the same sort may be objected, I answer, that by the Principles premised we are not deprived of any one thing in nature. Whatever we see, feel, hear, or anywise conceive or understand, remains as secure as ever, and is as real as ever. There is a *rerum natura,* and the distinction between realities and chimeras retains its full force. . . .

35. I do not argue against the existence of any one thing that we can apprehend, either by sense, or reflection. That the things I see with my eyes and touch with my hands do exist, really exist, I make not the least question. The only thing whose existence we deny is that which *philosophers* call Matter or corporeal substance. And in doing of this there is no damage done to the rest of mankind, who, I dare say, will never miss it. The Atheist, indeed, will want the color of an empty name to support his impiety; and the Philosophers may possibly find they have lost a great handle for trifling and disputation. (But that is all the harm that I can see done.)

36. If any man thinks this detracts from the existence or reality of things, he is very far from understanding what hath been premised in the plainest terms I could think of. Take here an abstract of what has been said: there are spiritual substances, minds, or human souls, which will or excite ideas in themselves at pleasure; but these are faint, weak, and unsteady in respect of others they perceive by sense: which, being impressed upon them according to certain rules or laws of nature, speak themselves the effects of a Mind more powerful and wise than human spirits. These latter are said to have *more reality* in them than the former; by which is meant that they are more affecting, orderly, and distinct, and that they are not fictions of the mind perceiving them. And in this sense the sun that I see by day is the real sun, and that which I imagine by night is the idea of the former. In

the sense here given of *reality,* it is evident that every vegetable, star, mineral, and, in general, each part of the mundane system, is as much a *real being* by our principles as by any other. Whether others mean anything by the term *reality* different from what I do, I entreat them to look into their own thoughts and see.

37. It will be urged that this much at least is true, to wit, that we take away all *corporeal substances.* To this my answer is, that if the word *substance* be taken in the vulgar sense, for a *combination* of sensible qualities, such as extension, solidity, weight, and the like—this we cannot be accused of taking away: but if it be taken in a philosophic sense, for the support of accidents or qualities without the mind—then, indeed, I acknowledge that we take it away, if one may be said to take away that which never had any existence, not even in the imagination.

38. But after all, say you, it sounds very harsh to say we eat and drink ideas, and are clothed with ideas. I acknowledge it does so—the word *idea* not being used in common discourse to signify the several combinations of sensible qualities which are called *things;* and it is certain that any expression which varies from the familiar use of language will seem harsh and ridiculous. But this doth not concern the truth of the proposition, which, in other words, is no more than to say we are fed and clothed with those things which we perceive immediately by our senses. The hardness or softness, the color, taste, warmth, figure, and such-like qualities, which combined together constitute the several sorts of victuals and apparel, have been shown to exist only in the mind that perceives

them: and this is all that is meant by calling them *ideas;* which word, if it was as ordinarily used as *thing,* would sound no harsher nor more ridiculous than it. I am not for disputing about the propriety but the truth of the expression. If, therefore, you agree with me that we eat and drink and are clad with the immediate objects of sense, which cannot exist unperceived or without the mind, I shall readily grant it is more proper or conformable to custom that they should be called *things* rather than *ideas.*

39. If it be demanded why I make use of the word *idea,* and do not rather in compliance with custom call them *things,* I answer, I do it for two reasons—first, because the term *thing,* in contradistinction to *idea,* is generally supposed to denote somewhat existing without the mind: secondly, because *thing* hath a more comprehensive signification than *idea,* including spirits, or thinking things, as well as ideas. Since, therefore, the objects of sense exist only in the mind, and are withal thoughtless and inactive, I chose to mark them by the word *idea,* which implies those properties.

40. But, say what we can, someone perhaps may be apt to reply, he will still believe his senses, and never suffer any arguments, how plausible soever, to prevail over the certainty of them. Be it so; assert the evidence of sense as high as you please, we are willing to do the same. That what I see, hear, and feel doth exist, that is to say, is perceived by me, I no more doubt than I do of my own being. But I do not see how the testimony of sense can be alleged as a proof for the existence of anything which is *not* perceived by sense. We are not for having any man turn sceptic and disbelieve his senses; on the contrary, we give them all the stress and assurance imaginable; nor are there any principles more opposite to Scepticism than those we have laid down. . . .

41. Secondly, it will be objected that there is a great difference betwixt real fire, for instance, and the idea of fire, betwixt dreaming or imagining oneself burnt, and actually being so. (If you suspect it to be only the idea of fire which you see, do but put your hand into it and you will be convinced with a witness.) This and the like may be urged in opposition to our tenets. To all which the answer is evident from what hath been already said; and I shall only add in this place that if real fire be very different from the idea of fire, so also is the real pain that it occasions very different from the idea of the same pain, and yet nobody will pretend that real pain either is, or can possibly be, in an unperceiving thing, or without the mind, any more than its idea.

QUESTIONS FOR DISCUSSION

1. Show how Berkeley tries to convince you that to be is to be perceived (*esse* is *percipi*) by examining his analysis of the meaning of the word "exist" as applied to a table, an odor, a color. Is there any important difference between the way he explains what it means for an odor or a color to exist and

the way he explains the meaning of saying that the table exists?

2. Berkeley holds that the notion of what is called Matter or corporeal substance involves a contradiction. What is the contradiction? How does Berkeley show it? Are you convinced?

3. Examine the proofs that Berkeley gives against the existence of Matter, or material substance.

4. Berkeley contends that his veiw is the natural or common sense position and that his opponents' view is "strange and unconvincing." Examine his reasoning. Do you agree?

5. Berkeley denies that corporeal substances exist outside the mind and holds that even if such substances did exist, we could never know of them. The position of his opponents who believe there are material substances outside the mind, and that we do know of their existence, he labels *skepticism*. Look up the word *skepticism* in an unabridged dictionary or philosophical encyclopedia and try to decide what Berkeley means by a skeptic, why he considers himself no skeptic, and why he is opposed to skepticism.

6. In denying the existence of Matter, Berkeley claims he is not arguing "against the existence of any one thing that we can apprehend, either by sense, or reflection." In that case, would you say there is a real or only a terminological difference of opinion between Berkeley and the materialists against whom he is arguing? Explain your answer.

David Hume (1711-1776)

6.2   An Inquiry
Concerning Human Understanding

SECTION IV

Sceptical Doubts Concerning the Operations of the Understanding

PART I

All the objects of human reason or inquiry may naturally be divided into two kinds, to wit, *Relations of Ideas,* and *Matters of Fact.* Of the first kind are the sciences of Geometry, Algebra, and Arithmetic; and in short, every affirmation which is either intuitively or demonstratively certain. *That the square of the hypothenuse is equal to the square of the two sides,* is a proposition which expresses a relation between these figures. *That three times five is equal to the half of thirty,* expresses a relation between these numbers. Propositions of this kind are discoverable by the mere operation of thought, without dependence on what is anywhere existent in the universe. Though there never were a circle or triangle in nature, the truths demonstrated by Euclid would forever retain their certainty and evidence.

From *An Inquiry Concerning Human Understanding* (1748).

Matters of fact, which are the second objects of human reason, are not ascertained in the same manner; nor is our evidence of their truth, however great, of a like nature with the foregoing. The contrary of every matter of fact is still possible; because it can never imply a contradiction, and is conceived by the mind with the same facility and distinctness, as if ever so conformable to reality. *That the sun will not rise tomorrow* is no less intelligible a proposition, and implies no more contradiction than the affirmation *that it will rise.* We should in vain, therefore, attempt to demonstrate its falsehood. Were it demonstratively false, it would imply a contradiction and could never be distinctly conceived by the mind.

It may, therefore, be a subject worthy of curiosity, to inquire what is the nature of that evidence which assures us of any real existence and matter of fact, beyond the present testimony of our senses, or the records of our memory. This part of philosophy, it is observable, has been little cultivated, either by the ancients or moderns; and, therefore, our doubts and errors, in the prosecution of so important an inquiry, may be the more excusable; while we march through such difficult paths without any guide or direction. They may even prove useful, by exciting curiosity, and destroying that implicit faith and security, which is the bane of all reasoning and free inquiry. The discovery of defects in the common philosophy, if any such there be, will not, I presume, be a discouragement, but rather an incitement, as is usual, to attempt something more full and satisfactory than has yet been proposed to the public.

All reasonings concerning matter of fact seem to be founded on the relation of *Cause and Effect.* By means of that relation alone we can go beyond the evidence of our memory and senses. If you were to ask a man why he believes any matter of fact which is absent; for instance, that his friend is in the country, or in France; he would give you a reason; and this reason would be some other fact; as a letter received from him, or the knowledge of his former resolutions and promises. A man finding a watch or any other machine in a desert island would conclude that there had once been men on that island. All our reasonings concerning fact are of the same nature. And here it is constantly supposed that there is a connection between the present fact and that which is inferred from it. Were there nothing to bind them together, the inference would be entirely precarious. The hearing of an articulate voice and rational discourse in the dark assures us of the presence of some person: Why? because these are the effects of the human make and fabric, and closely connected with it. If we anatomize all the other reasonings of this nature, we shall find that they are founded on the relation of cause and effect, and that this rela-

tion is either near or remote, direct or collateral. Heat and light are collateral effects of fire, and the one effect may justly be inferred from the other.

If we would satisfy ourselves, therefore, concerning the nature of that evidence, which assures us of matters of fact, we must inquire how we arrive at the knowledge of cause and effect.

I shall venture to affirm, as a general proposition, which admits of no exception, that the knowledge of this relation is not, in any instance, attained by reasonings *a priori;* but arises entirely from experience, when we find that any particular objects are constantly conjoined with each other. Let an object be presented to a man of ever so strong natural reason and abilities; if that object be entirely new to him, he will not be able, by the most accurate examination of its sensible qualities, to discover any of its causes or effects. Adam, though his rational faculties be supposed, at the very first, entirely perfect, could not have inferred from the fluidity and transparency of water that it would suffocate him, or from the light and warmth of fire that it would consume him. No object ever discovers, by the qualities which appear to the senses, either the causes which produced it, or the effects which will arise from it; nor can our reason, unassisted by experience, ever draw any inference concerning real existence and matter of fact.

This proposition, *that causes and effects are discoverable, not by reason but by experience,* will readily be admitted with regard to such objects as we remember to have once been altogether unknown to us, since we must be conscious of the utter inability, which we then lay under, of foretelling what would arise from them. Present two smooth pieces of marble to a man who has no tincture of natural philosophy; he will never discover that they will adhere together in such a manner as to require great force to separate them in a direct line, while they make so small a resistance to a lateral pressure. Such events, as bear little analogy to the common course of nature, are also readily confessed to be known only by experience; nor does any man imagine that the explosion of gunpowder, or the attraction of a loadstone, could ever be discovered by arguments *a priori*. In like manner, when an effect is supposed to depend upon an intricate machinery or secret structure of parts, we make no difficulty in attributing all our knowledge of it to experience. Who will assert that he can give the ultimate reason why milk or bread is proper nourishment for a man, not for a lion or a tiger?

But the same truth may not appear, at first sight, to have the same evidence with regard to events, which have become familiar to us from our first appearance in the world, which bear a close analogy to the whole course of nature, and which are supposed to depend on the simple qualities of objects, without any secret structure of parts. We are apt to imagine that we could discover these effects by the mere operation of our reason, without experience. We fancy, that were we brought on a sudden into this world, we could at first have inferred that one billiard ball would communicate motion to another upon impulse; and that we needed not to have waited for the event, in order to pronounce with certainty concern-

ing it. Such is the influence of custom, that, where it is strongest, it not only covers our natural ignorance, but even conceals itself, and seems not to take place, merely because it is found in the highest degree.

But to convince us that all the laws of nature, and all the operations of bodies without exception, are known only by experience, the following reflections may, perhaps, suffice. Were any object presented to us, and were we required to pronounce concerning the effect which will result from it, without consulting past observation, after what manner, I beseech you, must the mind proceed in this operation? It must invent or imagine some event, which it ascribes to the object as its effect; and it is plain that this invention must be entirely arbitrary. The mind can never possibly find the effect in the supposed cause, by the most accurate scrutiny and examination. For the effect is totally different from the cause, and consequently can never be discovered in it. Motion in the second billiard ball is a quite distinct event from motion in the first; nor is there anything in the one to suggest the smallest hint of the other. A stone or piece of metal raised into the air, and left without any support, immediately falls; but to consider the matter *a priori*, is there anything we discover in this situation which can beget the idea of a downward, rather than an upward, or any other motion, in the stone or metal?

And as the first imagination or invention of a particular effect, in all natural operations, is arbitrary, where we consult not experience; so must we also esteem the supposed tie or connection between the cause and effect, which binds them together, and renders it impossible that any other effect could result from the operation of that cause. When I see, for instance, a billiard ball moving in a straight line towards another; even suppose motion in the second ball should by accident be suggested to me, as the result of their contact or impulse; may I not conceive, that a hundred different events might as well follow from that cause? May not both these balls remain at absolute rest? May not the first ball return in a straight line, or leap off from the second in any line or direction? All these suppositions are consistent and conceivable. Why then should we give preference to one, which is no more consistent or conceivable than the rest? *All our reasonings a priori will never be able to show us any foundation for this preference.*

In a word, then, *every effect is a distinct event from its cause.* It could not, therefore, be discovered in the cause, and the first invention or conception of it, *a priori,* must be entirely arbitrary. And even after it is suggested, the conjunction of it with the cause must appear equally arbitrary; since there are always many other effects, which, to reason, must seem fully as consistent and natural. In vain, therefore, should we pretend to determine any single event, or infer any cause or effect, without the assistance of observation and experience.

Hence, we may discover the reason why no philosopher, who is rational and modest, has ever pretended to assign the ultimate cause of any natural operation, or to show distinctly the action of that power, which produces any single effect in the universe. It is confessed that the utmost effort of human reason is to reduce the principles, productive of natural phenomena, to a greater simplicity, and to resolve the many particular effects into a few general causes by means of reasonings from analogy, experience, and observation. But as to the causes of these general causes, we should in vain attempt their discovery; nor shall we ever be able to satisfy ourselves by any particular explication of them. These ultimate springs and principles are totally shut up from human curiosity and inquiry. Elasticity, gravity, cohesion of parts, communication of motion by impulse—these are probably the ultimate causes and principles which we shall ever discover in nature; and we may esteem ourselves sufficiently happy, if, by accurate inquiry and reasoning, we can trace up the particular phenomena to, or near to, these general principles. The most perfect philosophy of the natural kind only staves off our ignorance a little longer: as perhaps the most perfect philosophy of the moral or metaphysical kind serves only to discover larger portions of it. Thus the observation of human blindness and weakness is the result of all philosophy, and meets us at every turn, in spite of our endeavors to elude or avoid it.

Nor is geometry, when taken into the assistance of natural philosophy, ever able to remedy this defect, or lead us into the knowledge of ultimate causes, by all that accuracy of reasoning for which it is so justly celebrated. Every part of mixed mathematics proceeds upon the supposition that certain laws are established by nature in her operations; and abstract reasonings are employed, either to assist experience in the discovery of these laws, or to determine their influence in particular instances, where it depends upon any precise degree of distance and quantity. Thus, it is a law of motion, discovered by experience, that the moment or force of any body in motion is in the compound ratio or proportion of its solid contents and its velocity; and consequently, that a small force may remove the greatest obstacle or raise the greatest weight, if, by any contrivance or machinery, we can increase the velocity of that force, so as to make it an overmatch for its antagonist. Geometry assists us in the application of this law, by giving us the just dimensions of all the parts and figures which can enter into any species of machine; but still the discovery of the law itself is owing merely to experience, and all the abstract reasonings in the world could never lead us one step towards the knowledge of it. When we reason *a priori*, and consider merely any object or cause as it appears to the mind, independent of all observation, it never could suggest to us the notion of any distinct object, such as its effect; much less, show us the inseparable and inviolable connection between them. A man must be very sagacious who could discover by reasoning that crystal is the effect of heat, and ice of cold, without being previously acquainted with the operation of these qualities.

PART II

But we have not yet attained any tolerable satisfaction with regard to the question first proposed. Each solution still gives rise to a new question as difficult as the foregoing, and leads us on to farther inquiries. When it is asked, *What is the nature of all our reasonings concerning matter of fact?* the proper answer seems to be, that they are founded on the relation of cause and effect. When again it is asked, *What is the foundation of all our reasonings and conclusions concerning that relation?* it may be replied in one word, Experience. But if we still carry on our sifting humor, and ask, *What is the foundation of all conclusions from experience?* this implies a new question, which may be of more difficult solution and explication. Philosophers, that give themselves airs of superior wisdom and sufficiency, have a hard task when they encounter persons of inquisitive dispositions, who push them from every corner to which they retreat, and who are sure at last to bring them to some dangerous dilemma. The best expedient to prevent this confusion is to be modest in our pretensions; and even to discover the difficulty ourselves before it is objected to us. By this means, we may make a kind of merit of our very ignorance.

I shall content myself, in this section, with an easy task, and shall pretend only to give a negative answer to the question here proposed. I say then, that, even after we have experience of the operations of cause and effect, our conclusions from that experience are *not* founded on reasoning, or any process of the understanding. This answer we must endeavor both to explain and to defend.

It must certainly be allowed that nature has kept us at a great distance from all her secrets, and has afforded us only the knowledge of a few superficial qualities of objects, while she conceals from us those powers and principles on which the influence of those objects entirely depends. Our senses inform us of the color, weight, and consistence of bread; but neither sense nor reason can ever inform us of those qualities which fit it for the nourishment and support of a human body. Sight or feeling conveys an idea of the actual motion of bodies; but as to that wonderful force or power, which would carry on a moving body forever in a continued change of place, and which bodies never lose but by communicating it to others; of this we cannot form the most distant conception. But notwithstanding this ignorance of natural powers and principles, we always presume, when we see like sensible qualities, that they have like secret powers, and expect that effects, similar to those which we have experienced, will follow from them. If a body of like color and consistence with that bread, which we have formerly eaten, be presented to us, we make no scruple of repeating the experiment, and foresee, with certainty, like nourishment and support. Now this is a process of the mind or thought, of which I would willingly know the foundation. It is allowed on all hands that there is no known connection between the sensible qualities and the secret powers; and consequently, that the mind is not led to form such a conclusion concerning their constant and regular conjunction, by anything which it knows of their nature. As to past *Experience*, it can be allowed to give *direct* and *certain* information of those precise objects only, and that precise period of time, which fell under its cognizance: but why this experience should be extended to future times, and to other objects, which for aught we know, may be only in appearance similar; this is the main question on which I would insist. The bread, which I formerly ate, nourished me; that is, a body of such sensible qualities was, at that time, endued with such secret powers: but does it follow, that other bread must also nourish me at another time, and that like sensible qualities must always be attended with like secret powers? The consequence seems nowise necessary. At least, it must be acknowledged that there is here a consequence drawn by the mind; that there is a certain step taken; a process of thought, and an inference, which wants to be explained. These two propositions are far from being the same; *I have found that such an object has always been attended with such an effect*, and *I foresee, that other objects, which are, in appearance, similar, will be attended with similar effects*. I shall allow, if you please, that the one proposition may justly be inferred from the other: I know, in fact, that it always is inferred. But if you insist that the inference is made by a chain of reasoning, I desire you to produce that reasoning. The connection between these propositions is not intuitive. There is required a medium, which may enable the mind to draw such an inference, if indeed it be drawn by reasoning and argument. What that medium is, I must confess, passes my comprehension; and it is incumbent on those to produce it, who assert that it really exists, and is the origin of all our conclusions concerning matter of fact.

This negative argument must certainly, in process of time, become altogether convincing, if many penetrating and able philosophers shall turn their inquiries this way and no one be ever able to discover any connecting proposition or intermediate step which supports the understanding in this conclusion. But as the question is yet new, every reader may not trust so far to his own penetration as to conclude, because an argument escapes his inquiry, that therefore it does not really exist. For this reason it may be requisite to venture upon a more difficult task; and, enumerating all the branches of human knowledge, endeavor to show that none of them can afford such an argument.

All reasonings may be divided into two kinds, namely, demonstrative reasoning, or that concerning relations of ideas, and moral reasoning, or that concerning matter of fact and existence. That there are no demonstrative arguments in the case seems evident; since it implies no contradiction that the course of nature may change, and that an object, seemingly like those which we have experienced, may be attended with different or contrary effects. May I not clearly and distinctly conceive that a body, falling from the clouds, and which, in all other respects, resembles snow, has yet the taste of salt or feeling of fire? Is there any more intelligible proposition than to affirm that all the trees will flourish in December and January, and decay in May and June? Now whatever is intelligible, and can be distinctly conceived, implies no contradiction, and can never be proved false by any demonstrative argument or abstract reasoning a priori.

If we be, therefore, engaged by arguments to put trust in past experience, and make it the standard of our future judgment, these arguments must be probable only, or such as regard matter of fact and real existence, according to the division above mentioned. But that there is no argument of this kind, must appear, if our explication of that species of reasoning be admitted as solid and satisfactory. We have said that all arguments concerning existence are founded on the relation of cause and effect; that our knowledge of that

relation is derived entirely from experience; and that all our experimental conclusions proceed upon the supposition that the future will be conformable to the past. To endeavor, therefore, the proof of this last supposition by probable arguments, or arguments regarding existence, must be evidently going in a circle, and taking that for granted which is the very point in question.

In reality, all arguments from experience are founded on the similarity which we discover among natural objects, and by which we are induced to expect effects similar to those which we have found to follow from such objects. And though none but a fool or madman will ever pretend to dispute the authority of experience, or to reject that great guide of human life, it may surely be allowed a philosopher to have so much curiosity at least as to examine the principle of human nature, which gives this mighty authority to experience, and makes us draw advantage from that similarity which nature has placed among different objects. From causes which appear *similar* we expect similar effects. This is the sum of all our experimental conclusions. Now it seems evident that, if this conclusion were formed by reason, it would be as perfect at first, and upon one instance, as after ever so long a course of experience. But the case is far otherwise. Nothing so like as eggs; yet no one, on account of this appearing similarity, expects the same taste and relish in all of them. It is only after a long course of uniform experiments in any kind, that we attain a firm reliance and security with regard to a particular event. Now where is that process of reasoning which, from one instance, draws a conclusion so different from that which it infers from a hundred instances that are nowise different from that single one? This question I propose as much for the sake of information, as with an intention of raising difficulties. I cannot find, I cannot imagine any such, reasoning. But I keep my mind still open to instruction, if anyone will vouchsafe to bestow it on me.

Should it be said that, from a number of uniform experiments, we *infer* a connection between the sensible qualities and the secret powers; this, I must confess, seems the same difficulty, couched in different terms. The question still recurs, on what process of argument this *inference* is founded? Where is the medium, the interposing ideas, which join propositions so very wide of each other? It is confessed that the color, consistence, and other sensible qualities of bread appear not of themselves, to have any connection with the secret powers of nourishment and support. For otherwise we could infer these secret powers from the first appearance of these sensible qualities, without the aid of experience; contrary to the sentiment of all philosophers, and contrary to plain matter of fact. Here, then, is our natural state of ignorance with regard to the powers and influence of all objects. How is this remedied by experience? It only shows us a number of uniform effects resulting from certain objects, and teaches us that those particular objects, at that particular time, were endowed with such powers and forces. When a new object, endowed with similar sensible qualities, is produced, we expect similar powers and forces, and look for a like effect. From a body of like color and consistence with bread we expect like nourishment and support. But this surely is a step or progress of the mind, which

wants to be explained. When a man says, *I have found, in all past instances, such sensible qualities conjoined with such secret powers:* and when he says, *Similar sensible qualities will always be conjoined with similar secret powers,* he is not guilty of a tautology, nor are these propositions in any respect the same. You say that the one proposition is an inference from the other. But you must confess that the inference is not intuitive; neither is it demonstrative: of what nature is it, then? To say it is experimental, is begging the question. For all inferences from experience suppose, as their foundation, that the future will resemble the past, and that similar powers will be conjoined with similar sensible qualities. If there be any suspicion that the course of nature may change, and that the past may be no rule for the future, all experience becomes useless, and can give rise to no inference or conclusion. It is impossible, therefore, that any arguments from experience can prove this resemblance of the past to the future; since all these arguments are founded on the supposition of that resemblance. Let the course of things be allowed hitherto ever so regular; that alone, without some new argument or inference, proves not that, for the future, it will continue so. In vain do you pretend to have learned the nature of bodies from your past experience. Their secret nature, and consequently all their effects and influence, may change, without any change in their sensible qualities. This happens sometimes, and with regard to some objects: why may it not happen always, and with regard to all objects? What logic, what process of argument secures you against this supposition? My practice, you say, refutes my doubts. But you mistake the purport of my question. As an agent, I am quite satisfied in the point; but as a philosopher, who has some share of curiosity, I will not say scepticism, I want to learn the foundation of this inference. No reading, no inquiry has yet been able to remove my difficulty, or give me satisfaction in a matter of such importance. Can I do better than propose the difficulty to the public, even though, perhaps, I have small hopes of obtaining a solution? We shall at least, by this means, be sensible of our ignorance, if we do not augment our knowledge.

I must confess that a man is guilty of unpardonable arrogance who concludes, because an argument has escaped his own investigation, that, therefore, it does not really exist. I must also confess that, though all the learned, for several ages, should have employed themselves in fruitless search upon any subject, it may still, perhaps, be rash to conclude positively that the subject must, therefore, pass all human comprehension. Even though we examine all the sources of our knowledge, and conclude them unfit for such a subject, there may still remain a suspicion that the enumeration is not complete, or the examination not accurate. But with regard to the present subject, there are some considerations which seem to remove all this accusation of arrogance or suspicion of mistake.

It is certain that the most ignorant and stupid peasants—nay, infants; nay, even brute beasts—improve by experience, and learn the qualities of natural objects, by observing the effects which result from them. When a child has felt the sensation of pain from touching the flame of a candle, he will be careful not to put his hand near any candle; but will expect a similar effect from a cause which is similar in its sensible qualities and appearance. If you assert, therefore, that the understanding of the child is led into this conclusion by any process of argument or ratiocination, I may justly require you to produce that argument; nor have you any pretense to refuse so equitable a demand. You cannot say that the argument is abstruse, and may possibly escape your inquiry; since you confess that it is obvious to the capacity of a mere infant. If you hesitate, therefore, a moment, or if, after reflection, you produce any intricate or profound argument, you, in a manner, give up the question, and confess that it is not reasoning which engages us to suppose the past resembling the future, and to expect similar effects from causes which are, to appearance, similar. This is the proposition which I intended to enforce in the present section. If I be right, I pretend not to have made any mighty discovery. And if I be wrong, I must acknowledge myself to be, indeed, a very backward scholar; since I cannot now discover an argument which, it seems, was perfectly familiar to me long before I was out of my cradle.

SECTION V

Sceptical Solution of These Doubts

PART I

The passion for philosophy, like that for religion, seems liable to this inconvenience, that, though it aims at the correction of our manners and extirpation of our vices, it may only serve, by imprudent management, to foster a predominant inclination, and push the mind, with more determined resolution, towards that side which already *draws* too much, by the bias and propensity of the natural temper. It is certain that, while we aspire to the magnanimous firmness of the philosophic sage, and endeavor to confine our pleasures altogether within our own minds, we may, at last, render our philosophy like that of Epictetus, and other *Stoics*, only a more refined system of selfishness, and reason ourselves out of all virtue as well as social enjoyment. While we study with attention the vanity of human life, and turn all our thoughts towards the empty and transitory nature of riches and honors, we are, perhaps, all the while flattering our natural indolence, which, hating the bustle of the world and drudgery of business, seeks a pretense of reason to give itself a full and uncontrolled indulgence. There is, however, one species of philosophy which seems little liable to this inconvenience, and that because it strikes in with no disorderly passion of the human mind, nor can mingle itself with any natural affection or propensity; and that is the Academic or Sceptical philosophy. The academics always talk of doubt and suspense of judgment, of danger in hasty determinations, of confining to very narrow bounds the inquiries of the understanding, and of renouncing all speculations which lie not within the limits of common life and practice. Nothing, therefore, can be more contrary than such a philosophy to the supine indolence of the mind, its rash arrogance, its lofty pretensions, and its superstitious credulity. Every passion is mortified by it, except the love of truth; and that passion never is, nor can be, carried to too high a degree. It is surprising, therefore, that this philosophy, which, in almost every instance, must be harmless and innocent, should be the subject of so much groundless reproach and obloquy. But, perhaps, the very circumstance which renders it so innocent is what chiefly exposes it to the public hatred and resentment. By flattering no irregular passion, it gains few partisans: by opposing so many vices and follies, it raises to itself abundance of enemies, who stigmatize it as libertine, profane, and irreligious.

Nor need we fear that this philosophy, while it endeavors to limit our inquiries to common life, should ever undermine the reasonings of common life, and carry its doubts so far as to destroy all action, as well as speculation. Nature will always maintain her rights, and prevail in the end over any abstract reasoning whatsoever. Though we should conclude, for instance, as in the foregoing section, that, in all reasonings from experience, there is a step taken by the mind which is not supported by any argument or process of the understanding; there is no danger that these reasonings, on which almost all knowledge depends, will ever be affected by such a discovery. If the mind be not engaged by argument to make this step, it must be induced by some other principle of equal weight and authority; and that principle will preserve its influence as long as human nature remains the same. What that principle is may well be worth the pains of inquiry.

Suppose a person, though endowed with the strongest faculties of reason and reflection, to be brought on a sudden into this world; he would, indeed, immediately observe a continual succession of objects, and one event following another; but he would not be able to discover anything farther. He would not, at first, by any reasoning, be able to reach the idea of cause and effect; since the particular powers, by which all natural operations are performed, never appear to the senses; nor is it reasonable to conclude, merely because one event, in one instance, precedes another, that therefore the one is the cause, the other the effect. Their conjunction may be arbitrary and casual. There may be no reason to infer the existence of one from the appearance of the other. And in a word, such a person, without more experience, could never employ his conjecture or reasoning concerning any matter of fact, or be assured of anything beyond what was immediately present to his memory and senses.

Suppose, again, that he has acquired more experience, and has lived so long in the world as to have observed familiar objects or events to be constantly conjoined together; what is the consequence of this experience? He immediately infers the existence of one object from the appearance of the other. Yet he has not, by all his experience, acquired any idea or knowledge of the secret power by which the one object produces the other; nor is it, by any process of reasoning, he is engaged to draw this inference. But still he finds himself determined to draw it: and though he should be convinced that his understanding has no part in the operation, he would nevertheless continue in the same course of thinking. There is some other principle which determines him to form such a conclusion.

This principle is Custom or Habit. For wherever the repetition of any particular act or operation produces a propensity to renew the same act or operation, without being impelled by any reasoning or process of the understanding, we always say that this propensity is the effect of *Custom*. By employing that word, we pretend not to have given the ultimate reason of such a propensity. We only point out a principle of human nature, which is universally acknowledged, and which is well known by its effects. Perhaps we can push our inquiries no farther, or pretend to give the cause of this cause; but must rest contented with it as the ultimate principle, which we can assign, of all our conclusions from experience. It is sufficient satisfaction that we can go so far, without repining at the narrowness of our faculties because they will carry us no farther. And it is certain we here advance a very intelligible proposition at least, if not a true one, when we assert that, after the constant conjunction of two objects—heat and flame, for instance, weight and solidity—we are determined by custom alone to expect the one from the appearance of the other. This hypothesis seems even the only one which explains the difficulty, why we draw, from a thousand instances, an inference which we are not able to draw from one instance that is, in no respect, different from them. Reason is incapable of any such variation. The conclusions which it draws from considering one circle are the same which it would form upon surveying all the circles in the universe. But no man, having seen only one body move after being impelled by another, could infer that every other body will move after a like impulse. All inferences from experience, therefore, are effects of custom, not of reasoning.

Custom, then, is the great guide of human life. It is that principle alone which renders our experience useful to us, and makes us expect, for the future, a similar train of events with those which have appeared in the past. Without the influence of custom, we should be entirely ignorant of every matter of fact beyond what is immediately present to the memory and senses. We should never know how to adjust means to ends, or to employ our natural powers in the production of any effect. There would be an end at once of all action, as well as of the chief part of speculation.

But here it may be proper to remark that, though our conclusions from experience carry us beyond our memory and senses, and assure us of matters of fact which happened in the most distant places and most remote ages, yet some fact must always be present to the senses or memory, from which we may first proceed in drawing these conclusions. A man, who should find in a desert country the remains of pompous buildings, would conclude that the country had, in ancient times, been cultivated by civilized inhabitants; but did nothing of this nature occur to him, he could never form such an inference. We learn the events of former ages from history; but then we must peruse the volumes in which this instruction is contained, and thence carry up our inferences from one testimony to another, till we arrive at the eyewitnesses and spectators of these distant events. In a word, if we proceed not upon some fact, present to the memory or senses, our reasonings would be merely hypothetical; and however the particular links might be connected with each other, the whole chain of inferences would have nothing to support it, nor could we ever, by its means, arrive at the knowledge of any real existence. If I ask why you believe any particular matter of fact which you relate, you must tell me some reason; and this reason will be some other fact connected with it. But as you cannot proceed after this manner, *in infinitum*, you must at last terminate in some fact which is present to your memory or senses; or must allow that your belief is entirely without foundation.

What, then, is the conclusion of the whole matter? A simple one; though, it must be confessed, pretty remote from the common theories of philosophy. All belief of matter of fact or real existence is derived merely from some object, present to the memory or senses, and a customary conjunction between that and some other object. Or in other words; having found, in many instances, that any two kinds of objects—flame and heat, snow and cold—have always been conjoined together; if flame or snow be presented anew to the senses, the mind is carried by custom to expect heat or cold, and to *believe* that such a quality does exist and will discover itself upon a nearer approach. This belief is the necessary result of placing the mind in such circumstances. It is an operation of the soul, when we are so situated, as unavoidable as to feel the passion of love, when we receive benefits; or hatred, when we meet with injuries. All these operations are a species of natural instincts, which no reasoning or process of the thought and understanding is able either to produce or to prevent.

QUESTIONS FOR DISCUSSION

1. Give examples of what Hume calls Relations of Ideas from geometry, biology, physics, economics.
2. Give examples of Matters of Fact from the same areas.
3. In Hume's view are there any Matters of Fact that we can be sure of? Give his reasons.
4. Are Newton's laws Matters of Fact or Relations of Ideas?
5. In Hume's view, can an effect be inferred by valid reasoning once we know the cause? What kind of relation holds between cause and effect?
6. Explain what Hume means by Custom. What role does Custom play in his theory of knowledge?
7. Is Hume a skeptic? Defend your answer.

George Edward Moore (1873-1958)

6.3   A Defence of Common Sense

In what follows I have merely tried to state, one by one, some of the most important points in which my philosophical position differs from positions which have been taken up by *some* other philosophers. It may be that the points which I have had room to mention are not really the most important, and possibly some of them may be points as to which no philosopher has ever really differed from me. But, to the best of my belief, each is a point as to which many have really differed; although (in most cases, at

From *Contemporary British Philosophy*, J. Muirhead, ed. (New York: The Macmillan Company, 1924). Reprinted by permission of The Macmillan Company.

all events) each is also a point as to which many have agreed with me.

I. The first point is a point which embraces a great many other points. And it is one which I cannot state as clearly as I wish to state it, except at some length. The method I am going to use for stating it is this. I am going to begin by enunciating, under the heading (1), a whole long list of propositions, which may seem, at first sight, such obvious truisms as not to be worth stating: they are, in fact, a set of propositions, every one of which (in my own opinion) I *know*, with certainty, to be true. I shall, next, under the heading (2), state a single proposition which makes an assertion about a whole set of *classes* of propositions—each class being defined, as the class consisting of all propositions which resemble *one* of the propositions in (1) in a certain respect. (2), therefore, is a proposition which could not be stated, until the list of propositions in (1), or some similar list, had already been given. (2) is itself a proposition which may seem such an obvious truism as not to be worth stating: and it is also a proposition which (in my own opinion) I *know*, with certainty, to be true. But nevertheless, it is, to the best of my belief, a proposition with regard to which many philosophers have, for different reasons, differed from me; even if they have not directly denied (2) itself, they have held views incompatible with it. My first point, then, may be said to be that (2), together with all its implications, some of which I shall expressly mention, is true.

(1) I begin, then, with my list of truisms, every one of which (in my own opinion) I *know*, with certainty, to be true. The propositions to be included in this list are the following:

There exists at present a living human body, which is *my* body. This body was born at a certain time in the past, and has existed continuously ever since, though not without undergoing changes; it was, for instance, much smaller when it was born, and for some time afterwards, than it is now. Ever since it was born, it has been either in contact with or not far from the surface of the earth; and, at every moment since it was born, there have also existed many other things, having shape and size in three dimensions (in the same familiar sense in which it has), from which it has been *at various distances* (in the familiar

sense in which it is now at a distance both from that mantelpiece and from that bookcase, and at a greater distance from the bookcase than it is from the mantelpiece); also, there have (very often, at all events) existed some other things of this kind with which it was *in contact* (in the familiar sense in which it is now in contact with the pen I am holding in my right hand and with some of the clothes I am wearing). Among the things which have, in this sense, formed part of its environment (i.e., have been either in contact with it, or at *some* distance from it, however *great*) there have, at every moment since its birth, been large numbers of other living human bodies, each of which has, like it, (*a*) at some time been born, (*b*) continued to exist from some time after birth, (*c*) been, at every moment of its life after birth, either in contact with or not far from the surface of the earth; and many of these bodies have already died and ceased to exist. But the earth had existed also for many years before my body was born; and for many of these years, also, large numbers of human bodies had, at every moment, been alive upon it; and many of these bodies had died and ceased to exist before it was born. Finally (to come to a different class of propositions), I am a human being, and I have, at different times since my body was born, had many different experiences, of each of many different kinds: e.g., I have often perceived both my own body and other things which formed part of its environment, including other human bodies; I have not only perceived things of this kind, but have also observed facts about them, such as, for instance, the fact which I am now observing, that that mantelpiece is at present nearer to my body than that bookcase; I have been aware of other facts, which I was not at the time observing, such as, for instance, the fact, of which I am now aware, that my body existed yesterday and was then also for some time nearer to that mantelpiece than to that bookcase; I have had expectations with regard to the future, and many beliefs of other kinds, both true and false; I have thought of imaginary things and persons and incidents, in the reality of which I did not believe; I have had dreams; and I have had feelings of many different kinds. And, just as my body has been the body of a human being, namely myself, who has, during his lifetime, had many experiences of each of these (and other) different kinds; so, in the case of very many of the other human bodies which have lived upon the earth, each has been the body of a different human being, who has, during the lifetime of that body, had many different experiences of each of these (and other) different kinds.

(2) I now come to the single truism which, as will be seen, could not be stated except by reference to the whole list of truisms, just given in (1). This truism also (in my own opinion) I *know*, with certainty to be true; and it is as follows:

In the case of *very many* (I do not say *all*) of the human beings belonging to the class (which includes myself) defined in the following way, i.e., as human beings who have had human bodies, that were born and lived for some time upon the earth, and who have, during the lifetime of those bodies, had many different experiences of each of the kinds mentioned in (1), it is true that each has frequently, during the life of his body,

known, with regard to *himself* or *his* body, and with regard to some time earlier than any of the times at which I wrote down the propositions in (1), a proposition *corresponding* to each of the propositions in (1), in the sense that it asserts with regard to *himself* or *his* body and the earlier time in question (namely, in each case, the time at which he knew it), just what the corresponding proposition in (1) asserts with regard to *me* or *my* body and the time at which I wrote that proposition down.

In other words what (2) asserts is only (what seems an obvious enough truism) that each of *us* (meaning by "us," very many human beings of the class defined) has frequently *known*, with regard to *himself* or *his* body and the time at which he knew it, everything which, in writing down my list of propositions in (1), I was claiming to know about *myself* or *my* body and the time at which I wrote that proposition down, i.e., just as *I* knew (when I wrote it down) "There exists at present a living human body which is my body," so each of us has frequently known with regard to himself and some other time the different but corresponding proposition, which *he* could *then* have properly expressed by, "There exists *at present* a human body which is *my* body"; just as *I* know "Many human bodies other than mine have before now lived on the earth," so each of us has frequently known the different but corresponding proposition "Many human bodies other than *mine* have before *now* lived on the earth"; just as *I* know "Many human beings other than myself have before now perceived, and dreamed, and felt," so each of *us* has frequently known the different but corresponding proposition "Many human beings other than *myself* have before *now* perceived, and dreamed, and felt"; and so on, in the case of *each* of the propositions enumerated in (1).

I hope there is no difficulty in understanding, so far, what this proposition (2) asserts. I have tried to make clear by examples what I mean by "propositions *corresponding* to each of the propositions in (1)." And what (2) asserts is merely that each of us has frequently known to be true a proposition *corresponding* (in that sense) to each of the propositions in (1)—a *different* corresponding proposition, of course, at each of the times at which he knew such a proposition to be true.

But there remain two points, which, in view of the way in which some philosophers have used the English language, ought, I think, to be expressly mentioned, if I am to make quite clear exactly how much I am asserting in asserting (2).

The first point is this. Some philosophers seem to have thought it legitimate to use the word "true" in such a sense that a proposition which is partially false may nevertheless also be true; and some of these, therefore, would perhaps *say* that propositions like those enumerated in (1) are, in their view, true, when all the time they believe that every such proposition is partially false. I wish, therefore, to make it quite plain that I am not using "true" in any such sense. I am using it in such a sense (and I think this is the ordinary usage) that if a proposition is partially false, it follows that it is *not* true, though, of course, it may be *partially* true. I am maintaining, in short, that all the propositions in (1), and also many propositions corresponding to each of

these, are *wholly* true; I am asserting this in asserting (2). And hence, any philosopher, who does in fact believe, with regard to any or all of these classes of propositions, that every proposition of the class in question is partially false, is, in fact, disagreeing with me and holding a view incompatible with (2), even though he may think himself justified in *saying* that he believes some propositions belonging to all of these classes to be "true."

And the second point is this. Some philosophers seem to have thought it legitimate to use such expressions as, e.g., "The earth has existed for many years past," as if they expressed something which they really believed, when in fact they believe that every proposition, which such an expression would *ordinarily* be understood to express, is, at least partially, false; and all they really believe is that there is some *other* set of propositions, related in a certain way to those which such expressions do actually express, which, unlike these, really are true. That is to say, they use the expression "The earth has existed for many years past" to express, not what it would ordinarily be understood to express, but the proposition that some proposition, related to this in a certain way, is true; when all the time they believe that the proposition, which this expression would ordinarily be understood to express, is, at least partially, false. I wish, therefore, to make it quite plain that I was not using the expressions I used in (1) in any such subtle sense. I meant by each of them precisely what every reader, in reading them, will have understood me to mean. And any philosopher, therefore, who holds that any of these expressions, if understood in this popular manner, expresses a proposition which embodies some popular error, is disagreeing with me and holding a view incompatible with (2), even though he may hold that there is some *other*, true, proposition which the expression in question might be legitimately used to express.

In what I have just said, I have assumed that there is some meaning which is *the* ordinary or popular meaning of such expressions as "The earth has existed for many years past." And this, I am afraid, is an assumption which some philosophers are capable of disputing. They seem to think that the question "Do you believe that the earth has existed for many years past?" is not a plain question, such as should be met either by a plain "Yes" or "No," or by a plain "I can't make up my mind," but is the sort of question which can be properly met by: "It all depends on what you mean by 'the earth' and 'exists' and 'years': if you mean so and so, and so and so, and so and so, then I do; but if you mean so and so, and so and so, and so and so, or so and so, and so and so, and so and so, or so and so, and so and so, and so and so, then I don't, or at least I think it is extremely doubtful." It seems to me that such a view is as profoundly mistaken as any view can be. Such an expression as "The earth has existed for many years past" is the very type of an unambiguous expression, the meaning of which we all understand. Anyone who takes a contrary view must, I suppose, be confusing the question whether we understand its meaning (which we all certainly do) with the entirely different question whether we *know what it means*, in the sense that we are able to *give a correct analysis* of its meaning. The

question what is the correct analysis of *the* proposition meant *on any occasion* (for, of course, as I insisted in defining (2) a different proposition is meant at every different time at which the expression is used) by "The earth has existed for many years past" is, it seems to me, a profoundly difficult question, and one to which, as I shall presently urge, no one knows the answer. But to hold that we do not know what, in certain respects, is the analysis of what we understand by such an expression, is an entirely different thing from holding that we do not understand the expression. It is obvious that we cannot even raise the question how what we do understand by it is to be analyzed, unless we do understand it. So soon, therefore, as we know that a person who uses such an expression is using it in its ordinary sense, we understand his meaning. So that in explaining that I was using the expressions used in (1) in their ordinary sense (those of them which have an ordinary sense, which is not the case with quite all of them), I have done all that is required to make my meaning clear.

But now, assuming that the expressions which I have used to express (2) are understood, I think, as I have said, that many philosophers have really held views incompatible with (2). And the philosophers who have done so may, I think, be divided into two main groups. A. What (2) asserts is, with regard to a whole set of *classes* of propositions, that we have, each of us, frequently *known* to be true propositions belonging to *each* of these classes. And one way of holding a view incompatible with this proposition is, of course, to hold, with regard to one or more of the classes in question, that *no* propositions of that class *are* true—that all of them are, at least partially, false; since if, in the case of any one of these classes, *no* propositions of that class *are* true, it is obvious that nobody can have *known* any propositions of that class to be true, and, therefore, that *we* cannot have known to be true propositions belonging to *each* of these classes. And my first group of philosophers consists of philosophers who have held views incompatible with (2) for this reason. They have held, with regard to one or more of the classes in question, simply that no propositions of that class *are* true. Some of them have held this with regard to *all* the classes in question; some only with regard to *some* of them. But, of course, whichever of these two views they have held, they have been holding a view inconsistent with (2). B. Some philosophers, on the other hand, have not ventured to assert, with regard to *any* of the classes in (2), that no propositions of that class *are* true, but what they have asserted is that, in the case of some of these classes, no human being has ever *known*, with certainty, that any propositions of the class in question are true. That is to say, they differ profoundly from philosophers of group A, in that they hold that propositions of *all* these classes *may* be true; but, nevertheless, they hold a view incompatible with (2) since they hold, with regard to some of these classes, that none of us has ever *known* a proposition of the class in question to be true.

A. I said that some philosophers, belonging to this group, have held that no propositions belonging to *any* of the classes in (2) are wholly true, while others have only held this with regard to *some* of the classes in (2).

And I think the chief division of this kind has been the following. Some of the propositions in (1) (and, therefore, of course, all propositions belonging to the corresponding classes in (2) are propositions which cannot be true, unless some *material things* have existed and have stood *in spatial relations* to one another: that is to say, they are propositions which, *in a certain sense,* imply *the reality of material things,* and *the reality of Space.* For example, the proposition that my body has existed for many years past, and has, at every moment during that time been either in contact with or not far from the earth, is a proposition which implies both the *reality of material things* (provided you use "material things" in such a sense that to deny the reality of material things implies that no proposition which asserts that human bodies have existed, or that the earth has existed, is wholly true) and also the *reality of Space* (provided, again, that you use "Space" in such a sense that to deny the reality of Space implies that no proposition which asserts that anything has ever been in contact with or at a distance from another, in the familiar senses pointed out in (1), is wholly true). But others among the propositions in (1) (and, therefore, propositions belonging to the corresponding classes in (2)), do not (at least obviously) imply either the reality of material things or the reality of Space: e.g., the propositions that I have often had dreams, and have had many different feelings at different times. It is true that propositions of this second class do imply one thing which is also implied by all propositions of the first, namely that (*in a certain sense*) *Time is real,* and imply also one thing not implied by propositions of the first class, namely that (*in a certain sense*) *at least one Self is real.* But I think there are some philosophers, who, while denying that (in the senses in question) either material things or Space are real, have been willing to admit that Selves and Time are real, in the sense required. Other philosophers, on the other hand, have used the expression "Time is not real," to express some view that they held; and some, at least, of these have, I think, meant by this expression something which is incompatible with the truth of *any* of the propositions in (1)—they have meant, namely, that *every* proposition of the sort that is expressed by the use of "now" or "at present," e.g., "I am now both seeing and hearing" or "There exists at present a living human body," or by the use of a *past* tense, e.g., "I *have* had many experiences in the past," or "The earth *has* existed for many years," are, at least partially false.

All the four expressions I have just introduced, namely, "Material things are not real," "Space is not real," "Time is not real," "The Self is not real," are, I think, unlike the expressions I used in (1), really ambiguous. And it may be that, in the case of each of them, some philosopher has used the expression in question to express some view he held which was not incompatible with (2). With such philosophers, if there are any, I am not, of course, at present concerned. But it seems to me that the most natural and proper usage of each of these expressions is a usage in which it *does* express a view incompatible with (2); and, in the case of each of them, some philosophers have, I think, really used the expression in question to express such a view. All such philosophers have, therefore,

been holding a view incompatible with (2).

All such views, whether incompatible with *all* of the propositions in (1), or only with *some* of them, seem to me to be quite certainly false; and I think the following points are specially deserving of notice with regard to them:

(*a*) If *any* of the classes of propositions in (2) is such that no proposition of that class is true, then no philosopher has ever existed, and, therefore, none can ever have held with regard to any such class, that no proposition belonging to it is true. In other words, the proposition that some propositions belonging to each of these classes are true is a proposition which has the peculiarity, that, if any philosopher has ever denied it, it follows from the fact that he has denied it, that he must have been wrong in denying it. For when I speak of "philosophers" I mean, of course (as we all do), exclusively philosophers who have been human beings, with human bodies that have lived upon the earth, and who have at different times had many different experiences. If, therefore, there have been any philosophers, there have been human beings of this class; and if there have been human beings of this class, all the rest of what is asserted in (1) is certainly true too. Any view, therefore, incompatible with the proposition that many propositions corresponding to each of the propositions in (1) are true, can only be true, on the hypothesis that no philosopher has ever held any such view. It follows, therefore, that, in considering whether this proposition is true, I cannot consistently regard the fact that many philosophers, whom I respect, have, to the best of my belief, held views incompatible with it, as having any weight at all against it. Since, if I know that they have held such views, I am, *ipso facto*, knowing that they were mistaken; and, if I have no reason to believe that the proposition in question is true, I have still less reason to believe that they have held views incompatible with it; since I am more certain that they have existed and held *some* views, i.e., that the proposition in question is true, than that they have held any views incompatible with it.

(*b*) It is, of course, the case that all philosophers who have held such views have repeatedly, even in their philosophical works, expressed other views inconsistent with them: i.e., no philosopher has ever been able to hold such views consistently. One way in which they have betrayed this inconsistency, is by alluding to the existence of other philosophers. Another way is by alluding to the existence of the human race, and in particular by using "we" in the sense in which I have already constantly used it, in which any philosopher who asserts that "we" do so and so, e.g., that "*we* sometimes believe propositions that are not true," is asserting not only that he himself has done the thing in question, but that *very many other human beings, who have had bodies and lived upon the earth,* have done the same. The fact is, of course, that all philosophers have belonged to the class of human beings which exists only if (2) be true: that is to say, to the class of human beings who have frequently *known* propositions corresponding to each of the propositions in (1). In holding views incompatible with the proposition that propositions of all these classes are true, they have, therefore, been holding views incon-

sistent with propositions which they themselves *knew* to be true; and it was, therefore, only to be expected that they should sometimes betray their knowledge of such propositions. The strange thing is that philosophers should have been able to hold sincerely, as part of their philosophical creed, propositions inconsistent with what they themselves *knew* to be true; and yet, so far as I can make out, this has really frequently happened. My position, therefore, on this first point, differs from that of philosophers belonging to this group A, not in that I hold anything which they don't hold, but only in that I don't hold, as part of my philosophical creed, things which they do hold as part of theirs—that is to say, propositions inconsistent with some which they and I both hold in common. But this difference seems to me to be an important one.

(*c*) Some of these philosophers have brought forward, in favor of their position, arguments designed to show, in the case of some or all of the propositions in (1), that no propositions of that type can possibly be wholly true, because every such proposition entails both of two incompatible propositions. And I admit, of course, that if any of the propositions in (1) did entail both of two incompatible propositions it could not be true. But it seems to me I have an absolutely conclusive argument to show that none of them does entail both of two incompatible propositions. Namely this: All of the propositions in (1) are true; no true proposition entails both of two incompatible propositions; therefore, none of the propositions in (1) entails both of two incompatible propositions.

(*d*) Although, as I have urged, no

philosopher who has held with regard to any of these types of proposition that no propositions of that type are true, has failed to hold also other views inconsistent with his view in this respect, yet I do not think that the view, with regard to any or all of these types, that no proposition belonging to them is true, is *in itself* a self-contradictory view, i.e., entails both of two incompatible propositions. On the contrary, it seems to me quite clear that it *might* have been the case that Time was not real, material things not real, Space not real, selves not real. And in favor of my view that none of these things, which might have been the case, *is* in fact the case, I have, I think, no better argument than simply this—namely, that all the propositions in (1) are, in fact, true.

B. This view, which is usually considered a much more modest view than A, has, I think, the defect that, unlike A, it really is self-contradictory, i.e., entails both of two mutually incompatible propositions.

Most philosophers who have held this view, have held, I think, that though each of us knows propositions corresponding to *some* of the propositions in (1), namely to those which merely assert that *I* myself have had in the past experiences of certain kinds at many different times, yet none of us knows *for certain* any propositions either of the type (*a*) which assert the existence of *material things* or of the type (*b*) which assert the existence of *other* selves, beside myself, and that *they* also have had experiences. They admit that we do, in fact, *believe* propositions of both these types, and that they *may* be true: some would even say that we know them to be highly probable; but they

deny that we ever know them, *for certain,* to be true. Some of them have spoken of such beliefs as "beliefs of Common Sense," expressing thereby their conviction that beliefs of this kind are very commonly entertained by mankind: but they are convinced that these things are, in all cases, only *believed,* not known for certain; and some have expressed this by saying that they are matters of Faith, not of Knowledge.

Now the remarkable thing which those who take this view have not, I think, in general duly appreciated, is that, in each case, the philosopher who takes it is making an assertion about "us"— that is to say, not merely about himself, but about *many other human beings as well*. When he says, "No human being has ever *known* of the existence of other human beings," he is saying: "There have been many other human beings beside myself, and none of them (including myself) has ever known of the existence of other human beings." If he says: "These beliefs are beliefs of Common Sense, but they are not matters of *knowledge,*" he is saying: "There have been many other human beings, beside myself, who have shared these beliefs, but neither I nor any of the rest has ever known them to be true." In other words, he asserts with confidence that these beliefs *are* beliefs of Common Sense, and seems often to fail to notice that, *if* they are, they must be true; since the proposition that they are beliefs of Common Sense is one which logically entails propositions both of type (*a*) and of type (*b*); it logically entails the proposition that many human beings, beside the philosopher himself, have had human bodies, which lived upon the earth, and have had various experiences, including beliefs of this kind. This is why this position, as contrasted with positions of group A, seems to me to be self-contradictory. Its difference from A consists in the fact that it is making a proposition about *human knowledge* in general, and, therefore, is actually asserting the existence of many human beings, whereas philosophers of group A in stating their position are not doing this: they are only contradicting *other* things which they hold. It is true that a philosopher who says, "There have existed many human beings beside myself, and none of us has ever known of the existence of any human beings beside himself," is only contradicting himself if what he holds is, "There have *certainly* existed many human beings beside myself" or, in other words, "*I* know that there have existed other human beings beside myself." But this, it seems to me, is what such philosophers have in fact been generally doing. They seem to me constantly to betray the fact that they regard the proposition that those beliefs *are* beliefs of Common Sense, or the proposition that they themselves are not the only members of the human race, as not merely true, but *certainly* true; and *certainly* true it cannot be, unless one member, at least, of the human race, namely themselves, has *known* the very things which that member is declaring that no human being has ever known.

Nevertheless, my position that I *know*, with certainty, to be true all of the propositions in (1), is certainly not a position, the denial of which entails both of two incompatible propositions. If I do *know* all these propositions to be true, then, I think, it is quite certain that other human beings also have known corresponding propositions: that is to say (2) also *is* true, and I know it to be true. But do I really *know* all the propositions in (1) to be true? Isn't it possible that I merely believe them? Or know them to be highly probable? In answer to this question, I think I have nothing better to say than that it seems to me that I *do* know them, with certainty. It is, indeed, obvious that, in the case of most of them, I do not know them *directly:* that is to say, I only know them because, in the past, I have known to be true *other* propositions which were evidence for them. If, for instance, I do know that the earth had existed for many years before I was born, I certainly only know this because I have known other things in the past which were evidence for it. And I certainly do not know exactly what the evidence was. Yet all this seems to me to be no good reason for doubting that I do know it. We are all, I think, in this strange position that we do *know* many things, with regard to which we *know* further that we must have had evidence for them, and yet we do not know *how* we know them, i.e., we do not know what the evidence was. If there is any "we," and if we know that there is, this must be so: for that there is a "we" is one of the things in question. And that I do know that there is a "we," that is to say, that many other human beings, with human bodies, have lived upon the earth, it seems to me that I do know, for certain.

If this first point in my philosophical position, namely my belief in (2), is to be given any name, which has actually been used by philosophers in classifying the positions of other philosophers, it would have, I think, to be expressed by saying that I am one of those philosophers who have held that the "Common Sense view of the world" is, in certain fundamental features, *wholly* true. But it must be remembered that, according to me, *all* philosophers, without exception, have agreed with me in holding this: and that the real difference, which is commonly expressed in this way, is only a difference between those philosophers who have *also* held views inconsistent with these features in "the Common Sense view of the world," and those who have not.

The features in question (namely, propositions of any of the classes defined in defining (2)) are all of them features which have this peculiar property—namely, that *if we know that they are features in the "Common Sense view of the world," it follows that they are true:* it is self-contradictory to maintain that *we* know them to be features in the Common Sense view, and that yet they are not true; since to say that *we* know this is to say that they are true. And many of them also have the further peculiar property that, *if they are features in the Common Sense view of the world (whether "we" know this or not), it follows that they are true,* since to say that there is a "Common Sense view of the world" is to say that they are true. The phrases "Common Sense view of the world" or "Common Sense beliefs" (as used by philosophers) are, of course, extraordinarily vague; and, for all I know, there may be many propositions which may be properly called features in "the Common Sense view of the world" or "Common Sense beliefs" which are not true, and which deserve to be mentioned with the contempt with which some philosophers speak of "Common Sense beliefs." But to speak with contempt of those "Common Sense beliefs" which I have mentioned is quite certainly the height of absurdity. And there are, of course, enormous numbers of other features in "the Common Sense view of the world" which, if these are true, are quite certainly true too: e.g., that there have lived upon the surface of the earth not only human beings, but also many different species of plants and animals, etc., etc.

II. What seems to me the next in importance of the points in which my philosophical position differs from positions held by *some* other philosophers, is one which I will express in the following way. I hold, namely, that there is no good reason to suppose either (A) that *every* physical fact is *logically* dependent upon some mental fact or (B) that *every* physical fact is *causally* dependent upon some mental fact. In saying this, I am not, of course, saying that there *are* any physical facts which are wholly independent (i.e., both logically and causally) of mental facts: I do, in fact, believe that there are; but that is not what I am asserting. I am only asserting that there is *no good reason* to suppose the contrary; by which I mean, of course, that none of the human beings, who have had human bodies that lived upon the earth, have, during the lifetime of their bodies, had any good reason to suppose the contrary. Many philosophers have, I think, not only believed either that *every* physical fact is *logically* dependent upon some mental fact ("physical fact" and "mental fact" being understood in the sense in which I am using these terms) or that *every* physical fact is *causally* dependent upon some mental fact, or both, but also that they themselves had good reason for these beliefs. In this respect, therefore, I differ from them.

In the case of the term "physical fact," I can only explain how I am using it by giving examples. I mean by "physical facts," facts *like* the following: "That mantelpiece is at present nearer to this body than that bookcase is," "The earth has existed for many years past," "The moon has at every moment for many years past been nearer to the earth than to the sun," "That mantelpiece is of a light color." But, when I say "facts *like* these," I mean, of course, facts like them *in a certain respect;* and what this respect is I cannot define. The term "physical fact" is, however, in common use; and I think that I am using it in its ordinary sense. Moreover, there is no need for a definition to make my point clear; since among the examples I have given there are some with regard to which I hold that there is no reason to suppose *them* (i.e., these particular physical facts) either logically or causally dependent upon any mental fact.

"Mental fact," on the other hand, is a much more unusual expression, and I am using it in a specially limited sense, which, though I think it is a natural one, does need to be explained. There may be many other senses in which the term can be properly used, but I am only concerned with this one; and hence it is essential that I should explain what it is.

There may, possibly, I hold, be "mental facts" of three different kinds. It is only with regard to the first kind that I am sure that there are facts of that kind; but if there were any facts of either of the other two kinds, they would be "mental facts" in my limited sense, and, therefore, I must explain what is meant by the hypothesis that there are facts of those two kinds.

(a) My first kind is this. I am conscious now; and also I am seeing something now. These two facts are both of them mental facts of my first kind; and my first kind consists exclusively of facts which resemble one or other of the two *in a certain respect.*

(α) The fact that I am conscious now is obviously, in a certain sense, a fact, with regard to a particular individual and a particular time, to the effect that that individual is conscious at that time. And every fact which resembles this one in that respect is to be included in my first kind of mental fact. Thus the fact that I was also conscious at many different times yesterday is not itself a fact of this kind: but it entails that there *are* (or, as we should commonly say, because the times in question are past times, "were") many other facts of this kind, namely each of the facts, which, at each of the times in question, I could have properly expressed by "I am conscious *now.*" *Any* fact which is, in this sense, a fact with regard to an individual and a time (whether the individual be myself or another, and whether the time be past or present), to the effect that that individual *is* conscious at that time, is to be included in my first kind of mental fact: and I call such facts, facts of class (α).

(β) The second example I gave, namely, the fact that I am seeing something now, is obviously related to the fact that I am conscious now in a peculiar manner. It not only *entails* the fact that I am conscious now (for from the fact that I am seeing something it *follows* that I am conscious: I *could* not have been seeing anything unless I had been conscious, though I might quite well have been conscious without seeing anything) but it also is a fact, with regard to a *specific way* (or mode) of being conscious, to the effect that I am conscious in that way: in the same sense in which the proposition (with regard to any particular thing) "This is red" both entails the proposition (with regard to the same thing) "This is colored," and is also a proposition, with regard to a *specific way* of being colored, to the effect that that thing is colored in that way. And any fact which is related in this peculiar manner to any fact of class (a), is also to be included in my first kind of mental fact, and is to be called a fact of class (β). Thus the fact that I am hearing now is, like the fact that I am seeing now, a fact of class (β); and so is any fact, with regard to myself and a past time, which could at that time have been properly expressed by "I am dreaming now," "I am imagining now," "I am at present aware of the fact that . . . ," etc., etc. In short, any fact, which is a fact with regard to a particular individual (myself or another), a particular time (past or present), and *any particular kind of experience,* to the effect that that individual is having at that time an experience of that particular kind, is a fact of class (β): and only such facts are facts of class (β).

My first kind of mental facts consists exclusively of facts of classes (a) and (β), and consists of *all* facts of either of these kinds.

(b) That there are many facts of classes (a) and (β) seems to me perfectly certain. But many philosophers seem to me to have held a certain view with regard to the *analy-* *sis* of facts of class (a), which is such that, if it were true, there would be facts of another kind, which I should wish also to call "mental facts." I don't feel at all sure that this analysis is true; but it seems to me that it *may* be true; and since we can understand what is meant by the supposition that it is true, we can also understand what is meant by the supposition that there are "mental facts" of this second kind.

Many philosophers have, I think, held the following view as to the analysis of what each of us knows, when he knows (at any time) "I am conscious now." They have held, namely, that there is a certain intrinsic property (with which we are all of us familiar and which might be called that of "being an experience") which is such that, at any time at which any man knows "I am conscious now," he is knowing, with regard to that property and himself and the time in question, "There is occurring now an event which has this property (i.e., 'is an experience') and which is an experience of *mine,*" and such that this fact is what he expresses by "I am conscious now." And if this view is true, there must be many facts of each of three kinds, each of which I should wish to call "mental facts"; viz., (1) facts with regard to some event, which has this supposed intrinsic property, and to some time, to the effect that that event is occurring at that time, (2) facts with regard to this supposed intrinsic property and some time, to the effect that *some* event which has that property is occurring at that time, and (3) facts with regard to some property, which is a *specific way* of having the supposed intrinsic property (in the sense above explained in which "being red" is a specific way of "being colored") and some time, to the effect that some event which has that specific property is occurring at that time. Of course, there not only are not, but *cannot* be, facts of any of these kinds, unless there is an intrinsic property related to what each of us (on any occasion) expresses by "I am conscious now," in the manner defined above; and I feel very doubtful whether there is any such property; in other words, although I know for certain, both that I have had many experiences, and that I have had experiences of many different kinds, I feel very doubtful whether to say the first is the same thing as to say that there have been many events, each of which was an experience of mine, and whether to say the second is the same thing as to say that there have been many events, each of which was an experience of mine, and each of which also had a different property, which was a specific way of being an experience. The proposition that I have had experiences does not necessarily entail the proposition that there have been any events which were experiences; and I cannot satisfy myself that I am acquainted with any events of the supposed kind. But yet it seems to me possible that the proposed analysis of "I am conscious now" is correct: that I am really acquainted with events of the supposed kind, though I cannot see that I am. And *if* I am, then I should wish to call the three kinds of facts defined above "mental facts." Of course, if there are "experiences" in the sense defined, it would be possible (as many have held) that there *can* be no experiences which are not *some individual's* experiences; and in that case, any fact of any of these three kinds would be logically

dependent on, though not necessarily identical with, some fact of class (α) or class (β). But it seems to me also a possibility that, if there are "experiences," there might be experiences which did not belong to any individual; and, in that case, there would be "mental facts" which were neither identical with nor logically dependent on any fact of class (α) or class (β).

(*c*) Finally, some philosophers have, so far as I can make out, held that there are or may be facts which are facts with regard to some individual, to the effect that he is conscious, or is conscious in some specific way, but which differ from facts of classes (α) and (β), in the important respect that they are not facts *with regard to any time:* they have conceived the possibility that there may be one or more individuals, who are *timelessly* conscious, and timelessly conscious in specific modes. And others, again, have, I think, conceived the hypothesis that the intrinsic property defined in (b) may be one which does not belong only to *events*, but may also belong to one or more wholes, which do *not* occur at any time: in other words, that there may be one or more *timeless* experiences, which might or might not be the experiences of some individual. It seems to me very doubtful whether any of these hypotheses are even possibly true; but I cannot see for certain that they are not possible: and, if they are possible, then I should wish to give the name "mental fact" to any fact (if there were any) of any of the five following kinds, viz., (1) to any fact which is the fact, with regard to any individual, that he is *timelessly* conscious, (2) to any fact which is the fact, with regard to any individual, that he is *timelessly* conscious in any specific way, (3) to any fact which is the fact with regard to a *timeless* experience that it exists, (4) to any fact which is the fact with regard to the supposed intrinsic property "being an experience," that something timelessly exists which has that property, and (5) to any fact which is the fact, with regard to any property, which is a specific mode of this supposed intrinsic property, that something timelessly exists which has that property.

I have, then, defined three different kinds of facts, each of which is such that, if there *were* any facts of that kind (as there certainly *are*, in the case of the first kind), the facts in question *would* be "mental facts" in my sense; and to complete the definition of the limited sense in which I am using "mental facts," I have only to add that I wish also to apply the name to one *fourth* class of facts: namely, to any fact, which is the fact, with regard to any of these three kinds of facts, or any kinds included in them, *that there are facts of the kind in question;* i.e., not only will each individual fact of class (α) be, in my sense, a "mental fact," but also the general fact "that there are facts of class (α)," will itself be a "mental fact"; and similarly in all other cases: e.g., not only will the fact that I am now perceiving (which is a fact of class (β)) be a "mental fact," but also the general fact that *there are* facts, with regard to individuals and times, to the effect that the individual in question is perceiving at the time in question, will be a "mental fact."

A. Understanding "physical fact" and "mental fact" in the senses just explained, I hold, then, that there is no good reason to suppose that *every* physical fact is *logically* dependent upon some mental fact. And I use the phrase, with regard to two facts, F_1 and F_2, "F_1 is *logically dependent* on F_2," wherever and only where F_1 *entails* F_2, either in the sense in which the proposition "I am seeing now" *entails* the proposition "I am conscious now," or the proposition (with regard to any particular thing) "This is red" entails the proposition (with regard to the same thing) "This is colored," or else in the more strictly logical sense in which (for instance) the conjunctive proposition "All men are mortal, and Mr. Baldwin is a man" entails the proposition "Mr. Baldwin is mortal." To say, then, of two facts, F_1 and F_2, that F_1 is *not* logically dependent upon F_2, is only to say that F_1 *might* have been a fact, even if there had been no such fact as F_2; or that the conjunctive proposition "F_1 is a fact, but there is no such fact as F_2" is a proposition which is not self-contradictory, i.e., does not entail both of two mutually incompatible propositions.

I hold, then, that in the case of *some* physical facts, there is no good reason to suppose that there is some mental fact, such that the physical fact in question could not have been a fact unless the mental fact in question had also been one. And my position is perfectly definite, since I hold that this is the case with all the four physical facts, which I have given as examples of physical facts. For example, there is no good reason to suppose that there is any mental fact whatever, such that the fact that that mantelpiece is at present nearer to my body than that bookcase could not have been a fact, unless the mental fact in question had also been a fact; and, similarly, in all the other three cases.

In holding this I am certainly differing from some philosophers. I am, for instance, differing from Berkeley, who held that that mantelpiece, that bookcase, and my body are, all of them, either "ideas" or "constituted by ideas," and that no "idea" can possibly exist without being perceived.[1] He held, that is, that this physical fact is logically dependent upon a mental fact of my fourth class: namely, a fact which is the fact that there is at least one fact, which is a fact with regard to an individual and the present time, to the effect that that individual is now perceiving something. He does not say that this physical fact is logically dependent upon any fact which is a fact of any of my first three classes, e.g., on any fact which is the fact, with regard to a particular individual and the present time, that *that* individual is now perceiving something: what he does say is that the physical fact couldn't have been a fact, unless it had been a fact that there was *some* mental fact of this sort. And it seems to be that many philosophers, who would perhaps disagree either with Berkeley's assumption that my body is an "idea" or "constituted by ideas," or with his assumption that "ideas" cannot exist without being perceived, or with both, nevertheless would agree with him in thinking that this physical fact is logically dependent upon *some* "mental fact": e.g., they might say that it could not have been a fact, unless there had been, at some time or other, or, were timelessly, *some* "experience." Many, indeed, so far as I can make out, have held that *every* fact is logically dependent on every

other fact. And, of course, they have held in the case of their opinions, as Berkeley did in the case of his, that they had good reasons for them.

B. I also hold that there is no good reason to suppose that *every* physical fact is *causally* dependent upon some mental fact. By saying that F_1 is *causally* dependent on F_2, I mean only that F_1 *wouldn't* have been a fact unless F_2 had been; *not* (which is what "logically dependent" asserts) that F_1 *couldn't conceivably* have been a fact, unless F_2 had been. And I can illustrate my meaning by reference to the example which I have just given. The fact that that mantelpiece is at present nearer to my body than that bookcase, is (as I have just explained) so far as I can see, not *logically* dependent upon any mental fact; it *might* have been a fact, even if there had been no mental facts. But it certainly is *causally* dependent on many mental facts: my body *would* not have been here unless I had been conscious in various ways in the past; and the mantelpiece and the bookcase certainly *would* not have existed, unless other men had been conscious too.

But with regard to two of the facts, which I gave as instances of physical facts, namely, the fact that the earth has existed for many years past, and the fact that the moon has for many years past been nearer to the earth than to the sun, I hold that there is no good reason to suppose that these are *causally* dependent upon any mental fact. So far as I can see, there is no reason to suppose that there is any mental fact of which it could be truly said: unless this fact had been a fact, the earth would not have existed for many years past. And in holding this, again, I think I differ from some philosophers. I differ, for instance, from

---

[1] See selection 6.1.

those who have held that all material things were created by God, and that they had good reasons for supposing this.

III. I have just explained that I differ from those philosophers who have held that there is good reason to suppose that all material things were created by God. And it is, I think, an important point in my position, which should be mentioned, that I differ also from all philosophers who have held that there is good reason to suppose that there is a God at all, whether or not they have held it likely that he created all material things.

And similarly, whereas some philosophers have held that there is good reason to suppose that we, human beings, shall continue to exist and to be conscious after the death of our bodies, I hold that there is no good reason to suppose this.

IV. I now come to a point of a very different order.

As I have explained under I., I am not at all sceptical as to the *truth* of such propositions as "The earth has existed for many years past," "Many human bodies have each lived for many years upon it," i.e., propositions which assert the existence of material things: on the contrary, I hold that we all know, with certainty, many such propositions to be true. But I am very sceptical as to what, in certain respects, the correct *analysis* of such propositions is. And this is a matter as to which I think I differ from many philosophers. Many seem to hold that there is no doubt at all as to their *analysis*, nor, therefore, as to the analysis of the proposition "Material things have existed," in certain respects in which I hold that the analysis of the propositions in

question is extremely doubtful; and some of them, as we have seen, while holding that there is no doubt as to their *analysis*, seem to have doubted whether any such propositions are *true*. I, on the other hand, while holding that there is no doubt whatever that many such propositions are wholly true, hold also that no philosopher, hitherto, has succeeded in suggesting an analysis of them, as regards certain important points, which comes anywhere near to being certainly true.

It seems to me quite evident that the question how propositions of the type I have just given are to be analyzed, depends on the question how propositions of another and simpler type are to be analyzed. I know, at present, that I am perceiving a human hand, a pen, a sheet of paper, etc.; and it seems to me that I cannot know how the proposition "Material things exist" is to be analyzed, until I know how, in certain respects, these simpler propositions are to be analyzed. But even these are not simple enough. It seems to me quite evident that my knowledge that I am now perceiving a human hand is a deduction from a pair of propositions simpler still—propositions which I can only express in the form "I am perceiving *this*" and "*This* is a human hand." It is the analysis of propositions of the latter kind which seems to me to present such great difficulties, while nevertheless the whole question as to the *nature* of material things obviously depends upon their analysis. It seems to me a surprising thing that so few philosophers, while saying a great deal as to what material things *are* and as to what it is to perceive them, have attempted to give a clear account as to what precisely they suppose themselves to *know* (or to *judge,* in case they have held that we don't *know* any such propositions to be true, or even that no such propositions *are* true) when they know or judge such things as "This is a hand," "That is the sun," "This is a dog," etc., etc., etc.

Two things only seem to me to be quite certain about the analysis of such propositions (and even with regard to these I am afraid some philosophers would differ from me), namely, that whenever I know, or judge, such a proposition to be true, (1) there is always some *sense-datum* about which the proposition in question is a proposition—some sense-datum which is *a* subject (and, in a certain sense, the principal or ultimate subject) of the proposition in question, and (2) that, nevertheless, *what* I am knowing or judging to be true about this sense-datum is not (in general) that it is *itself* a hand, or a dog, or the sun, etc., etc., as the case may be.

Some philosophers have, I think, doubted whether there are any such things as other philosophers have meant by "sense-data" or "sensa." And I think it is quite possible that some philosophers (including myself, in the past) have used these terms in senses such that it is really doubtful whether there are any such things. But there is no doubt at all that there are sense-data, in the sense in which I am now using that term. I am at present seeing a great number of them, and feeling others. And in order to point out to the reader what sort of things I mean by sense-data, I need only ask him to look at his own right hand. If he does this he will be able to pick out something (and, unless he is seeing double, *only*

one thing) with regard to which he will see that it is, at first sight, a natural view to take that that thing is identical, not, indeed, with his whole right hand, but with that part of its surface which he is actually seeing, but will also (on a little reflection) be able to see that it is doubtful whether it can be identical with the part of the surface of his hand in question. Things *of the sort* (in a certain respect) of which this thing is, which he sees in looking at his hand, and with regard to which he can understand how some philosophers should have supposed it to *be* the part of the surface of his hand which he is seeing, while others have supposed that it can't be, are what I mean by "sense-data." I therefore define the term in such a way that it is an open question whether the sense-datum which I now see in looking at my hand, and which is a sense-datum of my hand, is or is not identical with that part of its surface which I am now actually seeing.

That what I know with regard to this sense-datum, when I know "This is a human hand," is not that it is *itself* a human hand, seems to me certain because I know that my hand has many parts (e.g., its other side, and the bones inside it), which are quite certainly *not* parts of this sense-datum.

I think it certain, therefore, that the analysis of the proposition, "This is a human hand" is, roughly at least, of the form "There is a thing, and only one thing, of which it is true both that it is a human hand and that *this surface* is a part of its surface." In other words, to put my view in terms of the phrase "theory of representative perception," I hold it to be quite certain that I do not *directly* perceive *my hand;* and that when I am said (as I may be correctly said) to "perceive" it, I "perceive" it means that I perceive (in a different and more fundamental sense) something which is (in a suitable sense) *representative* of it, namely, a certain part of its surface.

This is all that I hold to be *certain* about the analysis of the proposition "This is a human hand." We have seen that it includes in its analysis a proposition of the form "This is part of the surface of a human hand" (where "This," of course, has a different meaning from that which it has in the original proposition which has now been analyzed). But this proposition also is undoubtedly a proposition about the sense-datum, which I am seeing, which is a sense-datum *of* my hand. And hence, the further question arises: *What*, when I know "*This is part of the surface of* a human hand," am I knowing about the sense-datum in question? Am I, in this case, really knowing about the sense-datum in question that it *itself* is part of the surface of a human hand? Or, just as we found in the case of "This is a human hand," that what I was knowing about the sense-datum was certainly not that it *itself* was a human hand, so, is it perhaps the case, with this new proposition, that even here I am not knowing, with regard to the sense-datum, that it is *itself* part of the surface of a hand? And, if so, what is it that I am knowing about the sense-datum itself?

This is the question to which, as it seems to me, no philosopher has hitherto suggested an answer which comes anywhere near to being *certainly* true. There seem to me to be three, and

only three, alternative types of answer possible; and to any answer yet suggested, of any of these types, there seem to me to be very grave objections.

(1) Of the first type, there is but one answer: namely, that in this case what I am knowing really is that the sense-datum *itself* is part of the surface of a human hand. In other words that, though I don't perceive *my hand* directly, I do *directly* perceive part of its surface; that the sense-datum itself *is* this part of its surface and not merely something which (in a sense yet to be determined) "represents" this part of its surface; and that hence the sense in which I "perceive" this part of the surface of my hand, is not in its turn a sense which needs to be defined by reference to yet a third more ultimate sense of "perceive," which is the only one in which perception is direct, namely, that in which I perceive the sense-datum.

If this view is true (as I think it may just possibly be), it seems to me certain that we must abandon a view which has been held to be certainly true by most philosophers, namely, the view that our sense-data always really have the qualities which they sensibly appear to us to have. For I know that if another man were looking through a microscope at the same surface which I am seeing with the naked eye, the sense-datum which he saw would sensibly appear to him to have qualities very different from and incompatible with those which my sense-datum sensibly appears to me to have: and yet, if my sense-datum is identical with the surface we are both of us seeing, his must be identical with it also. My sense-datum can, therefore, be identical with this surface only on condition that it is identical with his sense-datum; and, since his sense-datum sensibly appears to him to have qualities incompatible with those which mine sensibly appears to me to have, his sense-datum can be identical with mine only on condition that the sense-datum in question either has not got the qualities which it sensibly appears to me to have, or has not got those which it sensibly appears to him to have.

I do not, however, think that this is a fatal objection to this first type of view. A far more serious objection seems to me to be that, when we see a thing double (have what is called "a double image" of it), we certainly have *two* sense-data, each of which is *of* the surface seen, and which cannot, therefore, both be identical with it; and that yet it seems as if, if any sense-datum is ever identical with the surface *of* which it is a sense-datum, each of these so-called "images" must be so. It looks, therefore, as if every sense-datum is, after all, only "representative" of the surface *of* which it is a sense-datum.

(2) But, if so, what relation has it to the surface in question?

This second type of view is one which holds that when I know "This is part of the surface of a human hand," what I am knowing with regard to the sense-datum which is *of* that surface, is, *not* that it is *itself* part of the surface of a human hand, but something of the following kind. There is, it says, *some* relation, R, such that what I am knowing with regard to the sense-datum is either "There is one thing and only one thing, of which it is true both that it is a part of the surface of a human hand, and that it has R to this sense-

datum," or else "There are a set of things, of which it is true both that that set, taken collectively, *are* part of the surface of a human hand, and also that each member of the set has R to this sense-datum, and that nothing which is not a member of the set has R to it."

Obviously, in the case of this second type, many different views are possible, differing according to the view they take as to what the relation R is. But there is only one of them which seems to me to have any plausibility; namely, that which holds that R is an ultimate and unanalyzable relation, which might be expressed by saying that "xRy" means the same as "y" is an appearance or manifestation of x." I.e., the analysis which this answer would give of "This is part of the surface of a human hand" would be "There is one and only one thing of which it is true, both that it is part of the surface of a human hand, and that this sense-datum is an appearance or manifestation of it."

To this view, also, there seem to me to be very grave objections, chiefly drawn from a consideration of the questions how we can possibly *know* with regard to any of our sense-data that there is one thing and one thing only which has to them such a supposed ultimate relation; and how, if we do, we can possibly *know* anything further about such things, e.g., of what size or shape they are.

(3) The third type of answer, which seems to me to be the only possible alternative if (1) and (2) are rejected, is the type of answer which J. S. Mill seems to have been implying to be the true one when he said that material things are "permanent possibilities of sensation." He seems to

have thought that when I know such a fact as "This is part of the surface of a human hand," what I am knowing with regard to the sense-datum which is the principal subject of that fact, is not that it is itself part of the surface of a human hand; nor yet, with regard to any relation, that *the* thing which has to it that relation is part of the surface of a human hand; but a whole set of hypothetical facts each of which is a fact of the form "If *these* conditions had been fulfilled, I should have been perceiving a sense-datum intrinsically related to *this* sense-datum in *this* way," "If *these* (other) conditions had been fulfilled, I should have been perceiving a sense-datum intrinsically related to *this* sense-datum in *this* (other) way," etc., etc.

With regard to this third type of view as to the analysis of propositions of the kind we are considering, it seems to me, again, just *possible* that it is a true one; but to hold (as Mill himself and others seem to have held) that it is *certainly*, or nearly certainly, true, seems to me as great a mistake, as to hold, with regard either to (1) or to (2), that they are *certainly*, or nearly certainly, true. There seem to me to be very grave objections to it; in particular the three, (*a*) that though, in general, when I know such a fact as "This is a hand," I certainly do know some hypothetical facts of the form "If *these* conditions had been fulfilled, I should have been perceiving a sense-datum of *this* kind, which would have been a sense-datum of the same surface of which *this* is a sense-datum," it seems doubtful whether any conditions with regard to which I know this are not themselves conditions of the form "If this and that

material thing had been in those positions and conditions . . . ," (*b*) that it seems again very doubtful whether there is any intrinsic relation, such that my knowledge that (under *these* conditions) I should have been perceiving a sense-datum of *this* kind, which would have been a sense-datum of the same surface of which *this* is a sense-datum, is equivalent to a knowledge, with regard to that relation, that I should, under those conditions, have been perceiving a sense-datum related by it to *this* sense-datum, and (*c*) that, if it were true, the sense in which a material surface is "round" or "square," would necessarily be utterly different from that in which our sense-data sensibly appear to us to be "round" or "square."

V. Just as I hold that the proposition "There are and have been material things" is quite certainly true, but that the question how this proposition is to be analyzed is one to which no answer that has been hitherto given is anywhere near certainly true; so I hold that the proposition "There are and have been many Selves" is quite certainly true, but that here again all the analyses of this proposition that have been suggested by philosophers are highly doubtful.

That I am now perceiving many different sense-data, and that I have at many times in the past perceived many different sense-data, I know for certain—that is to say, I know that there are mental facts of class (β), connected in a way which it is proper to express by saying that they are all of them facts about *me;* but how this kind of connection is to be analyzed, I do not know for certain, nor do I think that any other philosopher knows with any approach to certainty. Just as in the case of the proposition "This is part of the surface of a human hand," there are several extremely different views as to its analysis, each of which seems to me *possible*, but none nearly certain, so also in the case of the proposition "This, that and that sense-datum are all at present being perceived by *me*," and still more so in the case of the proposition "*I* am now perceiving this sense-datum, and *I* have in the past perceived sense-data of these other kinds." Of the *truth* of these propositions, there seems to me to be no doubt; but as to what is the correct analysis of them, there

seems to me to be the gravest doubt— the true analysis may, for instance, *possibly* be quite as paradoxical as is the third view given under IV as to the analysis of "This is part of the surface of a human hand"; but whether it *is* as paradoxical as this seems to me to be quite as doubtful as in that case. Many philosophers, on the other hand, seem to me to have assumed that there is little or no doubt as to the correct analysis of such propositions; and many of these, just reversing my position, have also held that the propositions themselves are not true.

QUESTIONS FOR DISCUSSION

1. After asserting a number of propositions that he says he knows are certainly true, Moore says that some philosophers in the past have disagreed with him either explicitly or implicitly. Give an example of a philosophical position which would be opposed to the position that Moore takes and show wherein they differ.

2. Show how Moore would argue against a philosopher who asserted that material things are not real. How do you suppose he would respond to Moore's criticism?

3. Show how Moore would argue against a philosopher who asserted that although it was commonly *believed* that material things do exist, nevertheless this was something none of us could *know*.

4. Does Moore think that a philosopher who asserts that "Time is not real" is contradicting himself? Why or why not?

5. Moore holds that he can know that a proposition is true, be certain of its truth, and yet not know its correct analysis. Could it not be argued that if he is in doubt as to the correct analysis of a proposition, he has no right to be certain of its truth? How do you think he would reply?

6. What do you think Moore means when he says he is *certain* of the truth of a proposition? In this connection, consider the following questions:
   a) Would it make sense to say today: "Last year I was certain that such and such was the case, but I see now I was mistaken"?
   b) Does it make sense to say: "I am certain that there are five books on my desk, but I may be mistaken"?

7. What does Moore mean by *sense-data*? Give examples.

Bertrand Russell (1872-1970)

6.4   Fact, Belief, Truth,
and Knowledge

The purpose of this chapter is to state in dogmatic form certain conclusions which follow from previous discussions together with the fuller discussions of *An Inquiry into Meaning and Truth*. More particularly, I wish to give meanings, as definite as possible, to the four words in the title of this chapter. I do not mean to deny that the words are susceptible of other equally legitimate meanings, but only that the meanings which I shall assign to them represent important concepts, which, when understood and distinguished, are useful in many philosophical problems, but when confused are a source of inextricable tangles.

A. FACT

"Fact," as I intend the term, can only be defined ostensively. Everything that there is in the world I call a "fact." The sun is a fact; Caesar's crossing of the Rubicon was a fact; if I have a toothache, my toothache is

a fact. If I make a statement, my making it is a fact, and if it is true there is a further fact in virtue of which it is true, but not if it is false. The butcher says, "I'm sold out, and that's a fact"; immediately afterward, a favored customer arrives and gets a nice piece of lamb from under the counter. So the butcher told two lies, one in saying he was sold out and the other in saying that his being sold out was a fact. Facts are what make statements true or false. I should like to confine the word "fact" to the minimum of what must be known in order that the truth or falsehood of any statement may follow analytically from those asserting that minimum. For example, if "Brutus was a Roman" and "Cassius was a Roman" each assert a fact, I should not say that "Brutus and Cassius were Romans" asserted a new fact. We have seen that the questions whether there are negative facts and general facts raise difficulties. These niceties, however, are largely linguistic.

I mean by a "fact" something which is there, whether anybody thinks so or not. If I look up a railway timetable and find that there is a train to Edinburgh at 10 A.M., then, if the timetable is correct, there is an actual train, which is a "fact." The statement in the timetable is itself a "fact," whether true or false, but it only *states* a fact if it is true, i.e., if there really is a train. Most facts are independent of our volitions; that is why they are called "hard," "stubborn," or "ineluctable." Physical facts, for the most part, are independent, not only of our volitions but even of our existence.

The whole of our cognitive life is, biologically considered, part of the process of adaptation to facts. This process is one which exists, in a greater or less degree, in all forms of life, but is not commonly called "cognitive" until it reaches a certain level of development. Since there is no sharp frontier anywhere between the lowest animal and the most profound philosopher, it is evident that we cannot say precisely at what point we pass from mere animal behavior to something deserving to be dignified by the name of "knowledge." But at every stage there is adaptation, and that to which the animal adapts itself is the environment of *fact*.

B. BELIEF

"Belief," which we have next to consider, has an inherent and inevitable vagueness, which is due to the continuity of mental development from the amoeba to *homo sapiens*. In its most developed form, which is that most considered by philosophers, it is displayed by the assertion of a sentence. After sniffing for a time, you exclaim, "Good heavens! The house is on fire." Or, when a picnic is in contemplation, you say, "Look at those clouds. There will be rain." Or, in a

train, you try to subdue an optimistic fellow-passenger by observing, "Last time I did this journey we were three hours late." Such remarks, if you are not lying, express beliefs. We are so accustomed to the use of words for expressing beliefs that it may seem strange to speak of "belief" in cases where there are no words. But it is clear that even when words are used they are not of the essence of the matter. The smell of burning first makes you believe that the house is on fire, and then the words come, not as *being* the belief but as a way of putting it into a form of behavior in which it can be communicated to others. I am thinking, of course, of beliefs that are not very complicated or refined. I believe that the angles of a polygon add up to twice as many right angles as the figure has sides diminished by four right angles, but a man would need superhuman mathematical intuition to be able to believe this without words. But the simpler kind of belief, especially when it calls for action, may be entirely unverbalized. When you are traveling with a companion, you may say, "We must run; the train is just going to start." But if you are alone you may have the same belief, and run just as fast, without any words passing through your head.

I propose, therefore, to treat belief as something that can be preintellectual, and can be displayed in the behavior of animals. I incline to think that, on occasion, a purely bodily state may deserve to be called a "belief." For example, if you walk into your room in the dark and someone has put a chair in an unusual place, you may bump into it, because your body believed there was no chair there. But the parts played by mind and body respectively in belief are not very important to separate for our present purposes. A belief, as I understand the term, is a certain kind of state of body or mind or both. To avoid verbiage, I shall call it a state of an organism, and ignore the distinction of bodily and mental factors.

One characteristic of a belief is that it has external reference, in the sense defined in a previous chapter. The simplest case, which can be observed behavioristically, is when, owing to a conditioned reflex, the presence of A causes behavior appropriate to B. This covers the important case of acting on information received: here the phrase heard is A, and what it signifies is B. Somebody says, "Look out, there's a car coming," and you act as you would if you saw the car. In this case you are believing what is signified by the phrase "a car is coming."

Any state of an organism which consists in believing something can, theoretically, be fully described without mentioning the something. When you believe "a car is coming," your belief consists in a certain state of the muscles, sense-organs, and emotions, together perhaps with certain visual images. All this, and whatever else may go to make up your belief, could, in theory, be fully described by a psychologist and physiologist working together, without their ever having to mention anything outside your mind and body. Your state, when you believe that a car is coming, will be very different in different circumstances. You may be watching a race, and wondering whether the car on which you have put your money will win. You may be waiting for the return of your son from captivity in the Far East. You may be trying to escape from the police. You may be suddenly roused from absent-mindedness while crossing the street. But although your total state will not be the same in these various cases, there will be something in common among them, and it is this something which makes them all instances of the belief that a car is coming. A belief, we may say, is a collection of states of an organism bound together by all having in whole or part the same external reference.

In an animal or a young child, believing is shown by an action or series of actions. The beliefs of the hound about the fox are shown by his following the scent. But in human beings, as a result of language and of the practice of suspended reactions, believing often becomes a more or less static condition, consisting perhaps in pronouncing or imagining appropriate words, together with one of the feelings that constitute different kinds of belief. As to these, we may enumerate: first, the kind of belief that consists in filling out sensations by animal inferences; second, memory; third, expectation; fourth, the kind of belief generated unreflectingly by testimony; and fifth, the kind of belief resulting from conscious inference. Perhaps this list is both incomplete and in part redundant, but certainly perception, memory, and expectation differ as to the kinds of feeling involved. "Belief," therefore, is a wide generic term, and a state of believing is not sharply separated from cognate states which would not naturally be described as believings.

The question what it is that is believed when an organism is in a state of believing is usually somewhat vague. The hound pursuing a scent is unusually definite, because his purpose is simple and he has no doubt as to the means; but a pigeon hesitating whether to eat out of your hand is in a much more vague and complex condition. Where human beings are concerned, language gives an illusory appearance of precision; a man may be able to express his belief in a sentence, and it is then supposed that the sentence is what he believes. But as a rule this is not the case. If you say, "Look, there is Jones," you are believing something, and expressing your belief in words, but what you are believing has to do with Jones, not with the name "Jones." You may, on another occasion, have a belief which *is* concerned with words. "Who is that very distinguished man who has just come in? That is Sir Theophilus Thwackum." In this case it is the name you want. But as a rule in ordinary speech the words are, so to speak, transparent; they are not what is believed, any more than a man is the name by which he is called.

When words merely *express* a belief which is about what the words mean, the belief indicated by the words is lacking in precision to the degree that the meaning of the words is lacking in precision. Outside logic and pure mathematics, there are no words of which the meaning is precise, not even such words as "centimeter" and "second." Therefore even when a belief is expressed in words having the greatest degree of precision of which empirical words are capable, the question as to what it is that is believed is still more or less vague.

This vagueness does not cease when a belief is what may be called "purely verbal," i.e., when what is believed is that a certain sentence is true. This

is the sort of belief acquired by schoolboys whose education has been on old-fashioned lines. Consider the difference in the schoolboy's attitude to "William the Conqueror, 1066" and "Next Wednesday will be a whole holiday." In the former case, he knows that that is the right form of words, and cares not a pin for their meaning; in the latter case, he acquires a belief about next Wednesday, and cares not a pin what words you use to generate his belief. The former belief, but not the latter, is "purely verbal."

If I were to say that the schoolboy is believing that the sentence "William the Conqueror, 1066" is "true," I should have to add that his definition of "truth" is purely pragmatic: a sentence is "true" if the consequences of uttering it in the presence of a master are pleasant; if they are unpleasant, it is "false."

Forgetting the schoolboy, and resuming our proper character as philosophers, what do *we* mean when we say that a certain sentence is "true"? I am not yet asking what is meant by "true"; this will be our next topic. For the moment I am concerned to point out that however "true" may be defined, the significance of "This sentence is true" must depend upon the significance of the sentence, and is therefore vague in exactly the degree in which there is vagueness in the sentence which is said to be true. We do not therefore escape from vagueness by concentrating attention on purely verbal beliefs.

Philosophy, like science, should realize that, while complete precision is impossible, techniques can be invented which gradually diminish the area of vagueness or uncertainty. However admirable our measuring apparatus may be, there will always remain some lengths concerning which we are in doubt whether they are greater than, less than, or equal to a meter; but there is no known limit to the refinements by which the number of such doubtful lengths can be diminished. Similarly, when a belief is expressed in words, there will always remain a band of possible circumstances concerning which we cannot say whether they would make the belief true or false, but the breadth of this band can be indefinitely diminished, partly by improved verbal analysis, partly by a more delicate technique in observation. Whether complete precision is or is not theoretically possible depends upon whether the physical world is discrete or continuous.

Let us now consider the case of a belief expressed in words all of which have the greatest attainable degree of precision. Suppose, for the sake of concreteness, that I believe the sentence "My height is greater than 5 ft., 8 ins., and less than 5 ft., 9 ins." Let us call this sentence "S." I am not yet asking what would make this sentence true, or what would entitle me to say that I know it; I am asking only: "What is happening in me when I have the belief which I express by the sentence S?" There is obviously no one correct answer to this question. All that can be said definitely is that I am in a state such as, if certain further things happen, will give me a feeling which might be expressed by the words "quite so," and that, now, while these things have not yet happened, I have the idea of their happening combined with the feeling expressed by the word "yes." I may, for instance, imagine myself standing against a wall on which there is a

scale of feet and inches, and in imagination see the top of my head between two marks on this scale, and toward this image I may have the feeling of assent. We may take this as the essence of what may be called "static" belief, as opposed to belief shown by action: static belief consists in an idea or image combined with a yes-feeling.

C. TRUTH

I come now to the definition of "truth" and "falsehood." Certain things are evident. Truth is a property of beliefs, and derivatively of sentences which express beliefs. Truth consists in a certain relation between a belief and one or more facts other than the belief. When this relation is absent, the belief is false. A sentence may be called "true" or "false" even if no one believes it, provided that if it were believed, the belief would be true or false as the case may be.

So much, I say, is evident. But what is not evident is the nature of the relation between belief and fact that is involved, or the definition of the possible fact that will make a given belief true, or the meaning of "possible" in this phrase. Until these questions are answered we have no adequate definition of "truth."

Let us begin with the biologically earliest form of belief, which is to be seen among animals as among men. The compresence of two kinds of circumstances, A and B, if it has been frequent or emotionally interesting, is apt to have the result that when A is sensibly present, the animal reacts as it formerly reacted to B, or at any rate displays some part of this reaction. In some animals this connection may be sometimes innate, and not the result of experience. But however the connection may be brought about, when the sensible presence of A causes acts appropriate to B, we may say that the animal "believes" B to be in the environment, and that the belief is "true" if B is in the environment. If you wake a man up in the middle of the night and shout, "Fire!," he will leap from his bed even if he does not yet see or smell fire. His action is evidence of a belief which is "true" if there is fire, and "false" otherwise. Whether his belief is true depends upon a fact which may remain outside his experience. He may escape so fast that he never acquires sensible evidence of the fire; he may fear that he will be suspected of incendiarism and fly the country, without ever inquiring whether there was a fire or not; nevertheless his belief remains true if there was the fact (namely fire) which constituted its external reference or significance, and if there was not such a fact his belief remained false even if all his friends assured him that there had been a fire.

The difference between a true and false belief is like that between a wife and a spinster: in the case of a true belief there is a fact to which it has a certain relation, but in the case of a false belief there is no such fact. To complete our definition of "truth" and "falsehood" we need a description of the fact which would make a given belief true, this description being one which applies to nothing if the belief is false. Given a woman of whom we do not know whether she is married or not, we can frame a description which will apply to her husband if she has one, and to nothing if she is a spinster. Such a description would

be: "the man who stood beside her in a church or registry office while certain words were pronounced." In like manner we want a description of the fact or facts which, if they exist, make a belief true. Such fact or facts I call the "verifier" of the belief.

What is fundamental in this problem is the relation between sensations and images, or, in Hume's terminology, between impressions and ideas. We have considered in a previous chapter the relation of an idea to its prototype, and have seen how "meaning" develops out of this relation. But given meaning and syntax, we arrive at a new concept, which I call "significance," and which is characteristic of sentences and of complex images. In the case of single words used in an exclamatory manner, such as "fire!" or "murder!," meaning and significance coalesce, but in general they are distinct. The distinction is made evident by the fact that words must have meaning if they are to serve a purpose, but a string of words does not necessarily have significance. Significance is a characteristic of all sentences that are not nonsensical, and not only of sentences in the indicative but also of such as are interrogative, imperative, or optative. For present purpose, however, we may confine ourselves to sentences in the indicative. Of these we may say that the significance consists in the description of the fact which, if it exists, will make the sentence true. It remains to define this description.

Let us take an illustration. Jefferson had a belief expressed in the words "There are mammoths in North America." This belief might have been true even if no one had seen one of these mammoths; there might, when he expressed the belief, have been just two in an uninhabited part of the Rocky Mountains, and they might soon afterward have been swept by a flood down the Colorado River into the sea. In that case, in spite of the truth of his belief, there would have been no evidence for it. The actual mammoths would have been facts, and would have been, in the above sense, "verifiers" of the belief. A verifier which is not experienced can often be described, if it has a relation known by experience to something known by experience; it is in this way that we understand such a phrase as "the father of Adam," which describes nothing. It is in this way that we understand Jefferson's belief about mammoths: we know the sort of facts that would have made his belief true; that is to say, we can be in a state of mind such that, if we had seen mammoths, we should have exclaimed, "Yes, that's what I was thinking of."

The significance of a sentence results from the meanings of its words together with the laws of syntax. Although meanings must be derived from experience, significance need not. I know from experience the meaning of "man" and the meaning of "wings," and therefore the significance of the sentence "There is a winged man," although I have no experience of what this sentence signifies. The significance of a sentence may always be understood as in some sense a description. When this description describes a fact, the sentence is "true"; otherwise it is "false."

It is important not to exaggerate the part played by convention. So long as we are considering beliefs, not the sentences in which they are expressed, convention plays no part at all. Suppose you are expecting to meet some person of whom you are fond, and whom you have not seen for some time. Your expectation may be quite wordless, even if it is detailed and complex. You may hope that he will be smiling; you may recall his voice, his gait, the expression of his eyes; your total expectation may be such as only a good painter could express, in paint, not in words. In this case you are expecting an experience of your own, and the truth or falsehood of your expectation is covered by the relation of idea and impression: your expectation is "true" if the impression, when it comes, is such that it might have been the prototype of your previous idea if the time order had been reversed. This is what we express when we say, "That is what I expected to see." Convention is concerned only in the translation of belief into language, or (if we are told something) of language into belief. Moreover the correspondence of language and belief, except in abstract matters, is usually by no means exact: the belief is richer in detail and context than the sentence, which picks out only certain salient features. You *say,* "I shall see him soon," but you *think,* "I shall see him smiling, but looking older, friendly, but shy, with his hair untidy and his shoes muddy"—and so on, through an endless variety of detail of which you may be only half aware.

The case of an expectation is the simplest from the point of view of defining truth and falsehood, for in this case the fact upon which truth or falsehood depends is about to be experienced. Other cases are more difficult.

Memory, from the standpoint of

our present problem, is closely analogous to expectation. A recollection is an idea, while the fact recollected was an impression; the memory is "true" if the recollection has to the fact that kind of resemblance which exists between an idea and its prototype.

Consider, next, such a statement as "You have a toothache." In any belief concerning another person's experience there may be the same sort of extraverbal richness that we have seen to be frequent in regard to expectations of our own experiences; you may, having recently had toothache, feel sympathetically the throbbing pangs that you imagine your friend to be suffering. Whatever wealth or paucity of imagination you may bring to bear, it is clear that your belief is "true" in proportion as it resembles the fact of your friend's toothache—the resemblance being again of the sort that can subsist between idea and prototype.

But when we pass on to something which no one experiences or has experienced, such as the interior of the earth, or the world before life began, both belief and truth become more abstract than in the above cases. We must now consider what can be meant by "truth" when the verifying fact is experienced by no one.

Anticipating coming discussions, I shall assume that the physical world, as it is independently of perception, can be known to have a certain structural similarity to the world of our percepts, but cannot be known to have any qualitative similarity. And when I say that it has structural similarity, I am assuming that the ordering relations in terms of which the structure is defined are spatio-temporal relations such as we know in our own experience. Certain facts about the physical world, therefore—those facts, namely, which consist of space-time structure—are such as we can imagine. On the other hand, facts as to the qualitative character of physical occurrences are, presumably, such as we cannot imagine.

Now, while there is no difficulty in supposing that there are unimaginable *facts,* there cannot be *beliefs,* other than general beliefs, of which the verifiers would be unimaginable. This is an important principle, but if it is not to lead us astray a little care is necessary as regards certain logical points. The first of these is that we may know a general proposition although we do not know any instance of it. On a large pebbly beach you may say, probably with truth, "There are pebbles on this beach which no one will ever have noticed." It is quite certainly true that there are finite integers which no one will ever have thought of. But it is self-contradictory to suppose such propositions established by giving instances of their truth. This is only an application of the principle that we can understand statements about all or some of the members of a class without being able to enumerate the members. We understand the statement "All men are mortal" just as completely as we should if we could give a complete list of men; for to understand this statement we need only understand the concepts "man" and "mortal" and what is meant by being an instance of them.

Now take the statement "There are facts which I cannot imagine." I am not considering whether this statement is true; I am only concerned to show that it is intelligible. Observe, in the first place, that if it is not intelligible, its contradictory must also be not intelligible, and therefore not true, though also not false. Observe, in the second place, that to understand the statement it is unnecessary to be able to give instances, any more than of the unnoticed pebbles or the numbers that are not thought of. All that is necessary is to understand the words and the syntax, which we do. The statement is therefore intelligible; whether it is true is another matter.

Take, now, the following statement: "There are electrons, but they cannot be perceived." Again I am not asking whether the statement *is* true, but what is meant by supposing it true or believing it to be true. "Electron" is a term defined by means of causal and spatio-temporal relations to events that we experience, and to other events related to them in ways of which we have experience. We have experience of the relation "parent," and can therefore understand the relation "great-great-great-grandparent," although we have no experience of this relation. In like manner we can understand sentences containing the word "electron," in spite of not perceiving anything to which this word is applicable. And when I say we can understand such sentences, I mean that we can imagine facts which would make them true.

The peculiarity, in such cases, is that we can imagine *general* circumstances which would verify our belief, but cannot imagine the particular facts which are instances of the general fact. I cannot imagine any particular fact of the form: "n is a number which will never have been thought of," for, whatever value I give to n, my statement becomes false by the very fact of my giving that value. But I can quite well imagine the general fact which gives truth to the statement "There are numbers which will never have been thought of." The reason is that general statements are concerned with intensions, and can be understood without any knowledge of the corresponding extensions.

Beliefs as to what is not experienced, as the above discussion has shown, are not as to unexperienced individuals, but as to classes of which no member is experienced. A belief must always be capable of being analyzed into elements that experience has made intelligible, but when a belief is set out in logical form it often suggests a different analysis, which would seem to involve components not known by experience. When such psychologically misleading analysis is avoided, we can say, quite generally: Every belief which is not merely an impulse to action is in the nature of a picture, combined with a yes-feeling or a no-feeling; in the case of a yes-feeling it is "true" if there is a fact having to the picture the kind of similarity that a prototype has to an image; in the case of a no-feeling it is "true" if there is no such fact. A belief which is not true is called "false."

This is a definition of "truth" and "falsehood."

D. KNOWLEDGE

I come now to the definition of "knowledge." As in the cases of "belief" and "truth," there is a certain inevitable vagueness and inexactitude in the conception. Failure to realize this has led, it seems to me, to important errors in the theory of knowledge. Nevertheless, it is well to be as precise as possible about the unavoidable lack of precision in the definition of which we are in search.

It is clear that knowledge is a subclass of true beliefs: every case of knowledge is a case of true belief, but not vice versa. It is very easy to give examples of true beliefs that are not knowledge. There is the man who looks at a clock which is not going, though he thinks it is, and who happens to look at it at the moment when it is right; this man acquires a true belief as to the time of day, but cannot be said to have knowledge. There is the man who believes, truly, that the last name of the Prime Minister in 1906 began with a B, but who believes this because he thinks that Balfour was Prime Minister then, whereas in fact it was Campbell Bannerman. There is the lucky optimist who, having bought a ticket for a lottery, has an unshakable conviction that he will win, and, being lucky, does win. Such instances can be multiplied indefinitely, and show that you cannot claim to have known merely because you turned out to be right.

What character in addition to truth must a belief have in order to count as knowledge? The plain man would say there must be sound evidence to support the belief. As a matter of common sense this is right in most of the cases in which doubt arises in practice, but if intended as a complete account of the matter it is very inadequate. "Evidence" consists, on the one hand, of certain matters of fact that are accepted as indubitable, and, on the other hand, of certain principles by means of which inferences are drawn from the matters of fact. It is obvious that this process is unsatisfactory unless we know the matters of fact and the principles of inference not merely by means of evidence, for otherwise we become involved in a vicious circle or an endless regress. We must therefore concentrate our attention on the matters of fact and the principles of inference. We may then say that what is known consists, first, of certain matters of fact and certain principles of inference, neither of which stands in need of extraneous evidence, and secondly, of all that can be ascertained by applying the principles of inference to the matters of fact. Traditionally, the matters of fact are those given in perception and memory, while the principles of inference are those of deductive and inductive logic.

There are various unsatisfactory features in this traditional doctrine, though I am not at all sure that, in the end, we can substitute anything very much better. In the first place, the doctrine does not give an intensional definition of "knowledge," or at any rate not a *purely* intensional definition; it is not clear what there is in common between facts of perception and principles of inference. In the second place, . . . it is very difficult to say what are facts of perception. In the third place, deduction has turned out to be much less powerful than was formerly supposed; it does not give new knowledge, except as to new forms of words for stating truths in some sense already known. In the fourth place, the methods of inference that may be called in a broad sense "inductive" have never been satisfactorily formulated; when formulated, even if completely true, they only give probability to their conclusions; moreover, in any possibly accurate form, they lack self-evidence, and are only to be believed, if at all, because they seem indispensable in reaching conclusions that we all accept.

There are, broadly speaking, three ways that have been suggested for coping with the difficulties in defining "knowledge." The first, and oldest, is to emphasize the concept of "self-evidence." The second is to abolish the distinction between premises and conclusions, and to say that knowledge is constituted by the coherence of a whole body of beliefs. The third and most drastic is to abandon the concept of "knowledge" altogether and substitute "beliefs that promote success"—and here "success" may perhaps be interpreted biologically. We may take Descartes, Hegel, and Dewey as protagonists of these three points of view.

Descartes holds that whatever I conceive clearly and distinctly is true. He believes that, from this principle, he can derive not only logic and metaphysics but also matters of fact, at least in theory. Empiricism has made such a view impossible; we do not think that even the utmost clarity in our thoughts would enable us to demonstrate the existence of Cape Horn. But this does not dispose of the concept of "self-evidence": we may say that what he says applies to conceptual evidence, but that there is also perceptual evidence, by means of which we come to know matters of fact. I do not think we can entirely dispense with self-evidence. If you slip on a piece of orange peel and hit your head with a bump on the pavement, you will have little sympathy with a philosopher who tries to persuade you that it is uncertain whether you are hurt. Self-evidence

also makes you accept the argument that if all men are mortal and Socrates is a man, then Socrates is mortal. I do not know whether self-evidence is anything except a certain firmness of conviction; the essence of it is that, where it is present, we cannot help believing. If, however, self-evidence is to be accepted as a guarantee of truth, the concept must be carefully distinguished from others that have a subjective resemblance to it. I think we must bear it in mind as relevant to the definition of "knowledge," but as not in itself sufficient.

Another difficulty about self-evidence is that it is a matter of degree. A clap of thunder is indubitable, but a very faint noise is not; that you are seeing the sun on a bright day is self-evident, but a vague blur in a fog may be imaginary; a syllogism in *Barbara* is obvious, but a difficult step in a mathematical argument may be very hard to "see." It is only for the highest degree of self-evidence that we should claim the highest degree of certainty.

The coherence theory and the instrumentalist theory are habitually set forth by their advocates as theories of *truth*. As such they are open to certain objections which I have urged elsewhere. I am considering them now not as theories of *truth* but as theories of *knowledge*. In this form there is more to be said for them.

Let us ignore Hegel, and set forth the coherence theory of knowledge for ourselves. We shall have to say that sometimes two beliefs cannot both be true, or, at least, that we sometimes believe this. If I believe simultaneously that A is true, that B is true, and that A and B cannot both be true, I have three beliefs which do not form a coherent group. In that case at least one of the three must be mistaken. The coherence theory in its extreme form maintains that there is only one possible group of mutually coherent beliefs, which constitutes the whole of knowledge and the whole of truth. I do not believe this; I hold, rather, to Leibniz's multiplicity of possible worlds. But in a modified form the coherence theory can be accepted. In this modified form it will say that all, or nearly all, of what passes for knowledge is in a greater or less degree uncertain; that if principles of inference are among the prima-facie materials of knowledge, then one piece of prima-facie knowledge may be inferrible from another, and thus acquire more credibility than it had on its own account. It may thus happen that a body of propositions, each of which has only a moderate degree of credibility on its own account, may collectively have a very high degree of credibility. But this argument depends upon the possibility of varying degrees of intrinsic credibility, and is therefore not a *pure* coherence theory. . . .

With respect to the theory that we should substitute for "knowledge" the concept "beliefs that promote success," it is sufficient to point out that it derives whatever plausibility it may possess from being halfhearted. It assumes that we can know (in the old-fashioned sense) what beliefs promote success, for if we cannot know this the theory is useless in practice, whereas its purpose is to glorify practice at the expense of theory. In practice, obviously, it is often very difficult to know what beliefs promote success, even if we have an adequate definition of "success."

The conclusion to which we seem to be driven is that knowledge is a matter of degree. The highest degree is found in facts of perception, and in the cogency of very simple arguments. The next highest degree is in vivid memories. When a number of beliefs are each severally in some degree credible, they become more so if they are found to cohere as a logical whole. General principles of inference, whether deductive or inductive, are usually less obvious than many of their instances, and are psychologically derivative from apprehension of their instances. Toward the end of our inquiry I shall return to the definition of "knowledge," and shall then attempt to give more precision and articulation to the above suggestions. Meanwhile let us remember that the question "What do we mean by 'knowledge'?" is not one to which there is a definite and unambiguous answer, any more than to the question "What do we mean by 'baldness'?"

QUESTIONS FOR DISCUSSION

1. Give Russell's definition of belief. Does this definition coincide with the ordinary notion of belief? If not, explain the difference(s).
2. What is the difference between a true belief and a false belief?
3. Explain the three views of knowledge associated respectively with the names of (a) Descartes, (b) Hegel, (c) Dewey.
4. What are Russell's criticisms of each of these views?

5. What criticism does Russell make of deduction as a means of attaining knowledge? Do you agree?
6. What criticism does Russell make of induction as a means of attaining knowledge?

Gilbert Ryle (1900-   )

6.5   Descartes' Myth

THE OFFICIAL DOCTRINE

There is a doctrine about the nature and place of minds which is so prevalent among theorists and even among laymen that it deserves to be described as the official theory. Most philosophers, psychologists, and religious teachers subscribe, with minor reservations, to its main articles and, although they admit certain theoretical difficulties in it, they tend to assume that these can be overcome without serious modifications being made to the architecture of the theory. It will be argued here that the central principles of the doctrine are unsound and conflict with the whole body of what we know about minds when we are not speculating about them.

The official doctrine, which hails chiefly from Descartes, is something like this. With the doubtful excep-

From *The Concept of Mind,* Chapters 1-2 (London: Hutchinson & Co., Ltd., 1949). Reprinted by permission of Hutchinson & Co., Ltd.

tions of idiots and infants in arms every human being has both a body and a mind. Some would prefer to say that every human being is both a body and a mind. His body and his mind are ordinarily harnessed together, but after death of the body his mind may continue to exist and function.

Human bodies are in space and are subject to the mechanical laws which govern all other bodies in space. Bodily processes and states can be inspected by external observers. So a man's bodily life is as much a public affair as are the lives of animals and reptiles and even as the careers of trees, crystals, and planets.

But minds are not in space, nor are their operations subject to mechanical laws. The workings of one mind are not witnessable by other observers; its career is private. Only I can take direct cognizance of the states and processes of my own mind. A person therefore lives through two collateral histories, one consisting of what happens in and to his body, the other consisting of what happens in and to his mind. The first is public, the second private. The events in the first history are events in the physical world, those in the second are events in the mental world.

It has been disputed whether a person does or can directly monitor all or only some of the episodes of his own private history; but, according to the official doctrine, of at least some of these episodes he has direct and unchallengable cognizance. In consciousness, self-consciousness, and introspection he is directly and authentically apprised of the present states and operations of his mind. He may have great or small uncertainties about concurrent and adjacent episodes in the physical world, but he can have none about at least part of what is momentarily occupying his mind.

It is customary to express this bifurcation of his two lives and of his two worlds by saying that the things and events which belong to the physical world, including his own body, are external, while the workings of his own mind are internal. This antithesis of outer and inner is, of course, meant to be construed as a metaphor, since minds, not being in space, could not be described as being spatially inside anything else, or as having things going on spatially inside themselves. But relapses from this good intention are common and theorists are found speculating how stimuli, the physical sources of which are yards or miles outside a person's skin, can generate mental responses, inside his skull, or how decisions framed inside his cranium can set going movements of his extremities.

Even when "inner" and "outer" are construed as metaphors, the problem how a person's mind and body influence one another is notoriously charged with theoretical difficulties. What the mind wills, the legs, arms, and the tongue execute; what affects the ear and the eye has something to do with what the mind perceives; grimaces and smiles betray the mind's moods; and bodily castigations lead, it is hoped, to moral improvement. But the actual transactions between the episodes of the private history and those of the public history remain mysterious, since by definition they can belong to neither series. They could not be reported among the happenings described in a person's autobiography of his inner life, nor could they be reported among those described in someone else's biography of that person's overt career. They can be inspected neither by introspection nor by laboratory experiment. They are theoretical shuttlecocks which are forever being bandied from the physiologist back to the psychologist and from the psychologist back to the physiologist.

Underlying this partly metaphorical representation of the bifurcation of a person's two lives, there is a seemingly more profound and philosophical assumption that there are two different kinds of existence or status. What exists or happens may have the status of physical existence, or it may have the status of mental existence. Somewhat as the faces of coins are either heads or tails, or somewhat as living creatures are either male or female, so, it is supposed, some existing is physical existing, other existing is mental existing. It is a necessary feature of what has physical existence that it is in space and time; it is a necessary feature of what has mental existence that it is in time but not in space. What has physical existence is composed of matter, or else is a function of matter; what has mental existence consists of consciousness, or else is a function of consciousness.

There is thus a polar opposition between mind and matter, an opposition which is often brought out as follows. Material objects are situated in a common field, known as "space," and what happens to one body in one part of space is mechanically connected with what happens to other bodies in other parts of space. But mental happenings occur in insulated fields, known as "minds," and there is, apart maybe from telepathy, no direct causal connection between what happens in one mind and what happens in another. Only through the medium of the public physical world can the mind of one person make a difference to the mind of another. The mind is its own place and in his inner life each of us lives the life of a ghostly Robinson Crusoe. People can see, hear, and jolt one another's bodies, but they are irremediably blind and deaf to the workings of one another's mind and inoperative upon them.

What sort of knowledge can be secured of the workings of a mind? On the one side, according to the official theory, a person has direct knowledge of the best imaginable kind of the workings of his own mind. Mental states and processes are (or are normally) conscious states and processes, and the consciousness which irradiates them can engender no illusions and leaves the door open for no doubts. A person's present thinkings, feelings, and willings, his perceivings,

rememberings, and imaginings are intrinsically "phosphorescent": their existence and their nature are inevitably betrayed to their owner. The inner life is a stream of consciousness of such a sort that it would be absurd to suggest that the mind whose life is that stream might be unaware of what is passing down it.

True, the evidence adduced recently by Freud seems to show that there exist channels tributary to this stream, which run hidden from their owner. People are actuated by impulses the existence of which they vigorously disavow; some of their thoughts differ from the thoughts which they acknowledge; and some of the actions which they think they will to perform they do not really will. They are thoroughly gulled by some of their own hypocrisies and they successfully ignore facts about their mental lives which on the official theory ought to be patent to them. Holders of the official theory tend, however, to maintain that anyhow in normal circumstances a person must be directly and authentically seized of the present state of workings of his own mind.

Besides being currently supplied with these alleged immediate data of consciousness, a person is also generally supposed to be able to exercise from time to time a special kind of perception, namely, inner perception, or introspection. He can take a (nonoptical) "look" at what is passing in his mind. Not only can he view and scrutinize a flower through his sense of sight and listen to and discriminate the notes of a bell through his sense of hearing; he can also reflectively or introspectively watch, without any bodily organ of sense, the current episodes of his inner life. This self-observation is also commonly supposed to be immune from illusion, confusion, or doubt. A mind's reports of its own affairs have a certainty superior to the best that is possessed by its reports of matters in the physical world. Sense-perceptions can, but consciousness and introspection cannot, be mistaken or confused.

On the other side, one person has no direct access of any sort to the events of the inner life of another. He cannot do better than make problematic inferences from the observed behavior of the other person's body to the states of mind which, by analogy from his own conduct, he supposes to be signalized by that behavior. Direct access to the workings of a mind is the privilege of that mind itself; in default of such privileged access, the workings of one mind are inevitably occult to everyone else. For the supposed arguments from bodily movements similar to their own to mental workings similar to their own would lack any possibility of observational corroboration. Not unnaturally, therefore, an adherent of the official theory finds it difficult to resist this consequence of his premises, that he has no good reason to believe that there do exist minds other than his own. Even if he prefers to believe that to other human bodies there are harnessed minds not unlike his own, he cannot claim to be able to discover their individual characteristics, or the particular things that they undergo and do. Absolute solitude is on this showing the ineluctable destiny of the soul. Only our bodies can meet.

As a necessary corollary of this general scheme there is implicitly prescribed a special way of construing our ordinary concepts of mental powers and operations. The verbs, nouns, and adjectives, with which in ordinary life we describe the wits, characters, and higher-grade performances of the people with whom we have to do, are required to be construed as signifying special episodes in their secret histories, or else as signifying tendencies for such episodes to occur. When someone is described as knowing, believing, or guessing something, as hoping, dreading, intending, or shirking something, as designing this or being amused at that, these verbs are supposed to denote the occurrence or specific modifications in his (to us) occult stream of consciousness. Only his own privileged access to this stream in direct awareness and introspection could provide authentic testimony that these mental-conduct verbs were correctly or incorrectly applied. The onlooker, be he teacher, critic, biographer, or friend, can never assure himself that his comments have any vestige of truth. Yet it was just because we do in fact all know how to make such comments, make them with general correctness and correct them when they turn out to be confused or mistaken, that philosophers found it necessary to construct their theories of the nature and place of minds. Finding mental-conduct concepts being regularly and effectively used, they properly sought to fix their logical geography. But the logical geography officially recommended would entail that there could be no regular or effective use of these mental-conduct concepts in our descriptions of, and prescriptions for, other people's minds.

THE ABSURDITY OF THE OFFICIAL DOCTRINE

Such in outline is the official theory. I shall often speak of it, with deliberate abusiveness, as "the dogma of the Ghost in the Machine." I hope to prove that it is entirely false, and false not in detail but in principle. It is not merely an assemblage of particular mistakes. It is one big mistake and a mistake of a special kind. It is, namely, a category-mistake. It represents the facts of mental life as if they belonged to one logical type or category (or range of types or categories), when they actually belong to another. The dogma is, therefore, a philosopher's myth. In attempting to explode the myth I shall probably be taken to be denying well-known facts about the mental life of human beings, and my plea that I aim at doing nothing more than rectify the logic of mental-conduct concepts will probably be disallowed as mere subterfuge.

I must first indicate what is meant by the phrase "category-mistake." This I do in a series of illustrations.

A foreigner visiting Oxford or Cambridge for the first time is shown a number of colleges, libraries, playing fields, museums, scientific departments, and administrative offices. He then asks, "But where is the University? I have seen where the members of the Colleges live, where the Registrar works, where the scientists experiment and the rest. But I have not yet seen the University in which reside and work the members of your University." It has then to be explained to him that the University is not another collateral institution, some ulterior counterpart to the colleges, laboratories and offices which he has seen. The University is just the way in which all that he has already seen is organized. When they are seen and when their co-ordination is understood, the University has been seen. His mistake lay in his innocent assumption that it was correct to speak of Christ Church, the Bodleian Library, the Ashmolean Museum, *and* the University, to speak, that is, as if "the University" stood for an extra member of the class of which these other units are members. He was mistakenly allocating the University to the same category as that to which the other institutions belong.

The same mistake would be made by a child witnessing the march-past of a division, who, having had pointed out to him such and such battalions, batteries, squadrons, etc., asked when the division was going to appear. He would be supposing that a division was a counterpart to the units already seen, partly similar to them and partly unlike them. He would be shown his mistake by being told that in watching the battalions, batteries, and squadrons marching past he had been watching the division marching past. The march-past was not a parade of battalions, batteries, squadrons, *and* a division; it was a parade of the battalions, batteries, and squadrons *of* a division.

One more illustration. A foreigner watching his first game of cricket learns what are the functions of the bowlers, the batsmen, the fielders, the umpires, and the scorers. He then says, "But there is no one left on the field to contribute the famous element of team-spirit. I see who does the bowling, the batting, and the wicket-keeping; but I do not see whose role it is to exercise *esprit de corps*." Once more, it would have to be explained that he was looking for the wrong type of thing. Team-spirit is not another cricketing-operation supplementary to all of the other special tasks. It is, roughly, the keenness with which each of the special tasks is performed, and performing a task keenly is not performing two tasks. Certainly exhibiting team-spirit is not the same thing as bowling or catching, but nor is it a third thing such that we can say that the bowler first bowls *and* then exhibits team-spirit or that a fielder is at a given moment *either* catching *or* displaying *esprit de corps*.

These illustrations of category-mistakes have a common feature which must be noticed. The mistakes were made by people who did not know how to wield the concepts *University, division,* and *team-spirit.* Their puzzles arose from inability to use certain items in the English vocabulary.

The theoretically interesting category-mistakes are those made by people who are perfectly competent to apply concepts, at least in the situations with which they are familiar, but are still liable in their abstract thinking to allocate those concepts to logical types to which they do not belong. An instance of a mistake of this sort would be the following story. A student of politics has learned the main differences between the British, the French, and the American Constitutions, and has learned also the differences and connections between the Cabinet, Parliament, the various Ministries, the Judicature, and the Church of England. But he still be-

comes embarrassed when asked questions about the connections between the Church of England, the Home Office, and the British Constitution. For while the Church and the Home Office are institutions, the British Constitution is not another institution in the same sense of that noun. So inter-institutional relations which can be asserted or denied to hold between the Church and the Home Office cannot be asserted or denied to hold between either of them and the British Constitution. "The British Constitution" is not a term of the same logical type as "the Home Office" and "the Church of England." In a partially similar way, John Doe may be a relative, a friend, an enemy, or a stranger to Richard Roe; but he cannot be any of these things to the Average Taxpayer. He knows how to talk sense in certain sorts of discussions about the Average Taxpayer, but he is baffled to say why he could not come across him in the street as he can come across Richard Roe.

It is pertinent to our main subject to notice that, so long as the student of politics continues to think of the British Constitution as a counterpart to the other institutions, he will tend to describe it as a mysteriously occult institution; and so long as John Doe continues to think of the Average Taxpayer as a fellow citizen, he will tend to think of him as an elusive insubstantial man, a ghost who is everywhere yet nowhere.

My destructive purpose is to show that a family of radical category-mistakes is the source of the double-life theory. The representation of a person as a ghost mysteriously ensconced in a machine derives from this argument. Because, as is true, a person's thinking, feeling, and purposive doing cannot be described solely in the idioms of physics, chemistry, and physiology, therefore they must be described in counterpart idioms. As the human body is a complex organized unit, so the human mind must be another complex organized unit, though one made of a different sort of stuff and with a different sort of structure. Or, again, as the human body, like any other parcel of matter, is a field of causes and effects, so the mind must be another field of causes and effects, though not (Heaven be praised) mechanical causes and effects.

THE ORIGIN OF THE CATEGORY-MISTAKE

One of the chief intellectual origins of what I have yet to prove to be the Cartesian category-mistake seems to be this. When Galileo showed that his methods of scientific discovery were competent to provide a mechanical theory which should cover every occupant of space, Descartes found in himself two conflicting motives. As a man of scientific genius he could not but endorse the claims of mechanics, yet as a religious and moral man he could not accept, as Hobbes accepted, the discouraging rider to those claims, namely that human nature differs only in degree of complexity from clockwork. The mental could not be just a variety of the mechanical.

He and subsequent philosophers naturally but erroneously availed themselves of the following escape-route. Since mental-conduct words are not to be construed as signifying the occurrence of mechanical processes, they must be construed as signifying the occurrence of non-mechanical processes; since mechanical laws explain movements in space as the effects of other movements in space, other laws must explain some of the non-spatial working of minds as the effects of other non-spatial workings of minds. The difference between the human behaviors which we describe as intelligent and those which we describe as unintelligent must be a difference in their causation; so, while some movements of human tongues and limbs are the effects of mechanical causes, others must be the effects of non-mechanical causes, i.e., some issue from movements of particles of matter, others from workings of the mind.

The differences between the physical and the mental were thus represented as differences inside the common framework of the categories of "thing," "stuff," "attribute," "state," "process," "change," "cause," and "effect." Minds are things, but different sorts of things from bodies; mental processes are causes and effects, but different sorts of causes and effects from bodily movements. And so on. Somewhat as the foreigner expected the University to be an extra edifice, rather like a college but also considerably different, so the repudiators of mechanism represented minds as extra centers of causal processes, rather like machines but also considerably different from them. Their theory was a para-mechanical hypothesis.

That this assumption was at the heart of the doctrine is shown by the fact that there was from the beginning felt to be a major theoretical difficulty in explaining how minds can influence and be influenced by bodies. How can a mental process, such as willing, cause spatial movements like the movements of the tongue? How can a physical change in the optic nerve have among its effects a mind's perception of a flash of light? This notorious crux by itself shows the logical mould into which Descartes pressed his theory of the mind. It was the self-same mould into which he and Galileo set their mechanics. Still unwittingly adhering to the grammar of mechanics, he tried to avert disaster by describing minds in what was merely an obverse vocabulary. The workings of minds had to be described by the mere negatives of the specific descriptions given to bodies; they are not in space, they are not motions, they are not modifications of matter, they are not accessible to public observation. Minds are not bits of clockwork, they are just bits of not-clockwork.

As thus represented, minds are not merely ghosts harnessed to machines, they are themselves just spectral machines. Though the human body is an engine, it is not quite an ordinary engine, since some of its workings are governed by another engine inside it—this interior governor-engine being one of a very special sort. It is invisible, inaudible, and it has no size or weight. It cannot be taken to bits and the laws it obeys are not those known to ordinary engineers. Nothing is known of how it governs the bodily engine.

A second major crux points the same moral. Since, according to the doctrine, minds belong to the same category as bodies and since bodies are rigidly governed by mechanical laws, it seemed to many theorists to follow that minds must be similarly governed by rigid non-mechanical laws. The physical world is a deterministic system, so the mental world must be a deterministic system. Bodies cannot help the modifications that they undergo, so minds cannot help pursuing the careers fixed for them. *Responsibility, choice, merit,* and *demerit* are, therefore, inapplicable concepts—unless the compromise solution is adopted of saying that the laws governing mental processes, unlike those governing physical processes, have the congenial attribute of being only rather rigid. The problem of the Freedom of the Will was the problem how to reconcile the hypothesis that minds are to be described in terms drawn from the categories of mechanics with the knowledge that higher-grade human conduct is not of a piece with the behavior of machines.

It is an historical curiosity that it was not noticed that the entire argument was broken-backed. Theorists correctly assumed that any sane man could already recognize the differences between, say, rational and non-rational utterances or between purposive and automatic behavior. Else there would have been nothing requiring to be salved from mechanism. Yet the explanation given presupposed that one person could in principle never recognize the difference between the rational and the irrational utterances issuing from other human bodies, since he could never get access to the postulated immaterial causes of some of their utterances. Save for the doubtful exception of himself, he could never tell the difference between a man and a robot. It would have to be conceded, for example, that, for all that we can tell, the inner lives of persons who are classed as idiots or lunatics are as rational as those of anyone else. Perhaps only their overt behavior is disappointing; that is to say, perhaps "idiots" are not really idiotic, or "lunatics" lunatic. Perhaps, too, some of those who are classed as sane are really idiots. According to the theory, external observers could never know how the overt behavior of others is correlated with their mental powers and processes, and so they could never know or even plausibly conjecture whether their applications of mental-conduct concepts to these other people were correct or incorrect. It would then be hazardous or impossible for a man to claim sanity or logical consistency even for himself, since he would be debarred from comparing his own performances with those of others. In short, our characterizations of persons and their performances as intelligent, prudent, and virtuous or as stupid, hypocritical, and cowardly could never have been made, so the problem of providing a special causal hypothesis to serve as the basis of such diagnoses would never have arisen. The question, "How do persons differ from machines?" arose just because everyone already knew how to apply mental-conduct concepts before the new causal hypothesis was introduced. This causal hypothesis could not, therefore, be the source of the criteria used in those applications. Nor, of course, has the causal hypothesis in any degree improved our handling of those criteria. We still distinguish good from bad arithmetic, politic from impolitic conduct, and fertile

from infertile imaginations in the ways in which Descartes himself distinguished them before and after he speculated how the applicability of these criteria was compatible with the principle of mechanical causation.

He had mistaken the logic of his problem. Instead of asking by what criteria intelligent behavior is actually distinguished from non-intelligent behavior, he asked, "Given that the principle of mechanical causation does not tell us the difference, what other causal principle will tell it us?" He realized that the problem was not one of mechanics and assumed that it must, therefore, be one of some counterpart to mechanics. Not unnaturally psychology is often cast for just this role.

When two terms belong to the same category, it is proper to construct conjunctive propositions embodying them. Thus a purchaser may say that he bought a left-hand glove and a right-hand glove, but not that he bought a left-hand glove, a right-hand glove, and a pair of gloves. "She came home in a flood of tears and a sedan-chair" is a well-known joke based on the absurdity of conjoining terms of different types. It would have been equally ridiculous to construct the disjunction, "She came home either in a flood of tears or else in a sedan-chair." Now the dogma of the Ghost in the Machine does just this. It maintains that there exist both bodies and minds; that there occur physical processes and mental processes; that there are mechanical causes of corporeal movements and mental causes of corporeal movements. I shall argue that these and other analogous conjunctions are absurd; but, it must be noticed, the argument will not show that either of the illegitimately conjoined propositions is absurd in itself. I am not, for example, denying that there occur mental processes. Doing long division is a mental process and so is making a joke. But I am saying that the phrase "there occur mental processes" does not mean the same sort of thing as "there occur physical processes," and, therefore, that it makes no sense to conjoin or disjoin the two.

If my argument is successful, there will follow some interesting consequences. First, the hallowed contrast between Mind and Matter will be dissipated, but dissipated not by either of the equally hallowed absorptions of Mind by Matter or of Matter by Mind, but in quite a different way. For the seeming contrast of the two will be shown to be as illegitimate as would be the contrast of "she came home in a flood of tears" and "she came home in a sedan-chair." The belief that there is a polar opposition between Mind and Matter is the belief that they are terms of the same logical type.

It will also follow that both Idealism and Materialism are answers to an improper question. The "reduction" of the material world to mental states and processes, as well as the "reduction" of mental states and processes to physical states and processes, presuppose the legitimacy of the disjunction "Either there exist minds or there exist bodies (but not both)." It would be like saying, "Either she bought a left-hand and a right-hand glove or she bought a pair of gloves (but not both)."

It is perfectly proper to say, in one logical tone of voice, that there exist minds and to say, in another logical tone of voice, that there exist bodies. But these expressions do not indicate two different species of existence, for "existence" is not a generic word like "colored" or "sexed." They indicate two different senses of "exist," somewhat as "rising" has different senses in "the tide is rising," "hopes are rising," and "the average age of death is rising." A man would be thought to be making a poor joke who said that three things are now rising, namely the tide, hopes, and the average age of death. It would be just as good or bad a joke to say that there exist prime numbers and Wednesdays and public opinions and navies; or that there exist both minds and bodies. In the succeeding chapters I try to prove that the official theory does rest on a batch of category-mistakes by showing that logically absurd corollaries follow from it. The exhibition of these absurdities will have the constructive effect of bringing out part of the correct logic of mental-conduct concepts.

HISTORICAL NOTE

It would not be true to say that the official theory derives solely from Descartes' theories, or even from a more widespread anxiety about the implications of seventeenth-century mechanism. Scholastic and Reformation theology had schooled the intellects of the scientists as well as of the laymen, philosophers, and clerics of that age. Stoic-Augustinian theories of the will were embedded in the Calvinist doctrines of sin and grace; Platonic and Aristotelian theories of the intellect shaped the orthodox doctrines of the immortality of the soul. Descartes was reformulating already prevalent theological doctrines of the soul in the new syntax of Galileo. The theologian's privacy of conscience became the philosopher's privacy of consciousness, and what had been the bogy of Predestination reappeared as the bogy of Determinism.

It would also not be true to say that the two-worlds myth did no theoretical good. Myths often do a lot of theoretical good, while they are still new. One benefit bestowed by the para-mechanical myth was that it partly superannuated the then prevalent para-political myth. Minds and their Faculties had previously been described by analogies with political superiors and political subordinates. The idioms used were those of ruling, obeying, collaborating, and rebelling. They survived and still survive in many ethical and some epistemological discussions. As, in physics, the new myth of occult Forces was a scientific improvement on the old myth of Final Causes, so, in anthropological and psychological theory, the new myth of hidden operations, impulses, and agencies was an improvement on the old myth of dictations, deferences, and disobediences. . . .

THE MOTIVES OF THE INTELLECTUALIST LEGEND

Why are people so strongly drawn to believe, in the face of their own daily experience, that the intelligent execution of an operation must embody two processes, one of doing and another of theorizing? Part of the answer is that they are wedded to the dogma of the ghost in the machine. Since doing is often an overt muscular affair, it is written off as a merely physical process. On the assumption of the antithesis between "physical" and "mental," it follows that muscular doing cannot itself be a mental operation. To earn the title "skillful," "cunning," or "humorous," it must, therefore, get it by transfer from another counterpart act occurring not "in the machine" but "in the ghost"; for "skillful," "cunning," and "humorous" are certainly mental predicates.

It is, of course, perfectly true that when we characterize as witty or tactful some piece of overt behavior, we are not considering only the muscular movements which we witness. A parrot might have made the same remark in the same situation without our crediting it with a sense of humor, or a lout might have done precisely what the tactful man did, without our thinking him tactful. But if one and the same vocal utterance is a stroke of humor from the humorist, but a mere noise-response when issuing from the parrot, it is tempting to say that we are ascribing wit, not to something that we hear, but to something else that we do not hear. We are accordingly tempted to say that what makes one audible or visible action witty, while another audibly or visibly similar action was not, is that the former was attended by another inaudible and invisible action which was the real exercise of wit. But to admit, as we must, that there may be no visible or audible difference between a tactful or witty act and a tactless or humorless one is not to admit that the difference is constituted by the performance or non-performance of some extra secret acts.

The cleverness of the clown may be exhibited in his tripping and tumbling. He trips and tumbles just as clumsy people do, except that he trips and tumbles on purpose and after much rehearsal and at the golden moment and where the children can see him and so as not to hurt himself. The spectators applaud his skill at seeming clumsy, but what they applaud is not some extra hidden performance executed "in his head." It is his visible performance that they admire, but they admire it not for being an effect of any hidden internal causes but for being an exercise of a skill. Now a skill is not an act. It is, therefore, neither a witnessable nor an unwitnessable act. To recognize that a performance is an exercise of a skill is indeed to appreciate it in the light of a factor which could not be separately recorded by a camera. But the reason why the skill exercised in a performance cannot be separately recorded by a camera is not that it is an occult or ghostly happening, but that it is not a happening at all. It is a disposition, or complex of dispositions, and a disposition is a factor of the wrong logical type to be seen or unseen, recorded or unrecorded. Just as the habit of talking loudly is not itself loud or quiet, since it is not the sort of term of which "loud" and "quiet" can be predicated, or just as a susceptibility to headaches is for the same reason not itself unendurable or endurable, so the skills, tastes, and bents which are exercised in overt or internal operations are not themselves overt or internal, witnessable or unwitnessable. The traditional theory of the mind has misconstrued the type-distinction between disposition and exercise into its mythical bifurcation of unwitnessable mental causes and their witnessable physical effects.

The clown's trippings and tumblings are the workings of his mind, for they are his jokes; but the visibly similar trippings and tumblings of a clumsy man are not the workings of that man's mind. For he does not trip on purpose. Tripping on purpose is both a bodily and a mental process, but it is not two processes, such as one process of purposing to trip and, as an effect, another process of tripping. Yet the old myth dies hard. We are still tempted to argue that if the clown's antics exhibit carefulness, judgment, wit, and appreciation of the moods of his spectators, there must be occurring in the clown's head a counterpart performance to that which is taking place on the sawdust. If he is thinking what he is doing, there must be occurring behind his painted face a cogitative shadow-operation which we do not witness, tallying with, and controlling, the bodily contortions which we do witness. Surely the thinking of thoughts is the basic activity of minds and surely, too, the process of thinking is an invisible and inaudible process. So how can the clown's visible and audible performance be his mind at work?

To do justice to this objection it is necessary to make a verbal concession. There has fairly recently come into general use a certain special sense of the words "mental" and "mind." We speak of "mental arithmetic," of "mind-reading," and of debates going on "in the mind," and it certainly is the case that what is in this sense mental is unwitnessable. A boy is said to be doing "mental arithmetic" when instead of writing down, or reciting aloud, the numerical symbols with which he is operating, he says them to himself, performing his calculations in silent soliloquy. Similarly, a person is said to be reading the mind of another when he describes truly what the other is saying or picturing to himself in auditory or visual images. That these are special uses of "mental" and "mind" is easily shown. For a boy who does his calculating aloud, or on paper, may be reasoning correctly and organizing his steps methodically; his reckoning is not the less a careful intellectual operation for being conducted in public instead of in private. His performance is, therefore, an exercise of a mental faculty in the normal sense of "mental."

Now calculating does not first acquire the rank of proper thinking when its author begins to do it with his lips closed and his hands in his pockets. The sealing of the lips is no part of the definition of thinking. A man may think aloud or half under his breath; he may think silently, yet with lip movements conspicuous enough to be read by a lip reader; or he may, as most of us have done since nursery days, think in silence and with motionless lips. The differences are differences of social and personal convenience, of celerity, and of facility. They need import no more differences into the coherence, cogency, or appropriateness of the intellectual operations performed than is imported into them by a writer's preference for pencils over pens, or for invisible ink over ordinary ink. A deaf and dumb person talks in manual signs. Perhaps, when he wants to keep his thoughts to himself, he makes these signs with his hands kept behind his back or under the table. The fact that these signs might happen to be observed by a Paul Pry would not lead us or their maker to say that he was not thinking.

This special use of "mental" and "mind" in which they signify what is done "in one's head" cannot be used as evidence for the dogma of the ghost in the machine. It is nothing but a contagion from that dogma. The technical trick of conducting our thinking in auditory word-images, instead of in spoken words, does indeed secure secrecy for our thinking, since the auditory imaginings of one person are not seen or heard by another (or, as we shall see, by their owner either). But this secrecy is not the secrecy ascribed to the postulated episodes of the ghostly shadow-world. It is merely the convenient privacy which characterizes the tunes that run in my head and the things that I see in my mind's eye.

Moreover, the fact that a person says things to himself in his head does not entail that he is thinking. He can babble deliriously, or repeat jingles in inner speech, just as he can in talking aloud. The distinction between talking sense and babbling, or between thinking what one is saying and merely saying, cuts across the distinction between talking aloud and talking to oneself. What makes a verbal operation an exercise of intellect is independent of what makes it public or private. Arithmetic done with pencil and paper may be more intelligent than mental arithmetic, and the public tumblings of the clown may be more intelligent than the tumblings which he merely "sees" in his mind's eye or "feels" in his mind's legs, if, as may or may not be the case, any such imaginings of antics occur.

QUESTIONS FOR DISCUSSION

1. Describe what Ryle calls "The Official Doctrine." Look back at Descartes' *Meditations* (selection 2.3) to see whether Ryle has correctly presented Descartes' views. Has he?
2. Why does Ryle regard the Official Doctrine as absurd?
3. What is a category mistake? Give some examples of category mistakes.
4. Explain what Ryle means by a para-mechanical hypothesis.
5. Explain in your own words what Ryle means by the Dogma of the Ghost in the Machine.

FURTHER READINGS FOR CHAPTER 6

Austin, John L., *Philosophical Papers,* J. O. Urmson and G. J. Warnock, eds. New York: Oxford University Press, 1961.

————, *Sense and Sensibilia,* G. J. Warnock, ed. New York: Oxford University Press, 1962.

*Ayer, A. J., *The Foundations of Empirical Knowledge.* New York: St. Martin's, n.d.

————, ed., *Logical Positivism.* New York: Free Press, 1958.

————, *Philosophical Essays.* New York: St. Martin's, 1954.

*————, *The Problem of Knowledge.* Harmondsworth, England: Penguin Books, n.d.

*Berkeley, George, *Three Dialogues Between Hylas and Philonous.* Indianapolis: Bobbs-Merrill, 1954.

Blanshard, Brand, *The Nature of Thought,* 2 vols. New York: Macmillan, 1940.

*Carnap, Rudolf, *Meaning and Necessity: A Study in Semantics and Model Logic.* Chicago: University of Chicago Press, 1958.

————, "The Methodological Character of Theoretical Concepts," in *The Foundations of Science and the Concepts of Psychology and Psychoanalysis,* Minnesota Studies in the Philosophy of Science, Vol. I, Herbert Feigl and Michael Scriven, eds. Minneapolis: University of Minnesota Press, 1956.

*Chappell, Vere C., ed., *The Philosophy of Mind.* Englewood Cliffs, N.J.: Prentice-Hall, 1962.

Chisholm, Roderick M., *Perceiving: A Philosophical Study.* Ithaca: Cornell University Press, 1957.

————, *Realism and the Background of Phenomenology.* New York: Free Press, n.d.

———

* Paperback edition.

*Descartes, René, *Essential Works of Descartes*, Lowell Bair, trans. New York: Bantam, 1966, 2nd ed.

Feigl, Herbert, and Wilfrid Sellars, eds., *Readings in Philosophical Analysis*. New York: Appleton-Century-Crofts, 1949.

Flew, Antony, ed., *Logic and Language*, 2 vols. New York: Philosophical Library, 1953.

*Hempel, Carl G., *Fundamentals of Concept Formation in Empirical Science*. Chicago: University of Chicago Press, 1952.

Hirst, R. J., *The Problems of Perception*. London: Allen & Unwin, 1959.

*Hume, David, *An Inquiry Concerning Human Understanding*. (Numerous editions available.)

*————, *Treatise of Human Nature*. New York: Doubleday, n.d.

*Kant, Immanuel, *Critique of Pure Reason*, 2nd rev. ed., F. M. Muller, trans. New York: Doubleday, n.d.

*————, *Prolegomena to Any Future Metaphysics*, L. W. Beck and Paul Carus, trans. Indianapolis: Bobbs-Merrill, n.d.

Leibniz, Gottfried Wilhelm von, *New Essays Concerning Human Understanding*, A. G. Langley, trans. LaSalle, Ill.: Open Court, n.d.

*Lewis, C. I., *Analysis of Knowledge and Valuation*. LaSalle, Ill.: Open Court, 1947.

*————, *Mind and the World Order*. New York: Dover, n.d.

Linsky, Leonard, ed., *Semantics and the Philosophy of Language*. Urbana: University of Illinois Press, 1952.

*Locke, John, *An Essay Concerning Human Understanding*, A. C. Fraser, ed., 2 vols. New York: Dover, 1959.

*Moore, George Edward, *Philosophical Papers*. New York: Collier Books, 1962.

*————, *Philosophical Studies*. Paterson, N.J.: Littlefield, Adams & Co., 1959.

*————, *Some Main Problems of Philosophy*. New York: Collier Books, n.d.

Pap, Arthur, *Semantics and Necessary Truth*. New Haven: Yale University Press, 1958.

*Plato, *Theatetus*, Benjamin Jowett, trans. Indianapolis: Bobbs-Merrill, 1959.

Quine, Willard van Orman, *Word and Object*. New York: John Wiley, 1960.

*Russell, Bertrand, *Human Knowledge: Its Scope and Limits*. New York: Simon & Schuster, 1962.

————, *An Inquiry into Meaning and Truth*. New York: Norton, 1940.

*————, *Our Knowledge of the External World*. New York: New American Library of World Literature, 1960.

*————, *Problems of Philosophy*. New York: Oxford University Press, 1912.

*Ryle, Gilbert, *The Concept of Mind*. New York: Barnes & Noble, 1950.

*Santayana, George, *Scepticism and Animal Faith*. New York: Dover, 1955.

*Spinoza, Benedict de, *On the Improvement of the Understanding*, J. Katz, trans. Indianapolis: Bobbs-Merrill, 1958.

Wisdom, John, *Other Minds*. New York: Philosophical Library, 1952.

Wittgenstein, Ludwig, *The Blue and Brown Books*. New York: Harper & Row, 1958.

————, *Philosophical Investigations*, G. E. M. Anscombe, trans. New York: Macmillan, 1953.

Chapter 7

THEORIES OF ART AND AESTHETICS

INTRODUCTION

To the realm of art and aesthetic experience one hesitates to bring critical reflection. Before the products of art we stand in rapture; the word that expresses our feelings is *ineffable,* and the ineffable is not prone to analysis. Yet if not at the moment of aesthetic experience, at a later time questions begin to rise. What was it that moved us so deeply upon hearing a certain musical piece? Why did we say that the painting we saw was beautiful? Has the ugly or the neutral any place in art? Why do we call certain objects works of art? Do they all have some common trait? Why is it that we consider certain works of art as great and others as inferior? Are there absolute standards of taste or are they merely relative? Has art any function in civilization, and if so, what is it? These and similar questions when fully analyzed become the basis of one's philosophy of art and aesthetics.

Before examining some of these questions we ought briefly to define our terms. Art, in its inclusive sense, refers to any manipulation of objects or events for any human purpose whatsoever. We speak of the art of masonry, the art of weaving, the art of speech, the art of writing, the art of politics, the art of war. Usually art is divided into two types: useful or technical art and fine art. Technical art refers to any human product that is useful for an end other than aesthetic effect. The central notion here is utility. Cars, machines, and tools are examples of technical art. Fine art, on the other hand, refers to products whose end is aesthetic effect, commonly referred to as beauty. A painting, a statue, a poem, a piece of music are examples of fine art. In the present discussion, art will be used in the sense of fine art unless otherwise specified. Similarly, the general meaning of aesthetics is much broader than the sense in which it will be used here. The word *aesthetic*, derived originally from the Greek, referred to anything that is perceptive. Gradually, however, it came to be applied to the realms of art and beauty. We shall therefore use the term to designate any experience that has relevance to art, whether the experience be that of the creative artist or of the appreciator. Some of the major theories of art and aesthetics will now be examined, and philosophic questions will be raised concerning the nature and function of art.

Art as Imitation and as Inspiration

One of the oldest theories of art is that art is essentially imitation. Plato gives expression to this theory, though it is not the only theory of art that he presents. Plato describes the art of painting, for example, as an imitation of appearances, say of a tree or a bed, with such similitude that one may mistake the copy for the real thing. In his words: "A painter will paint a cobbler, carpenter, or any other artist, though he knows nothing of their arts; and, if he is a good artist, he may deceive children or simple persons, when he shows them his picture of a carpenter from a distance, and they will fancy that they are looking at a real carpenter." [1] But it is just because the poets and the painters are imitators that they are incapable of discerning what is good and what is bad. In Plato's state there is no place for the artist. "When we have anointed him with myrrh, and set a garland upon his head, we shall send him away to another city."

In his *Poetics,* Aristotle presents a modified form of the imitation theory of art. For Aristotle, poetry springs from the instinct for harmony and rhythm. The instinct of imitation "is implanted in man from childhood, one difference between him and the other animals being that he is the most imitative of living creatures and through imitation he learns his earliest lessons." Aristotle not only finds the source of poetry in the mimetic instinct but he indicates that it is "also natural for all to delight in works of imitation."

Aristotle also refers to tragedy as an imitation "of men and action" (see selection 7.1). This view of tragedy calls for "lifelikeness" and "plausibility." A tragedy should have a "beginning, middle and end" and the connections should be "probable and necessary." Tragedy characteristically arouses the emotions of fear and pity; yet these emotions in tragedy give rise to "catharsis," which is pleasurable. Why catharsis is a pleasurable experience has been the source of many discussions. At least one of its aspects is the relief of emotional agitation.

The theory of art as imitation is too simple to be satisfactory. If art is merely an exact imitation of the original, why, as Socrates points out, should

---

[1] *The Republic,* Book X, translated by Benjamin Jowett.

we go to art? Is not the original much superior? A painting of a tree can never completely capture the colors and shape of the real tree. If fine art is merely an imitation, it is at best something second rate. Besides, the imitation theory of art fails to account for significant forms of art. Such major art forms as architecture, poetry, and music may occasionally make use of imitation—for instance in a floral motif or in a pastoral theme—but these imitations are minor aspects. Art is not so much an imitation as an enrichment of human experience through objective forms; imitation is passive, but art is essentially creative.

In the *Ion*, one of Plato's ironical dialogues, poetry is said to be the result not of logical processes but of inspiration. The poets are "simply inspired to utter that to which the Muse impels them, and that only." They speak not of themselves but utter the priceless words in a state of unconsciousness, for God himself is the speaker, and through them converses with us. Plato neither seriously entertains the inspirational view of poetry nor wholly rejects it. Yet he does make a distinction between rational knowledge and the inspired words of the poets.

Art as Insight into Reality

A more metaphysical theory of art holds that the aesthetic experience is a species of knowledge. Sometimes the claim is that the aesthetic experience is insight into some transcendental reality, independent of observed particular objects. Beauty, for example, in this view is not a mundane quality of certain objects in their natural environment but is a universal, something over and above all particular beautiful objects. And sometimes, though less frequently, the claim is that art and aesthetics are not so much insight into universals but rather into particular objects and situations. In both cases the fundamental belief is that art is a form of cognition.

Plato, who is the source of so many major theories of art, argues in some of his dialogues—especially in the *Symposium* and the *Phaedrus*—that beauty, with truth and goodness, is an eternal, changeless reality. Beauty belongs to the realm of Ideas or Forms, and these for him are perfect, absolute, immutable. A given beautiful object only partially expresses and vaguely reminds us of absolute beauty. Absolute beauty cannot be perceived in our ordinary experience. To attain it one must go through a spiritual struggle. In the *Symposium* Plato describes the steps of this ascent. To attain the final vision of absolute beauty one should begin early in life to be sensitive to physical beauty, then gradually go beyond physical beauty and learn to love the beauty of the soul, even when it is not expressed in outward comeliness. Next, one must learn to love beauty as revealed in laws and institutions, and then advance to "science." But even here you have not reached the end of the ascent. The final step is the one that will reward you with the vision of supreme beauty which was all along the object of your search. Beauty at this highest level is eternal and perfect, above mutability. Particular beautiful objects are mere echoes, imitations, reminders of the absolute beauty.

According to the classic view, art is a species of cognition. For Plato it is an apprehension of form, and for the later Platonist on this subject, like Schopenhauer, art is a way of securing knowledge of reality. Benedetto Croce retains the fundamental thesis that art is cognitive, though for him the object of knowledge is the individual thing and not the universal or the Idea in the Platonic sense. For Croce reality is spirit developing in several independent ways (see selection 7.2). The various aspects of reality do not have to be reduced to one another. In the activity of the spirit one may distinguish between contemplation and action. We perceive, know, and also act. The perceptive aspect of experience may be assigned to intuition; the intellectual aspect to concept formation. Art belongs to the realm of intuition. For Croce art is intuition, and intuition includes all that is concrete and immediate in experience. Intuition involves sense-data; it also involves memory, imagination, feeling. Croce also defines art as expression, but intuition and expression are identical for him. "To intuit is to express, and nothing else." Expression takes the form of images: color-images, line-images, word-images. These images are not mere passive impressions but are meaningful and charged with feeling. Aesthetic experience is thus expression in images; and the physical creative work of art, such as a painting, a statue, or a poem, is nothing but a copy of what the artist has experienced.

Alexander's elegant discussion on beauty [2] should be studied carefully as a corrective of Croce's neglect of the physical in his definition of art. Croce's interpretation of art in terms of intuition tends to drift toward extreme subjectivism. Alexander rightly points out that art both in its origin as well as in its creation depends on external material. As he expresses it: "Art grows out of craft and goes beyond it, when the worker handles his materials not, or not only, as a means of reaching a certain practical end but for their own sakes, and becomes contemplative instead of merely practical."

We need not examine here the basic ideas of Plato's and Croce's philosophical systems. The issues are complex and would lead us too far from the present subject. Yet it is important to note that valuable ideas of these philosophers about art and aesthetics can be retained without necessarily consenting to their theories of reality. Plato's insistence that the vision of beauty can be attained only through a spiritual ascent, and Croce's account of aesthetic experience as intuition and expression—both of these views have permanent value. One may accept the empirical insights of these philosophers into different phases of aesthetic experience without submitting to their more doubtful and speculative metaphysics.

[2] Samuel Alexander, *Beauty and Other Forms of Value* (New York: The Macmillan Company, 1933), pp. 15-26.

Art as Expression of Feeling and Desire

The view of art as insight into reality places absolute beauty above the mundane realm and emphasizes the vision and contemplation of this beauty. Yet to make art and its experience more intelligible and vital, greater continuity has to be established between art and other activities of life. Art occupies too wide an area of human life to be exclusively identified with the rare insights of geniuses. Some of the more recent theories of art make crucial the active, conative, and affective aspects. The play theory of art emphasizes activity, origins, functions. A variety of thinkers have found this theory of art fruitful. The theory has its beginnings in some of the Greek philosophers, but one who is interested in a more adequate presentation of this theory should go primarily to the writings of Schiller, Spencer, and Groos, where he will find its full development and implications.

Common to the more dominant recent theories which stress the conative and affective aspects is the claim that art is primarily concerned with the satisfaction and expression of desires and feelings. There are, of course, many variations within the general frame. One of the earlier proponents of this theory was Tolstoi. For Tolstoi, art is primarily the language of feeling, a means by which men transmit feeling in the same way that they transmit thought by speech. "Art is a human activity, consisting in this that one man consciously, by means of certain external signs, hands on to others feelings he has lived through, and that other people are infected by these feelings, and also experience them." The criterion of art is thus its degree of infectiousness, its ability to evoke in the observer or reader the feelings of the artist. These feelings are transmitted by means of movements, lines, colors, sounds, and words. The subject matter of art is as broad as life itself. The relation of man to his world is constantly taking on new aspects, and this fact provides unlimited material for artists. Yet the feelings connected with pleasure are quite limited, since they consist almost exclusively of pride, sex-expression, and weariness with life. In any case, they have long ago been interpreted by artists, so that their field is exhausted. In order to produce a real work of art, the artist must move on the level of the highest conception of humanity, and must experience the emotion that flowers on this level.

In DeWitt Parker's view, art is the imaginative expression of a wish (see selection 7.3). According to him wishes may be satisfied in two ways: in the real way and in the dream way. The first is the practical way: you satisfy your hunger by getting food. The second is the imaginary way—here "there is no acquisitive interaction with environment; the wish is satisfied by something that occurs entirely within myself, within my own mind and body in the realm of fantasy." Parker goes on to show some of the characteristics of dream experience, one being the "as if" attitude. Things seen in a daydream or in a dream at night are regarded "as if" they were actually real, not merely imaginary.

Parker applies his view of the imagination and the dream to various forms of art and tries to show that all are modes of make-believe which satisfy wishes both of the creator and beholder. That such arts as painting, sculpture, literature, and drama can be made to conform to his theory seems clear enough, but he claims the same conformity for music, the dance, and architecture.

Yet there are differences, for Parker, between ordinary dreams and art. A dream in the ordinary sense is an inner fact existing wholly in the realm of imagination, but art belongs also to the outer world, the world of the senses. In art the dream is given sensuous shape; it is expressed in colors, lines, sounds, and so on. The artist creates something external that can charm the senses. Yet despite the sensuous side of art, it does not leave the world of the imagination; rather the artist takes the senses into the imagination. A work of art possesses objectivity, the tang of reality, while still remaining a dream. Because of this objectivity, a work of art not only satisfies a wish as does any sort of dream, but it also becomes a means for "the clarification and communication of imagination." Art, for Parker, is expression, not the practical or scientific kind, but "expression for the sake of expression because in the process of expression a dream is embodied, a wish satisfied."

Finally, there is George Santayana's theory of "objectified pleasure." He first makes a distinction between the pleasures of the senses and the pleasure that is traceable to the sense of beauty. The former involves no assertion beyond the individual's experience, while the latter claims universality. When something gives me pleasure I do not assert that it must give pleasure to others too, but when I judge something to be beautiful my judgment means that "the thing is beautiful in itself, or . . . that it should seem so to everybody." Yet theoretically Santayana thinks it is difficult to defend the universality of aesthetic judgment. There is, for example, no universal agreement among men on aesthetic matters, and whatever agreement one does observe seems to stem from similarity of origin and circumstances. And, again, it is unreasonable to insist that what appears beautiful to one person ought to appear beautiful to another. How shall we, then, explain beauty's claim of universality? Santayana resorts to the psychological tendency to objectification. At an early stage of mental development the tendency of men was to objectify every sensation and emotion and thus consider them as qualities of external objects. In our own scientific era we tend to regard as qualities of objects only such qualities as extension and other physically measurable properties. Santayana believes that in our experience of beauty we have a survival of the primitive and prescientific tendency to objectification. The fact that we try to get others to share our aesthetic experience shows that we tend to regard beauty as being in the object rather than in our minds. Santayana thus reaches his definition: "Beauty is pleasure regarded as the quality of a thing."

Santayana's definition of beauty sums up a variety of ideas. First of all, beauty for Santayana is a value, that is, it is not the perception of a fact but rather of "an emotion, an affection of our volitional and appreciative nature." Secondly, beauty as value is something positive. In our appreciation of beauty we feel ourselves in the presence of something good. Thirdly, the pleasure we get from beauty is not derived from utility but from the immediate perception. For Santayana, beauty is ultimate good, "a positive value that is intrinsic; it is pleasure." Finally, the pleasure that comes from beauty, in contrast to the pleasure of the senses, tends to be objectified, thus appearing as the quality of things rather than as the mere experience of our private consciousness. The transition from the one to the other is gradual, yet the distinction is significant for Santayana. There is no sharp line between our ordinary sensations and our experiences of beauty; "it depends upon the degree of objectivity my feeling has attained at the moment whether I say it pleases me or it is beautiful." The more remote, interwoven, and inextricable the pleasure is, the more we tend to objectify it.

Santayana further expounds the concepts of the sublime, the comic, wit, humor, and the grotesque (see selection 7.4). The analysis of these concepts gives fuller meaning to his theory of art. The basic idea that runs through all his discussions is that the aesthetic effects of objects is always due to the emotional value of the consciousness. We merely attribute this value to the object by a projection which is the ground of its objectivity. The sublime is attained by emotional detachment and deliberation; wit is the result of quick association by similarity; the comic is attained by incongruity and degradation; the essence of humor lies in an amusing weakness combined with an amicable humanity; and the grotesque is produced by the exaggeration of one of the elements of an ideal type or by its combination with other types.

Interpretations of art in terms of desire, wish, and imagination make art and the aesthetic experience more intelligible than the other views that have been considered. They place the creative activity of the artist and the experience of the beholder in a natural setting; they establish a continuity between the biological drives or impulses and the idealized experiences we call aesthetic. In these views art retains all its ideal and creative qualities without becoming something transcendental or esoteric. Yet these interpretations leave many problems to be explored. What is an adequate conception of feeling, desire, imagination? What is the nature of the aesthetic mood? What is the relation between aesthetic symbol and symbol in general? What specific variations do these ideas assume in the different moods of art? These and similar questions need full analysis in the light of modern psychology and in terms of the techniques of the arts before the empirical theories of art can be wholly satisfactory.

Art, Standards, and Morality

We have been discussing various theories of art. But the philosophy of art entails many other problems: the analysis of form and expression; standards and criticism; the place of art in society; and the relation of art to science, religion, morality, and civilization. Of these problems we will examine two— standards in art, and the relation of art to morality.

C. J. Ducasse gives a clear and persuasive analysis of the issues involved in art criticism. He defends a relativistic view. "Beauty is relative to the individual observer. Beauty being . . . dependent upon the constitution of the individual observer, it will be as variable as the constitution. An object which one person properly calls beautiful will, with equal propriety, be not so judged by another" (selection 7.5). An extreme alternative to Ducasse's view would be the claim that there are absolute standards and truths of art that everyone must accept. Perhaps it may be possible to develop a theory of standards that would reconcile both positions; through long aesthetic experience we may develop certain functional absolutes in art that may help to regulate our taste and critical judgments.

The relation between art and morality is sensitively analyzed by R. B. Perry (selection 7.6), who points out that "the aesthetic life of man is embedded in his moral life." The aesthetic interest, though independent of morality, has a vital relation to it. "Because the aesthetic interest operates in the realm of the imagination, it enjoys a peculiar freedom to multiply and entertain ideal possibilities. It tends to emancipate men's minds from habit, authority, and status quo, and thus readily allies itself with the forces of progress and liberalization." On the other hand, the aesthetic interest may tend to be "a passive complacency, a narrow absorption, and an irresponsibility toward that very social organization on which aesthetic life itself depends." Aesthetic rapture may become "so obsessive as to make men indifferent to its evil effect—of commission or omission—on the lives of other men." How should one resolve this possible conflict arising between morality and art? This question is not easily answered. For Plato and Tolstoi, for instance, the demands of morality and religion must be the ruling factors. Yet Perry rightly refers to the dangers to which art may be exposed from moral and social controls. As he puts it: "Art will flourish best when it is allowed to germinate, grow and proliferate in obedience to its own nature." There may be occasions when the conflict between morality and art need not be settled by suppression of one interest in favor of the other, but rather by acceptance of the conflict as an inevitable part of experience—as something to be lived through and endured.

Aristotle (384-322 B.C.)

7.1   Tragedy

Let us proceed now to the discussion of Tragedy; before doing so, however, we must gather up the definition resulting from what has been said. A tragedy, then, is the imitation of an action that is serious and also, as having magnitude, complete in itself; in language with pleasurable accessories, each kind brought in separately in the parts of the work; in a dramatic, not in a narrative form; with incidents arousing pity and fear, wherewith to accomplish its catharsis of such emotions. Here by 'language with pleasurable accessories' I mean that with rhythm and harmony or song super-added; and by 'the kinds separately' I mean that some portions are worked out with verse only, and others in turn with song.

I. As they act the stories, it follows that in the first place the Spectacle (or stage-appearance of the actors) must be some part of the whole; and in the second Melody and Diction, these two being the means of their imitation. Here by 'Diction' I mean merely this, the composition of the verses; and by 'Melody', what is too completely understood to require explanation. But further: the subject represented also is an action; and the action involves agents, who must necessarily have their distinctive qualities both of character and thought, since it is from these that we ascribe certain qualities to their actions. There are in the natural order of things, therefore, two causes, Thought and Character, of their actions, and consequently of their success or failure in their lives. Now the action (that which was done) is represented in the play by the Fable or Plot. The Fable, in our present sense of the term, is simply this, the combination of the incidents, or things done in the story; whereas Character is what makes us ascribe certain moral qualities to the agents; and Thought is shown in all they say when proving a particular point or, it may be enunciating a general truth. There are six parts consequently of every tragedy, as a whole (that is) of such or such quality, viz. a Fable or Plot, Characters, Diction, Thought, Spectacle, and Melody; two of them arising from the means, one from the manner, and three from the objects of the dramatic imitation; and there is nothing else besides these six. Of these, its formative elements, then, not a few of the dramatists have made due use, as

From *De Poetica*. Oxford Translation of Aristotle, ed. W. D. Ross. Reprinted by permission of the Clarendon Press, Oxford.

every play, one may say, admits of Spectacle, Character, Fable, Diction, Melody, and Thought.

II. The most important of the six is the combination of the incidents of the story. Tragedy is essentially an imitation not of persons but of action and life, of happiness and misery. All human happiness or misery takes the form of action; the end for which we live is a certain kind of activity, not a quality. Character gives us qualities, but it is in our actions—what we do— that we are happy or the reverse. In a play accordingly they do not act in order to portray the Characters; they include the Characters for the sake of the action. So that it is the action in it, i.e. its Fable or Plot, that is the end and purpose of the tragedy; and the end is everywhere the chief thing. Besides this, a tragedy is impossible without action, but there may be one without Character. The tragedies of most of the moderns are characterless —a defect common among poets of all kinds, and with its counterpart in painting in Zeuxis as compared with Polygnotus; for whereas the latter is strong in character, the work of Zeuxis is devoid of it. And again: one may string together a series of character- istic speeches of the utmost finish as regards Diction and Thought, and yet fail to produce the true tragic effect; but one will have much better suc- cess with a tragedy which, however inferior in these respects, has a Plot, a combination of incidents, in it. And again: the most powerful elements of attraction in Tragedy, the Peripeties and Discoveries, are parts of the Plot. A further proof is in the fact that beginners succeed earlier with the Diction and Characters than with the construction of a story; and the same

may be said of nearly all the early dramatists. We maintain, therefore, that the first essential, the life and soul, so to speak, of Tragedy is the Plot; and that the Characters come second—compare the parallel in paint- ing, where the most beautiful colours laid on without order will not give one the same pleasure as a simple black-and-white sketch of a portrait. We maintain that Tragedy is primarily an imitation of action, and that it is mainly for the sake of the action that it imitates the personal agents. Third comes the element of Thought, i.e. the power of saying whatever can be said, or what is appropriate to the occasion. This is what, in the speeches in Tragedy, falls under the arts of Politics and Rhetoric; for the older poets make their personages discourse like statesmen, and the moderns like rhetoricians. One must not confuse it with Character. Character in a play is that which reveals the moral pur- pose of the agents, i.e. the sort of thing they seek or avoid, where that is not obvious—hence there is no room for Character in a speech on a purely indifferent subject. Thought, on the other hand, is shown in all they say when proving or disproving some particular point, or enunciating some universal proposition. Fourth among the literary elements is the Diction of the personages, i.e. as was before explained, the expression of their thoughts in words, which is practically the same thing with verse as with prose. As for the two remain- ing parts, the Melody is the greatest of the pleasurable accessories of Tragedy. The Spectacle, though an attraction, is the least artistic of all the parts, and has least to do with the art of poetry. The tragic effect is quite possible without a public performance and actors; and besides, the getting-up of the Spectacle is more a matter for the costumier than the poet.

Having thus distinguished the parts, let us now consider the proper construction of the Fable or Plot, as that is at once the first and the most important thing in Tragedy. We have laid it down that a tragedy is an imitation of an action that is complete itself, as a whole of some magnitude; for a whole may be of no magnitude to speak of. Now a whole is that which has beginning, middle, and end. A beginning is that which is not itself necessarily after anything else, and which has naturally something else after it; an end is that which is naturally after something itself, either as its necessary or usual consequent, and with nothing else after it; and a middle, that which is by nature after one thing and has also another after it. A well-constructed Plot, therefore, cannot either begin or end at any point one likes; beginning and end in it must be of the forms just described. Again: to be beautiful, a living creature, and every whole made up of parts, must not only present a certain order in its arrangement of parts, but also be of certain definite magnitude. Beauty is a matter of size and order, and therefore impossible either (1) in a very minute creature, since our perception becomes indistinct as it approaches instantaneity; or (2) in a creature of vast size—one, say, 1,000 miles long—as in that case, instead of the object being seen all at once, the unity and wholeness of it is lost to the beholder. Just in the same way, then, as a beautiful whole made up of parts, or a beautiful living creature, must be

of some size, but a size to be taken in by the eye, so a story or Plot must be of some length, but of a length to be taken in by the memory. As for the limit of its length, so far as that is relative to public performances and spectators, it does not fall within the theory of poetry. If they had to perform a hundred tragedies, they would be timed by water-clocks, as they are said to have been at one period. The limit, however, set by the actual nature of the thing is this: the longer the story, consistently with its being comprehensible as a whole, the finer it is by reason of its magnitude. As a rough general formula, 'a length which allows of the hero passing by a series of probable or necessary stages from misfortune to happiness, or from happiness to misfortune,' may suffice as a limit for the magnitude of the story.

The Unity of a Plot does not consist, as some suppose, in its having one man as its subject. An infinity of things befall that one man, some of which it is impossible to reduce to unity; and in like manner there are many actions of one man which cannot be made to form one action. One sees, therefore, the mistake of all the poets who have written a *Heracleid*, a *Theseid*, or similar poems; they suppose that, because Heracles was one man, the story also of Heracles must be one story. Homer, however, evidently understood this point quite well, whether by art or instinct, just in the same way as he excels the rest in every other respect. In writing an *Odyssey*, he did not make the poem cover all that ever befell his hero—it befell him, for instance, to get wounded on Parnassus and also to feign madness at the time of the call to arms, but the two incidents had no necessary or probable connexion with one another—instead of doing that, he took as the subject of the *Odyssey*, as also of the *Iliad*, an action with a Unity of the kind we are describing. The truth is that just as in the other imitative arts one imitation is always of one thing, so in poetry the story, as an imitation of action, must represent one action, a complete whole, with its several incidents so closely connected that the transposal or withdrawal of any one of them will disjoin and dislocate the whole. For that which makes no perceptible difference by its presence or absence is no real part of the whole.

From what we have said it will be seen that the poet's function is to describe, not the thing that has happened, but a kind of thing that might happen, i.e. what is possible as being probable or necessary. The distinction between historian and poet is not in the one writing prose and the other verse—you might put the work of Herodotus into verse, and it would still be a species of history; it consists really in this, that the one describes the thing that has been, and the other a kind of thing that might be. Hence poetry is something more philosophic and of graver import than history, since its statements are of the nature rather of universals, whereas those of history are singulars. By a universal statement I mean one as to what such or such a kind of man will probably or necessarily say or do—which is the aim of poetry, though it affixes proper names to the characters; by a singular statement, one as to what, say, Alcibiades did or had done to him. In Comedy this has become clear by this time; it is only when their Plot is already made up of probable incidents that they give it a basis of proper names, choosing for the purpose any names that may occur to them, instead of writing like the old iambic poets about particular persons. In Tragedy, however, they still adhere to the historic names; and for this reason: what convinces is the possible; now whereas we are not yet sure as to the possibility of that which has not happened, that which has happened is manifestly possible, else it would not have come to pass. Nevertheless even in Tragedy there are some plays with but one or two known names in them, the rest being inventions; and there are some with a single known name, e.g. Agathon's *Antheus*, in which both incidents and names are of the poet's invention; and it is no less delightful on that account. So that one must not aim at a rigid adherence to the traditional stories on which tragedies are based. It would be absurd, in fact, to do so, as even the known stories are only known to a few, though they are a delight none the less to all.

It is evident from the above that the poet must be more the poet of his stories or Plots than of his verses, inasmuch as he is a poet by virtue of the imitative element in his work, and it is actions that he imitates. And if he should come to take a subject from actual history, he is none the less a poet for that; since some historic occurrences may very well be in the probable and possible order of things; and it is in that aspect of them that he is their poet.

Of simple Plots and actions the episodic are the worst. I call a Plot episodic when there is neither probability nor necessity in the sequence of its episodes. Actions of this sort bad poets construct through their own fault, and good ones on account of the players. His work being for public performance, a good poet often stretches out a Plot beyond its capabilities, and is thus obliged to twist the sequence of incident.

Tragedy, however, is an imitation not only of a complete action, but also of incidents arousing pity and fear. Such incidents have the very greatest effect on the mind when they occur unexpectedly and at the same time in consequence of one another; there is more of the marvellous in them then than if they happened of themselves or by mere chance. Even matters of chance seem most marvellous if there is an appearance of design as it were in them; as for instance the statue of Mitys at Argos killed the author of Mitys' death by falling down on him when a looker-on at a public spectacle; for incidents like that we think to be not without a meaning. A Plot, therefore, of this sort is necessarily finer than others.

Plots are either simple or complex, since the actions they represent are naturally of this twofold description. The action, proceeding in the way defined, as one continuous whole, I call simple, when the change in the hero's fortunes takes place without Peripety or Discovery; and complex, when it involves one or the other, or both. These should each of them arise out of the structure of the Plot itself, so as to be the consequence, necessary or probable, of the antecedents. There is a great difference between a thing happening *propter hoc* and *post hoc.*

A Peripety is the change of the kind described from one state of things within the play to its opposite, and that too in the way we are saying, in the probable or necessary sequence of events; as it is for instance in *Oedipus:* here the opposite state of things is produced by the Messenger, who, coming to gladden Oedipus and to remove his fears as to his mother, reveals the secret of his birth. And in *Lynceus:* just as he is being led off for execution, with Danaus at his side to put him to death, the incidents preceding this bring it about that he is saved and Danaus put to death. A Discovery is, as the very word implies, a change from ignorance to knowledge, and thus to either love or hate, in the personages marked for good or evil fortune. The finest form of Discovery is one attended by Peripeties, like that which goes with the Discovery in *Oedipus.* There are no doubt other forms of it; what we have said may happen in a way in reference to inanimate things, even things of a very casual kind; and it is also possible to discover whether some one has done or not done something. But the form most directly connected with the Plot and the action of the piece is the first-mentioned. This, with a Peripety, will arouse either pity or fear—actions of that nature being what Tragedy is assumed to represent; and it will also serve to bring about the happy or unhappy ending. The Discovery, then, being of persons, it may be that of one party only to the other, the latter being already known; or both the parties may have to discover themselves. Iphigenia, for instance, was discovered to Orestes by sending the letter; and another Discovery was required to reveal him to Iphigenia.

Two parts of the Plot, then, Peripety and Discovery, are on matters of this sort. A third part is Suffering; which we may define as an action of a destructive or painful nature, such as murders on the stage, tortures, woundings, and the like. The other two have been already explained. . . .

The next points after what we have said above will be these: (1) What is the poet to aim at, and what is he to avoid, in constructing his Plots? and (2) What are the conditions on which the tragic effect depends?

We assume that, for the finest form of Tragedy, the Plot must be not simple but complex; and further, that it must imitate actions arousing fear and pity, since that is the distinctive function of this kind of imitation. It follows, therefore, that there are three forms of Plot to be avoided. (1) A good man must not be seen passing from happiness to misery, or (2) a bad man from misery to happiness. The first situation is not fear-inspiring or piteous, but simply odious to us. The second is the most untragic that can be; it has no one of the requisites of Tragedy; it does not appeal either to the human feeling in us, or to our pity, or to our fears. Nor, on the other hand, should (3) an extremely bad man be seen falling from happiness into misery. Such a story may arouse the human feeling in us, but it will not move us to either pity or fear; pity is occasioned by undeserved misfortune, and fear by that of one like ourselves; so that there will be nothing either piteous or fear-inspiring in the situation. There remains, then, the intermediate kind of personage, a man not pre-eminently virtuous and just, whose misfortune, however, is brought upon him not by vice and depravity but by some error

of judgment, of the number of those in the enjoyment of great reputation and prosperity; e.g. Oedipus, Thyestes, and the men of note of similar families. The perfect Plot, accordingly, must have a single, and not (as some tell us) a double issue; the change in the hero's fortunes must be not from misery to happiness, but on the contrary from happiness to misery; and the cause of it must lie not in any depravity, but in some great error on his part; the man himself being either such as we have described, or better, not worse, than that.

Fact also confirms our theory. Though the poets began by accepting any tragic story that came to hand, in these days the finest tragedies are always on the story of some few houses, on that of Alcmeon, Oedipus, Orestes, Meleager, Thyestes, Telephus, or any others that may have been involved, as either agents or sufferers, in some deed of horror. The theoretically best tragedy, then, has a Plot of this description. The critics, therefore, are wrong who blame Euripides for taking this line in his tragedies, and giving many of them an unhappy ending. It is, as we have said, the right line to take. The best proof is this: on the stage, and in the public performances, such plays, properly worked out, are seen to be the most truly tragic; and Euripides, even if his execution be faulty in every other point, is seen to be nevertheless the most tragic certainly of the dramatists. After this comes the construction of Plot which some rank first, one with a double story (like the *Odyssey*) and an opposite issue for the good and the bad personages. It is ranked as first only through the weakness of the audiences; the poets merely follow their public, writing as its wishes dictate. But the pleasure here is not that of Tragedy. It belongs rather to Comedy, where the bitterest enemies in the piece (e.g. Orestes and Aegisthus) walk off good friends at the end, with no slaying of any one by any one.

The tragic fear and pity may be aroused by the Spectacle; but they may also be aroused by the very structure and incidents of the play—which is the better way and shows the better poet. The Plot in fact should be so framed that, even without seeing the things take place, he who simply hears the account of them shall be filled with horror and pity at the incidents; which is just the effect that the mere recital of the story in *Oedipus* would have on one. . . .

The Dénouement should arise out of the Plot itself, and not depend on a stage-artifice, as in *Medea*, or in the story of the (arrested) departure of the Greeks in the *Iliad*. The artifice must be reserved for matters outside the play—for past events beyond human knowledge, or events yet to come, which require to be foretold or announced; since it is the privilege of the Gods to know everything. There should be nothing improbable among the actual incidents. If it be unavoidable, however, it should be outside the Tragedy, like the improbability in the *Oedipus* of Sophocles. But to return to the Characters. As Tragedy is an imitation of personages better than the ordinary man, we in our way should follow the example of good portrait-painters, who reproduce the distinctive features of a man, and at the same time, without losing the likeness, make him handsomer than he is. The poet in like manner, in portraying men quick or slow to anger, or with similar infirmities of character, must know how to represent them as such, and at the same time as good men, as Agathon and Homer have represented Achilles.

QUESTIONS FOR DISCUSSION

1. How does Aristotle apply the notion of imitation to the notion of tragedy? Do you find his theory convincing?
2. Discuss the possibility that though tragedy arouses pity and fear, it may accomplish the catharsis of these emotions.
3. What is the importance of the plot for Aristotle in relation to the character of the tragic hero?
4. What distinction does Aristotle make between the function of the poet and the function of the historian?
5. Discuss in some detail your interpretation of the concept of tragedy.

Benedetto Croce (1866-1952)

7.2   What Is Art?

The question as to what is art,—I will say at once, in the simplest manner, that art is *vision* or *intuition*. The artist produces an image or a phantasm; and he who enjoys art turns his gaze upon the point to which the artist has pointed, looks through the chink which he has opened, and reproduces that image in himself. "Intuition," "vision," "contemplation," "imagination," "fancy," "figurations," "representations," and so on, are words continually recurring, like synonyms, when discoursing upon art, and they all lead the mind to the same conceptual sphere which indicates general agreement.

But this reply, that art is intuition, obtains its force and meaning from all that it implicitly denies and from which it distinguishes art. What negations are implicit in it? I shall indicate the principal, or at least those that are the most important for us at this present moment of our culture.

It denies, above all, that art is a *physical fact:* for example, certain determined colours, or relations of colours: certain definite forms of

bodies; certain definite sounds, or relations of sounds; certain phenomena of heat or of electricity—in short, whatsoever be designated as "physical." The inclination toward this error of physicising art is already present in ordinary thought, and as children who touch the soap-bubble and would wish to touch the rainbow, so the human spirit, admiring beautiful things, hastens spontaneously to trace out the reasons for them in external nature, and proves that it must think, or believes that it should think, certain colours beautiful and certain other colours ugly, certain forms beautiful and certain other forms ugly. But this attempt has been carried out intentionally and with method on several occasions in the history of thought: from the "canons" which the Greek and Renaissance theoreticians and artists fixed for the beauty of bodies, through the speculations as to the geometrical and numerical relations of figures and sounds, down to the researches of the aestheticians of the nineteenth century (Fechner, for example), and to the "communications" presented in our day by the inexpert, at philosophical, psychological, and natural science congresses, concerning the relations of physical phenomena with art. And if it be

From *Breviary of Aesthetic* by Benedetto Croce, Chapter 1, in the *Book of the Opening of the Rice Institute,* vol. II. Reprinted by kind permission of Rice University.

asked why art cannot be a physical fact, we must reply, in the first place, that physical facts *do not possess reality,* and that art, to which so many devote their whole lives and which fills all with a divine joy, is *supremely real;* thus it cannot be a physical fact, which is something unreal. This sounds at first paradoxical, for nothing seems more solid and secure to the ordinary man than the physical world; but we, in the seat of truth, must not abstain from the good reason and substitute for it one less good, solely because the first should have the appearance of a lie; and besides, in order to surpass what of strange and difficult may be contained in that truth, to become at home with it, we may take into consideration the fact that the demonstration of the unreality of the physical world has not only been proved in an indisputable manner and is admitted by all philosophers (who are not crass materialists and are not involved in the strident contradictions of materialism), but is professed by these same physicists in the spontaneous philosophy which they mingle with their physics, when they conceive physical phenomena as products of principles that are beyond experience, of atoms or of ether, or as the manifestation of an Unknowable; besides, the matter itself of the materialists is a super-material principle. Thus physical facts reveal themselves, by their internal logic and by common consent, not as reality, but as a *construction of our intellect for the purposes of science.* Consequently, the question whether art be a physical fact must rationally assume this different signification: that is to say, *whether it be possible to construct art physically.* And this is certainly possible, for we indeed carry it out always, when, turning from the sense of a poem and ceasing to enjoy it, we set ourselves, for example, to count the words of which the poem is composed and to divide them into syllables and letters; or, disregarding the aesthetic effect of a statue, we weigh and measure it: a most useful performance for the packers of statues, as is the other for the typographers who have to "compose" pages of poetry; but most useless for the contemplator and student of art, to whom it is neither useful nor licit to allow himself to be "distracted" from his proper object. Thus art is not a physical fact in this second sense, either; which amounts to saying that when we propose to ourselves to penetrate its nature and mode of action, to construct it physically is of no avail.

Another negation is implied in the definition of art as intuition: if it be intuition, and intuition is equivalent to *theory* in the original sense of contemplation, art cannot be a utilitarian act; and since a utilitarian act aims always at obtaining a pleasure and therefore at keeping off a pain, art, considered in its own nature, has nothing to do with the *useful* and with *pleasure* and *pain,* as such. It will be admitted, indeed, without much difficulty, that a pleasure as a pleasure, any sort of pleasure, is not of itself artistic; the pleasure of a drink of water that slakes thirst, or a walk in the open air that stretches our limbs and makes our blood circulate more lightly, or the obtaining of a longed-for post that settles us in practical life, and so on, is not artistic. Finally, the difference between pleasure and art leaps to the eyes in the relations that are developed between ourselves and works of art, because the figure represented may be dear to us and represent the most delightful memories, and at the same time the picture may be ugly; or, on the other hand, the picture may be beautiful and the figure represented hateful to our hearts, or the picture itself, which we approve as beautiful, may also cause us rage and envy, because it is the work of our enemy or rival, for whom it will procure advantage and on whom it will confer new strength: our practical interests, with their relative pleasures and pains, mingle and sometimes become confused with art and disturb, but are never *identified* with, our aesthetic interest. At the most it will be affirmed, with a view to maintaining more effectively the definition of art as the pleasurable, that it is not the pleasurable in general, but a *particular* form of the pleasurable. But such a restriction is no longer a defence, it is indeed an abandonment of that thesis; for given that art is a particular form of pleasure, its distinctive character would be supplied, not by the pleasurable, but by what distinguishes that pleasurable from other pleasurables, and it would be desirable to turn the attention to that distinctive element—more than pleasurable or different from pleasurable. Nevertheless, the doctrine that defines art as the pleasurable has a special denomination (hedonistic aesthetic), and a long and complicated development in the history of aesthetic doctrines; it showed itself in the Graeco-Roman world, prevailed in the eighteenth century, reflowered in the second half of the nineteenth, and still enjoys much favour, being especially well received by beginners in aesthetic, who are above all struck by the fact

that art causes pleasure. The life of this doctrine has consisted of proposing in turn one or another class of pleasures, or several classes together (the pleasure of the superior senses, the pleasure of play, of consciousness of our own strength, of love, etc., etc.), or of adding to it elements differing from the pleasurable, the useful for example (when understood as distinct from the pleasurable), the satisfaction of cognoscitive and moral wants, and the like. And its progress has been caused just by this restlessness, and by its allowing foreign elements to ferment in its bosom, which it introduces through the necessity of somehow bringing itself into agreement with the reality of art, thus attaining to its dissolution as hedonistic doctrine and to the unconscious promotion of a new doctrine, or at least to drawing attention to its necessity. And since every error has its element of truth (and that of the physical doctrine has been seen to be the possibility of the physical "construction" of art as of any other fact), the hedonistic doctrine has its eternal element of truth in the placing in relief the hedonistic accompaniment, or pleasure, common to the aesthetic activity as to every form of spiritual activity, which it has not at all been intended to deny in absolutely denying the identification of art with the pleasurable, and in distinguishing it from the pleasurable by defining it as intuition.

A third negation, effected by means of the theory of art as intuition, is that art is a *moral act;* that is to say, that form of practical act which, although necessarily uniting with the useful and with pleasure and pain, is not immediately utilitarian and hedonistic, and moves in a superior spiritual sphere.

But the intuition, in so far as it is a theoretic act, is opposed to the practical of any sort. And in truth, art, as has been remarked from the earliest times, does not arise as an act of the will; good will, which constitutes the honest man, does not constitute the artist. And since it is not the result of an act of will, so it escapes all moral discrimination, not because a privilege of exemption is accorded to it, but simply because moral discrimination cannot be applied to art. An artistic image portrays an act morally praiseworthy or blameworthy; but this image, as image, is neither morally praiseworthy nor blameworthy. Not only is there no penal code that can condemn an image to prison or to death, but no moral judgment, uttered by a rational person, can make of it its object: we might just as well judge the square moral or the triangle immoral as the Francesca of Dante immoral or the Cordelia of Shakespeare moral, for these have a purely artistic function, they are like musical notes in the souls of Dante and of Shakespeare. Further, the moralistic theory of art is also represented in the history of aesthetic doctrines nor is it entirely dead today, though much discredited in the common opinion of our times, not only on account of its intrinsic demerit, but also, in some measure, owing to the moral demerit of certain tendencies of our times, which render possible, owing to psychological dislike, that refutation of it which should be made—and which we here make—solely for logical reasons. The end attributed to art, of directing the good and inspiring horror of evil, of correcting and ameliorating customs, is a derivation of the moralistic doctrine; and so is the demand addressed to artists to collaborate in the education of the lower classes, in the strengthening of the national or bellicose spirit of a people, in the diffusion of the ideals of a modest and laborious life; and so on. These are all things that art cannot do, any more than geometry, which, however, does not lose anything of its importance on account of its inability to do this; and one does not see why art should do so, either. That it cannot do these things was partially perceived by the moralistic aestheticians also; who very readily effected a transaction with it, permitting it to provide pleasures that were not moral, provided they were not openly dishonest, or recommending it to employ to a good end the dominion that, owing to its hedonistic power, it possessed over souls, to gild the pill, to sprinkle sweetness upon the rim of the glass containing the bitter draught—in short, to play the courtezan (since it could not get rid of its old and inborn habits), in the service of holy church or of morality: *meretrix ecclesiae.* On other occasions they have sought to avail themselves of it for purposes of instruction, since not only virtue but also science is a difficult thing, and art could remove this difficulty and render pleasant and attractive the entrance into the ocean of science—indeed, lead them through it as through a garden of Armida, gaily and voluptuously, without their being conscious of the lofty protection they had obtained, or of the crisis of renovation which they were preparing for themselves. We cannot now refrain from a smile when we talk of these theories, but should not forget that they were once a serious matter corresponding to a serious effort to understand the nature of art and to elevate the conception of it; and that among those who believed in it (to limit ourselves to Italian literature) were Dante and Tasso, Parini and Alfieri, Manzoni and Mazzini. And the moralistic doctrine of art was and is and will be perpetually beneficial by its very contradictions; it was and will be an effort, however unhappy, to separate art from the merely pleasing, with which it is sometimes confused, and to assign to it a more worthy post: and it, too, has its true side, because, if art be beyond morality, the artist is neither this side of it nor that, but under its empire, in so far as he is a man who cannot withdraw himself from the duties of man, and must look upon art itself—art, which is not and never will be moral—as a mission to be exercised as a priestly office.

Again (and this is the last and perhaps the most important of all the general negations that it suits me to recall in relation to this matter), with the definition of art as intuition, we deny that it has the character of *conceptual knowledge*. Conceptual knowledge, in its true form, which is the philosophical, is always realistic, aiming at establishing reality against unreality, or at lowering unreality by including it in reality as a subordinate moment of reality itself. But intuition means, precisely, indistinction of reality and unreality, the image with its value as mere image, the pure ideality of the image, and opposing the intuitive or sensible knowledge to the conceptual or intelligible, the aesthetic to the noetic, it aims at claiming the autonomy of this more simple and elementary form of knowledge, which has been compared to the dream (the dream, and not the sleep) of the theoretic life, in respect to which philosophy would be the waking. And indeed, whoever should ask, when examining a work of art, whether what the artist has expressed be metaphysically and historically true or false, asks a question that is without meaning, and commits an error analogous to his who should bring the airy images of the fancy before the tribunal of morality: without meaning, because the discrimination of true and false always concerns an affirmation of reality, or a judgment, but it cannot fall under the head of an image or of a pure subject, which is not the subject of a judgment, since it is without qualification or predicate. It is useless to object that the individuality of the image cannot subsist without reference to the universal, of which that image is the individuation, because we do not here deny that the universal, as the spirit of God, is everywhere and animates all things with itself, but we deny that the universal is rendered logically explicit and is thought in the intuition. Useless also is the appeal to the principle of the unity of the spirit, which is not broken, but, on the contrary, strengthened by the clear distinction of fancy from thought, because from the distinction comes opposition, and from opposition concrete unity. . . . Certainly art is symbol, all symbol—that is, all significant; but symbol of what? What does it mean? The intuition is truly artistic, it is truly intuition, and not a chaotic mass of images, only when it has a vital principle that animates it, making it all one with itself; but what is this principle?

The answer to such a question may be said to result from the examination of the greatest ideal strife that has ever taken place in the field of art (and is not confined to the epoch that took its name from it and in which it was predominant): the strife between *romanticism* and *classicism*. Giving the general definition, here convenient, and setting aside minor and accidental determinations, romanticism asks of art, above all, the spontaneous and violent effusion of the affections, of love and hate, of anguish and jubilation, of desperation and elevation; and is willingly satisfied and pleased with vaporous and indeterminate images, broken and allusive in style, with vague suggestions, with approximate phrases, with powerful and troubled sketches: while classicism loves the peaceful soul, the wise design, figures studied in their characteristics and precise in outline, ponderation, equilibrium, clarity; and resolutely tends toward *representation,* as the other tends toward *feeling.* And whoever puts himself at one or the other point of view finds crowds of reasons for maintaining it and for confuting the opposite point of view; because (say the romantics), What is the use of an art, rich in beautiful images, which, nevertheless, does not speak to the heart? And if it do speak to the heart, what is the use if the images be not beautiful? And the others will say, What is the use of the shock of the passions, if the spirit do not rest upon a beautiful image? And if the image be beautiful, if our taste be satisfied, what matters the absence of those emotions which can all of them be obtained outside art, and which life does not fail to provide, sometimes in greater quantity than we desire?— But when we begin to feel weary of the fruitless defence of both partial views; above all, when we turn away

from the ordinary works of art produced by the romantic and classical schools, from works convulsed with passion or coldly decorous, and fix them on the works, not of the disciples, but of the masters, not of the mediocre, but of the supreme, we see the contest disappear in the distance and find ourselves unable to call the great portions of these works, romantic or classic representative, because they are both classic and romantic, feelings and representations, a vigorous feeling which has become all most brilliant representation. Such, for example, are the works of Hellenic art, and such those of Italian poetry and art: the transcendentalism of the Middle Ages became fixed in the bronze of the Dantesque *terzina;* melancholy and suave fancy, in the transparency of the songs and sonnets of Petrarch; sage experience of life and badinage with the fables of the past, in the limpid *ottava rima* of Ariosto; heroism and the thought of death, in the perfect blank verse hendecasyllabics of Foscolo: the infinite variety of everything, in the sober and austere songs of Giacomo Leopardi. Finally (be it said in parenthesis and without intending comparison with the other examples adduced), the voluptuous refinements and animal sensuality of international decadentism have received their most perfect expression in the prose and verse of an Italian, D'Annunzio. All these souls were profoundly passionate (all, even the serene Lodovico Ariosto, who was so amorous, so tender, and so often represses his emotion with a smile); their works of art are the eternal flower that springs from their passions.

These expressions and these critical

judgments can be theoretically resumed in the formula, that what gives coherence and unity to the intuition is feeling: the intuition is really such because it represents a feeling, and can only appear from and upon that. Not the idea, but the feeling, is what confers upon art the airy lightness of the symbol: an aspiration enclosed in the circle of a representation—that is art; and in it the aspiration alone stands for the representation, and the representation alone for the aspiration. Epic and lyric, or drama and lyric, are scholastic divisions of the indivisible; art is always lyrical—that is, epic and dramatic in feeling. What we admire in genuine works of art is the perfect fanciful form which a state of the soul assumes; and we call this life, unity, solidity of the work of art. What displeases us in the false and imperfect forms is the struggle of several different states of the soul not yet unified, their stratification, or mixture, their vacillating method, which obtains apparent unity from the will of the author, who for this purpose avails himself of an abstract plan or idea, or of extra-aesthetic, passionate emotion. A series of images which seem to be, each in turn, rich in power of conviction, leaves us nevertheless deluded and diffident, because we do not see them generated from a state of the soul, from a "sketch" (as the painters call it), from a motive; and they follow one another and crowd together without that precise intonation, without that accent, which comes from the heart. And what is the figure cut out from the background of the picture or transported and placed against another background, what is the personage of drama or of romance outside his relation with all the other

personages and with the general action? And what is the value of this general action if it be not an action of the spirit of the author? The secular disputes concerning dramatic unity are interesting in this connection; they are first applied to the unity of "action" when they have been obtained from an extrinsic determination of time and place, and this finally applied to the unity of "interest," and the interest would have to be in its turn dissolved in the interest of the spirit of the poet—that is, in his intimate aspiration, in his feeling. The negative issue of the great dispute between classicists and romanticists is interesting, for it resulted in the negation both of the art which strives to distract and illude the soul as to the deficiency of the image with mere feeling, with the practical violence of feeling, with feeling that has not become contemplation, and of the art which, by means of the superficial clearness of the image, of drawing correctly false, of the word falsely correct, seeks to deceive as to its lack of inspiration and its lack of an aesthetic reason to justify what it has produced. A celebrated sentence uttered by an English critic, and become one of the commonplaces of journalism, states that "all the arts tend to the condition of music"; but it would have been more accurate to say that all the arts are music, if it be thus intended to emphasise the genesis of aesthetic images in feeling, excluding from their number those mechanically constructed or realistically ponderous. And another not less celebrated utterance of a Swiss semi-philosopher, which has had the like good or bad fortune of becoming trivial, discovers that "every landscape is a state of the soul"; which is indisputable, not because the landscape is landscape, but because the landscape is art.

Artistic intuition, then, is always *lyrical* intuition: this latter being a word that is not present as an adjective or definition of the first, but as a synonym, another of the synonyms that can be united to the several that I have mentioned already, and which, all of them, designate the intuition. And if it be some times convenient that instead of appearing as a synonym, it should assume the grammatical form of the adjective, that is only to make clear the difference between the intuition-image, or nexus of images (for what is called image is always a nexus of images, since image-atoms do not exist any more than thought-atoms), which constitutes the organism, and, as organism, has its vital principle, which is the organism itself,—between this, which is true and proper intuition, and that false intuition which is a heap of images put together in play or intentionally or for some other practical purpose, the connection of which, being practical, shows itself to be not organic, but mechanic, when considered from the aesthetic point of view. But the word *lyric* would be redundant save in this explicative or polemical sense; and art is perfectly defined when it is simply defined as *intuition*.

QUESTIONS FOR DISCUSSION

1. What does Croce mean by defining art as intuition?
2. What are the different meanings of intuition?
3. Discuss in some detail in what sense art for Croce is not physical fact, nor utilitarian function, nor moral act, nor conceptual knowledge.
4. Analyze with some illustrations the nature of the strife in the field of art between *romanticism* and *classicism*. Can this strife be reconciled?
5. What are some of the difficulties in Croce's neglect of the physical in his definition of art?

DeWitt H. Parker (1885-1949)

7.3   The Analysis of Art

For those who delight in thinking, the most fascinating problems are the most elusive. There is an initial discouragement in approaching them and a continuing humility, yet stronger than either is the attraction of their mystery and the hardihood of trying again where so many have failed. That shall be my excuse, as it has been others', for attempting the *pons asinorum* of defining art. No definition of so living a thing as art can be wholly adequate; yet a good definition should at least seize the distinctive characteristics of art, and thus make the mind more vividly aware of art against the background of things that are not art. The hope of framing such a definition has been greatly increased in recent years through the new insight into the nature of art which has come to us from several sources. Yet from none of these sources can one get precisely what a satisfactory theory of art should provide, namely, insight into the differentia, the distinguishing characteristics of art. The chief reason for their failure is the mistaken faith that some single, simple formula can contain the es-

From *The Analysis of Art* by DeWitt H. Parker, Chapter I. Reprinted by kind permission of the publishers, Yale University Press.

sence of art, whereas art is a very complex, and also a very special sort of thing, that requires a correspondingly complex formula to do it justice. Most of the statements that men have made about art are true enough, but unfortunately they are also true of many other things, or else leave out of account aspects of art equally essential. The well-known formulae that come to mind, the 'objectified pleasure' of Santayana; 'intuition' of Croce and Fiedler; the 'expression of feeling' of Véron and Tolstoy; 'significant form' of Clive Bell—these are, one and all, illuminating, but inadequate, either because they fit other things besides works of art or because they omit characteristics of art as important as those they emphasize. And yet one cannot reach the truth about art by merely piecing these and other descriptions together; for that would leave unrevealed the strikingly organic, unified nature of art. Only the sort of definition that would follow and unfold the living structure of art could be successful at all. For this reason, while gratefully making use of the ideas of others, I shall seek to describe art as good painters have always sought to paint nature, from the model rather than from mere information or academic canons and formulae.

We shall find that art has no inescapably threefold complexity, as imagination, as language, and as design, but that nevertheless it has its own unity and uniqueness.

That art belongs to the sphere of the imagination has long been recognized. It is true that this recognition has not been so complete and general as it should be, owing to the classical theory of art as 'imitation'; yet whereas the classical theory has always found difficulty in squaring itself with such obviously fantastic forms of art as *Alice in Wonderland* or the Barberini Faun, there is no trouble in finding a place for imitation within imagination. For, despite its creativeness, the imagination derives its elements from nature, and by reproducing nature can include it. Only recently, however, has the full significance of the imaginative character of art come to light. The now demonstrated kinship between art, daydreaming, dreaming at night, and mythology has opened new avenues of insight, and also, as we shall see, given rise to new problems and some false suggestions.

The most valuable result that has emerged is the proof that the imagination itself, including all its forms, not excepting art, is no independent, autonomous thing, functioning according to mechanical laws of similarity or contiguity, but is, in a sense, secondary, being always under the control of what, without too much misunderstanding, we may still venture to call a 'wish.' The imagination exists for a purpose, to provide satisfaction for moods and desires. That this is true of day-dreams is clear to every one; that it is also true of night-dreams has been rendered almost certain by Freud. There are two ways in which wishes may find satisfaction; one of which may be called the real way, and the other, the dream way. The first is the practical method, to appropriate from the environment what is needed. Thus I satisfy hunger by procuring food, or ambition by inducing other people to provide me with the place and advantages that I desire. In the second mode of satisfaction of wishes, there is no acquisitive interaction with the environment; the wish is satisfied by something that occurs entirely within myself, within my own mind and body, in the realm of my fantasy. And, strangely, this mode of satisfaction of a wish is as genuine as the other; for the time being, at least, my wish is fulfilled, and I am content. Theoretically, to every real satisfaction, there corresponds a possible imaginary, or ideal, satisfaction. So, we are told, hungry and thirsty men, crossing the desert, find satisfaction in dreaming that they are feasting, and in an idle hour every ambitious man dreams that he has won his prize, and every lover that his mistress has favored him. Any wish, frustrated or postponed or only partially satisfied, may generate a dream, a fantasy, in which it finds a substitute satisfaction. Thus it is that we 'get even' with fate, and, however bound by the world, achieve freedom in our dreams. The importance of such satisfactions in the life of man is immense; for whenever he is not busy doing things or planning to do them, he is secretly dreaming that he has done them successfully.

The typical characteristics of dream experiences are now pretty well known. One of the most fundamental of these we may call, after Vaihinger, the 'as if' attitude, the analogue of the 'conscious self-deception' (*bewusste*

Selbst-Täuschung) of Gross and Lange. Things seen in a dream, be it a day-dream or a dream at night, are to us 'as if' they were real; for the time being, at least, we do not treat them as imaginary, but as actual. And the interest that we take in them depends upon the fact that we do accept them as real. They must seem to us to be real or our wish would not be able to fulfil itself in them. Nevertheless, the acceptance of objects and occurrences in a dream as real is seldom entire; there is always, in the fringe of consciousness, an awareness that, after all, they are unreal. One part of ourselves believes in them, but another part refuses its assent; and it is this unique combination of belief and unbelief which creates the 'as if' attitude, the attitude of make-believe. There is a dissociation of certain elements of the mind, which form a little island of belief, from the wider sea of consciousness which maintains the point of view of ordinary life and condemns the dream as unreal. These two diverse points of view toward the same thing coexist in the same mind; so that it is almost true to say that we at once believe and do not believe. Sometimes one and sometimes another of the two attitudes will dominate; in dreams at night there is partial, if not complete, submergence of the doubter; complete submergence occurs only in the delusions of the insane, when dream passes into reality; in the day-dream the doubter is still active, but overruled for the time being by the dreamful believer; in art and in play there is equipoise, and we dream on, knowing full well and luminously that we are dreaming.

In accordance with the foregoing, it should be possible to show that works of art, as products of the imagi-nation, are at once characterized by the 'as if' attitude and are satisfactions of wishes. That the 'as if' attitude dominates the aesthetic appreciation of the normal types of painting and sculpture is evident. But even when we look at the Cézanne landscape . . . it is for us as if there were hills and trees and skies before us; great as the schematization is, they are to us as if they were real, and they evoke in us some, at least, of the interests and feelings called forth by real things. There is, as we shall see, absolutely no test of good drawing or painting except the capacity of the artist to make us believe; his work may be realistic or highly stylized, either method is good as art, so long as it creates an image in which we believe. Or when, for example, we look at MacMonnies' Bacchante, it is as if the divinely frenzied girl and her child were alive in our presence and we were witnesses of their ecstasy in the festival of the god. To induce us to make believe this is the triumph of the artist. But equally, when we look at Brancusi's Miss Pogany, for all the geometrization of the head, we get a feeling of reality. So, likewise, we demand of every novel and play, every dramatic and narrative poem, that it create the semblance of reality.

That such arts as painting, sculpture, literature, and the drama belong to the realm of the imagination seems clear enough, but music, the dance, and architecture do not so obviously belong there. The character of make-believe, of the 'as if' attitude, may seem to be absent. For is not music real sound, and the dance real motion, and a building real marble? And yet, so far as these things are beautiful, that is not the whole truth about them. Let us consider the dance first.

We must distinguish from the outset the aesthetic experience of the dancer from that of one who is watching the dance. Now the latter is clearly an imaginative experience; for when I watch a dance, I enjoy it fully only when it is as if I, too, were dancing; when, in the imagination, I move with the motions of the dancer, experiencing vicariously her ease and her joy. The dancer's experience is, of course, different. She really moves, no make-believe that. Yet, even so, her experience possesses the essential character of imagination. For it is a satisfaction of impulses through occurrences within her own mind and body. For the moment it is as if she were having her way, only not through some purposive adjustment to her environment, but through action within her own self. To be sure, that action is not confined to her mind, as it is with me who watch her, but overflows into the body; but who has ever set the limits of the mind or the body? And even in my case when I watch her, something more than the mind is really involved, for imagination tends to translate itself into action, and there are impulses to movement, inhibited for obvious reasons, all through my muscles. In this enlarged sense of imagination, therefore, which nevertheless retains its fundamental meaning as a satisfaction of desire from within the system of the mind and body, dancing belongs with the other arts to imagination.

The case is similar with music. And, in parallel fashion, let us distinguish between music which we ourselves make and music which we merely listen to. And let us, furthermore, confine our attention entirely to absolute music, where no definite ideas or images are summoned to mind. I exclude programme music, because it is obviously imaginative; one cannot listen to the Golliwogs' Cake Walk, for example, without having the experience as if the Golliwogs were dancing. Suppose, then, I just hum a tune, say the motif from the first movement of Beethoven's Second Symphony. Well, why do I hum it? Perhaps my neighbor does not understand, but I do: I hum the tune because it pleases me; because some wish, some emotion of mine, is satisfied thus—an emotion which I feel none the less strongly because I am unable to tell what it is about or just what it means. At all events, in this little world of sound that I am making, it is as if I were having my way perfectly, and that is enough reason for humming: I so seldom have my way in real life! Thus, as in dancing, I am securing the satisfaction of my wish, not through some practical relation to the environment, but by way of an occurrence that is entirely within my own mind and body, and, for the time being at least, it is for me as if the satisfaction were real; and that, let me say once more, is the essence of imagination. The fact that my wishes may be objectless, that I do not attach them to some fancied situation or happening, is irrelevant. But suppose now, instead of humming the tune, I listen to some one play it. Then, first of all, I apprehend what Hanslick called an arabesque, a pattern of sound. But my experience is richer than that. For on hearing the sound, various wishes, moods, emotions, are awakened in me, the same, in fact, that I felt when I, myself, hummed the tune, and these emotions and wishes find expression and fulfilment, as before, in the sounds. Thus there is no important difference in what happens within me whether I make or only listen to the music. Music is beautiful as a voice that I hear storming, sobbing, making merry, lamenting, rejoicing, as the case may be, and it is as if that voice were my own. Hence music, too, belongs to the world of the imagination, in the larger and truer sense.

The demonstration of the imaginative quality of beautiful architecture is not so simple, and in place of the scientific analysis that should be given I beg leave to report a personal experience, which is, I believe, universal. Whenever I am in the presence of a beautiful building, and especially when I am inside it, I seem not to be in the neighborhood of a mere thing. I am not alone, as I am alone when surrounded by buildings unbeautiful or indifferent, as when at night I walk down the undistinguished streets of a large city; on the contrary, I am richly companioned; I feel all about me a life variously and magnificently eloquent; uttering a meaning which, to be sure, I cannot put into words—any more than I can translate music into words—but which I seem to understand; a meaning that comes to me, not by the avenues of sound, but by that of sight, and through subtle arousals of imaginative touch and movement. Every beautiful building is not only fit to house, but itself possesses or is a personality; a personality as distinct, as unique, as the faces of friends. Amiens, Rheims, Ulm, St. Mark's; piles of stone, yes, of course; but how much more; and that more is, so tells my sober reason, mere make-believe, pure fancy; yet essen-

tial to beauty. A beautiful building makes us dream, becomes itself a dream. And what I have said of beautiful architecture applies, if in lower key, to beautiful specimens of the potter's art, to color paintings, to oriental carpets; if they have for us the quality of beauty, they are not dead things, but things possessed of an imagined life. When you look at an oriental carpet it may seem to you at first no more than a mere pattern of colors and lines, but as you linger over it, you observe a change. The lines begin to run or shoot like arrows, the colors tingle; everything seems to move, or if not moving rests—not really, of course, but in the mind, in the imagination. . . .

Thus far I have accepted the familiar comparison between art and dream, but certain differences between them are of the utmost importance. For a dream is an inner fact only, an affair wholly of the imagination, while a work of art belongs also to the outer world, to the senses. It is something to be seen, heard, perhaps even touched. A work of art is born only when imaginative vision is wedded to sensuous shape. The inner vision must be expressed, in the etymological meaning of the term, put out into color and line, word-sound or tone. To be an artist always involves being more than a dreamer or seer; it involves mastery of a material as well; the mere dreamers are only half artists. The painter is one who can translate his visions of nature into visible line and color; the poet is one fertile in words as well as in ideas; the sculptor does not exist until he is able to model. Art is a 'gift of tongues,' of language. The artist must be able to create, in the external world, something to charm the senses as well as to speak to the mind. It is as if the artist were not content to realize his wishes in the closed room of the imagination, but desired to step out into reality and find satisfaction there. Yet the artist never does, of course, achieve reality. In the words of Bacon, he submits the mere *shows* of things to the desires of the mind. He takes the senses into the imagination, he does not leave the world of the imagination. His work remains a show, a make-believe, to the end; or rather it makes of reality itself such a show. It is a play, not of images merely, as in a dream, but of sensations. These are chosen partly for their ability to embody the dream, but also for their own intrinsic beauty. Thus in a song, like Der Erlkönig, the musical tones are not merely an embodiment in sound of Goethe's ideas as Schubert made them his own; but independently, as mere sound, they are an expression of vague moods and desires; and the colors in a painting are not only the right colors from the point of view of representation, but beautiful on their own account, apart from any representation. A picture is, first of all, a pattern of expressive colors and lines, just as music is first of all an arabesque of beautiful sound. Thus the sense medium is itself a part of the dream and an expression of the artist's desire.

That, despite its sensuous side, a work of art remains within the sphere of imagination, can easily be seen from another point of view. Consider, for example, Vermeer's Young Woman with a Water Jug. The pigments and the canvas are, of course, physical objects, as real as sun and moon; no dream work, no mere imagination

they. Yet the paint and the canvas are relevant to the aesthetic experience only through what can be seen of them in the picture; as parts of the aesthetic object, they are only visual sensations in the mind of the beholder; they might as well be a hallucination. Moreover, the colors there are the colors of the woman's face, of her garments, of the casement and the map. Now admittedly all those things are not real; despite the convincing art of the painter, they are a make-believe, that is all. And notwithstanding their intrinsic beauty, the colors are, for aesthetic appreciation, constituents of these make-believe objects, nothing more.

Yet certain transformations accrue to the dream through sensuous embodiment; or, in order to avoid the possibility of misunderstanding (as if in artistic work the vision must precede expression when, as a matter of fact, the two usually go hand in hand), let me say rather that a dream expressed differs in important ways from a mere dream. It possesses a poignancy, an objectivity, an additional tang of reality, while remaining nevertheless a dream. Through its connection with the sense world, it is partly dissociated from the rest of the self, and so seems to be external, like the color or sound in which it is embodied. It belongs to the outer as well as to the inner world; it confronts us; it draws attention to itself; we are awake to it, not asleep in it, as we are in a dream. It is "the dream of a man awake." It possesses a steadiness, clarity, and independence that permit us to observe it, as we cannot observe a dream. In the experience of beauty there are two, the work of art and myself. This fact renders inadequate every comparison of the aesthetic experience to hypnosis or the mystical experience, where the distinction between subject and object disappears in utter oneness. So far may the process of dissociation go that the poet's passion is no longer felt as his own, after expression; and the novelist's characters, for all that they are bits of himself, may seem to be doing their own wills, not his. . . .

But even now our analysis of art is incomplete; for we have barely mentioned one of the most striking characteristics of art, aesthetic form or design. . . . By design I mean, of course, harmony, balance, rhythm, and the like. A poem is not only an expression of feeling, it is patterned words; a musical composition is not only an embodiment of mood, it has a very elaborate harmonic and rhythmic structure; a picture or statue is never merely the representation of some object in nature, it is besides a harmony of lines and colors and space elements. A beautiful building is never one that is merely well adapted to its purpose, it possesses besides proportion and expressive lines and space forms. No matter how interesting and noble be the imagination of the artist, without design there is no picture or statue or poem or beautiful building. Moreover, the fundamental principles underlying aesthetic design are universal; they are exemplified in primitive art as well as in civilized art; in oriental art as well as in occidental art; in the art of the black, the white, and the yellow man. Arguing from the universality of design some students of art, called formalists, have claimed that design was the essence of art, the very thing we call beauty.

Yet despite the importance of design in art, the claim of the formalist is unjustified. For the underlying impulse to art is the demand for satisfaction of wishes in the imagination; design is a necessary, not a sufficient, condition of beauty, as many a faultless but cold and meaningless work attests. Moreover, design is no independent thing, imposed as from the outside upon imaginative expression, but a perfectly natural and inevitable development of expression, when it is an end in itself. For . . . design is the form of all experience when it is satisfactory. Whenever experience is most delightful, it possesses rhythm, balance, unity in variety, and a cumulative movement—these are not peculiar to art, except in their perfect realization, and they are perfect there because the artist, unlike other men, has complete control of his material. Building up in the imagination a little world that shall satisfy his wishes, and embodying it in a medium over which, as expert technician, he is master, it would be strange if the artist did not give that world design. Design is the inevitable consummation of the artistic impulse. And it is right that artists and critics should place stress upon that which gives to art its perfection.

QUESTIONS FOR DISCUSSION

1. Discuss Parker's theory of art as the "imaginary satisfaction of wishes" and indicate its application to painting, architecture, and music.

2. What are the similarities and differences between art, dream, and daydream?
3. What are the different ways of satisfying wishes according to Parker? Analyze in some detail his notion of "as if."
4. What, according to Parker, are the characteristics of design in art?
5. Do you find any difficulties in Parker's theory of art?

George Santayana (1863-1952)

7.4   Expression and Art

THE LIBERATION OF SELF

Hitherto we have been considering those elements of a pathetic presentation which may mitigate our sympathetic emotion, and make it on the whole agreeable. These consist in the intrinsic beauties of the medium of presentation, and in the concomitant manifestation of various goods, notably of truth. The mixture of these values is perhaps all we have in mildly pathetic works, in the presence of which we are tolerably aware of a sort of balance and compensation of emotions. The sorrow and the beauty, the hopelessness and the consolation, mingle and merge into a kind of joy which has its poignancy, indeed, but which is far too passive and penitential to contain the louder and sublimer of our tragic moods. In these there is a wholeness, a strength, and a rapture, which still demands an explanation.

Where this explanation is to be

From *The Sense of Beauty* by George Santayana (1896).

found may be guessed from the following circumstance. The pathetic is a quality of the object, at once lovable and sad, which we accept and allow to flow in upon the soul; but the heroic is an attitude of the will, by which the voices of the outer world are silenced, and a moral energy, flowing from within, is made to triumph over them. If we fail, therefore, to discover, by analysis of the object, anything which could make it sublime, we must not be surprised at our failure. We must remember that the object is always but a portion of our consciousness: that portion which has enough coherence and articulation to be recognized as permanent and projected into the outer world. But consciousness remains one, in spite of this diversification of its content, and the object is not really independent, but is in constant relation to the rest of the mind, in the midst of which it swims like a bubble on a dark surface of water.

The aesthetic effect of objects is always due to the total emotional value of the consciousness in which they exist. We merely attribute this value to the object by a projection which is the ground of the apparent objectivity of beauty. Sometimes this value may be inherent in the process by which the object itself is perceived; then we have sensuous and formal beauty; sometimes the value may be due to the incipient formation of other ideas, which the perception of this object evokes; then we have beauty of expression. But among the ideas with which every object has relation there is one vaguest, most comprehensive, and most powerful one, namely, the idea of self. The impulses, memories, principles, and energies which we designate by that word baffle enumeration; indeed, they constantly fade and change into one another; and whether the self is anything, everything, or nothing depends on the aspect of it which we momentarily fix, and especially on the definite object with which we contrast it.

Now, it is the essential privilege of beauty to so synthesize and bring to a focus the various impulses of the self, so to suspend them to a single image, that a great peace falls upon that perturbed kingdom. In the experience of these momentary harmonies we have the basis of the enjoyment of beauty, and of all its mystical meanings. But there are always two methods of securing harmony: one is to unify all the given elements, and another is to reject and expunge all the elements that refuse to be unified. Unity by inclusion gives us the beautiful; unity by exclusion, opposition, and isolation gives us the sublime. Both are pleasures: but the pleasure of the one is warm, passive, and pervasive; that of the other cold,

imperious, and keen. The one identifies us with the world, the other raises us above it.

There can be no difficulty in understanding how the expression of evil in the object may be the occasion of this heroic reaction of the soul. In the first place, the evil may be felt; but at the same time the sense that, great as it may be in itself, it cannot touch us, may stimulate extraordinarily the consciousness of our own wholeness. This is the sublimity which Lucretius calls "sweet" in the famous lines in which he so justly analyzes it. We are not pleased because another suffers an evil, but because, seeing it is an evil, we see at the same time our own immunity from it. We might soften the picture a little, and perhaps make the principle even clearer by so doing. The shipwreck observed from the shore does not leave us wholly unmoved; we suffer, also, and if possible, would help. So, too, the spectacle of the erring world must sadden the philosopher even in the Acropolis of his wisdom; he would, if it might be, descend from his meditation and teach. But those movements of sympathy are quickly inhibited by despair of success; impossibility of action is a great condition of the sublime. If we could count the stars, we should not weep before them. While we think we can change the drama of history, and of our own lives, we are not awed by our destiny. But when the evil is irreparable, when our life is lived, a strong spirit has the sublime resource of standing at bay and of surveying almost from the other world the vicissitudes of this.

The more intimate to himself the tragedy he is able to look back upon with calmness, the more sublime that calmness is, and the more divine the ecstasy in which he achieves it. For the more of the accidental vesture of life we are able to strip ourselves of, the more naked and simple is the surviving spirit; the more complete its superiority and unity, and, consequently, the more unqualified its joy. There remains little in us, then, but that intellectual essence, which several great philosophers have called eternal and identified with the Divinity.

A single illustration may help to fix these principles in the mind. When Othello has discovered his fatal error, and is resolved to take his own life, he stops his groaning, and addresses the ambassadors of Venice thus:

Speak of me as I am: nothing extenuate,
Nor set down aught in malice: then, must you speak
Of one that loved, not wisely, but too well;
Of one not easily jealous, but, being wrought,
Perplexed in the extreme; of one whose hand,
Like the base Indian, threw a pearl away
Richer than all his tribe; of one whose subdued eyes,
Albeit unusèd to the melting mood,
Drop tears as fast as the Arabian trees
Their medicinal gum. Set you down this:
And say, besides, that in Aleppo once
When a malignant and a turbaned Turk
Beat a Venetian, and traduced the state,
I took by the throat the circumcisèd dog,
And smote him, thus.

There is a kind of criticism that would see in all these allusions, figures of speech, and wandering reflections, an unnatural rendering of suicide. The man, we might be told, should have muttered a few broken phrases, and killed himself without this pomp of declamation, like the jealous husbands in the daily papers. But the conventions of the tragic stage are more favorable to psychological truth than the conventions of real life. If we may trust the imagination (and in imagination lies, as we have seen, the test of propriety), this is what Othello would have felt. If he had not expressed it, his dumbness would have been due to external hindrances, not to the failure in his mind of just such complex and rhetorical thoughts as the poet has put into his mouth. The height of passion is naturally complex and rhetorical. Love makes us poets, and the approach of death should make us philosophers. When a man knows that his life is over, he can look back upon it from a universal standpoint. He has nothing more to live for, but if the energy of his mind remains unimpaired, he will still wish to live, and, being cut off from his personal ambitions, he will impute to himself a kind of vicarious immortality by identifying himself with what is eternal. He speaks of himself as he is, or rather as he was. He sums himself up, and points to his achievement. This I have been, says he, this I have done.

This comprehensive and impartial view, this synthesis and objectification of experience, constitutes the liberation of the soul and the essence of sublimity. That the hero attains it at the end consoles us, as it consoles him, for his hideous misfortunes. Our pity and terror are indeed purged;

we go away knowing that, however tangled the net may be in which we feel ourselves caught, there is liberation beyond, and an ultimate peace.

THE SUBLIME INDEPENDENT OF THE EXPRESSION OF EVIL

So natural is the relation between the vivid conception of great evils, and that self-asseration of the soul which gives the emotion of the sublime, that the sublime is often thought to depend upon the terror which these conceived evils inspire. To be sure, that terror would have to be inhibited and subdued, otherwise we should have a passion too acute to be incorporated in any object; the sublime would not appear as an aesthetic quality in things, but remain merely an emotional state in the subject. But this subdued and objectified terror is what is commonly regarded as the essence of the sublime, and so great an authority as Aristotle would seem to countenance some such definition. The usual cause of the sublime is here confused, however, with the sublime itself. The suggestion of terror makes us withdraw into ourselves: there with the supervening consciousness of safety or indifference comes a rebound, and we have that emotion of detachment and liberation in which the sublime really consists.

Thoughts and actions are properly sublime, and visible things only by analogy and suggestion when they induce a certain moral emotion; whereas beauty belongs properly to sensible things, and can be predicated of moral facts only by a figure of rhetoric. What we objectify in beauty is a sensation. What we objectify in the sublime is an act. This act is necessarily pleasant, for if it were not the sublime would be a bad quality and one we should rather never encounter in the world. The glorious joy of self-assertion in the face of an uncontrollable world is indeed so deep and entire, that it furnishes just that transcendent element of worth for which we were looking when we tried to understand how the expression of pain could sometimes please. It can please, not in itself, but because it is balanced and annulled by positive pleasures, especially by this final and victorious one of detachment. If the expression of evil seems necessary to the sublime, it is so only as a condition of this moral reaction.

We are commonly too much engrossed in objects and too little centred in ourselves and our inalienable will, to see the sublimity of a pleasing prospect. We are then enticed and flattered, and won over to a commerce with these external goods, and the consummation of our happiness would lie in the perfect comprehension and enjoyment of their nature. This is the office of art and of love; and its partial fulfillment is seen in every perception of beauty. But when we are checked in this sympathetic endeavor after unity and comprehension; when we come upon a great evil or an irreconcilable power, we are driven to seek our happiness by the shorter and heroic road; then we recognize the hopeless foreignness of what lies before us, and stiffen ourselves against it. We thus for the first time reach the sense of our possible separation from our world, and of our abstract stability; and with this comes the sublime.

But although experience of evil is the commonest approach to this attitude of mind, and we commonly become philosophers only after despairing of instinctive happiness, yet there is nothing impossible in the attainment of detachment by other channels. The immense is sublime as well as the terrible; and mere infinity of the object, like its hostile nature, can have the effect of making the mind recoil upon itself. Infinity, like hostility, removes us from things, and makes us conscious of our independence. The simultaneous view of many things, innumerable attractions felt together, produce equilibrium and indifference, as effectually as the exclusion of all. If we may call the liberation of the self by the consciousness of evil in the world, the Stoic sublime, we may assert that there is also an Epicurean sublime, which consists in liberation by equipoise. Any wide survey is sublime in that fashion. Each detail may be beautiful. We may even be ready with a passionate response to its appeal. We may think we covet every sort of pleasure, and lean to every kind of vigorous, impulsive life. But let an infinite panorama be suddenly unfolded; the will is instantly paralyzed, and the heart choked. It is impossible to desire everything at once, and when all is offered and approved, it is impossible to choose everything. In this suspense, the mind soars into a kind of heaven, benevolent but unmoved.

This is the attitude of all minds to which breadth of interest or length of years has brought balance and dignity. The sacerdotal quality of old age comes from this same sympathy in disinterestedness. Old men full of hurry and passion appear as fools, because we understand that their experience has not left enough mark upon their brain to qualify with the memory of other goods any object that may be now presented. We cannot venerate anyone in whom appreciation is not divorced from desire. And this elevation and detachment of the heart need not follow upon any great disappointment; it is finest and sweetest where it is the gradual fruit of many affections now merged and mellowed into a natural piety. Indeed, we are able to frame our idea of the Deity on no other model.

When the pantheists try to conceive all the parts of nature as forming a single being, which shall contain them all and yet have absolute unity, they find themselves soon denying the existence of the world they are trying to deify; for nature, reduced to the unity it would assume in an omniscient mind, is no longer nature, but something simple and impossible, the exact opposite of the real world. Such an opposition would constitute the liberation of the divine mind from nature, and its existence as a self-conscious individual. The effort after comprehensiveness of view reduces things to unity, but this unity stands out in opposition to the manifold phenomena which it transcends, and rejects as unreal.

Now this destruction of nature, which the metaphysicians since Parmenides have so often repeated (nature nevertheless surviving still), is but a theoretical counterpart and hypostasis of what happens in every man's conscience when the comprehensiveness of his experience lifts him into thought, into abstraction. The sense of the sublime is essentially mystical: it is the transcending of distinct perception in favor of a feeling of unity and volume. So in the moral sphere, we have the mutual cancelling of the passions in the breast that includes them all, and their final subsidence beneath the glance that comprehends them. This is the Epicurean approach to detachment and perfection; it leads by systematic acceptance of instinct to the same goal which the stoic and the ascetic reach by systematic rejection of instinct. It is thus possible to be moved to that self-enfranchisement which constitutes the sublime, even when the object contains no expression of evil.

This conclusion supports that part of our definition of beauty which declares that the values beauty contains are all positive; a definition which we should have had to change if we had found that the sublime depended upon the suggestion of evil for its effect. But the sublime is not the ugly, as some descriptions of it might lead us to suppose; it is the supremely, the intoxicatingly beautiful. It is the pleasure of contemplation reaching such an intensity that it begins to lose its objectivity, and to declare itself, what it always fundamentally was, an inward passion of the soul. For while in the beautiful we find the perfection of life by sinking into the object, in the sublime we find a purer and more inalienable perfection by defying the object altogether. The surprised enlargement of vision, the sudden escape from our ordinary interests and the identification of ourselves with something permanent and superhuman, something much more abstract and inalienable than our changing personality, all this carries us away from

the blurred objects before us, and raises us into a sort of ecstasy.

In the trite examples of the sublime, where we speak of the vast mass strength, and durability of objects, or of their sinister aspect, as if we were moved by them on account of our own danger, we seem to miss the point. For the suggestion of our own danger would produce a touch of fear; it would be a practical passion, or if it could by chance be objectified enough to become aesthetic, it would merely make the object hateful and repulsive, like a mangled corpse. The object is sublime when we forget our danger, when we escape from ourselves altogether, and live as it were in the object itself, energizing in imitation of its movement, and saying, "Be thou me, impetuous one!" This passage into the object, to live its life, is indeed a characteristic of all perfect contemplation. But when in thus translating ourselves we rise and play a higher personage, feeling the exhilaration of a life freer and wilder than our own, then the experience is one of sublimity. The emotion comes not from the situation we observe, but from the powers we conceive; we fail to sympathize with the struggling sailors because we sympathize too much with the wind and waves. And this mystical cruelty can extend even to ourselves; we can so feel the fascination of the cosmic forces that engulf us as to take a fierce joy in the thought of our own destruction. We can identify ourselves with the abstractest essence of reality, and, raised to that height, despise the human accidents of our own nature. Lord, we say, though thou slay me, yet will I trust in thee. The sense of suffering disappears in the sense of life and the imagination overwhelms the understanding.

THE COMIC

Something analogous takes place in the other spheres where an aesthetic value seems to arise out of suggestions of evil, in the comic, namely, and the grotesque. But here the translation of our sympathies is partial, and we are carried away from ourselves only to become smaller. The larger humanity, which cannot be absorbed, remains ready to contradict the absurdity of our fiction. The excellence of comedy lies in the invitation to wander along some by-path of the fancy, among scenes not essentially impossible, but not to be actually enacted by us on account of the fixed circumstances of our lives. If the picture is agreeable, we allow ourselves to dream it true. We forget its relations; we forbid the eye to wander beyond the frame of the stage, or the conventions of the fiction. We indulge an illusion which deepens our sense of the essential pleasantness of things.

So far, there is nothing in comedy that is not delightful, except, perhaps, the moment when it is over. But fiction, like all error or abstraction, is necessarily unstable; and the awakening is not always reserved for the disheartening moment at the end. Everywhere, when we are dealing with pretension or mistake, we come upon sudden and vivid contradictions; changes of view, transformations of apperception which are extremely stimulating to the imagination. We have spoken of one of these: when the sudden dissolution of our common habits of thought lifts us into a mystical contemplation, filled with the sense of the sublime; when the transformation is back to common sense and reality, and away from some fiction, we have a very different emotion. We feel cheated, relieved, abashed, or amused, in proportion as our sympathy attaches more to the point of view surrendered or to that attained.

The disintegration of mental forms and their reintegration is the life of the imagination. It is a spiritual process of birth and death, nutrition and generation. The strongest emotions accompany these changes, and vary infinitely with their variations. All the qualities of discourse, wit, eloquence, cogency, absurdity, are feelings incidental to this process, and involved in the juxtapositions, tensions, and resolutions of our ideas. Doubtless the last explanation of these things would be cerebral; but we are as yet confined to verbal descriptions and classifications of them, which are always more or less arbitrary.

The most conspicuous headings under which comic effects are gathered are perhaps incongruity and degradation. But clearly it cannot be the logical essence of incongruity or degradation that constitutes the comic; for then contradiction and deterioration would always amuse. Amusement is a much more directly physical thing. We may be amused without any idea at all, as when we are tickled, or laugh in sympathy with others by a contagious imitation of their gestures. We may be amused by the mere repetition of a thing at first not amusing. There must, therefore, be some nervous excitement on which the feeling of amusement directly depends, although this excitement may most often coincide with a sudden transition to an incongruous or meaner image. Nor can we suppose that particular ideational excitement to be entirely dissimilar to all others; wit is often hardly distinguishable from brilliancy, as humor from pathos. We must, therefore, be satisfied with saying vaguely that the process of ideation involves various feelings of movement and relation—feelings capable of infinite gradation and complexity, and ranging from sublimity to tedium and from pathos to uncontrollable merriment.

Certain crude and obvious cases of the comic seem to consist of little more than a shock of surprise: a pun is a sort of jack-in-the-box, popping from nowhere into our plodding thoughts. The liveliness of the interruption, and its futility, often please; *dulce est desipere in loco;* and yet those who must endure the society of inveterate jokers know how intolerable this sort of scintillation can become. There is something inherently vulgar about it; perhaps because our train of thought cannot be very entertaining in itself when we are so glad to break in upon it with irrelevant nullities. The same undertone of disgust mingles with other amusing surprises, as when a dignified personage slips and falls, or some disguise is thrown off, or those things are mentioned and described which convention ignores. The novelty and the freedom please, yet the shock often outlasts the pleasure, and we have cause to wish we had been stimulated by something which did not involve this degradation. So, also, the impossibility in plausibility which tickles the fancy in Irish bulls, and in wild

exaggerations, leaves an uncomfortable impression, a certain aftertaste of foolishness.

The reason will be apparent if we stop to analyze the situation. We have a prosaic background of common sense and everyday reality; upon this background an unexpected idea suddenly impinges. But the thing is a futility. The comic accident falsifies the nature before us, starts a wrong analogy in the mind, a suggestion that cannot be carried out. In a word, we are in the presence of an absurdity; and man, being a rational animal, can like absurdity no better than he can like hunger or cold. A pinch of either may not be so bad, and he will endure it merrily enough if you repay him with abundance of warm victuals; so, too, he will play with all kinds of nonsense for the sake of laughter and good fellowship and the tickling of his fancy with a sort of caricature of thought. But the qualm remains, and the pleasure is never perfect. The same exhilaration might have come without the falsification, just as repose follows more swiftly after pleasant than after painful exertions.

Fun is a good thing, but only when it spoils nothing better. The best place for absurdity is in the midst of what is already absurd—then we have the play of fancy without the sense of ineptitude. Things amuse us in the mouth of a fool that would not amuse us in that of a gentleman; a fact which shows how little incongruity and degradation have to do with our pleasure in the comic. In fact, there is a kind of congruity and method even in fooling. The incongruous and the degraded displease us even there, as by their nature they must at all times. The shock which they bring may sometimes be the occasion of a subsequent pleasure, by attracting our attention, or by stimulating passions, such as scorn, or cruelty, or self-satisfaction (for there is a good deal of malice in our love of fun); but the incongruity and degradation, as such, always remain unpleasant. The pleasure comes from the inward rationality and movement of the fiction, not from its inconsistency with anything else. There are a great many topsy-turvy worlds possible to our fancy, into which we like to drop at times. We enjoy the stimulation and the shaking up of our wits. It is like getting into a new posture or hearing a new song.

Nonsense is good only because common sense is so limited. For reason, after all, is one convention picked out of a thousand. We love expansion, not disorder, and when we attain freedom without incongruity we have a much greater and a much purer delight. The excellence of wit can dispense with absurdity. For on the same prosaic background of common sense, a novelty might have appeared that was not absurd, that stimulated the attention quite as much as the ridiculous, without so baffling the intelligence. This purer and more thoroughly delightful amusement comes from what we call wit.

WIT

Wit also depends upon transformation and substitution of ideas. It has been said to consist in quick association by similarity. The substitution must here be valid, however, and the similarity real, though unforeseen. Unexpected justness makes wit, as sudden incongruity makes pleasant foolishness. It is characteristic of wit to penetrate into hidden depths of things, to pick out there some telling circumstance or relation, by noting which the whole object appears in a new and clearer light. Wit often seems malicious because analysis in discovering common traits and universal principles assimilates things at the poles of being; it can apply to cookery the formulas of theology, and find in the human heart a case of the fulcrum and lever. We commonly keep the departments of experience distinct; we think the different principles hold in each and that the dignity of spirit is inconsistent with the explanation of it by physical analogy, and the meanness of matter unworthy of being an illustration of moral truths. Love must not be classed under physical cravings, nor faith under hypnotization. When, therefore, an original mind overleaps these boundaries, and recasts its categories, mixing up our old classifications, we feel that the values of things are also confused. But these depended upon a deeper relation, upon their response to human needs and aspirations. All that can be changed by the exercise of intelligence is our sense of the unity and homogeneity of the world. We may come to hold an object of thought in less isolated respect, and another in less hasty derision; but the pleasures we derive from all, or our total happiness and wonder, will hardly be diminished. For this reason the malicious or destructive character of intelligence must not be regarded as fundamental. Wit belittles one thing and dignifies another; and its comparisons are as often flattering as ironical.

The same process of mind that we observed in wit gives rise to those effects we call charming, brilliant, or inspired. When Shakespeare says,

Come and kiss me, *sweet and twenty,*
Youth's a stuff will not endure.

the fancy of the phrase consists in a happy substitution, a merry way of saying something both true and tender. And where could we find a more exquisite charm? So, to take a weightier example, when St. Augustine says the virtues of the pagans were *splendid vices,* we have—at least if we catch the full meaning—a pungent assimilation of contrary things, by force of a powerful principle; a triumph of theory, the boldness of which can only be matched by its consistency. In fact, a phrase could not be more brilliant, or better condense one theology and two civilizations. The Latin mind is particularly capable of this sort of excellence. Tacitus alone could furnish a hundred examples. It goes with the power of satirical and bitter eloquence, a sort of scornful rudeness of intelligence, that makes for the core of a passion or of a character, and affixes to it a more or less scandalous label. For in our analytical zeal it is often possible to condense and abstract too much. Reality is more fluid and elusive than reason, and has, as it were, more dimensions than are known even to the latest geometry. Hence the understanding, when not suffused with some glow of sympathetic emotion or some touch of mysticism, gives but a dry, crude image of the world. The quality of wit inspires more admiration than confidence. It is a merit we should miss little in anyone we love.

The same principle, however, can have more sentimental embodiments. When our substitutions are brought on by the excitement of generous emotion, we call wit inspiration. There is the same finding of new analogies, and likening of disparate things; there is the same transformation of our apperception. But the brilliancy is here not only penetrating, but also exalting. For instance:

Peace, peace, he is not dead, he doth
    not sleep,
He hath awakened from the dream
    of life:
'Tis we that wrapped in stormy visions
    keep
    With phantoms an unprofitable
    strife.

There is here paradox, and paradox justified by reflection. The poet analyzes, and analyzes without reserve. The dream, the storm, the phantoms, and the unprofitableness could easily make a satirical picture. But the mood is transmuted; the mind takes an upward flight, with a sense of liberation from the convention it dissolves, and of freer motion in the vagueness beyond. The disintegration of our ideal here leads to mysticism, and because of this effort towards transcendence, the brilliancy becomes sublime.

HUMOR

A different mood can give a different direction to the same processes. The sympathy by which we reproduce the feeling of another, is always very much opposed to the aesthetic attitude to which the whole world is merely a stimulus to our sensibility. In the tragic, we have seen how the sympathetic feeling, by which suffering is appreciated and shared, has to be overlaid by many incidental aesthetic pleasures, if the resulting effect is to be on the whole good. We have also seen how the only way in which the ridiculous can be kept within the sphere of the aesthetically good is abstracting it from its relations, and treating it as an independent and curious stimulus; we should stop laughing and begin to be annoyed if we tried to make sense out of our absurdity. The less sympathy we have with men, the more exquisite is our enjoyment of their folly: satirical delight is closely akin to cruelty. Defect and mishap stimulate our fancy, as blood and tortures excite in us the passions of the beast of prey. The more this inhuman attitude yields to sympathy and reason, the less are folly and error capable of amusing us. It would, therefore, seem impossible that we should be pleased by the foibles or absurdities of those we love. And in fact we never enjoy seeing our own persons in a satirical light, or anyone else for whom we really feel affection. Even in farces, the hero and heroine are seldom made ridiculous, because that would jar upon the sympathy with which we are expected to regard them. Nevertheless, the essence of what we call human is that amusing weaknesses should be combined with an amicable humanity. Whether it be in the way of ingenuity, or oddity, or drollery, the humorous person must have an absurd side, or be placed in an absurd situation. Yet this comic aspect, at which we ought to wince, seems to endear the character all the more. This is a parallel case to that of tragedy, where the depth of the woe we sympathize

with seems to add to our satisfaction. And the explanation of the paradox is the same. We do not enjoy the expression of evil, but only the pleasant excitements that come with it; namely, the physical stimulus and the expression of good. In tragedy, the misfortunes help to give the impression of truth, and to bring out the noble qualities of the hero, but are in themselves depressing, so much so that oversensitive people cannot enjoy the beauty of the representation. So also in humor, the painful suggestions are felt as such, and need to be overbalanced by agreeable elements. These come from both directions, from the aesthetic and the sympathetic reaction. On the one hand there is the sensuous and merely perceptive stimulation, the novelty, the movement, the vivacity of the spectacle. On the other hand, there is the luxury of imaginative sympathy, the mental assimilation of another congenial experience, the expansion into another life.

The juxtaposition of these two pleasures produces just that tension and complication in which the humorous consists. We are satirical, and we are friendly at the same time. The consciousness of the friendship gives a regretful and tender touch to the satire, and the sting of the satire makes the friendship a trifle humble and sad. Don Quixote is mad; he is old, useless, and ridiculous, but he is the soul of honor, and in all his laughable adventures we follow him like the ghost of our better selves. We enjoy his discomfitures too much to wish he had been a perfect Amadis; and we have besides a shrewd suspicion that he is the only kind of Amadis there can ever be in this world. At the same time it does us good to see the courage of his idealism, the ingenuity of his wit, and the simplicity of his goodness. But how shall we reconcile our sympathy with his dream and our perception of its absurdity? The situation is contradictory. We are drawn to some different point of view, from which the comedy may no longer seem so amusing. As humor becomes deep and really different from satire, it changes into pathos, and passes out of the sphere of the comic altogether. The mischances that were to amuse us as scoffers now grieve us as men, and the value of the representation depends on the touches of beauty and seriousness with which it is adorned.

THE GROTESQUE

Something analogous to humor can appear in plastic forms, when we call it the grotesque. This is an interesting effect produced by such a transformation of an ideal type as exaggerates one of its elements or combines it with other types. The real excellence of this, like that of all fiction, consists in re-creation; in the formation of a thing which nature has not, but might conceivably have offered. We call these inventions comic and grotesque when we are considering their divergence from the natural rather than their inward possibility. But the latter constitutes their real charm; and the more we study and develop them, the better we understand it. The incongruity with the conventional type then disappears, and what was impossible and ridiculous at first takes its place among recognized ideals. The cen-

taur and the satyr are no longer grotesque; the type is accepted. And the grotesqueness of an individual has essentially the same nature. If we like the inward harmony, the characteristic balance of his features, we are able to disengage this individual from the class into which we were trying to force him; we can forget the expectation which he was going to disappoint. The ugliness then disappears, and only the reassertion of the old habit and demand can make us regard him as in any way extravagant.

What appears as grotesque may be intrinsically inferior or superior to the normal. That is a question of its abstract material and form. But until the new object impresses its form on our imagination, so that we can grasp its unity and proportion, it appears to us as a jumble and distortion of other forms. If this confusion is absolute, the object is simply null; it does not exist aesthetically, except by virtue of materials. But if the confusion is not absolute, and we have an inkling of the unity and character in the midst of the strangeness of the form, then we have the grotesque. It is the half-formed, the perplexed, and the suggestively monstrous.

The analogy to the comic is very close, as we can readily conceive that it should be. In the comic we have this same juxtaposition of a new and an old idea, and if the new is not futile and really inconceivable, it may in time establish itself in the mind, and cease to be ludicrous. Good wit is novel truth, as the good grotesque is novel beauty. But there are natural conditions of organization, and we must not mistake every mutilation for the creation of a new form. The tendency of nature to establish well-marked species of animals shows what various combinations are most stable in the face of physical forces, and there is a fitness also for survival in the mind, which is determined by the relation of any form to our fixed method of perception. New things are, therefore, generally bad because, as has been well said, they are incapable of becoming old. A thousand originalities are produced by defect of faculty, for one that is produced by genius. For in the pursuit of beauty, as in that of truth, an infinite number of paths lead to failure, and only one to success.

QUESTIONS FOR DISCUSSION

1. Analyze Santayana's view that beauty is pleasure when regarded as the quality of a thing.
2. Critically discuss the meanings involved in this quotation from Santayana: "The aesthetic effect of objects is always due to the total emotional value of consciousness in which they exist. We merely attribute this value to the object of a projection which is the ground of the apparent objectivity of beauty."
3. Discuss in some detail Santayana's concept of the sublime.
4. Compare and contrast the notion of the comic, the humorous, and the grotesque.

C. J. Ducasse (1881-1969)

7.5 Standards of Criticism

1. *Criticism is (a) Judgment, (b) of Worth, (c) Mediate or Immediate, and (d) Respectively Fallible or Infallible.*

Criticism is judgment concerning questions of worth, value. All criticism involves reference to some char-

From *The Philosophy of Art* by C. J. Ducasse (New York: Dial Press, Inc., 1929). Reprinted by permission of the publisher.

acter, the possession of which by the object criticized is regarded by the critic as being in some way good, or the lack of it, bad. The object is then examined with respect to that character, and pronounced good or bad in the degree in which it possesses it or lacks it. Such a character so used constitutes a standard of criticism. The character used may be one the possession of which makes an object *mediately good;* or on the other hand it may be one that makes the object *immediately good.* The object is said to be mediately or instrumentally good, when the character used as standard of goodness, and possessed by the object, is that of being an adequate instrument to or a necessary condition of the production or preservation in certain other objects, or characters which confer upon those objects immediate goodness of some sort. An object, on the other hand, is said to be immediately good when the character used as standard of goodness, and possessed by the object, is that of being directly and immediately a source of active or passive pleasure to some conscious being. That is to say, the object is called immediately good when it is, to the sentient being in terms of whose point of view it is asserted to be good, a source of pleasure *directly through its* relation to him, and apart from any pleasure which it may also procure him indirectly through its actual or potential effects upon other objects. The conscious being in terms of whose point of view the assertion of immediate goodness is made may be one person or a class of persons; it may be oneself or someone else; it may be a self considered in some one only of its aspects, which may be an active or a passive one; or it may be a self, such only as it is at a given time or in given circumstances. But any doubt as to which such sort of self is referred to when goodness is predicated of anything, will leave the import of the predication hopelessly ambiguous.

The instrumental goodness of an object can be proved or disproved, if there is agreement as to the end, being a means to or condition of which constitutes the object's goodness; for it is then only a matter of showing whether or not the object does under the sort of conditions in view, cause or make possible in other objects effects of the sort desired. Thus it is possible to prove to someone who doubts or disbelieves it, that a given chisel is a good, or as the case may be, a bad chisel. As to instrumental goodness, mistakes can be made.

But the immediate goodness of an object cannot be proved or disproved to the self in terms of whose point of view immediate goodness is asserted to be possessed by the object. Such immediate goodness being a matter of the pleasure which *that* self experiences through his direct relation to the object, he himself is the final and infallible judge of it; for, as to pleasure, appearance and reality are identical. His actual pleasure or displeasure when in direct relation to the object, constitutes the proof or disproof *to others,* of any assertions or predictions that *they* may have made as to what, in terms of his point of view, is, or will turn out to be, immediately good. Such another, to whom the prediction may have been made, may of course be, or have been, living under the same skin as the self who verifies the prediction; but it cannot be strictly the same self.

10. *Beauty Is Relative to the Individual Observer.*

Beauty . . . was defined as the capacity of an object esthetically contemplated to yield feelings that are pleasant. This definition cannot be characterized simply either as objective, or as subjective. According to it, "beautiful" is an adjective properly predicable only of objects, but what that adjective does predicate of an object is that the feelings, of which it constitutes the esthetic symbol for a contemplating observer, are pleasurable. Beauty being in this definite sense dependent upon the constitution of the individual observer, it will be as variable as that constitution. That is to say, an object which one person properly calls beautiful will, with equal propriety, be not so judged by another, or indeed by the same person at a different time.

There is, then, no such thing as authoritative opinion concerning the beauty of a given object. There is only the opinion of this person or that; or the opinion of persons of some specified sort. When one has stated the opinion and mentioned the person or class of persons who hold it, one has gone as far as it is possible to go in the direction of a scientifically objective statement relating to the beauty of the object. When some matter (as that of beauty) is not of the sort which "is so," or "not so," in an *absolute* sense, the nearest approach that one can make to the wished-for absoluteness lies in furnishing, as fully as possible, the data to which the matter in question is *relative;* and this is what one does in the case of beauty when one indicates just who it happens to be, that judges the given object beautiful or the reverse.

All that was said above concerning esthetic connoisseurship, i.e., concerning superior capacity for experiencing difference in esthetic feeling in the presence of slight differences in the esthetic object, applies equally here, where differences in the pleasantness of the feelings are particularly in question. There are connoisseurs of beauty, or, more often, of particular sorts of beauty; but their judgments of beauty are "binding" on no one. Indeed, it is hard to see what could possibly be meant by "binding" in such a connection, unless it were an obligation on others to lie or dissemble concerning the esthetic feelings which, in fact, they have or do not have on a given occasion. There is, of course, such a thing as good taste, and bad taste. But good taste, I submit, means either my taste, or the taste of people who are to my taste, or the taste of people to whose taste I want to be. There is no objective test of the goodness or badness of taste, in the sense in which there is an objective test of the goodness or badness of a person's judgment concerning, let us say, the fitness of a given tool to a given task.

11. *Why We Have a Natural Inclination to Think Otherwise.*

What makes it so difficult for us to acknowledge that judgments of esthetic value, i.e., of beauty and ugliness which are truly judgments about objects, are not universally and necessarily valid, but on the contrary valid, except by chance, only for the individuals who make them, is that we are so constantly occupied otherwise with judgments concerning instrumental values. These have to do with relations of the object judged, *to other objects,* and such relations are socially observable, and the judgments concerning them socially valid. That a given railroad bridge is a good bridge can be proved or disproved by running over it such trains as we wished it to carry, and observing whether or not it does carry them. But there is no similar test by which the beauty of a landscape could be proved or disproved. Judgments of beauty (which is an immediate value) have to do with the relation of the object judged to the individual's own pleasure experience, of which he himself is the sole possible observer and judge. Judgments of beauty are, therefore, in this respect exactly on a par with judgments of the pleasantness of foods, wines, climates, amusements, companions, etc. Like these, they are ultimately matters of the individual's own taste. It is, of course, quite possible that two persons, or two million, should have similar tastes, i.e., should happen alike to find pleasure in a given food or wine, or to obtain pleasurable feelings in contemplating esthetically a given picture, melody, etc. But such community in the experience of pleasure even then remains a bare matter of fact concerning just the persons who have it in common, and leaves wholly untouched the equally bare fact that other persons—whether many, few, or only one —find not pleasure but displeasure in the very same objects. . . .

12. *Beauty Cannot Be Proved by Appeal to Consensus, or to the "Test of Time," or to the Type of Person Who Experiences It in a Given Case.*

In the light of what precedes, it is obvious that the familiar attempts to prove the beauty of certain works of art by appeal to the consensus of opinion, or to the test of continued approval through long periods of time in the life either of society or of the individual, are, like the appeal to the connoisseur's verdict, entirely futile. Such tests cannot possibly prove the object's beauty to those who do not perceive any in it; and to those who do, they are needless. They prove nothing whatever, except that beauty is found in the object . . . by such as do find it there.

We might attempt to rank beauties on the basis of the particular aspect of human nature, or type of human being, that experiences esthetic pleasure in given cases. This would lead to a classifying of beauties as, for instance, sentimental, intellectual, sexual, spiritual, utilitarian, sensuous, social, etc. We might well believe in some certain order of worth or dignity in the human faculties respectively concerned, but this would not lead to any esthetically objective ranking of beauties. To suggest it would be as ludicrous as a proposal to rank the worth of various religions according to the average cost of the vestments of their priests. For a ranking of beauties, there are available only such principles as the relative intensity of the pleasure felt, its relative duration, relative volume, and relative freedom from admixture of pain. These principles, however, do not in the least release us from the need of relying upon the individual's judgment; on the contrary, their application rests wholly upon it.

13. *Beauty Cannot Be Proved by Appeal to Technical Principles or Canons.*

It may yet be thought, however, that there are certain narrower and more technical requirements in the various fields of art, without the fulfilling of which no work can be beautiful. Among such alleged canons of beauty may be mentioned the rules of so-called "harmony" in music; various precepts concerning literary composition; unity; truth to nature; such requirements as consistency, relevance, and unambiguity; and so on. There are indeed "rules" or "principles" of that sort, some of which are, I will freely declare, valid for me; so that when I find myself confronted by flagrant violations of them, I am apt to feel rather strongly, and to be impatient or sarcastic about "that sort of stuff." And indeed, on occasions when I have found myself inadvertently guilty of having drawn some line or written some sentence in violation of my own esthetic canons, I have at times felt as ashamed of the line or the sentence as I should of having picked somebody's pocket. I admit having pronounced opinions about the beauty or ugliness of various things, and what is more, in many cases I am able to *give reasons* for my opinions.

But of what nature are those reasons? They are, ultimately, of the same nature as would be that offered by a man arguing that my pen had to fall when I let go of it a moment ago, *because of gravitation.* Gravitation is but the name we give to the general fact that unsupported objects *do* fall, and at a certain rate; but it is not a reason, or cause, or proof of that fact. To say that something always happens, is not to give any reason why it ever does. Therefore, when I say that a certain design is ugly because it is against the "law of symmetry," I am not giving a reason why it *had* to give me esthetic displeasure, but only mentioning the fact that it resembles in a stated respect certain others which, as a bare matter of fact, also do displease me.

This character which displeases me and many persons, may, however, please others. And what is more directly to the point, it not only may but it does—jazzy or uncouth though I may call the taste of such persons. But what most obstinately drives me to the acquisition of a certain, at least abstract, sense of humor concerning the ravening intolerance and would-be-authoritativeness of my own pet canons of beauty, is the fact that they have changed in the past, and that I see no reason why they should not change again in the future. For all I can see to prevent it, I may well tomorrow, next year, or in some future incarnation, burn what I esthetically adore today, and adore what I now would burn. If this happens, I have no doubt at all that I shall then smugly label the change a progress and a development of my taste; whereas today I should no less smugly describe the possibility of a change of that sort in me, as a possibility that my taste may go to the devil. And, let it be noted, the sole foundation upon which either of the two descriptions would rest, would be the fact that the describer *actually* possesses at the time the sort of taste which he does. Tastes can be neither proved nor refuted, but only "called names," i.e., praised or reviled.

Certain limited and empirical generalizations have been found possible concerning factors upon which the esthetic pleasure of most people, or of some kinds of people, appears to depend. Precarious generalizations of this sort may be found, for instance, in manuals of design and of pictorial composition, where they are often dignified by the name of "principles." People familiar with them may then be heard to say that a given picture, perhaps, is well composed and why; or that the tones, the masses, or the values are, as the case may be, well or ill balanced, and so on. Other statements that we may hear and which also imply "principles," would be that the color is clean, or else muddy; that the drawing is, perhaps, distorted; that the surfaces are well modelled; that the lines are rhythmical; that the color combinations are impossible; that the masses lack volume or solidity, etc. The words beauty and ugliness may not occur once, but it is nevertheless obvious that all such statements are not merely descriptive, but *critical*. They are not direct assertions of esthetic value or disvalue, viz., of beauty or ugliness, but, taking it as an obvious fact, they attempt to trace it to certain definite sorts of features in the work. The more intelligent and better-informed kind of art criticism is of this analytical and diagnostic sort, and there is nothing beyond this that the art critic could do.

All such comments, worded in the technical jargon of the particular craft, have the imposing sound of expert judgments based upon authoritative principles, and are likely to make the lay consumer of art feel very small and uninitiated. Therefore, it cannot be too much emphasized here that a given picture is not ugly because the composition of it, or the color combination in it, are against the rules; but that the rule against a given type of composition or of color combination is authoritative only because, or if, or for whom, or when, compositions or combinations of that type are *actually* found displeasing. All rules and can-

ons and theories concerning what a painting or other work of art should or should not be, derive such authority as they have over you or me or anyone else, solely from the capacity of such canons *to predict to us* that we shall feel esthetic pleasure here, and esthetic pain there. If a given rule predicts this accurately for a given person, that person's *actual* feeling of esthetic pleasure or displeasure then, proves that that rule *was* a valid one so far as *he* is concerned. That is, the feeling judges the rule, not the rule the feeling. The rule may not be valid for someone else, and it may at any time cease to be valid for the given person, since few things are so variable as pleasure. The *actual* experience of beauty or ugliness by somebody is the final test of the validity of all rules and theories of painting, music, etc., and that test absolutely determines how far, and when, and for whom any given rule or theory holds or does not hold.

The difference between the criticisms of the professionals, and those of the people who, having humbly premised that they "know nothing about art," find little more to say than that a given work is in their judgment beautiful, or as the case may be, ugly or indifferent;—the difference, I say, between the criticisms of professionals and of laymen is essentially that the former are able to trace the esthetic pleasure or displeasure which they feel, to certain features of the object, while the latter are not able to do it. From this, however, it does not in the least follow that the evaluations of the professionals ultimately rest on any basis less subjective and less a matter of individual taste than do those of the layman. Indeed, so far as the non-professionals really judge at all, i.e., do not merely echo an opinion which they have somehow been bluffed into accepting as authoritative, their judgment is based on the fact that they actually feel something. The artists and professional critics, on the other hand, are exposed to a danger which does not threaten people who know nothing of the factors on which esthetic pleasure or displeasure has in the past been found to depend for most people, or for some particular class of people—the danger, namely, of erecting such empirical findings into fixed and rigid rules, and of judging the work of art no longer by the esthetic pleasure it actually gives them, but by that which they think it "ought" to give them according to such rules. This danger is really very great, especially for the artist, who, in the nature of the case, is constantly forced to give attention to the technical means by which the objective expression of his feeling is alone to be achieved. Having thus all the time to solve technical problems, it is fatally easy for him to become interested in them for their own sake, and, without knowing it, to be henceforth no longer an artist expressing what he feels, but a restless virtuoso searching for new stunts to perform. This may be the reason why so many of the pictures displayed in our exhibits, although well-enough painted, make one feel as though one were receiving a special-delivery, registered, extra-postage letter, . . . just to say, perhaps, that after Thursday comes Friday!

Listening to the comments of artists and of some critics on a picture will quickly convince one that, strange as it sounds, they are as often as not almost incapable of seeing the picture about which they speak. What they see instead is brush work, values, edges, dark against light, colored shadows, etc. They are thus often not more but less capable than the untrained public of giving the picture *esthetic* attention, and of getting from it genuinely esthetic enjoyment. The theory that *esthetic* appreciation of the products of a given art is increased by cultivating an amateur's measure of proficiency in that art, is therefore true only so far as such cultivation results in more intimate and thoroughgoing *esthetic* acquaintance with the products of that art. This is likely to be the case in an interpretative art like music (not music-composing). But in an art which, like painting, is not so largely interpretative, and is at the same time dependent on rather elaborate technical processes, the amateur practitioner's attention is from the very first emphatically directed to these processes; and, when it is directed to extant works of art, it is directed to them as examples of a technique to be studied, not as esthetic objects to be contemplated. The danger is then that such technical matters will come to monopolize his attention habitually, and that even in the face of nature he will forget to look at her, wondering instead whether the water or the sky be the brighter, or what color would have to be used to reproduce the appearance of a given shadow. Attention to technique is, of course, indispensable to the acquisition of it; and mastery of technique is in turn necessary to the production of art on any but the most humble scale. The risk is that the outcome of technical training will be not mastery of technique, but slavery to it. This risk disappears only when the technical apparatus has become as intimately a part of the artist as the hand is of the body for ordinary purposes, and is used without requiring attention. The attention can then turn from the means to the ends of art, viz., to the objective expression of feeling. But the stage at which technique has so become second-nature as to be forgotten, is not often fully reached. With most artists, what we may call their technical *savoir-faire* creaks more or less, as does the social *savoir-faire* of people who have become emily-posted but lately. Like the nouveaux gentlemen, such artists are too conscious of their technical manners, and forget what they are for.

14. *Beauty and Accuracy of Representation.*

Among the special criteria by which the merit of works of art—especially paintings—is judged by many, there is one about which something should be said here, namely, accuracy of representation. Accuracy of representation is important from the standpoint of esthetic criticism only so far as beauty happens to be conditioned by it. Representation, in painting, is a relation between the perceptual varicolored canvas and the esthetic object, when that esthetic object is not simply a flat design as such, but contains imaginal and conceptual elements. Accuracy of representation of the intended esthetic object, by the perceptual canvas is thus not in itself an esthetic but a noematic merit. Nevertheless, it is a merit which is indispensable, since without it the intended esthetic object (in the sort of cases considered) would be set up before

the attention, either not at all, or only in altered form.

Accuracy of representation of the esthetic object is, of course, not at all the same thing as accuracy of representation of the model. An accurate representation of a model is, merely as such, not a work of art at all, but only a document—a piece of reliable information about the appearance of an existing object. If it is accurate, the copy will indeed have more or less the same esthetic import and value as the model itself, but that copy, as such, will none the less be only a work of imitative skill. It will not be a work of art unless it also constitutes the conscious objective expression of a feeling experienced by the painter. Accuracy of representation of the esthetic object, on the other hand, means only that the perceptual canvas sets up clearly before the ideational attention just the esthetic object that embodies the feeling which it is intended should be obtained in contemplation.

Photographic accuracy of drawing, and faithfulness of representation of persons or things, provokes the pleasure of recognition, and admiration of the painter's capacity to act as a color camera. But this does not mean that his work is a work of art; nor even that he has created something beautiful, if the object which he has "photographed" happens not to be so. On the other hand, the fact that various elements are out of drawing in some pictures in which the artist is expressing himself in terms of represented objects, does not mean that they are necessarily ugly. What is important for beauty is *not truth but plausibility*. A dramatic entity represented may in fact be distorted, but it is not on this account ugly if it does not *look* distorted. Contrariwise, if something which in fact is photographically accurate looks distorted or unplausible, it will be disagreeable in esthetic effect. The works of El Greco, who is famous for his distortions of drawing, illustrate this. Some people have thought that something was wrong with his eyes; but the true explanation of his distortions is much more probably his preoccupation with the design-aspect of his paintings. When his design needed a line or thing of a particular shape and size at a certain place, and the object represented at that place happened to be, say, a human leg incapable of the needed shape and size, then it was so much the worse for the leg. Either design or accuracy of representation had to be sacrificed, and in such cases El Greco did not hesitate to sacrifice the latter. Whether ugliness is produced thereby, however, depends on whether the sacrifice is obvious—the inaccuracy flagrant. In many places it is not; and it does not there constitute an esthetic fault. Where the distortion is not plausible, on the other hand, but thrusts itself upon our notice as distortion, it gives rise to ugliness and is, therefore, to that extent esthetically bad, whatever esthetic gains it may otherwise involve. Only the addicts of design, who are satisfied with but a half of what an esthetically complete beholder demands, fail to see this. On the other hand, to the painter who justifies this or that bad part of his picture by insisting that "nature looked just like that," the answer is that even if she did, she ought not to have so far as beauty was concerned. As often has been said, when truth is stranger than fiction, it does not make good fiction, but only news for the papers.

QUESTIONS FOR DISCUSSION

1. What is the distinction, according to Ducasse, between the object that is mediately good and the one that is immediately good? Illustrate.
2. Ducasse states that "beauty is relative to the individual observer." Critically analyze this statement.
3. Why doesn't the "test of time" or an appeal to "technical canons" prove for Ducasse the object's beauty? State your views on these issues.
4. In what sense, for Ducasse, is accuracy of representation an important standard in aesthetic criticism? Give some examples.
5. What would be the difficulties, if any, in Ducasse's relativistic theory of beauty?

Ralph Barton Perry (1876-1957)

7.6   Art and Morality

The aesthetic life of man is embedded in his total life, and its internal standard is only one among many standards by which it may be judged. The critique of art by external standards of education has played an important role in controversy over the place of art in civilization. The critique of art by religious standards played a considerable part in the rise of protestanism, and in disputes among protestant sects. The omission of these topics is practically compensated by the fact that these critiques are largely concerned with the relation of art to morality. The examination of the moral and cognitive critiques of art is more fundamental and calls for special consideration.

In the appraisal of man's major institutions of conscience, polity, law, and economy, the moral standard is internal. These forms of human life are essentially moral institutions, that is, their very being lies in their more or less successful solution of the problem created by the conflict of interests. The aesthetic activities and enjoyments, on the other hand, are only

From *Realms of Value* by Ralph Barton Perry (Cambridge, Mass.: Harvard University Press). © 1954 by the President and Fellows of Harvard College. Reprinted by permission of the publisher.

accidentally moral; they become so because the aesthetic interest is one among many interests with which it will conflict or harmonize, and because morality itself may be an object of the aesthetic interest.

It may be argued that these relations of the moral and the aesthetic are necessary and not accidental. Thus it may be argued that there is a positive correlation between the value of art and the moral character of the artist. But this is notoriously contrary to fact. Indeed the aesthetic interest seems peculiarly capable of flourishing in the absence of morality; indulgence of moral laxity is considered a price to pay for the contributions of artistic genius. It is by no means clear that an excess of passion beyond the bounds of virtue, and even extended to vices highly offensive to the conscience of the community, may not positively enhance artistic creativity. A distinguished musical critic has described Wagner's looseness of living, his sponging on his friends, his cruelty to his opponents, his infidelities, childish tantrums, ingratitude, egotism, insolence, and dishonesty. He was, in short, a moral monstrosity—a social parasite. It is clear that a society of Wagners could not exist. The writer goes on to say:

And the curious thing about this record is that it doesn't matter in the least. . . . When you consider what he wrote—thirteen operas and music dramas, eleven of them still holding the stage, eight of them unquestionably worth ranking among the world's great musico-dramatic masterpieces— when you listen to what he wrote, the debts and heartaches that people had to endure from him don't seem much of a price. . . . The miracle is that what he did in the little space of seventy years could have been done at all, even by a great genius. Is it any wonder that he had no time to be a man? [1]

It is often argued that art must choose a moral object; or that if it deals with human life at all, it must point a moral. William Dean Howells was a comparatively moderate exponent of this view:

If a novel flatters the passions, and exalts them above the principles, it is poisonous; it may not kill, but it will certainly injure; and this test will alone exclude an entire class of fiction, of which eminent examples will occur to all. Then the whole spawn of so-called unmoral romances, which imagine a world where the sins of sense are unvisited by the penalties following, swift or slow, but inexorably sure, in the real world, are deadly poison: these do kill.

This argument would seem to contradict the same writer's contention that fiction should be true to life. But are "sins of sense" invariably visited by penalties? Is the critic not representing what would happen in a just world? And if so, on what artistic ground can he demand that a writer omit the tragic fact that vice *is* sometimes rewarded and virtue penalized?

[1] D. Taylor, *Of Men and Music*, pp. 7-8.

There is a persistent strain of European thought which identifies the aesthetic and the moral through the principle of harmony:

Harmony, which might be called an aesthetic principle, is also the principle of health, of justice, and of happiness. Every impulse, not the aesthetic mood alone, is innocent and irresponsible in its origin and precious in its own eyes; but every impulse or indulgence, including the aesthetic, is evil in its effect, when it renders harmony impossible in the general tenor of life, or produces in the soul division and ruin.

But the aesthetic value of harmony and the moral value of harmony are not the same value. The aesthetic value of harmony is the enjoyment of the whole in contemplation; the moral value of harmony is benefit to the parts from nonconflict and coöperation.

The distinction between the aesthetic and moral standards paves the way to the understanding of their relations. Insofar as harmony is one of the constituents of beauty a moral society is beautiful, that is, good to contemplate. But many, indeed, most, harmonies fail to meet the requirements of morality; and are under no *aesthetic* obligation to do so. The moral standard is one of many external standards which are applicable to art.[2]

Assuming the aesthetic interest to have a peculiar and independent bias of its own, it may be asked how far this bias happily coincides with morality, and how far it diverges and re-

[2] There are indefinitely many external standards which are applicable to art—including, for example, the dealer's standard, and the collector's standard.

sists. The aesthetic interest, like the cognitive interest, is amenable to morality because it is non-preëmptive, that is, does not appropriate its object exclusively. In the act of enjoying its object it does not deprive other subjects of its enjoyment. On the contrary, its enjoyment is enhanced by participation. Not only does it possess this original innocence, but it disposes men to friendly association. Because it does not need to take away from other interests it is unlikely to be associated with combativeness—with an impulse to weaken or destroy competitors.

Because the aesthetic interest operates in the realm of the imagination, it enjoys a peculiar freedom to multiply and entertain ideal possibilities. It tends to emancipate men's minds from habit, authority, and the *status quo,* and thus readily allies itself with the forces of progress and liberalization. It can dream utopias without hindrance, and through giving them vividness and permanence can provide direction to the moral life and to all aspiration. It can add to the attractiveness of any goal, including the goal of harmonious happiness; and can thus provide an additional motivation for ends which would otherwise suffer from their remoteness or abstractness. Art provides symbols for the moral cause. In its symbolic role the aesthetic object helps to preserve the identity of the goal amidst the vicissitudes of fortune, and to make it clearly manifest. Like the flag it can be hauled up where it can be seen; like the flag it can rally armies, regiments, and companies, and their successive replacements, to the same standard. And finally, the aesthetic interest can fortify moral courage by compensating life's practical and theoretical failures, and enable men to face the grimmer aspects of reality by presenting them in their tragic beauty. It thus contributes to that general auspiciousness of outlook which constitutes happiness.

The same traits of the aesthetic interest which render it morally propitious account for its moral dangers. Its detachment from the competitive struggle does, it is true, render art comparatively innocent, but there is a selfishness of innocence which consists in a withdrawal from affairs. The aesthetic interest does, it is true, tend to non-aggression, but it may tend to a passive complacency, a narrow absorption, and an irresponsibility toward that very social organization on which the aesthetic life itself depends. In his Olympian detachment the artist or man of contemplation is likely to forget that Olympus rises from the plain of organized society and that he owes his privileges to those who guard its approaches.

Aesthetic rapture does not escape the danger which attends all raptures. It tends to be so obsessive as to make men indifferent to its evil effects—of commission or omission—on the lives of other men. Nero would not have been less morally blameworthy, if he had been Jascha Heifetz.

The aesthetic interest evades the problems of knowledge and action, instead of solving them; for their real solution it substitutes that pseudo-solution which is called "aestheticism" or "escapism." The aesthetic interest may render the ideal so vivid and reassuring that it is mistaken for the real: and men may perish from aesthetic illusion, as they die of thirst in the desert through the allurement of the mirage. Because the aesthetic interest renders the evil of life palatable it weakens the will to remove it.

Aesthetic enjoyment can add to the appeal of the good and strengthen the moral passion; but it can also strengthen evil passion. It has a promiscuity similar to that of science. "Music hath charms to soothe the savage breast"; but it has other charms, and may debase the civilized man to savagery. There are "Dorian and Phrygian harmonies" which incite men to courage and temperance, but there are also Lydian, Ionian, and other harmonies which incite men to voluptuousness, to idleness, or to sexual excesses.[3] The fine arts can be used to give force to any propaganda, whether totalitarian or democratic; the actor can play any part and give it dramatic value; the poet can make Satan more appealing than God.

The fact that art can be put to bad as well as to good uses, and that the aesthetic motive cannot be trusted, when left to itself, to take the side of the angels, raises the question of its social control. It cannot be controlled as effectively as science, nor is its control so deadly. Under the present regime of Soviet Russia art is explicitly subjected to the state and to Communist ideology, but we are told that "there are thinkers and artists, living perfectly respectable lives, but forever struggling to introduce into their official epics of stereotyped verbosity disguised glimpses of an inner vision personal to themselves."[4] And in art, at least, this struggle is more or less successful. Science is more readily controlled, because it depends on access to evidence, and on the facilities of organized experimentation. The "inner vision" escapes external control, and its disguise is not easily penetrated by the grosser eye of the censor. Whatever restrictions are placed on men's overt conduct, there is always food for aesthetic contemplation, and some room for the play of the imagination.

But in principle the objection to social control is the same in art as in science. The artist renders his particular form of service through being free to follow his particular vocation. Art appraised by rulers and police is no longer judged by its own standard. Art harnessed to ideology becomes a dependent interest, deriving its motive from an ulterior end. In proportion as it is thus enslaved, art is destroyed at its source; it can no longer give other interests that very enhancement for the sake of which it was controlled. The effect of control is likely to be wholly negative. It can destroy and prevent better than it can create. Art will flourish best when it is allowed to germinate, grow, and proliferate in obedience to its own nature.[5]

---

[4] E. Crankshaw, *Russia and the Russians,* 1948, p. 187.

[5] Political and ideological controls are not the only alien controls by which the aesthetic part of life may be frustrated. There is also a commercial control, less palpable, but all the more insidious.

---

[3] Plato's *Republic,* tr. by Jowett, Bk. III, 398-9.

QUESTIONS FOR DISCUSSION

1. According to Perry, what is the relation between art and morality? In what sense is art independent of morality?
2. In what different ways, for Perry, does art emancipate man's mind from habit, authority, and the status quo?
3. Discuss in some detail the alternative views on the issue of the social control of art. Should art be free of all control or, if not, to what degree and under what circumstances? State Perry's view on this issue.
4. Perry writes, "Aesthetic rapture does not escape the danger which attends all rapture." What might be some of the dangers of aesthetic rapture?

FURTHER READINGS FOR CHAPTER 7

Alexander, Samuel, *Beauty and Other Forms of Value*. New York: Macmillan, 1933.
*Aristotle, *Poetics*. (Numerous editions available.)
*Bell, Clive, *Art*. New York: G. P. Putnam's Sons, 1959.
Bosanquet, Bernard, *Three Lectures on Aesthetics*. New York: Macmillan, 1915.
*Dewey, John, *Art as Experience*. New York: G. P. Putnam's Sons, 1959.
Hegel, G. W. F., *The Philosophy of Fine Art*. New York: Harcourt Brace Jovanovich, 1921.
Housman, A. E., *The Name and Nature of Poetry*. New York: Cambridge University Press, n.d.
Lee, Vernon, *The Beautiful*. New York: Cambridge University Press, 1913.
Prall, David Wight, *The Aesthetic Analysis*. New York: Thomas Y. Crowell, 1936.

---

* Paperback edition.

Chapter 8

THE PHILOSOPHY
OF RELIGION

INTRODUCTION

Religion is an important aspect of human life. In some form or other it functions in every society; its symbols and activities exist throughout the world. Although something so complex and diverse may be difficult to describe, we can indicate its essential traits. First, it should be noted that the motives and driving forces in religion are the basic human wants and desires—survival, growth, well-being, self-realization. There is nothing distinctive in this phase of religion; and if all human desires could be naturally fulfilled, there would probably be no need of religion. Secondly, and more distinctively, religion involves belief in a supreme power or powers on whom human beings depend for their well-being. As man's wants grow, his need for greater gods grows. In earlier religions men worshiped a number of gods; in later religions men worshiped a supreme God. The reasons for this belief, then as now, are practical as well as intellectual. Thirdly, religion involves rituals that are believed to be ways of winning the favor of gods or God. Finally, it should be noted that religion, like all other major human activities, assumes a social, institutional form. The temple, the church, the synagogue, the "beloved community"—each form not only preserves the great religious traditions but makes it possible for religion to function in the group.

Such a rich and varied aspect of human life may be approached in different ways. The historical approach deals with the origins and development of religion. Where and when did religion begin? How did religion evolve from tribal to more universal forms? These and other historical questions may be of interest to some. The psychological approach deals with the mental or emotional basis of religion. Does religion satisfy some deep-seated psychological craving? What, in mental or emotional terms, is conversion, the mystic experience, worship? A third approach to religion is the sociological, which deals with religion as a social institution. What is the organization of this institution? How does it affect other institutions, and how, in turn, is it affected by them? All three approaches are necessary for a full understanding of religion.

Yet there remains another approach—sometimes called the philosophy of religion. This term may refer to the beliefs that a religious person or group entertains, or it may refer to the critical examination of these beliefs. It is in the latter sense that we will examine the philosophy of religion. Our examination may lead to a firmer attachment to religious beliefs or it may awaken doubts about them. In other words, we shall take the philosopher to be the seeker who inquires into the meaning of religious experience and into the truth of religious beliefs, rather than the dogmatic knower who tells us what to believe and what not to believe.

Religion and Theism

Various aspects of religion are material for philosophical reflection, but the one aspect of crucial importance is the idea of God. On this issue philosophers and theologians have engaged in the severest, most fundamental conflicts. Let us examine some of the major views on the idea of God.

Some conceive of God as a transcendent, supernatural being, a being believed to be a personal God. In the great monotheistic religions—Judaism, Christianity, Mohammedanism—the idea of a supernatural God is central. This view is usually called *theism*. In theism God is the creator and the sustainer of the world. There are, however, differences among the theists. Absolute theists maintain that God is all-knowing, all-good, and all-powerful; they feel that the object of worship must be infinite and ideal perfection. Other theists, primarily to meet the intellectual difficulties in the existence of evil, advocate belief in a finite God. According to them, as with William James, God is all-good but not all-powerful. What, one may ask, is the basis for belief in a theistic God, whether infinite *or* finite?

To validate belief in a supernatural personal God, the method of authority has sometimes been relied upon. The authority may be a sacred book, a religious institution, or a person. The authoritarian method has been influential in theistic religions and still has a firm hold on many people. There is, however, more than one authority, and different authorities conflict. Christians have their Bible, Jews their Talmud, Mohammedans their Koran. Which should be taken as *the* authority? But an even graver difficulty confronts the authoritarians: the need to justify, rationally, the claim of authority. Why should one accept authority? Especially those who are philosophically inclined tend to distrust authority, since they are committed to thinking for themselves and are reluctant to forego independence of judgment.

A second means of determining the truth of theism has been through the "proofs" of the existence of God. This argumentative method does not resort to authority, but claims that certain arguments can substantiate the existence of God. There are three arguments of this kind: (1) The cosmological argument, which affirms that the existence of nature demands a "first" cause, while this in turn is identified with God. In this argument one must determine whether the same demand does not attach to the "first" cause. (2) The teleological argument, which affirms that the designful structure and activities of nature prove the existence of a supreme designer. One must examine here whether nature is as designful as it is claimed to be, and even if designful, whether it is possible to explain design by causality or chance. (3) The ontological argument, which affirms that the idea of perfection that is attributed to God implies His existence, since a being that lacked existence would not be perfect. In analyzing this argument one must consider carefully whether the idea of perfection necessarily implies existence, or for that matter, whether existential truth can be established by mere logical argument. In the past these arguments were discussed by philosophers in great detail, and at present they are receiving new formulations which deserve careful study.

A third way of determining the truth of theism has been through moral and practical considerations. Kant and James are important representatives of this approach. According to Kant, man must act in accordance with moral law; therefore, he must be free to do so. Faith in freedom, therefore, is a necessary correlate of the existence of a moral law. And, again, since the ideal of moral perfection can be made real only through an unending series of acts, immortality is an imperative belief. Finally, since ultimately the determining factor in reality must be favorable to the absolute good of man, and thus provide immortality for him, belief in God is a moral necessity. According to James, the practical argument for God arises from the possibility of choice between two alternative conceptions that are equally logical. James argues that where knowledge in the strict sense of the word is impossible but where a choice between hypotheses is forced upon one in the interests of effective living, one has the right to make the choice. The religious question—namely, belief in God—presents to James such a genuine option. We have, therefore, the right to believe in God. This is James's famous doctrine of the "will to believe." Kant and James's approach to religion have appealed to many, especially to liberal theists. Yet the arguments upon which this approach is based should be closely examined. Is it true that morality demands that we postulate God, as Kant argues? Or is the theistic belief necessary for effective and dynamic living, as James insists? Or, again, have we the right to believe as we hope if our hope is not sufficiently borne out by the facts? These and similar questions must be fully explored before this approach can establish its validity.

Recently, the forms and meanings of language used in arguments for the existence of God have been examined, especially by the British analysts. J. J. C. Smart gives a clear account of these studies (see selection 8.3). The linguistic approach is of considerable help in evaluating the validity of the classical arguments.

A fourth way of determining the truth of theism has been suggested by Martin Buber in his influential book *I and Thou*. According to Buber the ultimate appeal of theism is not to the intellect but to the desire for a direct relation with God. This relation is not to an "It," but to a "Thou" that involves deep intrinsic values (see selection 8.7).

Religion and Mysticism

Mystics usually emphasize the oneness of all things and the union of the finite self with the infinite God. In the mystic vision there are not two things—God and the individual—but one. The seer and the seen are one; the finite individual is mingled with the Divine. "My Me is God, nor do I recognize any other Me, except God himself. My being is God, not by simple participation but by a true transformation." (St. Catherine of Genoa). This ultimate unity of things, the mystic claims, may be intuited but cannot be described. "The One is an Absolute transcending all thought." (Plotinus). He may be adored in silence, but He cannot be described by the intellect. The nearest descriptions are by negatives. "To God as Godhead, appertains neither will nor knowledge nor manifestations, nor anything that we can measure, or say, or conceive." (*Theologia Germanica*). Yet mystical pantheism on the whole tends to claim that God is all, rather than all is God. For the mystic, material objects in space as well as events in time are deceptive. The mystical vision leaves behind perceptual objects. "The soul to find God must go out from all things, and all things must be to it as if they existed not." (St. John of the Cross). Similarly, time vanishes. Past and present are like dreams for the mystic. Time and place are hindrances, for God is above them. "The soul has two eyes; the right beholds eternity, and the left eye, time. Both cannot perform their work at once. If the soul would see into eternity, the left eye must be closed." (*Theologia Germanica*). Finally, evil and ugliness do not come within the range of mystical contemplation; they are as if they were not. Since God is all, and God is absolutely good, there can be no evil. What seems evil is only an illusory appearance in the deluded mortal mind. "Evil is merely a negation and lies entirely outside the knowledge of God, who only knows and wills the good. . . . For God evil is not. It has existence only in the sphere of time." (Scotus Erigena).

Mystics are convinced that in their mystical experience they have direct contact and union with Divine Reality and that this Divine Reality or God is all. This claim, however, cannot be so easily settled. That there is a type of experience which corresponds to the so-called mystical experience may not be doubted, but the problem of interpreting this experience is difficult and controversial. Some regard the mystical experience as giving direct knowledge of a supernatural, divine being; others consider it as a union with an all-inclusive Reality; still others interpret it as an expression of an abnormal pathological state. It is also worth observing that different cultures have given different accounts of the mystics' claim. The account of Hindu mystics differs from that of neo-Platonic mystics, and the account of the latter, in turn, differs from that of later mystics.

Religion and Naturalism

There is a third view which insists that religion should be concerned neither with belief in a supernatural power nor with belief related to alleged perfection of reality as a whole. Instead, religion should limit itself to human hopes in the context of natural existence; if we must retain the word "God," it should be applied to some ideal phase of human experience, such as the hope for a better world, the aspiration for a happier society, the ideal of a nobler individual life. This philosophy of religion, which is sometimes called the naturalistic humanistic view, starts with the basic belief that only through science can questions of fact be determined. "That which science refuses to grant to religion is not its right to exist," writes Durkheim, "but its right to dogmatize upon the nature of things and the special competence which it claims for itself for knowing man and the world." It is true that there are supernaturalistic ideas of God, but these ideas, the naturalists argue, must be so reinterpreted that they will not rival scientific truth but become intelligible within the natural and social human setting. Though there are many types of naturalistic-humanistic philosophies of religion, they all agree in the denial of a supernaturalistic God; they differ in their specific formulation of religion and their idea of God.

About a hundred years ago Ludwig Feuerbach gave a naturalistic interpretation of religion by emphasizing its strictly human or psychological aspect. For Feuerbach, religion is man's earliest and indirect form of self-knowledge. Religion is "the childlike condition of humanity: in childhood a man is an object to himself under the form of another man." Consciousness of God, for Feuerbach, is "self-consciousness, knowledge of God is self-knowledge." Freud, in turn, gives a psychiatric description of religion. For the child, Freud argues, the mother is the first "love-object"; she was the first to satisfy its hunger. But the mother is soon superseded by the stronger father. And God, for Freud, is exalted-father. Gods have a threefold task:

to exorcise the terrors of nature, to reconcile one to the cruelty of fate, and to make amends for the sufferings that the communal life imposes on the individual. A more sociological interpretation is given by Emil Durkheim. For Durkheim, the idea of God is rooted in totemism. "The notion of the great god is due entirely to the sentiment . . . observed in the genesis of the most specifically totemic beliefs; this is the tribal sentiment. . . . Totemism was . . . elaborated in the body of a tribe which was to some degree conscious of its unity. . . . It is this same sentiment of a tribal unity which is expressed in the conception of a supreme God, common to the tribe as a whole."

Nietzsche is more violent and extreme in his reaction to Christianity and supernaturalism. For him God is dead, and the virtues of Christianity are vices (see selection 8.4). It is no new idea that God is dead; Xenophanes near the beginning of pagan thought, and Epicurus and Lucretius toward the end of it, had brought the same news. But it remained for Nietzsche to suggest that God died of pity. For Nietzsche, the Christian virtues of faith, hope, charity, and especially pity were vices. The Christian God is to be rejected, he is "the poor people's God," "one of the most corrupt concepts of God ever arrived at on earth." Everything "strong, brave, domineering, and proud has been eliminated out of it." The good life is that life which by the might of its superiority *can* both survive and *deserves* to survive. "The Superman is the meaning of the earth." Let your will say: "The Superman *shall* be the meaning of the earth."

In this country Santayana and Dewey have given interpretations of religion more strictly in terms of ideal human aspiration. For Santayana, science and religion have different functions, and the way to avoid conflict between these two enterprises is not to confuse their functions.[1] It is to science that one must turn for truth about matters of fact. The belief that religion may also convey literal truth is an impossible view for Santayana. Whenever religion attempts to give truth about the nature of the world, the result is pseudoscience or superstition. Santayana thus rejects all forms of supernaturalistic religion. What, then, is religion for Santayana? It is poetry or mythology. But for him the poetic conception has no disparaging implications. Religion as poetry has a moral function, and it is this function that defines religion. The poetic conception of religion also makes it possible for you to respect the fantastic beliefs of religions. The belief in animal gods or in certain eschatological expectations when regarded as myth can be appreciated as expressions of human pathos and desires. There should, therefore, be no conflict between religions on the ground that one is truer than another. At most, one religion may be better than another in the efficacy of its symbols. From Santayana's point of view it naturally follows that "God" is not

---

[1] George Santayana, *The Life of Reason* (New York: Charles Scribner's Sons, 1905), vol. 3, *Reason in Religion*, chapter 1.

the name for a transcendent, supernaturalistic being but rather the poetic symbol for human ideals of truth, beauty, and goodness. The different gods of religion symbolize different human ideals—Ahura Mazda that of goodness, Zeus that of power, and Yahweh that of justice, whereas the God of the great monotheistic religion symbolizes the unified ideal of perfection.

John Dewey, like Santayana, feels the necessity of giving a naturalistic account of religion that will preserve both the validity of science and the ideal values of religion. Dewey approaches his task by making a distinction between "religion" meaning organized, primarily supernatural religion, and "the religious," by which he means an attitude. What Dewey is anxious to preserve is the religious attitude, defined as a fundamental perspective that guides our action and gives direction to life. We may, therefore, reverse the usual statement and say that "whatever introduces genuine perspective is religious, not that religion is something that introduces it." The religious attitude as a pursuit of ideals refers to natural possibilities, that is, to possibilities which belong to natural things and to natural creatures. Dewey's naturalistic account of religion leads him to restate the traditional religious ideas. The term *God*, if it is to be used, stands for "the ideal ends that at a given time and place one acknowledges as having authority over his volition and emotion, the values to which one is supremely devoted." And, again, religious faith is used by Dewey not in relation to some alleged religious truths as being other than or superior to scientific truths, but as loyalty and steadfast adherence to one's ideals. Such a faith is obviously not opposed to science but is the result of free inquiry. The scientific attitude, when perfectly adhered to, is itself one of the ideals of this religious attitude.

Naturalistic-humanistic forms of religion lack the rich tradition and symbolism of the older forms. They also fail to give the same degree of guarantee as theism does for the final triumph of man's deep desires. Their strength seems to lie in not being in conflict with science and in offering more effective methods to ameliorate human conditions. Whether naturalistic forms of religion will ever become a significant factor in our civilization has yet to be determined.

God, Evil, and Immortality

The central problem of religion is the nature and existence of God. Most of the readings on religion are concerned with this issue. Yet a belief in God, especially a belief in a personal God, is not an isolated abstract problem; it has its vital relation to human destiny. This relationship becomes obvious in considering the problem of evil and the hope of immortality.

Let us first consider the problem of evil. That there is evil in our world—pain, suffering, injustice, and inevitable death—hardly demands argument. Even should evil be illusion, as some argue, there would still be the evil of illusion. The theological issue that has been a source of endless controversy through the ages is: How can one reconcile the existence of evil with a God that is perfect in power as well as in goodness?

The usual answer to this question has been that evil is in some sense less real than good is, and that evil is ultimately a means for the fruition of good. Some, for example, consider evil as necessary to "the good of the whole." There are many variations of this view: evil as good "in disguise," evil as "something torn of its context," evil as "illusory." Others think of evil as a means for the growth and strengthening of character. Hardship, sorrow, defeat have, it is claimed, their salutary effects. They are the means for "soul-making." Still others justify evil as something that heightens the danger and excitement of life. Without evil, life would be insipid; there would be no drama, no high tragedy of existence. All these theories in some way consider evil as a means for good.

W. H. Sheldon, in his attempt to defend the thesis that the existence of evil and perfection of God (in power and goodness) are not contradictory, does not resort to the view that evil is in some sense not fully real.[2] Evil for Sheldon is real, and he is not concerned with the question why evil is permitted. Sheldon's interest is primarily a negative one. As he puts it, "We have only a negative task; to show that the contradiction alleged is not necessary." Evil "being actual—need not imply any lack of perfection in the Divine nature." Sheldon tries to establish his claim through the highly dubious notion of reincarnation, through the more defensive notions that we do not know the given order of God's plan and purpose; that later experience includes and transmutes the earlier; that responsibility means acceptance of the consequences of one's acts. Sheldon presents his views fairly and persuasively.

Yet there are philosophers who reject Sheldon's formulation of the problem. William James and contemporary personal idealists like Brightman and Hartshorne try to ease the problem by claiming that God is all-good but not all-powerful. Brightman finds God's limitation in his own internal constitution, whereas Hartshorne finds it in the powers of His creatures, who try to thwart His purposes. Others, like Dewey, take a more radical step. Dewey limits the problem of evil to practical action. As he puts it: "The position of natural intelligence is that there exists a *mixture* of good and evil, and that reconstruction of the good which is indicated by ideal ends, must take place, if at all, through continued co-operative effort."

Hope in immortality is also vitally related to a belief in God and is a central dogma of the Christian religion. Of all evils death is the supreme evil, for it brings individual life to final, inevitable shipwreck. Religion with its ultimate optimism holds the faith that no final disaster can destroy man.

---

[2] W. H. Sheldon, *God and Polarity* (New Haven: Yale University Press, 1954), pp. 266-295.

The theologian Douglas C. Macintosh presents some of the weightiest arguments for immortality (see selection 8.9). Starting with the premise that conservation of spiritual values involves the conservation of persons, he first argues that mind is independent of physical body. And if mind is independent of body, it is plausible that it may exist and act when set free from the body at death. In the fact of human freedom Macintosh finds a more assured argument for the possibility of immortality. Human freedom being granted, it follows "that mind or the self acts in an originative manner." Mind for Macintosh is an agent and not a mere phenomenon. Finally, and more significantly from the theistic viewpoint, Macintosh finds assurance for immortality in the belief in God, that is, in a Power great enough and good enough to conserve the human individual in spite of bodily death. All these arguments for immortality deserve careful examination.

Yet here again the student of philosophy must examine other serious possible answers to the questions before he comes to a final decision. Moreover, he must ask which of the alternative theories does greater justice to human aspirations, to experience, to known facts. One such alternative view is found in Professor W. E. Hocking's philosophy. Hocking, a leading idealist of today, argues that immortality is not something assured but rather conditional on the type of life we live. "There is such a thing as losing one's soul; . . . the destiny of our own deeds, great and small, is an integral part of whatever future there may be for us. To deserve to endure is the only guarantee of enduring. I have no faith in an intrinsic indestructibility of the substance of consciousness. One life is given us; another may be acquired."

The Function of Religion

We have been analyzing and contrasting theistic, mystical, and naturalistic views of religion. But religion is not merely a matter of intellectual belief, it is a practical thing. Kant and James justify belief in God not on theoretical grounds, which they could not find, but on moral and practical grounds. Similarly, Spinoza, Santayana, and Dewey in different ways emphasize the practical aspect of religion. What, then, are the practical functions of religion that are common to all different religious interpretations? Only some of the major ones can be indicated here.

One such function is the integration of the individual life. An individual, as James defined him, "is a fighter for ends." Devotion to God or to a supreme ideal unifies and therefore integrates conflicting desires. The religious experience called salvation is primarily this process of unification of the self in the light of some inclusive and worthy object. Theists, mystics, and naturalists, in different ways, emphasize this function of religion. Yet one should evaluate this function of religion with a critical attitude. Some gods and some ends are not sufficiently moral or inclusive to be adequate objects of devotion. Therefore, in such inadequate religions, the unification of the self would tend to make a person fanatic, narrow, and arrogant. It is dangerous to assume that whatever is related to religion is thereby morally worthy. Actions motivated by religion must be examined critically, in the light of moral standards.

Another major function of religion is to idealize and sanctify social morals or customs. Religion sanctifies birth and death, marriage and celibacy, peace and war. Terms like "Father," "King of Kings," and "Lord," and expressions like "Kingdom of God" and "Blessed Community" are social in their implications. Sometimes religion has been socially beneficial by promoting philanthropy, education, and the arts, by pressing for greater economic equality, by opposing despotic political power, or by emphasizing internationalism. But at other times religion has been socially harmful, by opposing scientific thought and philosophic freedom, by defending vested economic interests, by sanctifying political tyranny, or by idealizing fanatic nationalism. Religious institutions are human institutions. Their social politics must always be examined in relation to secular, human interests. Religious institutions as social agencies must never be allowed special privileges, but must always remain subject to social criticism; at the same time they should be encouraged to use their power toward humane ends.

Still another function of religion is to express man's ultimate concern in terms of symbols. This function is best developed in the writings of Paul Tillich. He examines in detail the intention and meaning of religious symbols. For him, the language of faith "is the language of symbols. . . . Faith, understood as the state of being ultimately concerned, has no language other than symbols" (selection 8.8).

Finally, religion has the function of lending cosmic support to human aspirations. Life is so full of inscrutable evils and crushing tragedies that many find it almost impossible to face without belief in a power that will ultimately bring triumph. Theism provides this sanction in the form of a personal God who is benevolent and powerful; mysticism, in the perfection of the whole; and naturalistic religion, in the genuine possibilities for good in nature. As with the other functions of religion, this one, too, should not be accepted without critical scrutiny. It is true that certain religious beliefs, especially the belief in a personal God, have given hope and courage to many; yet these very beliefs have made many others unduly resigned to evil and suffering. Passively hoping that good must triumph over evil, human beings have failed to apply their intelligence to strengthen the good. Religion, to be satisfactory, must be intellectually acceptable and morally conducive to a worthy life.

Saint Anselm (1033-1109)

8.1   God and the Idea of Perfection

Truly there is a God, although the fool hath said in his heart, "There is no God."

And so, Lord, do thou, who dost give understanding to faith give me, so far as thou knowest it to be profitable, to understand that thou art as we believe; and that thou art that which we believe. And, indeed, we believe that thou art a being than which nothing greater can be conceived. Or is there no such nature, since the fool hath said in his heart, there is no God? (Psalms xiv. 1). But, at any rate, this very fool, when he hears of this being of which I speak —a being than which nothing greater can be conceived—understands what he hears, and what he understands is in his understanding; although he does not understand it to exist.

For, it is one thing for an object to be in the understanding, and another to understand that the object exists. When a painter first conceives of what he will afterwards perform, he has it in his understanding, but he does not yet understand it to be, because he has not yet performed it. But after he has made the painting, he both has

From *Proslogium*, Chapters 2-3. Translated by S. N. Deane (LaSalle, Ill.: The Open Court Publishing Company, 1961). Reprinted by permission of the publisher.

it in his understanding, and he understands that it exists, because he has made it.

Hence, even the fool is convinced that something exists in the understanding, at least, than which nothing greater can be conceived. For, when he hears of this, he understands it. And whatever is understood, exists in the understanding. And assuredly that, than which nothing greater can be conceived, cannot exist in the understanding alone. For, suppose it exists in the understanding alone: then it can be conceived to exist in reality; which is greater.

Therefore, if that, than which nothing greater can be conceived, exists in the understanding alone, the very being, than which nothing greater can be conceived, is one, than which a greater can be conceived. But obviously this is impossible. Hence, there is no doubt that there exists a being, than which nothing greater can be conceived, and it exists both in the understanding and in reality.

God cannot be conceived not to exist. —God is that, than which nothing greater can be conceived. —That which can be conceived not to exist is not God.

And it assuredly exists so truly, that it cannot be conceived not to exist.

For, it is possible to conceive of a being which cannot be conceived not to exist; and this is greater than one which can be conceived not to exist. Hence, if that, than which nothing greater can be conceived, can be conceived not to exist, it is not that, than which nothing greater can be conceived. But this is an irreconcilable contradiction. There is, then, so truly a being than which nothing greater can be conceived to exist, that it cannot even be conceived not to exist; and this being thou art, O Lord, our God.

So truly, therefore, dost thou exist, O Lord, my God, that thou canst not be conceived not to exist; and rightly. For, if a mind could conceive of a being better than thee, the creature would rise above the Creator; and this is most absurd. And, indeed, whatever else there is, except thee alone, can be conceived not to exist. To thee alone, therefore, it belongs to exist more truly than all other beings, and hence in a higher degree than all others. For, whatever else exists does not exist so truly, and hence in a less degree it belongs to it to exist. Why, then, has the fool said in his heart, there is no God. (Psalms xiv 1), since it is so evident, to a rational mind, that thou dost exist in the highest degree of all? Why, except that he is dull and a fool?

How the fool has said in his heart what cannot be conceived. —A thing may be conceived in two ways: (1) when the word signifying it is conceived; (2) when the thing itself is understood. As far as the word goes, God can be conceived not to exist; in reality he cannot.

But how has the fool said in his heart what he could not conceive; or how is it that he could not conceive what he said in his heart? since it is the same to say in the heart, and to conceive.

But, if really, nay, since really, he both conceived, because he said in his heart; and did not say in his heart, because he could not conceive; there is more than one way in which a thing is said in the heart or conceived. For, in one sense, an object is conceived, when the word signifying it is conceived; and in another, when the very entity, which the object is, is understood.

In the former sense, then, God can be conceived not to exist; but in the latter, not at all. For no one who understands what fire and water are can conceive fire to be water, in accordance with the nature of the facts themselves, although this is possible according to the words. So, then, no one who understands what God is can conceive that God does not exist; although he says these words in his heart, either without any or with some foreign, signification. For God is that than which a greater cannot be conceived. And he who thoroughly understands this, assuredly understands that this being so truly exists, that not even in concept can it be non-existent. Therefore, he who understands that God so exists, cannot conceive that he does not exist.

I thank thee, gracious Lord, I thank thee; because what I formerly believed by thy bounty, I now so understand by thine illumination, that if I were unwilling to believe that thou dost exist, I should not be able not to understand this to be true.

Saint Thomas Aquinas (1225?-1274?)

8.2 Whether God Exists

Objection 1. It seems that God does not exist: because if one of two contraries be infinite, the other would be altogether destroyed. But the word "God" means that He is infinite goodness. If, therefore, God existed, there would be no evil discoverable; but there is evil in the world. Therefore, God does not exist.

Objection 2. Further, it is superfluous to suppose that what can be accounted for by a few principles has been produced by many. But it seems that everything we see in the world can be accounted for by other principles, supposing God did not exist. For all natural things can be reduced to one principle, which is nature; and all voluntary things can be reduced to one principle, which is human reason, or will. Therefore, there is no need to suppose God's existence.

On the contrary, It is said in the person of God: *I am Who am* (Exod. iii. 14).

I answer that, The existence of God can be proved in five ways.

The first and more manifest way is the argument from motion. It is certain, and evident to our senses, that in the world some things are in motion. Now whatever is in motion is put in motion by another, for nothing can be in motion except it is in potentiality to that towards which it is in motion; whereas a thing moves inasmuch as it is in act. For motion is nothing else than the reduction of something from potentiality to actuality, except by something in a state of actuality. Thus that which is actually hot, as fire, makes wood, which is potentially hot, to be actually hot, and thereby moves and changes it. Now it is not possible that the same thing should be at once in actuality and potentiality in the same respect, but only in different respects. For what is actually hot cannot simultaneously be potentially hot; but it is simultaneously potentially cold. It is therefore impossible that in the same respect and in the same way a thing should be both mover and moved, i.e., that it should move itself. Therefore, whatever is in motion must be put in motion by another. If that by which it is put in motion be itself put in motion by another, and that by another again. But this cannot go on to infinity, because then there would be no first mover, and, consequently, no other mover; seeing that subsequent movers move only inasmuch as they

From *Summa Theologica,* Part I. Translated by Dominican Fathers of English Province (New York: Benziger Bros., Inc., 1947). Reprinted by permission of the publisher.

are put in motion by the first mover; as the staff moves only because it is put in motion by the hand. Therefore, it is necessary to arrive at a first mover, put in motion by no other; and this everyone understands to be God.

The second way is from the nature of the efficient cause. In the world of sense we find there is an order of efficient causes. There is no case known (neither is it, indeed, possible) in which a thing is found to be the efficient cause of itself; for so it would be prior to itself, which is impossible. Now in efficient causes it is not possible to go on to infinity, because in all efficient causes following in order, the first is the cause of the intermediate cause, and the intermediate is the cause of the ultimate cause, whether the intermediate cause be several, or one only. Now to take away the cause is to take away the effect. Therefore, if there be no first cause among efficient causes, there will be no ultimate, nor any intermediate cause. But if in efficient causes it is possible to go on to infinity, there will be no first efficient cause, neither will there be an ultimate effect, nor any intermediate efficient causes, all of which is plainly false. Therefore, it is necessary to admit a first efficient cause, to which everyone gives the name of God.

The third way is taken from possibility and necessity, and runs thus. We find in nature things that are possible to be and not to be, since they are found to be generated, and to corrupt, and consequently, they are possible to be and not to be. But it is impossible for these always to exist, for that which is possible not to be at some time is not. Therefore, if everything is possible not to be, then at one time there could have been nothing in existence. Now if this were true, even now there would be nothing in existence, because that which does not exist only begins to exist by something already existing. Therefore, if at one time nothing was in existence, it would have been impossible for anything to have begun to exist; and thus even now nothing would be in existence—which is absurd. Therefore, not all beings are merely possible, but there must exist something the existence of which is necessary. But every necessary thing either has its necessity caused by another, or not. Now it is impossible to go on to infinity in necessary things which have their necessity caused by another, as has already been proved in regard to efficient causes. Therefore, we cannot but postulate the existence of some being having of itself its own necessity, and not receiving it from another, but rather causing in others their necessity. This all men speak of as God.

The fourth way is taken from the gradation to be found in things. Among beings there are some more and some less good, true, noble, and the like. But "more" and "less" are predicated of different things, according as they resemble in their different ways something which is the maximum, as a thing is said to be hotter according as it more nearly resembles that which is hottest; so that there is something which is truest, something best, something noblest, and, consequently, something which is uttermost being; for those things that are greatest in truth are greatest in being, as it is written in *Metaph.ii.* Now the maximum in any genus is the cause of all in that genus; as fire, which is the maximum of heat, is the cause of all hot things. Therefore, there must also be something which is to all beings the cause of their being, goodness, and every other perfection; and this we call God.

The fifth way is taken from the governance of the world. We see that things which lack intelligence, such as natural bodies, act for an end, and this is evident from their acting always, or nearly always, in the same way, so as to obtain the best result. Hence it is plain that not fortuitously, but designedly, do they achieve their end. Now whatever lacks intelligence cannot move towards an end, unless it be directed by some being endowed with knowledge and intelligence; as the arrow is shot to its mark by the archer. Therefore, some intelligent being exists by whom all natural things are directed to their end; and this being we call God.

Reply Objection 1. As Augustine says (Enchir. XI): *Since God is the highest good, He would not allow any evil to exist in His works, unless His omnipotence and goodness were such as to bring good even out of evil.* This is part of the infinite goodness of God, that He should allow evil to exist, and out of it produce good.

Reply Objection 2. Since nature works for a determinate end under the direction of a higher agent, whatever is done by nature must needs be traced back to God, as to its first cause. So, also, whatever is done voluntarily must also be traced back to some higher cause other than human reason or will, since these can change and fail; for all things that are changeable and capable of defect must be traced back to an immovable and self-necessary first principle, as was shown in the body of the *Article.*

J. J. C. Smart (1902-   )

8.3   *The Existence of God*

This lecture is not to discuss whether God exists. It is to discuss reasons which philosophers have

From *New Essays in Philosophical Theology,* Anthony Flew and Alasdair McIntyre, eds. (New York: The Macmillan Company, 1956). First published by The Student Christian Movement Press, Ltd., London, 1955. Reprinted by permission of The Macmillan Company and SCM Press Ltd.

given for saying that God exists. That is, to discuss certain arguments.

First of all, it may be as well to say what we may hope to get out of this. Of course, if we found that any of the traditional arguments for the existence of God were sound, we should get out of our one hour this Sunday afternoon something of inestimable value, such as one never got out of any hour's work in our lives before. For we should have got out of one hour's work the answer to that question about which, above all, we want to know the answer. (This is assuming for the moment that the question "Does God exist?" is a proper question. The fact that a question is all right as far as the rules of ordinary grammar are concerned does not ensure that it has a sense. For example, "Does virtue run faster than length?" is certainly all right as far as ordinary grammar is concerned, but it is obviously not a meaningful question. Again, "How fast does time flow?" is all right as far as ordinary grammar is concerned, but it has no clear meaning. Now some philosophers would ask whether the question "Does God exist" is a proper question. The greatest danger to theism at the present moment does not come from people who deny the validity of the arguments for the existence of God, for many Christian theologians do not believe that the existence of God can be proved, and certainly nowhere in the Old or New Testaments do we find any evidence of people's religion having a metaphysical basis. The main danger to theism today comes from people who want to say that "God exists" and "God does not exist" are equally absurd. The concept of God, they would say, is a nonsensical one. . . .)

However, let us assume for the moment, that the question "Does God exist?" is a proper question. We now ask: Can a study of the traditional proofs of the existence of God enable us to give an affirmative answer to this question? I contend that it cannot. I shall point out what seems to me to be fallacies in the main traditional arguments for the existence of God. Does proving that the arguments

are invalid prove that God does not exist? Not at all. For to say that an argument is invalid is by no means the same thing as to say that its conclusion is false. Still, if we do find that the arguments we consider are all fallacious, what do we *gain* out of our investigation? Well, one thing we gain is a juster (if more austere) view of what philosophical argument can do for us. But, more important, we get a deeper insight into the logical nature of certain concepts, in particular, of course, the concepts of deity and existence. Furthermore, we shall get some hints as to whether philosophy can be of any service to theologians, and if it can be of service, some hints as to how it can be of service. I think that it can be, but I must warn you that many, indeed perhaps the majority, of philosophers today would not entirely agree with me here. . . .

One very noteworthy feature which must strike anyone who first looks at the usual arguments for the existence of God is the extreme brevity of these arguments. They range from a few lines to a few pages. St. Thomas Aquinas presents five arguments in three pages! Would it not be rather extraordinary if such a great conclusion should be got so easily? . . . It is my belief that in the case of any metaphysical argument it will be found that if the premises are uncontroversial the argument is unfortunately not valid, and that if the argument is valid the premises will unfortunately be just as doubtful as the conclusion they are meant to support.

With these warnings in mind let us proceed to the discussion of the three most famous arguments for the existence of God. These are:

(1) The Ontological Argument

(2) The Cosmological Argument
(3) The Teleological Argument

The first argument—the ontological argument—really has no premises at all. It tries to show that there would be a contradiction in denying that God exists. It was first formulated by St. Anselm and was later used by Descartes. It is not a convincing argument to modern ears, and St. Thomas Aquinas gave essentially the right reasons for rejecting it. However, it is important to discuss it, as an understanding of what is wrong with it is necessary for evaluating the second argument, that is, the cosmological argument. This argument does have a premise, but not at all a controversial one. It is that something exists. We should all, I think, agree to that. The teleological argument is less austere in manner than the other two. It tries to argue to the existence of God not purely *a priori* and not from the mere fact of *something* existing, but from the actual features we observe in nature, namely, those which seem to be evidence of design or purpose.

We shall discuss these three arguments in order. I do not say that they are the only arguments which have been propounded for the existence of God, but they are, I think, the most important ones. For example, of St. Thomas Aquinas' celebrated "Five Ways" the first three are variants of the cosmological argument, and the fifth is a form of the teleological argument.

The Ontological Argument. This as I remarked, contains no factual premis. It is a *reductio ad absurdum* of the supposition that God does not exist. Now *reductio ad absurdum* proofs are to be suspected whenever there is

doubt as to whether the statement to be proved is *significant.* For example, it is quite easy, as anyone who is familiar with the so-called Logical Paradoxes will know, to produce a not *obviously* nonsensical statement, such that both it *and* its denial imply a contradiction. So unless we are sure of the significance of a statement we cannot regard a *reductio ad absurdum* of its contradictory as proving its truth. This point of view is well known to those versed in the philosophy of mathematics; there is a well-known school of mathematicians, led by Brouwer, who refuse to employ *reductio ad absurdum* proofs. However, I shall not press this criticism of the Ontological Argument, for this criticism is somewhat abstruse (though it has been foreshadowed by Catholic philosophers, who object to the ontological argument by saying that it does not first show that the concept of an infinitely perfect being is a *possible* one). We are at present assuming that "Does God exist?" is a proper question, and if it is a proper question, there is no objection so far to answering it by means of a *reductio ad absurdum* proof. We shall content ourselves with the more usual criticisms of the ontological argument.

The ontological argument was made famous by Descartes. It is to be found at the beginning of his Fifth Meditation. As I remarked earlier, it was originally put forward by Anselm, though I am sorry to say that to read Descartes you would never suspect that fact! Descartes points out that in mathematics we can deduce various things purely *a priori*, "as for example," he says, "when I imagine a triangle, although there is not and perhaps never was in any place . . . one such figure, it remains true, nevertheless, that this figure possesses a certain determinate nature, form, or essence, which is . . . not framed by me, nor in any degree dependent on my thought, as appears from the circumstance, that diverse properties of the triangle may be demonstrated; for example, that its three angles are equal to two right, that its greatest side is subtended by its greatest angle, and the like." Descartes now goes on to suggest that just as having the sum of its angles equal to two right angles is involved in the idea of a triangle, so *existence* is involved in the very idea of an infinitely perfect being, and that it would, therefore, be as much of a contradiction to assert that an infinitely perfect being does not exist as it is to assert that the three angles of a triangle do not add up to two right angles or that two of its sides are not together greater than the third side. We may then, says Descartes, assert that an infinitely perfect being *necessarily* exists, just as we may say that two sides of a triangle are together *necessarily* greater than the third side.

This argument is highly fallacious. To say that a so-and-so exists is not in the least like saying that a so-and-so has such-and-such a property. It is not to amplify a concept but to say that a concept applies to something, and whether or not a concept applies to something cannot be seen from an examination of the concept itself. Existence is not a property. "Growling" is a property of tigers, and to say that "tame tigers growl" is to say something about tame tigers but to say "tame tigers exist" is not to say something about tame tigers but to say that there are tame tigers. Professor G. E. Moore once brought out the difference between existence and a property such as that of being

tame, or being a tiger, or being a growler, by reminding us that though the sentence "some tame tigers do not *growl*" makes perfect sense, the sentence "some tame tigers do not *exist*" has no clear meaning. The fundamental mistake in the ontological argument, then, is that it treats "exists" in "an infinitely perfect being exists" as if it ascribed a property existence to an infinitely perfect being, just as "is loving" in "an infinitely perfect being is loving" ascribes a property, or as "growl" in "tame tigers growl" ascribes a property: the verb "to exist" in "an infinitely perfect being exists" does not ascribe a property to something already conceived of as existing, but says that the concept of an infinitely perfect being applies to something. The verb "to exist" here takes us right out of the purely conceptual world. This being so, there can never be any *logical contradiction* in denying that God exists. It is worth mentioning that we are less likely to make the sort of mistake that the ontological argument makes if we use the expression "there is a so-and-so" instead of the more misleading form of words "a so-and-so exists."

I should like to mention another interesting, though less crucial, objection to Descartes' argument. He talks as though you can deduce further properties of, say, a triangle, by considering its definition. It is worth pointing out that from the definition of a triangle as a figure bounded by three straight lines you can only deduce trivialities, such as that it is bounded by more than one straight line, for example. It is not at all a contradiction to say that the two sides of a triangle are together not greater than the third side, or that its angles do not add up to two right angles.

To get a contradiction you have to bring in the specific axioms of Euclidean geometry. (Remember school geometry, how you used to prove that the angles of a triangle add up to two right angles. Through the vertex C of the triangle ABC you drew a line parallel to BA, and so you assumed the axiom of parallels for a start.) Definitions, by themselves, are not deductively potent. Descartes, though a very great mathematician himself, was profoundly mistaken as to the nature of mathematics. However, we can interpret him as saying that from the definition of a triangle, *together with the axioms of Euclidean geometry*, you can deduce various things, such as that the angles of a triangle add up to two right angles. But this just shows how pure mathematics is a sort of game with symbols; you start with a set of axioms, and operate on them in accordance with certain rules of inference. All the mathematician requires is that the axiom set should be *consistent*. Whether or not it has application to reality lies outside pure mathematics. Geometry is no fit model for a proof of real existence.

We now turn to the *Cosmological Argument*. This argument does at least seem more promising than the ontological argument. It does start with a factual premise, namely that something exists. The premise that something exists is indeed a very abstract one, but nevertheless it *is* factual; it does give us a foothold in the real world of things; it does go beyond the consideration of mere concepts. The argument has been put forward in various forms, but for present purposes it may be put as follows:

Everything in the world around us

is *contingent*. That is, with regard to any particular thing, it is quite conceivable that it might not have existed. For example, if you were asked why you existed, you could say that it was because of your parents, and if asked why they existed you could go still further back, but however far you go back you have not, so it is argued, made the fact of your existence really intelligible. For however far back you go in such a series you only get back to something which itself might not have existed. For a really satisfying explanation of why anything contingent (such as you or me or this table) exists, you must eventually begin with something which is not itself contingent, that is, with something of which we cannot say that it might not have existed, that is, we must begin with a necessary being. So the first part of the argument boils down to this. *If anything exists, an absolutely necessary being must exist. Something exists. Therefore, an absolutely necessary being must exist. . . .* the cosmological argument is radically unsound. The trouble comes much earlier than where Kant locates it. The trouble comes in the *first* stage of the argument. For the first stage of the argument purports to argue to the existence of a necessary being. And by "a necessary being" the cosmological argument means "a *logically* necessary being," i.e., "a being whose non-existence is inconceivable in the sort of way that a triangle's having four sides is inconceivable." The trouble is, however, that the concept of a logically necessary being is a self-contradictory concept, like the concept of a round square. For in the first place "necessary" is a predicate of *propositions*, not of things. That is, we can contrast *necessary* propositions, such as "3 +

2 = 5," "a thing cannot be red and green all over," "either it is raining or it is not raining," with *contingent* propositions, such as "Mr. Menzies is Prime Minister of Australia," "the earth is slightly flattened at the poles," and "sugar is soluble in water." The propositions in the first class are guaranteed solely by the rules for the use of the symbols they contain. In the case of the propositions of the second class, a genuine possibility of agreeing or not agreeing with reality is left open; whether they are true or false depends not on the conventions of our language but on reality. (Compare the contrast between "the equator is 90 degrees from the pole," which tells us nothing about geography but only about our map-making conventions, and "Adelaide is 55 degrees from the pole," which does tell us a geographical fact.) So no informative proposition can be logically necessary. Now since "necessary" is a word which applies primarily to propositions, we shall have to interpret "God is a necessary being" as "The proposition 'God exists' is logically necessary." But this *is* the principle of the ontological argument, and there is no way of getting round it this time in the way that we got out of Kant's criticism. No existential proposition can be logically necessary, for we saw that the truth of a logically necessary proposition depends only on our symbolism, or to put the same thing in another way, on the relationship of concepts. We saw, however, in discussing the ontological argument, that an existential proposition does not say that one concept is involved in another, but that a concept applies to something. An existential proposition must be very different from any logi-

cally necessary one, such as a mathematical one, for example, for the conventions of our symbolism clearly leave it open for us either to affirm or deny an existential proposition; it is not our symbolism but reality which decides whether or not we must affirm or deny it.

The demand that the existence of God should be *logically* necessary is thus a self-contradictory one. When we see this and go back to look at the first stage of the cosmological argument, it no longer seems compelling; indeed, it now seems to contain an absurdity. If we cast our minds back, we recall that the argument was as follows: that if we explain why something exists and is what it is, we must explain it by reference to something else, and we must explain that thing's being what it is by reference to yet another thing, and so on, back and back. It is then suggested that, unless we can go back to a logically necessary first cause, we shall remain intellectually unsatisfied. We should otherwise only get back to something which might have been otherwise, and with reference to which the same questions can again be asked. This is the argument, but we now see that in asking for a logically necessary first cause we are doing something worse than asking for the moon. It is only *physically* impossible for us to get the moon; if I were a few million times bigger I could reach out for it and give it to you. That is, I know what it would be *like* to give you the moon, though I cannot in *fact* do it. A logically necessary first cause, however, is not impossible in the way that giving you the moon is impossible; no, it is *logically* impossible. "Logically necessary being" is a self-contradictory expression like "round square." It is not any good saying that we would only be intellectually satisfied with a logically necessary cause, that nothing else would do. We can easily have an absurd wish. We should all like to be able to eat our cake and have it, but that does not alter the fact that our wish is an absurd and self-contradictory one. We reject the cosmological argument, then, because it rests on a thorough absurdity. . . .

The cosmological argument, we saw, failed because it made use of the absurd conception of a *logically* necessary being. We now pass to the third argument which I propose to consider. This is the *Teleological Argument.* It is also called "the Argument from Design." It would be better called the argument *to* design, as Kemp Smith does call it, for clearly that the universe has been designed by a great architect is to assume a great part of the conclusion to be proved. Or we could call it "the argument from apparent design." The argument is very fully discussed in Hume's *Dialogues concerning Natural Religion,* to which I should like to draw your attention. In these dialogues the argument is presented as follows: "Look round the world: contemplate the whole and every part of it: you will find it to be nothing but one great machine, subdivided into an infinite number of lesser machines. . . . The curious adapting of means to ends, throughout all nature, resembles exactly, though it much exceeds, the productions of human contrivance. . . . Since, therefore, the effects resemble each other, we are led to infer, by all the rules of analogy, that the causes also resemble; and that the Author of nature is somewhat

similar to the mind of man; though possessed of much larger faculties, proportioned to the grandeur of the work which he has executed."

This argument may at once be criticized in two ways: (1) We may question whether the analogy between the universe and artificial things like houses, ships, furniture, and machines (which admittedly are designed) is very close. Now in any ordinary sense of language, it is true to say that plants and animals have *not* been designed. If we press the analogy of the universe to a plant, instead of to a machine, we get to a very different conclusion. And why should the one analogy be regarded as any better or worse than the other? (2) Even if the analogy were close, it would only go to suggest that the universe was designed by a *very great* (not infinite) architect, and note, an *architect,* not a *creator.* For if we take the analogy seriously we must notice that we do not create the materials from which we make houses, machines and so on, but only *arrange* the materials.

This, in bare outline, is the general objection to the argument from design, and will apply to any form of it. In the form in which the argument was put forward by such theologians as Paley, the argument is, of course, still more open to objection. For Paley laid special stress on such things as the eye of an animal, which he thought must have been contrived by a wise Creator for the special benefit of the animal. It seemed to him inconceivable how otherwise such a complex organ, so well suited to the needs of the animal, should have arisen. Or listen to Henry More: "For why have we three joints in our legs and arms, as also in our fingers, but that it was much better than having two or four? And why are our fore-teeth sharp like chisels to cut, but our inward teeth broad to grind, [instead of] the fore-teeth broad and the other sharp? But we might have made a hard shift to have lived through in that worser condition. Again, why are the teeth so luckily placed, or rather, why are there not teeth in other bones as well as in the jawbones? For they might have been as capable as these. But the reason is, nothing is done foolishly or in vain; that is, there is a divine Providence that orders all things." This type of argument has lost its persuasiveness, for the theory of Evolution explains why our teeth are so luckily placed in our jawbones, why we have the most convenient number of joints in our fingers, and so on. Species which did not possess advantageous features would not survive in competition with those which did.

The sort of argument Paley and Henry More used is thus quite unconvincing. Let us return to the broader conception, that of the universe as a whole, which seems to show the mark of a benevolent and intelligent Designer. Bacon expressed this belief forcibly: "I had rather beleave all the Fables in the Legend and the Talmud and the Alcoran than that this Universal Frame is without a Minde." So, in some moods, does the universe strike us. But sometimes, when we are in other moods, we see it very differently. To quote Hume's dialogues again: "Look around this Universe. What an immense profusion of beings, animated and organized, sensible and active! You admire this prodigious variety and fecundity. But inspect a little more narrowly these living exist-

ences, the only beings worth regarding. How hostile and destructible to each other! How insufficient all of them for their own happiness! . . . the whole presents nothing but the idea of a blind Nature, impregnated by a great vivifying principle, and pouring forth from her lap, without discernment of parental care, her maimed and abortive children!" There is indeed a great deal of suffering, some part of which is no doubt attributable to the moral choices of men, and to save us from which would conflict with what many people would regard as the greater good of moral freedom, but there is still an immense residue of apparently needless suffering, that is, needless in the sense that it could be prevented by an omnipotent being. The difficulty is that of reconciling the presence of evil and suffering with the assertion that God is both omnipotent and benevolent. If we *already* believe in an omnipotent and benevolent God, then some attempt may be made to solve the problem of evil by arguing that the values in the world form a sort of organic unity, and that making any *part* of the world better would perhaps nevertheless reduce the value of the whole. Paradoxical though this thesis may appear at first sight, it is perhaps not theoretically absurd. If, however, evil presents a *difficulty* to the believing mind, it presents an *insuperable* difficulty to one who wishes to argue rationally from the world as we find it to the existence of an omnipotent and benevolent God. As Hume puts it: "Is the world considered in general, and as it appears to us in this life, different from what a man . . . would *beforehand* expect from a very powerful, wise, and benevolent Deity? It must be a strange prejudice to assert the contrary. And . . . thence I conclude, that, however consistent the world may be, allowing certain suppositions and conjectures, with the idea of such a Deity, it can never afford us an inference concerning his existence."

The teleological argument is thus extremely shaky, and in any case, even if it were sound, it would only go to prove the existence of a very great architect, not of an omnipotent and benevolent Creator.

Nevertheless, the argument has a fascination for us that reason cannot easily dispel. Hume, in his twelfth dialogue, and after pulling the argument from design to pieces in the previous eleven dialogues, nevertheless speaks as follows: "A purpose, an intention, a design strikes everywhere the most careless, the most stupid thinker; and no man can be so hardened in absurd systems as at all times to reject it . . . all the sciences almost lead us insensibly to acknowledge a first Author." Similarly Kant, before going on to exhibit the fallaciousness of the argument, nevertheless says of it: "This proof always deserves to be mentioned with respect. It is the oldest, the clearest, and the most accordant with the common reason of mankind. It enlivens the study of nature, just as it itself derives its existence and gains ever new vigor from that source. It suggests ends and purposes, where our observation would not have detected them by itself, and extends our knowledge of nature by means of the guiding-concept of a special unity, the principle of which is outside nature. This knowledge . . . so strengthens the belief in a supreme Author of nature that the belief acquires the force of an irresistible conviction." It is somewhat of a paradox that an invalid argument should command so much respect even from those who have demonstrated its invalidity. The solution of the paradox is perhaps somewhat as follows: The argument from design is no good as an argument. But in those who have the seeds of a genuinely religious attitude already within them, the facts to which the argument from design draws attention, facts showing the grandeur and majesty of the universe, facts that are evident to anyone who looks upwards on a starry night, and which are enormously multiplied for us by the advance of theoretical science, these facts have a powerful effect. But they only have this effect on the already religious mind, on the mind which has the capability of feeling the religious type of awe. That is, the argument from design is in reality no argument, or if it is regarded as an argument it is feeble, but it is a potent instrument in heightening religious emotions. . . .

QUESTIONS FOR DISCUSSION

Critically analyze the following issues involved in the major arguments for the existence of God.

1. Carefully state St. Anselm's argument for the existence of God. Does his argument involve any reference to fact or experience?

2. Can one establish an existential proposition from the meaning of the concept itself, as St. Anselm in his ontological argument tries to do? What is the distinction between the meaning of a concept and the application of a concept?

3. Is existence an attribute, as St. Anselm assumes it to be? What does it mean to say that a thing exists?

4. Is the notion of the First Mover or the First Cause a necessary one, as St. Thomas Aquinas asserts? What is the meaning of necessity? Does it apply to existence?

5. If everything must have a cause, why isn't God caused? And if God is self-caused why isn't nature self-caused?

6. Even if you establish the truth of the belief in the First Mover or the First Cause, does that prove the existence of a benevolent, righteous God?

7. Carefully state with illustrations the favorable aspects of St. Thomas Aquinas's claim that "some intelligent being exists by whom all natural things are directed to their end," and that "this being we call God."

8. Critically discuss the alternative interpretations of the apparent designful patterns in nature, whether chance or the evolutionary process. What would be the basis for choosing either of these interpretations?

9. Is the teleological argument adequate for dealing with the existence of evil, suffering, and frustration?

10. What are some of the difficulties, as pointed out by J. J. C. Smart, in connection with the ontological, cosmological, and teleological arguments for the existence of God?

11. Do the philosophical arguments for the existence of God in any way enhance one's faith in God?

Friedrich Nietzsche (1844-1900)

8.4   God Is Dead

WHAT OUR CHEERFULNESS SIGNIFIES

The most important of more recent events—that "God is dead," that the belief in the Christian God has become unworthy of belief—already begins to cast its first shadows over Europe. To the few at least whose eye, whose *suspecting* glance, is strong enough and subtle enough for this drama, some sun seems to have set, some old, profound confidence seems to have changed into doubt: our old world must seem to them daily more darksome, distrustful, strange and "old." In the main, however, one may say that the event itself is far too great, too remote, too much beyond most people's power of apprehension, for one to suppose that so much as the report of it could have *reached* them; not to speak of many who already knew *what* had taken place, and what must all collapse now that this belief had been undermined, —because so much was built upon it, so much rested on it, and had become one with it: for example, our entire European morality. This lengthy, vast and uninterrupted process of crumbling, destruction, ruin and overthrow which is now imminent: who has realised it sufficiently to-day to have to stand up as the teacher and herald of such a tremendous logic of terror, as the prophet of a period of gloom and eclipse, the like of which has probably never taken place on earth before? . . . Even we, the born riddle-readers, who wait as it were on the mountains posted 'twixt to-day and to-morrow, and engirt by their contradiction, we, the firstlings and premature children of the coming century, into whose sight especially the shadows which must forthwith envelop Europe *should* already have come—how is it that even we, without genuine sympathy for this period of gloom, contemplate its advent without any *personal* solitude or fear? Are we still, perhaps, too much under the *immediate effects* of the event—and are these effects, especially as regards *ourselves*, perhaps the reverse of what was to be expected—not at all sad and depressing, but rather like a new and indescribable variety of light, happiness, relief, enlivement, encouragement, and dawning day? . . . In fact, we philosophers and "free spirits" feel ourselves irradiated as by a new dawn by the report that the "old God is

From *Joyful Wisdom* by Friedrich Nietzsche. Translated by Thomas Common (1882).

dead"; our hearts overflow with gratitude, astonishment, presentiment and expectation. At last the horizon seems open once more, granting even that it is not bright; our ships can at last put out to sea in face of every danger; every hazard is again permitted to the discerner; the sea, *our* sea, again lies open before us; perhaps never before did such an "open sea" exist.—

Let us be on our guard against thinking that the world is a living being. Where could it extend itself? What could it nourish itself with? How could it grow and increase? We know tolerably well what the organic is; and we are to reinterpret the emphatically derivative, tardy, rare and accidental, which we only perceive on the crust of the earth, into the essential, universal and eternal, as those do who call the universe an organism? That disgusts me. Let us now be on our guard against believing that the universe is a machine; it is assuredly not constructed with a view to *one* end; we invest it with far too high an honour with the word "machine." Let us be on our guard against supposing that anything so methodical as the cyclic motions of our neighbouring stars obtains generally and throughout the universe; indeed a glance at the Milky Way induces doubt as to whether there are not many cruder and more contradictory motions there, and even stars with continuous, rectilinearly gravitating orbits, and the like. The astral arrangement in which we live is an exception; this arrangement, and the relatively long durability which is determined by it, has again made possible the exception of exceptions, the formation of organic life. The general character of the world, on the other hand, is to all

eternity chaos; not the absence of necessity, but in the sense of the absence of order, structure, form, beauty, wisdom, and whatever else our aesthetic humanities are called. Judged by our reason, the unlucky casts are far oftenest the rule, the exceptions are not the secret purpose; and the whole musical box repeats eternally its air, which can never be called a melody, —and finally the very expression, "unlucky cast" is already an anthropomorphising which involves blame. But how could we presume to blame or praise the universe! Let us be on our guard against ascribing to it heartlessness and unreason, or their opposites; it is neither perfect, nor beautiful, nor noble; nor does it seek to be anything of the kind, it does not at all attempt to imitate man! It is altogether unaffected by our aesthetic and moral judgments! Neither has it any self-preservative instinct, nor instinct at all; it also knows no law. Let us be on our guard against saying that there are laws in nature. There are only necessities: there is no one who commands, no one who obeys, no one who transgresses. When you know that there is no design, you know also that there is no chance: for it is only where there is a world of design that the word "chance" has a meaning. Let us be on our guard against saying that death is contrary to life. The living being is only a species of dead being, and a very rare species.—Let us be on our guard against thinking that the world eternally creates the new. There are no eternally enduring substances; matter is just another such error as the God of the Eleatics. But when shall we be at an end with our foresight and precaution! When will all these shadows of God cease to obscure us? When shall we have nature entirely undeified! When shall we be permitted to *naturalise* ourselves by means of the pure, newly discovered, newly redeemed nature?

THE MADMAN

Have you ever heard of the madman who on a bright morning lighted a lantern and ran to the market-place calling out unceasingly: "I seek God! I seek God!"—As there were many people standing about who did not believe in God, he caused a great deal of amusement. Why! is he lost? said one. Has he strayed away like a child? said another. Or does he keep himself hidden? Is he afraid of us? Has he taken a sea-voyage? Has he emigrated?—the people cried out laughingly, all in a hubbub. The insane man jumped into their midst and transfixed them with his glances. "Where is God gone?" he called out. "I mean to tell you! *We have killed him,*—you and I! We are all his murderers! But how have we done it? How were we able to drink up the sea? Who gave us the sponge to wipe away the whole horizon? What did we do when we loosened this earth from its sun? Whither does it now move? Whither do we move? Away from all suns? Do we not dash on unceasingly? Backwards, sideways, forwards, in all directions? Is there still an above and below? Do we not stray, as through infinite nothingness? Does not empty space breathe upon us? Has it not become colder? Does not night come on continually, darker and darker? Shall we not have to light lanterns in the morning? Do we not hear the noise of the grave-diggers who are burying God? Do we not smell the divine putrefaction?—for even Gods putrefy! God is dead! God remains dead! And we have killed him! How shall we console ourselves, the most murderous of all murderers? The holiest and mightiest that the world has hitherto possessed, has bled to death under our knife,—who will wipe the blood from us? With what water could we cleanse ourselves? What lustrums, what sacred games shall we have to devise? Is not the magnitude of this deed too great for us? Shall we not ourselves have to become Gods, merely to seem worthy of it? There never was a greater event,—and on account of it, all who are born after us belong to a higher history than any history hitherto!"—Here the madman was silent and looked again at his hearers; they also were silent and looked at him in surprise. At last he threw his lantern on the ground, so that it broke in pieces and was extinguished. "I come too early," he then said, "I am not yet at the right time. This prodigious event is still on its way, and is travelling,—it has not yet reached men's ears. Lightning and thunder need time, the light of the stars needs time, deeds need time, even after they are done, to be seen and heard. This deed is as yet further from them than the furthest star,— *and yet they have done it!*"—It is further stated that the madman made his way into different churches on the same day, and there intoned his *Requiem aeternam deo.* When led out and called to account, he always gave the reply: "What are these churches now, if they are not the tombs and monuments of God?"

QUESTIONS FOR DISCUSSION

1. What are Nietzsche's reasons, if any, for his claim that "God is dead"? Is he proclaiming a piece of news, expressing a wish, or arguing for a philosophic view?
2. Does Nietzsche assume that God was alive before he died? What caused God's death? How would one verify the belief that God is alive or that He is dead?
3. Critically examine Nietzsche's basic philosophic premises for his atheism. Are they tenable premises?

William James (1842-1910)

8.5   The Will to Believe

In the recently published Life by Leslie Stephen of his brother, Fitz-James, there is an account of a school to which the latter went when he was a boy. The teacher, a certain Mr. Guest, used to converse with his pupils in this wise: "Gurney, what is the difference between justification and sanctification?—Stephen, prove the omnipotence of God!" etc. In the midst of our Harvard freethinking and indifference we are prone to imagine that here at your good old orthodox College conversation continues to be somewhat upon this order; and to show you that we at Harvard have not lost all interest in these vital subjects, I have brought with me tonight something like a sermon on justification by faith to read to you—I mean

an essay in justification *of* faith, a defense of our right to adopt a believing attitude in religious matters, in spite of the fact that our merely logical intellect may not have been coerced. "The Will to Believe," accordingly, is the title of my paper.

I have long defended to my own students the lawfulness of voluntary adopted faith; but as soon as they have got well imbued with the logical spirit, they have as a rule refused to admit my contention to be lawful philosophically, even though in point of fact they were personally all the time chock-full of some faith or other themselves. I am all the while, however, so profoundly convinced that my own position is correct, that your invitation has seemed to me a good occasion to make my statements more clear. Perhaps your minds will be

From *The Will to Believe* (1896).

more open than those with which I have hitherto had to deal. I will be as little technical as I can, though I must begin by setting up some technical distinctions that will help us in the end.

I

Let us give the name of *hypothesis* to anything that may be proposed to our belief; and just as the electricians speak of live and dead wires, let us speak of any hypothesis as either *live* or *dead*. A live hypothesis is one which appeals as a real possibility to him to whom it is proposed. If I ask you to believe in the Mahdi, the notion makes no electric connection with your nature—it refuses to scintillate with any credibility at all. As an hypothesis it is completely dead. To an Arab, however (even if he be not one of the Mahdi's followers), the hypothesis is among the mind's possibilities: it is alive. This shows that deadness and liveness in an hypothesis are not intrinsic properties, but relations to the individual thinker. They are measured by his willingness to act. The maximum of liveness in an hypothesis means willingness to act irrevocably. Practically, that means belief; but there is some believing tendency wherever there is willingness to act at all.

Next, let us call the decision between two hypotheses an *option*. Options may be of several kinds. They may be—1, *living* or *dead;* 2, *forced* or *avoidable;* 3, *momentous* or *trivial;* and for our purposes we may call an option a *genuine* option when it is of the forced, living, and momentous kind.

1. A living option is one in which both hypotheses are live ones. If I

say to you: "Be a theosophist or be a Mohammedan," it is probably a dead option, because for you neither hypothesis is likely to be alive. But if I say: "Be an agnostic or be a Christian," it is otherwise: trained as you are, each hypothesis makes some appeal, however small, to your belief.

2. Next, if I say to you: "Choose between going out with your umbrella or without it," I do not offer you a genuine option, for it is not forced. You can easily avoid it by not going out at all. Similarly, if I say, "Either love me or hate me," "Either call my theory true or call it false," your option is avoidable. You may remain indifferent to me, neither loving nor hating, and you may decline to offer any judgment as to my theory. But if I say, "Either accept this truth or go without it," I put on you a forced option, for there is no standing place outside of the alternative. Every dilemma based on a complete logical disjunction, with no possibility of not choosing, is an option of this forced kind.

3. Finally, if I were Dr. Nansen and proposed to you to join my North Pole expedition, your option would be momentous; for this would probably be your only similar opportunity, and your choice now would either exclude you from the North Pole sort of immortality altogether or put at least the chance of it into your hands. He who refuses to embrace a unique opportunity loses the prize as surely as if he tried and failed. *Per contra,* the option is trivial when the opportunity is not unique, when the stake is insignificant, or when the decision is reversible if it later prove unwise. Such trivial options abound in the scientific life. A chemist finds an hypoth-

esis live enough to spend a year in its verification; he believes in it to that extent. But if his experiments prove inconclusive either way, he is quit for his loss of time, no vital harm being done.

It will facilitate our discussion if we keep all these distinctions well in mind. . . .

IV

The thesis I defend is, briefly stated, this: *Our passional nature not only lawfully may, but must, decide an option between propositions, whenever it is a genuine option that cannot by its nature be decided on intellectual grounds; for to say, under such circumstances, "Do not decide, but leave the question open," is itself a passional decision—just like deciding yes or no—and is attended with the same risk of losing the truth.* The thesis thus abstractly expressed will, I trust, soon become quite clear. . . .

VIII

And now, after all this introduction, let us go straight at our question. I have said, and now repeat it, that not only as a matter of fact do we find our passional nature influencing us in our opinions, but that there are some options between opinions in which this influence must be regarded both as an inevitable and as a lawful determinant of our choice.

I fear here that some of you my hearers will begin to scent danger, and lend an inhospitable ear. Two first steps of passion you have indeed had to admit as necessary—we must think so as to avoid dupery, and we must think so as to gain truth; but the surest path to those ideal consummations, you will probably consider, is from now onwards to take no further passional step.

Well, of course, I agree as far as the facts will allow. Wherever the option between losing truth and gaining it is not momentous, we can throw the chance of *gaining truth* away, and at any rate save ourselves from any chance of *believing falsehood*, by not making up our minds at all till objective evidence has come. In scientific questions, this is almost always the case; and even in human affairs in general, the need of acting is seldom so urgent that a false belief to act on is better than no belief at all. Law courts, indeed, have to decide on the best evidence attainable for the moment, because a judge's duty is to make law as well as to ascertain it, and (as a learned judge once said to me) few cases are worth spending much time over: the great thing is to have them decided on *any* acceptable principle, and got out of the way. But in our dealings with objective nature we obviously are recorders, not makers, of the truth; and decisions for the mere sake of deciding promptly and getting on to the next business would be wholly out of place. Throughout the breadth of physical nature facts are what they are quite independently of us, and seldom is there any such hurry about them that the risks of being duped by believing a premature theory need be faced. The questions here are always trivial options, the hypotheses are hardly living (at any rate not living for us spectators), the choice between believing truth or falsehood is seldom forced. The attitude of sceptical balance is, therefore, the absolutely wise one if we would escape mistakes. What difference, indeed, does it make to most of us whether we have or have not a theory of the Röntgen rays, whether we believe or not in mind-stuff, or have a conviction about the causality of conscious states? It makes no difference. Such options are not forced on us. On every account it is better not to make them, but still keep weighing reasons *pro et contra* with an indifferent hand.

I speak, of course, here of the purely judging mind. For purposes of discovery such indifference is to be less highly recommended, and science would be far less advanced than she is if the passionate desires of individuals to get their own faith confirmed had been kept out of the game. See for example the sagacity which Spencer and Weismann now display. On the other hand, if you want an absolute duffer in an investigation, you must, after all, take the man who has no interest whatever in its results: he is the warranted incapable, the positive fool. The most useful investigator, because the most sensitive observer, is always he whose eager interest in one side of the question is balanced by an equally keen nervousness lest he become deceived.[1] Science has organized this nervousness into a regular *technique,* her so-called method of verification; and she has fallen so deeply in love with the method that one may even say she has ceased to care for truth by itself at all. It is only truth as technically verified that interests her. The truth of truths might come in merely affirmative form, and she would decline to touch it. Such

truth as that, she might repeat with Clifford, would be stolen in defiance of her duty to mankind. Human passions, however, are stronger than technical rules. "Le coeur a ses raisons," as Pascal says, "que la raison ne connait pas"; and however indifferent to all but the bare rules of the game the umpire, the abstract intellect, may be, the concrete players who furnish him the materials to judge of are usually, each one of them, in love with some pet "live hypothesis" of his own. Let us agree, however, that wherever there is no forced option, the dispassionately judicial intellect with no pet hypothesis, saving us, as it does, from dupery at any rate, ought to be our ideal.

The question next arises: Are there not somewhere forced options in our speculative questions, and can we (as men who may be interested at least as much in positively gaining truth as in merely escaping dupery) always wait with impunity till the coercive evidence shall have arrived? It seems *a priori* improbable that the truth should be so nicely adjusted to our needs and powers as that. In the great boardinghouse of nature, the cakes and the butter and the syrup seldom come out so even and leave the plates so clean. Indeed, we should view them with scientific suspicion if they did.

IX

Moral questions immediately present themselves as questions whose solution cannot wait for sensible proof. A moral question is a question not of what sensibly exists, but of what is good, or would be good if it did exist. Science can tell us what exists; but to compare the *worths,* both of what

[1] Compare Wilfrid Ward's essay, "The Wish to Believe," in his *Witnesses to the Unseen* (New York: The Macmillan Company, 1893).

exists and of what does not exist, we must consult not science, but what Pascal calls our heart. Science herself consults her heart when she lays it down that the infinite ascertainment of act and correction of false beliefs are the supreme goods for man. Challenge the statement, and science can only repeat it oracularly, or else prove it by showing that such ascertainment and correction bring man all sorts of other goods which man's heart in turn declares. The question of having moral beliefs at all or not having them is decided by our will. Are our moral preferences true or false, or are they only odd biological phenomena, making things good or bad for *us*, but in themselves indifferent? How can your pure intellect decide? If your heart does not *want* a world of moral reality, your head will assuredly never make you believe in one. Mephistophelian scepticism, indeed, will satisfy the head's play-instincts much better than any rigorous idealism can. Some men (even at the student age) are so naturally cool-hearted that the moralistic hypothesis never has for them any pungent life, and in their supercilious presence the hot young moralist always feels strangely ill at ease. The appearance of knowingness is on their side, of *naïveté* and gullibility on his. Yet, in the inarticulate heart of him, he clings to it that he is not a dupe, and that there is a realm in which (as Emerson says) all their wit and intellectual superiority is no better than the cunning of a fox. Moral scepticism can no more be refuted or proved by logic than intellectual scepticism can. When we stick to it that there *is* truth (be it of either kind), we do so with our whole nature, and resolve to stand or fall by the results.

The sceptic with his whole nature adopts the doubting attitude; but which of us is the wiser, Omniscience only knows.

Turn now from these wide questions of good to a certain class of questions of fact, questions concerning personal relations, states of mind between one man and another. *Do you like me or not?*—for example. Whether you do or not depends, in countless instances, on whether I meet you half-way, am willing to assume that you must like me, and show you trust and expectation. The previous faith on my part in your liking's existence is in such cases what makes your liking come. But if I stand aloof, and refuse to budge an inch until I have objective evidence, until you shall have done something apt, as the absolutists says, *ad extorquendum assensum meum,* ten to one your liking never comes. How many women's hearts are vanquished by the mere sanguine insistence of some man that they *must* love him! he will not consent to the hypothesis that they cannot. The desire for a certain kind of truth here brings about that special truth's existence; and so it is in innumerable cases of other sorts. Who gains promotions, boons, appointments, but the man in whose life they are seen to play the part of live hypotheses, who discounts them, sacrifices other things for their sake before they have come, and takes risks for them in advance? His faith acts on the powers above him as a claim, and creates its own verification.

A social organism of any sort whatever, large or small, is what it is because each member proceeds to his own duty with a trust that the other members will simultaneously do theirs.

Wherever a desired result is achieved by the co-operation of many independent persons, its existence as a fact is a pure consequence of the precursive faith in one another of those immediately concerned. A government, an army, a commercial system, a ship, a college, an athletic team, all exist on this condition, without which not only is nothing achieved, but nothing is even attempted. A whole train of passengers (individually brave enough) will be looted by a few highwaymen, simply because the latter can count on one another, while each passenger fears that if he makes a movement of resistance, he will be shot before anyone else backs him up. If we believed that the whole car-full would rise at once with us, we should each severally rise, and train-robbing would never even be attempted. There are, then, cases where a fact cannot come at all unless a preliminary faith exists in its coming. *And where faith in a fact can help create the fact,* that would be an insane logic, which should say that faith running ahead of scientific evidence is the "lowest kind of immorality" into which a thinking being can fall. Yet such is the logic by which our scientific absolutists pretend to regulate our lives!

X

In truths dependent on our personal action, then, faith based on desire is certainly a lawful and possibly an indispensable thing.

But now, it will be said, these are all childish human cases, and have nothing to do with great cosmical matters, like the question of religious faith. Let us then pass on to that. Religions differ so much in their ac-

cidents that in discussing the religious question we must make it very generic and broad. What then do we now mean by the religious hypothesis? Science says things are; morality says some things are better than other things; and religion says essentially two things.

First, she says that the best things are the more eternal things, the overlapping things, the things in the universe that throw the last stone, so to speak, and say the final word. "Perfection is eternal"—this phrase of Charles Secrétan seems a good way of putting this first affirmation of religion, an affirmation which obviously cannot yet be verified scientifically at all.

The second affirmation of religion is that we are better off even now if we believe her first affirmation to be true.

Now, let us consider what the logical elements of this situation are *in case the religious hypothesis in both its branches be really true.* (Of course, we must admit that possibility at the outset. If we are to discuss the question at all, it must involve a living option. If for any of you religion be an hypothesis that cannot, by any living possibility be true, then you need go no farther. I speak to the "saving remnant" alone.) So proceeding, we see, first, that religion offers itself as a *momentous* option. We are supposed to gain, even now, by our belief, and to lose by our non-belief, a certain vital good. Secondly, religion is a *forced* option, so far as that good goes. We cannot escape the issue by remaining sceptical and waiting for more light, because, although we do avoid error in that way *if religion be untrue,* we lose the good, *if it be true,* just as certainly as if we positively chose to disbelieve. It is as if a man should hesitate indefinitely to ask a certain woman to marry him because he was not perfectly sure that she would prove an angel after he brought her home. Would he not cut himself off from that particular angel-possibility as decisively as if he went and married someone else? Scepticism, then, is not avoidance of option; it is option of a certain particular kind of risk. *Better risk loss of truth than chance of error*—that is your faith-vetoer's exact position. He is actively playing his take as much as the believer is; he is backing the field against the religious hypothesis, just as the believer is backing the religious hypothesis against the field. To preach scepticism to us as a duty until "sufficient evidence" for religion be found, is tantamount therefore to telling us, when in presence of the religious hypothesis, that to yield to our fear of its being error is wiser and better than to yield to our hope that it may be true. It is not intellect against all passions, then; it is only intellect with one passion laying down its law. And by what, forsooth, is the supreme wisdom of this passion warranted? Dupery for dupery, what proof is there that dupery through hope is so much worse than dupery through fear? I, for one, can see no proof; and I simply refuse obedience to the scientist's command to imitate his kind of option, in a case where my own stake is important enough to give me the right to choose my own form of risk. If religion be true and the evidence for it be still insufficient, I do not wish, by putting your extinguisher upon my nature (which feels to me as if it had after all some business in this matter), to forfeit my sole

chance in life of getting upon the winning side—that chance depending, of course, on my willingness to run the risk of acting as if my passional need of taking the world religiously might be prophetic and right.

All this is on the supposition that it really may be prophetic and right, and that even, to us who are discussing the matter, religion is a live hypothesis which may be true. Now, to most of us religion comes in a still further way that makes a veto on our active faith even more illogical. The more perfect and more eternal aspect of the universe is represented in our religions as having personal form. The universe is no longer a mere *It* to us, but a *Thou*, if we are religious; and any relation that may be possible from person to person might be possible here. For instance, although in one sense we are passive portions of the universe, in another we show a curious autonomy, as if we were small active centers on our own account. We feel, too, as if the appeal of religion to us were made to our own active good-will, as if evidence might be forever withheld from us unless we met the hypothesis half-way. To take a trivial illustration: just as a man who in a company of gentlemen made no advances, asked a warrant for every concession, and believed no one's word without proof, would cut himself off by such churlishness from all the social rewards that a more trusting spirit would earn—so here, one who should shut himself up in snarling logicality and try to make the gods extort his recognition willy-nilly, or not get it at all, might cut himself off forever from his only opportunity of making the gods' acquaintance. This feeling, forced on us we know not whence, that by obstinately believing that there are gods (although not to do so would be so easy both for our logic and our life) we are doing the universe the deepest service we can, seems part of the living essence of the religious hypothesis. If the hypothesis *were* true in all its parts, including this one, then pure intellectualism, with its veto on our making willing advances, would be an absurdity; and some participation of our sympathetic nature would be logically required. I, therefore, for one, cannot see my way to accepting the agnostic rules for truth-seeking, or willfully agree to keep my willing nature out of the game. I cannot do so for this plain reason, that *a rule of thinking which would absolutely prevent me from acknowledging certain kinds of truth if those kinds of truth were really there, would be an irrational rule.* That for me is the long and short of the formal logic of the situation, no matter what the kinds of truth might materially be.

I confess I do not see how this logic can be escaped. But sad experience makes me fear that some of you may still shrink from radically saying with me, *in abstracto*, that we have the right to believe at our own risk any hypothesis that is live enough to tempt our will. I suspect, however, that if this is so, it is because you have got away from the abstract logical point of view altogether, and are thinking (perhaps without realizing it) of some particular religious hypothesis which for you is dead. The freedom to "believe what we will" you apply to the case of some patent superstition; and the faith you think of is the faith defined by the schoolboy when he said, "Faith is when you believe something that you know ain't true." I can only

repeat that this is misapprehension. *In concreto,* the freedom to believe can only cover living options which the intellect of the individual cannot by itself resolve; and living options never seem absurdities to him who has them to consider. When I look at the religious question as it really puts itself to concrete men, and when I think of all the possibilities which both practically and theoretically it involves, then this command that we shall put a stopper on our heart, instincts, and courage, and *wait*—acting of course meanwhile more or less as if religion were *not* true [2]—till doomsday, or till such time as our intellect and senses working together may have raked in evidence enough—this command, I say, seems to me the queerest idol ever manufactured in the philosophic cave. Were we scholastic absolutists, there might be more excuse. If we had an infallible intellect with its objective certitudes, we might feel ourselves disloyal to such a perfect organ of knowledge in not trusting to it exclusively, in not waiting for its releasing word. But if we are empiricists, if we believe that no bell in us tolls to let us know for certain when truth is

---

[2] Since belief is measured by action, he who forbids us to believe religion to be true, necessarily also forbids us to act as we should if we did believe it to be true. The whole defense of religious faith hinges upon action. If the action required or inspired by the religious hypothesis is in no way different from that dictated by the naturalistic hypothesis, then religious faith is a pure superfluity, better pruned away, and controversy about its legitimacy is a piece of idle trifling, unworthy of serious minds. I myself believe, of course, that the religious hypothesis gives to the world an expression which specifically determines our reactions, and makes them in a large part unlike what they might be on a purely naturalistic scheme of belief.

in our grasp, then it seems a piece of idle fantasticality to preach so solemnly our duty of waiting for the bell. Indeed we *may* wait if we will—I hope you do not think that I am denying that—but if we do so, we do so at our peril as much as if we believed. In either case we *act*, taking our life in our hands. No one of us ought to issue vetoes to the other, nor should we bandy words of abuse. We ought, on the contrary, delicately and profoundly to respect one another's mental freedom: then only shall we bring about the intellectual republic; then only shall we have that spirit of inner tolerance without which all our outer tolerance is soulless, and which is empiricism's glory; then only shall we live and let live, in speculative as well as in practical things.

I began by a reference to Fitz-James Stephen; let me end by a quotation from him.

What do you think of yourself? What do you think of the world? . . . These are questions with which all must deal as it seems good to them. They are riddles of the Sphinx, and in some way or other we must deal with them. . . . In all important transactions of life we have to take a leap in the dark. . . . If we decide to leave the riddles unanswered, that is a choice; if we waver in our answer, that, too, is a choice: but whatever choice we make, we make it at our peril. If a man chooses to turn his back altogether on God and the future, no one can prevent him; no one can show beyond reasonable doubt that he is mistaken. If a man thinks otherwise and acts as he thinks, I do not see that any one can prove that *he* is mistaken. Each must act as he thinks best; and if he is wrong, so much the worse for him. We stand on a mountain pass in the midst of whirling snow and blinding mist, through which we get glimpses now and then of paths which may be deceptive. If we stand still we shall be frozen to death. If we take the wrong road we shall be dashed to pieces. We do not certainly know whether there is any right one. What must we do? "Be strong and of a good courage." Act for the best, hope for the best, and take what comes. . . . If death ends all, we cannot meet death better.[3]

---

[3] *Liberty, Equality, Fraternity,* 2nd ed. (London, 1874), p. 353.

QUESTIONS FOR DISCUSSION

1. What distinctions does James make between the following pairs of hypotheses as options: *alive* or *dead, forced* or *avoidable, momentous* or *trivial?* What bearing do these options have on religious beliefs?
2. What is James's central claim in *The Will to Believe?* Do you find this claim convincing?
3. James says, "There are . . . cases where a fact cannot come at all unless a preliminary faith exists in its coming." Discuss the meaning of this statement with some illustrations. Indicate its bearing on religious faith.
4. What is the specific nature of the religious hypothesis for James? Is James's pragmatic method adequate for establishing the truth of his hypothesis?

5. What would be the probable response of an orthodox religious person to William James's suggestion of the will to believe? How would an atheist respond? Whose stand do you favor?

John Dewey (1859-1952)

8.6 Faith and Its Object

All religions . . . involve specific intellectual beliefs, and they attach—some greater, some less—importance to assent to these doctrines as true, true in the intellectual sense. They have literatures held especially sacred containing historical material with which the validity of the religions is connected. They have developed a doctrinal apparatus it is incumbent upon "believers" (with varying degrees of strictness in different religions) to accept. They also insist that there is some special and isolated channel of access to the truths they hold.

No one will deny, I suppose, that the present crisis in religion is intimately bound up with these claims. The skepticism and agnosticism that are rife and that from the standpoint of the religionist are fatal to the religious spirit are directly bound up with the intellectual contents, historical, cosmological, ethical, and theological, asserted to be indispensable in everything religious. There is no need

From *A Common Faith* by John Dewey (New Haven: Yale University Press, 1934). Reprinted by permission of the publisher.

for me here to go with any minuteness into the causes that have generated doubt and disbelief, uncertainty and rejection, as to these contents. It is enough to point out that all the beliefs and ideas in question, whether having to do with historical and literary matters, or with astronomy, geology, and biology, or with the creation and structure of the world and man, are connected with the supernatural, and that this connection is the factor that has brought doubt upon them; the factor that from the standpoint of historic and institutional religions is sapping the religious life itself.

The obvious and simple facts of the case are that some views about the origin and constitution of the world and man, some views about the course of human history and personages and incidents in that history, have become so interwoven with religion as to be identified with it. On the other hand, the growth of knowledge and of its methods and tests has been such as to make acceptance of these beliefs increasingly onerous and even impossible for large numbers of cultivated men and women. With such persons, the result is that the more these ideas are used as the basis and justification of a religion, the more dubious that religion becomes.

Protestant denominations have largely abandoned the idea that particular ecclesiastic sources can authoritatively determine cosmic, historic, and theological beliefs. The more liberal among them have at least mitigated the older belief that individual hardness and corruption of heart are the causes of intellectual rejection of the intellectual apparatus of the Christian religion. But these denominations have also, with exceptions numerically insignificant, retained a certain indispensable minimum of intellectual content. They ascribe peculiar religious force to certain literary documents and certain historic personages. Even when they have greatly reduced the bulk of intellectual content to be accepted, they have insisted at least upon theism and the immortality of the individual.

It is no part of my intention to rehearse in any detail the weighty facts that collectively go by the name of the conflict of science and religion—a conflict that is not done away with by calling it a conflict of science with theology, as long as even a minimum of intellectual assent is prescribed as essential. The impact of astronomy not merely upon the older cosmogony of religion but upon elements of creeds dealing with historic events— witness the idea of ascent into heaven —is familiar. Geological discoveries have displaced creation myths which once bulked large. Biology has revolutionized conceptions of soul and mind which once occupied a central place in religious beliefs and ideas, and this science has made a profound impression upon ideas of sin, redemp-

tion, and immortality. Anthropology, history, and literary criticism have furnished a radically different version of the historic events and personages upon which Christian religions have built. Psychology is already opening to us natural explanations of phenomena so extraordinary that once their supernatural origin was, so to say, the natural explanation.

The significant bearing for my purpose of all this is that new methods of inquiry and reflection have become for the educated man today the final arbiter of all questions of fact, existence, and intellectual assent. Nothing less than a revolution in the "seat of intellectual authority" has taken place. This revolution, rather than any particular aspect of its impact upon this and that religious belief, is the central thing. In this revolution, every defeat is a stimulus to renewed inquiry; every victory won is the open door to more discoveries, and every discovery is a new seed planted in the soil of intelligence, from which grow fresh plants with new fruits. The mind of man is being habituated to a new method and ideal: There is but one sure road of access to truth—the road of patient, co-operative inquiry operating by means of observation, experiment, record, and controlled reflection.

The scope of the change is well illustrated by the fact that whenever a particular outpost is surrendered it is usually met by the remark from a liberal theologian that the particular doctrine or supposed historic or literary tenet surrendered was never, after all, an intrinsic part of religious belief, and that without it the true nature of religion stands out more clearly than before. Equally significant is the growing gulf between fundamentalists and liberals in the churches. What is not realized—although perhaps it is more definitely seen by fundamentalists than by liberals—is that the issue does not concern this and that piecemeal *item* of belief, but centers in the question of the method by which any and every item of intellectual belief is to be arrived at and justified.

The positive lesson is that religious qualities and values if they are real at all are not bound up with any single item of intellectual assent, not even that of the existence of the God of theism; and that, under existing conditions, the religious function in experience can be emancipated only through the surrender of the whole notion of special truths that are religious by their own nature, together with the idea of peculiar avenues of access to such truths. For were we to admit that there is but one method for ascertaining fact and truth—that conveyed by the word "scientific" in its most general and generous sense— no discovery in any branch of knowledge and inquiry could then disturb the faith that is religious. I should describe this faith as the unification of the self through allegiance to inclusive ideal ends, which imagination presents to us and to which the human will responds as worthy of controlling our desires and choices.

It is probably impossible to imagine the amount of intellectual energy that has been diverted from normal processes of arriving at intellectual conclusions because it has gone into rationalization of the doctrines entertained by historic religions. The set that has thus been given the general mind is much more harmful, to my mind, than are the consequences of any one particular item of belief, serious as have been those flowing from acceptance of some of them. The modern liberal version of the intellectual content of Christianity seems to the modern mind to be more rational than some of the earlier doctrines that have been reacted against. Such is not the case in fact. The theological philosophers of the Middle Ages had no greater difficulty in giving rational form to all the doctrines of the Roman church than has the liberal theologian of today in formulating and justifying intellectually the doctrines he entertains. This statement is as applicable to the doctrine of continuing miracles, penance, indulgences, saints, and angels, etc., as to the trinity, incarnation, atonement, and the sacraments. The fundamental question, I repeat, is not of this and that article of intellectual belief but of intellectual habit, method, and criterion.

One method of swerving aside the impact of changed knowledge and method upon the intellectual content of religion is the method of division of territory and jurisdiction into two parts. Formerly these were called the realm of nature and the realm of grace. They are now often known as those of revelation and natural knowledge. Modern religious liberalism has no definite names for them, save, perhaps, the division . . . between scientific and religious experience. The implication is that in one territory the supremacy of scientific knowledge must be acknowledged, while there is another region, not very precisely defined, of intimate personal experience wherein other methods and criteria hold sway.

This method of justifying the peculiar and legitimate claim of certain elements of belief is always open to the objection that a positive conclusion is drawn from a negative fact. Existing ignorance or backwardness is employed to assert the existence of a division in the nature of the subject-matter dealt with. Yet the gap may only reflect, at most, a limitation now existing but in the future to be done away wtih. The argument that because some province or aspect of experience has not yet been "invaded" by scientific methods, it is not subject to them, is as old as it is dangerous. Time and time again, in some particular reserved field, it has been invalidated. Psychology is still in its infancy. He is bold to the point of rashness who asserts that intimate personal experience will never come within the ken of natural knowledge.

It is more to the present point, however, to consider the region that is claimed by religionists as a special preserve. It is mystical experience. The difference, however, between mystic experience and the theory about it that is offered to us must be noted. The experience is a fact to be inquired into. The theory, like any theory, is an interpretation of the fact. The idea that by its very nature the experience is a veridical realization of the direct presence of God does not rest so much upon examination of the facts as it does upon importing into their interpretation a conception that is formed outside them. In its dependence upon a prior conception of the supernatural, which is the thing to be proved, it begs the question.

History exhibits many types of mystic experience, and each of these types is contemporaneously explained by the concepts that prevail in the culture and the circle in which the phenomena occur. There are mystic crises that arise, as among some North American Indian tribes, induced by fasting. They are accompanied by trances and semi-hysteria. Their purpose is to gain some special power, such perhaps as locating a person who is lost or finding objects that have been secreted. There is the mysticism of Hindu practice now enjoying some vogue in Western countries. There is the mystic ecstasy of Neoplatonism with its complete abrogation of the self and absorption into an impersonal whole of Being. There is the mysticism of intense aesthetic experience independent of any theological or metaphysical interpretation. There is the heretical mysticism of William Blake. There is the mysticism of sudden unreasoning fear in which the very foundations seem shaken beneath one—to mention but a few of the types that may be found.

What common element is there between, say, the Neoplatonic conception of a super-divine Being wholly apart from human needs and conditions and the medieval theory of an immediate union that is fostered through attention to the sacraments or through concentration upon the heart of Jesus? The contemporary emphasis of some Protestant theologians upon the sense of inner personal communion with God, found in religious expereince, is almost as far away from medieval Christianity as it is from Neoplatonism or Yoga. Interpretations of the experience have not grown from the experience itself with the aid of such scientific resources as may be available. They have been imported by borrowing without criticism from ideas that are current in the surrounding culture.

The mystic states of the shaman and of some North American Indians are frankly techniques for gaining a special power—*the* power as it is conceived by some revivalist sects. There is no especial intellectual objectification accompanying the experience. The knowledge that is said to be gained is not that of Being but of particular secrets and occult modes of operation. The aim is not to gain knowledge of superior divine power, but to get advice, cures for the sick, prestige, etc. The conception that mystic experience is a normal mode of religious experience by which we may acquire knowledge of God and divine things is a nineteenth-century interpretation that has gained vogue in direct ratio to the decline of older methods of religious apologetics.

There is no reason for denying the existence of experiences that are called mystical. On the contrary, there is every reason to suppose that, in some degree of intensity, they occur so frequently that they may be regarded as normal manifestations that take place at certain rhythmic points in the movement of experience. The assumption that denial of a particular interpretation of their objective content proves that those who make the denial do not have the experience in question, so that if they had it they would be equally persuaded of its objective source in the presence of God, has no foundation in fact. As with every empirical phenomenon, the occurrence of the state called mystical is simply an occasion for inquiry into its mode of causation. There is no more reason for convert-

ing the experience itself into an immediate knowledge of its cause than in the case of an experience of lightning or any other natural occurrence.

My purpose, then, in this brief reference to mysticism is not to throw doubt upon the existence of particular experiences called mystical. Nor is it to propound any theory to account for them. I have referred to the matter merely as an illustration of the general tendency to mark off two distinct realms in one of which science has jurisdiction, while in the other, special modes of immediate knowledge of religious objects have authority. This dualism as it operates in contemporary interpretation of mystic experience in order to validate certain beliefs is but a reinstatement of the old dualism between the natural and the supernatural, in terms better adapted to the cultural conditions of the present time. Since it is conception of the supernatural that science calls in question, the circular nature of this type of reasoning is obvious.

Apologists for a religion often point to the shift that goes on in scientific ideas and materials as evidence of the unreliability of science as a mode of knowledge. They often seem peculiarly elated by the great, almost revolutionary, change in fundamental physical conceptions that has taken place in science during the present generation. Even if the alleged unreliability were as great as they assume (or even greater), the question would remain: Have we any other recourse for knowledge? But in fact they miss the point. Science is not constituted by any particular body of subject-matter. It is constituted by a method, a method of changing beliefs by means of tested inquiry as well as of arriving at them. It is its glory, not its condemnation, that its subject-matter develops as the method is improved. There is no special subject-matter of belief that is sacrosanct. The identification of science with a particular set of beliefs and ideas is itself a hold-over of ancient and still current dogmatic habits of thought which are opposed to science in its actuality and which science is undermining.

For scientific method is adverse not only to dogma but to doctrine as well, provided we take "doctrine" in its usual meaning—a body of definite beliefs that needs only to be taught and learned as true. This negative attitude of science to doctrine does not indicate indifference to truth. It signifies supreme loyalty to the method by which truth is attained. The scientific-religious conflict ultimately is a conflict between allegiance to this method and allegiance to even an irreducible minimum of belief so fixed in advance that it can never be modified.

The method of intelligence is open and public. The doctrinal method is limited and private. This limitation persists even when knowledge of the truth that is religious is said to be arrived at by a special mode of experience, that termed "religious." For the latter is assumed to be a very special kind of experience. To be sure, it is asserted to be open to all who obey certain conditions. Yet the mystic experience yields, as we have seen, various results in the way of belief to different persons, depending upon the surrounding culture of those who undergo it. As a method, it lacks the public character belonging to the method of intelligence. Moreover, when the experience in question does

not yield consciousness of the presence of God, in the sense that is alleged to exist, the retort is always at hand that it is not a genuine religious experience. For by definition, only that experience *is* religious which arrives at this particular result. The argument is circular. The traditional position is that some hardness or corruption of heart prevents one from having the experience. Liberal religionists are now more humane. But their logic does not differ.

It is sometimes held that beliefs about religious matters are symbolic, like rites and ceremonies. This view may be an advance upon that which holds to their literal objective validity. But as usually put forward it suffers from an ambiguity. Of what are the beliefs symbols? Are they symbols of things experienced in other modes than those set apart as religious, so that the things symbolized have an independent standing? Or are they symbols in the sense of standing for some transcendental reality—transcendental because not being the subject-matter of experience generally? Even the fundamentalist admits a certain quality and degree of symbolism in the latter sense in objects of religious belief. For he holds that the objects of these beliefs are so far beyond finite human capacity that our beliefs must be couched in more or less metaphorical terms. The conception that faith is the best available substitute for knowledge in our present estate still attaches to the notion of the symbolic character of the materials of faith; unless by ascribing to them a symbolic nature we mean that these materials stand for something that is verifiable in general and public experience.

Were we to adopt the latter point of view, it would be evident not only that the intellectual articles of a creed must be understood to be symbolic of moral and other ideal values; but that the facts taken to be historic and used as concrete evidence of the intellectual articles are themselves symbolic. These articles of a creed present events and persons that have been made over by the idealizing imagination in the interest, at their best, of moral ideals. Historic personages in their divine attributes are materializations of the ends that enlist devotion and inspire endeavor. They are symbolic of the reality of ends moving us in many forms of experience. The ideal values that are thus symbolized also mark human experience in science and art and the various modes of human association: they mark almost everything in life that rises from the level of manipulation of conditions as they exist. It is admitted that the objects of religion are ideal in contrast with our present state. What would be lost if it were also admitted that they have authoritative claim upon conduct just because they are ideal? The assumption that these objects of religion exist already in some realm of Being seems to add nothing to their force, while it weakens their claim over us as ideals, in so far as it bases that claim upon matters that are intellectually dubious. The question narrows itself to this: Are the ideals that move us genuinely ideal or are they ideal only in contrast with our present estate?

The import of the question extends far. It determines the meaning given to the word "God." On one score, the word can mean only a particular Being. On the other score, it denotes the unity of all ideal ends arousing us to desire and actions. Does the unification have a claim upon our attitude and conduct because it is already, apart from us, in realized existence, or because of its own inherent meaning and value? Suppose for the moment that the word "God" means the ideal ends that at a given time and place one acknowledges as having authority over his volition and emotion, the values to which one is supremely devoted, as far as these ends, through imagination, take on unity. If we make this supposition, the issue will stand out clearly in contrast with the doctrine of religions that "God" designates some kind of Being having prior and therefore non-ideal existence.

The word "non-ideal" is to be taken literally in regard to some religions that have historically existed, to all of them as far as they are neglectful of moral qualities in their divine beings. It does not apply in the same *literal* way to Judaism and Christianity. For they have asserted that the Supreme Being has moral and spiritual attributes. But it applies to them none the less in that these moral and spiritual characters are thought of as properties of a particular existence and are thought to be of religious value for us because of this embodiment in such an existence. Here, as far as I can see, is the ultimate issue as to the difference between *a* religion and the religious as a function of experience.

The idea that "God" represents a unification of ideal values that is essentially imaginative in origin when the imagination supervenes in conduct is attended with verbal difficulties owing to our frequent use of the word "imagination" to denote fantasy and doubtful reality. But the reality of ideal ends as ideals is vouched for by their undeniable power in action. An ideal is not an illusion because imagination is the origin through which it is apprehended. For *all* possibilities reach us through the imagination. In a definite sense the only meaning that can be assigned the term "imagination" is that things unrealized in fact come home to us and have power to stir us. The unification effected through imagination is not fanciful, for it is the reflex of the unification of practical and emotional attitudes. The unity signifies not a single Being, but the unity of loyalty and effort evoked by the fact that many ends are one in the power of their ideal, or imaginative, quality to stir and hold us.

We may well ask whether the power and significance in life of the traditional conceptions of God are not due to the ideal qualities referred to by them, the hypostatization of them into an existence being due to a conflux of tendencies in human nature that converts the object of desire into an antecedent reality . . . with beliefs that have prevailed in the cultures of the past. For in the older cultures the idea of the supernatural was "natural," in the sense in which "natural" signifies something customary and familiar. It seems more credible that religious persons have been supported and consoled by the reality with which ideal values appeal to them than that they have been upborne by sheer matter of fact existence. That, when once men are inured to the idea of the union of the ideal and the physical, the two should be so bound together in emotion that

it is difficult to institute a separation, agrees with all we know of human psychology.

The benefits that will accrue, however, from making the separation are evident. The dislocation frees the religious values of experience once for all from matters that are continually becoming more dubious. With that release there comes emancipation from the necessity of resort to apologetics. The reality of ideal ends and values in their authority over us is an undoubted fact. The validity of justice, affection, and that intellectual correspondence of our ideas with realities that we call truth, is so assured in its hold upon humanity that it is unnecessary for the religious attitude to encumber itself with the apparatus of dogma and doctrine. Any other conception of the religious attitude, when it is adequately analyzed, means that those who hold it care more for force than for ideal values—since all that an Existence can add is force to establish, to punish, and to reward. There are, indeed, some persons who frankly say that their own faith does not require any guarantee that moral values are backed up by physical force, but who hold that the masses are so backward that ideal values will not affect their conduct unless in the popular belief these values have the sanction of a power that can enforce them and can execute justice upon those who fail to comply.

There are some persons, deserving of more respect, who say: "We agree that the beginning must be made with the primacy of the ideal. But why stop at this point? Why not search with the utmost eagerness and vigor for all the evidence we can find, such as is supplied by history, by presence of design in nature, which may lead on to the belief that the ideal is already extant in a Personality having objective existence?"

One answer to the question is that we are involved by this search in all the problems of the existence of evil that have haunted theology in the past and that the most ingenious apologetics have not faced, much less met. If these apologists had not identified the existence of ideal goods with that of a Person supposed to originate and support them—a Being, moreover, to whom omnipotent power is attributed—the problem of the occurrence of evil would be gratuitous. The significance of ideal ends and meanings is, indeed, closely connected with the fact that there are in life all sorts of things that are evil to us because we would have them otherwise. Were existing conditions wholly good, the notion of possibilities to be realized would never emerge.

But the more basic answer is that while if the search is conducted upon a strictly empirical basis there is no reason why it should not take place, as a matter of fact it is always undertaken in the interest of the supernatural. Thus it diverts attention and energy from ideal values and from the exploration of actual conditions by means of which they may be promoted. History is testimony to this fact. Men have never fully used the powers they possess to advance the good in life, because they have waited upon some power external to themselves and to nature to do the work they are responsible for doing. Dependence upon an external power is the counterpart of surrender of human endeavor. Nor is emphasis on exercising our own powers for good

an egoistical or a sentimentally optimistic recourse. It is not the first, for it does not isolate man, either individually or collectively, from nature. It is not the second, because it makes no assumption beyond that of the need and responsibility for human endeavor, and beyond the conviction that, if human desire and endeavor were enlisted in behalf of natural ends, conditions would be bettered. It involves no expectation of a millennium of good.

Belief in the supernatural as a necessary power for apprehension of the ideal and for practical attachment to it has for its counterpart a pessimistic belief in the corruption and impotency of natural means. That is axiomatic in Christian dogma. But this apparent pessimism has a way of suddenly changing into an exaggerated optimism. For according to the terms of the doctrine, if the faith in the supernatural is of the required order, regeneration at once takes place. Goodness, in all essentials, is thereby established; if not, there is proof that the established relation to the supernatural has been vitiated. This romantic optimism is one cause for the excessive attention to individual salvation characteristic of traditional Christianity. Belief in a sudden and complete transmutation through conversion and in the objective efficacy of prayer, is too easy a way out of difficulties. It leaves matters in general just about as they were before; that is, sufficiently bad so that there is additional support for the idea that only supernatural aid can better them. The position of natural intelligence is that there exists a *mixture* of good and evil, and that reconstruction in the direction of the good which is indicated by ideal ends, must take place, if at all, through continued co-operative effort. There is at least enough impulse toward justice, kindliness, and order so that if it were mobilized for action, not expecting abrupt and complete transformation to occur, the disorder, cruelty, and oppression that exist would be reduced.

The discussion has arrived at a point where a more fundamental objection to the position I am taking needs consideration. The misunderstanding upon which this objection rests should be pointed out. The view I have advanced is sometimes treated as if the identification of the divine with ideal ends left the ideal wholly without roots in existence and without support from existence. The objection implies that my view commits one to such a separation of the ideal and the existent that the ideal has no chance to find lodgment even as a seed that might grow and bear fruit. On the contrary, what I have been criticizing is the *identification* of the ideal with a particular Being, especially when that identification makes necessary the conclusion that this Being is outside of nature, and what I have tried to show is that the ideal itself has its roots in natural conditions; it emerges when the imagination idealizes existence by laying hold of the possibilities offered to thought and action. There are values, goods, actually realized upon a natural basis —the goods of human association, of art and knowledge. The idealizing imagination seizes upon the most precious things found in the climacteric moments of experience and projects them. We need no external

criterion and guarantee for their goodness. They are had, they exist as good, and out of them we frame our ideal ends.

Moreover, the ends that result from our projection of experienced goods into objects of thought, desire, and effort exist, only they exist *as* ends. Ends, purposes, exercise determining power in human conduct. The aims of philanthropists, of Florence Nightingale, of Howard, of Wilberforce, of Peabody, have not been idle dreams. They have modified institutions. Aims, ideals, do not exist simply in "mind"; they exist in character, in personality and action. One might call the roll of artists, intellectual inquirers, parents, friends, citizens who are neighbors, to show that purposes exist in an *operative* way. What I have been objecting to, I repeat, is not the idea that ideals are linked with existence and that they themselves exist, through human embodiment, as forces, but the idea that their authority and value depend upon some prior complete embodiment—as if the efforts of human beings in behalf of justice, or knowledge, or beauty, depended for their effectiveness and validity upon assurance that there already existed in some supernal region a place where criminals are humanely treated, where there is no serfdom or slavery, where all facts and truths are already discovered and possessed, and all beauty is eternally displayed in actualized form.

The aims and ideals that move us are generated through imagination. But they are not made out of imaginary stuff. They are made out of the hard stuff of the world of physical and social experience. The locomotive did not exist before Stevenson, nor the telegraph before the time of Morse. But the conditions for their existence were there in physical material and energies and in human capacity. Imagination seized hold upon the idea of a rearrangement of existing things that would evolve new objects. The same thing is true of a painter, a musician, a poet, a philanthropist, a moral prophet. The new vision does not arise out of nothing, but emerges through seeing, in terms of possibilities, that is, of imagination, old things in new relations serving a new end which the new end aids in creating.

Moreover, the process of creation is experimental and continuous. The artist, scientific man, or good citizen, depends upon what others have done before him and are doing around him. The sense of new values that become ends to be realized arises first in dim and uncertain form. As the values are dwelt upon and carried forward in action they grow in definiteness and coherence. Interaction between aim and existent conditions improves and tests the ideal; and conditions are at the same time modified. Ideals change as they are applied in existent conditions. The process endures and advances with the life of humanity. What one person and one group accomplish becomes the standing ground and starting point of those who succeed them. When the vital factors in this natural process are generally acknowledged in emotion, thought, and action, the process will be both accelerated and purified through elimination of that irrelevant element that culminates in the idea of the supernatural. When the vital factors

attain the religious force that has been drafted into supernatural religions, the resulting reinforcement will be incalculable.

These considerations may be applied to the idea of God, or, to avoid misleading conceptions, to the idea of the divine. This idea is, as I have said, one of ideal possibilities unified through imaginative realization and projection. But this idea of God, or of the divine, is also connected with all the natural forces and conditions —including man and human association—that promote the growth of the ideal and that further its realization We are in the presence neither of ideals completely embodied in existence nor yet of ideals that are mere rootless ideals, fantasies, utopias. For there are forces in nature and society that generate and support the ideals. They are further unified by the action that gives them coherence and solidity. It is this *active* relation between ideal and actual to which I would give the name "God." I would not insist that the name *must* be given. There are those who hold that the associations of the term with the supernatural are so numerous and close that any use of the word "God" is sure to give rise to misconception and be taken as a concession to traditional ideas.

They may be correct in this view. But the facts to which I have referred are there, and they need to be brought out with all possible clearness and force. There exist concretely and experimentally goods—the values of art in all its forms, of knowledge, of effort, and of rest after striving, of education and fellowship, of friendship and love, of growth in mind and body. These goods are there and yet they are relatively embryonic. Many persons are shut out from generous participation in them; there are forces at work that threaten and sap existent goods as well as prevent their expansion. A clear and intense conception of a union of ideal ends with actual conditions is capable of arousing steady emotion. It may be fed by every experience, no matter what its material.

In a distracted age, the need for such an idea is urgent. It can unify interests and energies now dispersed; it can direct action and generate the heat of emotion and the light of intelligence. Whether one gives the name "God" to this union, operative in thought and action, is a matter for individual decision. But the *function* of such a working union of the ideal and actual seems to me to be identical with the force that has in fact been attached to the conception of God in all the religions that have a spiritual content; and a clear idea of that function seems to me urgently needed at the present time.

The sense of this union may, with some persons, be furthered by mystical experiences, using the term "mystical" in its broadest sense. That result depends largely upon temperament. But there is a marked difference between the union associated with mysticism and the union which I had in mind. There is nothing mystical about the latter; it is natural and moral. Nor is there anything mystical about the perception or consciousness of such union. Imagination of ideal ends pertinent to actual conditions represents the fruition of a disciplined mind. There is, indeed, even danger that resort to mystical

experiences will be an escape, and that its result will be the passive feeling that the union of actual and ideal is already accomplished. But in fact this union is active and practical; it is a *uniting*, not something given.

One reason why personally I think it fitting to use the word "God" to denote that uniting of the ideal and actual which has been spoken of, lies in the fact that aggressive atheism seems to me to have something in common with traditional supernaturalism. I do not mean merely that the former is mainly so negative that it fails to give positive direction to thought, though that fact is pertinent. What I have in mind especially is the exclusive preoccupation of both militant atheism and supernaturalism with man in isolation. For in spite of supernaturalism's reference to something beyond nature, it conceives of this earth as the moral center of the universe and of man as the apex of the whole scheme of things. It regards the drama of sin and redemption enacted within the isolated and lonely soul of man as the one thing of ultimate importance. Apart from man, nature is held either accursed or negligible. Militant atheism is also affected by lack of natural piety. The ties binding man to nature that poets have always celebrated are passed over lightly. The attitude taken is often that of man living in an indifferent and hostile world and issuing blasts of defiance. A religious attitude, however, needs the sense of a connection of man, in the way of both dependence and support, with the enveloping world that the imagination feels is a universe. Use of the words "God" or "divine" to convey the union of actual with ideal may protect man from a sense of isolation and from consequent despair or defiance.

In any case, whatever the name, the meaning is selective. For it involves no miscellaneous worship of everything in general. It selects those factors in existence that generate and support our idea of good as an end to be striven for. It excludes a multitude of forces that at any given time are irrelevant to this function. Nature produces whatever gives reinforcement and direction but also what occasions discord and confusion. The "divine" is thus a term of human choice and aspiration. A humanistic religion, if it excludes our relation to nature, is pale and thin, as it is presumptuous, when it takes humanity as an object of worship. Matthew Arnold's conception of a "power not ourselves" is too narrow in its reference to operative and sustaining conditions. While it is selective, it is too narrow in its basis of selection—righteousness. The conception thus needs to be widened in two ways. The powers that generate and support the good as experienced and as ideal, work *within* as well as without. There seems to be a reminiscence of an external Jehovah in Arnold's statement. And the powers work to enforce other values and ideals than righteousness. Arnold's sense of an opposition between Hellenism and Hebraism resulted in exclusion of beauty, truth, and friendship from the list of the consequences toward which powers work within and without.

In the relation between nature and human ends and endeavors, recent science has broken down the older dualism. It has been engaged in this task for three centuries. But as long as the conceptions of science were strictly mechanical (mechanical in the sense of assuming separate things acting upon one another purely externally by push and pull), religious apologists had a standing ground in pointing out the differences between man and physical nature. The differences could be used for arguing that something supernatural had intervened in the case of man. The recent acclaim, however, by apologists for religion of the surrender by science of the classic type of mechanicalism [1] seems ill-advised from their own point of view. For the change in the modern scientific view of nature simply brings man and nature nearer together. We are no longer compelled to choose between explaining away what is distinctive in man through reducing him to another form of a mechanical model and the doctrine that something literally supernatural marks him off from nature. The less mechanical—in its older sense—physical nature is found to be, the closer is man to nature.

In his fascinating book, *The Dawn of Conscience,* James Henry Breasted refers to Haeckel as saying that the question he would most wish to have answered is this: Is the universe friendly to man? The question is an ambiguous one. Friendly to man in what respect? With respect to ease and comfort, to material success, to egoistic ambitions? Or to his aspiration to inquire and discover, to invent and create, to build a more secure order for human existence? In

---

[1] I use this term because science has not abandoned its beliefs in working mechanisms in giving up the idea that they are of the nature of a strictly mechanical contact of discrete things.

whatever form the question be put, the answer cannot in all honesty be an unqualified and absolute one. Mr. Breasted's answer, as an historian, is that nature has been friendly to the emergence and development of conscience and character. Those who will have all or nothing cannot be satisfied with this answer. Emergence and growth are not enough for them. They want something more than growth accompanied by toil and pain. They want final achievement. Others who are less absolutist may be content to think that, morally speaking, growth is a higher value and ideal than is sheer attainment. They will remember also that growth has not been confined to conscience and character; that it extends also to discovery, learning, and knowledge, to creation in the arts, to furtherance of ties that hold men together in mutual aid and affection. These persons at least will be satisfied with an intellectual view of the religious function that is based on continuing choice directed toward ideal ends.

For, I would remind readers in conclusion, it is the intellectual side of the religious attitude that I have been considering. I have suggested that the religious element in life has been hampered by conceptions of the supernatural that were imbedded in those cultures wherein man had little control over outer nature and little in the way of sure method of inquiry and test. The crisis today as to the intellectual content of religious belief has been caused by the change in the intellectual climate due to the increase of our knowledge and our means of understanding. I have tried to show that this change is not fatal to the religious values in our common experience, however adverse its impact may be upon historic religions. Rather, provided that the methods and results of intelligence at work are frankly adopted, the change is liberating.

It clarifies our ideals, rendering them less subject to illusion and fantasy. It relieves us of the incubus of thinking of them as fixed, as without power of growth. It discloses that they develop in coherence and pertinency with increase of natural intelligence. The change gives aspiration for natural knowledge a definitely religious character, since growth in understanding of nature is seen to be organically related to the formation of ideal ends. The same change enables man to select those elements in natural conditions that may be organized to support and extend the sway of ideals. All purpose is selective, and all intelligent action includes deliberate choice. In the degree in which we cease to depend upon belief in the supernatural, selection is enlightened and choice can be made in behalf of ideals whose inherent relations to conditions and consequences are understood. Were the naturalistic foundations and bearings of religion grasped, the religious element in life would emerge from the throes of the crisis in religion. Religion would then be found to have its natural place in every aspect of human experience that is concerned with estimate of possibilities, with emotional stir by possibilities as yet unrealized, and with all action in behalf of their realization. All that is significant in human experience falls within this frame.

QUESTIONS FOR DISCUSSION

1. What are Dewey's philosophic reasons for his rejection of supernaturalism? Do you find his reasons valid?
2. What method does Dewey suggest to establish the truth or falsity of religious beliefs? In what ways does he differ from fundamentalists, Thomists, and religious existentialists?
3. What is Dewey's notion of God? In what way is his notion of God similar to and yet different from the Judeo-Christian notion of God?
4. What is the nature of mystical experience? Does mystical experience establish the reality of the religious object? What is Dewey's view on this issue?
5. How does Dewey deal with the problem of evil? How does his method differ from that of the traditional religionists?

Martin Buber (1878-1956)

8.7   I and Thou

Men have addressed their eternal *Thou* with many names. In singing of Him who was thus named they always had the *Thou* in mind: the first myths were hymns of praise. Then the names took refuge in the language of *It;* men were more and more strongly moved to think of and to address their eternal *Thou* as an *It*. But all God's names are hallowed, for in them He is not merely spoken about, but also spoken to.

Many men wish to reject the word God as a legitimate usage, because

From *I and Thou* by Martin Buber, second edition, Part 3. Reprinted by permission of Charles Scribner's Sons and T. & T. Clark (Edinburgh).

it is so misused. It is indeed the most heavily laden of all the words used by men. For that very reason it is the most imperishable and most indispensable. What does all mistaken talk about God's being and works (though there has been, and can be, no other talk about these) matter in comparison with the one truth that all men who have addressed God had God Himself in mind? For he who speaks the word God and really has *Thou* in mind (whatever the illusion by which he is held), addresses the true *Thou* of his life, which cannot be limited by another *Thou*, and to which he stands in a relation that gathers up and includes all others.

But when he, too, who abhors the name, and believes himself to be godless, gives his whole being to addressing the *Thou* of his life, as a *Thou* that cannot be limited by another, he addresses God.

Every real relation with a being or life in the world is exclusive. Its *Thou* is freed, steps forth, is single, and confronts you. It fills the heavens. This does not mean that nothing else exists; but all else lives in *its* light. As long as the presence of the relation continues, this its cosmic range is inviolable. But as soon as a *Thou* becomes *It,* the cosmic range of the relation appears as an offence to the world, its exclusiveness as an exclusion of the universe.

In the relation with God unconditional exclusiveness and unconditional inclusiveness are one. He who enters on the absolute relation is concerned with nothing isolated any more, neither things nor beings, neither earth nor heaven; but everything is gathered up in the relation. For to step into pure relation is not to disregard everything but to see everything in the *Thou,* not to renounce the world but to establish it on its true basis. To look away from the world, or to stare at it, does not help a man to reach God; but he who sees the world in Him stands in His presence. "Here world, there God" is the language of *It;* "God in the world" is another language of *It;* but to eliminate or leave behind nothing at all, to include the whole world in the *Thou,* to give the world its due and its truth, to include nothing beside God but everything in him—this is full and complete relation.

Men do not find God if they stay in the world. They do not find Him if they leave the world. He who goes out with his whole being to meet his *Thou* and carries to it all being that is in the world, finds Him who cannot be sought.

Of course God is the "wholly Other"; but He is also the wholly Same, the wholly Present. Of course He is the *Mysterium Tremendum* that appears and overthrows; but He is also the mystery of the self-evident, nearer to me than my *I.*

If you explore the life of things and of conditioned being you come to the unfathomable, if you deny the life of things and of conditioned being you stand before nothingness, if you hallow this life you meet the living God.

Man's sense of *Thou,* which experiences in the relations with every particular *Thou* the disappointment of the change to *It,* strives out but not away from them all to its eternal *Thou;* but not as something is sought: actually there is no such thing as seeking God, for there is nothing in which He could not be found. How foolish and hopeless would be the man who turned aside from the course of his life in order to seek God; even though he won all the wisdom of solitude and all the power of concentrated being he would miss God. Rather is it as when a man goes his way and simply wishes that it might be the way: in the strength of his wish his striving is expressed. Every relational event is a stage that affords him a glimpse into the consummating event. So in each event he does not partake, but also (for he is waiting) does partake, of the one event. Waiting, not seeking, he goes his way;

hence he is composed before all things, and makes contact with them which helps them. But when he has *found,* his heart is not turned from them, though everything now meets him in the one event. He blesses every cell that sheltered him, and every cell into which he will yet turn. For this finding is not the end, but only the eternal middle, of the way.

It is a finding without seeking, a discovering of the primal, of origin. His sense of *Thou,* which cannot be satiated till he finds the endless *Thou,* had the *Thou* present to it from the beginning; the presence had only to become wholly real to him in the reality of the hallowed life of the world.

God cannot be inferred in anything—in nature, say, as its author, or in history as its master, or in the subject as the self that is thought in it. Something else is not "given" and God then elicited from it; but God is the Being that is directly, most nearly, and lastingly, over against us, that may properly only be addressed, not expressed.

Men wish to regard a feeling (called feeling of dependence, and recently, more precisely, creaturely feeling) as the real element in the relation with God. In proportion as the isolation and definition of this element is accurate, its unbalanced emphasis only makes the character of complete relation the more misunderstood.

What has already been said of love is even more unshakably valid here. Feelings are a mere accompaniment to the metaphysical and metapsychical fact of the relation, which is fulfilled not in the soul but between *I*

and *Thou.* A feeling may be considered ever so essential, it remains nevertheless subject to the dynamic of the soul, where one feeling is outstripped, outdone, and abolished by another. In distinction from relation a feeling has its place in a scale. But above all, every feeling has its place within a polar tension, obtaining its colour and significance not from itself alone, but also from the opposite pole: every feeling is conditioned by its opposite. Thus the absolute relation (which gathers up into reality all those that are relative, and is no more a part, as these are, but is the whole that completes and unifies them all), in being reduced to the status of an isolated and limited feeling, is made into a relative psychological matter.

If the soul is the starting-point of our consideration, complete relation can be understood only in a bipolar way, only as the *coincidentia oppositorum,* as the coincidence of oppositions of feeling. Of course, the one pole—suppressed by the person's basic religious attitude—often disappears from the reflective consciousness, and can only be recalled in the purest and most ingenuous consideration of the depths of the being.

Yes; in pure relation you have felt yourself to be simply dependent, as you are able to feel in no other relation—and simply free, too, as in no other time or place: you have felt yourself to be both creaturely and creative. You had the one feeling then no longer limited by the other, but you had both of them limitlessly and together.

You know always in your heart that you need God more than everything; but do you not know too that God needs you—in the fullness of His eternity needs you? How would man be, how would you be, if God did not need him, did not need you? You need God, in order to be—and God needs you, for the very meaning of your life. In instruction and in poems men are at pains to say more, and they say too much—what turgid and presumptuous talk that is about the "God who becomes"; but we know unshakably in our hearts that there is a becoming of the God that is. The world is not divine sport, it is divine destiny. There is divine meaning in the life of the world, of man, of human persons, of you and of me.

Creation happens to us, burns itself into us, recasts us in burning— we tremble and are faint, we submit. We take part in creation, meet the Creator, reach out to Him, helpers and companions.

Two great servants pace through the ages, prayer and sacrifice. The man who prays pours himself out in unrestrained dependence, and knows that he has—in an incomprehensible way—an effect upon God, even though he obtains nothing from God; for when he no longer desires anything for himself he sees the flame of his effect burning at its highest.—And the man who makes sacrifice?—I cannot despise him, this upright servant of former times, who believed that God yearned for the scent of his burnt-offering. In a foolish but powerful way he knew that we can and ought to give to God. This is known by him, too, who offers up his little will to God and meets Him in the grand will. "Thy will be done," he says, and says no more; but truth adds for him, "through me whom Thou needest."

What distinguishes sacrifice and prayer from all magic?—Magic desires to obtain its effects without entering into relation, and practises its tricks in the void. But sacrifice and prayer are set "before the Face," in the consummation of the holy primary word that means mutual action: they speak the *Thou,* and then they hear.

To wish to understand pure relation as dependence is to wish to empty one of the bearers of the relation, and hence the relation itself, of reality.

The world of *It* is set in the context of space and time.

The world of *Thou* is not set in the context of either of these.

Its context is in the Centre, where the extended lines of relations meet —in the eternal *Thou.*

In the great privilege of pure relation the privileges of the world of *It* are abolished. By virtue of this privilege there exists the unbroken world of *Thou:* the isolated moments of relations are bound up in a life of world solidarity. By virtue of this privilege formative power belongs to the world of *Thou:* spirit can penetrate and transform the world of *It.* By virtue of this privilege we are not given up to alienation from the world and the loss of reality by the *I*—to domination by the ghostly. Turning is the recognition of the Centre and the act of turning again to it. In this act of the being the buried relational power of man rises again, the wave that carries all the spheres of relation swells in living streams to give new life to our world.

Perhaps not to our world alone. For this double movement, of estrangement from the primal Source, in virtue of which the universe is sustained in the process of becoming, and of turning towards the primal Source, in virtue of which the universe is released in being, may be perceived as the metacosmical primal form that dwells in the world as a whole in its relation to that which is not the world—form whose twofold nature is represented among men by the twofold nature of their attitudes, their primary words, and their aspects of the world. Both parts of this movement develop, fraught with destiny, in time, and are compassed by grace in the timeless creation that is, incomprehensibly, at once emancipation and preservation, release and binding. Our knowledge of twofold nature is silent before the paradox of the primal mystery.

What is the eternal, primal phenomenon, present here and now, of that which we term revelation? It is the phenomenon that a man does not pass, from the moment of the supreme meeting, the same being as he entered into it. The moment of meeting is not an "experience" that stirs in the receptive soul and grows to perfect blessedness; rather, in that moment something happens to the man. At times it is like a light breath, at times like a wrestling-bout, but always—it *happens*. The man who emerges from the act of pure relation that so involves his being has now in his being something more that has grown in him, of which he did not know before and whose origin he is not rightly able to indicate. However the source of this new thing is classified in scientific orientation of the world, with its authorised efforts to establish an unbroken causality, we, whose concern is real consideration of the real, cannot have our purpose served with subconsciousness or any other apparatus of the soul. The reality is that we receive what we did not hitherto have, and receive it in such a way that we know it has been given to us. In the language of the Bible, "Those who wait upon the Lord shall renew their strength." In the language of Nietzsche, who in his account remains loyal to reality, "We take and do not ask who it is there that gives."

Man receives, and he receives not a specific "content" but a Presence, a Presence as power. This Presence and this power include three things, undivided, yet in such a way that we may consider them separately. First, there is the whole fullness of real mutual action, of the being raised and bound up in relation: the man can give no account at all of how the binding in relation is brought about, nor does it in any way lighten his life—it makes life heavier, but heavy with meaning. Secondly, there is the inexpressible confirmation of meaning. Meaning is assured. Nothing can any longer be meaningless. The question about the meaning of life is no longer there. But were it there, it would not have to be answered. You do not know how to exhibit and define the meaning of life, you have no formula or picture for it, and yet it has more certitude for you than the perceptions of your senses. What does the revealed and concealed meaning purpose with us, desire from us? It does not wish to be explained (nor are we able to do that) but only to be done by us. Thirdly, this meaning is not that of "another life," but that of this life of ours, not one of a world "yonder" but that of this world of ours, and it desires its confirmation in this life and in relation with this world. This meaning can be received, but not experienced; it cannot be experienced but it can be done, and this is its purpose with us. The assurance I have of it does not wish to be sealed within me, but it wishes to be born by me into the world. But just as the meaning itself does not permit itself to be transmitted and made into knowledge generally current and admissible, so confirmation of it cannot be transmitted as a valid Ought; it is not prescribed, it is not specified on any tablet, to be raised above all men's heads. The meaning that has been received can be proved true by each man only in the singleness of his being and the singleness of his life. As no prescription can lead us to the meeting, so none leads from it. As only acceptance of the Presence is necessary for the approach to the meeting, so in a new sense is it so when we emerge from it. As we reach the meeting with the simple *Thou* on our lips, so with the *Thou* on our lips we leave it and return to the world.

That before which, in which, out of which, and into which we live, even the mystery, has remained what it was. It has become present to us and in its presentness has proclaimed itself to us as salvation; we have "known" it, but we acquire no knowledge from it which might lessen or moderate its mysteriousness. We have come near to God, but not nearer to unveiling being or solving its riddle. We have felt release, but not discovered a "solution." We cannot approach others with what we have received, and say "You must know this, you must do this." We can only go, and confirm its truth. And this, too, is no "ought," but we can, we *must*.

This is the eternal revelation that is present here and now. I know of no revelation and believe in none whose primal phenomenon is not precisely this. I do not believe in a self-naming of God, a self-definition of God before men. The Word of revelation is *I am that I am*. That which reveals is that which reveals. That which is *is*, and nothing more. The eternal source of strength streams, the eternal contact persists, the eternal voice sounds forth, and nothing more.

QUESTIONS FOR DISCUSSION

1. How does Buber distinguish *It* from *Thou*? What is the bearing of this distinction on religion?
2. Buber says: "God cannot be inferred in anything—in nature, say, as its author, or in history as its master, or in the subject as the self that is thought in it . . . ; but God is the Being that is directly, most nearly, and lastingly, over against us, that may properly only be addressed, not expressed." Carefully examine the implications of these statements and their bearing on religion.
3. What is the nature of revelation for Buber, and what are its results?

Paul Tillich (1896-1965)

8.8 Symbols of Faith

THE MEANING OF SYMBOL

Man's ultimate concern must be expressed symbolically, because sybolic language alone is able to express the ultimate. This statement demands explanation in several respects. In spite of the manifold research about the meaning and function of symbols which is going on in contemporary philosophy, every writer who uses the term "symbol" must explain his understanding of it.

Symbols have one characteristic in common with signs; they point beyond themselves to something else. The red sign at the street corner points to the order to stop the movements of cars at certain intervals. A red light and the stopping of cars have essentially no relation to each other, but conventionally they are united as long as the convention lasts. The same is true of letters and numbers and partly even words. They point beyond themselves to sounds and meanings. They are given this special function by convention within a nation or by international conventions, as the mathematical signs.

Sometimes such signs are called symbols; but this is unfortunate because it makes the distinction between signs and symbols more difficult. Decisive is the fact that signs do not participate in the reality of that to which they point, while symbols do. Therefore, signs can be replaced for reasons of expediency or convention, while symbols cannot.

This leads to the second characteristic of the symbol: It participates in that to which it points: the flag participates in the power and dignity of the nation for which it stands. Therefore, it cannot be replaced except after an historic catastrophe that changes the reality of the nation which it symbolizes. An attack on the flag is felt as an attack on the majesty of the group in which it is acknowledged. Such an attack is considered blasphemy.

The third characteristic of a symbol is that it opens up levels of reality which otherwise are closed for us. All arts create symbols for a level of reality which cannot be reached in any other way. A picture and a poem reveal elements of reality which cannot be approached scientifically. In the creative work of art we encounter reality in a dimension which is closed for us without such works. The symbol's fourth characteristic not only opens up dimensions and elements of reality which otherwise would remain unapproachable but also unlocks dimensions and elements of our soul which correspond to the dimensions and elements of reality. A great play gives us not only a new vision of the human scene, but it opens up hidden depths of our own being. Thus we are able to receive what the play reveals to us in reality. There are within us dimensions of which we cannot become aware except through symbols, as melodies and rhythms in music.

Symbols cannot be produced intentionally—this is the fifth characteristic. They grow out of the individual or collective unconscious and cannot function without being accepted by the unconscious dimension of our being. Symbols which have an especially social function, as political and religious symbols, are created or at least accepted by the collective unconscious of the group in which they appear.

The sixth and last characteristic of the symbol is a consequence of the fact that symbols cannot be invented. Like living beings, they grow and they die. They grow when the situation is ripe for them, and they die when the situation changes. The symbol of the "king" grew in a special period of history, and it died in most parts of the world in our period. Symbols do not grow because people are longing for them, and they do not die because of scientific or practical criticism. They die because they can no longer produce response in the group where they originally found expression.

These are the main characteristics of every symbol. Genuine symbols are created in several spheres of man's cultural creativity. We have mentioned already the political and the artistic realm. We could add history and, above all, religion, whose symbols will be our particular concern.

RELIGIOUS SYMBOLS

We have discussed the meaning of symbols generally because, as we said, man's ultimate concern must be expressed symbolically! One may ask: Why can it not be expressed directly and properly? If money, success, or the nation is someone's ultimate concern, can this not be said in a direct way without symbolic language? Is it not only in those cases in which the content of the ultimate concern is called "God" that we are in the realm of symbols? The answer is that everything which is a matter of unconditional concern is made into a god. If the nation is someone's ultimate concern, the name of the nation becomes a sacred name and the nation receives divine qualities which far surpass the reality of the being and functioning of the nation. The nation then stands for and symbolizes the true ultimate, but in an idolatrous way. Success as ultimate concern is not the national desire of actualizing potentialities, but is readiness to sacrifice all other values of life for the sake of a position of power and social predominance. The anxiety about not being a success is an idolatrous form of the anxiety about divine condemnation. Success is grace; lack of success, ultimate judgment. In this way concepts designating ordinary realities become idolatrous symbols of ultimate concern.

The reason for this transformation of concepts into symbols is the character of ultimacy and the nature of faith. That which is the true ultimate transcends the realm of finite reality infinitely. Therefore, no finite reality can express it directly and properly. Religiously speaking, God transcends his own name. This is why the use of his name easily becomes an abuse or a blasphemy. Whatever we say about that which concerns us ultimately, whether or not we call it God, has a symbolic meaning. It points beyond itself while participating in that to which it points. In no other way can faith express itself adequately. The language of faith is the language of symbols. If faith were what we have shown that it is not, such an assertion could not be made. But faith, understood as the state of being ultimately concerned, has no language other than symbols. When saying this I always expect the question: Only a symbol? He who asks this question shows that he has not understood the difference between signs and symbols nor the power of symbolic language, which surpasses in quality and strength the power of any nonsymbolic language. One should never say "only a symbol," but one should say "not less than a symbol." With this in mind we can now describe the different kinds of symbols of faith.

The fundamental symbol of our ultimate concern is God. It is always present in any act of faith, even if the act of faith includes the denial of God. Where there is ultimate concern, God can be denied only in the name of God. One God can deny the

other one. Ultimate concern cannot deny its own character as ultimate. Therefore, it affirms what is meant by the word "God." Atheism, consequently, can only mean the attempt to remove any ultimate concern—to remain unconcerned about the meaning of one's existence. Indifference toward the ultimate question is the only imaginable form of atheism. Whether it is possible is a problem which must remain unsolved at this point. In any case, he who denies God as a matter of ultimate concern affirms God, because he affirms ultimacy in his concern. God is the fundamental symbol for what concerns us ultimately. Again it would be completely wrong to ask: So God is nothing but a symbol? Because the next question has to be: A symbol for what? And then the answer would be: For God! God is symbol for God. This means that in the notion of God we must distinguish two elements: the element of ultimacy, which is a matter of immediate experience and not symbolic in itself; and the element of concreteness, which is taken from our ordinary experience and symbolically applied to God. The man whose ultimate concern is a sacred tree has both the ultimacy of concern and the concreteness of the tree which symbolizes his relation to the ultimate. The man who adores Apollo is ultimately concerned, but not in an abstract way. His ultimate concern is symbolized in the divine figure of Apollo. The man who glorifies Jahweh, the God of the Old Testament, has both an ultimate concern and a concrete image of what concerns him ultimately. This is the meaning of the seemingly cryptic statement that God is the symbol of God. In this qualified sense God is the fundamental and universal content of faith.

It is obvious that such an understanding of the meaning of God makes the discussions about the existence or non-existence of God meaningless. It is meaningless to question the ultimacy of an ultimate concern. This element in the idea of God is in itself certain. The symbolic expression of this element varies endlessly through the whole history of mankind. Here again it would be meaningless to ask whether one or another of the figures in which an ultimate concern is symbolized does "exist." If "existence" refers to something which can be found within the whole of reality, no divine being exists. The question is not this, but: which of the innumerable symbols of faith is most adequate to the meaning of faith? In other words, which symbol of ultimacy expresses the ultimate without idolatrous elements? This is the problem, and not the so-called "existence of God"—which is in itself an impossible combination of words. God as the ultimate in man's ultimate concern is more certain than any other certainty, even that of one-self. God as symbolized in a divine figure is a matter of daring faith, of courage and risk.

God is the basic symbol of faith, but not the only one. All the qualities we attribute to him, power, love, justice, are taken from finite experiences and applied symbolically to that which is beyond finitude and infinity. If faith calls God "almighty," it uses the human experience of power in order to symbolize the content of its infinite concern, but it does not describe a highest being who can do as he pleases. So it is with all the other qualities and with all the actions, past, present, and future, which men attribute to God. They are symbols taken from our daily experience, and not information about what God did once upon a time or will do sometime in the future. Faith is not the belief in such stories, but it is the acceptance of symbols that express our ultimate concern in terms of divine actions.

Another group of symbols of faith are manifestations of the divine in things and events, in persons and communities, in words and documents. This whole realm of sacred objects is a treasure of symbols. Holy things are not holy in themselves, but they point beyond themselves to the source of all holiness, that which is of ultimate concern.

SYMBOLS AND MYTHS

The symbols of faith do not appear in isolation. They are united in "stories of the gods," which is the meaning of the Greek word "mythos"— myth. The gods are individualized figures, analogous to human personalities, sexually differentiated, descending from each other, related to each other in love and struggle, producing world and man, acting in time and space. They participate in human greatness and misery, in creative and destructive works. They give to man cultural and religious traditions, and defend these sacred rites. They help and threaten the human race, especially some families, tribes, or nations. They appear in epiphanies and incarnations, establish sacred places, rites, and persons, and thus create a cult. But they themselves are under the command and threat of a fate which is beyond everything that is. This is mythology as developed most impressively in ancient Greece. But many of these characteristics can be found in every mythology. Usually the mythological gods are not equals. There is a hierarchy, at the top of which is a ruling god, as in Greece; or a trinity of them, as in India; or a duality of them, as in Persia. There are savior-gods who mediate between the highest gods and man, sometimes sharing the suffering and death of man in spite of their essential immortality. This is the world of the myth, great and strange, always changing but fundamentally the same: man's ultimate concern symbolized in divine figures and actions. Myths are symbols of faith combined in stories about divine-human encounters.

Myths are always present in every act of faith, because the language of faith is the symbol. They are also attacked, criticized, and transcended in each of the great religions of mankind. The reason for this criticism is the very nature of the myth. It uses material from our ordinary experience. It puts the stories of the gods into the framework of time and space, although it belongs to the nature of the ultimate to be beyond time and space. Above all, it divides the divine into several figures, removing ultimacy from each of them without removing their claim to ultimacy. This inescapably leads to conflicts of ultimate claims, able to destroy life, society, and consciousness.

The criticism of the myth first rejects the division of the divine and goes beyond it to one God, although in different ways according to the different types of religion. Even one God is an object of mythological language, and if spoken about is drawn into the framework of time and space. Even He loses his ultimacy if made to be the content of concrete concern. Consequently, the criticism of the myth does not end with the rejection of the polytheistic mythology.

Monotheism also falls under the criticism of the myth. It needs, as one says today, "demythologization." This word has been used in connection with the elaboration of the mythical elements in stories and symbols of the Bible, both of the Old and the New Testaments—stories like those of the Paradise, of the fall of Adam, of the great Flood, of the Exodus from Egypt, of the virgin birth of the Messiah, of many of his miracles, of his resurrection and ascension, of his expected return as the judge of the universe. In short, all the stories in which divine-human interactions are told are considered as mythological in character, and objects of demythologization. What does this negative and artificial term mean? It must be accepted and supported if it points to the necessity of recognizing a symbol as a symbol and a myth as a myth. It must be attacked and rejected if it means the removal of symbols and myths altogether. Such an attempt is the third step in the criticism of the myth. It is an attempt which never can be successful, because symbol and myth are forms of the human consciousness which are always present. One can replace one myth by another, but one cannot remove the myth from man's spiritual life. For the myth is the combination of symbols of our ultimate concern.

A myth which is understood as a myth, but not removed or replaced, can be called a "broken myth." Christianity denies by its very nature any unbroken myth, because its presupposition is the first commandment: the affirmation of the ultimate as ultimate and the rejection of any kind of idolatry. All mythological elements in the Bible, and doctrine and liturgy should be recognized as mythological, but they should be maintained in their symbolic form and not be replaced by scientific substitutes. For there is no substitute for the use of symbols and myths: they are the language of faith.

The radical criticism of the myth is due to the fact that primitive mythological consciousness resists the attempt to interpret the myth of myth. It is afraid of every act of demythologization. It believes that the broken myth is deprived of its truth and of its convincing power. Those who live in an unbroken mythological world feel safe and certain. They resist, often fanatically, any attempt to introduce an element of uncertainty by "breaking the myth," namely, by making conscious its symbolic character. Such resistance is supported by authoritarian systems, religious or political, in order to give security to the people under their control and unchallenged power to those who exercise the control. The resistance against demythologization expresses itself in "literalism." The symbols and myths are understood in their immediate meaning. The material, taken from nature and history, is used in its proper sense. The character of the symbol to point beyond itself to something else is disregarded. Creation is taken as a magic act which happened once upon a time. The fall of Adam is localized on a special geographical point and attributed to a human individual. The virgin birth of the Messiah is understood in biological terms, resurrection and as-

cension as physical events, the second coming of the Christ as a telluric, or cosmic, catastrophe. The presupposition of such literalism is that God is a being, acting in time and space, dwelling in a special place, affecting the course of events and being affected by them like any other being in the universe. Literalism deprives God of his ultimacy and, religiously speaking, of his majesty. It draws him down to the level of that which is not ultimate, the finite and conditional. In the last analysis it is not rational criticism of the myth which is decisive but the inner religious criticism. Faith, if it takes its symbols literally, becomes idolatrous! It calls something ultimate which is less than ultimate. Faith, conscious of the symbolic character of its symbols, gives God the honor which is due him.

One should distinguish two stages of literalism, the natural and the reactive. The natural stage of literalism is that in which the mythical and the literal are indistinguishable. The primitive period of individuals and groups consists in the inability to separate the creations of symbolic imagination from the facts which can be verified through observation and experiment. This stage has a full right of its own and should not be disturbed, either in individuals or in groups, up to the moment when man's questioning mind breaks the natural acceptance of the mythological visions as literal. If, however, this moment has come, two ways are possible. The one is to replace the unbroken by the broken myth. It is the objectively demanded way, although it is impossible for many people who prefer the repression of their questions to the uncertainty which appears with the breaking of the myth.

They are forced into the second stage of literalism, the conscious one, which is aware of the questions but represses them, half consciously, half unconsciously. The tool of repression is usually an acknowledged authority with sacred qualities like the Church or the Bible, to which one owes unconditional surrender. This stage is still justifiable, if the questioning power is very weak and can easily be answered. It is unjustifiable, if a mature mind is broken in its personal center by political or psychological methods, split in his unity, and hurt in his integrity. The enemy of a critical theology is not natural literalism but conscious literalism with repression of and aggression toward autonomous thought.

Symbols of faith cannot be replaced by other symbols, such as artistic ones, and they cannot be removed by scientific criticism. They have a genuine standing in the human mind, just as science and art have. Their symbolic character is their truth and their power. Nothing less than symbols and myths can express our ultimate concern.

One more question arises, namely, whether myths are able to express every kind of ultimate concern. For example, Christian theologians argue that the word "myth" should be reserved for natural myths in which repetitive natural processes, such as the seasons, are understood in their ultimate meaning. They believe that if the world is seen as an historical process with beginning, end, and center, as in Christianity and Judaism, the term "myth" should not be used. This would radically reduce the realm in which the term would be applicable. Myth could not be understood as the language of our ultimate concern, but only as a discarded idiom of this language. Yet history proves that there are not only natural myths but also historical myths. If the earth is seen as the battleground of two divine powers, as in ancient Persia, this is an historical myth. If the God of creation selects and guides a nation through history toward an end which transcends all history, this is an historical myth. If the Christ—a transcendent, divine being—appears in the fullness of time, lives, dies, and is resurrected, this is an historical myth. Christianity is superior to those religions which are bound to a natural myth. But Christianity speaks the mythological language like every other religion. It is a broken myth, but it is a myth; otherwise Christianity would not be an expression of ultimate concern.

QUESTIONS FOR DISCUSSION

1. What are the characteristics of symbol as discussed by Tillich? Give examples.
2. Discuss in some detail Tillich's views on the nature of religious symbols and myths. Would a symbolic interpretation of religious beliefs strengthen or weaken those beliefs?
3. Analyze Tillich's statement: "Man's ultimate concern must be expressed symbolically, because symbolic language alone is able to express the ultimate."
4. What is the nature of Tillich's ultimate concern?

Douglas C. Macintosh (1877-1948)

8.9   Immortality

Moral optimism assumes man's right to an optimistic outlook on moral conditions. As a life-attitude it is moral and critical enough to recognize the unconditional imperative of the moral law, and at the same time normal and healthy-minded enough to rest assured that he whose life is consecrated to the moral ideal, to the discovery and performance of his duty, has a right to be nobly unconcerned as to what may happen to himself. What it logically involves is the faith that no absolute and final disaster can happen to man through purely external or physical events; that, even when outside forces have done their worst, no ultimate and irremediable evil, no final loss of spiritual values, can have befallen the will that was steadfastly devoted to the realization of the true ideal.

If we turn to human experience for confirmation of this conviction, we are confronted at once with the universal fact of physical death. Sooner or later each individual dies and disappears; only the race remains. Is this consistent with moral optimism? The ul-timate conservation of all absolute, that is, spiritual, values, in spite of physical death, is obviously involved in the morally optimistic faith upon which we have taken our stand; for only under such conditions could the moral will be justified in facing any possible physical event with equanimity.

But the adequate conservation of spiritual values necessarily involves the conservation of persons. If all genuine spiritual values are to be conserved without final loss, the death of the body cannot mean the end of personal existence. There are spiritual values, moral and social values particularly, but other values also, which are inseparably bound up with the existence of the individuals in and for whom they exist. Since the human individual is a free agent, as we have seen, he is able creatively to produce spiritual values. This means that, given ever new opportunity for activity, he would be of infinite value as a possible means of creating such values. In other words, by virtue of his moral personality, man is of potentially infinite value as a means. Thus we find reflective support for love's intuitive certainty of the infinite value of the individual as an end. There is a cynical proverb to the effect that love is blind,

Reprinted by permission of Charles Scribner's Sons from The Reasonableness of Christianity by Douglas Clyde Macintosh, pp. 64-73. © 1925 The Trustees of Lake Forest University; renewal © 1953.

and this may be true of some kinds of love. But all noble and true loves are glimpses into the infinite worth of the personal individual as such, and he who does not know from experience what true love is, is blind. Feeling has cognitive value, and, generally speaking, the true worth of personality is not discovered apart from love.

There is nothing more fundamental or essential in Christianity than this appreciation of the infinite value of the human individual, and it is in this essentially Christian insight that we find the true answer to latter-day speculations about a merely conditional immortality. Wherever a divine all-seeing love would find absolute values, actual or potential, there is something the conservation of which divine love imperatively demands. If personalities in whom such absolute values exist are allowed to sink into nothingness, then faith in the conservation of absolute values is mistaken, and moral optimism is an illusory dream.

We are aware that some high-minded persons would turn attention away from the individual to the race, urging that while the individual unit may cease to exist, the race will persist; that values produced by the individual will be conserved in the race. Now this is true enough of some of the spiritual values produced by the individual, but it is not true of all. In character and friendship are moral and social values which are inseparably bound up with the existence of the individual. Spiritual personality is of value as an end, and not merely as a means. We can view with composure the final disappearance of merely relative and instrumental values; but spiritual personality is of absolute value as an end. And spiritual

personality is always individual, even when it is also social. Wherefore the moral optimism which affirms the conservation of all spiritual values cannot be satisfied with the persistence of the race alone. Besides, in spite of the speculations of some thinkers, it remains doubtful whether without the immortality of the individual there can be any immortality for the race. If, then, at last upon the physically embodied race inhabiting this gradually cooling planet the "slow, sure doom" shall fall, without personal immortality all values of and for human personality, social as well as individual, will be as if they never had been, and moral optimism will have been all along a delusion and a lie.

Just what will be involved in the undiminished conservation of spiritual personality, with its absolute values, we may not be able to surmise, except in a general way. But there must of necessity be included not only continued existence of intelligence, with experience, selective memory, and thought, but moral activity with the development of character, and social relations, with the conservation of all true friendship and love. All this, with the vision beatific, moral optimism must postulate and the conservation of absolute values include. And with this, essential Christianity is in full accord. Apart from figurative and merely negative descriptions of the ideal future life, our Christian scriptures contain statements in terms of relationship to Christ which may be regarded as expressions of a more general truth. "To be with Christ"—this stands for ideal social relations. "We shall be like Him"—this means progressive realization of ideal character. "His servants shall serve Him"—this, taken with the words of the parable of judgment, "Inasmuch as ye have done it unto one of the least of these my brethren, ye have done it unto Me," can only mean ideal human activity along lines of social service. All of this is essentially Christian and all is logically involved in moral optimism, so that if the attitude we have so designated is reasonable and true, the same may be said of this vital and essentially Christian hope.

It will be seen that from the point of view of moral optimism the question as to whether the individual desires a future life is comparatively unimportant. Whether we desire immortality or not, the conservation of every person whose will is actually or even potentially moral is as imperative as the value of every such person is absolute. We may not want to live again; but as it is our duty to act morally whether we want to or not, so it is our duty to want to live again and to do in a future existence whatever good it may then be possible for us to accomplish. The desire to live forever is not a selfish or unworthy desire, if the extension of existence is not desired for unworthily selfish purposes. If to live is in itself better than not to live, to continue to live is similarly better than not to continue to live. It could never be right to refuse or not to desire further opportunity to develop and express the good will, and any adequate appreciation of the moral ideal with its categorical imperative must be accompanied by desire amounting to an absolute demand for opportunity progressively to realize that ideal.

We have seen that belief in human immortality is logically involved in moral optimism. We have also seen that moral optimism is normal and necessary for spiritual ends, so that, finding it theoretically permissible as far as we went into the matter, we have continued to regard it as a reasonable fundamental faith. With equal cogency we conclude that belief in immortality is reasonable also. But it is always true that the more general hypothesis is tested in the tests applied to the propositions logically deduced from it, and we may raise the further question whether belief in a future life, together with the moral optimism of which it is one expression, is still theoretically permissible when we come to look further into the facts of nature and human life. It is admitted that with the morally discerning and those who have known friendship dearer than life itself, the demand for immortality is too imperious for the hope to be given up for anything short of its refutation by indubitable facts of experience. But the question remains whether, in the light of modern science, such refutation may not be forthcoming.

It must be admitted that it is the opinion of some scientists that human consciousness depends upon the brain in such a way that without that organ the conscious existence of the individual would be impossible; but this is not the teaching of science itself. As William James, William McDougall, and other eminent psychologists have said, and as every psychologist who has not needlessly sold out to materialism knows, there are no known facts concerning the relation of consciousness to the brain which require us to believe that the physical organ is indispensably necessary for conscious survival. Consciousness is instrumental to the body, without doubt; but increasingly the inverse relationship tends to establish itself. More and more as development proceeds in the individual and in the race, brain and body come to be instrumental to mind, whose interests reach out far beyond the bodily organism and its physical environment. It is not necessarily an unreasonable interpretation of the facts, therefore, when mind is regarded as destined for a position of ultimate independence with reference to the present physical body. That normal faith of the healthy mind and moral will which we have called moral optimism, leading necessarily, as it does, to belief in human immortality, cannot be dismissed as forbidden by the facts. We who are still in the body have not yet verified the future life directly. The time for that will come when this earthly physical life is over. Whether we shall ever in this life verify the other life indirectly, through completely demonstrated communication from the departed, may well be doubted. When fraud, hallucination, and mere chance coincidence have been eliminated from the phenomena to which spiritists appeal, it seems always possible to regard the facts as due to subconscious activities of the medium and others present, and to telepathy between living persons. However, it may be remarked in passing that if mind in its relation to body is independent enough to make telepathy under certain conditions a fact, it seems not unreasonable to think that mind may be independent enough to continue to exist and act when set free from the body at death.

A more assured argument for the possibility of immortality is found in the fact of human freedom, already sufficiently established as morally certain. Human freedom being granted in the sense in which we have defined the term, it follows that mind or the self acts in an originative manner in and through the brain; and if the mind is independent enough to act thus creatively in and through the brain, it may conceivably be independent enough to act independently of this particular organism altogether. If mind is an agent and not a mere phenomenon, it may conceivably find or be furnished with another instrument when the one it is now using becomes no longer serviceable. In spite, then, of anything the pessimistic or doubting critic can show by appeal to reason or experience, belief in the undiminished survival of human personality is theoretically permissible and, in view of its foundation in moral optimism, presumably true. Considering, then, the central place the belief occupies in the Christian religious faith, we are in a position to claim, at this point also, further confirmation of essential Christianity as reasonable and so presumably true.

Before leaving the subject, however, one very important thing remains to be said. If we ask the secret of the persistence of belief in immortality in the absence of any absolute empirical demonstration of the truth of the doctrine, the answer is that, after an appreciation of the worth of human personality, the chief factor in the belief has been the idea of God, that is, of a Power great enough and good enough to conserve the human individual in spite of bodily death. If we can be adequately assured, through experience or argument, of the existence of such a Being, we can at the same time be reassured of the truth of immortality. If we can be assured that the Su-

preme Being in the universe loves man with an everlasting love, we can be assured that man is intended for everlasting life.

QUESTIONS FOR DISCUSSION

1. Discuss Macintosh's arguments in favor of immortality. In your discussion state clearly his basic premises and his theory of evidence for his belief in immortality.
2. The opinion of some scientists is that "human consciousness depends upon the brain in such a way that without that organ the conscious existence of the individual would be impossible." What is the alleged evidence in favor of or against this view? What is your view on this issue?
3. Is belief in immortality a necessary postulate for morality? Discuss the alternative view on this issue.

FURTHER READINGS FOR CHAPTER 8

Alexander, Samuel, *Space, Time and Deity,* vol. II. New York: Macmillan, 1920.

*Bergson, Henri, *Two Sources of Morality and Religion.* New York: Doubleday, 1954.

*Berkeley, George, *Three Dialogues Between Hylas and Philonous.* Indianapolis: Bobbs-Merrill, 1954.

Bronstein, Daniel J., and Harold Schulweis, eds., *Approaches to the Philosophy of Religion.* Englewood Cliffs, N.J.: Prentice-Hall, 1954.

*Durkheim, Emil, *The Elementary Forms of Religious Life,* Joseph W. Swain, trans. New York: Collier Books, n.d.

Foster, G. B., *The Function of Religion in Man's Struggle for Existence.* Chicago: University of Chicago Press, n.d.

*Frazer, J. G., *New Golden Bough,* Theodore H. Gaster, ed. New York: Doubleday, n.d.

*Freud, Sigmund, *The Future of an Illusion.* New York: Doubleday, 1957.

*Fromm, Erich, *Psychoanalysis and Religion.* New Haven: Yale University Press, 1959.

Hegel, Georg W. F., *Lectures on the Philosophy of Religion,* 3 vols., New York: Humanities Press, n.d.

Hocking, William E., *The Meaning of Immortality in Human Experience.* New York: Harper & Row, 1957.

*James, William, *Varieties of Religious Experience.* (Numerous editions available.)

---

* Paperback edition.

*Kant, Immanuel, *Religion Within the Limits of Reason Alone*. New York: Harper & Row, 1960.

*Kierkegaard, Soren, *The Journals of Kierkegaard, Alexander Dru,* ed. New York: Harper & Row, 1959.

Leuba, James H., *The Psychological Nature and Origin of Religion*. LaSalle, Ill.: Open Court, 1910.

Macintosh, Douglas C., *The Problem of Religious Knowledge*. New York: Harper & Row, 1940.

McTaggart, J. M. E., *Some Dogmas of Religion*. New York: McKay, 1930.

*Malinowski, Bronislaw, *Magic, Science and Religion*. New York: Doubleday, 1954.

*Mill, John Stuart, *The Nature and Utility of Religion*. Indianapolis: Bobbs-Merrill, 1958.

Montague, William P., *Belief Unbound*. New Haven: Yale University Press, 1930.

Pfeffer, Leo, *Church, State and Freedom*. Boston: Beacon Press, 1953.

*Plato, *Euthyphro*, F. J. Church and R. Cumming, trans. Indianapolis: Bobbs-Merrill, 1948.

Taylor, Alfred E., *Faith of a Moralist*. New York: Macmillan, 1930.

*Tillich, Paul, *The Religious Situation*. Cleveland: World Publishing, n.d.

Chapter 9

THEORIES OF REALITY

INTRODUCTION

We all observe many facts and go through many experiences, yet somehow we are not fully satisfied with isolated, piecemeal facts and experiences; we wish to tie them together and thus arrive at some sense of them as a whole. We make a big chart of life and existence not unlike an artist's outline sketch. We call the world good or bad, designful or chaotic, mental or material. Most of these charts or world-views, sometimes referred to as theories of reality or metaphysical systems, are mythical, fantastic, and intellectually irresponsible. Too often they are intense expressions of what we wish the world to be rather than interpretations of what the world really is. Still what we are all genuinely seeking is a critical, inclusive, and coherent perspective of the nature of things.

Metaphysics

Traditionally the pursuit of a comprehensive view of existence has been called *metaphysics*. The word literally means *after physics* and derives from the fact that Aristotle's writings on what he called "First Philosophy" (in which he considered the generic traits of existence), were located after his "Physics" treatise in early editions of Aristotle's works. Probably Aristotle never heard the term *metaphysics,* which was associated with his name for centuries and has acquired a variety of meanings. Sometimes it has stood for the study of some hidden reality beyond all possible experience, and therefore not empirically verifiable; sometimes it has stood for knowledge of the first causes of what is given in sensible experience; sometimes it has stood for the search for the "Real" or the "Whole"; and sometimes it has stood for the inquiry into the generic traits of existence as such.

Without getting involved in the disputes over the term, we can focus on the core that is common to all interpretations. All metaphysical pursuits seek to arrive at a generalized understanding of existence through which to chart a synthetic map of existence.

Historically, as mentioned earlier, there have been various formulations of the notion of metaphysics. For Aristotle metaphysics is a certain body of knowledge that examines being or existence as existence and "whatever belongs to existence merely because it is existence." In this interpretation, existence does not mean something other than particular existence, such as mountains, rivers, plants, animals, human beings, or stars. One need not turn from concrete objects to know what existence is. As S. P. Lamprecht points out in his interpretation of Aristotle's metaphysics, "Existence in general is the nature that the many, many concrete existences have in common. And it is the common nature of these many concrete existences with which the metaphysician is concerned." [1] As the physicist or the biologist generalizes about physical entities or living beings, so the metaphysician generalizes about the common nature of existence.

Metaphysics in a meaningful sense is the "first science." Not chronologically, for many sciences, like physics, astronomy, and biology, developed earlier. Metaphysics is logically prior to other sciences in the sense that its general propositions apply to all existences. A good illustration of Aristotle's notion of metaphysics as the study of the generic traits of existence is his discussion of actuality and potentiality (see selection 9.1). These categories are applicable not only to a few particular existences but to all empirically known existences.

Metaphysical pursuit has not remained within Aristotle's sober confines but has made many speculative ventures. Especially in the middle of the nineteenth century many idealistic systems claimed to have found the key to a complete and final comprehension of reality. Realism and pragmatism and later the analytic school and logical positivism challenged the supremacy of these claims.

The criticism of metaphysics was not something new—Kant and before him Hume had raised challenging questions. But recent attacks have become more widespread and persistent, the most violent and uncompromising being those of the logical positivists represented by A. J. Ayer.

Meaningful propositions, according to Ayer, are either analytic or empirical. A proposition is analytic when its truth depends on the definition of its symbols. "Either it is true or it is not true" and "All oculists are eye doctors" are true statements independent of experience, for their truth depends on the definition of their symbols. A proposition is empirical, according to Ayer, when its validity is "determined by the fact of experience"; it is verifiable. Every "empirical hypothesis must be relevant to some actual or possible

---

[1] Sterling P. Lamprecht, *The Metaphysics of Naturalism* (New York: Appleton-Century-Crofts, 1967), p. 6.

experience." Therefore a statement which is not relevant to any experience cannot be an empirical hypothesis.

Metaphysical propositions are neither analytic nor empirical; they are meaningless in the sense that they are neither tautologies like the propositions of mathematics or logic nor factual in content. Since they assert something about the nature of reality that transcends all possible sense experience, they cannot in principle be verified.[2]

H. H. Price finds value in the analytic school, but he thinks there is a place for metaphysics (see selection 9.2). The metaphysician should give us a unified reasoned outlook on the world. He need not give us new knowledge about matters of fact; his task is "to devise a conceptual scheme which brings out certain systematic relationships between the matters of fact we know already." The philosopher's job is to make things comprehensible, not to establish what things are. In short, there is synoptic clarity as well as analytic clarity.

Before studying the great historic metaphysical systems, your reading of William James's discussion of "The One and the Many" (selection 9.3) should give you a full sense of Price's idea of metaphysics as a conceptual synthesis. Should one comprehend the known facts as a single unified reality in the Absolute or as a more-or-less disjointed plurality?

Monistic philosophies have emphasized the relation of logical implications or the notion of a universal mind as an argument for organic unity. For a thoroughgoing empiricist the world is a mixture of oneness and multiplicity, relevance and irrelevance, conjunction and disjunction. As James says, " 'The world is One,' therefore, just so far as we experience it to be concatenated, One by as many definite conjunctions as appear. But then also *not* One by just as many definite dis-junctions as we find. The oneness and the manyness of it thus obtain in respects which can be separately named. It is neither a universe pure and simple nor a multiverse pure and simple."

Now that you have some idea of the metaphysical pursuit, you can proceed with the philosophic world-views of idealism, naturalism, process-philosophy, and existentialism. Although these philosophies are not the only possible ones, they are among the dominant theories.

Idealism

The idealist's central belief is that reality is of the nature of mind. Since mind has a number of aspects—perceiving, reasoning, and willing, idealists differ as to which of these aspects is the prime reality. Reality is for some a system of perceptions; for others, a coherent system of thought; and for still others, a form of will. There are also idealists who try to synthesize all

---

[2] For a full discussion, see A. J. Ayer, *Language, Truth and Logic* (New York: Dover Publications, Inc., 1952), pp. 33-45.

the aspects of mind into a system. The idealistic view might have been appropriately called Mentalism or Spiritualism, in the sense that the ultimate reality is said to be Mind or Spirit. Yet the name "idealism" has its own peculiar implications, for most idealists feel that ideals find a firmer footing in a universe that is basically mind rather than matter.

Idealism has a long history. Only a few of the landmarks will be mentioned. Long before its development in the West, idealism was the core of Vedantism and Brahmanism in India, and of certain Buddhistic sects in China. In the West, Plato was the first great idealist, though there was always a strong dualistic strain in his philosophy. Plato's idealism is not primarily mentalistic but logical. For him the real things are Ideas, but he meant by Ideas not mental states or images but objective forms, eternal essences, prototypes. For the development of mentalistic idealism one must go to Berkeley, who is often regarded as the true founder of modern idealism. His theory that the essence of objects depends upon perception has been the cornerstone of most idealistic arguments. Kant, though not an idealist in the strict sense of the word since he did not reduce the whole of reality to mind, made possible the development of absolute idealism through his doctrine that knowledge is in large part determined by the formal activity of the mind. Hegel is the outstanding figure in the development of post-Kantian idealism. For him reality is rational throughout, and the rational is real. The world, you might say, is a great thought-process, and to know the laws of thought you must know the laws of reality. Idealism spread to other countries, especially in the Hegelian form. In England, Green, Bradley, and Bosanquet were idealists; in Italy, Croce and Gentile; and in America, Royce and Howison.

As has just been indicated, idealism takes many forms. For metaphysical analysis, pluralistic idealism and monistic idealism are of special importance. Pluralistic idealism pictures the universe as a society of spirits. Although there may be a hierarchy of spirits culminating in a supreme Mind, individuality is never lost. God himself as a member of this society is limited in power. Pluralistic idealists, on the whole, emphasize the values of the personal life, such as freedom, individuality, change, reality of time. On the other hand, monistic idealists would unify reality in one supreme Mind or Self; they emphasize the dynamic relations and interactions that exist among different phases of reality. Monistic idealism tends to be eternalistic, deterministic, and optimistic. There have been many attempts to synthesize these polar extremes of idealism.

The first impression of idealism may be puzzling. It is not obvious that reality is a society of minds or a universal Mind. Surely common sense does not favor this philosophy. What, then, is the reasoning out of which the idealistic world-view takes its rise? The present discussion will be limited to some of Royce's arguments for idealism, since he is not only the most brilliant idealist this country has produced but also important because of his rich synthesis of the pluralistic and monistic forms of idealism. For Royce reality is a supreme Mind. This Mind he calls Self, God, Absolute, Logos. But in Royce's Absolute, individuals are not swallowed up; they are unique and indispensable parts of the whole. In such a universe nothing is dead. Nature as a whole and in its specific parts is conscious. As Royce puts it, "My hypothesis is that in case of Nature in general, as in the case of the particular portions of Nature known as our fellow men, we are dealing with phenomenal signs of a vast conscious process."

One argument that Royce offers for his idealism is based on the distinction he makes between the World of Description and the World of Appreciation. According to him, the World of Description, which is the world of science, deals "with a realm of abstraction—everywhere founded upon final truth although in itself not final." It is very much like describing a friend as a congeries of physical qualities, that is, by omitting what counts most—his character or his lovableness. Description emphasizes only quantitative relations and uniform laws. To understand reality fully you must go beyond and behind the World of Description. It is only through inner appreciation that we discover the irreplaceability of the one we love, the unity of our own selves, the social interdependence of individuals, and the organic inclusiveness of the Absolute.

Another of Royce's arguments in support of his idealism is the claim that mind is primary in the knowing process. This type of argument is fundamental for most idealists. Royce's formulation of it consists of two parts. Like Berkeley, he argues first that external objects depend on mind for their existence. No object can have meaning apart from the knower. This being so, the inference is drawn that objects cannot exist apart from the mind; that is, they are only ideas. What do we mean, Royce asks, by the shape of anything or by the size of anything? What is the meaning of any property that we give to the outer world? All these, he maintains, can be expressed only in terms of one's ideas. What, for instance, are trees or mountains but sensations of mind, and again, what are sound waves or ether waves but conceptions of the mind to explain the facts of nature? But the argument thus far merely attempts to establish the claim that external objects depend for their existence on mind; the reality of the Supreme Mind has not yet been proved. To prove this we must pass to the second part of Royce's argument. Our knowledge, he maintains, always looks beyond the immediate present. How do we recognize the objects in our environment if not by combining our perception of them with memories of them as perceived in the past? How do we recall a forgotten name if not by appealing to our larger self of memory that knows that name? In knowledge, Royce argues, we must always draw more on a larger self than on the immediate one. Again, how do we settle our arguments? There must be some common framework for arriving at the truth.

To escape conflict of aims or the relativity of human ideas, we must assume a self-consistent system of ideas; and this system is, for Royce, our deeper Self or the Absolute.

Royce's arguments raise many fundamental issues. As his argument maintains, science does possess abstraction and ideal construction. But do these involve neglect of facts? And, again, as his second argument points out, the known object as an object of knowledge is always related to mind. (This is sometimes called "the egocentric predicament.") But does this fact prove that the known object has no independent existence? These problems have been given a great deal of attention in modern philosophy, but no unanimous solution has as yet been reached.

Naturalism

According to this theory, nature is the whole of reality; that is, there is no other realm of reality beyond or behind nature; there is no supernatural. For the naturalist nature is all-inclusive; everything has its origin and career in nature. But what is this all-inclusive nature and how should you approach it to find its secret? A poet may find beauty in nature, a mystic an inner spirit, a practical man useful power; but the naturalist, though he does not deny the significance or value of these approaches to nature, insists that in order to know nature you must resort to the scientific method. Wherever knowledge is possible the naturalist is committed to the application of the scientific method. He claims that every area of nature—physical, biological, psychological, or social—must be approached by this method. This does not mean that the same specialized technique and instruments must be used in every area, but that the same general canons should be used to test the truth of every claim. Thus, for the naturalist, nature is what science says it is or, more precisely, what completed science will say it is.

Like other great metaphysical systems, naturalism has had a long history. In Western thought the Greek atomists Leucippus and Democritus were the first materialists.[3] According to them the world was composed of atoms that combined and recombined by necessity. The first modern materialist of note was Thomas Hobbes, who sought to reduce all events, including thought, to matter in motion. Before the French Revolution, materialism was vigorously advocated by Diderot, La Mettrie, Holbach, and others. But the great era of naturalism was the nineteenth century. The extensive developments in mathematics, physics, biology, psychology, sociology, and particularly Darwin's theory of evolution, gave a wide vogue to naturalism. Spencer tried to generalize the idea of evolution into a formula for the whole universe. Karl Marx, at one time an admirer of Hegel, turned Hegel's philosophy of history upside down by giving the chief role not to spirit but to material

---

[3] Historically, the terms naturalism and materialism have often been interchanged.

and economic conditions. Contemporary naturalism is more complex and varied than that of the nineteenth century. Among the leading contemporary naturalists are Dewey, Santayana, Alexander, and Russell.

There are different types of naturalists. Of these we shall examine the reductive and nonreductive types.

The reductive naturalist is one who thinks that everything in nature, living as well as nonliving, mental as well as nonmental, must be explained in the most basic, elementary physical terms. Traditionally, this ideal was to explain everything in terms of matter in motion or in terms of the laws of mechanics. In current thought, reductive naturalism, which is sometimes called mechanism, has a looser meaning. The reductive naturalist usually tries to explain biological, psychological, and sociological phenomena in "nothing but" physico-chemical terms—such as motion, electric charge, oxidation, and so on. From this point of view, such things as adaptation, thinking, loving, or the social will, have the same status as physico-chemical entities and processes. Sometimes materialists like Democritus, Hobbes, and certain extreme contemporary behaviorists are supposed to hold this view. In any case, those who uphold reductive naturalism are compelled to draw a distinction between appearance and reality, between illusion and true judgment. According to them all so-called biological or psychological occurrences should be regarded as mere appearance, since only physico-chemical occurrences can be granted the status of the real. But because life, mind, and society are conditioned by the physico-chemical medium, it does not necessarily follow that they can be wholly defined in terms of the concepts of this medium. The issue is an empirical one, and empirically, different modes of action are being observed—the physical, the biological, the psychological, and the social.

What might be called nonreductive naturalism differs from the reductive type by not reducing everything to physico-chemical terms. Alexander's philosophy is an example of this type, since Alexander not only states with clearness the major principles common to the nonreductive naturalists but also offers some original speculations of his own, which, though perhaps of doubtful validity, yield new perspectives.[4] As in the case of all other major metaphysical views, no one philosopher should be regarded as the definitive representative of naturalism. Though the exponents of any one type of philosophy hold certain major principles in common, there are always differences in emphasis, terminology, or speculation.

The crucial idea in Alexander's naturalistic metaphysics is emergence. The best way to understand this idea of emergence is to compare it with the central claim of reductive naturalism. Alexander, as an emergenist, agrees

---

[4] Samuel Alexander, *Space, Time, and Deity* (1920), Vols. I and II.

with the reductionists that living and mental beings are compounded of physico-chemical elements and that there is no vitalistic entity, such as *élan vital*. He also agrees with the reductionists that no biological or psychological phenomenon, such as adaptation, thinking, or willing, would be possible without physical conditions. But he disagrees with the reductionists' claim that these phenomena are "nothing but" or that their meaning can be wholly expressed in physico-chemical terms. He believes, on the contrary, that when certain elements are organized in a certain way, new distinctive qualities emerge that are not identifiable with the properties of the elements in their isolation. According to him, one should distinguish between the discrete properties of an object and its organizational properties. An object, for example, may exhibit no curvature when one examines it discretely, that is, point for point, yet it may exhibit the quality of curvature when examined organizationally. The same principle applies when defining a molecule, a cell, or a living organism. It is experience that must show what organizations should be described in terms of new distinctive qualities that result from the organization of their parts. Alexander also insists that "higher" levels of emergence could not have been predicted from a knowledge of the "lower" levels. For instance, antecedent to the emergence of life one could not have predicted the nature of life from a knowledge of atoms and molecules. Emergences are, for Alexander, new facts.

Moreover, according to him, there are different levels of emergence. Most emergent evolutionists agree that there are three levels of natural existence—matter, life, and mind. Alexander is more speculative on this point. For him the basic level of existence is space-time. This is the primal stuff of which all things consist. The next level is matter with its primary qualities—size, shape, motion. At still another level secondary qualities emerge, such as color and sound. These qualities have, for Alexander, a reality apart from our minds. Though they do not inhere in objects, as the primary qualities do, they belong to objects in relation to their surroundings—in relation to light in the case of color, in relation to air in the case of sound. Life comes at a still higher level. Life possesses certain unique qualities found only in the organism. Living organisms do not possess a new entity, but they are matter organized in a distinctive way. Yet living organisms have new emergent qualities. These are primarily the organic and kinesthetic senses: the motion of muscles and the sensations of hunger and thirst—qualities quite distinct from colors and sounds, since they inhere in organic bodies. The next higher level of emergence is mind. Yet mind is firmly embedded in nature and emerges only when certain physiological conditions concur. Mind has two main functions, contemplation and enjoyment. We contemplate objects about us as mere things external to us and to one another. We contemplate our bodies when we look at our hands and feet. But when we play a game we enjoy as well as contemplate our playing. Alexander's term *enjoyment* includes not only joy but also grief and, indeed, every experience of the inner life.

Is there any higher level of emergence than mind? Most naturalists would stop at mind; but Alexander believes that the universe is pressing forward toward still higher levels of emergence. He often uses the term *Deity* for the level above mind. His Deity does not belong to the past but to the future, as something not yet actual. And Alexander does not think of Deity in the singular. Should this higher level come into existence, there would be many individuals on this level to which the term would apply.

Alexander's naturalism is impressive and has many merits, although some of his ideas are highly speculative. Many find it hard to accept his claim that the basic stuff of existence is space-time. And many can find no evidence for his exciting idea that the universe is pressing forward to create a higher level of existence.

Sterling P. Lamprecht's discussion of naturalism (selection 9.5) is enlightening but free of speculative theories. He rejects supernaturalism and idealism of all sorts, and he is neither reductive as traditional materialists tend to be nor highly speculative as Alexander is. For him naturalism means deeper kinship with nature, with her "vast embracing forces and events from which come, surprisingly, all sorts of things, so that we meet new glories and fresh disasters at each precarious moment of our lives." This complex is our alma mater. It nourishes and fosters us, but it "also threatens and eventually destroys us."

Process-Philosophy

Whitehead's metaphysics is one of the most daring and magnificent philosophical creations of our time. As against the abstractions of nineteenth-century scientific materialism, he emphasizes concreteness and fidelity to experience. As against the irresponsible speculation of romanticists, he insists on the necessity of incorporating into one's philosophy matters of fact and the most exacting recent theories of science. As against many thin current philosophies, he richly weaves together varied aspects of experience: change with permanence, causality with teleology, science with religion, modern hopes with traditional values.

The key in Whitehead's interpretation of reality is process, and the title of his major work, *Process and Reality*, reminds us of this fact (see selection 9.6). The notion of process was eloquently expressed in early Greek philosophy by Heraclitus: "You cannot step twice into the same river; for fresh waters are ever flowing in upon us." In modern philosophy Bergson, James, Dewey, and Alexander have again made change or flux the central concept of philosophy. The transitoriness of everyday events, the principle of evolution, and the recent theories of matter, all favor such a view.

Whitehead's notion of process is rich and many-sided. First, process is a universal happening in the spatio-temporal world. Every point in nature is in the throes of change—some swifter, others slower. There are no permanent substances, no immutable material particles, no self-sufficient realities. In Whitehead's view, "becoming" attains greater importance metaphysically than "being." As he expresses it, "The world is always becoming, and as it becomes it passes away and perishes." Second, world process or becoming is not sheer flux, formless continuity, but is atomized, individualized into units of process. Passing events initiate new processes. The creative activity of emerging events brings together various elements of the prior events to form new syntheses that are characterized by new qualities and activities. In time these new syntheses disintegrate and become material for future events. This pattern of world-process is endless. Whitehead calls the units of process "actual entities." These are the ultimate facts of reality; there is no going behind them to anything more real. These units are not observable objects like stones, trees, or human beings; they are too microscopic and transitory. They are like a vibration or pulse; yet every object is nothing more than a complex grouping of these processes. Finally, a given process, and this is the most controversial aspect of Whitehead's suggestion, is not merely a physical event but rather a center or pulse of experience. Individualized processes are, if you like, miniatures of human experience. They have feelings and are guided by aims. Even atoms and molecules, for Whitehead, are composed of processes that possess inner experience. Thus nature is alive at every point. This does not mean that every process has "conscious" experience, but it does mean that all processes have experience in the widest sense of the term. Whitehead's metaphysics becomes essentially a type of panpsychism.

In the turmoil of the changing world there is still, for Whitehead, something permanent. All passing and perishing events exhibit certain qualities that are not exposed to the ravages of time. Fallen leaves that are carried away by the winds, joyous moods that are changed by succeeding events, have eternal characteristics. The same shade of green or the same oval contour observed in one of the drifting leaves may recur in the future; the same joyous mood may recur. Qualities like greenness, ovalness, or joyfulness, usually designated as "universals," Whitehead calls "eternal objects." Eternal objects, for him, do not emerge from nature to perish like other events—they invade nature, or *ingress* (to use his term) into the events of nature.

Whitehead's thought here, with some modifications, is similar to Plato's. Plato, in his attempt to reconcile the conflict between the changing and the changeless, the temporal and the eternal, had suggested the theory of Ideas or Forms. What one perceives, he claimed, are imperfect, perishing copies of immutable, eternal models. All straight lines, for example, as perceived by the senses are only crude repetitions of an ideal straight line. Similarly,

Whitehead's eternal objects are immutable. They are not confined to the spatio-temporal world, yet they may be exemplified in the transitory events of this world. But Whitehead's eternal objects, unlike Plato's Ideas, are not superior realities; they are, rather, possibilities of realization.

One further question: How does one explain the fact that eternal objects as possibilities are actualized in the world in a rational, orderly way? The world exhibits a rational order, yet it might have been a chaos. Events occur as if prescribed by certain standards, yet they might have been altogether capricious. Whitehead thinks reality must contain some principle of limitation or selection to make this orderliness possible. This principle of limitation or rationality he calls "God." To the question: "Why should there be this principle of rationality, this God?" no answer can be given, since God as the principle of rationality is the ground for the presence of everything. Not even God can account for His presence.

Yet Whitehead's God is not merely a metaphysical principle but an object to satisfy religious aspiration. His God is persuasive rather than coercive; not omnipotent, but a "fellow-sufferer who understands." He is "wisdom." He is the poet of the world "with tender patience leading it by his vision of truth, beauty and goodness."

Although Whitehead's metaphysics has scope, depth, and coherence, it has certain serious deficiencies. Scrupulously empirical whenever the matter under discussion permits, in attempting to fill the gaps in our knowledge Whitehead suggests ideas that are basically not verifiable. In this respect he partly revives the classic role of philosophy as something having access to knowledge that is not open to the uninitiated. But this role seems doubtful to many. Whitehead rightly points out that a true metaphysics must do justice to all phases of experience and that one's final interpretation of reality must escape the abstractions of the specific sciences; yet to achieve such an all-embracing philosophy it should not be necessary to go beyond natural, experimental knowledge. What we need is a more empirical metaphysics than Whitehead has offered.

Similarly unwarranted is his claim that reality must contain a principle of limitation, called God by him, as a ground for the actualization of possibilities. Unless you adhere to Whitehead's theories of eternal objects and actual entities, which are highly controversial, there is no need of going outside of nature to make sense of natural happenings. It is true that Whitehead's metaphysical God is free from most of the obscurities of the traditional gods. But this postulate gets you involved in the same difficulties as those that characterize every nonempirical philosophy.

Whitehead's metaphysics is an impressive alternative to naturalistic philosophy. To some, his philosophy may be a source for retaining beliefs that have been deeply disturbed by science; to others, his occasional flights beyond the natural world are untenable. Yet even the latter need not deprive themselves of Whitehead's rich and generous insights.

Existentialism

Existentialism is a very recent metaphysical system. At present it exerts considerable influence, primarily in religious and literary circles. Sören Kierkegaard (1813-1855) is considered its originator, though some of its basic ideas go back to Scholastic philosophy, to Fichte, and especially to Schopenhauer and Nietzsche. Contemporary existentialists belong to one of two camps: the theistic existentialists, such as Gabriel Marcel in France and Reinhold Niebuhr, Richard Kroner, and Paul Tillich in North America; and the atheistic existentialists, such as Martin Heidegger in Germany and Jean-Paul Sartre in France. Karl Jaspers, another major representative of existentialism, seems to occupy a middle position between the two camps. Existentialists as a group adhere to a common philosophic claim, though there are important differences among them. Sartre's discussion (selection 9.7) presents some of the major tenets of the existentialists, primarily of the atheistic type.

The primary doctrine of the existentialists, on which all seem to agree, is that existence is prior to essence. As Sartre expresses it: "What they (existentialists) have in common is that they think that existence precedes essence, or, if you prefer, that subjectivity must be the starting point." What does this obscure saying mean? In reading existentialist literature you have to be prepared for a pervasive fogginess. As antirationalists they are not primarily concerned with rational categories. Yet the attempt will be made to apply such categories.

In order to understand the doctrine that existence precedes essence, you must bear in mind that for most existentialists, the term *existence* is not used in its widest sense but refers to the existence of *man*. Existentialism is primarily a philosophy of man as a struggling and hopeful being. Sartre argues, clearly and eloquently, that man's fate or reality is not determined by a prior superimposed essence or universal plan, as most dogmatic religions and metaphysical systems maintain. But rather, man's fate is determined by his free decisions and actions. The chisel that carves essences into existence is man's free choice between alternative actions. And Sartre assumes absolute freedom for such actions.

Existentialism is thus a philosophy of crisis rather than a philosophy of pure contemplation. The existentialists assert that in life you must either take the reins or be destroyed. As Kierkegaard says: "*Both-And* is the road to hell," but "*Either-Or* is the key to heaven."

A second doctrine of the existentialists is that, as man must make choices and act, he is inevitably involved in anguish, forlornness, and despair. These and similar words, like terror, violence, death, and nothingness are favorites with the existentialists. Anguish, as Sartre describes it, is due to our feeling of responsibility in action, especially toward others; forlornness results from our knowledge that we live in a purposeless world in which all things perish, including oneself; despair comes from the realization that ultimately all events are contingent, that there are no certainties.

Finally, despite the fact that Sartre depicts a purposeless, precarious world, he is not a quietistic, pessimistic philosopher. Anguish, forlornness, and despair are spurs to heroic action and creative enterprise. As he says: "Being condemned in such a purposeless world, we must create (our values)."

Sartre has important philosophic insights, such as that reality has extra-rational (though not necessarily contrarational) aspects; that human beings have freedom; that our decisions shape our destiny. Yet one has to raise many questions. Is there any pure existence without essence? Do not even our free choices exhibit evidence of certain essences, that is, do they not exhibit character, significance? And, again, in what sense, if any, might one assume absolute freedom? Is Sartre neglecting many of the determinants—physical, psychological, social—of our actions? Finally, if you are not to be hampered by reason in crucial decisions, religious existentialists like Marcel and Niebuhr might ask Sartre: "Why not take the ultimate leap and have faith in God?" Analysis of these and similar questions would help you not only to obtain a fuller understanding of existentialism but also to clarify your own metaphysics.

The metaphysical systems that have been considered offer different world-views; yet they have one quality in common—the aim to understand fully the nature of things. It is not strange that equally great minds should arrive at different metaphysical views, for the task is complex and difficult.

Aristotle (384-322 B.C.)

9.1 Metaphysics

I. BEING

There is a science which investigates being as being and the attributes which belong to this in virtue of its own nature. Now this is not the same as any of the so-called special sciences; for none of these others deals generally with being as being. They cut off a part of being and investigate the attributes of this part— this is what the mathematical sciences for instance do. Now since we are seeking the first principles and the highest causes, clearly there must be some thing to which these belong in virtue of its own nature. If then our predecessors who sought the elements of existing things were seeking these same principles, it is necessary that the elements must be elements of being not by accident but just because it *is* being. Therefore it is of being as being that we also must grasp the first causes.

There are many senses in which a thing may be said to 'be,' but they are related to one central point, one definite kind of thing, and have not merely the *epithet* 'being' in common.

From *Metaphysics.* Oxford Translation of Aristotle, ed. W. D. Ross. Reprinted by permission of the Clarendon Press, Oxford.

Everything which is healthy is related to health, one thing in the sense that it preserves health, another in the sense that it is a symptom of health, another because it is capable of it. And that which is medical is relative to the medical art, one thing in the sense that it possesses it, another in the sense that it is naturally adapted to it, another in the sense that it is a function of the medical art. And we shall find other words used similarly to these. So, too, there are many senses in which a thing is said to be, but all refer to one starting-point; some things are said to be because they are substances, others because they are affections of substance, others because they are a process towards substance, or destructions or privations or qualities of substance, or productive or generative of substance, or of things which are relative to substance, or negations of some of these things or of substance itself. It is for this reason that we say even of non-being that it *is* non-being. As, then, there is one science which deals with all healthy things, the same applies in the other cases also. For not only in the case of things which have one common notion does the investigation belong to one science, but also in the case of things which are related to one common nature; for even these in a sense have one common notion. It is clear then that it is the work of one science also to study all things that are, *qua* being.—But everywhere science deals chiefly with that which is primary, and on which the other things depend, and in virtue of which they get their names. If, then, this is substance, it is of substances that the philosopher must grasp the principles and the causes.

II. THE FOUR CAUSES

'Cause' means (1) that from which (as immanent material) a thing comes into being, e.g. the bronze of the statue and the silver of the saucer, and the classes which include these. (2) The form or pattern, i.e. the formula of the essence, and the classes which include this (e.g. the ratio 2:1 and number in general are causes of the octave) and the parts of the formula. (3) That from which the change or the freedom from change first begins, e.g. the adviser is a cause of the action, and the father a cause of the child, and in general the maker a cause of the thing made and the change-producing of the changing. (4) The end, i.e. that for the sake of which a thing is, e.g. health is the cause of walking. For why does one walk? We say 'that one may be healthy,' and in speaking thus we think we have given the cause. The same is true of all the means that intervene before the end, when something else has put the process in motion (as e.g. thinning or purging or drugs or instruments intervene before health is reached); for all these are for the sake of the end, though they differ from one another in that some are instruments and others are actions.

These, then, are practically all the senses in which causes are spoken of, and as they are spoken of in several senses it follows that there are several causes of the same thing, and in no accidental sense, e.g. both the art of sculpture and the bronze are causes of the statue not in virtue of anything else but *qua* statue; not, however, in the same way, but the one as matter and the other as source of the movement. And things can be causes of one another, e.g. exercise of good condition, and the latter of exercise; not, however, in the same way, but the one as end and the other as source of movement.—Again, the same thing is sometimes a cause of contraries; for that which when present causes a particular thing, we sometimes charge, when absent, with the contrary, e.g. we impute the shipwreck to the absence of the steersman, whose presence was the cause of safety; and both —the presence and the privation—are causes as sources of movement.

All the causes now mentioned fall under four senses which are the most obvious. For the letters are the causes of syllables, and the material is the cause of manufactured things, and fire and earth and all such things are the causes of bodies, and the parts are causes of the whole, and the hypotheses are causes of the conclusion, in the sense that they are that out of which they respectively are made; but of these some are cause as *substratum* (e.g. the parts), others as *essence* (the whole, the synthesis, and the form). The semen, the physician, the adviser, and in general the agent, are all *sources of change* or of rest. The remainder are causes as the *end* and the good of the other things; for that, for the sake of which other things are, is naturally the best and the end of the other things; let us take it as making no difference whether we call it good or apparent good.

These, then, are the causes, and this is the number of their kinds, but the *varieties of* causes are many in number, though when summarized these also are comparatively few. Causes are spoken of in many senses, and even of those which are of the same kind some are causes in a prior and others in a posterior sense, e.g. both 'the physician' and 'the professional man' are causes of health, and 'the ratio 2:1' and 'number' are causes of the octave, and the classes that include any particular cause are always causes of the particular effect. Again, there are accidental causes and the classes which include these, e.g. while in one sense 'the sculptor' causes the statue, in another sense 'Polyclitus' causes it, because the sculptor happens to be Polyclitus: and the classes that include the accidental cause are also causes, e.g. 'man'—or in general 'animal'—is the cause of the statue, because Polyclitus is a man, and a man is an animal. Of accidental causes also some are more remote or nearer than others, as, for instance, if 'the white' and 'the musical' were called causes of the statue, and not only 'Polyclitus' or 'man.' But besides all these varieties of causes, whether proper or accidental, some are called causes as being able to act, others as acting, e.g. the cause of the house's being built is the builder, or the builder when building.—The same variety of language will be found with regard to the effects of causes, e.g. a thing may be called the cause of this statue or of a statue or in general of an image, and of this bronze or of bronze or of matter in general; and similarly in the case of accidental

effects. Again, both accidental and proper causes may be spoken of in combination, e.g. we may say not 'Polyclitus' nor 'the sculptor,' but 'Polyclitus the sculptor.'

Yet all these are but six in number, while each is spoken of in two ways: for (1) they are causes either as the individual, or as the class that includes the individual, or as the accidental, or as the class that includes the accidental, and these either as combined, or as taken simply; and (2) all may be taken as acting or as having a capacity. But they differ inasmuch as the acting causes and the individuals exist, or do not exist, simultaneously with the things of which they are causes, e.g. this particular man who is curing, with this particular man who is recovering health, and this particular builder with this particular thing that is being built; but the potential causes are not always in this case; for the house does not perish at the same time as the builder.

III. POTENTIALITY AND ACTUALITY

Since we have treated of the kind of potency which is related to movement, let us discuss actuality, its genus and its differentia. In the course of our analysis it will also become clear, with regard to the potential, that we not only ascribe potency to that whose nature it is to move something else, or to be moved by something else, either without qualification or in some particular way, but also use the word in another sense, in the pursuit of which we have discussed these previous senses. Actuality means the existence of the thing, not in the way which we express by 'potentially'; we say that potentially, for instance, a statue of Hermes is in the block of wood and the half-line is in the whole, because it might be separated out, and we call even the man who is not studying a man of science, if he is capable of actually studying a particular problem. Our meaning can be seen in the particular cases by induction, and we must not seek a definition of everything but be content to grasp the analogy,—that as that which is building is to that which is capable of building, so is the waking to the sleeping, and that which is seeing to that which has its eyes shut but has sight, and that which is shaped out of the matter to the matter, and that which has been wrought up to the unwrought. Let actuality be defined by one member of this antithesis, and 'the potential' by the other. But all things are not said in the *same sense* to exist actually, but only by analogy —as *A* is in *B* or to *B*, *C* is in *D* or to *D;* for some are as movement to potency, and the others as determinate substance to some sort of matter.

The infinite and the void and all similar things are said to exist potentially and actually in a different sense from that in which many other things are said so to exist, e.g. that which sees or walks or is seen. For of the latter class these predicates can at some time be truly asserted without qualification; for the seen is so called sometimes because it is being seen, sometimes because it is capable of being seen. But the infinite does not exist potentially in the sense that it will ever actually have separate existence; its separateness is only in knowledge. For the fact that division never ceases to be possible gives the result that this actuality exists potentially, but not that it exists separately.

QUESTIONS FOR DISCUSSION

1. Aristotle says that "there is a science which investigates being as being and the attributes which belong to this being in virtue of its own nature." Analyze and illustrate the meaning of this statement.
2. Carefully analyze, with examples, Aristotle's theory of four causes. In the light of your discussion formulate a definition of causality.
3. Discuss the meanings and relations of potentiality and actuality. Illustrate.

Henry H. Price (1899-   )

9.2   Clarity Is Not Enough

I think that there is one historical fact upon which we can all agree. In the period between the two wars it came to be very widely accepted, among professional philosophers at any rate, that clarification is the fundamental aim of Philosopy. Philosophy, it was often said, gives us no new knowledge; it only makes clear to us what we know already. The philosopher's task is to analyse the statements of science, of history and of common sense, including of course ethical statements, and I suppose religious statements too, though in practice not much attention was paid to these. The word "analysis," it is true, was sometimes associated with a particular school of philosophers, the so-called Cambridge school. But many Philosophers who did not subscribe to all the tenets and methods of that school would have agreed with this conception of Philosophy. For the purposes of this discussion, then, I propose to use the words "clarification" and "analysis" (both of which are metaphors after all) as if they were synonyms; and I

From *Proceedings of The Aristotelian Society*, Supplementary Volume XIX, © 1945, pp. 3-9, 20-30. Reprinted by permission of the Editor of The Aristotelian Society.

do not think that this will lead to any serious injustice or confusion.

But the statement that Philosophy "makes clear to us what we already know" is itself in need of interpretation. For in one sense of the word "know", what the philosopher had to clarify was not necessarily something known. It need not even be something true; it might just as well be something false. We start, for instance, by asking ourselves what exactly we are knowing when we know that there is a chair in the bedroom which is not at the moment observed by anyone. But it soon occurs to us that it makes no difference whether we do know this or not, or whether there is or is not as a matter of fact an unobserved chair there. What matters is merely what is *meant* by the statement "there is an unobserved chair in the bedroom." It does not matter whether this statement is true or false; whether it is known to be true, or only believed, or merely considered without either belief or disbelief. And a sentence of similar meaning which we are quite sure is false, e.g. "there is an unobserved crocodile on the roof", would do just as well. Thus the knowledge which has to be clarified is not, or not mainly, a knowledge of facts, but a knowledge of the meanings of statements. Similarly, it would be said that the moral philosopher's task is to ask what I *mean* by saying "I ought to keep the promise I have made to Jones"; even though in fact I have made no promise to Jones and know that I have not, or even though, knowing that I have made one, I know also that I ought not to keep it, owing to the demands of some more urgent duty.

Such is the programme of analytic or clarificatory philosophy. A very simple-minded person might feel some surprise at it. Is there any point in asking what such statements mean, since admittedly we already know their meaning to begin with? I remember a story about a celebrated authoress who addressed a meeting in Oxford, and made some very peculiar statements about the nature of literature. At the end an undergraduate got up and asked her what she had meant by one of them. She replied "You know English, don't you?" He had to admit that he did, and was silenced. But of course he ought not to have been silenced. (I do not think he can have been a student of Philosophy.) He ought to have said "Oh yes, in one sense I know perfectly well what you meant: but in another sense I do not, because I do not know it clearly." The original statement was puzzling or muddling in some way, and what he wanted was an equivalent statement, or set of statements which would not be puzzling or muddling. The new understanding with which the Analytic Philosopher provides us is not like that which we get when we learn a new technical terminology, e.g. that of Navigation or of Chemistry, though incidentally we may find ourselves acquiring one. It is like the new understanding which

we get when a puzzle is solved. The darkness, out of which we are to advance into light, is the darkness of perplexity, not of ignorance.

Hence the analytic conception of Philosophy developed very naturally into a "therapeutic" conception of it. The philosopher's job, it was said, is to cure us of muddles or headaches, generated by language; either by everyday language, or by the technical language of some science. But it would appear that nobody could suffer from headaches of that particular sort unless he were already a philosopher. The word "I" for example has caused many headaches, but the plain man does not suffer from any of them. And so we witness the curious spectacle of the professional philosopher deliberately and methodically causing the headaches which he is subsequently going to cure. The student spends the first year of his Philosophy course laboriously catching the disease, and then he spends the second year being cured of it. A strange sort of therapy! But unless things were done that way, the therapist would have no patients.

To this it would be replied that *some* of the headaches are sure to arise spontaneously, sooner or later, in almost everybody. To that extent everybody is by nature a philosopher. The disease, in a mild form, is endemic. But you can only be cured of it, if you catch it "good and proper." To say the same thing in a more old-fashioned way: philosophical problems arise spontaneously in everyone's mind sooner or later, when he begins to reflect upon himself and upon the world. But other people must teach us to state these problems in their most general form, to grasp the full implications of each problem and the connexion between one problem and another; that is why we study the History of Philosophy. When we have learned these things, but not before, we can profitably consider what solutions are possible.

But however the Analytic conception of Philosophy should be formulated—whether in a "therapeutic" way or in some other—it is clear that a good many people have become dissatisfied with it. Perhaps, as I have hinted already, this is one result of the general change in the climate of opinion which the second world-war has brought about. Our main task is to consider this dissatisfaction and to ask ourselves whether there are any good grounds for it. Perhaps those who feel it might state their case as follows. Philosophy, they might say, is admittedly a very difficult subject. To master it—if it can be mastered at all—takes a lifetime. To attain even a reasonable Honours standard in it takes two or three years. Now the individual, and the community as a whole, have only a limited amount of time and energy to spare. Is it really wise to spend so much of it on something so trivial as the analysis of sentences? It is a question of "priorities," of the optimum allocation of scarce resources. This spring-cleaning, this clearing up of the muddles which some of these sentences engender, is no doubt quite a good thing. But is it really a very important occupation? Should it not be left to a few, a very few, specialists who happen to have a talent for it? Is it a thing which every educated man should know something about, and quite a large number should know quite a lot? If Philosophy is only clarification, does it deserve the place it has traditionally had in a liberal education? It acquired

that place on the strength of a claim to be something much more than this. If that claim has now been abandoned, would it not be well for the claimant to stand down? Was it originally made at a time when Philosophy included much of what would be called Science today, and not only natural science, but also "human" sciences such as Psychology, Sociology, Economics?

To say the same thing less politely, we are being told that there is a danger that we shall lose both our readers and our pupils, if things go on as they have been going; that by our own confession, we ought to lose most of them; and that with the gradual spread of enlightened views of what Philosophy is, Philosophy will extinguish itself. Or at least, it will have to retire into a small and remote corner of the intellectual world, and an even smaller corner of the educational world, and there be left to cultivate its little garden, by the curious method of first planting weeds and then pulling them up again. And if the analysis of sentences is its sole job, can we honestly maintain that it deserves a more important place than this?

What answer shall we make to these candid friends? Up to a point, I think they can be answered. They have blackened the picture too much. Let us see what can be said on the other side.

In the first place, the complaint which is often made that "philosophers nowadays talk about nothing but words" is not altogether just. For one thing, the clarificatory conception of Philosophy need not be stated in a linguistic form at all. The analytical philosopher is not bound to maintain that the aim of Philosophy is just to analyse the meaning of sentences. He can equally well say that its aim is to analyse our experience, or again to analyse certain types or forms of fact: not of course certain individual facts, for example the fact that there is a table in the next room, but certain *types* of fact, of which this one is an instance. The antithesis between nonphilosophical knowledge which is concerned "with the world," and philosophical knowledge which is concerned "only with the sentences in which we talk about the world," is liable to mislead us; as if Philosophy were just Grammar or Lexicography, which no analytic philosopher really believes that it is. Words only matter because words are what we think with. So you could equally well say, as some clarificatory philosophers do say, that Philosophy is the analysis of certain very general and very fundamental concepts—such as Thing, Self, Cause, Duty—or that it is an analysis of categories. And then, in your definiton of Philosophy, you need not mention words or sentences at all.

If however you do think fit to mention them, there is nothing to be ashamed of in that. In all ages, philosophers have in fact been greatly concerned about words, whatever their official definition of Philosophy might be. I need only mention Socrates. If anyone was ever a "linguistic analyst," surely Socrates was. No one was more concerned with the unravelling of linguistically generated muddles, the curing of "headaches" arising from linguistic usages. Nor were his therapeutic methods very different from those which are practised today. We even observe that, like our modern practitioners, he usualy began by exacerbating the headaches which he then proceeded to cure. To be sure, he got little thanks for it from his contemporaries. We may suppose that a lot of them said "This verbal stuff is not Philosophy at all; it is not at all the sort of thing we used to get in the good old Ionian days." And persons who were concerned about the future of higher education accused him of corrupting the youth. Nevertheless, his successors have thought him not unworthy of admiration.

This brings me to another point which I have not hitherto mentioned. The clarificatory philosophers of the inter-war period were often accused of writing and speaking as if Philosophy had begun in the year 1900. It was said that they neglected the History of Philosophy; that they altogether ignored the "great problems" which our predecessors have handed down to us, and the solutions of them which our predecessors have offered; and that instead they concentrated on trivial and new-fangled puzzles of their own devising. Now perhaps some of them did neglect the History of Philosophy, though I do not think they all did (I seem to remember hearing a good deal of discussion of the views of Locke, Berkeley, Hume and Kant, for instance). But there was nothing in their principles which obliged them to neglect it. For clarification or analysis, even in the most strictly "verbalistic" interpretation of it, is as old, or almost as old, as Philosophy itself. In all periods from Socrates' time to our own, with the possible exception of the darkest part of the Dark Ages, clarification has been regarded as an essential part of the philosopher's job, though not generally as the whole of it. The practice of clarification has a long and very honourable history. And that history is relevant to our modern clarificatory techniques in two ways. It is worth studying for its own sake, as one of the monuments of human genius, and we shall study it more effectively if we have been taught to do some clarification for ourselves. The student of the Socratic dialogues will benefit from a reading of the works of Lord Russell or Professor Moore. Conversely, the modern clarifier who really wants to know the answers to the philosophical problems or muddles which puzzle him—some people speak as if there were something unscholarly and almost indecent in this desire for an answer, but for my part I disagree —the modern clarifier is surely very foolish if he neglects what has been said on the subject by the clarifiers of previous ages. Nor will he necessarily suppose that the analysts of the 19th or early 20th century have more to teach him than the analysts of the 4th or 5th century B.C. He will gladly accept any illumination he can get from any writer, however old or however new. Thus if the traditional "great problems" of Philosophy be problems of clarification—as many of them undoubtedly are—our modern clarifiers have every reason for studying them, and every reason also for studying what the great philosophers of the past have had to say about them. It is fair to add that if some modern clarifiers have looked with some suspicion on the History of Philosophy, their mistake has not been without excuse. For too often the History of Philosophy has been confounded with mere *Quellenforschung*. The clarifying philosopher is not interested in the question whether A borrowed such and such a theory from B or from C or from D. Why should he be? It is no concern of his. He only wants to

know what the theory in question is, and whether it is illuminating, no matter who invented it or when. . . .

In my opinion, the most that we can fairly say against our modern clarifiers on this head, is that they have sometimes paid too little attention to pre-verbal or non-verbal thinking. For we do also think in images as well as in words, and there is even a sense (I believe) in which we may be said to think "in" actions and motor attitudes, without even using images. And such pre-verbal thinking seems to me important, both in the Theory of Knowledge and in the Theory of Conduct. Of course you may refuse to call it thinking if you like, but it does seem to be a very important kind of symbolic cognition. Perhaps it has also been forgotten sometimes that when we do think in words, the language we use is by no means always the "full dress" language which would satisfy a grammarian or a governess; for example syntactical words like "and," "if," "some" are not always present. I do not think that these considerations are merely psychological (whatever exactly is meant by that abusive epithet) since they may well throw valuable light on what thinking is. Even if they were, it seems to me that they are not likely to be much studied in psychological laboratories, and if philosophers think it beneath them to discuss such subjects, they will not be discussed by any one at all.

Are we to conclude then that clarity *is* enough, and that the dissatisfaction widely aroused by the "clarificatory" conception of Philosophy is wholly, or almost wholly, unjustified? I do not think so. I think that clarification is a part of the philosopher's task; an indispensable part moreover, and one which he must be allowed to fulfil by whatever methods —verbalistic or other—may seem good to him. But I do not think that it is the whole of his task. And certainly clarification is not all that the educated public demands of him. Then what else does it demand, if clarification is the primary function alike of Moral Philosophy, Logic, and Theory of Knowledge? The simplest answer is "Metaphysics." Let us consider whether it is the right one.[1]

As we all know, Metaphysics was sadly blown upon in the second half of the inter-war period. Metaphysical statements were declared to be meaningless, not even false; indeed the adjective "metaphysical" became almost a term of abuse. To be sure, a number of the subjects previously included under Metaphysics might still be studied under other names, even by the most advanced thinkers. It was quite proper to study the notions of Substance and Cause, for example, provided one said one was studying the analysis of thing-propositions and causal propositions. You might still discuss the nature of the self or of Personal Identity, provided you called it "the analysis of 'I' sentences." You might even have been allowed to discuss the relation of Mind and Body, if you were prepared to change the label and say you wanted to talk about the relation between psychological statements and physiological statements. Thus although many of our modern Analysts would profess to have abolished Metaphysics, this rev-

olution—like others—is not quite such a clean sweep as it appears. And I think the revolutionaries themselves would admit this.

Nevertheless, they would insist that something has been abolished; and certainly there is something which has been rendered very unpopular among professional philosophers. It is *speculative* Metaphysics, the construction of metaphysical systems: what has been called "Philosophy in the grand manner." And perhaps those who tell us that clarity is not enough are really saying that the attempt to abolish speculative Metaphysics was a fundamental mistake, indeed a kind of intellectual suicide.

Is this because they are not convinced by the reasoning which purports to show that the sentences written by the speculative metaphysicians are meaningless? Partly, no doubt. It is indeed very difficult to decide just how much this reasoning establishes. I am inclined to think that in the last resort it only establishes this much: that it is illegitimate to argue to a conclusion concerning matters of fact if there are no matters of fact among your premises. But so far as I can see, the only important metaphysical argument which would be put out of court by this is the Ontological Argument for the existence of God. And although many constructors of metaphysical systems have used this argument, in one form or another, it is not true that they all have; and even when a speculative metaphysician does use the Ontological Argument, it is not necessarily true that his whole metaphysical system depends on it, so that a part of his system might still be sense even though another part might be nonsensical.

I think however that the main rea-

---

[1] Miss D. M. Emmet's recent book "The Nature of Metaphysical Thinking" (ch. 9, on Metaphysical Analogies) contains a number of points which are highly relevant to this section of my paper, which was unfortunately written before her book came into my hands.

son, or motive, behind these protests against the abolition of speculative Metaphysics is a different one. When the critics say that a philosopher ought to concern himself with the construction of metaphysical systems, or at least with the exposition of other people's metaphysical systems if he can construct none of his own, I think they mainly have in mind what I have called the interests of the consumer; that is, the needs of the educated public which reads philosophical books or is influenced by those who do, and sends its sons and daughters to philosophical lectures at universities. Now of course it is conceivable that even though the educated public does have these needs, it is impossible in principle that they should be satisfied; and the speculative metaphysicians who have professed to satisfy them in the past may have been confusing both themselves and their readers. But when we consider the long line of speculative metaphysicians from Plato to Whitehead, when we reflect that many of them were admittedly men of the very highest genius, can we really feel very comfortable about this conclusion? Or if we do feel comfortable about it, may we not be the victims of a kind of temporal parochialism? *Securus judicat orbis terrarum.* Is it not more likely that such men were talking sense (in *some* good sense of the word "sense") than that the arguments which purport to prove that they were talking nonsense are correct?

Moreover, this is not the first time that speculative Metaphysics has been abolished. The sceptics of the later Classical period abolished it. It revived in the form of Neoplatonism and of Christian metaphysical theol-

ogy. In the 18th century Hume abolished it, and Kant imposed the most drastic restrictions on it. But not for long. It arose again, more vigorous than ever, in the great speculative systems of the Romantic period. The Positivists and Agnostics of the later 19th century abolished it once more; and once more it revived in the speculative systems of Bergson, Alexander and Whitehead. If what I called the needs of the consumer are in principle incapable of being satisfied (as the modern anti-speculators assert) we may nevertheless be pretty confident that fresh attempts will in fact be made to satisfy them in the future, whether we like it or not. It looks as if there were a kind of rhythm in the history of human thought on metaphysical subjects. A long period of speculative thinking is followed by a shorter period of criticism and agnosticism, and then speculative thinking begins again in a different form. At the moment we happen to be living in one of the critical and agnostic periods; and perhaps the widespread complaint that "clarity is not enough" is itself one of the symptoms that the period is approaching its end. Certainly in other departments of human thought and culture the "debunking" which went on in the inter-war period has begun to look a little old-fashioned; as the saying is, it begins to "date." I suspect that if the complainants are asking for a revival of speculative metaphysics, they will in fact get what they want in the end, though they may not get it from the present generation of professional philosophers; and perhaps they will not get it from professional philosophers at all, but from other and less well-qualified persons.

But what exactly are these "needs

of the consumer" which—if I am right —are what the critics of the purely clarificatory conception of Philosophy are mainly concerned about? And how would these needs be satisfied by a system of speculative metaphysics? What the consumer mainly needs, I think, is a *Weltanschauung*, a unified outlook on the world. This is what he is asking for when he asks the philosopher for wisdom or guidance, or a clue to "the meaning of the Universe"; and this is what the analytic philosophers are failing to give him. I am afraid he is not particularly interested in the arguments by which this or that world outlook is recommended; at any rate not in the detail of them. But he is not wholly disinterested in them either. For the outlook which he demands has to be a *reasoned* outlook. If it is supported merely by the *ipse dixit* of some authority, or by the dictates of the heart, it will not satisfy him, or not for long. But the reasoning which supports it need not be the sort of reasoning which the anti-metaphysical philosophers disapprove of. It need not be that "pure thought" which tries to establish existential conclusions by means of wholly a priori premises. In every one of his arguments, the speculator might use one empirical premise at least. Nor is it at all necessary that any of his arguments should be completely demonstrative. His conclusions must be recommended by reasoning; but they need not be strictly proved, in a way which would satisfy a professor of Formal Logic.

Does this amount to saying that what is demanded of the speculative metaphysician is a kind of explanatory hypothesis, capable of accounting for all the main types of facts which are empirically known to us? That is one

way of putting it, but perhaps the word "hypothesis" may mislead us. For one thing, his hypothesis—if you call it that—must be more comprehensive than any scientific or historical hypothesis. It must cover all the main departments of human experience, including experiences which it is not fashionable nowadays for philosophers to talk about: religious and mystical experience, for instance, and the queer or "supernormal" experiences which psychical researchers investigate, such as telepathy and precognition. Moreover his theory will not, I think, be capable of conclusive refutation by future empirical data. New empirical facts may turn up which are (as we say) "difficult to reconcile with it"; but by sufficiently ingenious interpretation it will always be possible to explain them away. Indeed even the word "theory" is not altogether a suitable one, for it has come to be used mainly in a scientific sense ("the Evolution Theory" "the Quantum Theory"). For the same reason words like "explain" and "account for" may be misleading. "Explanation" has come to mean primarily *causal* explanation, or at any rate explanation in terms of inductively established regularities of sequence, whether deterministic or statistical. And this is not the speculative metaphysician's business. It would be better to say that what we demand of him is just a unifying conception, or to use some still vaguer expression like "point of view" or "outlook": thus we speak of the theocentric point of view of the Mediaeval Schoolmen, or the biocentric outlook of Bergson.

This has some bearing on a very puzzling question: in what sense can a system of speculative metaphysics be called true or false? I do not think that the words "true" and "false" are rightly applicable to the sentences in which the metaphysician formulates his speculative theses, though they do of course apply to the statements which he makes in support of them. In saying this, I am not agreeing with those who maintain that a system of speculative metaphysics is just an expression of emotion, akin to a work of art. There is some force in this analogy, no doubt. But I think a much better one would be a map or chart. This is a kind of picture, if you like, and it may well have aesthetic merits. But it is also something more. It is a systematic representation of a certain set of geographical facts. And the question whether this or that stretch of green paint or blue ink shall be put in or left out, or what shape it shall have, is not settled by the emotions of the map-maker. It is settled by two considerations in conjunction: by the geographical facts on the one hand (is it empirically true that there is a wood here, and a brook there?) and on the other by the principle of representation which he has adopted.

Now two maps of the same tract of territory may be very different indeed. If your map of the world is a school-room globe, it will differ in many ways from a flat map constructed according to Mercator's projection; on a one-inch map a main road may be broader than the river Thames, whereas on a six-inch map it will be the other way round. But we do not say on that account that the Mercator map is "wrong" and the Schoolroom globe "right," nor that the six-inch map is "right" and the one-inch map is "wrong."

It seems to me that systems of speculative metaphysics differ from each other in somewhat the same way. We may regard them as alternative modes of conceptual arrangement by which the body of empirical data is systematically ordered: for example, the speculative system of Alexander is a mode of conceiving the universe as a hierarchical arrangement, ordered by means of the three notions of space-time, quality and emergence. What the metaphysician has to show is that his method or arrangement—his principle of systematic representation—is a possible one, that the facts can be ordered in accordance with it, but not that it is the only one possible; no more than Mercator has to show that his method of projection is the one and only "right" one and all the others "wrong." We may of course find that a particular metaphysical system leaves out some of the facts altogether; not because the metaphysician was unaware of them (if that is all, the defect can be remedied by his successors) but because in the system of representaion which he has adopted they cannot be put in, just as in some types of maps there is no way of representing telegraph lines or level-crossings. Religious experience has been omitted by some metaphysicians in this way, moral experience by others; while "supernormal" experiences, such as telepathy, have been omitted by almost all. Or we may find that his system of representation is so obscure that we cannot see how to apply it to new facts which he himself did not know; or still worse, we cannot see how he applied it himself to the old ones he did know. But though we may discover defects of these sorts in a particular metaphysical system, we ought not to say on that account that it is wrong, or false, or that it has been refuted (as the

Phlogiston Theory has been refuted). We ought rather to say, and indeed we often do say, that it is inadequate or unsatisfactory in this or that respect, though perhaps satisfactory in others; which is much like what we say of Mercator's map of Greenland. And we shall then look about for another metaphysical system which is more illuminating. But in the meantime we shall not just throw the old ones into the waste-paper basket, on the ground that it has been "refuted," for the notion of refutation does not apply in this case. On the contrary, we shall continue to study it carefully, in order to get all the illumination out of it that we can; only, we shall hope to invent another (or rediscover an ancient one) which will illuminate more comprehensively. Thus the choice between different systems of speculative metaphysics is not a choice between the true and the false, at least in the ordinary sense of those words. It is rather a choice between the less good and the better, or even between several things which are good, but good in different ways. And even a little illumination is much better than none at all.

Let us now return to the needs of the consumer. What he is alleged to need is a unified conceptual scheme of the sort I have been trying to describe. And I think it is true that he does need it. When the ordinary educated man speaks of "a philosophy," it is a conceptual scheme of this kind which he has in mind. Such a scheme, he thinks, will provide him with the wisdom which philosophers are traditionally supposed to supply. He needs, as it were, a map of the universe so far as our empirical information has disclosed it; and not a map

of the physical world only, but one which makes room for all the known aspects of the universe, physical, spiritual, and whatever others there may be. He needs it nowadays more than ever, since for good reasons or bad the Christian metaphysical scheme has lost its hold over him; and Science does not give him what he wants either, since he feels (in my opinion rightly) that there are a number of very important questions on which Science has nothing to say. And he complains that just when his need is greatest, the philosophers are refusing to satisfy it. The prevalence of the purely clarificatory conception of Philosophy prevents them from even making the attempt. They will not even discuss and expound for his benefit the speculative systems of the past, so that he may avail himself of such illumination and guidance as these old fashioned "maps of the universe" have to offer. It is true that they are not by any means uninterested in the history of Philosophy, as I have argued already. But they *are* uninterested in the history of speculative Metaphysics.

It would seem then that the complaint "clarity is not enough" is in one important respect justified, in so far as the contemporary clarifying philosophers have neglected speculative Metaphysics, which is one of the things which philosophers are traditionally paid to know about. They have neglected it, not of course through mere laziness or inadvertence, but on principle, because they have thought that the speculative metaphysician is trying to do something which is from the nature of the case impossible: namely, to establish conclusions about matters of fact by means of purely *a priori* premises. But if I am right, that is not what he is trying to do, except in occasional moments of aberration. He is trying to do something much less extravagant and much more important: to produce a unified conceptual scheme under which all the known types of empirical fact may be systematically arranged. And there is nothing in this enterprise which even the most sensitive philosophical conscience need object to.

Yet if this be so, it might be said, the statement that clarity is not enough is hardly the best way of formulating the legitimate complaints of the consumer. For, it may be suggested, there are more sorts of clarity than one. The function of the map-maker, to whom I have compared the speculative metaphysician, is surely in a sense to make things clear which were not clear before. And the speculative metaphysician, at least as I have conceived him, could even accept the dictum that "Philosophy gives us no new knowledge, but only makes clear to us what we already know." For certainly it is not his function to give us new information about matters of fact, but rather to devise a conceptual scheme which brings out certain systematic relationships between the matters of fact we know already—including those queer and puzzling ones about which we know only a little. His job is to make things comprehensible, not to establish what things are. In short, is there not such a thing as *synoptic* clarity, as well as analytical clarity? And if we are careful to remember that the word "clarity" covers both of them, could we not conclude that clarity *is* enough after all?

Perhaps we could. But I should like to add a final word of caution, and it is probably the most shocking of all the shocking things I have said this evening. It has been maintained that whatever can be said at all, can be said clearly; from which it follows that if a thing cannot be said clearly, then it cannot be said at all. We should all like to believe this. It presents itself as a kind of charter of liberation, lifting a vast load of twaddle and muddle from our shoulders. But I think we ought not to accept this freedom which is offered to us, until we have considered carefully what the word "can" means in this context. I am afraid that it only means "can in principle," not "can in practice." A man may be saying something, even something of fundamental importance, and yet it may be quite impossible for *him* to say it clearly, and impossible equally for any of his contemporaries; and this not through lack of cleverness on his part or theirs, but simply because the existing terminology is not adequate for the task. We must not however allow ourselves to conclude—as this dictum might tempt us to, unless carefully interpreted—that he would have done better not to speak at all. There may very well be some things which in the terminology available at the time can only be said obscurely; either in a metaphor, or (still more disturbing) in an oxymoron or a paradox, that is, in a sentence which breaks the existing terminological rules and is in its literal meaning absurd. The man who says them may of course be just confused. But it is possible that he is saying something important; or he may be confused in some degree, and yet he may at the same time be saying something important. Nevertheless, his successors may be able to divine what he is trying to convey. The terminological rules may eventually be changed. And the wild metaphor or outrageous paradox of today may become the platitude of the day after tomorrow. The old saying that a philosopher's reach should exceed his grasp has no doubt been grossly abused in the past, and has enabled many solemn muddles to masquerade as profound truths. But it is not a wholly silly statement all the same. And the denial or neglect of it may be even more deleterious than the abuse of it. I think we are in danger of neglecting it. If we do, we shall only succeed in being clear at the expense of being superficial; and in our zeal to "disinfect" our language from muddles, we shall only succeed in sterilising it. To use another analogy, we shall have made its rules so rigid that it becomes a strait jacket, and prevents us even from asking questions which ought to be asked and from undertsanding the non-professional outsider who (in a confused way, very likely) is trying to ask them.

Has it not happened sometimes that an important question was first asked by poets and religious teachers and other unphilosophical persons, who were blissfully ignorant of the terminological rules which the philosophers of their day had laid down? "Nonsense! Nonsense!" says the professional philosopher, when he is told of the question these people have asked. But his successors a generation or two later may call it unconscious wisdom or untutored insight; and having altered the terminological rules so as to make the question a permissible one, they may spend their professional lives in looking for the answer. In that case the philosopher who said "Nonsense!" will appear a little ridiculous. Let us take care that this does not happen to ourselves, and let us not allow our zeal for "tightening up language," to run away with us. Even though we allow for the distinction between analytic clarity and synoptic clarity, it may still be true that clarity is not enough.

QUESTIONS FOR DISCUSSION

1. Discuss the program of the analytic school as the clarification of ideas and the "therapeutic" cure of muddles generated by language.
2. What are the reasons of the analytic school for rejecting the claims of speculative metaphysics? Do you find these reasons convincing?
3. Discuss Price's views on the analytic school, both the favorable and the unfavorable. To what degree do you agree with Price?
4. Carefully analyze Price's saying that the function of a metaphysician is "to devise a conceptual scheme which brings out certain systematic relationships between matters of fact we know already. . . . His job is to make things comprehensible, not to establish what things are."

William James (1842-1910)

9.3   The One and the Many

Philosophy has often been defined as the quest or the vision of the world's unity. Few persons ever challenge this definition, which is true as far as it goes, for philosophy has indeed manifested above all things its interest in unity. But how about the *variety* in things? Is that such an irrelevant matter? If instead of using the term philosophy, we talk in general of our intellect and its needs, we quickly see that unity is only one of them. Acquaintance with the details of fact is always reckoned, along with their reduction to system, as an indispensable mark of mental greatness. Your "scholarly" mind, of encyclopedic, philological type, your man essentially of *learning*, has never lacked for praise along with your philosopher. What our intellect really aims at is neither variety nor unity taken singly, but *totality*. In this, acquaintance with reality's diversities is as important as understanding their connection. Curiosity goes *pari passu* with the systematizing passion.

In spite of this obvious fact the unity of things has always been considered more *illustrious*, as it were, than their variety. When a young man first conceives the notion that the whole world forms one great fact, with all its parts moving abreast, as it were, and interlocked, he feels as if he were enjoying a great insight, and looks superciliously on all who still fall short of this sublime conception. Taken thus abstractly as it first comes to one, the monistic insight is so vague as hardly to seem worth defending intellectually. Yet probably everyone in this audience in some way cherishes it. A certain abstract monism, a certain emotional response to the character of oneness, as if it were a feature of the world not co-ordinate with its manyness, but vastly more excellent and eminent, is so prevalent in educated circles that we might almost call it a part of philosophic common sense. Of *course* the world is One, we say. Empiricists, as a rule, are as stout monists of this abstract kind as rationalists are.

The difference is that the empiricists are less dazzled. Unity doesn't blind them to everything else, doesn't quench their curiosity for special facts, whereas there is a kind of rationalist who is sure to interpret abstract unity mystically and to forget everything else, to treat it as a principle; to admire and worship it, and thereupon to come to a full stop intellectually.

From *Pragmatism* (1907).

"The world is One!"—the formula may become a sort of number-worship. "Three" and "seven" have, it is true, been reckoned sacred numbers; but, abstractly taken, why is "one" more excellent than "forty-three," or than "two million and ten"? In this first vague conviction of the world's unity, there is so little to take hold of that we hardly know what we mean by it.

The only way to get forward with our notion is to treat it pragmatically. Granting the oneness to exist, what facts will be different in consequence? What will the unity be known as? The world is One—yes, but *how* one? What is the practical value of the oneness for *us?*

Asking such questions, we pass from the vague to the definite, from the abstract to the concrete. Many distinct ways in which a oneness predicated of the universe might make a difference, come to view. I will note successively the more obvious of these ways.

1. First, the world is at least *one subject of discourse*. If its manyness were so irremediable as to permit *no* union whatever of its parts, not even our minds could "mean" the whole of it at once: they would be like eyes trying to look in opposite directions. But in point of fact we mean to cover the whole of it by our abstract term "world" or "universe," which expressly intends that no part shall be left out. Such unity of discourse carries obviously no farther monistic specifications. A "chaos," once so named, has as much unity of discourse as a cosmos. It is an odd fact that many monists consider a great victory scored for their side when pluralists say "the universe is many." " 'The Universe'!"

they chuckle—"his speech betrayeth him. He stands confessed of monism out of his own mouth." Well, let things be one in so far forth! You can then fling such a word as universe at the whole collection of them, but what matters it? It still remains to be ascertained whether they are one in any further or more valuable sense.

2. Are they, for example, *continuous?* Can you pass from one to another, keeping always in your one universe without any danger of falling out? In other words, do the parts of our universe *hang together,* instead of being like detached grains of sand?

Even grains of sand hang together through the space in which they are embedded, and if you can in any way move through such space, you can pass continuously from number one of them to number two. Space and time are thus vehicles of continuity by which the world's parts hang together. The practical difference to us, resultant from these forms of union, is immense. Our whole motor life is based upon them.

3. There are innumerable other parts of practical continuity among things. Lines of *influence* can be traced by which they hang together. Following any such line you pass from one thing to another till you may have covered a good part of the universe's extent. Gravity and heat-conduction are such all-uniting influences, so far as the physical world goes. Electric, luminous and chemical influences follow similar lines of influence. But opaque and inert bodies interrupt the continuity here, so that you have to step round them, or change your mode of progress if you wish to get farther on the day. Practically, you have then lost your uni-

verse's unity, *so far as it was constituted by those first lines of influence.*

There are innumerable kinds of connection that special things have with other special things; and the *ensemble* of any one of these connections forms one sort of *system* by which things are conjoined. Thus men are conjoined in a vast network of *acquaintanceship.* Brown knows Jones, Jones knows Robinson, etc.; and *by choosing your farther intermediaries rightly* you may carry a message from Jones to the Empress of China, or the Chief of the African Pigmies, or to anyone else in the inhabited world. But you are stopped short, as by a nonconductor, when you choose one man wrong in this experiment. What may be called love-systems are grafted on the acquaintance-system. A loves (or hates) B; B loves (or hates) C, etc. But these systems are smaller than the great acquaintance-system that they presuppose.

Human efforts are daily unifying the world more and more in definite systematic ways. We found colonial, postal, consular, commercial systems, all the parts of which obey definite influences that propagate themselves within the system but not to facts outside of it. The result is innumerable little hangings-together of the world's parts within the larger hangings-together, little worlds, not only of discourse but of operation, within the wider universe. Each system exemplifies one type or grade of union, its parts being strung on that peculiar kind of relation, and the same part may figure in many different systems, as a man may hold various offices and belong to several clubs. From this "systematic" point of view, therefore, the pragmatic value of the world's

unity is that all these definite networks actually and practically exist. Some are more enveloping and extensive, some less so; they are superposed upon each other; and between them all they let no individual elementary part of the universe escape. Enormous as is the amount of disconnection among things (for these systematic influences and conjunctions follow rigidly exclusive paths), everything that exists is influenced in *some* way by something else, if you can only pick the way out rightly. Loosely speaking, and in general, it may be said that all things cohere and adhere to each other *somehow,* and that the universe exists practically in reticulated or concatenated forms which make of it a continuous or "integrated" affair. Any kind of influence whatever helps to make the world one, so far as you can follow it from next to next. You may then say that "the world *is* One" —meaning in these respects, namely, and just so far as they obtain. But just as definitely is it *not* One, so far as they do not obtain; and there is no species of connection which will not fail, if, instead of choosing conductors for it you choose non-conductors. You are then arrested at your very first step and have to write the world down as a pure *many* from that particular point of view. If our intellect had been as much interested in disjunctive as it is in conjunctive relations, philosophy would have equally successfully celebrated the world's *disunion.*

The great point is to notice that the oneness and the manyness are absolutely co-ordinate here. Neither is primordial or more essential or excellent than the other. Just as with space, whose separating of things seems exactly on a par with its uniting of them, but sometimes one function and sometimes the other is what comes home to us most, so, in our general dealings with the world of influences, we now need conductors and now need non-conductors, and wisdom lies in knowing which is which at the appropriate moment.

4. All these systems of influence or non-influence may be listed under the general problem of the world's *causal unity*. If the minor causal influences among things should converge towards one common causal origin of them in the past, one great first cause for all that is, one might then speak of the absolute causal unity of the world. God's *fiat* on creation's day has figured in traditional philosophy as such an absolute cause and origin. Transcendental Idealism, translating "creation" into "thinking" (or "willing to think") calls the divine act "eternal" rather than "first," but the union of the many here is absolute, just the same—the many would not *be*, save for the One. Against this notion of the unity of origin of all things there has always stood the pluralistic notion of an eternal self-existing many in the shape of atoms or even of spiritual units of some sort. The alternative has doubtless a pragmatic meaning, but perhaps as far as these lectures go, we had better leave the question of unity of origin unsettled.

5. The most important sort of union that obtains among things, pragmatically speaking, is their *generic unity*. Things exist in kinds, there are many specimens in each kind, and what the "kind" implies for one specimen, it implies also for every other specimen of that kind. We can easily conceive that every fact in the world might be singular, that is, unlike any other fact and sole of its kind. In such a world of singulars our logic would be useless, for logic works by predicating of the single instance what is true of all its kind. With no two things alike in the world, we should be unable to reason from our past experiences to our future ones. The existence of so much generic unity in things is thus perhaps the most momentous pragmatic specification of what it may mean to say "the world is One." *Absolute* generic unity would obtain if there were one *summum genus* under which all things without exception could be eventually subsumed. "Beings," "thinkables," "experiences," would be candidates for this position. Whether the alternatives expressed by such words have any pragmatic significance or not, is another question which I prefer to leave unsettled just now.

6. Another specification of what the phrase "the world is One" may mean is *unity of purpose*. An enormous number of things in the world subserve a common purpose. All the man-made systems, administrative, industrial, military, or what not, exist each for its controlling purpose. Every living being pursues its own peculiar purposes. They co-operate, according to the degree of their development, in collective or tribal purposes, larger ends thus enveloping lesser ones, until an absolutely single, final, and climacteric purpose subserved by all things without exception might conceivably be reached. It is needless to say that the appearances conflict with such a view. Any resultant, as I said in my third lecture, *may* have been purposed in advance, but none of the results we actually know in this world have in point of

fact been purposed in advance in all their details. Men and nations start with a vague notion of being rich, or great, or good. Each step they make brings unforeseen chances into sight, and shuts out older vistas, and the specifications of the general purpose have to be daily changed. What is reached in the end may be better or worse than what was proposed, but it is always more complex and different.

Our different purposes also are at war with each other. Where one can't crush the other out, they compromise; and the result is again different from what anyone distinctly proposed beforehand. Vaguely and generally, much of what was purposed may be gained; but everything makes strongly for the view that our world is incompletely unified teleologically and is still trying to get its unification better organized.

Whoever claims *absolute* teleological unity, saying that there is one purpose that every detail of the universe subserves, dogmatizes at his own risk. Theologians who dogmatize thus find it more and more impossible, as our acquaintance with the warring interests of the world's parts grows more concrete, to imagine what the one climacteric purpose may possibly be like. We see, indeed, that certain evils minister to ulterior goods, that the bitter makes the cocktail better, and that a bit of danger or hardship puts us agreeably to our trumps. We can vaguely generalize this into the doctrine that all the evil in the universe is but instrumental to its greater perfection. But the scale of the evil actually in sight defies all human tolerance; and transcendental idealism, in the pages of a Bradley or a Royce,

brings us no farther than the book of Job did—God's ways are not our ways, so let us put our hands upon our mouth. A God who can relish such superfluities of horror is no God for human beings to appeal to. His animal spirits are too high. In others words the "Absolute" with his one purpose, is not the man-like God of common people.

7. *Aesthetic union* among things also obtains, and is very analogous to teleological union. Things tell a story. Their parts hang together so as to work out a climax. They play into each other's hands expressively. Retrospectively, we can see that although no definite purpose presided over a chain of events, yet the events fell into a dramatic form, with a start, a middle, and a finish. In point of fact all stories end; and here again the point of view of a many is the more natural one to take. The world is full of partial stories that run parallel to one another, beginning and ending at odd times. They mutually interlace and interfere at points, but we cannot unify them completely in our minds. In following your life-history, I must temporarily turn my attention from my own. Even a biographer of twins would have to press them alternately upon his reader's attention.

It follows that whoever says that the whole world tells one story utters another of those monistic dogmas that a man believes at his risk. It is easy to see the world's history pluralistically, as a rope of which each fibre tells a separate tale; but to conceive of each cross-section of the rope as an absolutely single fact, and to sum the whole longitudinal series into one being living an undivided life, is harder. We have, indeed, the analogy of embryology to help us. The microscopist makes a hundred flat cross-sections of a given embryo, and mentally unites them into one solid whole. But the great world's ingredients, so far as they are beings, seem like the rope's fibres, to be discontinuous, cross-wise, and to cohere only in the longitudinal direction. Followed in that direction they are many. Even the embryologist, when he follows the *development* of his object, has to treat the history of each single organ in turn. *Absolute* aesthetic union is thus another barely abstract ideal. The world appears as something more epic than dramatic.

So far, then, we see how the world is unified by its many systems, kinds, purposes, and dramas. That there is more union in all these ways than openly appears is certainly true. That there *may* be one sovereign purpose, system, kind, and story, is a legitimate hypothesis. All I say here is that it is rash to affirm this dogmatically without better evidence than we possess at present.

8. The *great* monistic *denkmittel* for a hundred years past has been the notion of *the one Knower*. The many exist only as objects for his thought—exist in his dream, as it were; and *as he knows* them, they have one purpose, form one system, tell one tale for him. This notion of an *all enveloping noetic unity* in things is the sublimest achievement of intellectualist philosophy. Those who believe in the Absolute, as the All-Knower is termed, usually say that they do so for coercive reasons, which clear thinkers cannot evade. The Absolute has far-reaching practical consequences, to some of which I drew attention in my second lecture. Many

kinds of difference important to us would surely follow from its being true. I cannot here enter into all the logical proofs of such a Being's existence, farther than to say that none of them seem to me sound. I must therefore treat the notion of an All-Knower simply as an hypothesis, exactly on a par logically with the pluralist notion that there is no point of view, no focus of information extant, from which the entire content of the universe is visible at once. "God's conscience," says Professor Royce,[1] "forms in its wholeness one luminously transparent conscious moment"—this is the type of noetic unity on which rationalism insists. Empiricism on the other hand, is satisfied with the type of noetic unity that is humanly familiar. Everything gets known by *some* knower along with something else; but the knowers may in the end be irreducibly many, and the greatest knower of them all may yet not know the whole of everything, or even know what he does know at one single stroke: he may be liable to forget. Whichever type obtained, the world would still be a universe noetically. Its parts would be conjoined by knowledge, but in the one case the knowledge would be absolutely unified, in the other it would be strung along and overlapped.

The notion of one instantaneous or eternal Knower—either adjective here means the same thing—is, as I said, the great intellectualist achievement of our time. It has practically driven out that conception of "Substance" which earlier philosophers set such store by, and by which so much unify-

---

[1] "The Conception of God," *Philosophical Union of the University of California, Bulletin No. 15* (1895).

ing work used to be done—universal substance which alone has being in and from itself, and of which all the particulars of experience are but forms to which it gives support. Substance has succumbed to the pragmatic criticisms of the English school. It appears now only as another name for the fact that phenomena as they come are actually grouped and given in coherent forms, the very forms in which we finite knowers experience or think them together. These forms of conjunction are as much parts of the tissue of experience as are the terms which they connect; and it is a great pragmatic achievement for recent idealism to have made the world hang together in these directly representable ways instead of drawing its unity from the "inherence" of its parts—whatever that may mean—in an unimaginable principle behind the scenes.

"The world is One," therefore, just so far as we experience it to be concatenated, One by as many definite conjunctions as appear. But then also *not* One by just as many definite *disjunctions* as we find. The oneness and and the manyness of it thus obtain in respects which can be separately named. It is neither a universe pure and simple nor a multiverse pure and simple. And its various manners of being One suggest, for their accurate ascertainments, so many distinct programs of scientific work. Thus the pragmatic question "What is the oneness known as? What practical difference will it make?" saves us from all feverish excitement over it as a principle of sublimity and carries us forward into the stream of experience with a cool head. The stream may indeed reveal far more connection and union than we now suspect, but we are not entitled on pragmatic principles to claim absolute oneness in any respect in advance.

QUESTIONS FOR DISCUSSION

1. How and in what sense, according to James, is the universe "one" and "many"?
2. James says, "Philosophy has often been defined as the quest or vision of the world's unity." Is this definition of philosophy true? If so, what different types of unity have philosophers suggested? If not, what alternative visions of the world have been suggested?
3. In what way is the causal relation an expression of the "one" and the "many"?
4. The phrase "the world is One" may mean the unity of purpose. What might be this unifying purpose? Or is there such a unifying purpose?
5. What would be the pragmatic consequences of believing in a monistic or a pluralistic universe?

Josiah Royce (1855-1916)

9.4   Reality and Idealism

Idealism has two aspects. It is, for the first, a kind of analysis of the world, an analysis which so far has no absolute character about it, but which undertakes, in a fashion that might be acceptable to any skeptic, to examine what you mean by all the things, whatever they are, that you believe in or experience. This idealistic analysis consists merely in a pointing out, by various devices, that the world of your knowledge, whatever it contains, is through and through such stuff as ideas are made of, that you never in your life believed in anything definable *but* ideas, that, as Berkeley put it, "this whole choir of heaven and furniture of earth" is nothing for any of us but a system of ideas which govern our belief and conduct. Such idealism has numerous statements, interpretations, embodiments: forms part of the most various systems and experiences, is consistent with Berkeley's theism, with Fichte's ethical absolutism, with Professor Huxley's agnostic empiricism, with Clifford's mind-stuff theory, with countless other theories that have used such idealism as a part of their scheme. In this aspect idealism is al-

From *The Spirit of Modern Philosophy* (1892), Lecture XI.

ready a little puzzling to our natural consciousness, but it becomes quickly familiar, in fact almost commonplace, and seems after all to alter our practical faith or to solve our deeper problems very little.

The other aspect of idealism is the one which gives us our notion of the absolute Self. To it the first is only preparatory. This second aspect is the one which from Kant, until the present time, has formed the deeper problem of thought. Whenever the world has become more conscious of its significance, the work of human philosophy will be, not nearly ended (Heaven forbid an end!), but for the first time fairly begun. For then, in critically estimating our passions, we shall have some truer sense of whose passions they are.

I begin with the first and the less significant aspect of idealism. Our world, I say, whatever it may contain, is such stuff as ideas are made of. This preparatory sort of idealism is the one that, as I just suggested, Berkeley made prominent, and, after a fashion, familiar. I must state it in my own way, although one in vain seeks to attain novelty in illustrating so frequently described a view.

Here, then, is our so-real world of the senses, full of light and warmth and sound. If anything could be solid and external, surely, one at first will say, it is this world. Hard facts, not mere ideas, meet us on every hand. Ideas any one can mould as he wishes. Not so facts. In ideas, socialists can dream out Utopias, disappointed lovers can imagine themselves successful, beggars can ride horses, wanderers can enjoy the fireside at home. In the realm of facts, society organizes itself as it must, rejected lovers stand for the time defeated, beggars are alone with their wishes, oceans roll drearily between home and the wanderer. Yet this world of fact is, after all, not entirely stubborn, not merely hard. The strenuous will can mould facts. We can form our world, in part, according to our ideas. Statesmen influence the social order, lovers woo afresh, wanderers find the way home. But thus to alter the world we must work, and just because the laborer is worthy of his hire, it is well that the real world should thus have such fixity of things as enables us to anticipate what facts will prove lasting, and to see of the travail of our souls when it is once done. This, then, is the presupposition of life, that we work in a real world, where house walls do not melt away as in dreams, but stand firm against the winds of many winters, and can be felt as real. We do not wish to find facts wholly plastic; we want them to be stubborn, if only the stubbornness be not altogether unmerciful. Our will makes constantly a sort of agreement with the world, whereby, if the world will continually show some respect to the will, the will shall consent to be strenuous in its industry. Interfere with the reality of my world, and you therefore take the very life and heart out of my will.

The reality of the world, however, when thus defined in terms of its stubbornness, its firmness as against the will that has not conformed to its laws, its kindly rigidity in preserving for us the fruits of our labors—such reality, I say, is still something wholly unanalyzed. In what does this stubbornness consist? Surely, many different sorts of reality, as it would seem, may be stubborn. Matter is stubborn when it stands in hard walls against us, or rises in vast mountain ranges before the path-finding explorer. But minds can be stubborn also. The lonely wanderer, who watches by the seashore the waves that roll between him and his home, talks of cruel facts, material barriers that, just because they *are* material, and not ideal, shall be the irresistible foes of his longing heart. "In wish," he says, "I am with my dear ones, but alas, wishes cannot cross oceans! Oceans are material facts, in the cold outer world. Would that the world of the heart were all!" But alas! to the rejected lover the world of the heart *is* all, and that is just his woe. Were the barrier between him and his beloved only made of those stubborn material facts, only of walls or of oceans, how lightly might his will erelong transcend them all! Matter stubborn! Nay, it is just an idea that now opposes him—just an idea, and that, too, in the mind of the maiden he loves. But in vain does he call this stubborn bit of disdain a merely ideal fact. No flint was ever more definite in preserving its identity and its edge than this disdain may be. Place me for a moment, then, in an external world that shall consist wholly of ideas—the ideas, namely, of other people about me, a world of maidens who shall scorn me, of old friends who shall have learned to hate me, of angels who shall condemn me, of God who shall judge me. In what piercing north winds, amidst what fields of ice, in the labyrinths of what tangled forests, in the depths of what thick-walled dungeons, on the edges of what tremendous precipices, should I be more genuinely in the presence of stubborn and unyielding facts than in that conceived world of ideas! So, as one sees, I by no means deprive my world of stubborn reality, if I merely call it a world of ideas. On the contrary, as every teacher knows, the ideas of the people are often the most difficult of facts to influence. We were wrong, then, when we said that whilst matter was stubborn, ideas could be moulded at pleasure. Ideas are often the most implacable of facts. Even my own ideas, the facts of my own inner life, may cruelly decline to be plastic to my wish. The wicked will that refuses to be destroyed—what rock has often more consistency for our senses than this will has for our inner consciousness! The king, in his soliloquy in *Hamlet*—in what an unyielding world of hard facts does he not move! and yet they are now only inner facts. The fault is past; he is alone with his conscience:

> What rests?
> Try what repentance can. What can it not?
> Yet what can it, when one cannot repent?
> O wretched state! O bosom black as death!
> O limèd soul, that, struggling to be free,
> Art more engaged!

No, here are barriers worse than any material chains. The world of ideas has its own horrible dungeons and chasms. Let those who have refuted Bishop Berkeley's idealism by the wonder why he did not walk over every precipice or into every fire if these things existed only in his idea, let such, I say, first try some of the fires and the precipices of the inner life, ere they decide that dangers cease to be dangers as soon as they are called ideal, or even subjectively ideal in me.

Many sorts of reality, then, may be existent at the heart of any world of facts. But this bright and beautiful sense-world of ours—what, amongst these many possible sorts of reality, does that embody? Are the stars and the oceans, the walls and the pictures, real as the maiden's heart is real—embodying the ideas of somebody, but none the less stubbornly real for that? Or can we make something else of their reality? For, of course, that the stars and the oceans, the walls and the pictures have *some* sort of stubborn reality, just as the minds of our fellows have, our analysis so far does not for an instant think of denying. Our present question is, what sort of reality? Consider, then, in detail, certain aspects of the reality that seems to be exemplified in our sense-world. The sublimity of the sky, the life and majesty of the ocean, the interest of a picture—to what sort of real facts do these belong? Evidently here we shall have no question. So far as the sense-world is beautiful, is majestic, is sublime, this beauty and dignity exist only for the appreciative observer. If they exist beyond him, they exist only for some other mind, or as the thought and embodied purpose of some universal soul of nature. A man who sees the same world, but who has no eye for the fairness of it, will find all the visible facts, but will catch nothing of their value. At once, then, the sublimity and beauty of the world are thus truths that one who pretends to insight ought to see, and they are truths which have no meaning except for such a beholder's mind, or except as embodying the thought of the mind of the world. So here, at least, is so much of the outer world that is ideal, just as the coin or the jewel or the banknote or the bond has its value, not alone in its physical presence, but in the idea that it symbolizes to a holder's mind, or to the relatively universal thought of the commercial world. But let us look a little deeper. Surely, if the objects yonder are unideal and outer, odors and tastes and temperatures do not exist in these objects in just the way in which they exist in us. Part of the being of these properties, at least, if not all of it, is ideal and exists for us, or at best is once more the embodiment of the thought or purpose of some world-mind. About tastes you cannot dispute, because they are not only ideal but personal. For the benumbed tongue and palate of diseased bodily conditions, all things are tasteless. As for temperatures, a well-known experiment will show how the same water may seem cold to one hand and warm to the other. But even so, colors and sounds are at least in part ideal. Their causes may have some other sort of reality; but colors themselves are not in the things, since they change with the light that falls on the things, vanish in the dark (whilst the things remained unchanged), and differ for different eyes. And as for sounds, both the pitch and the quality of tones depend for us upon certain interesting peculiarities of our hearing organs, and exist in nature only as voiceless sound waves trembling through the air. All such

sense qualities, then, are ideal. The world yonder may—yes, must—have attributes that give reasons why these qualities are thus felt by us; for so we assume. The world yonder may even be a mind that thus expresses its will to us. But these qualities need not, nay, cannot resemble the ideas that are produced in us, unless, indeed, that is because these qualities have placed as ideas in some world-mind. Sound waves in the air are not like our musical sensations; nor is the symphony as we hear it and feel it any physical property of the strings and the wind instruments; nor are the ether vibrations that the sun sends us like our ideas when we see the sun; nor yet is the flashing of moonlight on the water as we watch the waves a direct expression of the actual truths of fluid motion as the water embodies them.

Unless, then, the real physical world yonder is itself the embodiment of some world-spirit's ideas, which he conveys to us, unless it is real only as the maiden's heart is real, namely, as itself a conscious thought, then we have so far but one result: that real world (to repeat one of the commonplaces of modern popular science) is in itself, apart from somebody's eyes and tongue and ears and touch, neither colored nor tasteful, neither cool nor warm, neither light nor dark, neither musical nor silent. All these qualities belong to our ideas, being indeed none the less genuine facts for that, but being in so far ideal facts. We must see colors when we look, we must hear music when there is playing in our presence; but this *must* is a must that consists in a certain irresistible presence of an idea in us under certain conditions. *That* this idea must come is, indeed, a truth as unalterable, once more, as the king's settled remorse in *Hamlet*. But like this remorse, again, it exists as an ideal truth, objective, but through and through objective *for* somebody, and not *apart from* anybody. What this truth implies we have yet to see. So far it is only an ideal truth for the beholder, with just the bare possibility that behind it all there is the thought of a world-spirit. And, in fact, *so* far we must all go together if we reflect.

But now, at this point, the Berkeleyan idealist goes one step further. The real outside world that is still left unexplained and unanalyzed after its beauty, its warmth, its odors, its tastes, its colors, and its tones, have been relegated to the realm of ideal truths, what do you now *mean* by calling it real? No doubt it *is* known as somehow real, but *what* is this reality *known as* being? If you know that this world is still there and outer, as by hypothesis you know, you are bound to say *what* this outer character implies for your thought. And here you have trouble. Is the outer world, as it exists outside of your ideas, or of anybody's ideas, something having shape, filling space, possessing solidity, full of moving things? That would in the first place seem evident. That sound isn't outside of me, but the sound waves, you say, are. The colors are ideal facts; but the ether waves don't need a mind to know them. Warmth is ideal, but the physical fact called heat, this playing to and fro of molecules, is real, and is there apart from any mind. But once more, *is* this so evident? What do I *mean* by the shape of anything, or by the size of anything? Don't I mean just the idea of shape or of size

that I am obliged to get under certain circumstances? What is the meaning of any property that I give to the real outer world? How can I express that property except in case I think it in terms of my ideas? As for the sound waves and the ether waves, what are they but things ideally conceived to explain the facts of nature? The conceptions have doubtless their truth, but it is an ideal truth. What I mean by saying that the things yonder have shape and size and trembling molecules, and that there is air with sound waves, and ether with light waves in it—what I *mean* by all this is that experience forces upon me, directly or indirectly, a vast system of ideas, which may indeed be founded in truth beyond me, which in fact *must* be founded in such truth if my experience has any sense, but which, like my ideas of color and of warmth, are simply expressions of how the world's order must appear to me, and to anybody constituted like me. Above all, is this plain about space? The real things I say, outside of me, fill space, and move about in it. But what do I mean by space? Only a vast system of ideas which experience and my own mind force upon me. Doubtless these ideas have a validity. They have *this* validity, that I, at all events, when I look upon the world, am bound to see it in space, as much bound as the king in *Hamlet* was, when he looked within, to see himself as guilty and unrepentant. But just as his guilt was an idea—a crushing, an irresistible, an overwhelming idea—but still just an idea, so, too, the space in which I place my world is one great formal idea of mine. That is just why I can describe it to other people. "It has three dimensions," I say, "length, breadth, depth." I describe each. I form, I convey, I construct, an idea of it through them. I know space, as an idea, very well. I can compute all sorts of unseen truths about the relations of its parts. I am sure that you, too, share this idea. But, then, for all of us alike it is just an idea; and when we put our world into space, and call it real there, we simply think one idea into another idea, not voluntarily, to be sure, but inevitably, and yet without leaving the realms of ideas.

Thus, all the reality that *we* attribute to our world, in so far as *we* know and can tell what we mean thereby, becomes ideal. There is, in fact, a certain system of ideas, forced upon us by experience, which we have to use as the guide of our conduct. This system of ideas we can't change by our wish; it is for us as overwhelming a fact as guilt, or as the bearing of our fellows towards us, but we know it only *as* such a system of ideas. And we call it the world of matter. John Stuart Mill very well expressed the puzzle of the whole thing, as we have now reached the statement of this puzzle, when he called matter a mass of "permanent possibilities of experience" for each of us. Mill's definition has its faults, but is a very fair beginning. You know matter as something that either now gives you this idea or experience, or that would give you some other idea or experience under other circumstances. A fire, while it burns, is for you a permanent possibility of either getting the idea of an agreeable warmth, or of getting the idea of a bad burn, and you treat it accordingly. A precipice amongst mountains

is a permanent possibility of your experiencing a fall, or of your getting a feeling of the exciting or of the sublime in mountain scenery. You have no experience just now of the tropics or of the poles, but both tropical and polar climates exist in your world as permanent possibilities of experience. When you call the sun 92,000,000 miles away, you mean that between you and the sun (that is, between your present experience and the possible experience of the sun's surface) there would inevitably lie the actually inaccessible, but still numerically conceivable series of experiences of distance expressed by the number of miles in question. In short, your whole attitude towards the real world may be summed up by saying: "I have experiences now which I seem bound to have, experiences of color, sound, and all the rest of my present ideas; and I am also bound by experience to believe that in case I did certain things (for instance, touched the wall, traveled to the tropics, visited Europe, studied physics), I then should get, in a determinate order, dependent wholly upon *what* I have done, certain other experiences (for instance, experiences of the wall's solidity, or of a tropical climate, or of the scenes of a European tour, or of the facts of physics)." And this acceptance of actual experience, this belief in possible experience, constitutes all that you mean by your faith in the outer world.

But, you say, Is not, then, all this faith of ours after all well founded? Isn't there really something yonder that corresponds in fact to this series of experiences in us? Yes, indeed, there no doubt is. But what if this, which so shall correspond without us to the ideas within us, what if this hard and fast reality should itself be a system of ideas, outside of our minds but not outside of every mind? As the maiden's disdain is outside the rejected lover's mind, unchangeable so far for him, but not on that account the less ideal, not the less a fact in a mind, as, to take afresh a former fashion of illustration, the price of a security or the objective existence of this lecture is an ideal fact, but real and external for the individual person—even so why might not this world beyond us, this "permanent possibility of experience," be in essence itself a system of ideal experiences of some standard thought of which ours is only the copy? Nay, must it not be such a system in case it has any reality at all? For, after all, isn't this precisely what our analysis brings us to? Nothing whatever can I say about my world yonder that I do not express in terms of mind. *What* things are, extended, moving, colored, tuneful, majestic, beautiful, holy, *what* they are in any aspect of their nature, mathematical, logical, physical, sensuously pleasing, spiritually valuable, all this must mean for me only something that I have to express in the fashion of ideas. The more I am to know my world, the more of a mind I must have for the purpose. The closer I come to the truth about the things, the more ideas I get. Isn't it plain, then, that *if* my world yonder is anything knowable at all, it must be in and for itself essentially a mental world? Are my ideas to *resemble* in any way the world? Is the truth of my thought to consist in its *agreement* with reality? And am I thus capable, as common sense supposes, of *conforming* my

ideas to things? Then reflect. What can, after all, so well agree with an idea as another idea? To what can things that go on in my mind conform unless it be to another mind? If the more my mind grows in mental clearness, the nearer it gets to the nature of reality, then surely the reality that my mind thus resembles must be in itself mental.

After all, then, would it deprive the world here about me of reality, nay, would it not rather save and assure the reality and the knowableness of my world of experience, if I said that this world, as it exists outside of my mind, and of any other human minds, exists in and for a standard, a universal mind, whose system of ideas simply constitutes the world? Even if I fail to prove that there is such a mind, do I not at least thus make plausible that, as I said, our world of common sense has no fact in it which we cannot interpret in terms of ideas, so that this world is throughout such stuff as ideas are made of? To say this, as you see, in nowise deprives our world of its due share of reality. If the standard mind knows now that its ideal fire has the quality of burning those who touch it, and if I in my finitude am bound to conform in my experiences to the thoughts of this standard mind, then in case I touch that fire I shall surely get the idea of a burn. The standard mind will be at least as hard and fast and real in its ideal consistency as is the maiden in her disdain for the rejected lover; and I, in presence of the ideal stars and the oceans, will see the genuine realities of fate as certainly as the lover hears his fate in the voice that expresses her will.

I need not now proceed further

with an analysis that will be more or less familiar to many of you. . . . What I have desired thus far is merely to give each of you, as it were, the sensation of being an idealist in this first and purely analytical sense of the word idealism. The sum and substance of it all is, you see, this: you know your world in fact as a system of ideas about things, such that from moment to moment you find this system forced upon you by experience. Even matter, you know just as a mass of coherent ideas that you cannot help having. Space and time, as you think them, are surely ideas of yours. Now, what more natural than to say that *if* this be so, the real world beyond you must in itself be a system of somebody's ideas? If it is, then you can comprehend what its existence means. If it isn't, then since all you can know of it is ideal, the real world must be utterly unknowable, a bare *x*. Minds I can understand, because I myself am a mind. An existence that has no mental attribute is wholly opaque to me. So far, however, from such a world of ideas, existent beyond me in another mind, seeming to coherent thought essentially *un*real, ideas and minds and their ways, are, on the contrary, the hardest and stubbornest facts that we can name. *If* the external world is in itself mental, then, be this reality a standard and universal thought, or a mass of little atomic minds constituting the various particles of matter, in any case, one can comprehend what it is, and will have at the same time to submit to its stubborn authority as the lover accepts the reality of the maiden's moods. If the world *isn't* such an ideal thing, then indeed all our science, which is through and through concerned with our mental interpretations of things, can neither have objective validity, nor make satisfactory progress towards truth. For as science is concerned with ideas, the world beyond all ideas is a bare *x*. . . .

But with this result we come in presence of a final problem. All this, you say, depends upon my assurance that there is, after all, a real and therefore an essentially knowable and rational world yonder. Such a world would have to be in essence a mind, or a world of minds. But after all, how does one ever escape from the prison of the inner life? Am I not in all this merely wandering amidst the realm of my own ideas? *My* world, of course, isn't and can't be a mere *x*, an essentially unknowable thing, just because it *is my* world, and I have an idea of it. But then does not this mean that *my* world is, after all, forever just *my* world, so that I never get to any truth beyond myself? Isn't this result very disheartening? My world is thus a world of ideas, but alas! how do I then ever reach those ideas of the minds beyond me?

The answer is a simple, but in one sense a very problematic one. You, in one sense, namely, never *do* or can get beyond your own ideas, nor ought you to wish to do so, because in truth all those other minds that constitute your outer and real world are in essence one with your own self. This whole world of ideas is essentially *one* world, and so it is essentially the world of one self and *That art Thou.*

The truth and meaning of this deepest proposition of all idealism is now not at all remote from us. The considerations, however, upon which it depends are of the dryest possible sort, as commonplace as they are deep.

Whatever objects you may think about, whether they are objects directly known to you, or objects infinitely far removed, objects in the distant stars, or objects remote in time, or objects near and present—such objects, then, as a number with fifty places of digits in it, or the mountains on the other side of the moon, or the day of your death, or the character of Cromwell, or the law of gravitation, or a name that you are just now trying to think of and have forgotten, or the meaning of some mood or feeling or idea now in your mind —all such objects, I insist, stand in a certain constant and curious relation to your mind whenever you are thinking about them—a relation that we often miss because it is so familiar. What is this relation? Such an object, while you think about it, needn't be, as popular thought often supposes it to be, the *cause* of your thoughts concerning it. Thus, when you think about Cromwell's character, Cromwell's character isn't just now *causing* any ideas in you—isn't, so to speak, doing anything to you. Cromwell is dead, and after life's fitful fever his character is a very inactive thing. Not as the *cause*, but as the *object* of your thought is Cromwell present to you. Even so, if you choose now to think of the moment of your death, that moment is somewhere off there in the future, and you can make it your object, but it isn't now an active cause of your ideas. The moment of your death has no present physical existence at all, and just now causes nothing. So, too, with the mountains on the other side of the moon. When you make them the object of your

thought, they remain indifferent to you. They do not affect you. You never saw them. But all the same you can think about them.

Yet this thinking *about* things is, after all, a very curious relation in which to stand to things. In order to think *about* a thing, it is *not* enough that I should have an idea in me that merely resembles that thing. This last is a very important observation. I repeat, it is *not* enough that I should merely have an idea in me that resembles the thing whereof I think. I have, for instance, in me the idea of a pain. Another man has a pain just like mine. Say we both have toothache; or have both burned our fingertips in the same way. Now my idea of pain is just like the pain in him, but I am not on that account necessarily thinking about *his* pain, merely because what I am thinking about, namely my own pain, resembles his pain. No; to think about an object you must not merely have an idea that resembles the object, but you must *mean* to have your idea resemble that object. Stated in other form, to think of an object you must consciously aim at that object, you must pick out that object, you must already in some measure possess that object enough, namely, to identify it as what you mean. But how can you *mean* how can you *aim at,* how can you *possess,* how can you *pick out,* how can you *identify* what is not already present in essence to your own hidden self? Here is surely a deep question. When you aim at yonder object, be it the mountains in the moon or the day of your death, you really say, "I, as my real self, as my larger self, as my complete consciousness, already in deepest truth possess that object, have it, own it, identify it. And that, and that alone, makes it possible for me in my transient, my individual, my momentary personality, to mean yonder object, to inquire about it, to be partly aware of it and partly ignorant of it." You can't mean what is utterly foreign to you. You mean an object, you assert about it, you talk about it, yes, you doubt or wonder about it, you admit your private and individual ignorance about it, only in so far as your larger self, your deeper personality, your total of normal consciousness already *has* that object. Your momentary and private wonder, ignorance, inquiry or assertion, about the object, implies, asserts, presupposes, that your total self is in full and immediate possession of the object. This, in fact, is the very nature of that curious relation of a thought to an object which we are now considering. The self that is doubting or asserting, or that is even feeling its private ignorance about an object, and that still, even in consequence of all this, is *meaning*, is *aiming* at such object, is in essence identical with the self for which this object exists in its complete and consciously known truth.

So paradoxical seems this final assertion of idealism that I cannot hope in one moment to make it very plain to you. It is a difficult topic, about which I have elsewhere printed a very lengthy research,[1] wherewith I cannot here trouble you. But what I intend by thus saying that the self which thinks about an object, which really,

---

[1] See *The Religious Aspect of Philosophy* (Boston: Houghton Mifflin Company, 1885), Chapter 11, "The Possibility of Error," pp. 384-435.

even in the midst of the blindest ignorance and doubt concerning its object still means the object—that this self is identical with the deeper self which possesses and truly knows the object—what I intend hereby I can best illustrate by simple cases taken from your own experience. You are in doubt, say, about a name that you have forgotten, or about a thought that you just had, but that has now escaped you. As you hunt for the name or the lost idea, you are all the while sure that you mean just one particular name or idea and no other. But you don't yet know what name or idea this is. You try and reject name after name. You query, "Was this what I was thinking of, or this?" But after searching, you erelong find the name or the idea, and now at once you *recognize* it. "Oh, that," you say, "was what I meant all along, only—I didn't know what I meant." Did not know? Yes, in one sense you knew all the while—that is, your deeper self, your true consciousness knew. It was your momentary self that did not know. But when you found the long-sought name, recalled the lost idea, you recognized it at once, because it was all the while your own, because you, the true and larger self, who owned the name or the idea and were aware of what it was, now were seen to include the smaller and momentary self that sought the name or tried to recall the thought. Your deeper consciousness of the lost idea was all the while there. In fact, did you not presuppose this when you sought the lost idea? How can I mean a name, or an idea, unless I, in truth, am the self who knows the name, who possesses the idea? In hunting for the name or the lost idea, I am hunting for my own thought. Well, just so I know nothing about the far-off stars in detail, but in so far as I mean the far-off stars at all, as I speak of them, I am identical with that remote and deep thought of my own that already knows the stars. When I study the stars, I am trying to find out what I really mean by them. To be sure, only experience can tell me, but that is because only experience can bring me into relation with my larger self. The escape from the prison of the inner self is simply the fact that the inner self is through and through an appeal to a larger self. The self that inquires, either inquires without meaning, or if it has a meaning, this meaning exists in and for the larger self that knows.

Here is suggestion of what I mean by Synthetic Idealism. No truth, I repeat, is more familiar. That I am always meaning to inquire into objects beyond me, what clearer fact could be mentioned? That only in case it is already I who, in deeper truth, in my real and hidden thought, *know* the lost object yonder, the object whose nature I seek to comprehend, that only in this case I can truly *mean* the thing yonder—this, as we must assert, is involved in the very idea of *meaning*. That is the logical analysis of it. You can mean what your deeper self knows; you cannot mean what your deeper self doesn't know. To be sure, the complete illustration of this most critical insight of idealism belongs elsewhere. Few see the familiar. Nothing is more common than for people to think that they mean objects that have nothing to do with themselves. Kant it was, who, despite his things in themselves, first showed us that no-

body really means an object, really knows it, or doubts it, or aims at it, unless he does so by aiming at a truth that is present to his own larger self. Except for the unity of my true self, taught Kant, I have no objects. And so it makes no difference whether I know a thing or am in doubt about it. So long as I really *mean* it, that is enough. The self that *means* the object is identical with the larger self that possesses the object, just as when you seek the lost idea you are already in essence with the self that possesses the lost idea.

In this way I suggest to you the proof which a rigid analysis of the logic of our most commonplace thought would give for the doctrine that in the world there is but *one* Self, and that it is *his* world which we all alike are truly meaning, whether we talk of one another or of Cromwell's character or of the fixed stars or of the far-off aeons of the future. The relation of my thought to its object has, I insist, this curious character, that *unless* the thought and its object are part of one larger thought, I can't even be *meaning* that object yonder, can't even be in error about it, can't even doubt its existence. You, for instance, are part of one larger self with me, or else I can't even be meaning to address you as outer beings. You are part of one larger self along with the most mysterious or most remote fact of nature, along with the moon, and all the hosts of heaven, along with all truth and all beauty. Else could you not even intend to speak of such objects beyond you. For whatever you speak of you will find that your world is meant by you as just your world. Talk of the unknowable, and it forthwith becomes your unknowable, your problem, whose solution, unless the problem be a mere nonsense question, your larger self must own and be aware of. The deepest problem of life is, "What is this deeper self?" And the only answer is, *It is the self that knows in unity all truth.* This, I insist, is no hypothesis. It is actually the presupposition of your deepest doubt. And that is why I say: Everything finite is more or less obscure, dark, doubtful. Only the Infinite Self, the problem-solver, the complete thinker, the one who knows what we mean even when we are most confused and ignorant, the one who includes us, who has the world present to himself in unity, before whom all past and future truth, all distant and dark truth is clear in one eternal moment, to whom far and forgot is near, who thinks the whole of nature, and in whom are all things, the Logos, the world-possessor—only his existence, I say, is perfectly sure. . . .

QUESTIONS FOR DISCUSSION

1. Analyze in detail the meaning of and the arguments in favor of the saying that the " 'whole choir of heaven and furniture of the earth' is nothing for any of us but a system of ideas which govern our beliefs and conduct."
2. What would be a realist's or a pragmatist's position in regard to the status of alleged external objects? Could you give some of their reasons for rejecting the idealist's assertion that the so-called external objects are nothing but our ideas?
3. What is the meaning and the function of the Absolute Self in Royce's philosophy?
4. Discuss Royce's arguments in favor of the Absolute Self.
5. What would be a pluralist's difficulties with the idea of the Absolute Self? Is the Absolute Self open to human experience, or is it a speculative hypothesis?

Sterling P. Lamprecht (1890-1973)

9.5   The Meaning of Naturalism

Naturalism is not a term with a standard meaning. Few philosophic terms, if indeed any of them, have settled and established meanings that all who use them are sure to respect. Philosophers may well envy mathematicians for the ease with which they have become possessed of terms which mean precisely the same thing to all who are competent to carry on mathematical discussions. No one, not even a layman in the field of mathematics, need be in any doubt concerning the meaning of sine and cosine, of hypotenuse and parabola. It is quite different with philosophical discussions. Even the ablest philosophers often have to spend many hours in discovering the meaning attached by their fellows to terms used in debate and argument. A long book would be required to comment on the variety of meanings the term idea has had in its history from Socrates to John Dewey; and any one who introduces that word into his treatment of epistemology or metaphysics is almost certain to produce confusion. The confusion may be cleared up by

From *The Metaphysics of Naturalism* by Sterling P. Lamprecht. © 1967. Reprinted by permission of Appleton-Century-Crofts, Educational Division, Meredith Corporation.

sufficient explanation, or at least some headway towards clarity may be won. Similarly with such terms as substance, attribute, soul, mind, duty, beauty, and so on. And perhaps even more difficulty is caused by the various words which end in "ism," such as idealism, realism, rationalism, formalism, instrumentalism. This same confusion, perhaps to a more bewildering degree, is attached to the term naturalism.

No one is entitled to insist that the meaning he wishes to give to any philosophic word is the correct meaning. Therefore, in speaking in the title of this essay about the meaning of naturalism, no hint is intended that at last a final linguistic pronouncement is to be made to which all writers of philosophy ought hereafter to conform. The hope is rather the more plausible and modest one of promoting understanding of current trends in American philosophical thought. For not a few writers in this century in the United States have been willing, even eager, to call themselves naturalists. They have not all been in agreement upon details of their opinions and theories. Nonetheless, they have seemed to have a feeling of kinship among themselves. This feeling is not sheer partisanship. It is a feeling based upon confidence that one's fellows in the field of philosophical speculation, even when unfortunately mistaken on certain specific points, are yet oriented aright, can be expected in time to reconsider their views and perhaps correct their errors, and will be meticulously fair to one's own efforts to reach the truth.

A minimum amount of kinship among naturalists has always been due to their common rejection of supernaturalism and idealisms of all sorts. But there is a broader ground for the feeling of kinship than that, even if this broader ground is hard to define. The feeling of kinship has been usually generated by a conviction, not at all clearly realized by all its adherents, that we human beings are surrounded by, are involved in, and are ourselves a part of, for better or worse—or rather for better *and* worse—a vast embracing complex of forces and events from which come, surprisingly, all sorts of things, so that we meet new glories and fresh disasters at each precarious moment of our lives and may meet even more surprising things anon if, indeed, we survive to meet anything at all. This complex is what Lucretius called *alma mater*. It does undoubtedly nourish or foster us. But not always nor exclusively. It also threatens and eventually destroys us.

Normally today people call this complex the natural world or, simply, nature. And naturalism is the metaphysical theory which maintains that everything that exists comes into being, endures for a time, and then passes away because of the interactions of the things and forces of the natural world. Nature is not a single thing and does not do a simple act. Perhaps one should not refer to nature as "it," but should rather say "they." But linguistic correctness requires us to refer to any antecedent which is singular rather than plural as "it." So nature or the complex of interacting things about us is an "it." We ought always to remember that this "it" is many things, some that favor men's welfare and others that prove to be calamitous to men. In both its beneficial and its harmful contents, it embraces us, conditions us, and both provides us with such opportunities as we shall ever enjoy and sets up such dire limitations as we shall sooner or later find to mark the bounds of our finitude.

Such, I believe, is the essential position American naturalists today share. Doubtless much analysis and development are requisite to turn this position into a well-rounded metaphysical theory. And, doubtless, each naturalist, in making his particular analysis and development, will part company with his fellow-naturalists on certain moot points. I have given in the successive essays of this volume the kind of analysis and development I favor. I can make no claim to have formulated views which will win wide acceptance by other naturalists. But the basic conviction I have defined is, I believe, the common conception which runs through not only my own thinking but the thinking of almost all contemporary naturalists.

There are certain linguistic confusions in the use of the word nature which perhaps require comment at this point. Three such linguistic confusions will be noted, in the hope that the naturalist's terminology may be clarified.

We all use such expressions as "the realm of nature" and "the nature of things." But the word nature has not the same meaning in these two expressions. When we speak of the realm of nature, we refer to the constantly changing world. No situation in nature is fixed. We may speak poetically of the eternal hills, but the hills seem to remain unchanged only to a hasty glance or only in contrast to more rapid alterations of other natural situations. Columnists in the journals, bankers in their counting houses, soldiers near the battle line, indeed all of us everywhere and at all times, know that we face situations in more or less constant flux. There is nothing fixed about any natural situation. A situation would not be natural if it were static. The columnist, if he is shrewd, tries to analyze the factors that are impinging on the changing situation he is describing, so that he may infer the trend in public affairs. The banker watches the rise and fall of values in the stock market, so that his investments may be sound in the days ahead. The soldier, if alert, takes careful note of the advance or withdrawal of the enemy, the flight of planes over his head, the chance of reinforcements and of fresh supplies of munitions. All situations in nature are subject to sudden intrusions of unexpected factors as well as to transformations in the interplay of internal factors. A happy adjustment to a natural situation means adjustment to what the situation is in the process of becoming, to what the potentialities of the momentarily actual situation are, to what the immediate future—even, if possible, the more distant future—is likely to become.

When, however, we speak of the nature of things, we are trying to sum up selected aspects of things or events in formulae which can be learned and repeated and memorized as tools of knowledge. For example, the chemist may speak of the nature of sodium; the physicist, of the nature of gravitation; the politician, of the nature of democracy. These natures do not change. We may well, because we have incorrectly summed up the nature of our subject-matter, change our minds about the things and events around us, giving up the nature once chosen as descriptive of some phase of the world around us and choosing some other nature as a nearer approach to the truth. But in this sense of the word nature, one nature never changes into another nature; no one of these natures, indeed, ever changes in any respect at all. These natures are not, to speak strictly, things in the world that exists, nor are they events that occur in that world. They are abstractions utilized for the purpose of interpreting things and events; they are ideal entities the status of which is logical but not metaphysical. Our formulation of them, our thinking about them, our uses of them, are all natural events in the existing world. But they, as terms of discourse about things and events, are of a different order of being. Plato called them ideas; Santayana called them essences; others have called them subsistences. But whatever they be called, they ought never to be confused with the dynamic existences that change and pulsate through the successive stages of their history in time.

Naturalists may indeed entertain a theory concerning these abstract or ideal natures, just as they may entertain theories about political institutions or methods of securing world peace. After all, naturalists are human beings whose thinking may not always be confined to metaphysical problems. But naturalism as a type of metaphysical position is an effort to deal with nature in the sense of the host of changing existences. A natural object is an object which is involved in interaction with other objects which are also natural objects. A natural event is an event in which an object acquires or loses such qualities or relations as interaction with other objects causes it to undergo. The natural world, or the realm of nature, is the totality of natural objects and natural events that includes as well as surrounds ourselves and seems to stretch far beyond the ranges of our discernment in both spatial and temporal extent. The natural world is a vast realm of existing materials with their latent potentialities and of existing agents with their forceful capacities or potencies, such that, when any of the agents operate on any of the materials, the kind of thing we properly call natural effects will come to pass. The usage of the adjective natural with such nouns as object, event, effect, and world is a consistent development of a set of correlated and consistent meanings.

A second source of linguistic confusion has occurred because of the way in which we all, naturalists and others, are frequently prone to draw a contrast between nature and art. For certain purposes this manner of speech is quite apt. Sounds, we may say, are natural events, and music is an achievement of art. So the masses of stone in a quarry are a natural resource, and a handsome building is a work of art. The cries and calls of animals are natural expressions of emotions, and human languages—to say nothing of the diction and style of great literature—are products of art. These and all such contrasts between the natural materials that exist prior to human activity and the refashioned materials that come from human activities expended upon these natural materials—these and all such contrasts may be shown to be of great philosophic significance; they contribute to a philosophy of civilization. But however philosophically important these contrasts may be for some purposes, they are a sheer impertinence when applied to a metaphysical problem. Both the raw materials utilized in the arts and the finished products into which these materials are transformed can be pointed to as illustrations of metaphysical principles. Neither the one nor the other has any privileged status in metaphysical analysis.

The meaning the term nature has when nature and art are contrasted with each other is not that which the term has in the naturalist's discussion of metaphysics. Nature and art (in the senses those terms have when set in contrast with or in opposition to each other) are selected elements within the great complex of nature (in the sense that term has in legitimate metaphysical discussions). All the arts arise out of the natural potentialities of natural materials when some of these potentialities are brought into actuality by the natural capacities or potencies of natural agents who are endowed with trained and imaginative intelligence. Shakespeare's oft-quoted lines from *A Winter's Tale* express the point with eloquence as well as with precision.[1]

> Yet nature is made better by no mean,
> But nature makes that mean: so, over that art
> Which you say adds to nature, is an art
> That nature makes.

Not everyone would customarily use the word art in as inclusive a sense as that in which Shakespeare here uses it. Most people would choose to limit the word art to those human practices in which human foresight guides a change within the natural world. Yet Shakespeare's lines contain a meaning that is vitally important for metaphysics. An unusual extension of meaning of a word can be enlightening, and this Shakespearean instance of such extension is a case in point. For the most sophisticated human practices we call arts and the most exalted products of these practices are akin to what non-human agents and forces at times chance to bring to pass. Living things came into existence through the operation of forces which, to the best of our knowledge and in a high degree of probability, were not alive, much less intelligent and endowed with foresight or purpose. Plant life and animal life develop without guidance by conscious agents, though, of course, we human agents may intervene to direct some minor phase or the later stages of that long evolutionary development. Such natural activities of unthinking agents may well be called exhibits of "an art that nature makes." And the metaphysician may properly and quickly add that no human arts would ever have been possible, had not nature, prior to the historic appearance of the elementary forms of our human arts, already been the kind of system in which transformations of materials could give rise, and occasionally have actually given rise, to novel and significant accomplishments.

When the term nature is used to mean existential materials devoid of artistic potentialities, and when the term art must then mean processes imposed upon a recalcitrant nature, a weird metaphysical dualism ensues. But there exists no such thing as nature in that sense, and there occurs no such activity as art in that sense. The application of a legitimate contrast between nature and art to the formulation of a metaphysical system means the denigration of nature and the elevation of art to an unwholesome (because a fanciful) eminence. Nature ought not to be romantically idealized, because it contains all evils, all crimes, all ugliness. But neither ought it to be made the whipping boy of theologies and schemes of salvation which seek to rescue mankind from a horror in which, actually, he never existed. Better far it is to take the middle way with Santayana in his famous phrase: "Everything ideal has a natural basis and everything natural an ideal development." [2]

We may therefore say, in summary of this discussion of the import of the contrast between nature and art, that in legitimate usages of the various words, nature is a creator of many arts and all human arts are realizations of some of nature's vast potentialities. The most glorious manifestations of the arts are also manifestations of latent possibilities within nature. Art is sometimes shoddy, and

---

[1] Act IV, scene 4, lines 89-92.

[2] *The Life of Reason*, Vol. I (New York: Scribner, 1905-6), p. 21.

so, here and there, is nature. Art is sometimes magnificent, and so, here and there, is nature. The emergence of the fine arts is evidence of some, though probably not of all, of nature's capacities. Nature is the matrix of whatever is fine in existential developments as well as of whatever is base. More of nature's capacities may still be latent and may emerge in later times. But of the emergence of further accomplishments than those not actualized, we may have hopes but can have no assurance.

A third source of linguistic confusion arises when a contrast is drawn between nature and spirit. Much the same kind of criticism needs to be made of this contrast as has just been made of the contrast between nature and art. But before giving this criticism, we need to determine the meaning we may profitably give to the word spirit. For as used by one person or another, or in one human culture or another, the word spirit ranges in meaning from the most untutored of superstitions to the most lofty of moral insights.

In what anthropologists call primitive culture the belief in spirits is often found. The brook runs because animated by the brook spirit; the sun shines because animated by the sun spirit or the spirit of light; and so forth. These spirits have to be propitiated by men unless men would risk the spirits' displeasure and hence their own disasters. Much of the religious beliefs and practices of primitive peoples is concerned with spirits. The souls of the dead, too, are often thought of as spirits which may guard their families or tribes but may also haunt those who do not feed them or give the desired care and respect.

Spirits sometimes develop into gods. The Greek gods of course had bodies of fine stature, beauty, and more-than-natural skills; and so it has been with the gods of other social groups. But in other cases the gods have been disembodied spirits, uncontaminated by association with material forms. For with growth of belief in spirits has normally gone a tendency to denigrate matter and, indeed, the whole realm of nature, so that the natural is deemed inferior and only spirit is regarded as superior. Even if, as is sometimes the case, some spirits are regarded as dangerous, even as evil (hence as demons or devils), their status as spirits gives them more-than-natural powers and techniques of control.

The theologies of what are referred to as advanced religions are greatly influenced by the concept of spirit. Similiarly philosophies written by those who stand in these religious traditions incorporate ideas which stem from the more primitive beliefs. Such, it may fairly be said, are the *res cogitans* of Descartes and the "spiritual substances" of Locke. In spite of the sophistication of these great thinkers, their doctrines about spiritual beings are but survivals of ancient superstitions, clothed in the context of new interests and made plausible by incorporation in systems of important ideas.

Now naturalists, we may properly say, reject all such notions of spirits, disembodied souls, non-material personal gods, and more-than-natural agencies. The grounds for the rejection of these notions are a lack of evidence adequate to support these notions. Nature, in the course of its diverse ramifications and developments, brings all sorts of things to pass. Antecedently to investigation, there is nothing which might not, in theory at least, be deemed a possible development within nature. But though no one, be he naturalist or opponent of naturalism, has any philosophical or scientific right to set *a priori* limits to the capacities of natural agencies and forces, neither can he, be he naturalist or opponent of naturalism, assume the right to people the existent world with fancies or fantasies. Every assertion that a certain thing or type of thing actually exists requires evidence to support it. Conclusive proof is often impossible to achieve, and men must frequently rest satisfied with probabilities. But probability is the outcome of an impartial weighing of evidence, and differs enormously from credulity stemming from a wish-to-believe or an emotional preference for one thing against another. A sound naturalism is impossible except when leashed to a determined purpose to apply dispassionately the most stringent methods of empiricism. Testimony about such things as Poltergeister and ghosts and other non-material (hence, spiritual) existences has proved untenable time and time again. And the arguments for the gods (or God), while more dignified as they occur in the Judaic-Christian tradition, are not empirically satisfactory.[3] Hence naturalists seem thoroughly justified in rejecting the existence of spirits of all stages of primitive and advanced cultures.

While the many shades of mean-

---

[3] The arguments and the alleged evidence can not be examined in this place. A little more examination is given in [my] essay entitled "Naturalism and Religion."

ing of the word spirit can not even be listed in this essay, much less analyzed and discussed, one other meaning of the term ought to receive attention. This meaning is one that naturalists, at least many naturalists, are glad to affirm. We speak of the spirit of democracy, the spirit of fair play, the spirit of justice, and so forth. We also speak of the life of the spirit. In these usages we are dealing with what most surely is existential and hence is a factor in certain morally approved situations. The spirit of fair play (or any other such spirit) does not occur except as an ingredient in the life of a conscious and responsible person. This spirit is a qualitative aspect of a person's life or of an institution's administrative procedure. The person or the institution must exist in order then to manifest the spirit. Apart from persons and institutions a spirit in this sense of the term could not be an agent in society, but would be "reduced" to the status of an abstract principle: it would then preferably be referred to, not as the spirit of fair play, but as fair play or justice or whatever principle one is engaged in defining. Just as shape by or in itself is not an existent thing, but an aspect of the manner in which many things exist, so spirit is not an existent thing by itself but an aspect in the lives of certain existent things. But as an aspect in the lives of certain existent things, it is most surely itself existent too.

The phrase "the life of the spirit" deserves attention at this point. There is the greedy life, the sensual life, the commercial life, the moral life, the spiritual life. The spiritual life, or the life of the spirit, is a qualitatively supreme life: such, at least, it has been defined as and spoken of in the greatest cultural traditions of mankind. The phrase, like many other terms used in philosophical writings, has no standard meaning. But among the possible meanings, one may be affirmed as not merely consistent with the naturalistic position, but requisite to any discerning naturalism. There are many legitimate goals of human endeavor; there are many desirable goods men may and, indeed, ought to seek. In practice, distraction often occurs in human actions. A single chosen goal, desirable in its context in a man's life, may become so emphasized as to thwart the realization of other goals of equal or even higher value. There is then a dire need for balance, for recognition of levels of value, for a planned hierarchy of goods. The architectonic arrangement of ideals in a systematic synthesis is the only safeguard against such pursuit of one good as to eventuate in a neglect of other goods, perhaps of the best goods. And conscious adherence to that inclusive vision of ideal possibilities is the spiritual life. To remember the inclusive ideal while occupied with seizing the partial good is to give a heightened excellence to the partial good and a redeeming grace to those who, at the same time, see clearly their moral limitations and their need of moral compromises.

Naturalists differ from certain other groups of metaphysicians in that they insist that spirit, in the sense in which we may legitimately speak of the life of the spirit, is as much a part of nature as anything else. Like color or like magnetism, it emerges within nature in specific ways and at specific times. Like color and like magnetism, it is not omnipresent. But to treat nature and spirit as two different realms of being is to separate an achievement from the grounds of its occurrence.

It was said above, before discussion of the way in which nature and art, and also nature and spirit, are frequently spoken of as disparate and even antithetical, that nature is intended by naturalists as a term referring to all that exists and all that occurs. But it means something additional to that synoptic manner of referring to the whole of existence. That additional meaning is that, among the vast resources of the existential world, there are to be found the generating materials and forces of all that has ever been actual in the past, all that is now actual, all that will ever be actual, and, doubtless, of much else that might become actual if alternate and incompatible potentialities had not been actualized instead. The conditions for the appearance of any and every object are some of the materials and forces within the complex of nature's vast resources. The conditions for the survival of any and every object are materials and forces that sustain, feed, assist or at least tolerate those objects. The conditions for the destruction or ending of any and every object are the lack of sustaining aids or, as is often the case, the overt assault of different and existentially unreconcilable objects. The beginning, the continued being, and the passing away of each and every thing are consequences of the operation of some of nature's potent factors.

How much unity there is in nature remains an open question which a naturalist has no adequate means for deciding. Spinoza believed that the whole of nature's manner of generating the many types of "modes" could be formulated—though he, indeed, would be the last to claim he could himself sum up that formulation—in one logically compact set of propositions. There is something stirring in Spinoza's faith in the involvement of every part of the cosmos in every other part. And Spinoza's faith may be true. We certainly do not know, and we can not know, that the faith is false. We go along with Spinoza in scientific practice. That is, we seek, so far as we can, to put together our many conclusions about the nature of things in an ordered body of rounded truths. We even speak, perhaps too glibly but ever hopefully, of the *system* of nature. There certainly have been discovered certain systems of truths that display the character of segments of nature, and there may ideally be an inclusive system of these lesser systems. But just as there are gaps in our knowledge of nature, so there seem to be loose ends and unconnected occurrences in nature itself. It may not be even theoretically possible for a world that is full of contingency and of incompatible potentialities to be described in one set of logically related propositions. The history of scientific discoveries suggests, however, and suggests quite persuasively, that it pays to carry on investigations in the spirit of him who ever hopes for a more ordered knowledge.

In the listing of the many, many things and many, many kinds of things we encounter in nature, the naturalist comes to no end and believes that it is humanly impossible to come to an end. Other metaphysicians seem to suppose that they may sum up existence in a neat formula. The naturalist rejects such suppositions and is always alert for some new development and some new exhibition of nature's fertility of productive powers. Alone among metaphysicians the naturalist is not subject to Hamlet's response to his friend: [4]

> There are more things in heaven and
>   earth, Horatio,
> Then are dreamt of in your philosophy.

History does not repeat itself, and nature is not exhausted by its manifold developments to date. What materialists and idealists and dualists and others find, the naturalist also is glad to acknowledge to be where and when those things are found. But the naturalist is never ready to grant that the kinds of existence which other metaphysicians list bring to an end the manifestations of nature's cosmic resources.

For a naturalist, the word nature is neither a eulogistic nor a dyslogistic term. Vast power and vast resources may receive admiration from most men; for there is something both amazing and dazzling about sheer bigness. But one can be amazed and dazzled by what one does not therefore approve. Nature is not a moral matter at all. Our human reactions to nature *are* a moral matter, however. But that is because we are what we are, not because nature is subject to moral judgments.

There are two virtues that naturalists ought to be proud to exhibit towards nature. One of these looks towards the origin of human life and human society, and the other looks towards future possibilities.

---

[4] *Hamlet,* Act I, scene 5, lines 166-167.

The first of these two virtues may be called piety. It is piety in a very special sense of that word—the sense Santayana gives it when he defines it as "man's reverent attachment to the sources of his being and the steadying of life by that attachment." [5] The sources of our being are manifold. Among them are father, mother, family, teachers, friends, institutions of school and of government, country, and so forth. But before all these legitimate grounds of piety is that system of nature from which these many other grounds themselves come. Nature is the paramount ground of a wise and discerning piety. Without piety to nature, morality is exposed to whim and caprice. Sound morality can not be formulated in terms of abstract principles which have no reference to where we are, by what we are surrounded, by what we are conditioned, by what we may utilize as raw materials of our enterprises, by the obstacles in our path, by the opportunities in nature's potentialities and by the limits of those natural potentialities. Nature's contingency is the occasion of some of the disasters that hamper us and is also the ground of our genuine freedom.[6] "Piety," Santayana goes on to say, "is the spirit's acknowledgment of its incarnation." [7] Without piety towards nature, morality runs the risk of irrelevance. We surely ought not to act as if we were in a different kind of world from what actually (and potentially) is around us. We ought not to feel re-

sentment at our inevitable mortality, anger at storm or drought, ill humor at intrusion of unanticipated factors into our carefully planned arrangements. We are children of nature and nature is our *alma mater*. Piety towards nature is an insurance against flippant disregard of the conditions of achievement. We excel, if we excel at all, by learning to make the most of nature's opportunities while yet taking the adversities of nature's ways with a degree of grace.

The second of the two virtues naturalists ought to exhibit towards nature is courage. What is at any moment is not what inevitably and continuously must be. Change is always at hand. Novelty may appear. Other metaphysicians who accept the course of events as the working out of an imposed plan often find the good life in submission. Nature for them is a summons to acquiescence. For the naturalist nature is rather a challenge to creativity. Optimism may be and often is foolish; but despair is craven. Even if some planetary catastrophe made our earth uninhabitable by such creatures as men, nature, as we know full well, is fertile in producing living forms and may produce conscious and rational living things again in some other parts of its far reaches. Even during the comparative balance and stability of forces in our present solar system, the emergence of new ways of living is pressing upon mankind in rapid succession. The timid person is one of nature's failures. Nature is such that its denizens can prosper only if they love adventure. Without love of adventure men become victims of dull routine or even of destructive decay. Many types of philosophers other than naturalists give strong evidence of a

---

[5] *Reason in Religion*, Vol. III of *The Life of Reason*, p. 179.
[6] See [my] essay entitled "Metaphysical Background of the Problem of Freedom."
[7] *Reason in Religion*, p. 184.

love of adventure and a superb courage in facing life's exigencies. But the naturalist puts a reasoned metaphysics behind adventure and courage, a metaphysics that makes adventure inevitable and courage requisite.

Naturalism is primarily a term for a type of metaphysics; and it perhaps ought not to be extended to cover an ethical theory, too. But the greatest philosophers have always found significant intellectual bearings of a metaphysics upon all other branches of philosophical speculation. Aristotle and Spinoza are notable illustrations of this fact. And in the sense in which naturalism has here been defined and defended, Aristotle and Spinoza are two of the most conspicuous naturalists in the history of western philosophical traditions. It does not therefore seem without warrant to end a discussion of naturalism with some comment on its bearing upon ethical principles. No system of metaphysics has an exclusive right to claim consistency with whatever ethical principles the metaphysicians may deem true. But some metaphysical systems, though they may be such that ethical principles are consistent therewith (in the sense, at least, that the principles are not inconsistent) do not lead significantly to the ethical principles. Naturalism, in the meaning given the term in the essays of this volume, makes piety to nature and courage to face nature's contingencies and potentialities requisite for any rational inhabitant of our existential system of things and events. Whatever bearing naturalism may have for other ethical ideals and principles, it is a metaphysical position which gives at least these two virtues a sanction arising from the very nature of things.

QUESTIONS FOR DISCUSSION

1. Discuss in detail the main ideas of Lamprecht's naturalistic philosophy. Critically examine his arguments.
2. What are the objections of the supernaturalists to naturalism? Do you find their objections acceptable?
3. How does Lamprecht distinguish between "the realm of nature" and "the nature of things," and also between "nature and art"?
4. Is there any place, if any, in Lamprecht's naturalism for the notion of spirit? If so, what meaning and function does he give to the notion of spirit?
5. Lamprecht says, "There are two virtues that naturalists ought to be proud to exhibit toward nature." What are these two virtues? Are these virtues tenable in other metaphysical systems? What is the relation of one's metaphysics to one's ethics?

Alfred North Whitehead (1861-1947)

9.6 Process-Philosophy

MATTER AND PROCESS

The notion of empty space, the mere vehicle of spatial interconnections has been eliminated from recent science. The whole spatial universe is a field of force, or in other words, a field of incessant activity. The mathematical formulae of physics express the mathematical relations realized in this activity.

The unexpected result has been the elimination of bits of matter, as the self-identical supports for physical properties. . . . Matter has been identified with energy, and energy is sheer activity; the passive substratum composed of self-identical enduring bits of matter has been abandoned, so far as concerns any fundamental description. Obviously this notion expresses an important derivative fact. But it has ceased to be the presupposed basis of theory. The modern point of

From *Religion in the Making* by Alfred North Whitehead, © 1935 by The Macmillan Company, renewed 1954 by Evelyn Whitehead, and *Modes of Thought* by Alfred North Whitehead, © 1938 by The Macmillan Company, renewed 1966 by T. North Whitehead. Reprinted with permission of The Macmillan Company. This selection was prepared by Albert Lataner, former member of the Philosophy Department, City College of New York.

view is expressed in terms of energy, activity, and the vibratory differentiations of space-time. Any local agitation shakes the whole universe. The distant effects are minute, but they are there. The concept of matter presupposed simple location. Each bit of matter was self-contained, localized in a region with a passive, static network of spatial relations, entwined in a uniform relational system from infinity to infinity and from eternity to eternity. But in the modern concept the group of agitations which we term matter is fused into its environment. There is no possibility of a detached, self-contained local existence. The environment enters into the nature of each thing. Some element in the nature of a complete set of agitations may remain stable as those agitations are propelled through a changing environment. But such stability is only the case in a general, average way. This average fact is the reason why we find the same chair, the same rock, and the same planet, enduring for days, or for centuries, or for millions of years. In this average fact then time-factor takes the aspect of endurance, and change is a detail. The fundamental fact, according to the physics of the present day, is that the environment with its peculiarities seeps into the group-agitation which we call matter and the group-agitations extend their character to the environment. In truth, the notion of the self-contained particle of matter, self-sufficient within its local habitation, is an abstraction. Now an abstraction is nothing else than the omission of part of the truth. The abstraction is well-founded when the conclusions drawn from it are not vitiated by the omitted truth.

This general deduction from the modern doctrine of physics vitiates many conclusions drawn from the application of physics to other sciences, such as physiology, or even such as physics itself. For example, when geneticists conceive genes as the determinants of heredity, the analogy of the old concept of matter sometimes leads them to ignore the influence of the particular animal body in which they are functioning. They presuppose that a pellet of matter remains in all respects self-identical whatever be its changes of environment. So far as modern physics is concerned, any characteristic may, or may not, effect changes in the genes, changes which are as important in certain respects, though not in others. Thus no a priori argument as to the inheritance of characters can be drawn from the mere doctrine of genes. In fact, recently physiologists have found that genes are modified in some respects by their environment. The presuppositions of the old common sense view survive, even when the view itself has been abandoned as a fundamental description.

LIFE

The doctrine that I am maintaining is that neither physical nature nor life can be understood unless we fuse them together as essential factors in the composition of "really real" things whose interconnections and individual characters constitute the universe.

The first step in the argument must be to form some concept of what life can mean. Also, we require that the deficiencies in our concept of physical nature should be supplied by its fusion with life. And we require that, on the other hand, the notion of life should involve the notion of physical nature.

Now as a first approximation the notion of life implies a certain absoluteness of self-enjoyment. This must mean a certain immediate individuality, which is a complex process of appropriating into a unity of existence the many data presented as relevant by the physical processes of nature. Life implies the absolute, individual self-enjoyment arising out of this process of appropriation. I have, in my recent writings, used the word "prehension" to express this process of appropriation. Also, I have termed each individual act of immediate self-enjoyment an "occasion of experience." I hold that these unities of existence, these occasions of experience, are the really real things which in their collective unity compose the evolving universe, ever plunging into the creative advance.

This concept of self-enjoyment does not exhaust that aspect of process here termed "life." Process for its intelligibility involves the notion of a creative activity belonging to the very essence of each occasion. It is the process of eliciting into actual being factors in the universe which antecedently to that process exist only in the mode of unrealized potentialities.

The process of self-creation is the transformation of the potential into the actual, and the fact of such transformation includes the immediacy of self-enjoyment.

Thus in conceiving the function of life in an occasion of experience, we must discriminate the actualized data presented by the antecedent world, the non-actualized potentialities which lie ready to promote their fusion into a new unity of experience, and the immediacy of self-enjoyment which belongs to the creative fusion of those data with those potentialities. This is the doctrine of the creative advance whereby it belongs to the essence of the universe, that it passes into a future. It is nonsense to conceive of nature as a static fact, even for an instant devoid of duration. There is no nature apart from transition and there is no transition apart from temporal duration. This is the reason why the notion of an instant of time, conceived as a primary simple fact, is nonsense.

But even yet we have not exhausted the notion of creation which is essential to the understanding of nature. We must add yet another character to our description of life. This missing characteristic is "aim." By this term "aim" is meant the exclusion of the boundless wealth of alternative potentiality, and the inclusion of that definite factor of novelty which constitutes the selected way of entertaining those data in that process of unification. The aim is at that complex of feeling which is the enjoyment of those data in that way. "That way of enjoyment" is selected from the boundless wealth of alternatives. It has been aimed at for actualizations in that process.

Thus the characteristics of life are absolute self-enjoyment, creative activity, aim. Here "aim" evidently involves the entertainment of the purely ideal so as to be directive of the creative process. Also the enjoyment belongs to the process and is not a characteristic of any static result. The aim is at the enjoyment belonging to the process.

MIND

. . . . "Cogito, ergo sum" is wrongly translated, "I think, therefore I am." It is never bare thought or bare existence that we are aware of. I find myself as essentially a unity of emotions, enjoyments, hopes, fears, regrets, valuations of alternatives, decisions—all of them subjective reactions to the environment as active in my nature. My unity—which is Descartes' "I am"—is my process of shaping this welter of material into a consistent pattern of feeling. The individual enjoyment is what I am in my role of a natural activity, as I shape the activities of the environment into a new creation, which is myself at this moment; and yet, as being myself, it is a continuation of the antecedent world. If we stress the role of the environment, this process is causation. If we stress the role of my immediate pattern of active enjoyment, this process is self-creation. If we stress the role of the conceptual anticipation of the future whose existence is a necessity in the nature of the present, this process is the teleological aim at some ideal in the future. This aim, however, is not really beyond the present process. For the aim at the future is an enjoyment in the present. It thus effectively conditions the immediate self-creation of the new creature.

We can now again ask the final

question as put forward at the close of the former lecture. Physical science has reduced nature to activity, and has discovered abstract mathematical formulae which are illustrated in these activities of Nature. But the fundamental question remains, How do we add content to the notion of bare activity? This question can only be answered by fusing life with nature.

In the first place, we must distinguish life from mentality. Mentality involves conceptual experience, and is only one variable ingredient in life. The sort of functioning here termed "conceptual experience" is the entertainment of possibilities for ideal realization in abstraction from any sheer physical realization. The most obvious example of conceptual experience is the entertainment of alternatives. Life lies below this grade of mentality. Life is the enjoyment of emotion, derived from the past and aimed at the future. It is the enjoyment of emotion which was then, which is now, and which will be then. This vector character is of the essence of such entertainment.

The emotion transcends the present in two ways. It issues from, and it issues towards. It is received, it is enjoyed, and it is passed along, from moment to moment. Each occasion is an activity of concern, in the Quaker sense of that term. It is the conjunction of transcendence and immanence. The occasion is concerned, in the way of feeling and aim, with things that in their own essence lie beyond it; although these things in their present functions are factors in the concern of that occasion. Thus each occasion, although engaged in its own immediate self-realization, is concerned with the universe.

The process is always a process of modification by reason of the numberless avenues of supply, and by reason of the numberless modes of qualitative texture. The unity of emotion, which is the unity of the present occasion, is a patterned texture of qualities, always shifting as it is passed into the future. The creative activity aims at preservation of the components and at preservation of intensity. The modifications of pattern, the dismissal into elimination, are in obedience to this aim.

NATURE

A rough division can be made of six types of occurrences in nature. The first type is human existence, body and mind. The second type includes all sorts of animal life, insects, the vertebrates, and other genera. In fact, all the various types of animal life other than human. The third type includes all vegetable life. The fourth type consists of the single living cells. The fifth type consists of all large-scale inorganic aggregates, on a scale comparable to the size of animal bodies, or larger. The sixth type is composed of the happenings on an infinitesimal scale, disclosed by the minute analysis of modern physics.

Now all of these functionings of Nature influence each other, require each other, and lead on to each other. The list has purposely been made roughly, without any scientific pretension. The sharp-cut scientific classifications are essential for scientific method. But they are dangerous for philosophy. Such classification hides the truth that the different modes of natural existence shade off into each other. There is the animal life with its central direction of a society of cells, there is the vegetable life with its organized republic of cells, there is the cell life with its organized republic of molecules, there is the large-scale inorganic society of molecules with its passive acceptance of necessities derived from spatial relations, there is the infra-molecular activity which has lost all trace of the passivity of inorganic nature on a larger scale.

In this survey some main conclusions stand out. One conclusion is the diverse modes of functioning which are produced by diverse modes of organization. The second conclusion is the aspect of continuity between these different modes. There are border-line cases, which bridge the gaps. Often the border-line cases are unstable, and pass quickly. But span of existence is merely relative to our habits of human life. For infra-molecular occurrence, a second is a vast period of time. A third conclusion is the difference in the aspect of nature according as we change the scale of observation. Each scale of observation presents us with average effects proper to that scale.

. . . . In so far as conceptual mentality does not intervene, the grand patterns pervading the environment are passed on with the inherited modes of adjustment. Here we find the patterns of activity studied by the physicists and chemists. Mentality is merely latent in all these occasions as thus studied. In the case of inorganic nature any sporadic flashes are inoperative so far as our powers of discernment are concerned. The lowest stages of effective mentality, controlled by the inheritance of physical pattern, involve the faint direction of emphasis by unconscious ideal aim. The various examples of the higher forms of life exhibit the variety of grades of effectiveness of mentality. In the social habits of animals, there is evidence of flashes of mentality in the past which have degenerated into physical habits. Finally, in the higher mammals and more particularly in mankind, we have clear evidence of mentality habitually effective. In our own experience, our knowledge consciously entertained and systematized can only mean such mentality, directly observed.

. . . . In these lectures I have not entered upon systematic metaphysical cosmology. The object of the lectures is to indicate those elements in our experience in terms of which such a cosmology should be constructed. The key notion from which such construction should start is that the energetic activity considered in physics is the emotional intensity entertained in life.

GOD

Unlimited possibility and abstract creativity can procure nothing. The limitation, and the basis arising from what is already actual, are both of them necessary and interconnected.

Thus the whole process itself, viewed at any stage as a definite limited fact which has issued from the creativity, requires a definite entity, already actual among the formative elements, as an antecedent ground for the entry of the ideal forms into the definite process of the temporal world.

But such a complete aboriginal actuality must differ from actuality in process of realization in respect to the blind occasions of perceptivity which issue from process and require process. These occasions build up the physical world which is essentially in transition.

God, who is the ground antecedent to transition, must include all possibilities of physical value conceptually, hereby holding the ideal forms apart in equal, conceptual realization of knowledge. Thus, as concepts, they are grasped together in the synthesis of omniscience.

The limitation of God is his goodness. He gains his depth of actuality by his harmony of valuation. It is not true that God is in all respects infinite. If He were, He would be evil as well as good. Also, this unlimited fusion of evil with good would mean mere nothingness. He is something decided and is thereby limited.

He is complete in the sense that his vision determines every possibility of value. Such a complete vision coordinates and adjusts every detail. Thus his knowledge of the relationships of particular modes of value is not added to, or disturbed, by the realization in the actual world of what is already conceptually realized in his ideal world. This ideal world of conceptual harmonization is merely a description of God himself. Thus the nature of God is the complete conceptual realization of the realm of ideal forms. The kingdom of heaven is God. But these forms are not realized by him in mere bare isolation, but as elements in the value of his conceptual experience. Also, the ideal forms are in God's vision as contributing to his complete experience, by reason of his conceptual realization of their possibilities as elements of value in any creature. Thus God is the one systematic, complete fact, which is the antecedent ground conditioning every creative act.

The depths of his existence lie beyond the vulgarities of praise or of power. He gives to suffering its swift insight into values which can issue from it. He is the ideal companion who transmutes what has been lost into a living fact within his own nature. He is the mirror which discloses to every creature its own greatness.

The kingdom of heaven is not the isolation of good from evil. It is the overcoming of evil by good. This transmutation of evil into good enters into the actual world by reason of the inclusion of the nature of God, which includes the ideal vision of each actual evil so met with a novel consequent as to issue in the restoration of goodness.

God has in his nature the knowledge of evil, of pain, and of degradation, but it is there as overcome with what is good. Every fact is what it is, a fact of pleasure, of joy, of pain, or of suffering. In its union with God that fact is not a total loss, but on its finer side is an element to be woven immortally into the rhythm of mortal things. Its very evil becomes a stepping-stone in the all-embracing ideals of God.

Every event on its finer side introduces God into the world. Through it his ideal vision is given a base in actual fact to which He provides the ideal consequent, as a factor saving the world from the self-destruction of evil. The power by which God sustains the world is the power of himself as the ideal. He adds himself to the actual ground from which every creative act takes its rise. The world lives by its incarnation of God in itself.

He transcends the temporal world, because He is an actual fact in the nature of things. He is not there as derivative from the world; He is the actual fact from which the other formative elements cannot be torn apart.

But equally it stands in his nature that He is the realization of the ideal conceptual harmony by reason of which there is an actual process in the total universe—an evolving world which is actual because there is order.

The abstract forms are thus the link between God and the actual world. These forms are abstract and not real, because in themselves they represent no achievement of actual value. Actual fact always means fusion into one perceptivity. God is one such conceptual fusion, embracing the concept of all such possibilities graded in harmonious, relative subordination. Each actual occasion in the temporal world is another such fusion. The forms belong no more to God than to any one occasion. Apart from these forms, no rational description can be given either of God or of the actual world. Apart from God, there would be no actual world; and apart from the actual world with its creativity, there would be no rational explanation of the ideal vision which constitutes God.

Each actual occasion gives to the creativity which flows from it a definite character in two ways. In one way, as a fact, enjoying its complex of relationships with the rest of the world, it contributes a ground—partly good and partly bad—for the creativity to fuse with a novel consequent, which will be the outcome of its free urge. In another way, as transmuted in the nature of God, the ideal consequent as it stands in his vision is also added. Thus God in the world is the perpetual vision of the road which leads to the deeper realities.

QUESTIONS FOR DISCUSSION

1. In what sense is reality a creative process in Whitehead's philosophy?
2. What does Whitehead mean when he says that "the deficiencies in our concept of physical nature should be supplied by its fusion with life"? Do you find this suggestion acceptable?
3. Critically discuss Whitehead's theories of life and mind.
4. Critically examine Whitehead's statement, "God is the complete conceptual realization of the realm of ideal forms." Also his statement, "The power by which God sustains the world is the power of himself as the ideal."

Jean-Paul Sartre (1905-   )

9.7   Existentialism

What is meant by the term *existentialism?*

Most people who use the word would be rather embarrassed if they had to explain it, since now that the word is all the rage, even the work of a musician or painter is being called existentialist. . . . It seems that for want of an advance-guard doctrine analogous to surrealism, the kind of people who are eager for scandal and flurry turn to this philosophy which in other respects does not at all serve their purposes in this sphere.

Actually, it is the least scandalous, the most austere of doctrines. It is intended strictly for specialists and philosophers. Yet it can be defined easily. What complicates matters is that there are two kinds of existentialist; first, those who are Christian, among whom I would include Jaspers and Gabriel Marcel, both Catholic; and on the other hand, the atheistic existentialists, among whom I class Heidegger, and then the French existentialists and myself. What they have in common is that they think that existence precedes essence, or, if

From *Existentialism Is a Humanism* by Jean-Paul Sartre. © Philosophical Library, Inc., 1947. Reprinted by permission of Philosophical Library.

you prefer, that subjectivity must be the starting point.

Just what does that mean? Let us consider some object that is manufactured, for example, a book or a paper-cutter: here is an object which has been made by an artisan whose inspiration came from a concept. He referred to the concept of what a paper-cutter is and likewise to a known method of production, which is part of the concept, something which is, by and large, a routine. Thus, the paper-cutter is at once an object produced in a certain way and, on the other hand, one having a specific use; and one cannot postulate a man who produces a paper-cutter but does not know what it is used for. Therefore, let us say that, for the paper-cutter, essence—that is, the ensemble of both the production routines and the properties which enable it to be both produced and defined—precede existence. Thus, the presence of the paper-cutter or book in front of me is determined. Therefore, we have here a technical view of the world whereby it can be said that production precedes existence.

When we conceive God as the Creator, He is generally thought of as a superior sort of artisan. Whatever doctrine we may be considering, whether one like that of Descartes or that of Leibnitz, we always grant that will more or less follows understanding or, at the very least, accompanies it, and that when God creates He knows exactly what He is creating. Thus, the concept of man in the mind of God is comparable to the concept of paper-cutter in the mind of the manufacturer, and, following certain techniques and a conception, God produces man, just as the artisan, following a definition and a technique, makes a paper-cutter. Thus, the individual man is the realization of a certain concept in the divine intelligence.

In the eighteenth century, the atheism of the *philosophes* discarded the idea of God, but not so much for the notion that essence precedes existence. To a certain extent, this idea is found everywhere; we find it in Diderot, in Voltaire, and even in Kant. Man has a human nature: this human nature, which is the concept of the human, is found in all men, which means that each man is a particular example of a universal concept, man. In Kant, the result of this universality is that the wild-man, the natural man, as well as the bourgeois, are circumscribed by the same definition and have the same basic qualities. Thus, here too the essence of man precedes the historical existence that we find in nature.

Atheistic existentialism, which I represent, is more coherent. It states that if God does not exist, there is at least one being in whom existence precedes essence, a being who exists before he can be defined by any concept, and that this being is man, or as Heidegger says, human reality. What is meant here by saying that existence precedes essence? It means that, first of all, man exists, turns up, appears on the scene, and, only afterwards, defines himself. If man, as the existentialist conceives him, is indefinable, it is because at first he is nothing. Only afterward will he be something, and he himself will have made what he will be. Thus, there is no human nature, since there is no God to conceive it. Not only is man what he conceives himself to be, but he is also only what he wills himself to be after this thrust toward existence.

Man is nothing else but what he makes of himself. Such is the first principle of existentialism. It is also what is called subjectivity, the name we are labeled with when charges are brought against us. But what do we mean by this, if not that man has a greater dignity than a stone or table? For we mean that man first exists, that is, that man first of all is the being in the future. Man is at the start a plan which is aware of itself, rather than a patch of moss, a piece of garbage, or a cauliflower; nothing exists prior to this plan; there is nothing in heaven; man will be what he will have planned to be. Not what he will want to be. Because by the word "will" we generally mean a conscious decision, which is subsequent to what we have already made of ourselves. I may want to belong to a political party, write a book, get married; but all that is only a manifestation of an earlier, more spontaneous choice that is called "will." But if existence really does precede essence, man is responsible for what he is. Thus, existentialism's first move is to make every man aware of what he is and to make the full responsibility of his existence rest on him. And when we say that a man is responsible for himself, we do not only mean that he is responsible for his own individuality, but that he is responsible for all men.

The word subjectivism has two meanings, and our opponents play on the two. Subjectivism means, on the one hand, that an individual chooses and makes himself; and, on the other, that it is impossible for man to transcend human subjectivity. The second of these is the essential meaning of existentialism. When we say that man chooses his own self, we mean that every one of us does likewise; but we also mean by that that in making this choice he also chooses all men. In fact, in creating the man that we want to be, there is not a single one of our acts which does not at the same time create an image of man as we think he ought to be. To choose to be this or that is to affirm at the same time the value of what we choose, because we can never choose evil. We always choose the good, and nothing can be good for us without being good for all.

If, on the other hand, existence precedes essence, and if we grant that we exist and fashion our image at one and the same time, the image is valid for everybody and for our whole age. Thus, our responsibility is much greater than we might have supposed, because it involves all mankind. If I am a workingman and choose to join a Christian trade-union rather than be a communist, and if by being a member I want to show that the best thing for man is resignation, that the kingdom of man is not of this world, I am not only involving my own case—I want to be resigned for everyone. As a result, my action has involved all humanity. To take a more individual matter, if I want to marry, to have children; even if this marriage depends solely on my own circumstances or passion or wish, I am involving all

humanity in monogamy and not merely myself. Therefore, I am responsible for myself and for everyone else. I am creating a certain image of man of my own choosing. In choosing myself, I choose man.

This helps us understand what the actual content is of such rather grandiloquent words as anguish, forlornness, despair. As you will see, it's all quite simple.

First, what is meant by anguish? The existentialists say at once that man is anguish. What that means is this: the man who involves himself and who realizes that he is not only the person he chooses to be, but also a law-maker who is, at the same time, choosing all mankind as well as himself, cannot help escape the feeling of his total and deep responsibility. Of course, there are many people who are not anxious; but we claim that they are hiding their anxiety, that they are fleeing from it. Certainly, many people believe that when they do something, they themselves are the only ones involved, and when someone says to them, "What if everyone acted that way?" they shrug their shoulders and answer, "Everyone doesn't act that way." But really, one should always ask himself, "What would happen if everybody looked at things that way?" There is no escaping this disturbing thought except by a kind of double-dealing. A man who lies and makes excuses for himself by saying "not everybody does that," is someone with an uneasy conscience, because the act of lying implies that a universal value is conferred upon the lie.

Anguish is evident even when it conceals itself. This is the anguish that Kierkegaard called the anguish of Abraham. You know the story: an

angel has ordered Abraham to sacrifice his son; if it really were an angel
who has come and said, "You are
Abraham, you shall sacrifice your
son," everything would be all right.
But everyone might first wonder, "Is
it really an angel, and am I really
Abraham? What proof do I have? . . .

Now, I'm not being singled out as
an Abraham, and yet at every moment I'm obliged to perform exem-
plary acts. For every man, everything
happens as if all mankind had its eyes
fixed on him and were guiding itself
by what he does. And every man
ought to say to himself, "Am I really
the kind of man who has the right
to act in such a way that humanity
might guide itself by my actions?"
And if he does not say that to himself,
he is masking his anguish.

There is no question here of the
kind of anguish which would lead to
quietism, to inaction. It is a matter
of a simple sort of anguish that anybody who has had responsibilities is
familiar with. For example, when a
military officer takes the responsibility
for an attack and sends a certain number of men to death, he chooses to do
so, and in the main he alone makes
the choice. Doubtless, orders come
from above, but they are too broad;
he interprets them, and on this interpretation depend the lives of ten or
fourteen or twenty men. In making
a decision he cannot help having a
certain anguish. All leaders know this
anguish. That doesn't keep them from
acting; on the contrary, it is the very
condition of their action. For it implies that they envisage a number of
possibilities, and when they choose
one, they realize that it has value only
because it is chosen. We shall see that
this kind of anguish, which is the
kind that existentialism describes, is

explained, in addition, by a direct responsibility to the other men whom
it involves. It is not a curtain separating us from action, but is part of
action itself.

When we speak of forlornness, a
term Heidegger was fond of, we mean
only that God does not exist and that
we have to face all the consequences
of this. The existentialist is strongly
opposed to a certain kind of secular
ethics which would like to abolish
God with the least possible expense.
About 1880, some French teachers
tried to set up a secular ethics which
went something like this: God is a
useless and costly hypothesis; we are
discarding it; but, meanwhile, in order for there to be an ethics, a society,
a civilization, it is essential that certain values be taken seriously and that
they be considered as having an *a
priori* existence. It must be obligatory,
a priori, to be honest, not to lie, not
to beat your wife, to have children,
etc., etc. So we're going to try a little
device which will make it possible to
show that values exist all the same,
inscribed in a heaven of ideas, though
otherwise God does not exist. In other
words—and this, I believe, is the tendency of everything called reformism
in France—nothing will be changed if
God does not exist. We shall find ourselves with the same norms of honesty, progress, and humanism, and we
shall have made of God an outdated
hypothesis which will peacefully die
off by itself.

The existentialist, on the contrary,
thinks it very distressing that God
does not exist, because all possibility
of finding values in a heaven of ideas
disappear along with Him; there can
no longer be an *a priori* Good, since
there is no infinite and perfect consciousness to think it. Nowhere is it

written that the Good exists, that we must be honest, that we must not lie; because the fact is we are on a plane where there are only men. Dostoievsky said, "If God didn't exist, everything would be possible." That is the very starting point of existentialism. Indeed, everything is permissible if God does not exist, and as a result man is forlorn, because neither within him nor without does he find anything to cling to. He can't start making excuses for himself.

If existence really does precede essence, there is no explaining things away by reference to a fixed and given human nature. In other words, there is no determinism, man is free, man is freedom. On the other hand, if God does not exist, we find no values or commands to turn to which legitimize our conduct. So, in the bright realm of values, we have no excuse behind us, no justification before us. We are alone, with no excuses.

That is the idea I shall try to convey when I say that man is condemned to be free. Condemned, because he did not create himself, yet, in other respects is free; because, once thrown into the world, he is responsible for everything he does. The existentialist does not believe in the power of passion. He will never agree that a sweeping passion is a ravaging torrent which fatally leads a man to certain acts and is therefore an excuse. He thinks that man is responsible for his passion.

The existentialist does not think that man is going to help himself by finding in the world some omen by which to orient himself. Because he thinks that man will interpret the omen to suit himself. Therefore, he thinks that man, with no support and no aid, is condemned every moment to invent man. Ponge, in a very fine article, has said, "Man is the future of man." That's exactly it. But if it is taken to mean that this future is recorded in heaven, that God sees it, then it is false, because it would really no longer be a future. If it is taken to mean that, whatever a man may be, there is a future to be forged, a virgin future before him, then this remark is sound. But then we are forlorn.

To give you an example which will enable you to understand forlornness better, I shall cite the case of one of my students who came to see me under the following circumstances: his father was on bad terms with his mother, and, moreover, was inclined to be a collaborationist; his older brother had been killed in the German offensive of 1940, and the young man, with somewhat immature but generous feelings, wanted to avenge him. His mother lived alone with him, very much upset by the half-treason of her husband and the death of her older son; the boy was her only consolation.

The boy was faced with the choice of leaving for England and joining the Free French Forces—that is, leaving his mother behind—or remaining with his mother and helping her to carry on. He was fully aware that the woman lived only for him and that his going-off—and perhaps his death— would plunge her into despair. He was also aware that every act that he did for his mother's sake was a sure thing, in the sense that it was helping her to carry on, whereas every effort he made toward going off and fighting was an uncertain move which might run aground and prove completely useless; for example, on his way to England he might, while passing through Spain, be detained indefinitely in a Spanish camp; he might reach

England or Algiers and be stuck in an office at a desk job. As a result, he was faced with two very different kinds of action: one, concrete, immediate, but concerning only one individual; the other concerned an incomparably vaster group, a national collectivity, but for that very reason was dubious, and might be interrupted en route. And, at the same time, he was wavering between two kinds of ethics. On the one hand, an ethics of sympathy, of personal devotion; on the other, a broader ethics, but one whose efficacy was more dubious. He had to choose between the two.

Who could help him choose? Christian doctrine? No. Christian doctrine says, "Be charitable, love your neighbor, take the more rugged path, etc., etc." But which is the more rugged path? Whom should he love as a brother? The fighting man or his mother? Which does the greater good, the vague act of fighting in a group, or the concrete one of helping a particular human being to go on living? Who can decide *a priori?* Nobody. No book of ethics can tell him. The Kantian ethics says, "Never treat any person as a means, but as an end." Very well, if I stay with my mother, I'll treat her as an end and not as a means; but by virtue of this very fact, I'm running the risk of treating the people around me who are fighting, as means, and, conversely, if I go to join those who are fighting, I'll be treating them as an end, and, by doing that, I run the risk of treating my mother as a means.

If values are vague, and if they are always too broad for the concrete and specific case that we are considering, the only thing left for us is to trust our instincts. That's what this young man tried to do; and when I saw him,

he said, "In the end, feeling is what counts. I ought to choose whichever pushes me in one direction. If I feel that I love my mother enough to sacrifice everything else for her—my desire for vengeance, for action, for adventure—then I'll stay with her. If, on the contrary, I feel that my love for my mother isn't enough, I'll leave."

But how is the value of a feeling determined? What gives his feeling for his mother value? Precisely the fact that he remained with her. I may say that I like so-and-so well enough to sacrifice a certain amount of money for him, but I may say so only if I've done it. I may say, "I love my mother well enough to remain with her" if I have remained with her. The only way to determine the value of this affection is, precisely, to perform an act which confirms and defines it. But, since I require this affection to justify my act, I find myself caught in a vicious circle. . . .

As for despair, the term has a very simple meaning. It means that we shall confine ourselves to reckoning only with what depends upon our will, or on the ensemble of probabilities which make our action possible. When we want something, we always have to reckon with probabilities. I may be counting on the arrival of a friend. The friend is coming by rail or streetcar; this supposes that the train will arrive on schedule, or that the streetcar will not jump the track. I am left in the realm of possibility; but possibilities are to be reckoned with only to the point where my action comports with the ensemble of these possibilities, and no further. The moment the possibilities I am considering are not rigorously involved by my action, I ought to disengage myself from them, because no God, no scheme, can adapt the world and its possibilities to my will. When Descartes said, "Conquer yourself rather than the world," he meant essentially the same thing.

The Marxists to whom I have spoken reply, "You can rely on the support of others in your action, which obviously has certain limits because you're not going to live forever. That means: rely on both what others are doing elsewhere to help you, in China, in Russia, and what they will do later on, after your death, to carry on the action and lead it to its fulfillment, which will be the revolution. You even *have* to rely upon that, otherwise you're immoral." I reply at once that I will always rely on fellow fighters insofar as these comrades are involved with me in a common struggle, in the unity of a party or a group in which I can more or less make my weight felt; that is, one whose ranks I am in as a fighter and whose movements I am aware of at every moment. In such a situation, relying on the unity and will of the party is exactly like counting on the fact that the train will arrive on time or that the car won't jump the track. But, given that man is free and that there is no human nature for me to depend on, I cannot count on men whom I do not know by relying on human goodness or man's concern for the good of society. I don't know what will become of the Russian revolution; I may make an example of it to the extent that at the present time it is apparent that the proletariat plays a part in Russia that it plays in no other nation. But I can't swear that this will inevitably lead to a triumph of the proletariat. I've got to limit myself to what I see.

Given that men are free, and that tomorrow they will freely decide what man will be, I cannot be sure that, after my death, fellow fighters will carry on my work to bring it to its maximum perfection. Tomorrow, after my death, some men may decide to set up Fascism, and the others may be cowardly and muddled enough to let them do it. Fascism will then be the human reality, so much the worse for us.

Actually, things will be as man will have decided they are to be. Does that mean that I should abandon myself to quietism? No. First, I should involve myself; then, act on the old saw, "Nothing ventured, nothing gained." Nor does it mean that I shouldn't belong to a party, but rather that I shall have no illusions and shall do what I can. For example, suppose I ask myself, "Will socialization, as such, ever come about?" I know nothing about it. All I know is that I'm going to do everything in my power to bring it about. Beyond that, I can't count on anything. Quietism is the attitude of people who say, "Let others do what I can't do." The doctrine I am presenting is the very opposite of quietism, since it declares, "There is no reality except in action." Moreover, it goes further, since it adds, "Man is nothing else than his plan; he exists only to the extent that he fulfills himself; he is, therefore, nothing else than the ensemble of his acts, nothing else than his life."

QUESTIONS FOR DISCUSSION

1. Analyze Sartre's assertion that "existence precedes essence, or if you prefer, that subjectivity must be the starting point."
2. Why does absolute freedom cause anguish, anxiety, and forlornness in Sartre? Are we absolutely free in our actions? What are the limits, if any, of our freedom?
3. Sartre says, "For every man, everything happens as if all mankind had its eyes fixed on him and were guiding itself by what he does. And every man ought to say to himself, 'Am I really the kind of man who has the right to act in such a way that humanity might guide itself by my actions?'" Clarify the meaning of this quotation. Do you agree with Sartre?
4. Contrast the essentialist's and the existentialist's views on the nature of man. Could these two views be synthesized?

FURTHER READINGS FOR CHAPTER 9

Bergson, Henri, *Creative Evolution*. New York: Modern Library, 1944.

Bradley, Francis H., *Appearance and Reality*. New York: Oxford University Press, 1930.

*Dewey, John, *Experience and Nature*. LaSalle, Ill.: Open Court, n.d.

*Leibniz, Gottfried Wilhelm von, *Discourse on Metaphysics*, G. R. Montgomery, trans. LaSalle, Ill.: Open Court, n.d.

*Plato, *Timeaus*, Benjamin Jowett, trans. Indianapolis: Bobbs-Merrill, 1959.

*Royce, Josiah, *The World and the Individual*, 2 vols. New York: Dover, 1959.

Sheldon, Wilmon H., *God and Polarity*. New Haven: Yale University Press, 1954.

*Spinoza, Benedict de, *Ethics*, William H. White, trans., Part I. New York: Hafner, 1953.

*Whitehead, Alfred North, *Process and Reality*. New York: Harper & Row, n.d.

---

* Paperback edition.

Appendix **A**

BIOGRAPHICAL DATA

Anselm, Saint (1033-1109), born in Aosta (Italy); became an abbot in 1078; was Archbishop of Canterbury from 1093 until his death. The two works for which he is famous are *The Monologium* and *The Proslogium*. His ontological argument for the existence of God has attracted philosophers like Descartes and Spinoza, and been criticized by Kant and others.

Aquinas, Saint Thomas (1225-1274), born in Roccasicca (lower Italy), received his education at the Monte Cassino Abbey and in Naples, Cologne, and Paris; taught theology in Paris (1256-72) and several years in Rome and other cities. Generally regarded as the greatest of the Scholastic theologians. His two major works are *Summa Theologica* and *Summa Contra Gentiles*, which respectively synthesized Aristotelian and Christian doctrines, and attempted to answer the objections against Catholicism.

Aristotle (384-322 B.C.), son of a physician, studied in Plato's Academy for twenty years before founding his own more empirical school, the Lyceum. He tutored Alexander the Great. Wrote on logic, ethics, aesthetics, metaphysics, biology, physics, psychology, politics; had an enormous influence on medieval Hebrew, Arabic, and Christian philosophers, especially on St. Thomas Aquinas and his later scholastic followers. *The Works of Aristotle,* ed. W. D. Ross (1908-28).

Ayer, Sir Alfred Jules (1910-   ), Wykeham Professor of Logic, Oxford University, Fellow of New College and of the British Academy; author of *Language, Truth and Logic* (1936), *Foundations of Empirical Knowledge* (1940), *The Concept of Person* (1963), *The Origins of Pragmatism* (1969).

Bacon, Sir Francis (1561-1626), British statesman, essayist, philosopher. Criticized traditional scholastic philosophy as barren; he wanted philosophers to do more observing and classifying instead of a priori reasoning, as he felt this could lead to important discoveries, such as scientists were making. He described his method in a series of volumes, the most important of which are *Advancement of Learning* (1605), *Novum Organum* (1620), *New Atlantis* (1624).

Bergson, Henri (1859-1941), French speculative philosopher; born in the year of publication of Darwin's *Origin of Species,* he was much influenced by the theory of evolution. His most important work, *Creative Evolution,* appeared in English in 1911. Other works include *The Two Sources of Morality and Religion* (1935), *The Creative Mind* (1946).

Berkeley, George (1685-1753), Anglican bishop of Cloyne, vigorously opposed materialism and atheism; called his view "the immaterial hypothesis," although he is usually referred to as a subjective idealist. His philosophy is a strange combination of empiricism and idealism, of immaterialism and common sense. Author of *An Essay towards a New Theory of Vision* (1709), *A Treatise Concerning the Principles of Human Knowledge* (1710), *Three Dialogues between Hylas and Philonous* (1713), *Alciphron, or the Minute Philosopher* (1733).

Berlin, Sir Isaiah (1909-   ), President of Wolfson College (Oxford) since 1966. First Secretary of the British Embassy in Washington (1942-46) and Moscow (1945). Professor of Humanities at City University of New York; author of *Karl Marx* (1939), *The Hedgehog and the Fox* (1957), *Historical Inevitability* (1958), *Four Essays on Liberty* (1969).

Broad, Charlie Dunbar (1887-   ), British philosopher; attended Trinity College (Cambridge), where he was influenced by F. H. Bradley, W. McTaggart, W. E. Johnson, Bertrand Russell, and G. E. Moore. The latter's *Refutation of Idealism*, he says, "knocked the bottom out of my youthful subjective idealism." Author of *Perception, Physics and Reality* (1914), *Scientific Thought* (1923), *Mind and Its Place in Nature* (1925), *Five Types of Ethical Theory* (1930), *Examination of McTaggart's Philosophy* (2 vols. 1933, 1938), *Religion, Philosophy and Psychical Research* (1953).

Buber, Martin (1878-1956), educated in Austria and Germany; in later years, Professor of Philosophy at the Hebrew University in Jerusalem. The outstanding representative of the Judaic-existentialist trend, which he combined with the Hassidic tradition in his religious philosophy, educational and psychological theory, social philosophy. Author of *I and Thou* (1937), *Eclipse of God* (1951).

Campbell, Norman (1880-1949), British engineer and philosopher of science. Graduate and Fellow of Trinity College (Cambridge); research staff of General Electric (1911-44). Author of *Physics: The Elements* (1920), *What is Science?* (1921), *Measurement* (1928), *Photo-Electric Cells* (1929, 1934). Honorary Fellow of Leeds University.

Croce, Benedetto (1866-1952), Italian philosopher, statesman, literary critic, and historian; was an advocate of Absolute Idealism; Senator and Minister of Education, and a major figure in defense of liberalism during the period of Fascism. Editor of *La Critica;* wrote extensively on aesthetics, metaphysics, and historical theory. Author of *Aesthetic* (1909), *Philosophy of the Practical* (1913), *History as the Story of Liberty* (1941).

Descartes, René (1596-1650), French mathematician, scientist, philosopher, has exerted an enormous influence on modern and contemporary philosophy. His *Discourse on Method* (1637) and *Meditations on First Philosophy* (1641) are among the most readable of philosophical writings. Other works include *Principles of Philosophy* (1644), *The Passions of the Soul* (1649), *Objections* and *Replies* (to the *Meditations*).

Dewey, John (1859-1952), social psychologist, educator, philosopher, graduate of University of Vermont (1879), Ph.D. Johns Hopkins University (1884), where he met C. S. Peirce, G. S. Morris, and Thorstein Veblen. Taught at universities of Minnesota, Michigan, Chicago, where he worked with G. H. Mead, and Columbia, where he met Jane Adams. Author of *Psychology* (1887), *School and Society* (1899), *Ethics* (with J. H. Tufts, 1908), *Democracy and Education* (1916), *Human Nature and Conduct* (1922), *Experience and Nature* (1925), *The Quest for Certainty* (1929), *Art as Experience* (1934), *Logic: the Theory of Inquiry* (1938), *Problems of Men* (1946).

Ducasse, Curt J. (1881-1969), born in France, educated at the Lycée in Bordeaux and later at the Abbotsholme School in England; continued his studies at the University of Washington and at Harvard University. Taught for many years at Brown University, retiring in 1958. Author of many articles in metaphysics, theory of knowledge, and philosophy of art on a relativistic basis. His books include *The Philosophy of Art* (1930), *Nature, Mind and Death* (1949).

Gilson, Etienne (1884-   ), French philosopher and historian of philosophy; Professor of the History of Mediaeval Philosophy at the Sorbonne; one of the founders of the Institute of Mediaeval Philosophy at Toronto (1929); author of *The Spirit of Mediaeval Philosophy* (1936), *Modern Philosophy, Descartes to Kant* (1962), *The Philosopher and Theology* (1962), *Painting and Reality* (1955), *The Spirit of Thomism* (1964).

Ginsberg, Morris (1889-1970), Professor and Head of Department of Sociology at London School of Economics for twenty-five years; President of the Aristotelian Society (1942-43); Fellow of the British Academy (1953); author of *On the Diversity of Morals* (1956), *Evolution and Progress* (1961), *Nationalism: A Reappraisal* (1961), *On Justice in Society* (1965).

Hare, Richard M. (1919-   ), Fellow of Balliol College (Oxford), where he has taught Ethics for many years. Author of *Freedom and Reason* (1963), and of articles and reviews in *Mind*. *The Language of Morals* (1952) includes an abridgment of his winning dissertation for the T. H. Green Moral Philosophy Prize at Oxford.

Hegel, Georg W. F. (1770-1831), German philosopher, educated in theology at Tübingen; Professor of Philosophy at Jena, Heidelberg, and Berlin; at first a follower of Schelling. During Napoleonic occupation, wrote *Phenomenology of Mind* (1807). Author of *Science of Logic* (1812-16), *Encyclopedia of the Philosophical Sciences* (1817), *Philosophy of Right* (1821), and books on philosophy of history, philosophy of religion, history of philosophy, and aesthetics.

Hobbes, Thomas (1588-1679), graduate of Oxford University, tutor of Prince Charles, lived in exile in France (1640-51); his materialism offended churchmen. His complete works (11 vols.) include *De Cive* (1642), *Leviathan* (1651), *De Corpore Politico* (1650), *De Homine* (1658), and *Behemoth* (1680).

Hume, David (1711-1776), British philosopher, historian and essayist, whose views on causality stimulated Kant to construct his "critical philosophy"; noted for his development of the empiricism of Locke and Berkeley and for his skepticism. Author of *Treatise on Human Nature* (1739), *Inquiry into Human Understanding* (1748), *Dialogues on Natural Religion* (1779), *Inquiry Concerning the Principles of Morals* (1751).

James, William (1842-1910), American philosopher and psychologist, received his M.D. from Harvard in 1869, lectured there on anatomy and physiology until

1880, when he joined the Department of Psychology and Philosophy; amended and popularized Peirce's pragmatism in a series of books which include *The Will to Believe and other essays in popular philosophy* (1897), *The Varieties of Religious Experience* (1902), *Pragmatism* (1907), *Essays in Radical Empiricism* (1912).

Kant, Immanuel (1724-1804), born in Königsberg and never traveled from it. In 1770 he became Professor of Logic and Metaphysics at the University of Königsberg while under the influence of the rationalism of Leibniz and Wolff (his "precritical" period). After studying Hume, he wrote his famous *Critique of Pure Reason* (1st ed. 1781; 2nd ed. 1787), *Foundations of the Metaphysics of Morals* (1785), *Critique of Practical Reason* (1788), and *Critique of Judgment* (1790). His *Religion within the Limits of Mere Reason* (1793-94) was censored by the state. His *Philosophy of Right* and *Essay on Perpetual Peace* contain his philosophy of law and constructive view of international relations and world peace. His humanism aimed to avoid dogmatic rationalism and skepticism, and appealed to the necessity of a universal sense of duty and good will, treating all individuals as ends in themselves (see Categorical Imperative).

King, Rev. Martin Luther (1929-1968), Ph.D. Boston University (1955), D.D. Crozer Theological Seminary (1959), recipient of many honorary degrees and of the Nobel Peace Prize in 1964. President of the Southern Christian Leadership Conference; author of *Stride Toward Freedom* (1956), *Why We Can't Wait* (1964), and *Where Do We Go From Here* (1967). Killed by an assassin's bullet April 4, 1968.

Lamprecht, Sterling P. (1890-1973), born in Cleveland; attended Williams College, Harvard University, The Union Theological School, and Columbia University; taught at Amherst College until his retirement; one of the outstanding American naturalist philosophers; author of *Nature and History* (1950), *The Metaphysics of Naturalism* (1967).

Macintosh, Douglas C. (1877-1948), born in Toronto; for many years Professor of Theology and the Philosophy of Religion at the Yale School of Religion; major contribution was the development of theology as an empirical science; author of *The Problem of Knowledge* (1915), *Theology as an Empirical Science* (1919), *The Problem of Religious Knowledge* (1940).

Marx, Karl (1818-1883), born in Germany, lived in London after 1850; wrote his Ph.D. thesis (1842) on Greek atomistic philosophy; editor of *Rheinische Zeitung* (1842) which was suppressed in 1843; joined F. Engels in Paris to develop theory of socialism; criticized Proudhon (1847); founded the First International Workingmen's Association (1864). Author of *Communist Manifesto* (1847), *Das Kapital* (1867), *Civil War in France* (1871), *Critique of Political Economy* (1859).

Mill, John Stuart (1806-1873), educated privately by his father (James Mill) and by Jeremy Bentham; after 1823 he worked in civil service (India House) while studying political economy, logic, music criticism, and social ethics; author of *Systems of Logic* (1843), *Principles of Political Economy* (1848), *Essay on Liberty* (1858), *Utilitarianism* (1863). With Harriet Taylor he advocated reforms in emancipation of women, labor organizations, and cooperatives.

Moore, George Edward (1873-1958), British philosopher, frankly admitted that the world and the sciences would not have suggested any philosophical problems to him; what did stimulate him to philosophize was what other philosophers said about the world or the sciences. He attended Cambridge with Bertrand Russell, who persuaded him to major in philosophy. Editor of *Mind* (1921-47). Most of his books are collections of articles or lectures; they include *Principia Ethica* (1903), *Philosophical Studies* (1922); *Some Main Problems of Philosophy* (lectures of 1910-11) was published in 1953; *Philosophical Papers* (1959) contains two of the most famous of his writings, "A Defence of Common Sense" and "Proof of An External World."

Nagel, Ernest (1901-   ), John Dewey Professor of Philosophy at Columbia University (1955-66), where he still teaches; Professor at Graduate Center, City University of New York (1970-71); author of *On the Logic of Measurement* (Ph.D. dissertation, 1931); *Introduction to Logic and Scientific Method* (with M. R. Cohen, 1932), *Sovereign Reason* (1954), *Logic Without Metaphysics* (1957), *Gödel's Proof* (with J. R. Newman, 1958), *The Structure of Science* (1960).

Nietzsche, Friedrich W. (1844-1900), a German romantic philosopher, was born in Röcken, a Prussian province of Saxony; his academic training was in theology and classical languages and literature at the University of Bonn; the influence of Schopenhauer's philosophy led him away from both theological studies and traditional Christianity. Granted a professorship at Basle, he resigned in 1879 because of poor health; author of *The Birth of Tragedy* (1872), *Thus Spoke Zarathustra* (1883 ff), *Beyond Good and Evil* (1886), *Genealogy of Morals* (1887).

Parker, DeWitt (1885-1949) studied at Harvard under Josiah Royce, William James, and George Santayana. Taught two years at the University of California, but most of his life at the University of Michigan. His creative work centered on the philosophy of value, including aesthetics and the philosophy of art. Author of *The Principles of Aesthetics* (1920), *Experience and Substance* (1941).

Peirce, Charles S. (1839-1914), son of mathematician Benjamin Peirce; graduate of Harvard (1859), M.A. in chemistry; astronomer and mathematical physicist for U.S. Coast Geodetic Survey; lecturer in Logic at Johns Hopkins University (his only teaching post, 1879-83); author of *Photometric Researches* (1878); edited *Johns Hopkins Studies in Logic* (1882); published articles on logic, mathematics, scientific method, and pragmatism in *Journal of Speculative Philosophy, Monist, Nation, Popular Science Monthly,* Baldwin's *Dictionary of Philosophy,* and *Century Dictionary.* Harvard has published eight volumes of his *Collected Papers* (1931-58).

Perry, Ralph B. (1876-1957), Ph.D., Harvard (1899), where he was Professor (1913-46); one of the leading "neo-Realists" in the theory of knowledge; made a major contribution in his relativistic *General Theory of Value* (1926); also deeply concerned with the ideals of democracy in public life; author of *The Thought and Character of William James* (1935), *The Moral Economy* (1909), *The Present Conflict of Ideals* (1918), *Realms of Value* (1954).

Price, Henry H. (1899-   ), educated at New College (Oxford), and connected for many years with Oxford University; his major philosophic interests have been in the problems and theories of perception and thought; author of *Perception* (1932), *Truth and Corrigibility* (1936), *Thinking and Experience* (1953).

Plato (427-347 B.C.), of noble parentage, a pupil and friend of Socrates; after a disappointing stay at the court of Dionysius in Sicily, he founded in Athens a philosophical school, the Academy, with emphasis on mathematics and logical analysis, using dialogue form and the Socratic method of examining opinions. Three of his dialogues, *Apology, Crito, Phaedo,* feature Socrates' trial and death; others are: *Euthyphro* on religion, *Charmides* on courage, *Lysis* on friendship, *Theaetetus* on knowledge, *Republic* on the ideal state, *Laws* on practical government, *Timaeus* on cosmology, *Parmenides* on the Eleatic metaphysics, *Symposium* on love, *Phaedrus* on the idea of beauty.

Poincaré, Henri (1854-1912), one of the greatest philosophical mathematicians; member of the French Academy; discovered Fuchsian and Abelian functions; author of *Science and Hypothesis* (1902), *Science and Method* (1904), *The Value of Science* (1908), and works on mathematical physics.

Royce, Josiah (1855-1916), born in Grass Valley, California; studied at the University of California and at Leipzig and Göttingen; received Ph.D. at Johns Hopkins University; began his teaching career at the University of California; taught for many years (1882-1916) at Harvard University; his Absolute Idealism is a unique synthesis of pluralism and monism; author of *The World and the Individual* (1900), *The Philosophy of Loyalty* (1908), *The Problem of Christianity* (1913).

Russell, Earl Bertrand (1872-1970), British philosopher, mathematician, and educationist, one of the most prolific, versatile, and influential philosophers of all time; he wrote on logic, psychology, mathematics, metaphysics, epistemology, ethics, politics, philosophy of science, social philosophy, religion, history of philosophy, philosophy of education. Some of his writings are highly technical, e.g., *Principles of Mathematics* (1903) and the monumental *Principia Mathematica* (with A. N. Whitehead, 3 vols. 1910-13); others are popular or semipopular, e.g., *Unpopular Essays* (1950), *The Autobiography of Bertrand Russell* (3 vols.). A good volume for the beginning student would be *Problems of Philosophy* (1912); more advanced readings are in *Logic and Knowledge,* R. C. Marsh, ed. (1956). Russell's views of his predecessors and some contemporaries are expressed in *A History of Philosophy* (1946).

Ryle, Gilbert (1900-   ), Wayneflete Professor of Metaphysics, Oxford University; Fellow of Magdalen College; editor of *Mind* since 1947; author of *The Concept of Mind* (1949), *Dilemmas* (1954), *Plato's Progress* (1965).

Samuel, Viscount Edwin H. (1870-1963), Lecturer in Philosophy, Oxford University; author of *Philosophy and the Ordinary Man* (1932), *Practical Ethics* (1935), *Essays in Physics* (1950), *In Search of Reality* (1957).

Santayana, George (1863-1952), born in Madrid of Spanish parents; emigrated to the United States, where he attended the Boston Latin School and Harvard University. He taught at Harvard as the colleague of William James and Josiah Royce, and spent the latter part of his life in Italy. Eminent as a poet, essayist, novelist, and philosopher; author of a classic, the five-volume *Life of Reason* (1905), a naturalistic and materialistic interpretation of the life of the spirit; he was one of six "critical realists"; other books include *Scepticism and Animal Faith* (1923) and the four-volume *Realms of Being* (1927-40).

Sartre, Jean-Paul (1905-   ), born in Paris; began training in philosophy in Paris and continued in Germany, where he came under the influence of Heidegger and Husserl; taught at Le Havre and Paris. A German prisoner during World War II, he was later released because of poor health. Widely known as an atheistic Marxist existentialist, gifted essayist and playwright, emphasizing man's forlornness and anguish, and the unavoidable role of free choice; author of *Being and Nothingness* (1943), *Existentialism* (1946).

Smart, J. J. C. (1920-   ), educated at the University of Glasgow and at Oxford, Professor of Philosophy at the University of Adelaide in Australia; author of *An Outline of a System of Utilitarian Ethics* (1961), and *Problems of Space and Time* (1964).

Spinoza, Benedict de (1632-1677), born in Amsterdam of Marrano Jews; excommunicated for criticizing Biblical stories of angels, miracles, and anthropomorphic God; made a living as lens-grinder while writing a Hebrew grammar, an exposition of Descartes' philosophy, an *Ethics, demonstrated in geometric order,* an unfinished essay on *Improvement of the Understanding,* and a *Tractatus Theologico-Politicus* (on religion and representative government).

Stace, Walter T. (1886-1971), British and American philosopher, born in London, graduated from Trinity College, Dublin in 1908; taught at Princeton from 1932 until he retired in 1955; President of the American Philosophical Association in 1949; author of *The Theory of Knowledge and Existence* (1932), *The Concept of Morals* (1937), *The Destiny of Western Man* (1942), *Time and Eternity* (1952), *Religion and the Modern Mind* (1952). Although an empiricist all his life, Stace was attracted to mysticism, which he tried to reconcile with empiricism in his book *Mysticism and Philosophy* (1960).

Tillich, Paul (1886-1965), born in Germany; attended the Universities of Berlin, Tübingen, Halle, and Breslau; taught at several German universities, Harvard University, the University of Chicago, and the Union Theological Seminary in New York. One of the most influential Protestant theologians, he fused existentialism with essentialism using a historical approach; author of *The Interpretation of History* (1936), *Systematic Theology* (2 vols.), *The Courage To Be* (1952).

Waismann, Friedrich (1896-1959), member of the Vienna Circle, friend and disciple of Wittgenstein, whose views he reported at its meetings. Author of *Introduction to Mathematical Thinking* (1951), and *The Principles of Linguistic Philosophy* (1965).

Waldman, Louis (1892-   ), well known labor lawyer and a leader of the Bar; an acknowledged expert in labor-management relations, industrial welfare, and pension programs; he has had an extensive practice in civil and criminal law, with cases involving labor, corporate matters, civil liberties; he is also an authority on social movements in this and other countries. Author of many works, including *Labor Lawyer,* an autobiography; past President and life trustee of the Brooklyn Bar Association; past Chairman of the Committee on Civil Rights of the New York State Bar Association, and a member of its Executive Committee.

Whitehead, Alfred N. (1861-1947), British philosopher of science, mathematician and metaphysician; taught at Cambridge and University of London, and then at Harvard University (1924-37). Author of *A Treatise on Universal Algebra* (1898), *An Introduction to Mathematics* (1911), *Science and the Modern World* (1925), *The Aims of Education* (1929), *Process and Reality* (1929), *Adventures of Ideas* (1933), *Modes of Thought* (1938), and *Principia Mathematica* (with Bertrand Russell, 3 vols. 1910-13).

GLOSSARY OF
PHILOSOPHICAL TERMS

Absolute   1. Not relative; unconditioned; independent; unchanging.   2. An important term in the philosophies of idealists such as Schelling, Hegel, Coleridge, Bradley, Bosanquet, Bergson, Royce, in whose view the Absolute is a unity, unconditioned, and the only ultimately real thing. See *Idealism.*

Absolutism   Opposed to relativism. In ethics, the view that there are moral rules or principles that are the same for all cultures and for all individuals. In aesthetics, the view that beauty is not in the eye of the beholder, that it is not relative to personal valuations or to an individual's experience, but is an objective, unvarying property of things. See *Relativism.*

Ad hoc   A hypothesis is said to be *ad hoc* if it is specially devised for the purpose of explaining a particular set of circumstances, but cannot be supported by independent evidence. Such a hypothesis does not really explain anything, although it may appear to do so.

Ad hominem   Literally "to the man," instead of to the point; name calling or character assassination as an easy substitute for reasoning. In logic, the *ad hominem* is a fallacy of irrelevance.

Analytic   A proposition is said to be analytic if it is true because of definitions or because of its logical form. It is sometimes defined as a proposition whose denial would involve a self-contradiction. Analytic truths are necessarily true, and cannot be refuted by any observation. Examples: (1) *Squares are equilateral;* (2) *All fathers have at least one child;* (3) *From truths only truths can validly be deduced.* Propositions that are not analytic are called *synthetic.* See *A priori.*

A priori   A proposition is said to be *a priori* if its truth can be determined by thought alone, without empirical investigation. All analytic truths are *a priori.* Most philosophers believe that all *a priori* truths are analytic, but some hold, agreeing with Kant, that there are synthetic *a priori* truths.

A posteriori   Based on experience, or experiment; not *a priori.*

Atheism   The belief that a supernatural Being does not exist; in this sense, Spinoza was an atheist, although the concept of God plays an important role in his *Ethics.* In a wider sense, atheism involves a denial that God, in any sense, exists. In this sense, Spinoza was not an atheist. The atheist should not be identified with the agnostic, who simply says that he doesn't know whether God exists or not. In traditional philosophy God is frequently required to perform certain metaphysical, ethical, or epistemological functions, e.g., to create the universe, to judge human actions, to guarantee certain truths, etc. But Pierre-Simon Laplace (1749-1827), French astronomer and mathematician, gave comfort to the atheists when he said of God, "I have no need of such a hypothesis." Napoleon replied: "It is a useful idea nonetheless!"

Categorical imperative   Kant's supreme principle of morality; a command that does not depend on conditions, as does a hypothetical imperative. Example of a hypothetical imperative: *If you want peace, you ought to be willing to compromise.* Kant's categorical imperative (in all its three forms) has no *if* clause. It commands categorically: *Act only in such a way that you can want the maxim of your act to become a universal law of nature. Treat each person as an end in himself, never simply as a means.*

Category   A basic classification. Aristotle listed ten categories: (1) Substance, (2) Quantity, (3) Quality, (4) Relation, (5) Place, (6) Time, (7) Position, (8) State, (9) Activity, (10) Passivity. For Kant, categories were conceptions of the mind used in interpreting what is given in sense-perception. Gilbert Ryle, contemporary British philosopher, has introduced the phrase "category mistake" to describe a certain kind of absurdity produced by a confusion of categories (see selection 6.5).

Causality (Causation)   Aristotle distinguished four causes: efficient, final, formal, and material. What is called the principle of causality could be formulated as: *Every event has a cause.* Causality is generally thought to be uniform, i.e., similar causes have similar effects. David Hume challenged the rationalist view that causation was based on the idea of logical necessity; instead he attributed our belief in the cause-effect relationship to a mental habit or custom (see selection 6.2).

Chance   A chance event is sometimes defined as an event without a cause, sometimes as an event whose cause is unknown. Charles S. Peirce, rejecting a belief in universal determinism, held that chance events do occur in nature. See *Tychism, Free will, Determinism.*

Common Sense   Truths of Common Sense are supposed to be those indubitable truths which arise from our natural endowment and which all men have in common. Every once in a while some philosopher undertakes to defend Common Sense from the encroachments and assaults made on it by other philosophers (see selection 6.3 from Moore).

Conditional   An "if . . . then" statement; for example: *If men were angels, government would be unnecessary.* Also called an implication, or a material implication, or a hypothetical.

Contradictory The contradictory of a proposition is another proposition so related to the first that both cannot be true and both cannot be false; one must be true and one false. Example: (1) *All a priori propositions are analytic;* (2) *Some a priori propositions are synthetic (not analytic).* Contradictories should be distinguished from *contraries,* which can both be false; for example: (1) *All great poets are philosophers;* (2) *No great poets are philosophers.*

Conventionalism The view that rules, definitions, and scientific laws are the result of human conventions, and that alternatives are always possible. See Poincaré, selection 5.2.

Cosmology A branch of metaphysics in which an attempt is made to understand the universe as a whole, setting forth the most general laws which govern it. A. N. Whitehead's *Process and Reality* is subtitled *An Essay in Cosmology.*

Darwinism The theory of evolution developed by Charles Darwin (1809-1882), see *Origin of Species* (1859); a monumental scientific achievement that had many philosophical implications and influences in ethics, philosophy of religion, social philosophy, and metaphysics.

Deduction The derivation of a conclusion which follows necessarily from certain premises. For example, from the premises: (1) *No logical empiricists are Platonists,* and (2) *Carnap was a logical empiricist,* there follows by a simple deduction, the conclusion: *Carnap was not a Platonist.* See *Induction.*

Deontology The "science" of duty, a branch of knowledge that deals systematically with moral obligations.

Determinism The view that all events, including human actions, occur according to established laws, and are the necessary results of previous events. Some determinists would add that they are the *inevitable* results. There are many varieties of determinism—logical, ethical, theological, physical, psychological, historical, etc.

Dialectic In Plato's dialogues, the question and answer technique used by Socrates to forge definitions of important Ideas such as Piety, Knowledge, Courage, Beauty, etc. Hegel's dialectic is a historical process in three stages, (1) Thesis, (2) Antithesis, (3) Synthesis. Ideas first pass into their opposites, and in the next stage a higher unity is achieved.

Dilemma A term used by logicians that refers to a form of argument containing two conditional premises and a set of alternatives, called the horns of the dilemma, leading to an unpalatable conclusion. For example, A witness may find himself in the following dilemma: If he tells the truth, he will incriminate himself, and if he answers falsely he will perjure himself; hence, he must either incriminate or perjure himself. Sometimes it is possible to escape between the horns, perhaps by taking the fifth amendment.

Duty An important concept of obligation in ethics, especially in the philosophy of Kant. See *Deontology, Categorical imperative.*

Empiricism As opposed to rationalism (q.v.), the view that experience rather than reason is the source of human knowledge. One empiricist slogan was that nothing is in the intellect which was not previously in the senses. John Locke, a British empiricist, denied that any of our ideas is innate. Modern empiricists include David Hume, John Stuart Mill, John Dewey, Bertrand Russell, and the logical Empiricists such as Rudolf Carnap, Hans Reichenbach, Moritz Schlick, Otto Neurath, Herbert Feigl.

Epistemology   The theory of knowledge. See Chapter 6.

Ethics   A branch of philosophy dealing with the rightness or wrongness of human actions, with moral obligation, principles of morality and their justification (meta-ethics). See Chapter 3.

Evil, problem of   A famous theological problem or dilemma: how to reconcile the existence of evil, or what appears to be unnecessary suffering, with that of a benevolent and omnipotent deity.

Evolution   See *Darwinism.*

Existentialism   A philosophical movement embracing such diverse philosophers as Socrates, Pascal, Kant; but more frequently referring to the views of Kierkegaard, Dostoyevsky, Sartre, Heidegger, and, in theology, Barth, Tillich, Buber, Bultmann. Some existentialists are theists while others, Sartre, for example, are avowed atheists or Marxists. The most common existentialist themes concern the notion of commitment, the ultimate importance of the individual, the concept of man's freedom.

Fallacy   1. *Formal.* An error in reasoning; a violation of a rule or principle of logic.   2. *Material.* An error in reasoning resulting from linguistic confusion, ambiguity, vagueness, or irrelevance.

Free will   A will capable of making genuine choices between alternatives; not coerced; not determined by external causes. See *Determinism.*

Idea   A concept, a representation or presentation of sense. In Platonism, one of the archetypes, or patterns, of which existing things are imperfect copies; in pragmatism, a plan or purpose of action. See *Idealism, Platonism, Pragmatism.*

Ideal   Existing as a pattern, or archetypal idea, pertaining to perfection of kind; existing as a perfect example or desirable goal.

Idealism   A type of philosophy in which Ideas are the basic or ultimate reality, as in Plato. Idealists regard reality as essentially spiritual, or the embodiment of mind or reason. For subjective idealism, see selection 6.1 from Berkeley. Absolute idealism is exemplified by Hegel, Bradley, Royce (see *Absolute,* definition 2). For objective idealism, see Peirce's *Collected Papers,* vol. VI.

Induction   Reasoning that yields conclusions which do not necessarily follow, but are nevertheless plausible or statistically probable on the evidence given, is called inductive reasoning. Reasoning based on analogy, sampling, or on the assumption that the future will resemble the past are inductive.

Intuition   A faculty of the mind supposedly capable of discerning truth without the use of inference or analysis. Bergson calls intuition a kind of intellectual sympathy (see selection 2.4).

Justice   The principle of rectitude and fair dealing of men with each other; "to each his due" (*suum cuique*). In Plato, each person attending well to his station and its duties.

Karma   In Hinduism and Buddhism, the whole ethical consequence of one's acts considered as fixing one's lot in the future existence. In a general sense, fate or destiny.

Knowledge   The act or state of understanding; clear and adequate perception of truth.

Logic   The science that deals with the canons and criteria of validity in thought and demonstration; the science of the normative formal principles of reckoning.

Logos   The rational principle in the universe; in Heraclitus, that which is at once the moving and regulating principle in things; in the Gospel of Saint John, the Word as the beginning and divine end of all things.

Materialism   Anything which considers the facts of the universe to be sufficiently explained by the existence and nature of matter.

Mechanism   The doctrine that natural processes are rigidly determined and capable of explanation by the laws of physics and chemistry.

Meliorism   The doctrine that the world tends to become better and that man has the power of aiding its betterment; opposed to pessimism.

Metaphysics   That division of philosophy which includes ontology, or the science of being, and cosmology, or the science of the fundamental causes and processes in things.

Mysticism   The doctrine or belief that direct knowledge of God, of spiritual truth, is attainable through immediate intuition or insight and in a way differing from ordinary sense perception or reasoning.

Natural law   Discernible to reason, as distinguished from law laid down in codes by State, Church, etc., hence deriving its validity from the inherent nature of things and persons; see *Natural rights*.

Natural rights   Those rights that are esteemed to belong to a man by the law of nature, especially the right to life, liberty, property, and the pursuit of happiness (e.g., in the Declaration of Independence of 1776).

Naturalism   The doctrine which expands conceptions drawn from the natural sciences into a world view, denying that anything in reality has a supernatural significance.

Neo-Platonism   The philosophy of a group of thinkers (e.g., Plotinus and his followers) of the early Christian era who endeavored to reconcile the teachings of Plato and Aristotle with Oriental conceptions. In the seventeenth century in England, the Cambridge neo-Platonists were Henry More and Ralph Cudworth.

Nirvana   In Hinduism, extinction of the flame of life; final emancipation; reunion with Brahma. In Buddhism, the abnegation of passion, hatred, and delusion. This emancipation involves a beatific spiritual condition, and freedom from the necessity of future transmigration.

Noumenon   An object of purely rational apprehension as opposed to sense-perceptible phenomenon in Kantianism; an object which is conceived by reason but could not be given in sense experience; an unknowable object whose existence is theoretically problematic. See *Phenomenon.*

Nous Mind, especially the mind as rational; the reason; the highest intellect; God regarded as the World Reason. Anaxagoras was the author of the doctrine of reason or *Nous* as world principle.

Ontology The science of being or reality; the branch of knowledge that investigates the nature, essential properties, and relations of being, as such.

Ontological argument An argument for the existence of God from the nature of His being, commonly stated thus: God is a Being than which a greater cannot be conceived, but an idea which existed only in the mind would not be so great as the one that existed in reality as well as in the mind; therefore God must be thought as necessarily existing.

Organicism The doctrine that life and living processes are the manifestation of an activity possible only in virtue of the state of autonomous organization of the system, rather than because of its individual components. Opposed to mechanism.

Phenomenon An object of sense perception as distinguished from an ultimate reality. This meaning is due to Kant's absolute separation of the thing-in-itself from the object of experience, or phenomenon. See *Noumenon.*

Phenomenalism The theory that limits positive or scientific knowledge to phenomena only. The theory that we know only phenomena and that there is no existence except the phenomenal.

Phenomenology Intuitive description of actual phenomena, with avoidance of all interpretation, explanation, or evaluation.

Platonism The philosophy of Plato; especially his doctrine that the true or ultimate reality consists of transcendent universals, corresponding to perfect concepts such as may be exemplified in mathematics. Actual things are but copies of universals or ideas. These ideas are objects of true knowledge, and they can be apprehended by an innate power of soul, called reminiscence.

Pluralism Contrasted with monism and dualism. The doctrine that there is more than one kind of ultimate reality (and, usually, more than two). Reality, for the pluralist, is not organic but is composed of a plurality of independent entities, whether material or spiritual or both.

Positivism A system of philosophy originated by Auguste Comte (1789-1857), which excluded everything but the natural phenomena or properties of knowable things, together with their invariable relations of coexistence and succession, as occurring in time and space. All other types of explanation are repudiated as "theological" or "metaphysical."

Pragmatism American movement in philosphy founded by C. S. Peirce and William James and continued by John Dewey, C. I. Lewis, and others. In Europe pragmatism is represented by G. Vailati, Maurice Blondel, F. R. Ramsey, Hans Vaihinger. Characteristic doctrines of this movement are that the meaning of conceptions is to be sought in their logical consequences and practical bearings, that the function of thought is to guide action, and that all claims to truth are preeminently to be tested by the operations of verifying the consequences of beliefs by regarding them as hypotheses.

Rationalism   As opposed to empiricism, makes reason and universal ideas and categories a source of *a priori* knowledge, e.g., in formal logic and pure mathematics, ethics, aesthetics, and theology. Plato, Anselm, Descartes, Spinoza, Leibniz, Chr. Wolff, and Hegel are classical rationalists. Not to be confused with rationalization, the psychological use of dubious reasons concealing true motives.

Realism   Opposed to nominalism, regards universal ideas to be objective (Platonic Realism); opposed to idealism, views truth and external objects as independent of the mind's opinions or sensations. Critical realism interposes sense-data or images between the mind and the objects they represent; naïve realism claims objects are directly perceived; neo-realism asserts a one-to-one correspondence between ideas and particulars perceived or universals conceived.

Reductionism   The view that all biological or mental phenomena (including secondary and tertiary qualities) are reducible to physical or primary properties.

Relativism   The view that truth and values are dependent on and vary with each individual's opinions, desires, or preferences; opposed to absolutism (q.v.).

Renaissance   Cultural period between Middle Ages and seventeenth century reviving classical models in art, science, and philosophy with the liberation of individuals from the medieval yoke of authority and tradition.

Scholasticism   Medieval philosophy and learning of Judaic, Christian, and Moslem culture in subordination to theology.

Scientific method   Use of hypothesis, deduction, and induction in experimental inquiry aimed at establishing truth and resolution of conflicting opinions.

Scientism   Dogmatic insistence that only the results of science can serve as truths or guides to living; an extreme form of positivism (q.v.).

Skepticism   (Pyrrhonian) skepticism denies truth, knowledge, or communicability of ideas; relative (Academic) skepticism admits truth, but doubts its certainty or independence of thought.

Social contract   Theory that the logical basis and justification of the State is the agreement of individuals to obey the laws laid down by those to whom they have delegated the power to make and enforce laws for the protection of life, liberty, and personal property (Hobbes, Locke, Spinoza, and Rousseau).

Solipsism   Theory that only the self and its mental states and thoughts are real.

Spirit   Pure thought or eternal mind whose reality is superior to material objects or sensory pleasures (cf. Berkeley and Hegel); "Spirit of the Age" or *Zeitgeist* (q.v.); for "world spirit" see *Weltgeist*.

Stoicism   The ethical school of Zeno, Epictetus, Cicero, and others, stressing self-control, primacy of reason in nature, universal determinism or natural law and natural rights, avoidance of pain and "follow nature" as ethical guides.

Subjectivism   Theory that only the mind and its sensations or thoughts are real (cf. Berkeley: "to be is to be perceived"); existence, truth, and values are relative to the individual's sensations, opinions, and desires.

Substance   That which exists by itself and is known through itself, independent of anything else (cf. Spinoza). Descartes posited Thought and Extension as two substances. Leibniz posited an infinite hierarchy of monads as substances.

Transcendentalism   Belief in a higher (spiritual) order of understanding and religious values (cf. Plato, Kant, Hegel, Emerson).

Truth   Relation of ideas or statements to observable things or to what statements designate; correspondence and coherence are used as criteria of judging claims to truth.

Tychism   C. S. Peirce's term for the theory that chance or unpredictable contingency is an essential feature (a *vera causa*) of nature and experience.

Understanding   Kant's basis of the universal categories required for conceiving the laws of nature, e.g., causation. Max Weber made it a special faculty required for the social sciences as distinct from the type of observations employed in the natural sciences.

Unity of science   A positivistic program for unifying the sciences by a common logic and empiricistic methodology. Also posited by monistic philosophies.

Universals   Abstract ideas, classes, or general truths having either finite instances (e.g., all living humans) or an infinite range (e.g., points on a line, number of possible worlds or combinations of numbers, past or future moments of time).

Utilitarianism   Doctrine that the moral aim of all social legislation is "the greatest happiness for the greatest number of people" (cf. Bentham and Mill).

Value judgments   Statements or hypotheses about what is good or beautiful, desirable or admirable, or worthy of approval or not.

Verifiability principle   Methodological rule that statements about the world are meaningless if they are not verifiable as true or false by actual or possible observation (cf. positivism).

Virtue   In Greek philosophy (*areté*) excellence of performance; in Roman thought, manliness; in Renaissance era (e.g., in Machiavelli), cunning; in Christian thought, abstinence from sensuous pleasure and obeying the ten commandments; in Spinoza, virtue is its own reward.

Vitalism   View that opposes the reduction of living processes and properties to purely physical and chemical ones, on the ground that life and the soul are unique.

Volksgeist   Spirit (q.v.) of a people rooted in its traditions, language, folkways (cf. Herder, Hegel).

Weltgeist   Universal spirit ruling the world and history of the rise and fall of nations (cf. Hegel).

Zeitgeist   Spirit of the times; characteristics of a cultural period.

INDEX